8C

maths links

Teacher's Guide

Chris Green
Kim Frazer
Sheelagh Raw

OXFORD
UNIVERSITY PRESS

OXFORD
UNIVERSITY PRESS

Great Clarendon Street, Oxford OX2 6DP

Oxford University Press is a department of the University of Oxford.
It furthers the University's objective of excellence in research, scholarship, and
education by publishing worldwide in

Oxford   New York

Auckland   Cape Town   Dar es Salaam   Hong Kong   Karachi
Kuala Lumpur   Madrid   Melbourne   Mexico City   Nairobi
New Delhi   Shanghai   Taipei   Toronto

With offices in

Argentina   Austria   Brazil   Chile   Czech Republic   France   Greece
Guatemala   Hungary   Italy   Japan   Poland   Portugal   Singapore
South Korea   Switzerland   Thailand   Turkey   Ukraine   Vietnam

© Oxford University Press

British Library Cataloguing in Publication Data

Data available

ISBN: 978-0-19-915309-1
10 9 8 7 6 5 4 3 2

Printed in United Kingdom by Synergie Basingstoke

Paper used in the production of this book is a natural, recyclable product made
from wood grown in sustainable forests. The manufacturing process conforms to
the environmental regulations to the country of origin.

Acknowledgments
The editors would like to thank Pete Crawford and Charlie Bond
for their excellent work on this book.

About this book

This Teacher's Guide conforms to the renewed Framework for Teaching Mathematics, for first teaching in 2008. The book is designed to accompany MathsLinks Students' Book 8C, which targets Year 8 students who have achieved level 5 at KS2 – the aim is to consolidate level 6 and extend to level 7 as Year 8 progresses.

The series authors are experienced teachers and maths advisers who have an excellent understanding of the KS3 Framework and programme of study, and so are well qualified to help you successfully deliver the Year 8 curriculum in your classroom.

This book is organised by chapter, which have been structured into lesson plans to enable you to deliver the learning objectives in each of the five strands of progression:

- Mathematical processes and applications
- Number
- Algebra
- Geometry
- Statistics

Topics are clearly levelled, enabling you to assess students' progress both collectively and individually. Misconceptions are highlighted and intervention strategies are suggested throughout to anticipate and remove barriers to learning.

For those following a condensed KS3 programme, a Fast-track route through the material is provided, along with a suggested scheme of work for Year 1-2.

In addition, full answers are given to the accompanying student book and homework book exercises.

The CD-ROM attached to this book contains all of the lesson plans in customisable Word format, to enable you to create your own lessons to suit your students' needs; also included on the CD are the answers in pdf format, suitable for whole-class display.

PLTS	Personal, learning and thinking skills	MPA	Mathematical processes and applications	I	Introduction
				CS	Case study
IE	Independent enquirers	1.1	Representing	UAM	Using and applying mathematics
CT	Creative thinkers	1.2	Analysing – use mathematical reasoning		
				SSM	Shape space measure
RL	Reflective learners	1.3	Analysing – use appropriate mathematical procedures	HD	Handling data
TW	Team workers			NNS	Numbers and the number system
SM	Self-managers	1.4	Interpreting and evaluating		
EP	Effective participators	1.5	Communicating and reflecting		

Contents

1 Integers

Objectives

- Extend mental methods of calculation, working with fractions, factors, powers and roots **5**
- Use the prime factor decomposition of a number **5**
- Use index notation for integer powers **5**
- Use the function keys (on a calculator) for powers and roots **5**
- Recognise the equivalence of 0.1, $\frac{1}{10}$ and 10^{-1} **5**
- Use efficient methods to add and subtract fractions **6**
- Use ICT to estimate square roots and cube roots **6**
- Know and use the index laws for multiplication and division of positive integer powers **6**

Introduction

The focus of this chapter is on extending the use of different types of number. Students add, subtract, multiply and divide negative numbers; find factors and primes, including the prime factor decomposition of a number; begin to use LCM and HCF to add, subtract and simplify fractions; find square and cube roots using a calculator and using prime factors; use index notation and begin to use the rules of indices to multiply and divide numbers written in index form.

The student book discusses the importance of prime numbers in the message sent into space by the Arecibo radio telescope in 1974. Prime numbers and their properties were first studied by mathematicians in Ancient Greece. They can be used to solve problems and, more recently, for encryption, for example in credit card transactions. In nature, some animals and insects exhibit behaviour related to prime numbers. There is more information about encryption using prime numbers at http://www.cpaadvisor.us/sub/8_encryption.htm (EP, TW).

Fast-track

1c, e

Level

MPA

1.1	1b, c, d, e
1.2	1a, b, d, f
1.3	1a, b, c, d, e, f
1.4	1a, b, c, d, e, f
1.5	1b, c, d, e

PLTS

IE	1a, b, c, d, e, f
CT	1a, b, c, d, e, f
RL	1a, b, c, e, f
TW	1I, b, c, d
SM	1a, b, c, d, e, f
EP	1I, b, d, e, f

Extra Resources

1   Start of chapter presentation
1a Animation: Positive and negative numbers
1a Consolidation sheet
1c Animation: Factor trees
1c Animation: HCF and LCM
1d Worked solution: Q4a
1d Consolidation sheet
1e Animation: Square roots
1e Worked solution: Q3a
1e Consolidation sheet

    Assessment: chapter 1

- Order decimals .... (L5)
- Add, subtract, multiply and divide integers .... (L5)

Useful resources
Number line
(-10 to 110)
Sheet music

••

Starter – Guess my number

Choose a number with one decimal place between -15 and 115.

Invite students to guess the number.

After each guess say whether the next guess should be higher or lower (1.2).

Can be extended by increasing the number of decimal places.

Teaching notes

A time counter begins to count down from 10 seconds to minus 10 seconds in thousandths of a second. Three people separately have a go at stopping the timer exactly on zero. Suggest three times and decide who is closest by comparing place value.

When adding and subtracting with negatives, many students confuse the rules. '*Two minuses make a plus*' is a common misconception, but -3 1 -6 makes a negative result (RL). Emphasise that '*adding a negative*' means '*take away*' but '*subtracting a negative*' means add. The first number is where you **start**, the second number is **how far** you move. Using the number line as an aid, students should write down question/working/answer. For example, -3 1 -6 → -3 2 6 → -9.

When multiplying and dividing ensure students realise the rules are different from adding and subtracting (RL). The rules '*signs different, so negative*', '*signs same, so positive*' can be used. Multiplying by -1 can be seen as a reflection in the number line about zero. This can help explain why minus 3 minus gives a positive result.

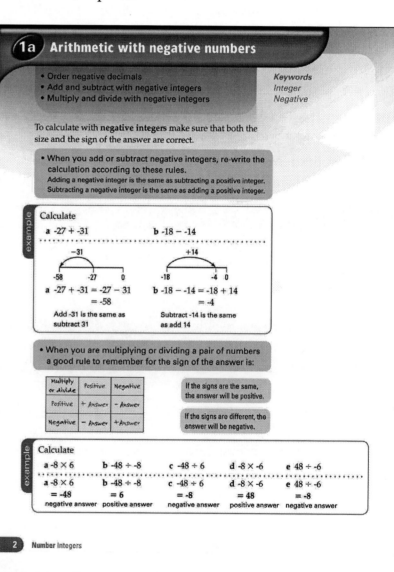

Plenary

Add the numbers 1, -2, 3, -4, *etc.* up to a certain limit. Is there a quick way to find the result? Is the rule different if the last number is odd or even? Encourage students to examine the positive and negative numbers as two different sets. If the sequence summed to 100 could you tell what the last number was? (199) (IE) (1.4)

Simplification

Give students a copy of a number line and encourage them to write on it to help with ordering numbers and also adding and subtracting.

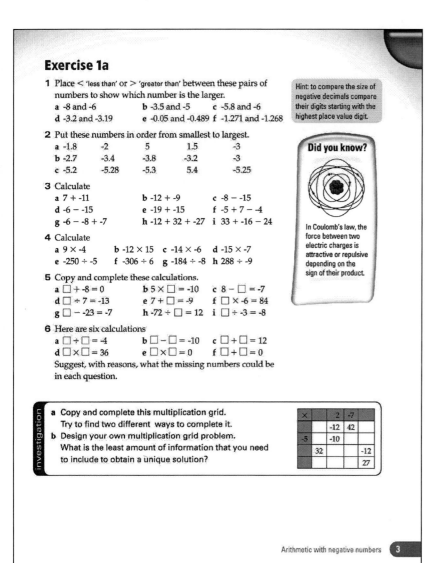

Exercise 1a

1 Place < 'less than' or > 'greater than' between these pairs of numbers to show which number is the larger.

   a -8 and -6   **b** -3.5 and -5   **c** -5.8 and -6

   d -3.2 and -3.19   **e** -0.05 and -0.489 **f** -1.271 and -1.268

> Hint: to compare the size of negative decimals compare their digits starting with the highest place value digit.

2 Put these numbers in order from smallest to largest.

   a -1.8   -2   5   1.5   -3

   b -2.7   -3.4   -3.8   -3.2   -3

   c -5.2   -5.28 -5.3   5.4   -5.25

> **Did you know?**
>
> In Coulomb's law, the force between two electric charges is attractive or repulsive depending on the sign of their product.

3 Calculate

   a 7 + -11   **b** -12 + -9   **c** -8 − -15

   d -6 − -15   **e** -19 + -15   **f** -5 + 7 − -4

   g -6 − -8 + -7   **h** -12 + 32 + -27 **i** 33 + -16 − 24

4 Calculate

   a 9 × -4   **b** -12 × 15 **c** -14 × -6 **d** -15 × -7

   e -250 ÷ -5 **f** -306 ÷ 6 **g** -184 ÷ -8 **h** 288 ÷ -9

5 Copy and complete these calculations.

   a ☐ + -8 = 0   **b** 5 × ☐ = -10   **c** 8 − ☐ = -7

   d ☐ ÷ 7 = -13   **e** 7 + ☐ = -9   **f** ☐ × -6 = 84

   g ☐ − -23 = -7   **h** -72 ÷ ☐ = 12 **i** ☐ ÷ -3 = -8

6 Here are six calculations

   a ☐ ÷ ☐ = -4   **b** ☐ − ☐ = -10   **c** ☐ + ☐ = 12

   d ☐ × ☐ = 36   **e** ☐ × ☐ = 0   **f** ☐ + ☐ = 0

   Suggest, with reasons, what the missing numbers could be in each question.

investigation

a Copy and complete this multiplication grid.
Try to find two different ways to complete it.

b Design your own multiplication grid problem.
What is the least amount of information that you need to include to obtain a unique solution?

×		2	-7
		-12	42
-5		-10	
	32		-12
			27

Arithmetic with negative numbers   **3**

Extension

Investigate negative numbers to a power. This could lead onto the difference between odd and even powers. Take care with the notation -2^2 and $(-2)^2$ have different meanings. Can students tell why? (RL, CT)

Exercise 1a commentary

All questions (1.3)

Question 1 – Students may need help remembering which way the , . signs go. Could think of a crocodiles jaws opening wider 'eating the larger number'.

Question 2 – Ask students which integer the decimal is closest to. Students often find the concept of negative decimals difficult.

Question 3 – Emphasise the importance of writing the question/working/answer down the page to avoid errors.

Question 4 – Students may need help here. All divisions are exact. Ask students to calculate positive answers and then think about signs.

Question 5 – Answers can be checked by asking a partner to work out the answer, for example **5a**, ask 'what is 8 1 -8?'

Question 6 – Encourage students to be descriptive, they can use examples to help explain the required patterns.

Question 7 – Ask, 'what is the product of 4, 5, 6?'

Challenge – The term product may need mentioning. The number 27 is the key, why would 27 and 1 be difficult to use? (SM) (1.2)

Assessment Criteria – NNS, level 5: order negative numbers in context. Calculating, level 5: solve simple problems involving ordering, adding, subtracting negative numbers in context.

Links

Bring in some sheet music for the class to use. The inequality signs are similar to the musical symbols *crescendo* (becoming louder) and *decrescendo* or *diminuendo* (becoming softer). Ask the class to find examples on the music.

- Use factors and primes   (L5)
- Extend mental methods of calculation, working with factors   (L5)

Useful resources
Calculator
List of integers: 10 000 to 10 050
Examples of each divisibility test

Starter – The answer is -1.2

Ask students to write down questions where the answer is -1.2. Score 1 point for an addition question, 2 points for a subtraction question, 3 for a multiplication or division question (CT).

Teaching notes

Ask the students how can they tell if a number divides exactly by 2, 5 or 10. Do students know any ways of telling if a number divides by other numbers? Introduce the divisibility tests and try one of them. Which do students think is the most complex? (EP)

Define the term **factor**. Show how listing a number's factors in pairs quickly helps complete the set of all factors. How will you know when you have them all? Listing factors in ascending order from two different ends is very helpful (1.5).

Which of these statements define prime numbers?

–an odd number but not 3, 9, 15, 21, etc.

–a number with exactly two factors

–a number whose factors are only 1 and itself.

Perform a divisibility test on 157 (prime), why don't you have to check beyond 12?

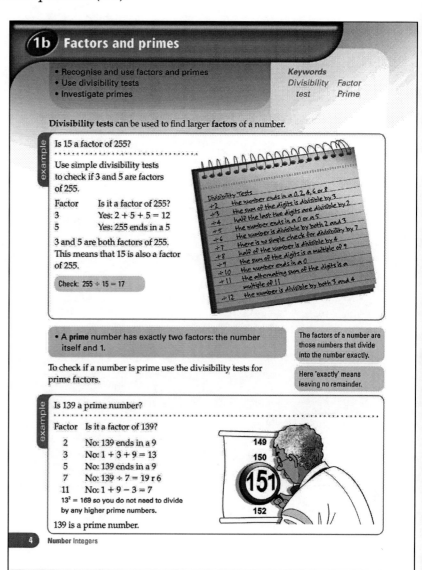

Plenary

Could the knowledge about primes gained from the challenge help in answering question **3**? All the numbers turn out to be multiples of 6 ± 1, so does this mean they are all prime? Challenge students to give an example where a multiple of 6 ± 1 is not prime. (25 is the lowest number).

Simplification

Provide students with an example of each divisibility test to help with applying them for question **1**.

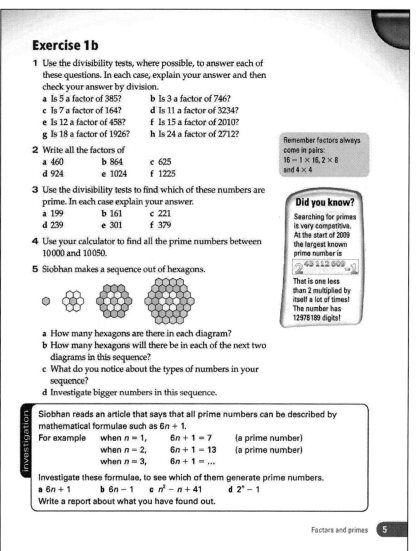

Exercise 1b

1 Use the divisibility tests, where possible, to answer each of these questions. In each case, explain your answer and then check your answer by division.
   a Is 5 a factor of 385?   b Is 3 a factor of 746?
   c Is 7 a factor of 164?   d Is 11 a factor of 3234?
   e Is 12 a factor of 458?   f Is 15 a factor of 2010?
   g Is 18 a factor of 1926?   h Is 24 a factor of 2712?

2 Write all the factors of
   a 460   b 864   c 625
   d 924   e 1024   f 1225

3 Use the divisibility tests to find which of these numbers are prime. In each case explain your answer.
   a 199   b 161   c 221
   d 239   e 301   f 379

4 Use your calculator to find all the prime numbers between 10 000 and 10 050.

5 Siobhan makes a sequence out of hexagons.

   a How many hexagons are there in each diagram?
   b How many hexagons will there be in each of the next two diagrams in this sequence?
   c What do you notice about the types of numbers in your sequence?
   d Investigate bigger numbers in this sequence.

> **investigation**
>
> Siobhan reads an article that says that all prime numbers can be described by mathematical formulae such as $6n + 1$.
> For example   when $n = 1$, $6n + 1 = 7$ (a prime number)
>   when $n = 2$, $6n + 1 = 13$ (a prime number)
>   when $n = 3$, $6n + 1 = ...$
>
> Investigate these formulae, to see which of them generate prime numbers.
> a $6n + 1$ b $6n - 1$ c $n^2 - n + 41$ d $2^n - 1$
> Write a report about what you have found out.

Remember factors always come in pairs:
$16 = 1 \times 16, 2 \times 8$ and 4×4

Did you know?

Searching for primes is very competitive. At the start of 2009 the largest known prime number is

$2^{43\,112\,609} - 1$

That is one less than 2 multiplied by itself a lot of times! The number has 12 978 189 digits!

Extension

How long would it take to write out the largest known prime number if you did not have to work it out, just copy it? Students could use a calculator or estimate without a calculator. Use the example in the student book of 12 978 189 digits. Between 2 and 4 months. How can students estimate the speed that they can write down digits? (CT) (1.1)

Exercise 1b commentary

All questions (1.3)

Question 1 – Use the divisibility tests to check a potential factor if possible. Challenge students about alternative ways to check a factor, short division or subtracting known multiples of the factor.

Question 2 – List factors in pairs. A calculator could be used since these are time consuming.

Question 3 – A calculator could be used to find the square root.

Question 4 – Provide students with a printed list of integers 10 000 to 10 050 and encourage elimination of multiples of 2, 3, 5, *etc.* first. For those left, use a calculator to check for factors from the list below.

Question 5 – Centred hexagonal numbers, $1 + 3n(n - 1)$. Make sure students look at how the sum is built up, not just the total. They appear to be primes, but the 8th term is 169 (13^2) (IE, RL) (1.2).

Investigation – Eratosthenes sieve implies all primes are in fact a multiple of 6 ± 1, with the exception of 2 and 3. For part **d**, Mersenne primes, see the **Did you know?** (TW, SM, IE) (1.1, 1.4)

Assessment Criteria – NNS, level 4: recognise and describe number relationships including multiple, factor and square.

Links

Bring in some dictionaries for the class to use. The word *divisibility* has 5 i's, the word *indivisibilities* has 7. Ask the class to find other words with at least 4 i's. Some examples include *infinitesimal* (4), *impossibilities* (5), *invisibility* (5) and *indistinguishability* (6). The dictionary will probably not include *supercalifragilisticexpialidocious* (7)!

- Find the prime factor decomposition of a number   (L5)
- Use the prime factor decomposition of a number   (L6)
- Use index notation for integer powers   (L5)

Useful resources
Calculator

Starter – Make 1 to 15

Throw three dice and ask students to make one number between 1 and 15 inclusive using all three scores and any operation(s). Throw again; students make another number between 1 and 15. Repeat until all the numbers have been made by a student.

Teaching notes

Challenge students to find the prime factors of a number. How can the number be made by multiplying these prime factors? Can every integer be written as the product (multiplication) of prime factors? Not -1, 0, 1.

Look at two methods for finding the product of prime factors. A factor tree and repeated division. Which method is easiest? Does it depend on the number you are starting with? Ask students for a strategy to break down large numbers quickly. Ask why this method might be called prime factor decomposition. Decompose means breaking down into pieces (1.5).

Ask how having the product of prime factors can help in the finding of all the factors of a number. In the example in the student book of 140, how can you list the combinations of prime factors in an organised way to ensure no factor is missed?(CT, RL)

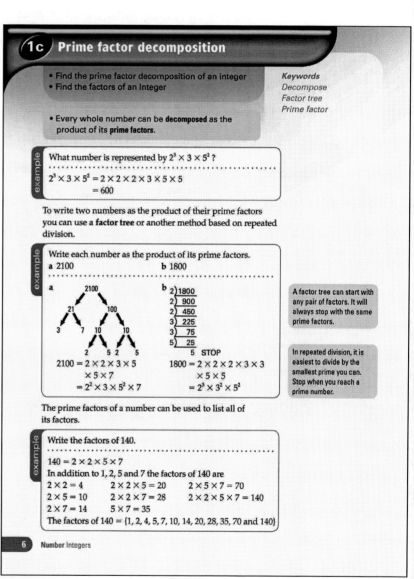

Plenary

Look at the number sequence 2, 6, 30, 210. Challenge students to find the next two numbers in the sequence; no calculators allowed. (2310, 30 030). After a few minutes give students the hint that they should try to write each term as the product of its prime factors. (2, 2×3, $2 \times 3 \times 5$, $2 \times 3 \times 5 \times 7$). How many terms would you need to find before you had a value over one billion? Encourage students to use estimates, for example, $30\,000 \times 20 \times 20 \times 20 \times 30$ when multiplying by 17, 19, 23 and 29. (ten terms) (IE) (1.3)

Simplification

When finding prime factor decompositions encourage students to check that the numbers at the ends of the branches are in the prime number list. Give the list of primes from 2 to 11.

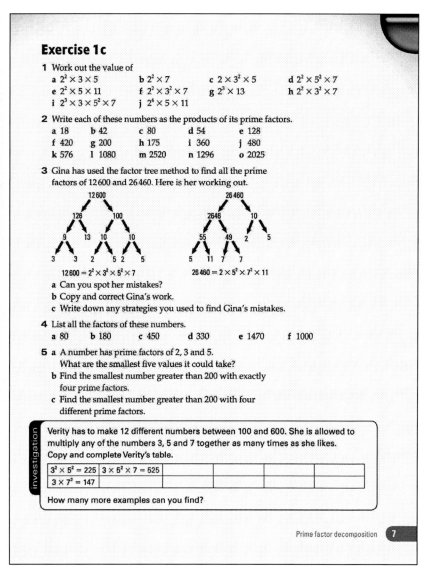

Exercise 1c

1 Work out the value of
a $2^2 \times 3 \times 5$ b $2^2 \times 7$ c $2 \times 3^2 \times 5$ d $2^2 \times 5^2 \times 7$
e $2^2 \times 5 \times 11$ f $2^2 \times 3^2 \times 7$ g $2^3 \times 13$ h $2^2 \times 3^2 \times 7$
i $2^3 \times 3 \times 5^2 \times 7$ j $2^4 \times 5 \times 11$

2 Write each of these numbers as the products of its prime factors.
a 18 b 42 c 80 d 54 e 128
f 420 g 200 h 175 i 360 j 480
k 576 l 1080 m 2520 n 1296 o 2025

3 Gina has used the factor tree method to find all the prime factors of 12 600 and 26 460. Here is her working out.

$12\,600 = 2^2 \times 3^2 \times 5^2 \times 7$ $26\,460 = 2 \times 5^2 \times 7^2 \times 11$
a Can you spot her mistakes?
b Copy and correct Gina's work.
c Write down any strategies you used to find Gina's mistakes.

4 List all the factors of these numbers.
a 80 b 180 c 450 d 330 e 1470 f 1000

5 a A number has prime factors of 2, 3 and 5.
What are the smallest five values it could take?
b Find the smallest number greater than 200 with exactly four prime factors.
c Find the smallest number greater than 200 with four different prime factors.

investigation

Verity has to make 12 different numbers between 100 and 600. She is allowed to multiply any of the numbers 3, 5 and 7 together as many times as she likes. Copy and complete Verity's table.

$3^2 \times 5^2 = 225$	$3 \times 5^2 \times 7 = 525$				
$3 \times 7^2 = 147$					

How many more examples can you find?

Prime factor decomposition **7**

Extension

What is the prime factor decomposition of 1 trillion? Hint that you could first try 10, then 100, then 1000 *etc*. What about a google (10^{100}) and a googolplex (10^{google})? (CT) (1.4)

Exercise 1c commentary

All questions (1.3)

Question 1 – Ensure students are not multiplying when they should be powering, for example, doubling when they should be squaring.

Question 2 – Challenge students to work in pairs. One student to use repeated division, the other to use the factor tree. Which process works best? (1.5)

Question 3 – Encourage use of a calculator to check for the error. Ask students if they would have decomposed the number differently?

Question 4 – Encourage students to use large factors to break down the number quicker rather than start from 2 (1.1).

Question 5 – A combination of logic and trial and improvement will be required (IE, RL).

Challenge – Use combinations of prime factors to create different results. Encourage a systemic approach. Do you allow just one number to be used repeatedly? (SM)

Links

The message sent by the Arecibo radio telescope (see Check-In page) consisted of 1679 0s and 1s, or bits. An alien trying to decipher the message would need to identify the prime factors of 1679, arrange the characters in a 23 × 73 rectangle and replace each 0 by a blank space and each 1 by a solid space. The deciphered message forms a picture showing the integers from 1 – 10, the chemical make-up of DNA, a stick man, a diagram of the solar system and an image of the telescope. There is a picture of the deciphered message at http://en.wikipedia.org/wiki/Arecibo_message (TW).

- Use highest common factors and lowest common multiples (L6)
- Use efficient methods to add and subtract fractions (L6)

Useful resources

Calculator

List of products of prime factors for integers up to 100

Starter – Prime calculations!

Ask students questions involving prime numbers less than 30. For example,

Two prime numbers that have a difference of 9? (2, 11)
Three prime numbers that have a total of 45? (5, 17, 23)
Two prime numbers with a product of 65? (5, 13)
Sum of first four prime numbers? (17)

Teaching notes

Explain what is meant by factor and HCF. Use small number examples to illustrate that the HCF is the product of the common prime factors. Show how a Venn diagram can illustrate this more clearly. Explain what is meant by a multiple and LCM. Use small examples and ask if the Venn diagram can also prove useful for LCM (1.1).

When two numbers are drawn in a Venn diagram using their prime factors, you could think of the overlapping circles like a person's face. If you spike up their hair and stick out their tongue, what numbers will you be using? The LCM and HCF.

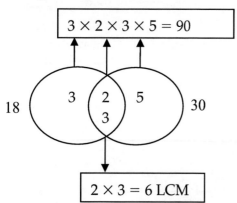

Give simple examples of simplifying and adding fractions. How can HCF and LCM help with these types of questions? What happens when the HCF and LCM are not used when working with fractions? Ask students what method they think computers use to deal with fractions? Why? (EP) (1.5)

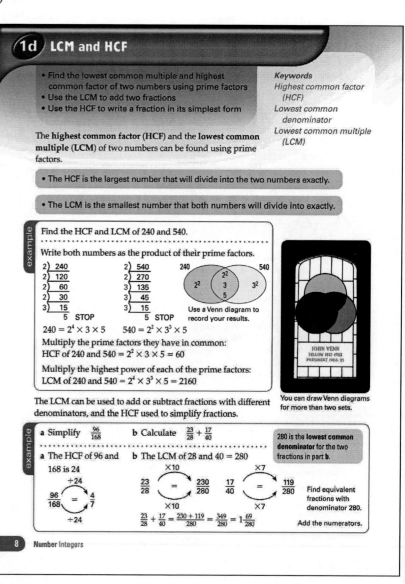

Plenary

The LCM of any two consecutive integers above zero is the product of the two numbers. Is this statement 'always true', 'sometimes true', 'never true'. Encourage students to investigate in a systematic way. While students may find that this is true for all the examples they try, does this prove that the statement is always true? It is in fact always true (1.4).

Simplification

The questions can be very time consuming, students could be provided with a list of prime factor decompositions up to 100 to help with many of the questions. The numbers in questions **4** could be replaced by numbers from question **2** in spread **1c** for which the prime factor decompositions already exist.

All questions (1.3)

Question 1 – For parts **a**, **b**, **e** students could be allowed to use inspection, for the other parts a Venn diagram is likely to work best.

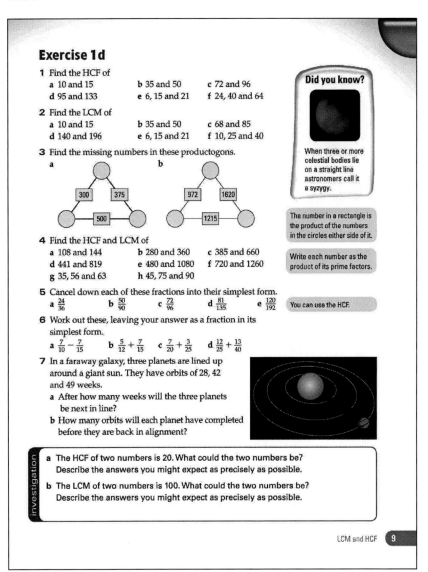

Exercise 1d

1 Find the HCF of
a 10 and 15   b 35 and 50   c 72 and 96
d 95 and 133   e 6, 15 and 21   f 24, 40 and 64

2 Find the LCM of
a 10 and 15   b 35 and 50   c 68 and 85
d 140 and 196   e 6, 15 and 21   f 10, 25 and 40

3 Find the missing numbers in these productogons.

a   [300] [375] [500]

b   [972] [1620] [1215]

4 Find the HCF and LCM of
a 108 and 144   b 280 and 360   c 385 and 660
d 441 and 819   e 480 and 1080   f 720 and 1260
g 35, 56 and 63   h 45, 75 and 90

5 Cancel down each of these fractions into their simplest form.
a $\frac{24}{36}$ b $\frac{50}{90}$ c $\frac{72}{96}$ d $\frac{81}{135}$ e $\frac{120}{192}$

6 Work out these, leaving your answer as a fraction in its simplest form.
a $\frac{7}{10} - \frac{7}{15}$ b $\frac{5}{12} + \frac{7}{15}$ c $\frac{7}{20} + \frac{3}{25}$ d $\frac{12}{25} + \frac{13}{40}$

7 In a faraway galaxy, three planets are lined up around a giant sun. They have orbits of 28, 42 and 49 weeks.
a After how many weeks will the three planets be next in line?
b How many orbits will each planet have completed before they are back in alignment?

Did you know?

When three or more celestial bodies lie on a straight line astronomers call it a syzygy.

The number in a rectangle is the product of the numbers in the circles either side of it.

Write each number as the product of its prime factors.

You can use the HCF.

investigation
a The HCF of two numbers is 20. What could the two numbers be? Describe the answers you might expect as precisely as possible.
b The LCM of two numbers is 100. What could the two numbers be? Describe the answers you might expect as precisely as possible.

LCM and HCF   9

Extension

Explore the ways in which LCM and HCF can be used with decimals. Students should begin by looking at how a decimal might be decomposed using a factor tree. Do the same rules apply for decimals and integers? Encourage students to set a challenge for a partner (IE, CT).

Exercise 1d commentary

Question 2 – For parts **a**, **b** students could be allowed to use inspection, for the other parts a Venn diagram is likely to work best (IE).

Question 3 – Investigate using prime factors. Encourage students to use trial and error to complete the puzzle. Is there only one solution?

Question 4 – Venn diagrams are likely to work best for each part.

Question 5 – Encourage students to use the HCF, although in practice it is likely to be faster to use repeated cancelling.

Question 6 – Parts **a**–**c** could be achieved by inspection, part **d** could make use a Venn diagram or use lists of multiples.

Question 7 – Practical application of LCM. Allow a calculator for this question. Hint: find the LCM (IE).

Investigation – Encourage use of a Venn diagram. Suggest students find the smallest answers first, then steadily larger numbers. Are there a finite (how many) or an infinite number of solutions (SM) (1.2).

Assessment Criteria – NNS, level 5: reduce a fraction to its simplest form by canceling common factors. Calculating, level 6: add and subtract fractions by writing them with a common denominator.

Links

Venn diagrams were invented by John Venn in around 1880. He was a fellow and lecturer in moral sciences at Cambridge University and wrote several books on logic. A stained glass window at Gonville and Caius College, Cambridge commemorates him. For more information see, http://en.wikipedia.org/wiki/John_venn (TW).

- Use the function keys (on a calculator) for powers and roots (L6)
- Use ICT to estimate square roots and cube roots (L6)

Useful resources
Calculator

Starter – Multiple factors

Write the following numbers on the board: 30, 125, 75, 16, 48. Ask students

Which numbers are factors of 5000? (only 125)
What is the lowest common multiple of the 5 numbers? (6000)
What is the largest square number that is a factor of 5000? (2500) *etc.*

Teaching notes

Ask students what is meant by *square* and *cube*. Include negative examples. Ask what is meant by *square root*. Why is their a positive and negative square root? What other types of roots might there be? Conclude that *cube roots* work in a similar way to square roots.

Investigate these functions on a calculator. Note that almost all scientific calculators have a cube function, but slightly less have a cube root function. Some students may need to be shown how to do a third root.

Ask students to work out 'the square of -4' using the correct function on the calculator. Most students will probably obtain -16, although some calculators insert brackets around the negative value automatically. How can we ensure that the calculator correctly squares -4? Insert brackets around the negative number (RL).

Explore the link between area/length/perimeter and square roots. Imagine a square field, the side length is 5m, the perimeter is 20 m, the area is 25 m². Ask students if any two of these measurements can be found by knowing the third (CT).

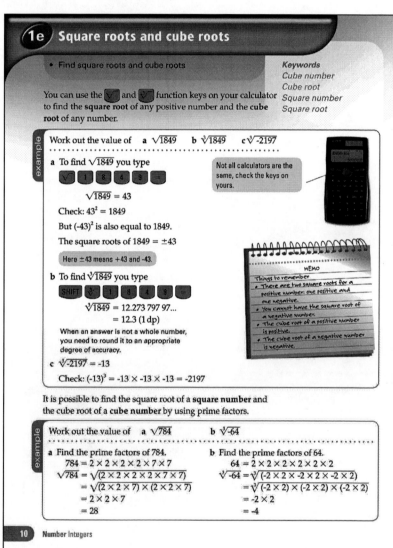

Plenary

A method for finding an approximation to a square root is as follows. Suppose $x \sim n^2$ is a close approximation, that is $\sqrt{x} \approx n$, then a better approximation is

$$\sqrt{x} \approx n - \frac{(n-x)}{2n}$$

Try finding $\sqrt{15}$ starting from $n^2 = 4^2 = 16$.

$$\sqrt{15} \approx 4 - \frac{(16-15)}{2 \times 4} = 4 - \frac{1}{8} = 3\frac{7}{8}$$

How good is the estimate? Check using a calculator (1.3)

Simplification

Ensure students are not confusing doubling with squaring. At the start of the exercise encourage students to check answers by repeated multiplication.

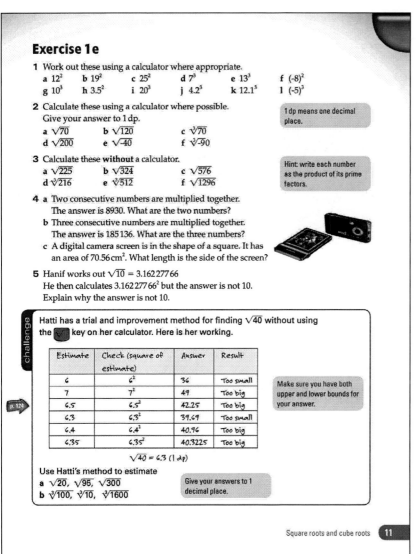

Exercise 1e

1 Work out these using a calculator where appropriate.
   a 12^2 b 19^2 c 25^2 d 7^3 e 13^3 f $(-8)^2$
   g 10^3 h 3.5^2 i 20^3 j 4.2^3 k 12.1^3 l $(-5)^3$

2 Calculate these using a calculator where possible.
  Give your answer to 1 dp.

> 1 dp means one decimal place.

   a $\sqrt{70}$ b $\sqrt{120}$ c $\sqrt[3]{70}$
   d $\sqrt{200}$ e $\sqrt{-40}$ f $\sqrt[3]{-90}$

3 Calculate these **without** a calculator.

> Hint: write each number as the product of its prime factors.

   a $\sqrt{225}$ b $\sqrt{324}$ c $\sqrt{576}$
   d $\sqrt[3]{216}$ e $\sqrt[3]{512}$ f $\sqrt{1296}$

4 a Two consecutive numbers are multiplied together.
    The answer is 8930. What are the two numbers?
   b Three consecutive numbers are multiplied together.
    The answer is 185 136. What are the three numbers?
   c A digital camera screen is in the shape of a square. It has
    an area of 70.56 cm². What length is the side of the screen?

5 Hanif works out $\sqrt{10} = 3.162\,277\,66$
  He then calculates $3.162\,277\,66^2$ but the answer is not 10.
  Explain why the answer is not 10.

challenge

Hatti has a trial and improvement method for finding $\sqrt{40}$ without using the ■ key on her calculator. Here is her working.

Estimate	Check (square of estimate)	Answer	Result
6	6^2	36	Too small
7	7^2	49	Too big
6.5	6.5^2	42.25	Too big
6.3	6.3^2	39.69	Too small
6.4	6.4^2	40.96	Too big
6.35	6.35^2	40.3225	Too big

> Make sure you have both upper and lower bounds for your answer.

$\sqrt{40} = 6.3$ (1 dp)

Use Hatti's method to estimate
  a $\sqrt{20}$, $\sqrt{95}$, $\sqrt{300}$
  b $\sqrt[3]{100}$, $\sqrt[3]{10}$, $\sqrt[3]{1600}$

> Give your answers to 1 decimal place.

Square roots and cube roots   **11**

Extension

A large cube is made from many smaller cubes. How many smaller cubes are on each face if the large cube contains 4913 smaller cubes? (Answer 17² 5 289). Allow a calculator to be used (IE, SM) (1.1).

Exercise 1e commentary

All questions (1.3)

Question 1 – Encourage students to use the proper functions on their calculators rather than repeated multiplication.

Question 2 – Be aware than some calculators do not have a ▣ key.

Question 3 – Use the number 36 to help explain how the method works.

Question 4 – Apply roots to practical problems. Compare the product of two consecutive numbers with the square root of the product. What do you notice? (1.4)

Question 5 – Ask students 'what do you think calculators do if the answer has more digits than can be displayed?' (1.5)

Investigation – Encourage an organised approach and the writing down of the trials. Why do you need to test to 2 dp when only looking for the solution to 1 dp?

Links

Bring in some sheets of A3, A4 and A5 paper and other ISO sizes if available. Ask the class to measure the paper and calculate the ratio of the length to the width for each size. The ratio is $\sqrt{2}$: 1 or 1.4142 : 1 in all cases. Now fold a sheet of A4 in half and compare with a sheet of A5. (same size). ISO paper sizes are designed so that A0 has an area of one square meter but with a length to width ratio of $\sqrt{2}$: 1. When a sheet of A0 is cut in half, it makes two smaller sheets size A1, each with a length to width ratio of $\sqrt{2}$: 1. There is a chart illustrating ISO paper sizes at http://en.wikipedia.org/wiki/Image:A_size_illustration.svg (EP)

- Recognise the equivalence of 0.1, 1/10 and 10^{-1} (L5)
- Know and use the index laws for multiplication and division of positive integer powers (L6)

Useful resources
Calculator
Multi-link cubes

Starter – Square calculations!

Ask students questions involving square numbers up to 144. For example,

Two square numbers that have a difference of 27? (36, 9)
Three square numbers that have a total of 101? (1, 36, 64)
Two square numbers with a product of 441? (9, 81)
Sum of first five square numbers? (55)

Teaching notes

Ask students why we need indices. Establish that they are a useful short hand for repeated multiplication and a neat way of writing large numbers, for example, 100 trillion is 10^{14}. Introduce the use of the power button, giving its different appearance on various calculators.

Investigate the patterns in the powers of 10 sequence in the student book. What is the meaning of the zero and negative powers. Challenge students to produce a similar list using a different base; include zero and negative powers (CT).

Sometimes we don't want to calculate an answer exactly, but would rather write it as a power. For example, $3^2 \times 3^3 = 243$, but 3^5 gives the same answer and is easier to work out. Ask students how this can be done – adding the indices. Establish that you are multiplying 3, but the number of 3s that are being multiplied is $3 + 2$ so 5. Note, avoid saying 'the number of times you are multiplying 3 is 5, since the meaning of *times* is ambiguous' Illustrate as $3^3 \times 3^2 = 3 \times 3 \times 3 \times 3 \times 3 = 3^5$

Construct a similar example for division and show that the indices subtract because you are cancelling a common factor from the numerator and denominator (1.4).

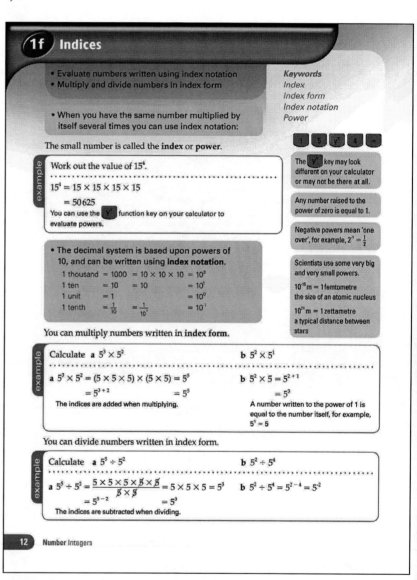

Plenary

If you put 1 penny on the first square of a chess board and then 2p on the next, 4p on the next, *etc.*, how much money would you put on the last square? Allow students to exhaust themselves (with or without a calculator) before suggesting the use of indices to express the solution. (2^{63} p, about ten million trillion pence, or £14 million for everyone on Earth!) What is this exactly in pounds? (£2^{61}/25) (CT) (1.2).

Simplification

Students without a scientific calculator will find need to use repeated multiplication for questions **1** to **5**. Leaving out question **1e**, **h**, **i**. To improve understanding of the ÷ rule for indices, show students how it is related to simplifying fractions.

All questions (1.3)

Question 1 – Encourage the use of the 'power' function on a calculator. Do any of the results from this question surprise you? Parts **e**, **h**, **i**? Why are the answers 1, 1, 0.01?

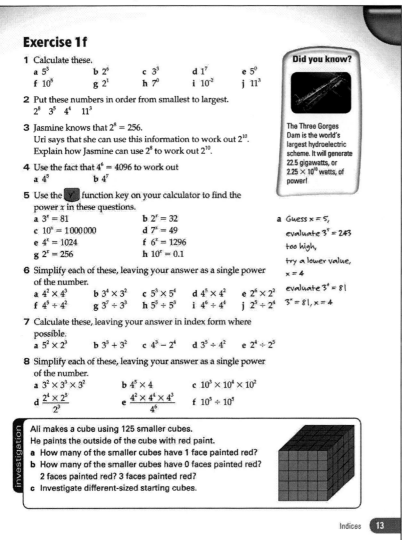

Exercise 1f

1 Calculate these.

  a 5^3 **b** 2^6 **c** 3^3 **d** 1^7 **e** 5^0

  f 10^5 **g** 2^1 **h** 7^0 **i** 10^{-2} **j** 11^3

2 Put these numbers in order from smallest to largest.

  2^8 3^5 4^4 11^3

3 Jasmine knows that $2^8 = 256$.
Uri says that she can use this information to work out 2^{10}.
Explain how Jasmine can use 2^8 to work out 2^{10}.

4 Use the fact that $4^6 = 4096$ to work out

  a 4^8 **b** 4^7

5 Use the ☐ function key on your calculator to find the power x in these questions.

  a $3^x = 81$ **b** $2^x = 32$

  c $10^x = 1\,000\,000$ **d** $7^x = 49$

  e $4^x = 1024$ **f** $6^x = 1296$

  g $2^x = 256$ **h** $10^x = 0.1$

6 Simplify each of these, leaving your answer as a single power of the number.

  a $4^2 \times 4^3$ **b** $3^4 \times 3^2$ **c** $5^3 \times 5^4$ **d** $4^5 \times 4^2$ **e** $2^6 \times 2^2$

  f $4^5 \div 4^2$ **g** $3^7 \div 3^3$ **h** $5^5 \div 5^3$ **i** $4^6 \div 4^4$ **j** $2^5 \div 2^4$

7 Calculate these, leaving your answer in index form where possible.

  a $5^2 \times 2^3$ **b** $3^3 + 3^2$ **c** $4^3 - 2^4$ **d** $3^5 \div 4^2$ **e** $2^4 \div 2^5$

8 Simplify each of these, leaving your answer as a single power of the number.

  a $3^2 \times 3^3 \times 3^2$ **b** $4^5 \times 4$ **c** $10^3 \times 10^4 \times 10^2$

  d $\dfrac{2^4 \times 2^5}{2^3}$ **e** $\dfrac{4^2 \times 4^4 \times 4^3}{4^6}$ **f** $10^3 \div 10^5$

> **investigation**
>
> Ali makes a cube using 125 smaller cubes.
> He paints the outside of the cube with red paint.
> **a** How many of the smaller cubes have 1 face painted red?
> **b** How many of the smaller cubes have 0 faces painted red?
>   2 faces painted red? 3 faces painted red?
> **c** Investigate different-sized starting cubes.

Did you know?

The Three Gorges Dam is the world's largest hydroelectric scheme. It will generate 22.5 gigawatts, or 2.25×10^{10} watts, of power!

a Guess $x = 5$,
evaluate $3^5 = 243$
too high,
try a lower value,
$x = 4$
evaluate $3^4 = 81$
$3^x = 81$, $x = 4$

Indices **13**

Extension

There is a special button on a scientific calculator that can help solve problems like question **5**. It is the 'log' button. See if students can see how to use it to find 'x'. For example, part **a** $3^x = 81$. Already found $x = 4$ by trial and improvement. How can 'log' help? Log 81 = 1.9084….. log 3 = 0.4771…. How can the answer '4' be made from these? (IE)

Exercise 1f commentary

Question 2 – Ask why some students might get this question wrong. Could they put the base numbers or indices in size order?

Question 3 and **4** – What is meant by 2^{10} and 2^8 or 4^5, 4^7 and 4^6?

Question 5 – Encourage students to use the power button and not repeated multiplication. Part **h** involving a negative power may provoke further discussion.

Question 6 – Challenge students to explain why you add and subtract the indices (EP) (1.2).

Question 7 – Emphasise that the same base is needed to use the indices rules. Encourage students to check that this is true. For example, $5^2 \times 2^3 = 25 \times 8 = 200$ but $\neq 10^5$.

Question 8 – What happens when no index is written? For example, 4 means 4^1. Can you have negative indices? See part **f**.

Investigation – Allow students to make errors in the 125 cube, but improve their solution by looking at the 27 and 64 cube problems and trying to spot a pattern in the results. Multi-link cubes would be useful in helping to visualise the problem (SM, RL) (1.2).

Links

The traditional nursery rhyme below is a riddle that can be investigated using indices.

As I was going to St. Ives (1)
I met a man with 7 wives
Each wife had 7 sacks
Each sack had 7 cats
Each cat had 7 kits
Kits, cats, sacks, wives
How many were going to St. Ives?
$\left(1 + 1 + 7 + 7^2 + 7^3 + 7^4 = 2802\right)$

Of course the answer to the riddle is actually 1 as everyone else is on their way back!

1a

1 Put these numbers in order from smallest to largest.

a -0.5 -3 2 0.5 -2

b -2.5 -3.5 -4.5 -1.5 -0.5

c -4.5 -4.6 -5 -5.2 3

2 Calculate

a $5 + -10$ b $-11 + -13$ c $-6 - -18$ d $-5 - -12$

e $-17 + -13$ f $13 + -19$ g $-24 + -23$ h $-35 - -38$

i $48 - -52$ j $-37 + -35.5$ k $-7 - 8 - -9$ l $-7 - -8 - -9$

3 Calculate

a 7×-9 b -8×9 c -11×-7 d -13×-9

e -12×15 f 17×-15 g -18×13 h -19×-9

i -15×-23 j -21×19 k $-150 \div -6$ l $-231 \div 7$

m $-216 \div -8$ n $-306 \div -9$ o $372 \div -12$ p $-345 \div -15$

1b

4 Write all the factors of

a 200 b 288 c 289 d 300 e 440 f 256

g 500 h 639 i 777 j 999 k 1000 l 2304

5 Use the divisibility tests to see which of these numbers are prime.
In each case explain your answer.

a 401 b 413 c 419 d 437 e 451 f 479

1c

6 Write each of these numbers as the product of its prime factors.

a 22 b 46 c 84 d 58 e 132 f 104

g 185 h 425 i 205 j 181 k 366 l 309

m 489 n 585 o 1089 p 2529 q 1305 r 3025

7 Use prime factors to list all the factors of these numbers.

a 60 b 96 c 110 d 165 e 430 f 600

g 950 h 1225 i 2116 j 1764 k 3136 l 3969

1d

8 Find the HCF and LCM of

a 100 and 120 b 144 and 192 c 210 and 240 d 336 and 378

e 315 and 495 f 616 and 728 g 40, 56 and 72 h 48, 80 and 176

9 Cancel down each of these fractions into its simplest form.

You can use the HCF.

a $\frac{35}{49}$ **b** $\frac{100}{120}$ **c** $\frac{144}{192}$ **d** $\frac{210}{240}$ **e** $\frac{105}{175}$

f $\frac{234}{273}$ **g** $\frac{210}{378}$ **h** $\frac{96}{528}$ **i** $\frac{477}{583}$ **j** $\frac{198}{858}$

10 Work out these, leaving your answer as a fraction in its simplest form.

a $\frac{6}{7} - \frac{3}{14}$ **b** $\frac{7}{16} + \frac{1}{4}$ **c** $\frac{3}{5} + \frac{1}{10}$ **d** $\frac{6}{13} + \frac{12}{39}$

e $\frac{13}{15} - \frac{5}{6}$ **f** $\frac{7}{24} + \frac{17}{30}$ **g** $\frac{8}{15} + \frac{7}{40}$ **h** $\frac{7}{30} + \frac{11}{25}$

11 Calculate these using a calculator. Give your answers to 1 dp.

a $\sqrt{11}$ **b** $\sqrt{111}$ **c** $\sqrt[3]{111}$ **d** $\sqrt[3]{-1111}$ **e** $\sqrt{-9}$ **f** $\sqrt[3]{91}$

12 **a** Three consecutive numbers are multiplied together. The result is -1716.
What are the three numbers?

b Two consecutive numbers are multiplied together. The result is 1806.
Give the two possible pairs of consecutive numbers.

13 Calculate these without a calculator.

Try writing each number as the product of its prime factors.

a $\sqrt{256}$ **b** $\sqrt{441}$ **c** $\sqrt{729}$
d $\sqrt[3]{1728}$ **e** $\sqrt[3]{3375}$ **f** $\sqrt{2025}$

14 Use the y^x function key on your calculator to find the power x in these questions.

a $3^x = 2187$ **b** $2^x = 512$ **c** $4^x = 65\,536$ **d** $5^x = 15\,625$

e $10^x = 1$ **f** $7^x = 16\,807$ **g** $4^x = 1$ **h** $6^x = 7776$

i $2^x = 16$ **j** $2^x = 0.5$

15 Simplify each of these, leaving your answer as a single power of the number.

a $2^3 \times 2^4$ **b** $7^4 \times 7^8$ **c** $4^3 \times 4^9$ **d** $3^5 \times 3^0$ **e** $6^5 \times 6^5$

f $2^5 \div 2^3$ **g** $2^7 \div 2^7$ **h** $4^5 \div 4^4$ **i** $3^6 \div 3$ **j** $10^5 \div 10^6$

16 Calculate these, leaving your answer in index form where possible.

a $3^4 \times 4^3$ **b** $2^3 + 4^2$ **c** $5^3 - 2^4$ **d** $4^5 \div 2^2$ **e** $3^2 \times 3^2$

17 Simplify each of these, leaving your answer as a single power of the number.

a $5^3 \times 5^3 \times 5^3$ **b** $3^5 \times 3^5 \times 3^5$ **c** $10^4 \times 10^4 \times 10^4$

d $(2^4)^3$ **e** $(5^3)^3$ **f** $8^9 \div 8^9$

g $\dfrac{3^4 \times 3^3}{3^2}$ **h** $\dfrac{2^2 \times 2^4 \times 2^6}{2^8}$ **i** $10^3 \div 10^3$

1 Summary

Assessment criteria

- Recognise and describe number relationships including multiple, factor and square   Level 4
- Order negative numbers in context   Level 5
- Solve simple problems involving ordering, adding, subtracting negative numbers in context   Level 5
- Reduce a fraction to its simplest form by cancelling common factors   Level 5
- Add and subtract fractions by writing them with a common denominator   Level 6

Question commentary

Example	
The example illustrates a typical problem about indices. Emphasise that the index tells you how many times to multiply the base by itself. In part **b**, emphasise that 8^5 is $8^4 \times 8$ by asking students to write out 8^4 and 8^5 as $8 \times 8 \times 8 \times 8$ and $8 \times 8 \times 8 \times 8 \times 8$. Ask questions such as "How would you write 8 in index form?"	**a** $2^5 = 2 \times 2 \times 2 \times 2 \times 2$ $\quad = 32$ $5^2 = 5 \times 5 = 25$ **b** $8^5 = 8 \times 8^4$ $\quad = 8 \times 4096$ $\quad = 32\,768$

Past question	
The question asks students to complete a table showing sums and products of signed integers. To complete the sum column, it may help some students to sketch a number line. When completing the product column, encourage students to calculate the answer as if both numbers are positive, and then work out what the sign of the product should be. Ask probing questions such as "Does addition always make numbers bigger?" and "Does subtraction always make numbers smaller?"	**Answer** **Level 6** **2**

Level 6

2

3	6	9	18
5	-3	2	-15
-8	3	-5	-24

Development and links

The work on LCM and HCF is developed in Chapter 4 when students add, subtract and simplify further fractions. Squares and cubes are used in work on area in Chapter 2 and volume in

Chapter 14 and students will find further square and cube roots in Chapter 10. Index notation and its use in algebra is developed further in Chapter 5 where students will also multiply a negative term over a bracket and use the HCF to factorise expressions.

Lowest common factors and highest common multiples are used in fraction work and in algebra to factorise equations and formulae. This has links with work with scientific formulae in science and multiples of fractional quantities in food technology and resistant materials. Indices are also important in science when dealing with units. Students will work with negative numbers in science and geography when working with concepts such as temperature, electric charge and height above or below sea level.

Objectives

- Solve problems involving measurements in a variety of contexts... **5**
- Know the definition of a circle and the names of its parts **5**
- Know and use the formulae for the circumference and area of a circle.. **6**

Introduction

The focus of this chapter is on measurement and finding areas of shapes. The chapter begins by reviewing knowledge of metric units of measurement, reading and interpreting scales on measuring instruments and rough metric equivalents of imperial units of length, mass and capacity. Students then use formulae to find areas of rectangles, triangles, parallelograms and trapeziums. The topic extends to finding the circumference and area of a circle.

The student book discusses the importance of using correct units when measuring distances. Students will often forget to give units with an answer, especially when giving the results of calculations. It should be emphasised that without units, a measurement is ambiguous and incomplete. There are many historical systems of units, but the SI (Systeme International d'Unites) of metric units is now recognised and used in most countries of the World. There is more information about systems of measurement at http://en.wikipedia.org/wiki/Units_of_measurement

Fast-track

2d

Level

MPA

1.1	2a, b, c, d, e
1.2	2a, e, f
1.3	2a, b, c, d, e, f
1.4	2b, c, d, e, f
1.5	2a, b, c

PLTS

IE	2a, b, c, d, e, f
CT	2a, c, d, e, f
RL	2c, d, e, f
TW	2a, b, e, f
SM	2c, d
EP	2a, b, c, e, f

Extra Resources

2   Start of chapter presentation

2b Starter: Metric unit matching

2c Animation: Areas

2d Worked solution: Q1a

2d Consolidation sheet

2e Animation: Circumference of a circle

2e Worked solution: Q3a

2e Consolidation sheet

2f Animation: Area of a circle

2f Consolidation sheet

Assessment: chapter 2

- Choose and use units of measurement to measure, estimate, calculate and solve problems in a range of contexts (L5)
- Convert one metric unit to another (L5)
- Solve problems involving measurements in a variety of contexts (L5)

Useful resources
250 ml and 1 litre bottle filled.

Starter – Powers of ten

Write 10.72 on the board.
Ask students what answer you will get if you multiply the number by 10^3, 10^2, 10^4.
Repeat with different start numbers.
Can be extended by using division.

Teaching notes

Ask students to suggest a number of different measures, which are metric and which are imperial? Are any measurements neither? (time). Students could fill in a list of metric measures. How many were known?

When converting between measures, place value can speed up the process. Examine what each digit represents in a measurement. For example, 2.304 km in metres. An analogy could be made with pounds and pence (CT) (1.1).

An alternative approach is to use multiplication and division by a power of ten. Look at the examples in the student book, challenge students to explain how to tell which of multiplication or division is needed (EP) (1.5).

Some students may rely on the answer being of the correct order of magnitude. Encourage students to consider if the answer is sensible.

Estimation of the mass of everyday objects can be difficult. For small objects students can be encouraged to relate mass to water. Pass round a litre bottle and equate this to 1 kg or 1000 g. For larger objects the mass of a student is helpful. Average for a year 8 student is around 40 to 50 kg.

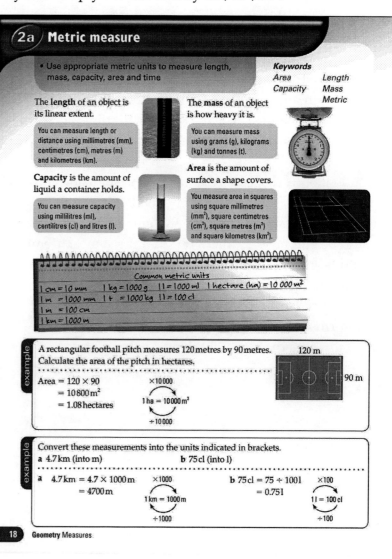

Plenary

Match the English coins to their corresponding approximate masses in grams listed here is ascending order.

3.3, 3.6, 5.0, 6.5, 7.1, 8.0, 9.5, 12.0

(5p, 1p, 20p, 10p, 2p, 50p, £1, £2 respectively)

Slot machines use a coins weight to help identify it (EP) (1.2).

Simplification

Students who find it difficult to appreciate the varying values of measures depending on place value, may find it useful to use equivalence to help further their understanding. For example, 0.2 kg = how many grams? Begin with 1 kg = 1000 g. Divide by 10 → 0.1 kg = 100 g.

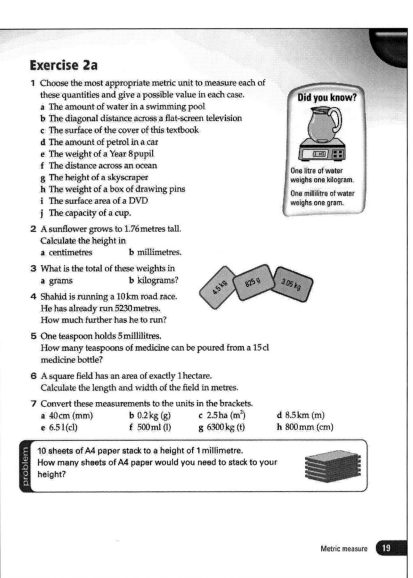

Exercise 2a

1 Choose the most appropriate metric unit to measure each of these quantities and give a possible value in each case.
  a The amount of water in a swimming pool
  b The diagonal distance across a flat-screen television
  c The surface of the cover of this textbook
  d The amount of petrol in a car
  e The weight of a Year 8 pupil
  f The distance across an ocean
  g The height of a skyscraper
  h The weight of a box of drawing pins
  i The surface area of a DVD
  j The capacity of a cup.

Did you know?

One litre of water weighs one kilogram.

One millilitre of water weighs one gram.

2 A sunflower grows to 1.76 metres tall. Calculate the height in
  a centimetres   b millimetres.

3 What is the total of these weights in
  a grams   b kilograms?

4.5 kg   825 g   3.05 kg

4 Shahid is running a 10 km road race. He has already run 5230 metres. How much further has he to run?

5 One teaspoon holds 5 millilitres. How many teaspoons of medicine can be poured from a 15 cl medicine bottle?

6 A square field has an area of exactly 1 hectare. Calculate the length and width of the field in metres.

7 Convert these measurements to the units in the brackets.
  a 40 cm (mm)   b 0.2 kg (g)   c 2.5 ha (m²)   d 8.5 km (m)
  e 6.5 l (cl)   f 500 ml (l)   g 6300 kg (t)   h 800 mm (cm)

problem 10 sheets of A4 paper stack to a height of 1 millimetre. How many sheets of A4 paper would you need to stack to your height?

Metric measure **19**

Extension

Investigate the use of prefixes in measurements. What examples can pupils find? For example mega tonne bomb or gigabytes of computer memory (IE). Some commonly used prefixes are

kilo	10^3	thousands	milli	10^{-3}	thousandths
Mega	10^6	millions	micro	10^{-6}	millionths
Giga	10^9	billions	nano	10^{-9}	billionths
Terra	10^{12}	trillions	pico	10^{-12}	trillionths

Exercise 2a commentary

All questions (1.1)

Question 1 – This question could be a good way to promote class debate. A homework could be set for pupils to investigate how close their estimates are (1.2).

Questions 2 to 5 – Ask students what each digit represents, emphasise the importance of place value (1.3).

Question 6 – Encourage students to sketch a hectare to help find the side lengths (1.3).

Question 7 – Again ask students what each digit means to build appreciation of the importance of place value (1.3).

Problem – Encourage students to give an estimate at the outset. What method will be used for measuring height? How accurately can a person's height be measured? How could you accurately measure the width of one sheet of paper? (1.2)

Assessment Criteria – SSM, level 5: solve problems involving the conversion of units and make sensible estimates of a range of measures in relation to everyday situations.

Links

Measurement of length was originally based on the human body. The ancient Egyptians used a unit called a cubit, which was the length of an arm from the elbow to the fingertips. As everybody's arm was a different length, the Egyptians developed the standard Royal cubit and preserved this length as a black granite rod. Other measuring sticks were made the same length as this rod. There is a picture of a cubit rod at http://www.globalegyptianmuseum.org/detail.aspx?id=4424 (TW, EP) (1.1)

2b Imperial Measure

- Know rough metric equivalents of imperial measures in common use, such as miles, pounds (lb) and pints (L5)
- Read and interpret scales on a range of measuring instruments (L5)

Useful resources
Calculator
Packet of biscuits

Starter – Metric pairs

Write the following measurements on the board:

0.01 g, 0.1 g, 0.1 kg, 1 g, 1 kg, 1t, 10 mg, 10 g, 100 mg, 100 g, 1000 mg, 1000 g, 1000 kg, 10 000 mg.

Ask students to find the equivalent pairs.

Can be extended by asking students to make their own equivalent pairs for capacity or length.

Teaching notes

Some rhymes maybe useful here:-

A litre of water's a pint and three quarters.

Two and a quarter pounds of jam is round about a kilogram.

A meter measures three foot three it's longer than a yard you see.

An unusual way to remember that 5 miles ≈ 8 km is as follows.

- Find a student in the class who lives about 5 miles from school, this is best done using an online map for the whole class to see.
- Send that student outside the classroom and ask them to act out something that they do at home. For example, watching TV, cutting the grass.
- Give every member of the remaining class a biscuit and ask them to scratch 'km' onto their biscuit.
- Explain that the whole class is now going to 'walk' five miles to the student's house. Take the class to where the student is pretending to be at home.
- When you get there ask the students 'what have they done so far?' 'walked 5 miles!'
- Now ask them all to eat their biscuits. Now ask 'what have they done so far?' Establish that they have all **'Walked 5 miles and ate (8) km'**

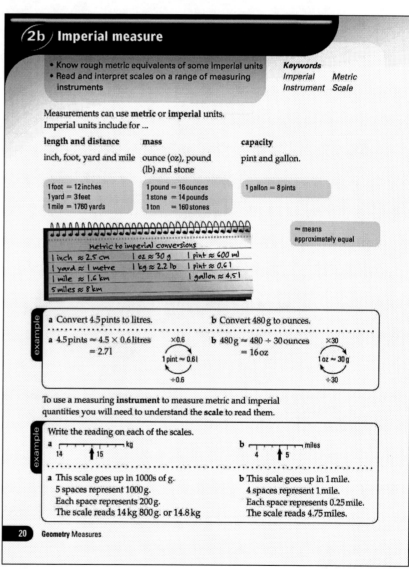

Plenary

Using a list of measure conversions with blanks, ask students to fill in as many gaps as they can based on the lesson. Ask students if they have any particular ways of recalling the measures now. Many students maybe able to draw on outside experiences, for example, the kitchen, athletics, fishing, where they maybe using metric and imperial measures (EP) (1.5).

Simplification

Students who find it difficult to decide whether multiplication or division is appropriate may find it easier to use a proportional method. For example, change 70 miles into km.

$$\times 70 \begin{array}{c} 1 \text{ mile } \approx 1.6 \text{ km} \\ \downarrow \qquad \downarrow \\ 70 \text{ miles} \approx 112 \text{ km} \end{array} \times 70$$

All questions (1.3)

Question 1 – Encourage students to show their method of calculation. Are any answers approximations?

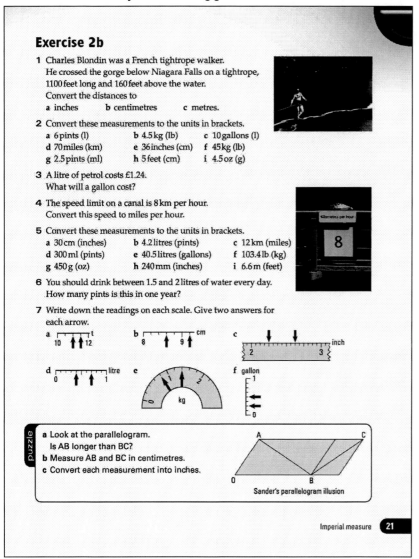

Exercise 2b

1 Charles Blondin was a French tightrope walker. He crossed the gorge below Niagara Falls on a tightrope, 1100 feet long and 160 feet above the water. Convert the distances to
   a inches   b centimetres   c metres.

2 Convert these measurements to the units in brackets.
   a 6 pints (l)   b 4.5 kg (lb)   c 10 gallons (l)
   d 70 miles (km)   e 36 inches (cm)   f 45 kg (lb)
   g 2.5 pints (ml)   h 5 feet (cm)   i 4.5 oz (g)

3 A litre of petrol costs £1.24. What will a gallon cost?

4 The speed limit on a canal is 8 km per hour. Convert this speed to miles per hour.

5 Convert these measurements to the units in brackets.
   a 30 cm (inches)   b 4.2 litres (pints)   c 12 km (miles)
   d 300 ml (pints)   e 40.5 litres (gallons) f 103.4 lb (kg)
   g 450 g (oz)   h 240 mm (inches)   i 6.6 m (feet)

6 You should drink between 1.5 and 2 litres of water every day. How many pints is this in one year?

7 Write down the readings on each scale. Give two answers for each arrow.
   a t   b cm   c inch   d litre   e kg   f gallon

puzzle
   a Look at the parallelogram. Is AB longer than BC?
   b Measure AB and BC in centimetres.
   c Convert each measurement into inches.

Sander's parallelogram illusion

Imperial measure   21

Extension

Most drivers used to measure a car's economy by stating the number of miles to the gallon that could be achieved. Today many people still continue to use this, but in the future people may well state the number of km to the litre. How would you covert miles/gallon to km/litre? Multiply by approximately 0.35 (0.354006…) Best progress maybe made by students constructing their own examples of a car's economy (IE) (1.4).

Exercise 2b commentary

Question 2 – Discourage the use of a calculator when a mental method is possible. Remind students to include units in their answers.

Question 3 – Petrol used to be sold in gallons; the price about 30 years ago was under £1 a gallon. By what factor has the price increased?

Question 4 – Which is easiest to use: 1 mile ≈ 1.6 km, 1 km ≈ $\frac{5}{8}$ mile, 5 miles ≈ 8 km ?

Question 5 – Which one of the measurements given in the question is not a common way of expressing an amount? Part **f**. Why?

Question 6 – Encourage a use of an estimate, for example, $2 \times 350 = 700$ litres. Use 1 litre ≈ 2 pints.

Question 7 – The two answers could be a combination of metric and imperial (1,1).

Puzzle – Encourage students to give an instinctive answer before they measure them. The class could be asked to vote on which is longest. Once it is established that they are in fact the same length, ask why it is that BC appears shorter.

Assessment Criteria – SSM, level 5: read and interpret scales on a range of measuring instruments, explaining what each labelled division represents.

Links

The United States has its own system of weights and measures which is largely similar to the imperial system. Yards, feet, inches and pounds are all in everyday use, however, the US pint and gallon are both smaller than the imperial pint and gallon. For more information see http://home.clara.net/brianp/usa.html or http://en.wikipedia.org/wiki/ Imperial_units (TW, EP)

- Calculate the area and perimeter of shapes made from rectangles (L5)
- Derive and use the formula for the area of a triangle (L6)

Useful resources
Calculator
Square grid paper

Starter – Estimation

Draw lines on the board.

Ask students to estimate the length of the lines in cm.

Ask how much this would be in inches.

Use a scoring system for the estimations, for example, within 10% score 3 points, within 20% score 1 point. Bonus points for correct metric to imperial conversion.

Teaching notes

What is meant by area? Do not accept answers that just relate to 'the space inside'. Draw a rectangle with dimensions 3 by 4. The area is 12. But 12 what? Establish that area is just '*the number of squares inside a shape*'. Once the individual squares are drawn in place ask why do we multiply the two side lengths of the rectangle together? Invite answers that explain the way that multiplication totals up the rows by the columns, that is, a quick way to add up all the squares (1.5).

What strategies could be used with compound shapes? Sketch a few examples made from rectangles? Is there more than one way to subdivide a shape? Does it matter how you cut the shape up? (RL)

Cut your original rectangle in half through the diagonal. What is the area of the resulting triangle? Establish that this area is exactly half of the rectangle around it. How can the area of any triangle be found? Look at the way in which a rectangle around the triangle always gives twice the area of the triangle. Introduce the formula area

$$= \frac{\text{base} \times \text{perpendicular height}}{2}$$

(CT) (1.4)

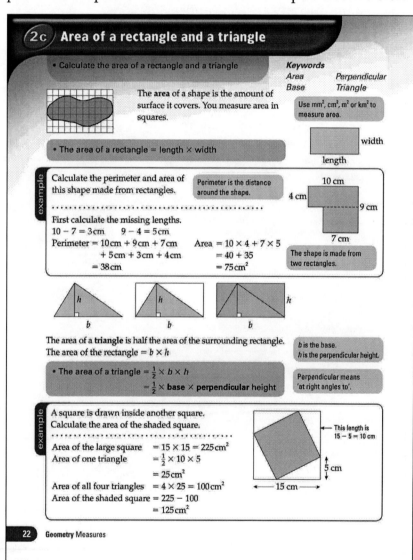

Plenary

Can the students write a formula for the side length given the area and one of the side lengths. Will the formula be different for a rectangle and a right angled triangle? What about a square?

Simplification

Students could use pre-printed copies of questions, some of which are draw full size on cm square grids. Students should feel free to annotate the drawings.

All questions (1.3)

Question 1 – Cutting up the shapes is likely to be the best approach. Some students may prefer to draw a bounding rectangle and subtract to find the area. Some students will incorrectly find the perimeter unless they label every edge.

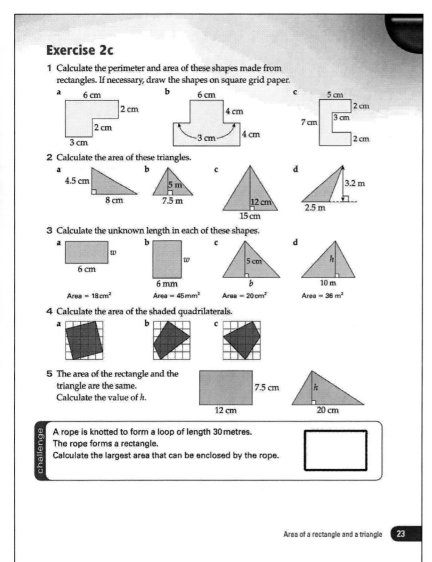

Extension

A regular hexagon has a perimeter of 60 cm. Why is it difficult to find the area? The hint that six congruent equilateral triangles make a regular hexagon. Encourage students to sketch the shape and discover what lengths they can. The problem is that, although two lengths are known, they are not perpendicular. Encourage a student to explain to others what information can be found and what information is still missing (EP) (1.5).

Exercise 2c commentary

Question 2 – Ask students why the perpendicular height has to be given. Ensure units are properly given.

Question 3 – How can you make sure your answer is correct? Discuss checking methods.

Question 4 – Why will counting squares be a poor method? Before commencing the question challenge students to put the areas in order of size. Students to check if they are correct.

Question 5 – What are the advantages/disadvantages of a trial and improvement method? (1.5) Encourage students to check their final solution.

Challenge – An isoperimetric problem. Encourage systematically listing possible lengths, widths and calculated areas. The function $y = x(15 - x)$ gives the area (y) for given widths (x). Plotting a few values graphically could establish the shape of the graph. ($7.5^2 = 56.25$ m²) (IE, SM) (1.1, 1.2)

Assessment Criteria – SSM, level 5: understand and use the formula for the area of a rectangle and distinguish area from perimeter. SSM, level 6: deduce and use the formula for the area of a triangle.

Links

An area of 10 000 m² is called a hectare and is often used to measure land areas. Measure or estimate the size of the classroom. What fraction is this of a hectare? Estimate how many hectares the school field or other local open space covers. The O₂ complex in Greenwich has a ground area of over 80 000m². How many hectares is this? There is information on the O₂ at, http://en.wikipedia.org/wiki/The_O2 (EP).

- Derive and use the formulae for the area of a parallelogram and trapezium

Useful resources

(L6)

Starter – Calculating height

Give the area and base of triangles and ask students for the heights, for example,

Area = 18 cm² and base = 3 cm (12 cm)
Area = 24 cm² and base = 6 cm (8 cm)
Area = 25 cm² and base = 10 cm (5 cm)

Can be extended by using numbers that will generate decimal heights.

Teaching notes

Remind students that area represents the number of squares inside a shape. Look at a parallelogram, base = 4, perpendicular height = 3. Why is it awkward to find the exact area? Show how the triangle at one end of the parallelogram can be moved to the other end to form a rectangle. What is the area of the rectangle? 4 × 3 = 12. Draw a general parallelogram and establish the formula for the area.
Area = *base × perpendicular height*

Draw a trapezium and ask students for suggestions for methods for finding the area. These may include breaking up the shape into two triangles and a rectangle. Why will this not work? Show how two identical trapeziums can fit together to form a parallelogram. How can the area of the parallelogram be found? Establish that the trapezium is just half of the area of the parallelogram. How is the base of the parallelogram made? From the sum of the two parallel sides of the trapezium. Establish the formula (CT), Area =

$$\frac{\text{sum of parallel sides} \times \text{perpendicular height}}{2}$$

This rhyme may aid remembering the formula

'Half the sum of the parallel sides, times the distance between them, that's how you calculate, the area of a trap-eee-zum'

sung to the tune of 'half a pound of tuppeny rice'

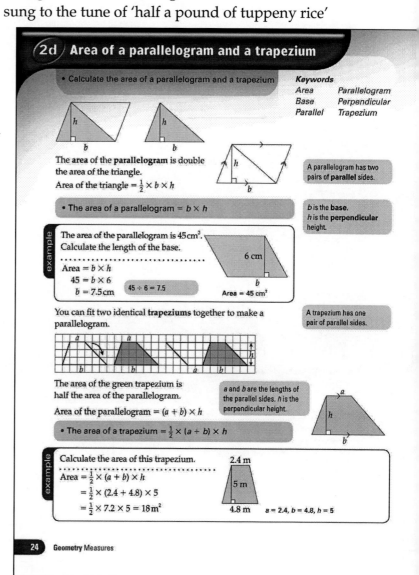

Plenary

Can a formula be constructed to find the area of a wall like the one in question **4**? Imagine that the width and overall height are always the same (*x*) and the shorter side height is different (*y*). You can split the area as a rectangle and a triangle or as two identical trapezia.

$$\text{Area} = xy + \frac{x(x - y)}{2} \quad \text{or} \quad = \frac{x(x + y)}{2} \quad (CT).$$

Simplification

Provide students with a print out of the exercise and encourage them to label the base, perpendicular height etc. before performing the calculations. Check that the student has correctly identified the required measurements before they begin using the formulae.

All the questions can be done without a calculator, but one could prove useful in checking the answers for question **3**.

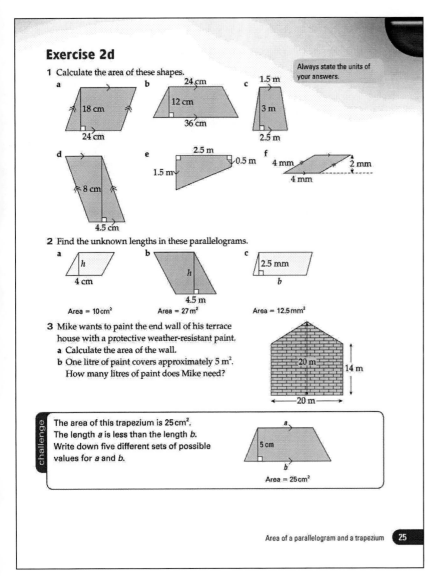

Extension

Challenge students to provide a formula for the area of a kite. Do you need to know all the side lengths or the diagonal lengths or a mixture? Formulae is (width × height) / 2 where the width and height are the lengths of the two diagonals. Students might adopt the method of a bounding rectangle or subdivide into smaller triangles (CT) (1.4).

Exercise 2d commentary

All questions (1.3)

Question 1 – Students need to be able to correctly identify a parallelogram and trapezium in any orientation. Encourage the procedure of (i) writing formula. (ii) substituting in values. (iii) working out answer.

Question 2 – Students should check their answer using their formulae for area (RL).

Question 3 – A sketch may help to avoid an error by correctly identifying the dimensions of the rectangle and triangle or two trapezia. Encourage students to split up the compound shape, however some students might alternatively draw a rectangle round the whole shape and subtract the area of two triangles.

Challenge – At first a trial and improvement method would be suitable. Examination of the formula with the area and height substituted in should lead to a discussion about the value of $a + b$ (=10). If you only allow integers then there are only four possible solutions. How many solutions are there all together? (SM, IE) (1.1)

Assessment Criteria –SSM, level 6, deduce and use the formula for the area of a parallelogram.

Links

The Trapezium cluster is a bright cluster of stars in the constellation of Orion discovered by Galileo in 1617. The four brightest stars form the shape of a trapezium. There is more information about the Trapezium cluster at http://en.wikipedia.org/wiki/Trapezium_cluster and at http://www.astropix.com/HTML/B_WINTER/TRAPEZ.HTM

- Know the definition of a circle and the names of its parts (L5)
- Know and use the formula for the circumference of a circle (L6)

Useful resources

Calculator
pi to 100 dp

Starter – Area bingo

Write a list of areas on the board, for example, 88, 12, 20, 36, 132, 54, 28, 24, 96, 45, 18, 49 cm²

Ask students to draw a 3 × 3 grid and enter nine areas from the list.

Give information such as:

The base of a triangle is 3 cm, the height is 8 cm.

The base of a parallelogram is 14 cm, the height is 3.5 cm.

The winner is the first student to cross out all their areas.

Teaching notes

Introduce the parts of a circle: radius, diameter, circumference and arc. What abbreviations do students think mathematicians use for the first three? (TW, EP)

There is a connection between the diameter and the circumference of a circle, the same connection for every circle. Give a set of examples and ask students to use a calculator to try to find the connection. (note that the circumferences have been rounded to 1 dp)

Diameter (cm)	10	5	1	3
Circumference (cm)	31.4	15.7	3.1	9.4

Agree the answer is multiplication by about 3.1 to 3.2; it is not possible to get an exact answer.

Introduce students to the symbol for Pi and examine its value to 9 dp. State the equation for finding the circumference: $C = \pi d$. The alternative formula involving radius could also be looked at.

Give examples of circumference calculations for a given diameter/radius, using $\pi = 3.14$. Emphasise the structure of the calculation

- Write formula
- Substitute in values
- Work out the answer

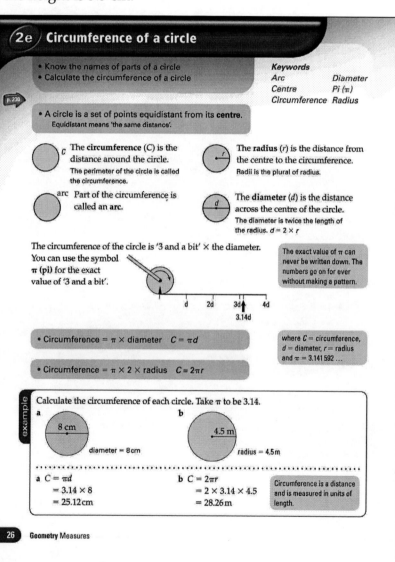

Plenary

Who in the class can memorise pi to the greatest number of decimal places? Display the value to 100 places (RL).

Simplification

Provide students with a table to help record their working. For example

Pi (3.14)	Diameter	Circumference (remember the units)
3.14	3 cm	3.14 × 3 = 9.42 cm

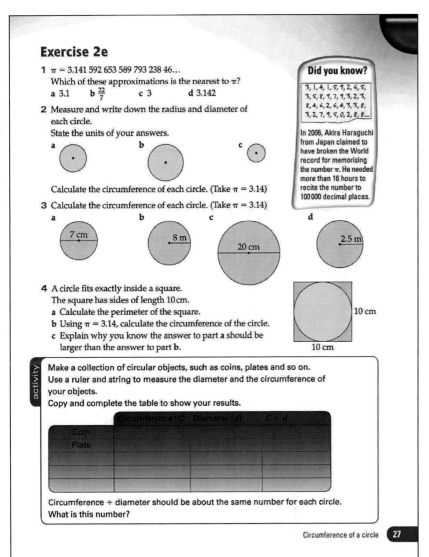

Exercise 2e

1 $\pi = 3.141\ 592\ 653\ 589\ 793\ 238\ 46...$
   Which of these approximations is the nearest to π?
   a 3.1   b $\frac{22}{7}$ c 3   d 3.142

2 Measure and write down the radius and diameter of each circle.
   State the units of your answers.
   a   b   c

   Calculate the circumference of each circle. (Take $\pi = 3.14$)

3 Calculate the circumference of each circle. (Take $\pi = 3.14$)
   a 7 cm   b 8 m   c 20 cm   d 2.5 m

4 A circle fits exactly inside a square.
   The square has sides of length 10 cm.
   a Calculate the perimeter of the square.
   b Using $\pi = 3.14$, calculate the circumference of the circle.
   c Explain why you know the answer to part **a** should be larger than the answer to part **b**.

   10 cm
   10 cm

Did you know?

3, 1, 4, 1, 5, 9, 2, 6, 5,
3, 5, 8, 9, 7, 9, 3, 2, 3,
8, 4, 6, 2, 6, 4, 3, 3, 8,
3, 2, 7, 9, 5, 0, 2, 8, 8...

In 2006, Akira Haraguchi from Japan claimed to have broken the World record for memorising the number π. He needed more than 16 hours to recite the number to 100 000 decimal places.

activity
Make a collection of circular objects, such as coins, plates and so on. Use a ruler and string to measure the diameter and the circumference of your objects.
Copy and complete the table to show your results.

	Circumference (C)	Diameter (d)	C ÷ d
Coin			
Plate			

Circumference ÷ diameter should be about the same number for each circle.
What is this number?

Circumference of a circle **27**

Extension

One way to calculate the value of pi is to using the Gregory-Liebnitz series. Calculate $\frac{4}{1}$ to get your first approximation, then calculate $\frac{4}{1} - \frac{4}{3}$ to get a better approximation. Next calculate $\frac{4}{1} - \frac{4}{3} + \frac{4}{5}$ to get a third and improved approximation. How far can you approximate pi to?
$\pi = \frac{4}{1} - \frac{4}{3} + \frac{4}{5} - \frac{4}{7} + \frac{4}{9} - \frac{4}{11}$ (convergence is very slow).
If this went of forever, would it give you the 'correct' value of pi? (Yes) (CT) (1.3)

Exercise 2e commentary

All questions (1.3)

Question 1 – Students may need reminding how to convert a fraction into a decimal using a calculator. Take every opportunity to reinforce the fact that the fraction line is also a dividing line.

Question 2 – When measuring the radius and diameter, one can be worked out from the other. If the centre dot were absent, which one can be measured more accurately? (diameter)

Question 3 – Encourage students to (i) write the formula, (ii) substitute in values, (iii) work out the answer. Note that the units vary.

Question 4 – An annotated diagram will help to connect the side length of the square with the diameter of the circle. Drawing a chord across a quadrant of the circle/diagonal of the square may help to answer part **c**. (1.1)

Activity – When finding a value for pi experimentally, why don't you always get the same answer? Why don't you get the exact value of pi? Do larger objects give a closer approximation? (IE) (1.2, 1.4)

Assessment Criteria – SSM, level 6: know and use the formula for the circumference of a circle.

Links

Stone circles can be found across the British Isles with the most famous example at Stonehenge in Wiltshire. The circles vary in size and are not always completely circular but they all date from about 3,000 BC to 1500 BC. Their exact purpose is unknown but there are often burial mounds nearby. There is a map showing all the stone circles in the UK at http://www.megalith.ukf.net/bigmap.htm

- Know the definition of a circle and the names of its parts (L5)
- Know and use the formula for the area of a circle (L6)

Useful resources
Calculator

Starter – Match up

Write the following measurements on the board:

Circumference: 60 cm, 176 cm, 113 cm, 88 cm, 22 cm, 25 cm

radius: 14 cm, 4 cm, 18 cm

diameter: 56 cm, 19 cm, 7 cm

Ask students to find the equivalent pairs.

Can be extended by changing some of the units.

Teaching notes

Introduce the parts of a circle: chord, segment and sector.

There is a connection between the radius and the area of a circle, the same connection for every circle. Give a set of examples and ask students to use a calculator to try to find the connection. (note that the areas have been rounded to 1 dp) You could hint that the value of radius^2 needs to be used. For example,

Radius (cm)	10	5	1	3
Area (cm^2)	314.2	78.5	3.1	28.3

Agree the answer is multiplication by π and radius^2. State the equation for finding the area: $A = \pi r^2$. Give examples of area calculations for a given radius/diameter, using π = 3.14. Emphasise the structure of the calculation

- Write formula
- Substitute in values
- Work out the answer

Point out the common error in calculating the area: multiplying π and *r* and then squaring that answer rather than just squaring the value of *r* (RL).

The **Did you know?** shows the obverse of a Field's medal – the mathematician's 'Nobel prize'.

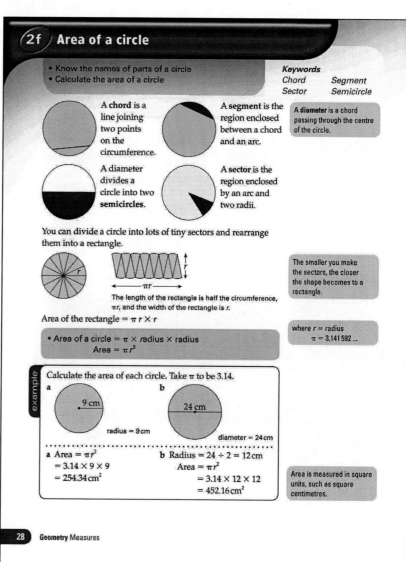

Plenary

A rhyme may help remember the formulae for area and circumference. It can include two diagrams or hand actions.

If a ring round the moon you see, use the formula πd.

If the hole needs to be repaired, use the formula πr².

An alternative plenary could ask the following question: is the perimeter of a semicircle half the perimeter of the whole circle? Investigate (1.2).

Simplification

Provide students with a table to help record their working. For example,

Pi (π)	Radius	Circumference (remember the units)
π	3 cm	$\pi \times 3^2 = 28.3 \text{ cm}^2$

Encourage the use of the $\boxed{\pi}$ key. All questions (1.3)

Question 1 – Reinforce the concept that area is just the number of squares of a specific size inside a shape. Why use a formula? Using a formula is just a progression that allows for a more accurate answer?

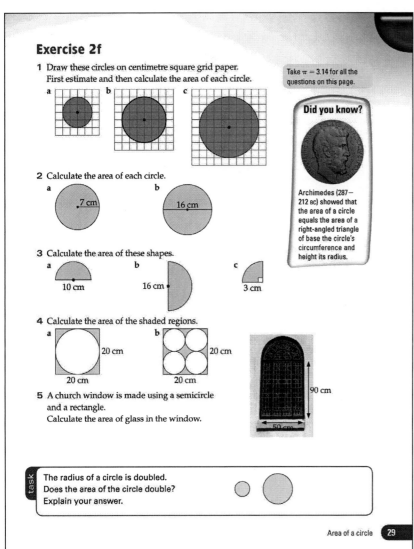

Extension

How can the circumference of a circle be calculated if only the area is know? Investigate. (CT) (1.2)

Exercise 2f commentary

Question 2 – Encourage students to use the three steps from the notes. The most common error is to calculate $(\pi \times r)^2$. Remind students of the rules of BIDMAS (RL).

Question 3 – Encourage students to sketch the whole circle. This may help reduce the confusion over the radius and diameter measure. Finding the area of the whole circle first is a good procedure.

Question 4 – Encourage the use of sketches and an orderly approach to setting out workings. When the area of one shape is found, a sketch of the shape it relates to could be drawn beside the answer (IE).

Question 5 – Some students will find it difficult to see the diameter as being equal to the width of the window. Ask students to label the length of every side they can.

Task – Students maybe surprised by this result. It can be reinforced by looking at the dimensions of a full sized snooker table (4.5 by 9 feet) and a half sized table. Compare the areas using diagrams to reinforce the fact that the area is not doubled.

Assessment Criteria – SSM, level 6: know and use the formula for the area of a circle.

Links

Since 1988, Pi Day has been celebrated around the World on 14th March, which coincidentally was also Einstein's birthday. In Americans write the date as 3/14. On Pi day, people eat pies and pizzas and march around circular spaces. There is more information at http://www.pidayinternational. org/index.htm and at http:// news.bbc.co.uk/2/hi/uk_news/ magazine/7296224. stm (TW, EP).

2a

1 Calculate the number of 10 cm lengths of string that can be cut from a 5 m ball of string.

2 Convert these measurements to the units indicated in brackets.
   a 8.5 l (ml)   **b** 456 mm (cm)   **c** 8.5 ha (m²)   **d** 25 cl (ml)   **e** 4.2 t (kg)

2b

3 Convert these measurements to the units indicated in brackets.
   a 27.5 kg (lbs)   **b** 120 cm (inches)   **c** 135 g (oz)
   d 750 ml (pints)   **e** 850 miles (km)

4 Write down each reading on the scales.
   Give an answer for each arrow.

a    b    c

2c

5 Six identical rectangles are arranged in the shape of a large rectangle.

Calculate the area of one of the rectangles.

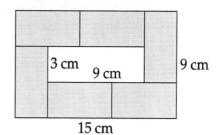

6 The area of all these triangles is 40 cm².
   Calculate the unknown values.

a   b 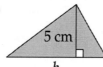   c   d

2d

7 Calculate the areas of the parallelogram and trapezia.

a 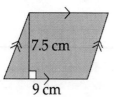   b 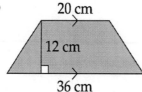   c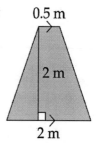

8 The area of the parallelogram and the trapezium are the same.
Calculate the value of *h*.

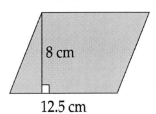
8 cm

12.5 cm

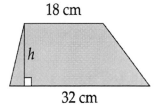
18 cm

h

32 cm

9 A penny-farthing was a type of bike used in the 19th century.

The diameter of the large wheel is 120 cm and is 3 times larger than the diameter of the small wheel.

Calculate

a the diameter of the small wheel

b the circumference of the small wheel

c the circumference of the large wheel.

The large wheel turns one complete revolution.

d How many times will the small wheel turn?

Use π = 3.14 for the remaining questions on this page.

10 Six equilateral triangles of side 6 cm are arranged to form a hexagon.

A circle is drawn passing through the vertices of the hexagon.

Calculate the circumference of the circle.

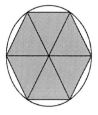

11 A circular pond has a radius of 5 metres.
Calculate the surface area of the water.

12 The 'No entry' sign consists of a white rectangle on a red circle of radius 30 cm.
The rectangle has dimensions of 50 cm by 11.5 cm.
Calculate the red area of the sign.

2 Summary

Assessment criteria

- Solve problems involving the conversion of units and make sensible estimates of a range of measures in relation to everyday situations **Level 5**

- Read and interpret scales on a range of measuring instruments, explaining what each labelled division represents **Level 5**

- Understand and use the formula for the area of a rectangle and distinguish area from perimeter **Level 5**

- Deduce and use formulae for the area of a triangle and parallelogram **Level 6**

- Know and use the formulae for the circumference and area of a circle **Level 6**

Question commentary

Example	The example asks students to calculate the perimeter of a semicircle given its diameter. Some students will find the length of the arc and neglect to add the diameter. Emphasise that units must be given with the final answer. The problem can be extended by asking students to find the area of the semicircle.	$$\text{Perimeter} = 20 + \frac{1}{2} \times 3.14 \times 20$$ $$= 51.4\ \text{cm}$$
Past question	The question requires students to find the area of a parallelogram drawn inside a rectangle. Some students will use the formula to find the area, but others may find the area of the rectangle and subtract the areas of the two triangles. Ask questions such as "Why do you have to multiply the base by the perpendicular height to find the area of a parallelogram?" Emphasise that units must be given with the final answer.	**Answer** **Level 6** **2** 35 cm² (units must be given)

Development and links

This topic is developed in Chapter 14 where students find further areas and circumferences of circles and extend to finding the surface area of a prism. Students will use measures when interpreting scale drawings and maps in Chapter 9 and constructing triangles and bisectors in Chapter 14. The properties of triangles, quadrilaterals and other polygons are investigated in Chapter 6.

Students will use area in many curriculum subjects, for example measuring areas of land in geography, using cross-sectional areas of wires, pipes and materials in design technology, using quadrats to give a sample area in biology and designing clothing projects in textiles. Students will encounter a range of SI units in science, where the skill of reading measuring scales accurately is especially important.

3 Probability

Statistics

Objectives

Level

- Identify all the mutually exclusive outcomes of an experiment.. **5/6**
- Know that the sum of probabilities of all mutually exclusive outcomes is 1 and use this when solving problems..................... **6**
- Interpret results involving uncertainty and prediction **6**
- Compare experimental and theoretical probabilities in a range of contexts **7**
- Appreciate the difference between mathematical explanation and experimental evidence.. **7**
- Justify the mathematical features drawn from a context and the choice of approach... **7**

Introduction

In this chapter students develop their knowledge of theoretical probability by calculating the probabilities of mutually exclusive events and listing outcomes for two successive events using tree diagrams and sample space diagrams. The topic extends to estimating probabilities based on an experiment or simulation. Students consider the effect of sample size on experimental probabilities, compare experimental probabilities with theoretical probabilities and simulate experimental data using a model.

The student book discusses the factors that affect the chance of success of a medical procedure. When taking risks, we are more likely to take the risk if there is a high probability of the action being successful. For example, if there is an eight out of ten chance that an operation will cure a medical condition, we are more likely to risk having the operation than if there is only a one in ten chance of success. Although an event may be random and unpredictable, probability gives an idea of the patterns that are likely to occur (EP).

Fast-track
3a, b, c, d, e

MPA

1.1 3a, b, c, d, e, e^2, CS
1.2 3a, b, c, d, e, e^2, CS
1.3 3b, c, d, e, e^2, CS
1.4 3b, c, e, e^2, CS
1.5 3a, b, c, e, e^2, CS

PLTS

IE 3a, b, c, d, e^2, CS
CT 3a, b, c, d, e, e^2, CS
RL 3c, d, e, e^2, CS
TW 3b, d, e^2, CS
SM 3a, b, c, e, e^2, CS
EP 3I, a, b, c, d, e, e^2, CS

Extra Resources

3   Start of chapter presentation
3b   Consolidation sheet
3c   Starter: Complimentary probability matching
3d   Starter: Probability time challenge
3e   Consolidation sheet
$3e^2$ Simulation: Coin tossing
$3e^2$ Consolidation sheet
    Maths life: Dice

    Assessment: chapter 3

Statistics Probability   **33**

- Identify all the mutually exclusive outcomes of an experiment   (L5)
- Use diagrams and tables to record in a systematic way all possible mutually exclusive outcomes for single events and for two successive events   (L6)

Useful resources

Starter – Stamps

A package costs 60 pence to post.
Ask students how many ways 60 pence can be made using 5p and 7p stamps.
$(12 \times 5p, 5 \times 5p + 5 \times 7p)$
Challenge students to find the largest postage amount that cannot be made using 5p and 7p stamps. (23p)
What about 5p and 11p stamps? (39p)

Teaching notes

In a football match there are three possible results for a team, win, lose and draw. If a team plays two matches, how can we list all the possible outcomes? Discuss suitable ways of abbreviating the outcomes. How can you set about listing all the outcomes in an organised way? Why is this necessary? How many possible outcomes are there for the two matches? $(3 \times 3 = 9)$. How many would it be for 3 matches? (27)

Give an example of the usefulness of a *sample space diagram* for two independent events in a two-way table. For example, a spinner (1–3) and a dice (1–4). Add the scores.

Ask questions like 'what is the probability of scoring over 5?'

What advantage does the sample space have over simply listing the outcomes? Is it possible to calculate answers to questions like these without a sample space? Would you recommend it?

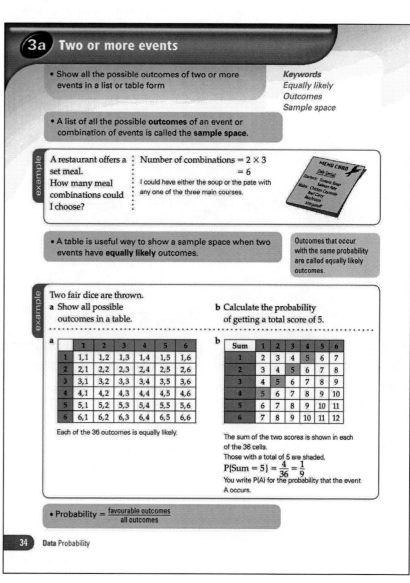

3a Two or more events

- Show all the possible outcomes of two or more events in a list or table form

Keywords
Equally likely
Outcomes
Sample space

- A list of all the possible **outcomes** of an event or combination of events is called the **sample space**.

A restaurant offers a set meal.
How many meal combinations could I choose?

Number of combinations = 2×3
= 6
I could have either the soup or the pate with any one of the three main courses.

- A table is useful way to show a sample space when two events have **equally likely** outcomes.

Outcomes that occur with the same probability are called equally likely outcomes.

Two fair dice are thrown.
a Show all possible outcomes in a table.
b Calculate the probability of getting a total score of 5.

a
	1	2	3	4	5	6
1	1,1	1,2	1,3	1,4	1,5	1,6
2	2,1	2,2	2,3	2,4	2,5	2,6
3	3,1	3,2	3,3	3,4	3,5	3,6
4	4,1	4,2	4,3	4,4	4,5	4,6
5	5,1	5,2	5,3	5,4	5,5	5,6
6	6,1	6,2	6,3	6,4	6,5	6,6

Each of the 36 outcomes is equally likely.

b
Sum	1	2	3	4	5	6
1	2	3	4	5	6	7
2	3	4	5	6	7	8
3	4	5	6	7	8	9
4	5	6	7	8	9	10
5	6	7	8	9	10	11
6	7	8	9	10	11	12

The sum of the two scores is shown in each of the 36 cells.
Those with a total of 5 are shaded.
$P\{\text{Sum} = 5\} = \frac{4}{36} = \frac{1}{9}$
You write P(A) for the probability that the event A occurs.

- Probability = $\frac{\text{favourable outcomes}}{\text{all outcomes}}$

34   Data Probability

Plenary

What is the most likely score when you roll two unbiased six sided dice numbered 1 to 6 and add the scores of the two dice? Would listing all possible outcomes help? Establish that the most likely score is 7, but it is not likely (probability being $\frac{1}{6}$). Does it make sense that 7 is the most likely outcome, but it is not likely to happen? (1.5)

Simplification

Establish meaningful abbreviations for the outcomes and discuss a logical approach to listing. For example, with coins, no heads, then one head, then two heads, *etc.*

Encourage fractions to be used to express probability, but accept that decimals could sometimes be used.

Questions 1 and **2** – Some students may need help deciding how to list outcomes. Part **1b ii** can be used to discuss the difference between HT and TH.

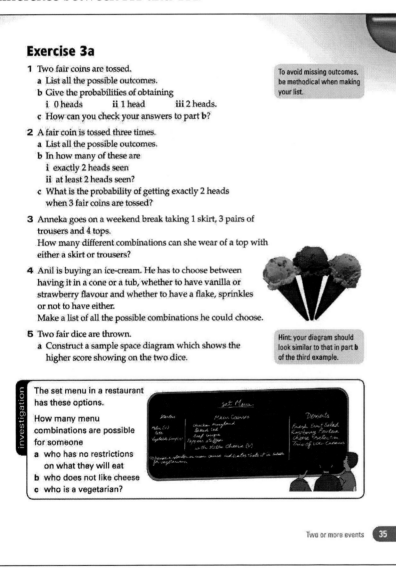

Exercise 3a

1 Two fair coins are tossed.
   a List all the possible outcomes.
   b Give the probabilities of obtaining
      i 0 heads   ii 1 head   iii 2 heads.
   c How can you check your answers to part **b**?

To avoid missing outcomes, be methodical when making your list.

2 A fair coin is tossed three times.
   a List all the possible outcomes.
   b In how many of these are
      i exactly 2 heads seen
      ii at least 2 heads seen?
   c What is the probability of getting exactly 2 heads when 3 fair coins are tossed?

3 Anneka goes on a weekend break taking 1 skirt, 3 pairs of trousers and 4 tops.
   How many different combinations can she wear of a top with either a skirt or trousers?

4 Anil is buying an ice-cream. He has to choose between having it in a cone or a tub, whether to have vanilla or strawberry flavour and whether to have a flake, sprinkles or not to have either.
   Make a list of all the possible combinations he could choose.

5 Two fair dice are thrown.
   a Construct a sample space diagram which shows the higher score showing on the two dice.

*Hint: your diagram should look similar to that in part **b** of the third example.*

investigation

The set menu in a restaurant has these options.

How many menu combinations are possible for someone
a who has no restrictions on what they will eat
b who does not like cheese
c who is a vegetarian?

Two or more events   **35**

Extension

Set the following problem. There are 60 possible meals you can choose if you have one item from each course. There is a choice for each course. No course has more than 5 choices. Two of the courses have the same number of choices. How many courses are there? (4 courses: 2, 2, 3, and 5 choices for each course) (IE, SM) (1.2)

Exercise 3a commentary

Question 3 – A sketch of the girl may help. The skirt and trousers will need to be considered as forming 4 different options.

Question 4 – Encourage abbreviations: C or T/V or S/F, Sp or N. Try to find a link between the number of possible outcomes for each event separately and for the total number of possible outcomes in questions **1–4** (CT) (1.2).

Question 5 – An example may be needed to help explain what is required: if a 4 and 6 are thrown, then record a 6 in the sample space for the higher score (1.1).

Investigation – Encourage students to calculate the number of outcomes without listing. Still allow listing if necessary, but challenge them to see if they can work out how the answer could have been achieved without listing. *Pate* may need explaining (CT) (1.2).

Assessment Criteria – HD, level, 6: find and record all mutually exclusive outcomes for single events and two successive events in a systematic way.

Links

Dice that are deliberately biased are called crooked or loaded dice. Dice can be loaded by adding a small amount of metal to one side or by manufacturing the dice with a hollow gap inside so that one side is lighter than the others. One way of testing for a loaded die is to drop it several times into a glass of water. If it is hollow it will float with the hollow side uppermost; if it is weighted, it will sink with the same number always facing down.

- Use tree diagrams to represent outcomes for two or more events (L6)

Useful resources
Bare tree diagrams

Starter − Ice cream

Ask students how many different combinations of ice cream they could make choosing two different flavours from the following seven flavours: vanilla, strawberry, toffee, mint choc, pistachio, coconut and banana ($\frac{7 \times 6}{2} = 21$)

What is the probability of choosing an ice cream with strawberry in it? ($\frac{6}{21} = \frac{2}{7}$)

Teaching notes

Explain that in a school register a student can be marked P for present, A for absent or L for late. Ask students to say how many possible combinations of marks there are for the entries for two lessons ($3 \times 3 = 9$) and how to list them all. Anticipate lists, such as PP, PA,…, or a two-way table. Did anyone come up with a tree diagram? Can they explain how to draw one? Show how one is drawn, focusing on the correct labeling of each tier of branches and the ends of each branch (TW).

Challenge students to draw a tree diagram for two successive tosses of a coin. State that the coin is biased and P(heads) = ¼. What is P(tails)? (1 − ¼ = ¾). Suppose the coin is tossed twice 64 times. How often do you expect heads to occur on the first toss? (¼ × 64 = 16). How often do you expect to get two heads? (¼× 16 = 4) Can students say how often the other outcomes are most likely to occur? Show how to find the probability of two heads (4/64 = 1/16) and challenge students to find the probabilities of the other three combinations (P(HT) = 12/64 = 3/16, P(TH)= 12/64 = 3/16 and P(TT) = 36/64 = 9/16) (CT) (1.4)

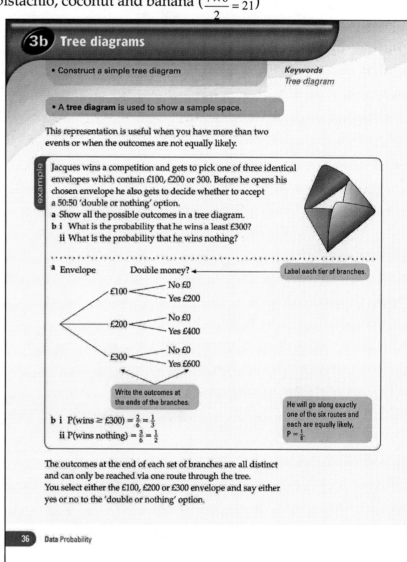

Plenary

Explain the scenario in the 'Monty Hall problem' as introduced in the **Did you know?** Ask students to say if they would swap envelopes or not. Then discuss the reasons for their choices. Again ask if students would swap (EP) (1.5). The advantage to swapping can be seen by carefully listing all options. Essentially you have a 1/3 chance of initially guessing the car (don't swap) or 2/3 chance of guessingly wrongly but then the unopened envelope is guaranteed to contain the car (do swap). See the discussion at http://en.wikipedia.org/wiki/Monty_hall_problem

Simplification

Have available bare tree diagrams so that students can focus on deciding how to label them correctly. If drawing a diagram by hand it is often useful to start at the end of the tree to help ensure enough space is available.

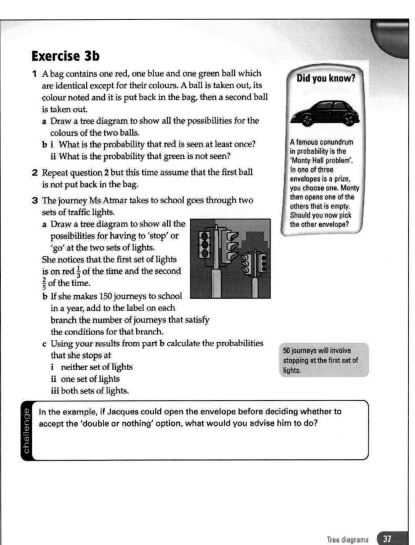

Exercise 3b

1 A bag contains one red, one blue and one green ball which are identical except for their colours. A ball is taken out, its colour noted and it is put back in the bag, then a second ball is taken out.
   a Draw a tree diagram to show all the possibilities for the colours of the two balls.
   b i What is the probability that red is seen at least once?
      ii What is the probability that green is not seen?

2 Repeat question 2 but this time assume that the first ball is not put back in the bag.

3 The journey Ms Atmar takes to school goes through two sets of traffic lights.
   a Draw a tree diagram to show all the possibilities for having to 'stop' or 'go' at the two sets of lights.
   She notices that the first set of lights is on red $\frac{1}{3}$ of the time and the second $\frac{2}{5}$ of the time.
   b If she makes 150 journeys to school in a year, add to the label on each branch the number of journeys that satisfy the conditions for that branch.
   c Using your results from part b calculate the probabilities that she stops at
      i neither set of lights
      ii one set of lights
      iii both sets of lights.

Did you know?

A famous conundrum in probability is the 'Monty Hall problem'. In one of three envelopes is a prize, you choose one, Monty then opens one of the others that is empty. Should you now pick the other envelope?

50 journeys will involve stopping at the first set of lights.

challenge
In the example, if Jacques could open the envelope before deciding whether to accept the 'double or nothing' option, what would you advise him to do?

Extension

Ask students to look at question **3** and see if they can relate the final probabilities to those along the set of branches followed (the product for independent events). This way of approaching the probabilities can be reinforced with further numerical examples (IE, SM) (1.2).

Exercise 3b commentary

All questions (1.3).

Question 1 – Check that students correctly label each set of branches 'first/second ball' and write the outcomes at the end of the branches 'red/blue/green' or 'R/B/G'.

Question 2 – This will involve a '3 × 2 tree diagram'. Introduce the language of with and without replacement and take the opportunity to discuss the idea of independent events.

Question 3 – Students may require further explanation with part **b**. Ask how students could check their answers to part **c**. (Probabilities should sum to 1) (CT) (1.1)

Challenge – This is an opportunity to discuss the *expectation*, which does not change, though considerations such as having a guaranteed £300 may change students' choices (EP) (1.5).

Key Indicator – HD, level 6: find and record all possible mutually exclusive outcomes for single events and two successive events in a systematic way.

Links

On the 10th December 1868 the railway engineer J.P. Knight installed the world's first traffic lights outside the British houses of parliament. It employed semaphore arms and red and green gas lamps which were manually turned around by a policeman. The use of red, amber and green to code levels of satisfaction is widely used in the civil service's *RAG rating* and has been adopted by the Food Standards Agency to indicate the healthiness of foods, see

http://www.eatwell.gov.uk/foodlabels/trafficlights/

- Identify all the mutually exclusive outcomes of an experiment (L6)
- Know that the sum of probabilities of all mutually exclusive outcomes is 1 and use this when solving problems (L6)

Useful resources
Dice

Starter – Dice bingo

Ask students to draw a 3 × 3 grid and enter nine numbers from 2 to 12 inclusive, duplicates allowed.

Throw two dice. Students add the scores and cross out the total if they have it in their grid (only one number at a time).

The winner is the first student to cross out all numbers.

Teaching notes

Give examples of events that are *mutually exclusive*. For example, rolling less than 3, rolling 5 or more on a dice. Show how it helps to list all the primitive outcomes that make up an event, {1, 2} and {5, 6}, and checking for common entries.

When two events take place it can be difficult to think about all the possible outcomes. The previous teaching notes used both a list and a tree diagram to look at all possible outcomes. Introduce a sample space that makes use of a two way table for rolling two dice. For example, two four sided dice where you add the scores together. Ask questions that relate to mutually exclusive events, for example, P(score less than 2 OR over 3), and show how this can be obtained by counting.

This could lead to a discussion of P(A or B) = P(A) + P(B) for mutually exclusive events. Why doesn't it work for non-mutually exclusive events? How could you fix the *double counting* problem? (CT, RL) (1.2)

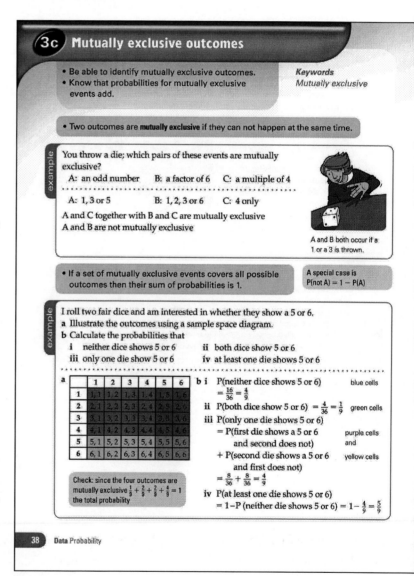

Plenary

When it's sunny people are less depressed. Does this mean that peoples' depression is effected by sunlight? Does this mean that the sunlight is affected by peoples' depression? Are the two dependent? Can you use the term mutually exclusive here? If so, are the events mutually exclusive? (EP) (1.5)

Simplification

Reinforce the idea that mutually exclusive means 'both events can't both happen at the same time'. Give the simple example that when you roll a dice the events (i) less than 3, (ii) over 4, are mutually exclusive because they can't both happen. BUT (i) rolling even, (ii) over 3, can both happen, so these events are not mutually exclusive.

Exercise 3c

1 For each of the following pairs of events say whether or not they are mutually exclusive.
  a i March 2nd will be the hottest day of next year.
    ii it will snow on March 2nd next year.
  b the total score when three ordinary dice are thrown will be
    i prime   ii even
  c a rugby player can play international rugby for
    i New Zealand   ii Ireland.

2 A red and a blue dice are thrown together.
  a Which pairs of the following events are mutually exclusive?
    A the sum of the scores is odd
    B the red and the blue dice show the same score
    C the total score is less than 5
    D the red dice is at least 3 more than the blue dice.
  b Give three more pairs of mutually exclusive events.
    Define any new events that you use.

3 A die is thrown twice and whether the score is even or odd is recorded each time.
  a Draw a sample space diagram to represent this situation.
  b Calculate the probability that the **product** of the scores showing is even.
  c Using the answer to part **b**, write down the probability that the product of the scores is odd.

4 A fair coin is tossed three times.
  a Draw a tree diagram to show all the possible outcomes.
  b Use your tree diagram to calculate the probability of getting
    i exactly 2 heads.   ii at least 2 heads.
  c The event 'not at least 2 heads' is the same as '0 or 1 head'.
    i Use the tree diagram to calculate the probability of getting 0 or 1 head.

puzzle

Without making a new list, answer the following.
a i If I toss a coin 4 times and list all possible outcomes, many are there?   *Hint: look back at the list in questions 1 and 2, spread 3a*
  ii How many of these would have exactly 1 head?
b If the coin was tossed 5 times how many possible outcomes would a complete list contain?
  How many of these would have exactly 1 head?
c Can you see any way to generalise to say what these would be if there were 10 tosses?

Mutually exclusive outcomes 39

Extension

If a coin is tossed n times, what is the probability of obtaining heads every time? $\left(\frac{1}{2^n}\right)$ (CT) (1.2, 1.4)

Exercise 3c commentary

Question 1 – Encourage students to list the prime numbers up to 18 for part **b**. How could you score 2?

Question 2 – What is a quick way to record all possible outcomes? Encourage the use of a two-way table as a sample space. Students will need to check six pairs of events (SM).

Question 3 – Encourage the use of suitable abbreviations. How would the results change if you looked at the sum rather than product of the scores? (1.3)

Question 4 – When is listing all possible outcomes a more efficient method than using a tree diagram? In part **c**, students may need help thinking through the logic (1.3).

Puzzle – How can the number of possible outcomes be investigated for different numbers of coins. How can a rule be found? The most successful students are likely to look at the number of outcomes for 1, 2 and 3 coins first (IE) (1.1, 1.3).

Assessment Criteria – HD, level 6: know that the sum of probabilities of all mutually exclusive outcomes is 1 and use this when solving problems.

Links

An impossible object is a type of optical illusion where the brain interprets a 2-D image as a 3-D object that cannot exist. Often the brain interprets different parts of the drawing in different ways which are incompatible with each other. There is a demonstration of an impossible object at http://www.michaelbach.de/ot/cog_imposs1/index.html and further examples at http://lookmind.com/illusions.php?cat=1

- Compare estimated experimental probabilities with theoretical probabilities, recognising that
  - if an experiment is repeated the outcome may, and usually will, be different (L5)
  - increasing the number of times an experiment is repeated generally leads to better estimates of probability (L5)

Useful resources
A piece of English text with frequency table
Drawing pins

Starter – Higher or lower

Using either a set of playing cards or a set of numbered cards, show students the first card and ask whether they think the next card will be higher or lower. Repeat several times. (As necessary, agree the values of face cards in advance). Can be extended by being more specific, for example, the chance of the next card being a square number.

Teaching notes

How likely is a drawing pin to land on its side or its head? How could the probability be discovered? Discuss the fact that only the *experimental probability* could be calculated. How many trials should be undertaken?

Conduct the drawing pin experiment to see what the experimental probability of 'side' and 'head' are? How should the experiment be conducted? Give students a few initial unrecorded trials to allow them to consider the problem. Ideas such as 'dropping from the same height' or 'dropping onto the same surface' might be considered. Once the rules are established, conduct the experiment and record the results (IE).

Analyse the results. How many trials did students use? How many are needed for a reliable estimate? Discuss the fact that more trials mean a better estimate. Is it fair to pull all the results together for the whole class? (1.3)

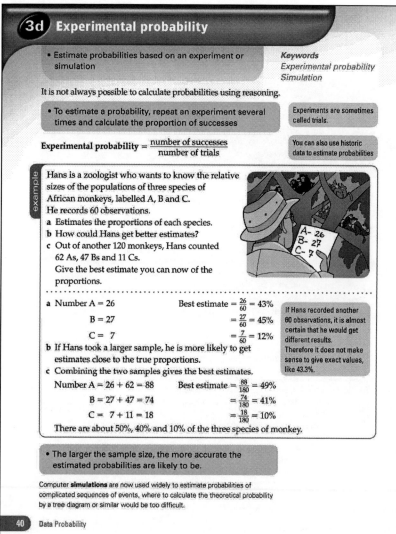

3d Experimental probability

- Estimate probabilities based on an experiment or simulation

Keywords
Experimental probability
Simulation

It is not always possible to calculate probabilities using reasoning.

- To estimate a probability, repeat an experiment several times and calculate the proportion of successes

Experiments are sometimes called trials.

$$\text{Experimental probability} = \frac{\text{number of successes}}{\text{number of trials}}$$

You can also use historic data to estimate probabilities

Hans is a zoologist who wants to know the relative sizes of the populations of three species of African monkeys, labelled A, B and C. He records 60 observations.
a Estimates the proportions of each species.
b How could Hans get better estimates?
c Out of another 120 monkeys, Hans counted 62 As, 47 Bs and 11 Cs. Give the best estimate you can now of the proportions.

A- 26
B- 27
C- 7

a Number A = 26 Best estimate $= \frac{26}{60} = 43\%$
  B = 27 $= \frac{27}{60} = 45\%$
  C = 7 $= \frac{7}{60} = 12\%$

If Hans recorded another 60 observations, it is almost certain that he would get different results. Therefore it does not make sense to give exact values, like 43.3%.

b If Hans took a larger sample, he is more likely to get estimates close to the true proportions.
c Combining the two samples gives the best estimates.
  Number A = 26 + 62 = 88 Best estimate $= \frac{88}{180} = 49\%$
  B = 27 + 47 = 74 $= \frac{74}{180} = 41\%$
  C = 7 + 11 = 18 $= \frac{18}{180} = 10\%$
  There are about 50%, 40% and 10% of the three species of monkey.

- The larger the sample size, the more accurate the estimated probabilities are likely to be.

Computer **simulations** are now used widely to estimate probabilities of complicated sequences of events, where to calculate the theoretical probability by a tree diagram or similar would be too difficult.

40 Data Probability

Plenary

The order of frequency for letter usage in the English language in descending order is ETAONIRSH. Choose a piece of English text and check this. The class could be subdivided and the whole class' results pooled. Why might the class result not agree? The longer the text, the more reliable the findings (TW).

Simplification

A pre-prepared piece of text could be used with an adjacent partially formed frequency table. This would offer an easier read than the student book.

Question 1 – Some students may think the actual times are significant. What would be the use of knowing these? (Finding average arrival time) (1.3)

Question 2 – This will take time; consider restricting to a part of the page or have students pool results from different sections. EAOIU is the actual order of frequency in descending order for the English language. Would students have predicted this? (TW) (1.1, 1.3)

Exercise 3d

1 Keith has a swipe card to enter the building he works in. The system records the time the card is first used each day. He is supposed to be at work by 8.30 am.
Over a month the times recorded were:

8.27	8.24	8.27	8.31	8.30	8.26	8.25	8.29	8.32	8.26	8.28
8.31	8.25	8.27	8.26	8.35	8.26	8.24	8.27	8.27	8.25	8.27

Estimate the probability that Keith is late for work on a randomly chosen day.

2 a Make up a tally chart and frequency table for the number of times the vowels (a, e, i, o and u) appear on the page facing this one.
  b Give an estimate of the probability of a vowel in English being an e.

Did you know?

The relative frequency of letters and letter combinations is used to crack secret ciphers.

3 Choose another page from this book at random.
  a Would you expect the proportion of vowels which are e to be the same on that page?
  b Repeat question 2 for that page.
  c Is the answer the same?
  d How could you get a more reliable estimate of the probability of a vowel being an e?

4 a What is the probability that the page number of a page chosen at random from the first chapter of this book will contain the digit 1?
  b Could this be used as an estimate of the probability that a page chosen at random from the book will contain the digit 1?

5 How could you estimate the probability of
  a being struck by lightening
  b it raining on your next birthday
  c Liverpool winning the next premiership league title?

discussion If you used a story book for children or a university history textbook, instead of this textbook, would you expect the estimate of the probability of a vowel being e to be the same, or higher, or lower?

Extension

How could you estimate the probability of becoming Prime Minister? What sort of information might you wish to find? For example, number of Prime Ministers, number of female, age. What would increase your probability of becoming Prime Minister? For example, joining a political party, watching the news, being on the school council, *etc.* (IE)

Exercise 3d commentary

Question 3 – Encourage students to use their experience from question 2 to improve their method for this question (CT). For example, reorganise the group (1.3).

Question 4 – Encourage some working to be shown that convinces the reader. What is the numbering for chapter **1**/whole book? Discourage counting all individual pages. Encourage the seeking of a short cut (RL) (1.2).

Question 5 – Emphasise that some probabilities can't be found by experiment or by listing equally likely outcomes. Historical records give an idea, but why might they give a poor estimate? Changing circumstances (1.5).

Discussion – What varies when you consider books that are easier or harder to read? Word length, use of unusual words, size of print, number of pages, *etc.* (1.2)

Assessment Criteria – HD, level 5: understand that different outcomes may result from repeating an experiment

Links

A substitution cipher conceals a message by consistently replacing one letter with another. This results in the frequency of the encrypted and original letters being the same. In English text, the most common letter is E, followed by T and A. Code breakers compare the relative frequencies in regular and the encrypted text to try to match original and substituted letters. An example is the cipher used in the Babbington plot, which is featured in the **Did you know?** For more information see http://simonsingh.net/The_Black_Chamber/frequencyanalysis.html (EP)

- Interpret results involving uncertainty and prediction (L6)
- Compare experimental and theoretical probabilities in a range of contexts (L7)

Useful resources
Calculator
Dice
Blue tack

Starter – Probability jumble

Write a list of anagrams on the board and ask students to unscramble them. Possible anagrams are

ANCHEC, COMETOU, TEENV, LIRAT, RODMAN, SLIPSOMBIE, KELLIY, TRAINCE
(chance, outcome, event, trial, random, impossible, likely, certain)

Can be extended by asking students to make a probability word search.

Teaching notes

Discuss the fact that a fair coin does not necessarily give 50 heads and 50 tails after being thrown 100 times. Why is this? Although 50 heads and 50 tails is the most likely outcome, it's not likely to happen. Encourage students to use the term random in their explanations (EP) (1.5).

What do students think is an estimate of the probability of 50 heads and 50 tails; choose from $\frac{22}{25}$, $\frac{8}{25}$, $\frac{2}{25}$ $\cdot$ $\left(\frac{2}{25}\right)$

Look at the example in the student book relating to the ancient burial. Discuss the sample sizes in parts **a** and **b**.

How should probability be expressed? Options are fractions, decimals, percentages, ratio? Discuss the advantages and disadvantages of each method. For example, decimals allow an easy comparison between different events. Note that ratio is generally not used in maths for probability, but is normally used on horse racing (EP).

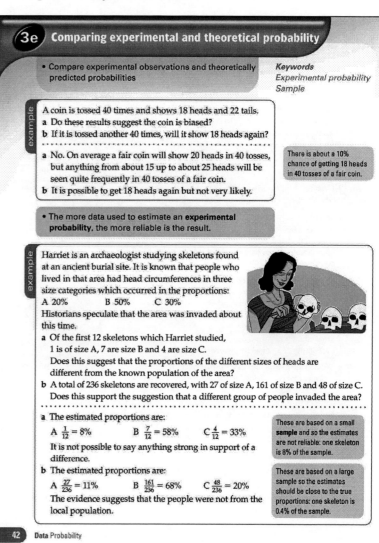

3e Comparing experimental and theoretical probability

- Compare experimental observations and theoretically predicted probabilities

Keywords
Experimental probability
Sample

A coin is tossed 40 times and shows 18 heads and 22 tails.
a Do these results suggest the coin is biased?
b If it is tossed another 40 times, will it show 18 heads again?

a No. On average a fair coin will show 20 heads in 40 tosses, but anything from about 15 up to about 25 heads will be seen quite frequently in 40 tosses of a fair coin.
b It is possible to get 18 heads again but not very likely.

There is about a 10% chance of getting 18 heads in 40 tosses of a fair coin.

- The more data used to estimate an **experimental probability**, the more reliable is the result.

Harriet is an archaeologist studying skeletons found at an ancient burial site. It is known that people who lived in that area had head circumferences in three size categories which occurred in the proportions:
A 20%   B 50%   C 30%
Historians speculate that the area was invaded about this time.
a Of the first 12 skeletons which Harriet studied, 1 is of size A, 7 are size B and 4 are size C.
Does this suggest that the proportions of the different sizes of heads are different from the known population of the area?
b A total of 236 skeletons are recovered, with 27 of size A, 161 of size B and 48 of size C.
Does this support the suggestion that a different group of people invaded the area?

a The estimated proportions are:
A $\frac{1}{12}$ = 8%   B $\frac{7}{12}$ = 58%   C $\frac{4}{12}$ = 33%
It is not possible to say anything strong in support of a difference.

These are based on a small sample and so the estimates are not reliable: one skeleton is 8% of the sample.

b The estimated proportions are:
A $\frac{27}{236}$ = 11%   B $\frac{161}{236}$ = 68%   C $\frac{48}{236}$ = 20%
The evidence suggests that the people were not from the local population.

These are based on a large sample so the estimates should be close to the true proportions: one skeleton is 0.4% of the sample.

42   Data Probability

Plenary

Examine a graph of experimental probability for the throwing of one coin and recording the number of heads. Record results after every five trials. Use a decimal value for experimental probability. What do you notice about the graph? (1.1)

Simplification

Allow students to generate their own data for question **1** and ask them to calculate probabilities after 1, 4, 10, 20, 40, 100 trials. How does the reliability of their results change?

All questions (CT) (1.1, 1.4)

Question 1 – Does experimental probability give the 'correct answer' for the probability? Is this experiment well suited to experimental probability? Suggest listing all possible outcomes. How will this help? (1.3, 1.5)

Exercise 3e

1 Darrell says that the chance of getting 1 head when you toss 2 fair coins is $\frac{1}{3}$. Ekaterina says he is wrong, and she will prove it to him. She tosses a pair of fair coins 40 times and the table shows the outcomes.

Number of heads	0	1	2
Frequency	8	21	11

a Do you think Darrell is right that the probability of getting 1 head is $\frac{1}{3}$?
b Has Ekaterina proved that Darrell is wrong?

2 Dr McDonald is overseeing a drug trial. He has given one group of patients drug A, another drug B and a third group a placebo. His results are shown in the table.

	Drug A	Drug B	Placebo
Number in trial	96	10	36
Number cured	72	7	17

Write a short report for Dr McDonald saying whether you think the drugs are effective and how a future drug trial might be improved.

A placebo is a 'dummy' medicine.

3 Kenny is testing a set of roulette wheels to see if they are biased. He spins each wheel 60 times and records how often the ball lands in one of three groups of numbers.

	1–12	13–24	25–36
Wheel 1	23	22	15
Wheel 2	17	19	22
Wheel 3	16	17	27
Wheel 4	20	18	22

a Calculate the theoretical probability of landing in each of the three groups of numbers.
b For each wheel, calculate the experimental probabilities of landing in each of the three groups of numbers.
c Should Kenny recommend that the casino continues to use these wheels?
d For each wheel, do the experimental probabilities add up to 1?

A European roulette wheel has numbers from 0 to 36 equally spaced around its edge.

> **task** If Ekaterina had tossed the pair of coins 4000 times in question **1**, would this have been a proof that Darrell is wrong?
> Can you think of any way to provide a **proof** in a situation like this?

Comparing experimental and theoretical probability 43

Extension

Would securing pieces of blue tack to the face of three sides of a dice cause it to be biased? Investigate. Consideration should be given to how the blue tack is secured and to which faces. Also to the number of trials. Also, is the dice biased to start with? (IE, SM)

Exercise 3e commentary

Question 2 – The term 'placebo' may need defining. Calculator could be used to find percentage success. Could drug B (70%) be more effective than drug A (75%)? Why is the number of trials important? (1.3)

Question 3 – Writing the probabilities as fractions is likely to offer the most straightforward approach. Encourage students to double check their additions or check with a partner. The distinction between the 'wheels' and the 'groups of numbers' may need explaining. Note that the number 'zero' is not included in the record of results (RL) (1.2, 1.3).

Discussion – What does an increased number of trials give you in terms of experimental probability? A more reliable answer, but not the exact answer (EP) (1.5).

Assessment Criteria – HD, level 7: understand relative frequency as an estimate of probability and use this to compare outcomes of an experiment.

Links

Many superstitions are based on the belief that a particular action can bring good or bad luck and so increase the chance of an event happening. For example, breaking a mirror is supposed to bring seven years bad luck and catching a falling leaf on the first day of autumn prevents catching a cold during the winter. How many other superstitions do the class know? The origins of some common superstitions are explained at http://www.allsands.com/history/originscommons_ssd_gn.htm

3e² Simulating experimental data

- Appreciate the difference between mathematical explanation and experimental evidence **(L7)**
- Justify the mathematical features drawn from a context and the choice of approach **(L7)**

Useful resources
Calculator with a random function
List of random numbers sheet
Website www.random.org

Starter – BIDMAS bingo

Ask students to draw a 3 × 3 grid and enter nine numbers from 20 to 40 inclusive, duplicates allowed.

Using a calculator (or dice), generate three random numbers from 1 to 6.

Students cross out one of their numbers if they can make it using the numbers and the standard arithmetic operations; they should write their calculation in the square.

The winner is the first student to cross out all numbers.

Teaching notes

Simulation is used to help model traffic flow and reduce congestion on the roads, c.f. the **extension** activity. Look at an example of traffic flow at a set of lights or road junction. Use probabilities that are multiples of $\frac{1}{6}$ at each junction. How can a calculator be used to help model the roll of a dice? Note that some calculators actually have a 'dice function'. Other calculators will have to use the R# or similar function (1.3).

Run the simulation. Where do the first 10 cars end up? What do you predict will happen for the first 40 cars? Run the simulation and encourage students to comment on the results (EP) (1.5).

If the simulation was run again, would the results be totally different?

How can the calculator be used to generate the outcome of heads or tails from a coin? What about an integer from 1 to 10?

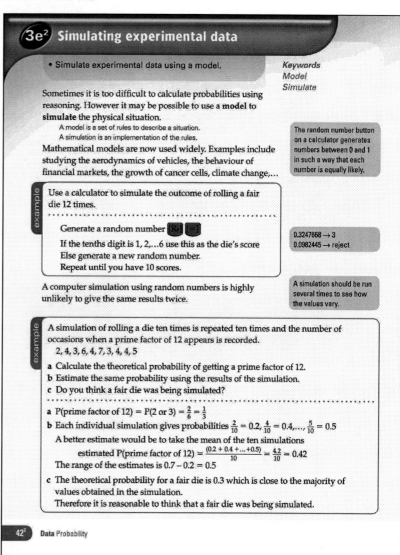

Plenary

Investigate the types of random numbers you can generate using the website www.random.org

Simplification

Provide students with a list of random integers from 1 to 10. How can this help to decide a coin toss? When working through the exercise ensure students understand that they should work through the sheet in order without missing or repeating a position.

All questions (IE, CT) (1.1, 1.3)

Question 1 – Encourage students to explore the random function on their calculator but use the suggestion in the student book example if no more elaborate option is available. Part **b ii** may need discussion of an efficient rule (1.5).

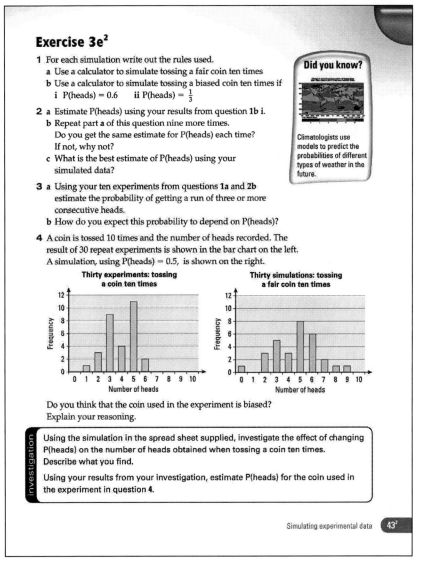

Exercise 3e²

1. For each simulation write out the rules used.
   a Use a calculator to simulate tossing a fair coin ten times
   b Use a calculator to simulate tossing a biased coin ten times if
      i P(heads) = 0.6   ii P(heads) = $\frac{1}{3}$

2. a Estimate P(heads) using your results from question **1b i**.
   b Repeat part **a** of this question nine more times.
      Do you get the same estimate for P(heads) each time? If not, why not?
   c What is the best estimate of P(heads) using your simulated data?

3. a Using your ten experiments from questions **1a** and **2b** estimate the probability of getting a run of three or more consecutive heads.
   b How do you expect this probability to depend on P(heads)?

4. A coin is tossed 10 times and the number of heads recorded. The result of 30 repeat experiments is shown in the bar chart on the left. A simulation, using P(heads) = 0.5, is shown on the right.

Did you know?

Climatologists use models to predict the probabilities of different types of weather in the future.

Thirty experiments: tossing a coin ten times

Thirty simulations: tossing a fair coin ten times

Do you think that the coin used in the experiment is biased? Explain your reasoning.

investigation

Using the simulation in the spread sheet supplied, investigate the effect of changing P(heads) on the number of heads obtained when tossing a coin ten times. Describe what you find.

Using your results from your investigation, estimate P(heads) for the coin used in the experiment in question **4**.

Simulating experimental data 43²

Extension

Four cars arrive at a cross roads. Each car has an equal probability of turning right, left or going straight on. Use a simulation to find an estimate of the probability that three of the cars turn down the same road. Note that a car can't do a 'U turn'. Theoretical probability is $\frac{8}{27}$ (0.30 to 2 dp), simulation should give a close approximation if number of trials is sufficient (IE, SM) (1.1, 1.4).

Exercise 3e² commentary

Question 2 – Emphasise that the process is random, which means that a simulation won't necessarily give the same result twice. What advantage do you gain from a greater number of trials? Students should record the entire results of the simulation for question **3**. Generating results could be done as a group activity (TW).

Question 3 –. If their results did not show a run of 3 heads, does this mean the estimate should be zero? (RL) (1.2)

Question 4 – The graphs may need some explanation of what they show. The coin is tossed 300 times; does this give a reliable number of trials? If the experiment is thought to use a biased coin, is it biased towards heads or tails?

Investigation – Ask students to be descriptive: comment on the shape of the graph, bunching of results, highest and lowest parts, *etc*. The average number of heads obtained, 117/300=0.39, gives a good estimate of P(heads)=0.4 (SM) (1.4)

Key Indicator – UAM, level 7: refine or extend the mathematics used to generate fuller solutions.

Links

Understanding how the Earth's future climate may change is now a pressing task given mans influence. Simulations are used but these make several assumptions and the effects of small changes to them need to be tested to be sure of any results. The distributed computing project climateprediction.net allows ordinary people to donate idle time on their personal computers to helping to solve this challenge. For details and how to get involved see http://www.climateprediction.net/index.php (EP).

1 A spinner with 3 equal sections coloured red, green and white is spun twice.
  a List all the possible outcomes.
  b In how many of these do you get a red and a green?
  c In how many of these do you not get a white?

2 Two fair dice are thrown.
  a Construct a sample space diagram which shows the product of the scores showing on the two dice.
  b What is the probability that the product is at least 20?

3 A lunch menu includes 3 starters, 4 main courses and 2 desserts.
  How many different menu combinations are there for someone who can eat anything on the menu?

4 A bag contains one black, one white and one purple ball which are identical except for their colours. A ball is taken out, its colour noted and then replaced before a second ball is taken out.
  a Draw a tree diagram to show the possibilities of the colurs of the two balls.
  b **i** What is the probability that the two balls are a black and white?
    ii What is the probability that the two balls are the same colour?

5 A white and a black dice are thrown together and the events A to D are defined as
    A the sum of the scores is even
    B the white and the black dice show different scores
    C the total score is less than 3
    D the difference between the scores is not more than 1.
  Explain why these pairs of events are mutually exclusive or not
  i A and B   **ii** B and D   **iii** B and C

6 The faces of a regular tetrahedron are labelled 1–4 and those of a regular octahedron 1–8. They are both rolled and the number on the bottom face is counted.
  a List all possible outcomes.
  b Use your list to calculate the probabilities that
    i both show prime numbers   **ii** only one shows a prime number.
  c Without looking at your list, what is the probability that neither shows a prime number?

7 Jorge is making stakes which should be about 1.3 m long.
The lengths of a number of stakes he has made are listed below.

1.27, 1.24, 1.27, 1.31, 1.30, 1.26, 1.25, 1.29, 1.32, 1.26, 1.28
1.31, 1.25, 1.27, 1.26, 1.35, 1.26, 1.24, 1.27, 1.27, 1.25, 1.27

   a Estimate the probability that one of his stakes is longer than 1.3 m.
   b Explain how a better estimate of this probability could be made.

8 How could you estimate the following probabilities?
   a A vowel chosen at random in French is an `a´.
   b The National Lottery has a single jackpot winner in the next draw.
   c Seeing at least 1 six when 3 dice are thrown together.

9 A trainee in a bank is surprised at how often transactions he sees start
with the digit 1. He does a quick tally of 100 transactions.

first digit	1	2	3	4	5	6	7	8	9
frequency	33	19	14	10	6	5	3	4	6

Do you think 1 to 9 are equally likely to occur as the first digit of
transactions?

10 An otherwise fair die is biased so that 5 and 6 are both three times as
likely to occur as the digits 1–4.
   a What are the individual probabilities of obtaining the numbers 1–6?
   b Use a calculator to simulate rolling such a die three times. Write
down the rules which you use and your results.
   c Repeat your simulation nine more times and use the results to
estimate the average sum of the three scores.
   d How could you improve the accuracy of your estimate?

- Use connections with related contexts to improve the analysis of a situation or problem (L6)
- Look for and reflect on other approaches and build on previous experience of similar situations and outcomes (L6)

Useful resources
Strips of card
Various dice (not all cubes)
Models of polyhedra
Nets for polyhedra
Zohn Ahl and Gins game boards

Background

Most people are familiar with cubic dice but there are other ways of randomly producing scores for games and other shapes of dice that can be used. The first part of this case study looks at two games from other cultures that use marked sticks in different ways to generate the scores (TW). By placing the student in unfamiliar situations, the intention is to look afresh at the likelihoods involved when throwing the sticks. There are direct parallels with more familiar coin tossing situations but many students will not initially spot this and it would be best not to mention it until they have worked out what happens with the sticks. The final part looks at dice of other shapes; some students might be aware of these from role playing games. The focus is to use the idea of fairness to explore regular solids (EP).

Teaching notes

Show an ordinary (cubic) die and remind the students that, assuming it is fair, it will have equal probabilities of landing on any one of its numbers. Then look at the section about stick dice and explain how the sticks, marked on one side but not the other, are used in different numbers to generate a range of scores. It would be helpful to have a set of homemade stick dice to show. Explain how the sticks are used and ask, what scores can be thrown using three sticks marked in this way? Establish that you can score 0, 1, 2 and 3.

Maths Life

Dice
Many games use dice to give them an element of chance. The dice are usually cubes, but they don' have to be.

STICK DICE
Sticks can be used to generate scores in the same way as we use dice. Stick dice have been found in Egyptian tombs and are still in use in many parts of the world today.

The sticks are usually marked on one side but not on the other. The sticks are thrown, the number of marked sides showing are counted and that number is used as the score.

What scores could be thrown using these three sticks?

What scores could be thrown with four sticks?

ZOHN AHL
Zohn Ahl is an ancient game that uses 4 sticks to decide the moves. Although thousands of years old, it is still played by the Kiowa Indians in Oklahoma.

As with many ancient games, it is often marked out on the ground or on an animal hide. The stone in the middle is to prevent cheating! The sticks are dropped onto the stone so that they scatter randomly.

The game uses this scoring system to make moves:

number of marked sides showing	number of spaces to move
1	1
2	2
3	3
4	6
0	10

46 MathsLife

Ask students to make their own stick dice (made from strips of thin wood or stiff card) and investigate how likely the various scores are. Can they explain the pattern that they see? You might need to suggest that they list all the possible ways of making the scores. Some students might benefit from colouring their marked sides in different ways to make it more obvious that there is more than one way of making some of the scores. Once they have found out the likelihood of throwing the various scores they should be able to work out what will happen if they were to use four marked sticks before they actually use them. Once they have worked out what they think will happen, they should then test their ideas by adding a fourth stick to their set and throwing the stick dice a sufficient number of times to see if the distribution of scores matches their prediction (IE) (1.1, 1.2).

Teaching notes continued

The game of Zohn Ahl uses four sticks and a scoring system to determine the moves. What do you notice about the scoring system? Does anything strike you as being not as you might expect it to be? Discuss how throwing a 4 or a 0 are equally likely but result in you moving a different number of spaces. The same is true for 1 and 3. Do you think this is fair? Some students might not. Question whether it is any less fair than throwing a 1 or a 6 on a normal dice, which are equally likely to happen, and then moving a different number of spaces (RL) (1.2, 1.5). Students could be allowed to play the game if a marked board is provided.

At this stage it might be best just to look quickly at the Gins game to see that it is another game that uses sticks for dice but that it uses them in a slightly different way as the sticks each have different markings and the scores are determined by the actual markings that are showing. If time permits, students could investigate the possible outcomes and likelihoods for this game (SM).

Move on to the section showing dice of other shapes. Ask if shapes need to be regular to be fair? What is a regular solid? Is a hexahedron (essentially two back-to-back tetrahedrons) with identical equilateral triangle faces regular? What is the difference with an octahedron? (CT) (1.4)

If you have any materials that allow you to make these shapes or have both the shapes in a set of solids, then it is worth having them available. Look at the hexahedron and consider how many faces and/or edges meet at each vertex. You will find that sometimes it is four and sometimes just three. Compare this with the octahedron where it is always four. You could also look at the angles between the faces on the two solids. On the octahedron they will all be the same (you could cut a profile that fits to show this) but on the hexahedron they will differ.

Can students see why there are only five regular solids. Agree that three or more faces must meet at a vertex. What options are there starting from a square? Three meet to give a cube (four are flat, five overlap). Similarly three pentagons meet to start a dodecahedron. Using equilateral triangles, 3/4/5 meet to start a tetrahedron/octahedron/icosahedron (CT) (1.2).

Extension

Provide nets (with tabs) on card for students to cut out and build their own regular polyhedra. Are theset dice fair? Can students invent their own shapes that result in fair dice when tested? (CT) (1.3)

Alternatively, students could research other older games to see what other methods of generating random moves have been used over the years and in different cultures (IE, TW).

3 Summary

Assessment criteria

- Understand that different outcomes may result from repeating an experiment — **Level 5**
- Find and record all mutually exclusive outcomes for single events and two successive events in a systematic way — **Level 6**
- Know that the sum of probabilities of all mutually exclusive events is 1 and use this when solving problems — **Level 6**
- Understand relative frequency as an estimate of probability and use this to compare outcomes of an experiment — **Level 7**
- Refine or extend the mathematics used to generate fuller solutions — **Level 7**

Question commentary

Example

The example asks students to draw a diagram to show the possible outcomes when two different spinners are spun at the same time. The answer is shown in the form of a sample space diagram but a tree diagram would be equally valid.

a

		\multicolumn{3}{c}{A}
		1	3	5
	2	(2, 1)	(2, 3)	(2, 5)
B	4	(4, 1)	(4, 3)	(4, 5)
	6	(6, 1)	(6, 3)	(6, 5)

b $P(\text{sum} = 7) = \dfrac{3}{9} = \dfrac{1}{3}$

Past question

The question is an example of a question about probability. Students may find this question confusing as no exact numbers of counters are given and there are many possible answers. In case of difficulty, encourage a trial and improvement approach. Choose a number for the number of red counters and use this to find the number of white counters. Make sure that a value for the number of yellow counters can be found to satisfy the condition that more than a quarter of all the counters are red.

Answer

Level 6

2 General solution: n red, $2n$ white, $< n$ yellow. For example, 5, 10, 1

Development and links

This topic links with the equivalence of decimals, fractions and percentages developed in Chapter 4. The topic of probability is extended further in Year 9.

Experimental probability links with work on data projects and comparison of experimental results with theoretical results in science. Students will use probability and sample space diagrams when studying inherited characteristics such as eye colour in biology. Probability is important in PSHE where students learn to make risk/reward assessments for events in their own lives. All forms of gambling are based on probability including buying a Lottery ticket and speculating on the Stock Exchange.

4 Fractions, decimals and percentages

Objectives

- Extend mental methods of calculation, working with percentages **5**
- Solve problems involving percentage changes **6**
- Use efficient methods to add, subtract, multiply and divide fractions, interpreting division as a multiplicative inverse........... **7**
- Cancel common factors before multiplying or dividing **7**

Introduction

In this chapter, students consolidate and extend skills in working with decimals, fractions and percentages. They use knowledge of lowest common multiples and highest common factors gained in chapter 1 to add, subtract, multiply and divide fractions, cancelling before multiplying. They calculate and solve problems using percentage changes and convert between and order fractions, decimals and percentages.

The student book discusses the development of Arabic numerals and the importance of good notation in efficient calculation. Arabic numerals are also known as Hindu-Arabic numbers as they originated in India, but were later used by Arabs who introduced them to Europe in the tenth century. Being able to calculate efficiently is vital in daily life. It is hard to imagine a shopping receipt, a recipe or a bank statement with all the numbers written as roman numerals. There is more information about the history of Arabic numerals at http://www-history.mcs.st-andrews.ac.uk/HistTopics/Arabic_numerals.html (TW).

⚡ast-track

4b, c

Level

MPA

1.1	4a, b, d, e, f
1.2	4a, b, c, d, e, f
1.3	4a, b, c, d, e, f
1.4	4b, c, d, e, f
1.5	4a, b, c, d, e, f

PLTS

IE	4b, c, d, e, f
CT	4a, b, c, d, e, f
RL	4b, c, d, f
TW	4I, a, b
SM	4e, f
EP	4c, d, e, f

Extra Resources

4   Start of chapter presentation

4a   Animation: Fractions and decimals

4b   Starter Factors and multiples T or F

4b   Animation: Adding fractions

4b   Worked solution: Q2d

4b   Consolidation sheet

4d   Consolidation sheet

4e   Worked solution: Q2a

4f   Starter: Fraction-decimal matching

4f   Animation: Fractions, decimals and percentages

Assessment: chapter 4

- Convert terminating decimals to fractions.   (L5) *Useful resources*
- Use division to convert a fraction to a decimal   (L5) *Calculator*
- Order fractions by converting them to decimals   (L5)

Starter – Decimal grid

Write nine decimal numbers in a 3 × 3 grid. Ask students to find

the sum of the top row

the product of the top left number and bottom right number

the difference between the middle left and middle right numbers, etc.

Can be differentiated by the number of decimal places in the chosen numbers.

Teaching notes

Use place value to remind students of the meaning of decimals. The place value columns could be written out and headings given. For example, 0.3 has a '3' in the 'tenths' column, so it represents '3 tenths' or $\frac{3}{10}$. Discuss how we write decimals that have digits in more than 1 column. Include examples that simplify.

How can the process be reversed, what should fractions be out of to make them easy to recognise as decimals? Use examples of fractions that have denominators easily converted to powers of ten.

What about awkward fractions? Discuss the method of short division and why many students end up calculating the reciprocal instead. How can a calculator be used? What if the decimal does not terminate? Discuss how to represent recurring decimals.

When ordering fractions and decimals, will it be easier to convert them all to fractions or decimals to allow for comparison?

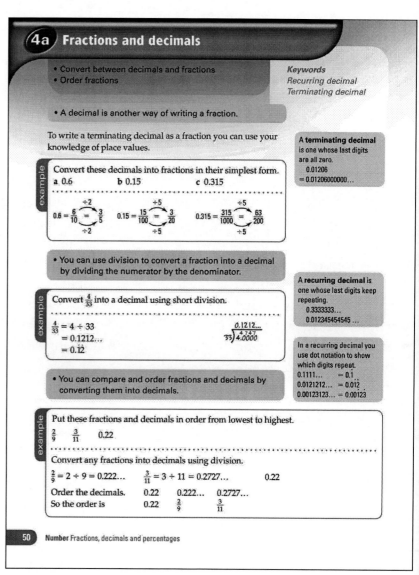

Plenary

When you look at a fraction in its simplest form, there is a way to tell if it will produce a recurring or termination decimal. Give examples of both. For example, $\frac{1}{5}, \frac{7}{8}, \frac{3}{20}$ (terminating). $\frac{2}{7}, \frac{4}{15}, \frac{5}{12}$ (recurring). Can students give further examples of either? Can students spot how to tell? Answer, look at the product of prime factors of the denominator. If it is made of only 2s and 5s then the fraction will be terminating, otherwise it's recurring (CT) (1.2, 1.5).

Simplification

Allow a calculator for all parts. Encourage students to use it not only to convert fractions to decimals, but also to check their answers. Remind students of the place value names tenths, hundredths, *etc*.

All questions (1.1, 1.3)

Question 1 – Encourage working to show how simplifying has been done.

Question 2 – Fort parts **e**, **i** and **j** encourage students to first simplify if possible.

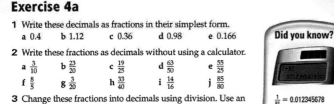
Extension

If $\frac{1}{3}$ is 0.33333…. what is the decimal equivalent of $\frac{2}{3}$ and $\frac{3}{3}$? Are 0.999999…. and 1 the same value? What would this mean about the fractional equivalent of 0.29999….? Same as 0.3 = $\frac{3}{10}$. Make up other recurring decimals that recur with a 9 and challenge students to convert them to fractions (CT) (1.2).

Exercise 4a commentary

Question 3 – Can be done without a calculator to practice short division if desired.

Question 4 – Use of a calculator sensible here. Ensure students compare each decimal place separately. Some reminder of the inequality signs maybe needed.

Question 5 – Very challenging without a calculator. Why is converting all values to a decimal easier than converting to a fraction?

Question 6 – Calculator useful to convert fractions to decimals. The term *variable* may need explaining. The two sided inequality may need explaining. For example, $3 < x < 7$ and x is a whole number. What could x be?

Question 7 – Encourage the use of earlier parts of this question to help inform the later parts. For example, double part **a** to find part **c**.

Challenge – Trial and improvement is likely to be effective. What fraction is the value close to? Over half, below three quarters. Does this help reduce the search?

Assessment Criteria – NNS, level 5: use equivalence between fractions and order fractions and decimals.

Links

Show the class an imperial foot-long ruler. Foot-long rulers are marked in inches and fractions of inches. What does each division on the ruler represent? ($\frac{1}{8}$", $\frac{1}{16}$" or $\frac{1}{32}$", depending on the ruler) How are different-sized divisions distinguished? (different length lines) A printable ruler can be found at http://www.vendian.org/mncharity/dir3/paper_rulers/UnstableURL/ruler_foot_a4.pdf (TW).

- Use efficient methods to add and subtract fractions   (L7)

Useful resources
*Calculator with a
fraction function*

Starter – Sums and products

Challenge students to find two numbers.

with a sum of 1.1 and a product of 0.24 (0.3, 0.8)
with a sum of 0.12 and a product of 0.0035 (0.05, 0.07)
with a sum of 0.76 and a product of 0.042 (0.06, 0.7)
with a sum of 1.29 and a product of 0.108, *etc* (0.09, 1.2)

Teaching notes

Re-enforce the concept of adding and subtracting fractions using shaded parts of diagrams. Discuss common misconceptions. For example, $\frac{2}{7} + \frac{3}{7} = \frac{5}{14}$ (RL)

How can fractions with different denominators be added and subtracted? Use a range of examples that require either one or both denominators to be converted. When fractions are converted, will the overall answer change?

How can fractions greater than one whole be written? Look at examples of both 'top heavy/improper fractions' and 'mixed fractions'. Re-enforce the concept with shaded diagrams.

How can fractions be added and subtracted when mixed fractions are used? Look at both the method in the student book and the method of treating the whole number parts separately. What are the advantages and disadvantages of both methods?

Include examples where the integer parts are large and the fractional parts cause a negative fraction. For example, $23\frac{3}{5} - 7\frac{5}{7}$. What is the best strategy? (RL) (1.5)

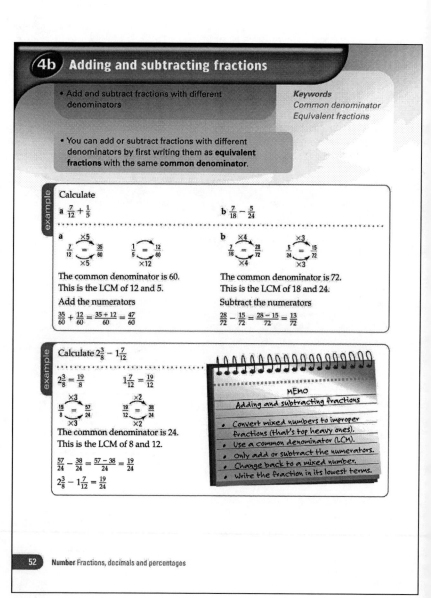

Plenary

If I add $\frac{1}{2}$ then $\frac{1}{4}$ then $\frac{1}{8}$ and continue adding fractions in this pattern, what happens to my answer? Encourage students to look for a pattern in the consecutive results that eliminates the need to keep finding a common denominator (sum first n term $= 2^{n-1}/2^n$) (CT) (1.2, 1.3).

Simplification

Finding a common denominator can be challenging for large numbers. Where needed, a calculator could be used to speed up the process of writing out lists of multiples to find a common multiple.

All questions (1.3)

Question 1 – Part **d** can be tackled by 'borrowing' from the first whole number. Ask students if they have an alternative method. For example, using a negative fraction to assist (1.5).

Question 2 – The lowest common denominator is the product of the denominators in all but part **h**. Students could use a calculator or choose a few parts from this question to reduce the time needed

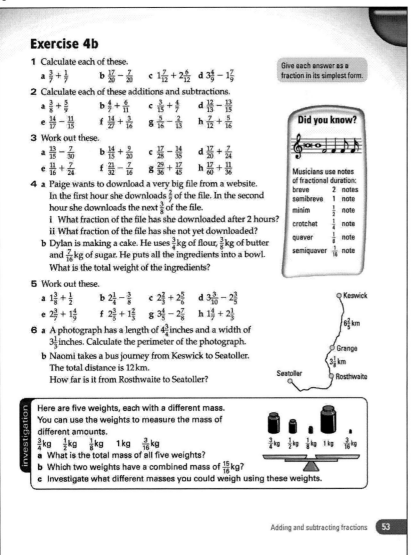

Extension

The diagonal length of a square of side 1 unit was thought by the ancient Babylonians (over three thousand years ago) to be roughly worked out by the following calculation, can you find the answer as a mixed fraction. Use a calculator to check the approximation.   ($\sqrt{2} = 1.41421356$ 8 dp)

$1 + \frac{24}{60} + \frac{51}{60^2} + \frac{10}{60^3} = 1\frac{8947}{21600} = 1.41421296$ (TW) (1.3)

Exercise 4b commentary

Question 3 – Encourage students to look for the lowest common denominator, or at least a common denominator that does not involve an unnecessarily large value.

Question 4 – Encourage students to form a line of working to express what they are calculating (1.1).

Question 5 – Parts **b**, **d** and **g**, are more difficult. Encourage more than one approach; see the examples (1.4).

Question 6 – What alternative methods can be used? In part **a**, did anyone add the two sides of the rectangle, then double (1.1).

Investigation – What common denominator should we use? Putting more than one mass on one side allows use to weigh different masses, but there are some you can't weigh in this way. Can you think of another way, using the same 5 masses in order to weigh $\frac{1}{16}, \frac{4}{16}, \frac{6}{16}, \frac{7}{16}, \frac{9}{16}, \frac{11}{16}, \frac{15}{16}$ kg. Answer, all can be achieved by putting masses on each side (IE, CT).

Assessment Criteria – Calculating, level 6: add and subtract fractions by writing them with a common denominator Calculating, level 7: add and subtract fractions.

Links

The Ancient Egyptians represented all their fractions as the sum of a number of unit fractions, where all the unit fractions are different. All positive rational numbers can be represented by Egyptian fractions. More information about Egyptian fractions, including a calculator to convert a fraction to an Egyptian fraction can be found at http://www.mcs.surrey.ac.uk/Personal/R.Knott/Fractions/egyptian.html (TW).

- Multiply and divide an integer by a fraction (L6)
- Use efficient methods to multiply and divide fractions, interpreting division as a multiplicative inverse (L7)
- Cancel common factors before multiplying or dividing (L7)

Useful resources
Die

Starter – Dice fractions

Ask students to draw six boxes representing the numerators and denominators of three fractions side by side. Throw a die six times. After each throw, ask students to place the score in one of their boxes. Students score points if the first fraction is bigger than the second fraction which in turn is bigger than the third fraction.

Teaching notes

When a fraction is multiplied what happens to the two numbers? For example, $\frac{2}{10} \times 3$ means what? $\left(\frac{6}{30}\right)$ Use shaded diagrams to establish the meaning. What possible error might some students make? Why is this incorrect?

What is the meaning of $\frac{3}{4}$ of 20? How can it be represented as a calculation? The word 'of' can be look at as meaning multiply, so $\frac{3}{4} \times 20$. Look at how this calculation can be simplified like the first example.

How can two fractions be multiplied? Use shaded diagrams to explain why this method works. Show how cancelling first can help.

How can two fractions be divided? What does $4 \div \frac{2}{5}$ mean? Express in words. Use diagrams to show that it is equivalent to multiplication by 5 and division by 2. Effectively the fraction has been 'turned upside down'. The following rhyme could useful to help divide with fractions: 'the one you are dividing by, turn upside down and multiply'.

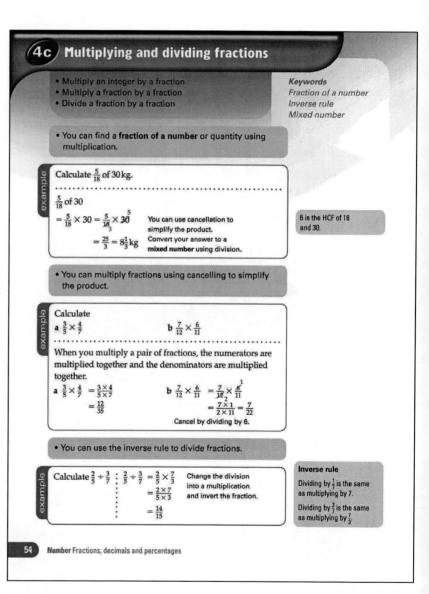

4c Multiplying and dividing fractions

- Multiply an integer by a fraction
- Multiply a fraction by a fraction
- Divide a fraction by a fraction

Keywords
Fraction of a number
Inverse rule
Mixed number

- You can find a **fraction of a number** or quantity using multiplication.

example

Calculate $\frac{5}{18}$ of 30 kg.

$\frac{5}{18}$ of 30

$= \frac{5}{18} \times 30 = \frac{5}{18} \times \overset{5}{\cancel{30}}$ You can use cancellation to simplify the product.

$= \frac{25}{3} = 8\frac{1}{3}$ kg   Convert your answer to a mixed number using division.

6 is the HCF of 18 and 30.

- You can multiply fractions using cancelling to simplify the product.

example

Calculate

a $\frac{3}{5} \times \frac{4}{7}$ b $\frac{7}{12} \times \frac{6}{11}$

When you multiply a pair of fractions, the numerators are multiplied together and the denominators are multiplied together.

a $\frac{3}{5} \times \frac{4}{7} = \frac{3 \times 4}{5 \times 7}$ b $\frac{7}{12} \times \frac{6}{11} = \frac{7}{\cancel{12}_2} \times \frac{\cancel{6}^1}{11}$

$= \frac{12}{35}$ $= \frac{7 \times 1}{2 \times 11} = \frac{7}{22}$

Cancel by dividing by 6.

- You can use the inverse rule to divide fractions.

example

Calculate $\frac{2}{5} \div \frac{3}{7}$: $\frac{2}{5} \div \frac{3}{7} = \frac{2}{5} \times \frac{7}{3}$ Change the division into a multiplication and invert the fraction.

$= \frac{2 \times 7}{5 \times 3}$

$= \frac{14}{15}$

Inverse rule
Dividing by $\frac{1}{7}$ is the same as multiplying by 7.
Dividing by $\frac{3}{7}$ is the same as multiplying by $\frac{7}{3}$.

54   **Number** Fractions, decimals and percentages

Plenary

Check that the **challenge** outcome also holds true for negative fractions by trying a few examples. It works for any positive or negative fraction or integer. A very able student may be able to prove this (IE, CT) (1.3, 1.4).

Simplification

Minimising the number of things to remember will simplify this exercise. Changing the integers to fractions over '1' will make multiplication easier. Not cancelling down before multiplication will allow the correct answer to be achieved, but point out that cancelling down needs to be looked at.

All questions (1.3)

Question 1 – Watch for students multiplying both the numerator and denominator. Use shaded diagrams to re-enforce the fact that only the numerator is changed (RL).

Question 2 – Some students may find it easier to make a single fraction first, and then cancel down. For example,

$$15 \times \frac{13}{25} = \frac{\cancel{15}^3 \times 13}{\cancel{25}_5} = \frac{3 \times 13}{5} = \frac{39}{5} = 7\frac{4}{5}$$

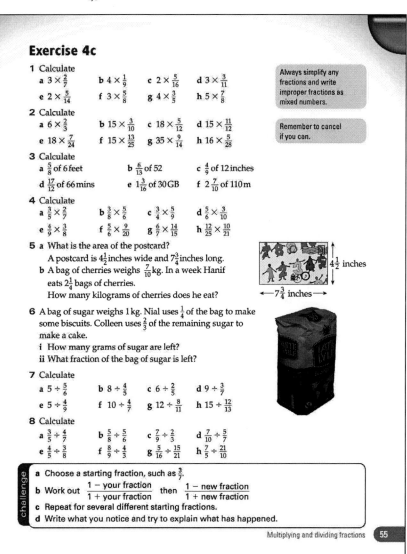

Exercise 4c

1 Calculate
a $3 \times \frac{2}{7}$ b $4 \times \frac{1}{9}$ c $2 \times \frac{5}{16}$ d $3 \times \frac{3}{11}$
e $2 \times \frac{5}{14}$ f $3 \times \frac{5}{8}$ g $4 \times \frac{3}{5}$ h $5 \times \frac{7}{8}$

> Always simplify any fractions and write improper fractions as mixed numbers.

2 Calculate
a $6 \times \frac{2}{3}$ b $15 \times \frac{3}{10}$ c $18 \times \frac{5}{12}$ d $15 \times \frac{11}{12}$
e $18 \times \frac{7}{24}$ f $15 \times \frac{13}{25}$ g $35 \times \frac{9}{14}$ h $16 \times \frac{5}{28}$

> Remember to cancel if you can.

3 Calculate
a $\frac{5}{8}$ of 6 feet   b $\frac{6}{13}$ of 52   c $\frac{4}{9}$ of 12 inches
d $\frac{17}{12}$ of 66 mins   e $1\frac{3}{16}$ of 30 GB   f $\frac{7}{10}$ of 110 m

4 Calculate
a $\frac{3}{5} \times \frac{2}{7}$ b $\frac{3}{8} \times \frac{5}{6}$ c $\frac{3}{4} \times \frac{5}{9}$ d $\frac{5}{6} \times \frac{3}{10}$
e $\frac{4}{9} \times \frac{3}{8}$ f $\frac{5}{6} \times \frac{9}{20}$ g $\frac{6}{7} \times \frac{14}{15}$ h $\frac{12}{25} \times \frac{10}{21}$

5 a What is the area of the postcard?
A postcard is $4\frac{1}{2}$ inches wide and $7\frac{3}{4}$ inches long.
b A bag of cherries weighs $\frac{7}{10}$ kg. In a week Hanif eats $2\frac{1}{4}$ bags of cherries.
How many kilograms of cherries does he eat?

$4\frac{1}{2}$ inches
$\leftarrow 7\frac{3}{4}$ inches $\rightarrow$

6 A bag of sugar weighs 1 kg. Nial uses $\frac{1}{4}$ of the bag to make some biscuits. Colleen uses $\frac{2}{3}$ of the remaining sugar to make a cake.
i How many grams of sugar are left?
ii What fraction of the bag of sugar is left?

7 Calculate
a $5 \div \frac{5}{6}$ b $8 \div \frac{4}{5}$ c $6 \div \frac{2}{5}$ d $9 \div \frac{3}{7}$
e $5 \div \frac{4}{9}$ f $10 \div \frac{4}{7}$ g $12 \div \frac{8}{11}$ h $15 \div \frac{12}{13}$

8 Calculate
a $\frac{3}{5} \div \frac{4}{7}$ b $\frac{5}{8} \div \frac{5}{6}$ c $\frac{7}{9} \div \frac{2}{3}$ d $\frac{7}{10} \div \frac{5}{7}$
e $\frac{4}{5} \div \frac{3}{8}$ f $\frac{8}{9} \div \frac{4}{3}$ g $\frac{5}{16} \div \frac{15}{21}$ h $\frac{7}{5} \div \frac{21}{10}$

challenge
a Choose a starting fraction, such as $\frac{3}{7}$.
b Work out $\dfrac{1 - \text{your fraction}}{1 + \text{your fraction}}$ then $\dfrac{1 - \text{new fraction}}{1 + \text{new fraction}}$
c Repeat for several different starting fractions.
d Write what you notice and try to explain what has happened.

Multiplying and dividing fractions   55

Extension

The √2 can be calculated as a 'continued fraction' which caries on for ever! How far can students get calculating √2? (1.3)

$11 \dfrac{1}{21\frac{1}{2}} = 1\frac{2}{5}$, $11 \dfrac{1}{21\frac{1}{21\frac{1}{2}}} = 1\frac{5}{12}$, $1\frac{12}{29}$, ...

$1 + \cfrac{1}{2 + \cfrac{1}{2 + \cfrac{1}{2 + \cfrac{1}{2 + \cfrac{1}{2 + \cfrac{1}{\dots}}}}}}$

Exercise 4c commentary

Question 3 – Remind students that 'of' means multiply.

Question 4 – Encourage students to try to cancel down before, rather than after, multiplying. Challenge students to try a question both ways and comment on the most efficient method for them (1.5).

Question 5 – Some students may try to deal with the integer and fractional parts separately as can be done with addition and subtraction. Encourage experimentation and ask for students conclusions.

Question 6 – Students maybe tempted to add rather than multiply the fractions. Why is multiplying the correct procedure? Is it easier to work in kg or grams in part **a**?

Question 7 and **8** –. Some students may find it helps to turn the integer into a fraction over '1'.

Challenge – Encourage students to begin with simple fractions and to hypothesise about the result (1.4).

Assessment Criteria – Calculating, level 6: calculate fractions of quantities (fraction answer), multiply and divide an integer by a fraction. Calculating, level 7: multiply and divide fractions.

Links

Meteorologists use fractions to estimate the amount of cloud covering the sky. The entire sky is divided into eighths and they estimate how many eighths or oktas of the sky are covered in cloud. 0/8 oktas means that the sky is clear/ completely covered by cloud. There is more information about the symbols used to show cloud cover on weather charts at http://www.metoffice.gov.uk/education/secondary/students/charts.html (EP).

- Calculate percentages and find the outcome of a given percentage increase or decrease (L6/7)
- Extend mental methods of calculation working with percentages (L5)
- Solve problems involving percentage changes (L6)

Useful resources
Calculator

Starter – Fraction sort

Write the following fractions on the board.

$$\frac{14}{49} \quad \frac{2}{12} \quad \frac{7}{42} \quad \frac{18}{30} \quad \frac{10}{35} \quad \frac{4}{24} \quad \frac{21}{35} \quad \frac{6}{21} \quad \frac{5}{30} \quad \frac{24}{40} \quad \frac{4}{14} \quad \frac{15}{25}$$

Ask students to sort the fractions into three sets of equivalent fractions. Can be extended by asking students to make up their own fraction sort puzzle.

Teaching notes

As a paired activity (TW), write the figure £120 in the centre of an A3 sheet and circle it. Write 100% at the edge of the circle. Branch of from the circle and create another percentage of £120, for example, 50% = £60. Explain that different percentages can be found by drawing in multiple branches, branches off other branches or combining results. Challenge students to come up with as many as possible including unusual ones, for example, $3\frac{1}{4}\%$.

A percentage of an amount can be found using a calculator. When would a calculator be useful? Ensure students are confident expressing percentages as decimals. Look at the method of decimal multiplication as outlined in the first example. Encourage students to show the stages of their working. Consider a discussion of the method of performing a percentage change with just one multiplication. For example, ×1.23 for a 23% increase or × 0.77 for a 23% decrease.

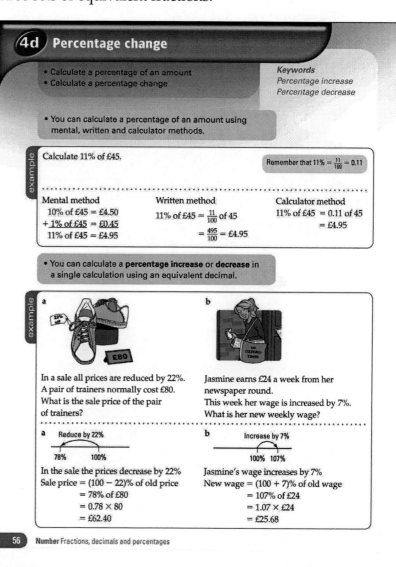

Plenary

Choose a simple starting amount. Increase it by a specific simple percentage. Now decrease the new amount by the same percentage. Why don't you get back to the original amount? What calculation do you have to do to increase then decrease by the same percentage? Encourage students to consider both the equivalent fraction and equivalent decimal method from the worked example. Make clear that multiplication and division are reverse processes.

Simplification

For percentage decreases, ask 'what percentage is left? Therefore what percentage are you trying to find?' Encourage the use of decimal multiplication for percentage change, but allow the practice of adding or subtracting the required percentage.

All questions (1.3)

Question 1 – Encourage students to try all three methods. Remind students that 'of' means multiply (1.1, 1.5).

Question 2 – An opportunity to explore payment schemes Why are monthly payments generally more expensive ? (EP)

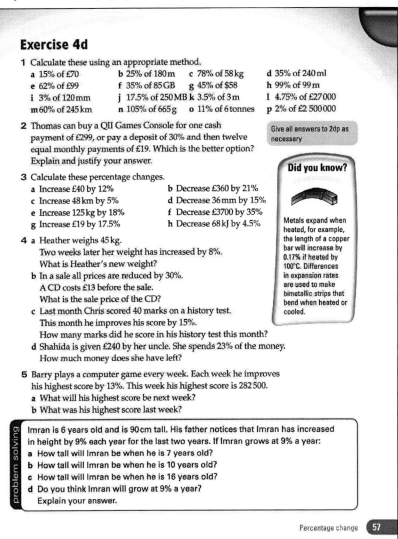

Extension

How can these two answers be written?

a Increase £50 by x %. $\qquad$ $50 + \frac{x}{2}$ or $\frac{(100 + x)}{2}$

b Increase £y by x %. $\qquad$ $y + \frac{xy}{100}$ or $\frac{(100y + xy)}{100}$.

An algebraic approach is likely to be very difficult, encourage an investigation approach with various values for x. Part **b** is even more demanding and will be beyond most students (CT) (1.2, 1.4).

Exercise 4d commentary

Question 3 – Ensure students make use of the decimal multiplication method for at least some of these examples as it is used in the future.

Question 4 – For these practical applications of percentage increase and decrease, get students to check to see if the answer is reasonable.

Question 5 – A function machine/arrow diagram may help students to realise how the reverse process of works. Students who subtract 13% for part **b** should check their answer by adding on 13% (CT, RL) (1.1).

Problem solving – Encourage an organised approach in laying out the working, identifying the age and height. How do you think growth rates change during your childhood? Why can't you find 9% of 90 cm and just multiply by the number of years that pass to find the increase? (IE, RL)

Assessment Criteria – Calculating, level 5: use a calculator where appropriate to calculate fractions/percentages of quantities/measurements. Calculating, level 6: calculate percentages and find the outcome of a given percentage increase or decrease. Calculating, level 7: calculate the result of any proportional change using multiplicative methods.

Links

Forests are important to the World environment as they absorb carbon emissions but every year vast areas are lost to logging and agricultural clearance. A table showing the total percentage loss of primary forest, those undisturbed by human activity, for 17 countries from 1990 to 2005 can be found at http://rainforests.mongabay.com/primary_annual. html

- Calculate an original amount when given the transformed amount after a percentage change (L8)
- Use calculators for reverse percentage change calculations by doing an appropriate division (L8)

Useful resources
Calculator

• •

Starter – Half-way fractions

Ask students to find the fraction that is half-way between
$\frac{3}{5}$ and $\frac{7}{10}$, $\frac{3}{8}$ and $\frac{1}{2}$, $\frac{1}{3}$ and $\frac{5}{6}$, $\frac{1}{4}$ and $\frac{1}{3}$.
Can be extended by asking for other fractions in the given ranges.
Can be differentiated by the choice of fractions.
Answers: $\frac{13}{20}$, $\frac{7}{16}$, $\frac{7}{12}$, $\frac{7}{24}$.

Teaching notes

How can a percentage increase be performed on a calculator in one step? Since the new amount is over 100%, a decimal of over 1 can be used as the multiplier. If this is illustrated on an arrow diagram, then a discussion could follow as to the method of reversing the initial percentage increase. Explain this in terms of a 'reverse process'.

Consider examples of percentage decrease in the same way. If an amount is decreased by 15%, what percentage is being found? What multiplication is required? Once the change has been applied, how can it be reversed?

Why is a percentage increase by 10% not reversed by a percentage decrease of 10%?

Look at practical problems of finding the new amount using a single decimal multiplier. Look at practical problems of finding the original amount that require the use of the reverse process. Could these sorts of questions be solved without a calculator? Look at a possible example.

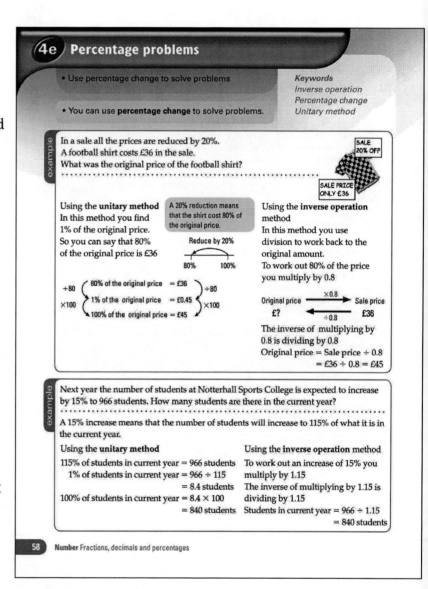

4e **Percentage problems**

• Use percentage change to solve problems

Keywords
Inverse operation
Percentage change
Unitary method

• You can use **percentage change** to solve problems.

In a sale all the prices are reduced by 20%.
A football shirt costs £36 in the sale.
What was the original price of the football shirt?

Using the **unitary method**
In this method you find 1% of the original price.
So you can say that 80% of the original price is £36

A 20% reduction means that the shirt cost 80% of the original price.

Reduce by 20%

80%   100%

÷80   ×100   80% of the original price = £36   ÷80   ×100
1% of the original price = £0.45
100% of the original price = £45

Using the **inverse operation** method
In this method you use division to work back to the original amount.
To work out 80% of the price you multiply by 0.8

Original price   ×0.8   Sale price
£?   ÷0.8   £36

The inverse of multiplying by 0.8 is dividing by 0.8
Original price = Sale price ÷ 0.8
= £36 ÷ 0.8 = £45

Next year the number of students at Notterhall Sports College is expected to increase by 15% to 966 students. How many students are there in the current year?

A 15% increase means that the number of students will increase to 115% of what it is in the current year.

Using the **unitary method**
115% of students in current year = 966 students
1% of students in current year = 966 ÷ 115
= 8.4 students
100% of students in current year = 8.4 × 100
= 840 students

Using the **inverse operation** method
To work out an increase of 15% you multiply by 1.15
The inverse of multiplying by 1.15 is dividing by 1.15
Students in current year = 966 ÷ 1.15
= 840 students

58   **Number** Fractions, decimals and percentages

Plenary

An amount is increase by 44% over 2 years. If the increase was the same each year, what was the yearly percentage increase? (12%). Repeat for 21%. (10%). Is there a better way to find the answer than trial and improvement? This need not be followed to using $\sqrt{1.44}$ or $\sqrt{1.21}$. Investigation of how to achieve × 1.44 in 2 equal multiplications would demonstrate a clear understanding (CT) (1.2, 1.3).

Simplification

Provide students with an arrow diagram to help reinforce the reverse operation of percentage change. For example,

original × 1.2 → new amount increased by 20%

original amount before 20% increased ← new amount ÷ 1.2

All questions (EP) (1.3)

Question 1 – Showing an arrow between columns to demonstrate the method of increasing by 4% may help to inform students of the reverse process. × 1.04.

Question 2 – Encourage the use of both multiplicative and ratio methods. Ask students, what percentage does the amount in the question represent? (1.1, 1.5)

Exercise 4e

1 Jackson decides to increase the wages of everybody in his factory by 4%.
  Copy and complete his new payroll list.

Name	Old wage	New wage
James	£300	
Bernie	£275	
Vikki		£520
Rufus		£364

2 a A pair of trainers are on sale for £84 which is 70% of the original price.
    What was the original price of the trainers?
  b A computer has been reduced in price by 25% to £345.
    What was the original price of the computer?
  c A packet of McDitty's chocolate fingers is increased in mass. The label says that the packet is now 35% bigger. The weight of the packet is now 324 g.
    What was the original weight of a packet of McDitty's chocolate fingers?

3 a Gareth bought a computer game in a sale and saved £5. The label said that it was a 25% reduction.
    What was the original price of the computer game?
  b Mandy bought a box of cereal on Monday. On Friday she bought a box of the same cereal but with 30% extra free. Mandy worked out that she got an extra 150 g of cereal in the new packet.
    How much cereal was there in the original packet?

4 Violet and Nita each bought an identical coat from the same shop. Violet bought hers on Saturday when there was 20% off the original price. Nita bought hers on Monday when there was 30% off the original price. Violet paid £15 more than Nita.
  a What was the original price of the coat?
  b How much did Violet pay for the coat?
  c How much did Nita pay for the coat?

investigation

The population of the Earth in the year 2007 was 6649 million.
a If the population of the Earth has increased by 2% a year, what was the population of the Earth in 2006?
b What was the population of the Earth in the year 2000?
c Investigate the population of the Earth at different times in history.

Percentage problems 59

Extension

Solve question **4** using an algebraic method. Call the initial value x. A decimal multiplication method is useful here and students may need prompting to form an equation. For example, $0.8x = 0.7x + 15$. (CT) (1.1, 1.4)

Exercise 4e commentary

Question 3 – How does the question differ from **1** and **2**? The amount of the change is given rather than the new or original amount. How will this change the way the question is handled?

Question 4 – A trial and improvement approach is a good initial method. Some students will accept that 10% = £15, but is this correct? Encourage students to check their final solution (IE, RL).

Investigation – Encourage the efficient use of a calculator. It may be appropriate to introduce the power function. For further investigation look at http://en.wikipedia.org/wiki/World_Population.Also, students might like to see what the population would have been in the year AD 864 if a 2% increase has continued throughout history. Take off the 2% increase (÷ 1.02) 1143 times. The population is just below 1! (SM, IE)

Assessment Criteria – calculating, level 8: use percentages to solve problems involving the calculation of the original quantity given the result of a proportional change.

Links

The Consumer Price Index (CPI) is an official measure of the average price of goods and services including travel costs, food, heating and household goods. The index number is calculated each month by finding the price of a sample of goods that a typical household might buy, and comparing the price to a reference value. The percentage change in the CPI from the previous month is a measure of inflation. The latest figures for the CPI can be found at http://www.statistics.gov.uk/cci/nugget.asp?ID=19 (EP)

- Use the equivalence of fractions, decimals and percentages to compare proportions (L6)
- Interpret percentage as the 'so many hundredths of' and express one given number as a percentage of another (L6)

Useful resources
Calculator

Starter – Percentage bingo

Ask students to draw a 3 × 3 grid and enter nine amounts from the following list:
£2, £3, £4, £5, £6, £7, £8, £9, £10, £11, £12, £13, £14, £15, £16, £17
Give questions, for example, 12% of £75, 68% of £25, 44% of £25.
Winner is the first student to cross out all 9 amounts.
(Hint: 12% of 75 = 75% of 12.)

Teaching notes

If a fraction is out of 10 or 100, *etc.* show how place value tells us the decimal equivalent. Look to see if the denominators can be easily converted. What does a fraction need to be out of to see it as a percentage?

The other conversions between decimals, fractions and percentages are covered in the previous spreads in chapter 4.

Look at examples of expressing one amount as the percentage of another amount. Include calculator and non calculator examples. Encourage students to see the decimal solution as a percentage rather than relying on a further multiplication by 100. For example, express 4 as a percentage of 15: $4 \div 15 = 0.26666...$ which is 27%. Express 3 as a percentage of 20: $\frac{3}{20} = \frac{15}{100} = 15\%$

Look at examples of finding the percentage change. Emphasise that the change is **always** out of the **original**.

Percentage change $= \frac{\text{change}}{\text{original}}$.

But this gives a decimal. What is the last step? Convert the decimal to a percentage.

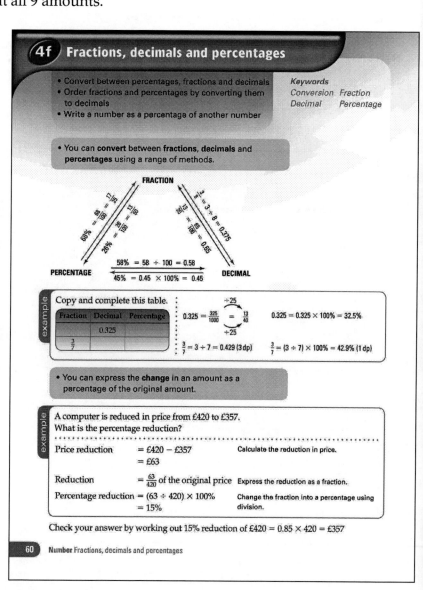

Plenary

Another use of percentages is in percentage errors. For example, attendance at a football game is 20 454 but a paper might quote 20 000. How might you calculate the percentage error? Ask students to estimate the size of the percentage error. Which value seems correct to divide by? True value or error value? Answer 2.22% (2dp) but students will get 2.27% if they divide by the wrong amount. (CT, EP) (1.3)

Simplification

Avoid simply giving students an algorithm to use. Focus on the meaning and understanding of fractions, decimals and percentages. For example, what does the line in a fraction mean when using a calculator? What does the first decimal place of a decimal tell us about the percentage it represents? Before you find the 'percentage increase', it makes sense to find the 'increase' etc.

All questions (1.3)

Question 1 – To improve technique, encourage students to only use a calculator when necessary. For example, converting $\frac{7}{12}$.

Extension

A pub might buy a pint of lemonade for 20p and a pint of larger or beer of 80p and sell them both for £2 each. What percentage profit is this? (900% and 150%) Try this without a calculator. Why do pubs charge a similar price for soft drinks and alcoholic drinks if the percentage profit is so different? How much of the difference is due to tax? (EP)

Exercise 4f commentary

Question 2 – What factors apart from the score in a test will give an indication of how well you have done? Discuss class average, position in class, last year's results, difficulty of the test, *etc.* (1.5).

Question 3 – Encourage students to check their result by working out the new amount from the answer they achieve for the percentage change. Allow students to use a mental method of finding convenient percentages of the original amount and combining them to try to find the percentage change (RL).

Question 4 –Challenge students to work without using a calculator. Encourage them to show how their fraction is being simplified (CT) (1.2).

Investigation – How could you investigate whether people are better or worse off based on this table of figures. Discuss the relevance of the salary and house increases in particular (IE, SM, EP).

Assessment Criteria – NNS, level 6: use the equivalence of fractions, decimals and percentages to compare proportions.

Links

Bring in some newspapers or magazines for the class to use. Ask students to find any article or advertisement where a decimal, percentage or fraction is used. Which format is used most frequently? Would the article or advertisement have the same affect if, for example, a decimal was used in place of a percentage, or a percentage in place of a fraction? Are there any examples where a conversion has been used? (EP) (1.1, 1.5)

4a

1 Change these fractions into decimals using division. Use an appropriate method.

> Give your answers to 5 decimal places where appropriate.

a $\frac{9}{16}$　　　**b** $\frac{5}{17}$　　　**c** $\frac{3}{13}$　　　**d** $\frac{6}{7}$　　　**e** $\frac{11}{19}$

2 Place < or > between these pairs of numbers to show which number is the largest.

a $0.4 \square \frac{3}{7}$　　**b** $\frac{6}{13} \square \frac{7}{15}$　　**c** $\frac{5}{8} \square 0.6$　　**d** $0.39 \square \frac{7}{19}$

3 Put these fractions and decimals in order from lowest to highest.

a $\frac{8}{13}$　　0.623　　$\frac{5}{8}$　　0.63　　**b** $\frac{3}{13}$　　$\frac{4}{17}$　　0.229　　0.23

4b

4 Work out

a $\frac{12}{15} - \frac{7}{18}$　　**b** $\frac{13}{15} + \frac{11}{25}$　　**c** $\frac{14}{27} + \frac{13}{18}$　　**d** $\frac{7}{14} + \frac{7}{21}$

e $\frac{13}{16} + \frac{7}{20}$　　**f** $\frac{24}{35} - \frac{5}{28}$　　**g** $\frac{23}{36} + \frac{7}{54}$　　**h** $\frac{13}{60} + \frac{8}{15}$

> In your answers, convert any improper fractions to mixed numbers and write fractions in their simplest form.

5 Hector has $2\frac{1}{2}$ litres of water. Jenny has $\frac{3}{5}$ of a litre of blackcurrant cordial. They mix the two drinks together. What is the total amount of liquid?

6 Work out

a $2\frac{1}{5} + \frac{1}{3}$　　**b** $1\frac{1}{4} - \frac{5}{8}$　　**c** $3\frac{2}{5} + 1\frac{2}{3}$　　**d** $2\frac{5}{8} - 1\frac{11}{12}$

4c

7 Calculate

a $\frac{3}{4}$ of 5 yards　　**b** $\frac{5}{12}$ of 60 kg　　**c** $\frac{3}{8}$ of 20 mm　　**d** $\frac{4}{13}$ of 39 km

e $1\frac{5}{16}$ of 40 miles　　**f** $3\frac{7}{8}$ of 200 m^2　　**g** $1\frac{5}{12}$ of 340 ml　　**h** $3\frac{8}{25}$ of 1 century

8 Calculate

a $\frac{4}{7} \times \frac{5}{3}$　　**b** $\frac{2}{5} \times \frac{3}{8}$　　**c** $\frac{5}{6} \times \frac{4}{5}$　　**d** $\frac{7}{8} \times \frac{3}{4}$

e $\frac{14}{15} \times \frac{12}{35}$　　**f** $\frac{12}{35} \times \frac{15}{21}$　　**g** $\frac{27}{16} \times \frac{32}{18}$　　**h** $\frac{5}{8} \times \frac{24}{15}$

> Use cancellation whenever possible.

9 Calculate

a $4 \div \frac{4}{7}$　　**b** $12 \div \frac{4}{3}$　　**c** $16 \div \frac{8}{9}$　　**d** $10 \div \frac{5}{7}$

e $3 \div \frac{5}{11}$　　**f** $14 \div \frac{7}{4}$　　**g** $15 \div \frac{10}{11}$　　**h** $18 \div \frac{9}{13}$

10 Calculate

a $\frac{4}{7} \div \frac{5}{8}$　　**b** $\frac{6}{9} \div \frac{6}{7}$　　**c** $\frac{8}{11} \div \frac{3}{4}$　　**d** $\frac{8}{13} \div \frac{4}{7}$

e $\frac{5}{6} \div \frac{4}{9}$　　**f** $\frac{9}{10} \div \frac{3}{5}$　　**g** $\frac{3}{14} \div \frac{12}{35}$　　**h** $\frac{8}{9} \div \frac{32}{45}$

11 Calculate these percentage changes.
   a Increase £50 by 28%   **b** Decrease £640 by 45%
   c Increase 180 km by 6%   **d** Decrease 270 mm by 3.5%
   e Increase 85 kg by 8%   **f** Decrease £9 000 000 by 1.2%

12 **a** Monica earns £35 each weekend, working in her mum's shop.
     Next weekend her pay will be increased by 4%.
     How much will Monica earn next weekend?
   b In a sale all prices are reduced by 15%.
     A DVD costs £12.49 before the sale.
     What is the sale price of the DVD?

13 **a** A computer is on sale for £330 which is 60% of the original price.
     What was the original price of the computer?
   b A Porsche 911 increased in price from 1982 to 2007 by 263%.
     The price for a Porsche 911 in 2007 was £60 621.
     What was the price of the Porsche in 1982?

14 **a** Kerry bought a mobile phone in a sale and saved £12.
     The label said that it was a 15% reduction.
     What was the original price of the mobile phone?
   b In a special offer, a packet of biscuits says that it contains 20% extra.
     The weight of the packet is 64 g heavier than it was before the special offer.
     How much did the packet of biscuits used to weigh?

15 Copy and complete this table.
Show clearly your working out.

> Give your answers as
> - decimals to 4 decimal places
> - percentages to 2 decimal place
> - fractions in their simplest form.

Fraction	Decimal	Percentage
$\frac{7}{15}$		
	0.995	
		12.5%
$\frac{4}{13}$		
	1.0377	

16 **a** A CD costs £13. In a sale the price is reduced to £11.44.
     What is the percentage reduction?
   b A computer is reduced in price from £880 to £836.
     What is the percentage reduction?

4 Summary

Assessment criteria

- Use equivalence between fractions and order fractions and decimals — Level 5
- Use a calculator where appropriate to calculate fractions/percentages of quantities/measurements — Level 5
- Add and subtract fractions by writing them with a common denominator, calculate fractions of quantities (fraction answers), multiply and divide an integer by a fraction — Level 6
- Calculate percentages and find the outcome of a given percentage increase or decrease — Level 6
- Add, subtract, multiply and divide fractions — Level 7
- Calculate the result of any proportional change using multiplicative methods — Level 7

Question commentary

Example

The example illustrates a Level 6 question on percentages. Some students may try to subtract the percentages first and give an answer equivalent to 3% of the number of girls. Emphasise that the percentage gives the proportion of left-handed children in each group but does not give information about the number of children in each group. The example uses the calculator method to find the percentages but a written or mental method is equally valid.

$$\text{girls} = 0.12 \times 27\,000 = 3240$$
$$\text{boys} = 0.09 \times 23\,900 = \frac{2151}{1089}$$

Past question

The question asks students to calculate with fractions. In part **a**, students may find the LCM of 5 and 10, or simplify $\frac{6}{10}$ first by cancelling. Emphasise that the answer should be given as a mixed number in its simplest form. Students can use their answer for part **b** to answer part **c**. This method is more intuitive than the usual multiplicative method and students should check that both methods give the same answer. Ask probing questions such as "Can you explain why dividing one fraction by another does not always give a smaller answer?"

Answer

Level 6

2 a $1\frac{4}{5}$

b 20

c 4 with correct working

Development and links

Students will calculate further percentage changes in Chapter 12 where the topic is developed to using fractions, decimals and percentages to compare proportions.

Fractions, decimals and percentages are used throughout the curriculum, especially when working with ratio and proportion, and analysing the results of statistical enquiries. Students will use fractions, decimals and percentages for measure in design technology, for recipes and recipe conversion in food technology, for pie charts and statistical analysis in geography, and for comparing concentrations of liquids in science. Outside school, students will use percentage change to calculate interest due on bank and building society accounts, to calculate VAT and to calculate price increases and reductions.

Objectives

	Level
• Use index notation for integer powers	**6**
• Substitute numbers into expressions and formulae	**6**
• Construct and solve linear equations with integer coefficients (with and without brackets, negative signs anywhere in the equation, positive or negative solution)	**6**
• Derive a formula and, in simple cases, change its subject	**6/7**
• Simplify or transform algebraic expressions by taking out single-term common factors	**7**
• Use formulae from mathematics and other subjects	**7**

MPA

1.1	5b, e
1.2	5a, c, d, e, f
1.3	5a, b, c, d, e, f
1.4	5a, b, d, e, f
1.5	5a, b, c, d, e, f

PLTS

IE	5b, c, d, e, f
CT	5a, b, d, e, f
RL	5a, d, e
TW	5I, d, e, f
SM	
EP	5I, b, e, f

Introduction

The focus of this chapter is on using and manipulating symbols in expressions and formulae. Students use index notation, simplify expressions, factorise expressions and multiply a negative term over a bracket. The chapter develops to include deriving formulae, substituting values into formulae, changing the subject of a formula and using real-life formulae.

The student book illustrates a quotation from Galileo Galilei about the language of mathematics. Algebra is a universal language used for hundreds of years and links across the curriculum to ICT, history, English and modern foreign languages. Scientists use the language of algebra to write formulae to describe the behaviour of the World around them. Translating problems into the language of algebra makes them quicker to write and easier to solve. Galileo was a famous mathematician, scientist, philosopher and astronomer and has been called the Father of Science. There is more information about Galileo Galilei at http://www.bbc.co.uk/history/historic_figures/galilei_galileo.shtml (TW, EP).

Extra Resources

5	Start of chapter presentation
5b	Consolidation sheet
5c	Animation: Multiplying brackets
5c	Worked solution: Q3a
5c	Consolidation sheet
5d	Starter Factors and multiples T or F
5d	Animation: Factorisation
5e	Consolidation sheet
5f	Starter: Collecting like terms T or F
5f	Worked solution: Q3d
	Assessment: chapter 5

Fast-track

5a, c, d, e, f

- Use index notation for integer powers (L6)
- Use index notation with negative powers (L7)
- Substitute numbers into expressions and formulae (L6)

Useful resources

Calculator for the extension

Starter – What is my number?

I am greater than 3^3 and…

I am less than 4^3 and…

I am a multiple of 7 and…

I have exactly 3 factors. (49)

Can be extended by asking students which clue could have been omitted and asking them to make up their own puzzles.

Teaching notes

Look at how indices can be used to abbreviate repeated multiplication. An example of prime factor decomposition could be used.

What is the meaning of a power of zero or a negative power? Look at the sequence of results for the powers of 2 from 2 cubed downwards.

$$\begin{array}{cccccc} \div 2 & \div 2 & \div 2 & \div 2 & \div 2 & \div 2 \end{array}$$
$$2^3 \rightarrow 2^2 \rightarrow 2^1 \rightarrow 2^0 \rightarrow 2^{-1} \rightarrow 2^{-2} \rightarrow 2^{-3}$$
$$\begin{array}{ccccccc} =8 & =4 & =2 & =? & =? & =? & =? \end{array}$$

Following the pattern means that $2^0 = 1$. What will other number to the power of zero produce? What about the negative powers? Establish that the negative part of the power is causing the number to 'turn upside down' know as the *reciprocal*. What role is the number playing? Establish that this works in the same way as an ordinary power. Include fractional examples of negative integer powers.

Remind students of the rules of BIDMAS and look at examples of substituting values into algebraic expressions. Include negative values raised to a power.

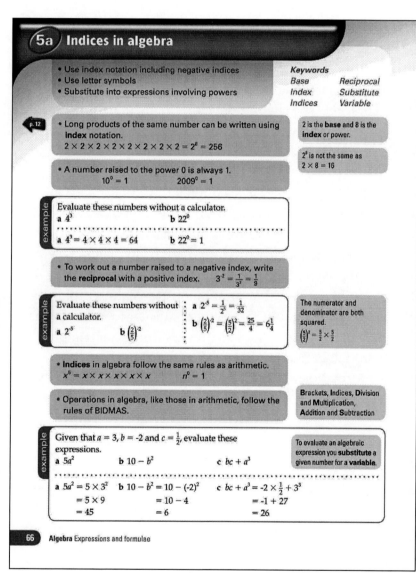

Plenary

Explore other examples of the type in question **3**. What misconceptions can students come up with? (RL) (1.5)

Simplification

Constant reminder of the rules of BIDMAS will help students. Also encourage the writing out of expressions in full and discuss why this is not going to be efficient in the future. Allow students to pass over the negative indices if necessary. Can be covered again next academic year.

All questions (RL) (1.3)

Question 1 – Likely mistakes are, to treat the index like a multiplication and to assume a negative number remains negative when raised to an index.

Question 2 – Encourage students to perform the power first, then think about what a negative index means. Students may still naturally think of a negative index as making a negative result.

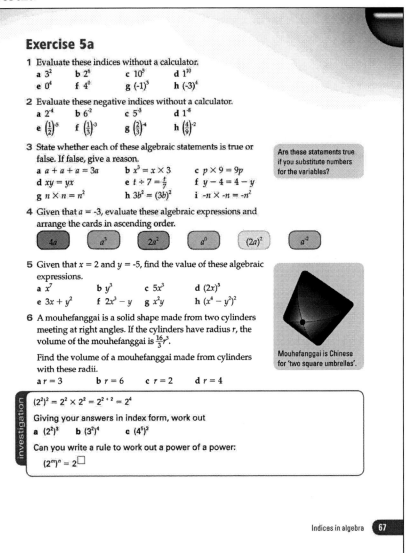

Exercise 5a

1 Evaluate these indices without a calculator.
   a 3^2 b 2^6 c 10^5 d 1^{10}
   e 0^4 f 4^0 g $(-1)^3$ h $(-3)^4$

2 Evaluate these negative indices without a calculator.
   a 2^{-4} b 6^{-2} c 5^{-3} d 1^{-8}
   e $\left(\frac{1}{2}\right)^{-5}$ f $\left(\frac{1}{3}\right)^{-3}$ g $\left(\frac{2}{3}\right)^{-4}$ h $\left(\frac{4}{9}\right)^{-2}$

3 State whether each of these algebraic statements is true or false. If false, give a reason.
   a $a + a + a = 3a$ b $x^3 = x \times 3$ c $p \times 9 = 9p$
   d $xy = yx$ e $t \div 7 = \frac{t}{7}$ f $y - 4 = 4 - y$
   g $n \times n = n^2$ h $3b^2 = (3b)^2$ i $-n \times -n = -n^2$

   Are these statements true if you substitute numbers for the variables?

4 Given that $a = -3$, evaluate these algebraic expressions and arrange the cards in ascending order.

   $4a$ a^3 $2a^2$ a^0 $(2a)^2$ a^{-2}

5 Given that $x = 2$ and $y = -5$, find the value of these algebraic expressions.
   a x^7 b y^3 c $5x^3$ d $(2x)^3$
   e $3x + y^2$ f $2x^3 - y$ g x^2y h $(x^4 - y^2)^2$

6 A mouhefanggai is a solid shape made from two cylinders meeting at right angles. If the cylinders have radius r, the volume of the mouhefanggai is $\frac{16}{3}r^3$.

   Find the volume of a mouhefanggai made from cylinders with these radii.
   a $r = 3$ b $r = 6$ c $r = 2$ d $r = 4$

   Mouhefanggai is Chinese for 'two square umbrellas'.

   investigation
   $(2^2)^2 = 2^2 \times 2^2 = 2^{2+2} = 2^4$

   Giving your answers in index form, work out
   a $(2^3)^3$ b $(3^2)^4$ c $(4^5)^3$

   Can you write a rule to work out a power of a power:
   $(2^m)^n = 2^{\square}$

Extension

Investigate the pattern 64^3, 64^2, 64^1, 64^0. What link can you see? Can you use this pattern to predict the value of $64^{\frac{1}{2}}$ and $64^{\frac{1}{3}}$ (8 and 4). Encourage students to be creative in their ideas, but don't necessarily lead onto formal discussion of roots (CT).

Exercise 5a commentary

Question 3 – After students attempt this question, encourage them to check their results by choosing a value to substitute. Advise students that 0, 1, 2 are not always the best values to choose, but they should still choose simple numbers (1.2).

Questions 4 and **5** – Real care will need to be taken with a^3, a^{-2} and $(x^4 - y^2)^2$, encourage use of brackets when substituting in a negative number.

Question 6 – Parts **c** and **d** leave fractional answers. If students are familiar with multiplying fractions by integers, encourage them to leave the answers as mixed fraction. Take care that students don't calculate $\frac{16 \; 3 \; r^3}{3 \; 3 \; r^3}$

Investigation – Encourage students to write out these in full to help appreciate what is being calculated. For example, $(2^2)^3 = 2^2 \times 2^2 \times 2^2 = 2 \times 2 \times 2 \times 2 \times 2 \times 2 = 2^6$. What incorrect answer might a student put? (CT) (1.4)

Assessment Criteria – Algebra, level 5: Use simple formulae involving one or two operations. Algebra, level 7: substitute numbers into expressions and formulae.

Links

A mnemonic is a memory aid which uses words and letters to jog the memory. The order of operations can be recalled using BI/ODMAS. (Brackets, Indices/pOwers, Multiplication and Division, Addition and Subtraction). Some well-known mnemonics are *Richard of York Gave Battle In Vain* (colours of the rainbow), and the rhyme *Thirty Days hath September…* (How many other mnemonics can the class remember?

- Simplify or transform linear expressions by collecting like terms (L6)
- Simplify simple algebraic fractions to produce linear expressions (L8)

Useful resources

Starter – ABC

Each letter of the alphabet represents a number:

$a = 1, b = 2, c = 3, d = 4, e = 5$, etc.

Challenge students to decode the following message

$(3e - 2) (t - s) (2j) \left(\frac{p}{b}\right) (dg - i) (c^2) (3f + a^2) \left(\frac{r}{c}\right) (3g) (d^2 - b)$

Can be extended by asking students to code their own message. (maths is fun)

Teaching notes

Look at examples of adding and subtracting algebraic terms. Include terms like x, y, x^2, constants, xy, yx. Some students may need reminding that x^2 means $x \times x$. Why can some terms be put together and other can't?

Look at examples of multiplying algebraic terms. Can the order of the multiplication be rearranged? For example, is $3ab \times 2a$ the same as $3 \times 2 \times a \times a \times b$? Use numerical examples to justify that multiplication can be done in any order, for example, $3 \times 4 = 4 \times 3$. Establish the common procedure of dealing with the numbers followed by the letters.

Look at examples of algebraic division. Insist on the expressions being written one over the other. Include examples similar to those in question **4**. Show how terms can be cancelled out. Compare this with the method for simplifying vulgar fractions.

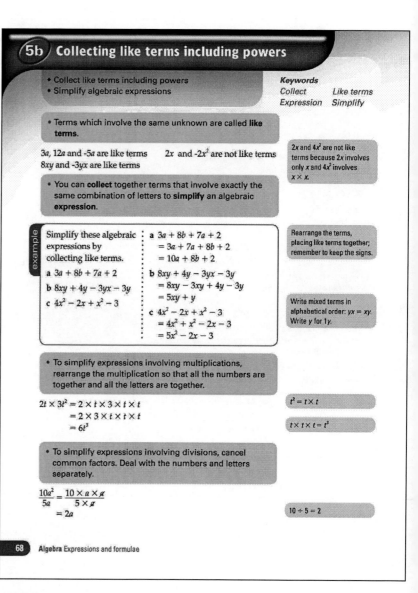

Plenary

Look at question **5** again. How could you express the volume of a cuboid that is twice as high as it is wide, and twice as long as it is high? Encourage a sketch and the possible use of numerical values before introducing algebra. (width $= x$, volume $= 8x^3$) (CT) (1.1,1.3)

Simplification

Ask students to try to explain in words what they think an expression means. Encourage a checking approach using a simple value for substitution into the question and simplified expression.

All questions (1.3)

Question 1 – The last fraction may cause some discussion. It can be written in an alternative way, but is it simpler? Compare with $2(y + 4)$ and $2y + 8$ or $1\frac{1}{3}$ and $\frac{4}{5}$ is this simplification or just an alternative way to express the answer? (1.5)

Question 2 – For part **g**, ask, when letters are multiplied the other way around, do they still make the same value? Use any numerical example to re-enforce this concept.

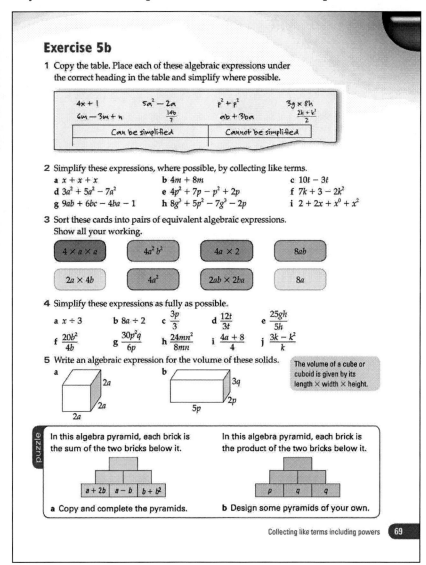

Exercise 5b

1 Copy the table. Place each of these algebraic expressions under the correct heading in the table and simplify where possible.

$4x + 1$	$5a^2 - 2a$	$p^2 + p^2$	$3g \times 8h$
$6m - 3m + n$	$\frac{14b}{7}$	$ab + 3ba$	$\frac{2k + k^2}{2}$

Can be simplified	Cannot be simplified

2 Simplify these expressions, where possible, by collecting like terms.
 a $x + x + x$ b $4m + 8m$ c $10t - 3t$
 d $3a^2 + 5a^2 - 7a^2$ e $4p^2 + 7p - p^2 + 2p$ f $7k + 3 - 2k^2$
 g $9ab + 6bc - 4ba - 1$ h $8g^3 + 5p^2 - 7g^3 - 2p$ i $2 + 2x + x^0 + x^2$

3 Sort these cards into pairs of equivalent algebraic expressions. Show all your working.

$4 \times a \times a$	$4a^2 b^2$	$4a \times 2$	$8ab$
$2a \times 4b$	$4a^2$	$2ab \times 2ba$	$8a$

4 Simplify these expressions as fully as possible.
 a $x \div 3$ b $8a \div 2$ c $\frac{3p}{3}$ d $\frac{12t}{3t}$ e $\frac{25gh}{5h}$
 f $\frac{20b^2}{4b}$ g $\frac{30p^2q}{6p}$ h $\frac{24mn^2}{8mn}$ i $\frac{4a + 8}{4}$ j $\frac{3k - k^2}{k}$

5 Write an algebraic expression for the volume of these solids.
 a   b

The volume of a cube or cuboid is given by its length × width × height.

In this algebra pyramid, each brick is the sum of the two bricks below it.

$a + 2b$	$a - b$	$b + b^2$

a Copy and complete the pyramids.

In this algebra pyramid, each brick is the product of the two bricks below it.

p	q	q

b Design some pyramids of your own.

Collecting like terms including powers   69

Extension

Two of the following can be simplified, two cannot. Explain why (IE, EP) (1.2, 1.3).

$\frac{4x \, 1 \, 8y}{6x \, 1 \, 2p}, \frac{10x \, 1 \, 8y}{5x \, 1 \, 2p}, \frac{1000x \, 1 \, 9y}{100x \, 1 \, 100p}, \frac{10x \, 1 \, 8xy}{5x \, 1 \, 2xp}$ (1st and 4th).

Exercise 5b commentary

Question 3 – Re-enforce the idea that multiplication can be achieved in any order, conventionally the numbers are multiplied in front of the letters., for example, $2ab \times 2ab = 2 \times 2 \times a \times a \times b \times b$.

Question 4 – Look at this question in a number of different ways. **i** Each separate term in the numerator is divided by the denominator. **ii** A common term in the numerator will cancel with the same common term in the denominator. **iii** The numerator and denominator can both be divided by a common term. Each of these approaches suits different parts of this question. Explore them all (1.4).

Question 5 – Students may need reminding of the concept of volumes of cuboids by multiplication. A sketch of a cuboid 2 by 3 by 4 split into unit cubes will help re-enforce this.

Puzzle – Ensure students use the simplification skills they have been practicing in the exercise. Some students may need to be reminded of the terms 'sum' and 'product'.

Links

People who collect and study postage stamps are called philatelists. Some philatelists collect stamps from a particular country while others collect stamps showing a particular theme such as trains, birds or insects. All postage stamps show the country of issue except those from Great Britain which carry an image of the head of the ruling monarch. There are collections of stamps showing insects at http://www.bugsonstamps.com/country_master.htm
and of birds at http://www.bird-stamps.org/

- Multiply a single term over a bracket. (L6)
- Derive a formula (L6)

Useful resources

•••

Starter – Power products

Draw a 4×4 table on the board. Label the columns 2^4 2^{-3} 2^3 3^{-2}.
Label the rows 2^2 2^{-2} 3^5 3^2.

Ask students to fill in the table with the products, for example,
the top row in the table would read $2^6, 2^{-1}, 2^5, 2^2 \times 3^{-2}$.

Can be differentiated by the choice of powers.

Teaching notes

What does multiplying a bracket by a number represent? For example, $3(x + 4)$. Explain that this is just repeated addition $x + 4 + x + 4 + x + 4$. What does this simplify to and how could the answer be found without the need to write out all the working? Establish that the term outside the bracket multiplies **every** term inside the bracket.

Include examples that like those used in questions **1** and **3**. Students may need reminding of the rules for multiplying with negatives.

For examples like those in questions **3** and **6**, encourage students to tackle the expansion of brackets in one line rather than split up the work into two separate parts. This is likely to reduce mistakes, especially when dealing with a negative multiplier.

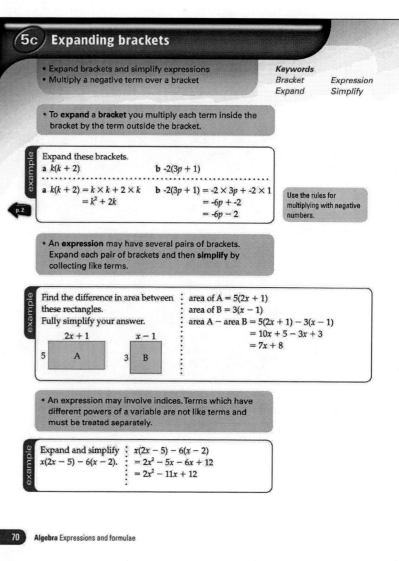

5c Expanding brackets

- Expand brackets and simplify expressions
- Multiply a negative term over a bracket

Keywords
Bracket   Expression
Expand   Simplify

- To **expand** a **bracket** you multiply each term inside the bracket by the term outside the bracket.

example
Expand these brackets.
a $k(k + 2)$ **b** $-2(3p + 1)$

a $k(k + 2) = k \times k + 2 \times k$
           $= k^2 + 2k$

b $-2(3p + 1) = -2 \times 3p + -2 \times 1$
              $= -6p + -2$
              $= -6p - 2$

Use the rules for multiplying with negative numbers.

- An **expression** may have several pairs of brackets. Expand each pair of brackets and then **simplify** by collecting like terms.

example
Find the difference in area between these rectangles.
Fully simplify your answer.

$2x + 1$ $x - 1$

5 [A]   3 [B]

area of $A = 5(2x + 1)$
area of $B = 3(x - 1)$
area A – area B $= 5(2x + 1) - 3(x - 1)$
                    $= 10x + 5 - 3x + 3$
                    $= 7x + 8$

- An expression may involve indices. Terms which have different powers of a variable are not like terms and must be treated separately.

example
Expand and simplify
$x(2x - 5) - 6(x - 2)$.

$x(2x - 5) - 6(x - 2)$
$= 2x^2 - 5x - 6x + 12$
$= 2x^2 - 11x + 12$

70   **Algebra** Expressions and formulae

Plenary

In the expressions $(3x + 4) + (7x - 2)$ and $4 - (3x + 1)$ what number are the brackets being multiplied by? Establish that 1 and -1 are being used. Expand and simplify. Why aren't the '1s' written in? Are there other examples of the number '1' not being written in? x rather than x^1 (1.3).

Simplification

Use arrows to re-enforce the fact that the term in front of the brackets is multiplying each term inside the bracket. Highlight that negative signs make dealing with brackets more challenging. Build confidence with the positive multipliers first. Questions **1a–f, 2, 3a–d, 4** and **5**.

All questions (1.3)

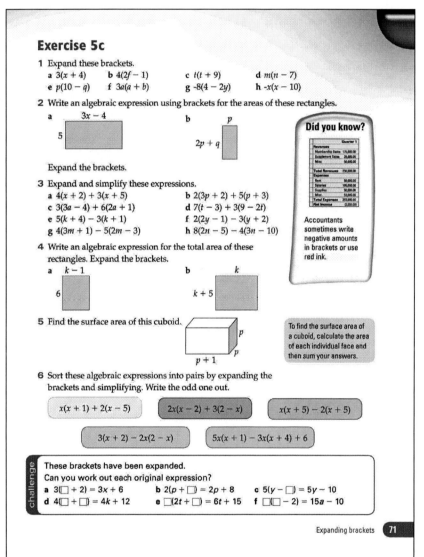

Exercise 5c

1 Expand these brackets.
 a $3(x + 4)$ b $4(2f - 1)$ c $t(t + 9)$ d $m(n - 7)$
 e $p(10 - q)$ f $3a(a + b)$ g $-8(4 - 2y)$ h $-x(x - 10)$

2 Write an algebraic expression using brackets for the areas of these rectangles.
 a $3x - 4$
 5
 b p
 $2p + q$

Did you know?

Quarter 1
Revenue
Membership Sales
Supplement Sales
Misc
Total Revenues
Expenses
Rent
Salaries
Supplies
Misc
Total Expenses
Net Income

Accountants sometimes write negative amounts in brackets or use red ink.

Expand the brackets.

3 Expand and simplify these expressions.
 a $4(x + 2) + 3(x + 5)$ b $2(3p + 2) + 5(p + 3)$
 c $3(3a - 4) + 6(2a + 1)$ d $7(t - 3) + 3(9 - 2t)$
 e $5(k + 4) - 3(k + 1)$ f $2(2y - 1) - 3(y + 2)$
 g $4(3m + 1) - 5(2m - 3)$ h $8(2n - 5) - 4(3n - 10)$

4 Write an algebraic expression for the total area of these rectangles. Expand the brackets.
 a $k - 1$
 6
 b k
 $k + 5$

5 Find the surface area of this cuboid.
 p
 p
 $p + 1$

To find the surface area of a cuboid, calculate the area of each individual face and then sum your answers.

6 Sort these algebraic expressions into pairs by expanding the brackets and simplifying. Write the odd one out.

| $x(x + 1) + 2(x - 5)$ | $2x(x - 2) + 3(2 - x)$ | $x(x + 5) - 2(x + 5)$ |

| $3(x + 2) - 2x(2 - x)$ | $5x(x + 1) - 3x(x + 4) + 6$ |

challenge

These brackets have been expanded.
Can you work out each original expression?
 a $3(\square + 2) = 3x + 6$ b $2(p + \square) = 2p + 8$ c $5(y - \square) = 5y - 10$
 d $4(\square + \square) = 4k + 12$ e $\square(2t + \square) = 6t + 15$ f $\square(\square - 2) = 15a - 10$

Expanding brackets   71

Extension

Expand and simplify $-(-3 - 4x) - (-2 - 4x)(-5)$. Ask, what makes this very challenging? Ask, what is each bracket being multiplied by? ($-16x - 7$). Encourage various methods of tackling this expression (1.3, 1.5).

Exercise 5c commentary

Question 1 – Students may need reminding of the rule for multiplying two negatives.

Questions 2 and **4** – Does it matter which way round the expressions are written?
For example, $5(3x - 4)$ or $(3x - 4)5$

Questions 3 and **6** – Successes is most likely to come from tackling these questions together. Encourage students to set out workings down the page. Ask, what is the second bracket being multiplied by? Establish that this could be a negative value. Is there a term that is not involved with the brackets?

Question 5 – The term 'surface area' may need explanation. Some students might like to make use of a net and write in the areas (IE).

Challenge – Encourage students to check their solutions by multiplying out the brackets. In these examples, is there only one solution? Can students make up an algebraic expression that can be put into brackets in more than one way? (1.2)

Assessment Criteria – Algebra, level 5: construct, express in symbolic form, and use simple formulae involving one or two operations. Algebra, level 7: derive a formula.

Links

Bring in some written text (books, magazines) for the class to use. Ask the students to find examples of the use of brackets in the text. Round brackets (also known as *parentheses*) are often used for explanations or to add to the information already given. They can also be used for translations and abbreviations. What is the purpose of the brackets in the examples?

- Simplify or transform algebraic expressions by taking out single-term common factors (L7)
- Construct and solve linear equations with integer coefficients (with and without brackets, negative signs anywhere in the equation, positive or negative solution) (L6)

Useful resources

Starter – Expressions

$a = 2, b = 3, c = 5$

Ask students for expressions that have a value of 24

For example, $3(b + c)$, $c^2 + a - b$

Encourage students to think of interesting expressions!
Can be extended by changing the target number or values of a, b and c.

Teaching notes

Students may need reminding about HCF, possibly covered previously in spread **1d**. Include algebraic examples (1.2).

Look at the expansion of a simple bracket, for example, $3(x + 4) = 3x + 12$. Is it possible work backwards? Look at $3x$ and 12. What factors do they both share? Show how this leads to the 'common factor' being put outside the bracket. What must the common factor be multiplied by to produce the correct result?

Look at examples where there is more than one common factor. Does this mean that there is more than one way to factorise? How can you tell which common factor to use? By using the highest common factor you are 'fully factorising'.

Include examples where the HCF is actually one of the terms, for example, $3x + 9xy$.

What error might students make here? Putting the HCF of $3x$ outside the bracket does not mean it has been 'removed', it still needs to make $3x$ when expanded, so what multiplication is needed? $3x(? + 3y)$.

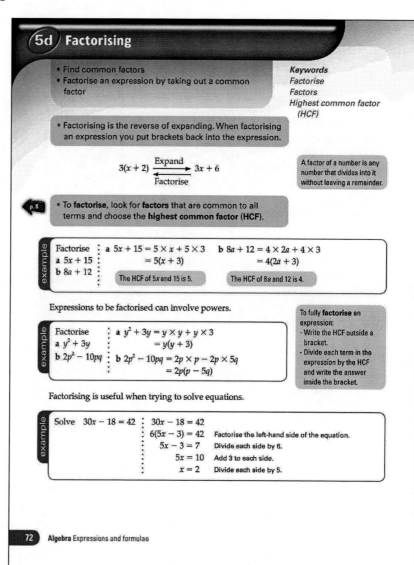

Plenary

Look at question **4** again. Do the students think they might make similar mistakes? If so, which ones? (RL) (1.5)

Simplification

Show how the expressions can be split into their prime and algebraic factors. What common groups can be seen in each term?

For example, $6xy - 18x = 2 \times 3 \times x \times y - 2 \times 3 \times 3 \times x$, can then see that $2 \times 3 \times x$ is common to both terms.

All questions (1.3)

Question 1 – Discourage the listing of all the factors, a mental approach is likely to be more effective in this whole exercise. Use words like 'what is the biggest thing that is in each term?' Remind students that it can be a number, or letter, or both.

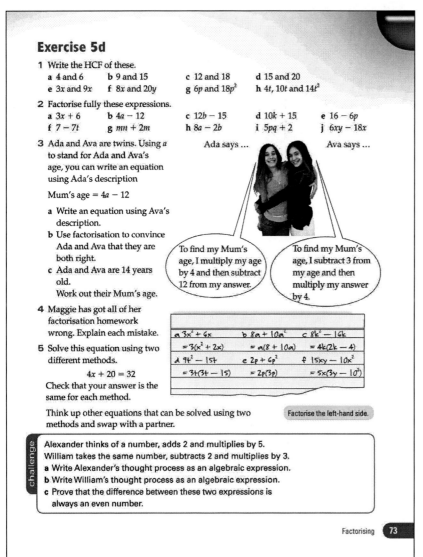

Exercise 5d

1 Write the HCF of these.
  a 4 and 6   **b** 9 and 15   **c** 12 and 18   **d** 15 and 20
  e $3x$ and $9x$ **f** $8x$ and $20y$ **g** $6p$ and $18p^2$ **h** $4t$, $10t$ and $14t^2$

2 Factorise fully these expressions.
  a $3x + 6$ **b** $4a - 12$ **c** $12b - 15$ **d** $10k + 15$ **e** $16 - 6p$
  f $7 - 7t$ **g** $mn + 2m$ **h** $8a - 2b$ **i** $5pq + 2$ **j** $6xy - 18x$

3 Ada and Ava are twins. Using a to stand for Ada and Ava's age, you can write an equation using Ada's description

Ada says …   Ava says …

Mum's age $= 4a - 12$

  a Write an equation using Ava's description.
  b Use factorisation to convince Ada and Ava that they are both right.
  c Ada and Ava are 14 years old.
  Work out their Mum's age.

To find my Mum's age, I multiply my age by 4 and then subtract 12 from my answer.

To find my Mum's age, I subtract 3 from my age and then multiply my answer by 4.

4 Maggie has got all of her factorisation homework wrong. Explain each mistake.

a $3x^2 + 6x$	b $8a + 10a^2$	c $8k^2 - 16k$
$= 3(x^2 + 2x)$	$= a(8 + 10a)$	$= 4k(2k - 4)$
d $9t^2 - 15t$	e $2p + 6p^2$	f $15xy - 10x^2$
$= 3t(3t - 15)$	$= 2p(3p)$	$= 5x(3y - 10^2)$

5 Solve this equation using two different methods.

$$4x + 20 = 32$$

Check that your answer is the same for each method.

Factorise the left-hand side.

Think up other equations that can be solved using two methods and swap with a partner.

challenge

Alexander thinks of a number, adds 2 and multiplies by 5.
William takes the same number, subtracts 2 and multiplies by 3.
  a Write Alexander's thought process as an algebraic expression.
  b Write William's thought process as an algebraic expression.
  c Prove that the difference between these two expressions is always an even number.

Factorising   73

Extension

A cuboid has a length 2 m shorter than its width, but a height twice as high as its width. Write a fully factorised expression for its volume. Allow students to make their own choices how to label their cuboid. [width $= x$, volume $= 2x^2(x - 2)$] (IE)

Exercise 5d commentary

Question 2 – Encourage students to check answers by expanding brackets. If their answer expands correctly, does this mean they are correct? No. Why not? Encourage students to compare answers to see if they have factorised as fully as each other.

Question 3 – Can students answers for part **a** be factorised? Is there any other part of this question that can be factorised? (1.2)

Question 4 – Encourage students to try to explain what it is that Maggie thought she was doing correctly (RL).

Question 5 – What can both sides be divided by once the left hand side is factorised fully? When forming an example for a partner, look at the way in which the original question was made to be able to factorise (TW) (1.4).

Challenge – Students may be unsure which way round to subtract in order to find the difference. Encourage both ways around to be tried. The result $2x + 16$ or $-2x - 16$ is not immediately obvious as an even value. Allow informal approaches to proving it's even, not necessarily through factorization (IE, CT).

Assessment Criteria – Algebra, level 6: construct and solve linear equations with integer coefficients, using an appropriate method.

Links

Bring in some dictionaries for the class to use. The word *bracket* can have several meanings and can be used as a noun or a verb. What do the meanings have in common? (group or hold something together)

- Use formulae from mathematics and other subjects (L7)
- Derive a formula (L6)

Useful resources
Calculator

Starter – Priceless!

If A costs 2p, B costs 4p, C costs 6p *etc.* How much is your name worth?
Are you more expensive than the person beside you?
Which of your school subjects is worth the most?
What topic in maths is worth 92p? (algebra)

Teaching notes

Remind students of the rules of BIDMAS give examples of substitution into formulae. Include examples that involve fractions and powers. Include examples similar to those in question **1**.

Is there a difference between the way in which $-p^2$ and $-p \times -p$ would be calculated? Show how the rule of BIDMAS, specifically indices before subtraction, means that the two expressions are not the same (RL).

Examine some of the formulae used in physics for measuring speed/ distance/time/acceleration (EP).

$v = u + at$ $\qquad\qquad v^2 = u^2 + 2as$

$s = ut + \frac{1}{2}\,at^2$

$s = \frac{t(v\,1\,u)}{2}$ $\qquad\qquad s = vt - \frac{1}{2}\,at^2$

Experiment with both non-calculator and calculator methods of evaluation. How are negative numbers and fractions to be correctly put into a calculator? Note that there is a wide variation in how calculators deal with these more complex operations. Encourage good practice when dealing with negatives and fractions. The negative function (–) or +/- should be used instead of the subtraction button. Fractions and negative numbers should be put into brackets if they are raised to a power. Some calculators automatically do this, others do not (1.5).

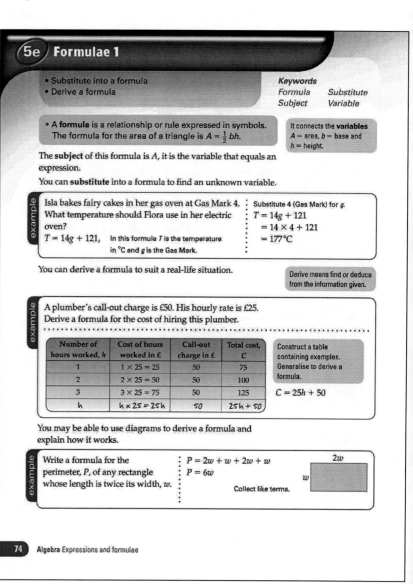

5e Formulae 1

- Substitute into a formula
- Derive a formula

Keywords
Formula Substitute
Subject Variable

- A **formula** is a relationship or rule expressed in symbols. The formula for the area of a triangle is $A = \frac{1}{2}bh$.

It connects the **variables** A = area, b = base and h = height.

The **subject** of this formula is A, it is the variable that equals an expression.

You can **substitute** into a formula to find an unknown variable.

example

Isla bakes fairy cakes in her gas oven at Gas Mark 4. What temperature should Flora use in her electric oven?

$T = 14g + 121$, In this formula T is the temperature in °C and g is the Gas Mark.

Substitute 4 (Gas Mark) for g.
$T = 14g + 121$
$= 14 \times 4 + 121$
$= 177°C$

You can derive a formula to suit a real-life situation.

Derive means find or deduce from the information given.

example

A plumber's call-out charge is £50. His hourly rate is £25. Derive a formula for the cost of hiring this plumber.

Number of hours worked, h	Cost of hours worked in £	Call-out charge in £	Total cost, C
1	$1 \times 25 = 25$	50	75
2	$2 \times 25 = 50$	50	100
3	$3 \times 25 = 75$	50	125
h	$h \times 25 = 25h$	50	$25h + 50$

Construct a table containing examples. Generalise to derive a formula.

$C = 25h + 50$

You may be able to use diagrams to derive a formula and explain how it works.

example

Write a formula for the perimeter, P, of any rectangle whose length is twice its width, w.

$P = 2w + w + 2w + w$
$P = 6w$

Collect like terms.

Plenary

The formula for the time (in seconds) it takes for a person on a swing to go forwards then backwards to the same point is given by $T \approx 2\sqrt{L}$. What might L stand for? (length of the chain in metres). What measurements do not matter in this formula? Mass of the person; is this a surprise? Work out the time for various sensible lengths of chain. An improved formula is $T = 2\pi \sqrt{\frac{L}{9.81}}$. How close are the answers you just calculated when you use this formula? (EP) (1.3)

Simplification

Ask students to explain what is being asked for in the formulae. What operations are being done and in what order. Make use of the rules of BIDMAS. Encourage the formal approach of writing down the question, substituting in values and calculating the answer in stages.

This exercise could be achieved with or without a calculator depending on the required focus. All questions (1.3)

Question 1 – What does a fraction next to a letter mean? Recall the rules for multiplying a fraction by an integer.

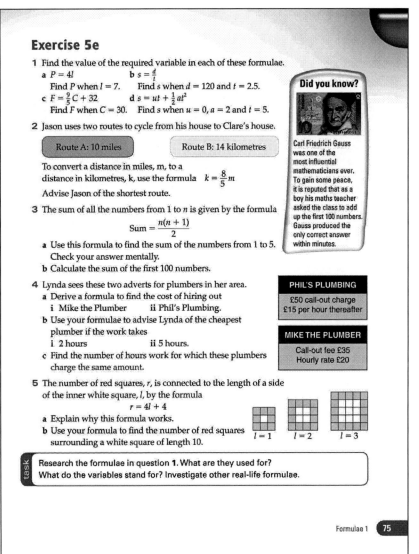

Exercise 5e

1 Find the value of the required variable in each of these formulae.
   a $P = 4l$ b $s = \frac{d}{t}$
       Find P when $l = 7$.   Find s when $d = 120$ and $t = 2.5$.
   c $F = \frac{9}{5}C + 32$ d $s = ut + \frac{1}{2}at^2$
       Find F when $C = 30$.   Find s when $u = 0$, $a = 2$ and $t = 5$.

2 Jason uses two routes to cycle from his house to Clare's house.

   | Route A: 10 miles | | Route B: 14 kilometres |

   To convert a distance in miles, m, to a distance in kilometres, k, use the formula $k = \frac{8}{5}m$

   Advise Jason of the shortest route.

Did you know?

Carl Friedrich Gauss was one of the most influential mathematicians ever. To gain some peace, it is reputed that as a boy his maths teacher asked the class to add up the first 100 numbers. Gauss produced the only correct answer within minutes.

3 The sum of all the numbers from 1 to n is given by the formula
   $$\text{Sum} = \frac{n(n+1)}{2}$$
   a Use this formula to find the sum of the numbers from 1 to 5. Check your answer mentally.
   b Calculate the sum of the first 100 numbers.

4 Lynda sees these two adverts for plumbers in her area.
   a Derive a formula to find the cost of hiring out
      i Mike the Plumber   ii Phil's Plumbing.
   b Use your formulae to advise Lynda of the cheapest plumber if the work takes
      i 2 hours   ii 5 hours.
   c Find the number of hours work for which these plumbers charge the same amount.

   PHIL'S PLUMBING
   £50 call-out charge
   £15 per hour thereafter

   MIKE THE PLUMBER
   Call-out fee £35
   Hourly rate £20

5 The number of red squares, r, is connected to the length of a side of the inner white square, l, by the formula
   $$r = 4l + 4$$
   a Explain why this formula works.
   b Use your formula to find the number of red squares surrounding a white square of length 10.
   $l = 1$ $l = 2$ $l = 3$

   task Research the formulae in question 1. What are they used for? What do the variables stand for? Investigate other real-life formulae.

Formulae 1   75

Extension

The formula in question **1c** is used for finding the temperature in degrees Fahrenheit when the temperature in degrees centigrade is given. Can the formula be written in reverse? $C = \frac{5(F - 32)}{9}$. An arrow diagram/function machine may help to re-enforce the inverse processes required (EP).

Exercise 5e commentary

Question 2 – Challenge students to write the formula so that it converts into kilometres from miles instead.

Question 3 – Is it quicker to expand the brackets in this formula before evaluating it? In pairs, students could try both methods to see which is more effective (TW) (1.4).

Question 4 – An opportunity to use a graphical package and plot each formula $y = 20x + 35$ and $y = 15x + 50$. What does the intersection show? (IE, CT) (1.1)

Question 5 – Match the white squares with red ones around the sides. What about the corners? (1.2)

Task – A hint could be given by drawing a square, a car, the sun and a rocket blasting off. Internet searches could be used for the formulae; how could divide, squared and ½ be entered?

Assessment Criteria – Algebra, level 5: construct, express in symbolic form, and use simple formulae involving one or two operations. Algebra, level 7: use formulae from mathematics and other subjects. Algebra, level 7: derive a formula.

Links

The amount of energy (calorific value) contained in domestic gas depends on its composition. To make sure that everybody pays the same price for their energy, companies test the gas and publish the calorific value for each area. This is then used in a formula to convert the volume of gas used as measured by the gas meter to the amount of energy used by a household. There is more information at http://www.nationalgrid.com/uk/Gas/Data/misc/reports/description/ (EP).

• In simple cases, change (a formula's) subject   (L7)   *Useful resources*

Starter – T, S or F

Write the following on the board and ask students which are always **T**rue, **S**ometimes true, always **F**alse:

$$x^2 = (-x^2) \quad \text{(S, only if } x = 0)$$
$$2(x - 3) = 2x - 3 \quad \text{(F)}$$
$$x - y = y - x \quad \text{(S, only if } x = y)$$
$$x^2 > x \quad \text{(S, not true if } -1 \le x \le 1)$$
$$3(2x + 4) = 2(3x + 6) \text{(F)}$$

Ask students to justify their answers using substitution.

Teaching notes

Look back at the methods of solving linear equations. By performing an operation on each side of the equations, the equation can be solved. The x is finally made to be 'on its own'. In one way we could say we are *rearranging* the equation to make x the *subject* (1.2).

Look at an example of a simple formula. What is the subject at the moment? How can it be rearranged to make one of the other letters the subject? Can the methods used for solving linear equations be used to rearrange formulae? Use examples that require operations of $+, -, \times, \div$.

How can formulae that have brackets be rearranged? If appropriate, draw on the work covered in spread **5c**.

Is there more than one way to rearrange formulae? Will the final answer be the same? Look at such an example and examine two possible ways of expressing the solution (1.5).

$$p = 2(x + y) \quad p = 2(x + y)$$

$$p = 2x + 2y \quad \frac{p}{2} = x + y$$

$$p = 2y = 2x \quad \frac{p}{2} - y = x$$

$$\frac{p - 2y}{2} = x$$

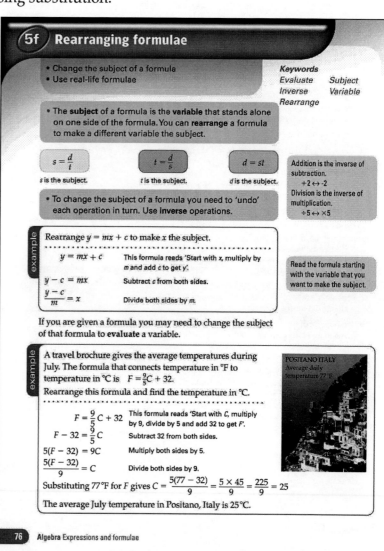

Plenary

Can the formulae from the plenary in spread **5e** be rearranged to make L the subject? Particularly discuss the problem with the square root (1.3, 1.4).

Simplification

Keep asking students, what is stopping the subject from being on its own? How can we 'get rid' of this?

Writing down the formula to be rearranged, showing working on both sides and working down the page is a clear and useful procedure. All questions (1.3)

Question 1 – Ask students to look for opportunities to simplify. Ask, what is being done to the intended subject?

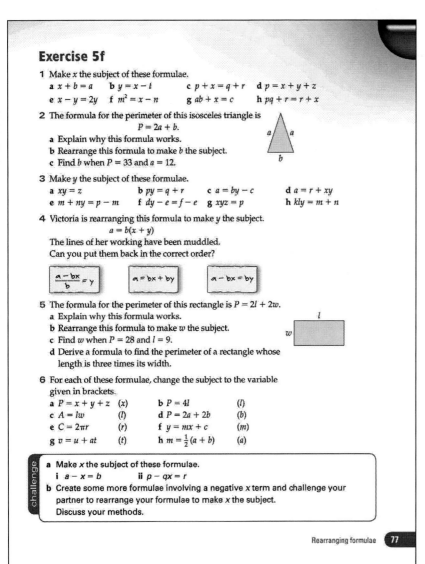

Exercise 5f

1 Make x the subject of these formulae.
  a $x + b = a$ **b** $y = x - t$ **c** $p + x = q + r$ **d** $p = x + y + z$
  e $x - y = 2y$ **f** $m^2 = x - n$ **g** $ab + x = c$ **h** $pq + r = r + x$

2 The formula for the perimeter of this isosceles triangle is
$$P = 2a + b.$$
  a Explain why this formula works.
  b Rearrange this formula to make b the subject.
  c Find b when $P = 33$ and $a = 12$.

3 Make y the subject of these formulae.
  a $xy = z$ **b** $py = q + r$ **c** $a = by - c$ **d** $a = r + xy$
  e $m + ny = p - m$ **f** $dy - e = f - e$ **g** $xyz = p$ **h** $kly = m + n$

4 Victoria is rearranging this formula to make y the subject.
$$a = b(x + y)$$
  The lines of her working have been muddled.
  Can you put them back in the correct order?

  $\dfrac{a - bx}{b} = y$ $a = bx + by$ $a - bx = by$

5 The formula for the perimeter of this rectangle is $P = 2l + 2w$.
  a Explain why this formula works.
  b Rearrange this formula to make w the subject.
  c Find w when $P = 28$ and $l = 9$.
  d Derive a formula to find the perimeter of a rectangle whose length is three times its width.

6 For each of these formulae, change the subject to the variable given in brackets.
  a $P = x + y + z$ (x) **b** $P = 4l$ (l)
  c $A = lw$ (l) **d** $P = 2a + 2b$ (b)
  e $C = 2\pi r$ (r) **f** $y = mx + c$ (m)
  g $v = u + at$ (t) **h** $m = \frac{1}{2}(a + b)$ (a)

challenge
  a Make x the subject of these formulae.
    i $a - x = b$ **ii** $p - qx = r$
  b Create some more formulae involving a negative x term and challenge your partner to rearrange your formulae to make x the subject. Discuss your methods.

Extension

How can x be made the subject in $3x + xy = p$. Allow students to try various methods before suggesting factorisation. Can students make up similar examples of these types? Encourage students to test their partners (IE, TW) (1.5).

Exercise 5f commentary

Question 2 – Encourage students to give a full answer using a proper sentence.

Question 3 – What happens in parts **g** and **h** if you first perform a division by a single letter? Why in further progress difficult?

Question 4 – Does this question have to be done by expanding the brackets first?

Question 5 – When deriving a formula, encourage students to use a diagram rather than leap to a solution. What mistake might a diagram help you prevent? Alternatively, students might attempt to find a formula mentally and check using a diagram.

Question 6 – Ask, what is being done to the intended subject? Do you have to perform more than one operation to each side at one time? Does it matter if you don't expand the brackets?

Challenge – Make the point that negative xs cause problems in equations and formulae, it is best to 'get rid of them' a.s.a.p. How do you get of $-x$? Create examples where the negative x term can't be got rid of immediately. For example, $3(y - 2x) = p$ (CT) (1.2).

Assessment Criteria – Algebra, level 7: derive a formula and, in simple cases, change its subject.

Links

Albert Einstein's famous formula $E = mc^2$ says that mass can be converted into energy. The amount of energy contained in a piece of matter can be found by multiplying the mass m by the square of the speed of light, c. This means that, in theory, there is enough energy in a grain of sand to boil 10 million kettles (EP).

1 Evaluate these numbers without a calculator.

a 5^2 **b** 3^4 **c** 2^8 **d** 6^0

e 4^{-3} **f** 8^{-2} **g** $\left(\frac{1}{2}\right)^{-7}$ **h** $\left(\frac{3}{4}\right)^{-2}$

2 Given that $m = 3$ and $n = -2$, find the value of these algebraic expressions.

a m^2 **b** n^3 **c** $2m^3$ **d** $6n^2$

e $(2n)^2$ **f** $3m + n^4$ **g** mn^2 **h** $(m^2 - n^2)^2$

3 Simplify these expressions, where possible, by collecting like terms.

a $3x + 8x - 2x$ **b** $4a^2 - 6a^2 + 10a^2$ **c** $10m + 7n - 3n - 5m$

d $4p^2 + 8 - 3p$ **e** $12ab - 6ba + ab$ **f** $3g^3 - 4g^3 + 2g^2$

4 Simplify these expressions as fully as possible.

a $\dfrac{20x}{5}$ **b** $\dfrac{12y}{4y}$ **c** $\dfrac{21pq}{7q}$

d $\dfrac{30k^2}{18k}$ **e** $\dfrac{24gh^2}{16h}$ **f** $\dfrac{3b + 12}{3}$

5 Use brackets to write an expression for the area of this rectangle.
Then expand the brackets.

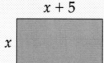

6 Expand and simplify these expressions.

a $5(a + 2) + 3(a + 4)$ **b** $3(4x + 1) + 6(2x - 1)$

c $3(4p + 3) + 7(1 - p)$ **d** $5(3b - 2) - 2(4b + 1)$

e $8(m + 2) - 3(2m - 3)$ **f** $6(4n - 3) - 4(5n - 4)$

g $x(x + 3) + 4(x - 2)$ **h** $y(2y - 5) - y(y - 3)$

7 Factorise fully these expressions.

a $2x + 4$ **b** $5y + 20$ **c** $6g - 2$ **d** $8t - 12$

e $18 - 15k$ **f** $10p + 15q$ **g** $7a + ab$ **h** $15mn - 9n$

8 a Three consecutive numbers are summed. Using n to
represent the first of these numbers, write and simplify
an algebraic expression.

> Use factorisation.

b Prove that the sum of three consecutive numbers is always equal to
three times the middle number.

9 Entry to the Cheeky Monkeys play barn costs £3.50 per child. Accompanying adults are free.

  a Work out the cost of one child paying 4 visits to Cheeky Monkeys.

  b Derive a formula to work out the cost, C, of one child paying n visits to Cheeky Monkeys.

A parent or carer can spend £10 for membership of Cheeky Monkeys for one year. Members pay only £2.50 entry fee per child.

  c Derive a formula to work out the cost, C, of one child paying n visits to Cheeky Monkeys if their parent or carer is a member.

  d Sam takes her only daughter, Aysha, to Cheeky Monkeys once a month. Work out whether or not it is worth Sam becoming a member of Cheeky Monkeys.

10 The diagrams show a pattern of red and white tiles.

  a Write a formula to connect the number of white tiles, w, with the number of red tiles, r.

  b Explain why this formula works.

  c Use your formula to find the number of red tiles surrounding 100 white tiles.

11 Make x the subject of each of these formulae.

  a $p = x + r$ **b** $a + b = x - c$ **c** $x + 3y = z$

  d $3p + x = 5p$ **e** $a = x - a^2$ **f** $x - mn = p + mn$

12 Make y the subject of each of these formulae.

  a $m = ny$ **b** $b^2y = a$ **c** $p + 3 = qy$

  d $g = fy + h$ **e** $aby = x$ **f** $y(\pi + 2) = r$

5 Summary

Assessment criteria

- Construct, express in symbolic form and use simple formulae
  involving one or two operations.   Level 5
- Construct and solve linear equations with integer coefficients
  using an appropriate method   Level 6
- Substitute numbers into expressions and formulae   Level 7
- Use formulae from mathematics and other subjects   Level 7
- Derive a formula and, in simple cases, change its subject   Level 7

Question commentary

Example	The example illustrates a straightforward question about rearranging simple formulae. Encourage students to discuss the problems in terms of inverse operations. In case of difficulty, it may help to discuss the problems in terms of function machines.	**a** $f = g + 6$ **b** $q = \dfrac{p}{3}$
Past question	The question requires students to write algebraic expressions to describe the steps in a number puzzle. Some students may find this question daunting. Emphasise the idea that the puzzle is being translated into a different language. In the first step to be completed, some students may add the number 5 instead of the symbol n. Ask students how they can check each expression. Encourage students to substitute the value 5 into each expression to check that the resulting value is the same as that given in the example column.	**Answer** **Level 6** **2** $2n + 4, n + 2, n$

Development and links

The topic of algebra is developed further in Chapter 7 where students will solve equations with a negative algebraic term on one or both sides. Powers and indices are extended to include the index laws in Chapter 10. The topic of substituting into and rearranging formulae is developed further in Chapter 13.

Students will encounter algebra in areas of the curriculum where formulae are used, especially in technology and in science where formulae are used extensively to describe the physical world. The language of algebra is used for computer programming in ICT. Algebra can be used to solve many of the number puzzles that appear in newspapers, magazines and puzzle books.

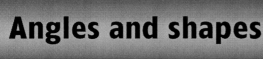

Objectives

Introduction

This chapter consolidates and develops Year 7 knowledge of angle. The chapter reviews angles at a point and on parallel and intersecting lines and the properties of triangles, quadrilaterals and polygons and students use these properties to solve problems. Students consider congruence and explore the properties of 3-D shapes using 2-D representations including nets and plan and elevation views.

The student book discusses the Eiffel Tower in Paris which has to be extremely strong to withstand all weather conditions. The properties of shapes are very important in building, both for strength and for aesthetic design. Designers use plans and elevations to show how the completed building will look. Some examples of the use of shapes in various structures can be found at http://www.architecture.com/WhatsOn/Exhibitions/AtTheVictoriaAndAlbertMuseum/ArchitectureGallery/Structures/Introduction.aspx

⇶ast-track

All spreads

Level

Extra Resources

- Solve problems using properties of angles, of parallel and intersecting lines, and of triangles and other polygons, justifying inferences and explaining reasoning with diagrams and text   (L6)

Useful resources
Protractor
World map (showing latitude and longitude)

Starter – Angle estimation

Draw a mixture of acute, obtuse and reflex angles on the board.

Ask students to estimate the size of each angle in degrees then measure the angles.

Students score 6 points for an exact answer, 4 points for within 10° and 2 points for within 15°.

Teaching notes

Look at examples of angles at a point and on a straight line. What are the rules for the angle sum? Look at examples of vertically opposite angles. Are the rules for these three types of angles linked? Show their relationship to each other using an example of intersecting lines.

Draw a pair of parallel lines. Draw a *transversal*, a line that crosses the pair. What angles have been made? Ask students to measure the angles. Are some of the angles equal? Which ones? Are some of the angles equal and in the same position in relation to the parallel line and intersecting line? These angles 'match up' or *correspond* known as *corresponding angles*.

Are there angles that are equal but are on *alternate sides* of the intersecting line? Look particularly at angles inside the parallel lines. These are known as *alternate angles*.

How many pairs or corresponding and alternate angles are there for one pair of parallel lines and transversal? (4 pairs and 2 pairs) (CT)

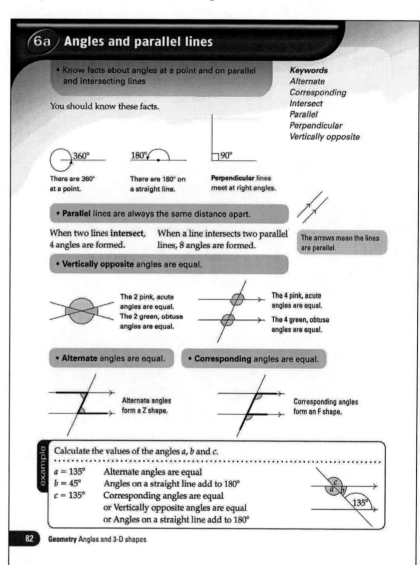

Plenary

Discuss how longitude and latitude are used to fix your position on Earth. What do students know? Which one measures horizontally and which one vertically? What range of angles does each measure have? How are they written? (EP) (1.5)

Simplification

Provide students with a copy of the exercise and encourage the use on annotation. Allow students to arrive at the results by not necessarily following the most efficient root. For example, calculate any of the angles in the question to help work towards the result.

All questions (IE) (1.2)

Question 1 – Ask students to give a simple statement of which rule they used: 'angles at a point = 360°', 'angles on a straight line = 180°' 'vertically opposite. angles are equal'.

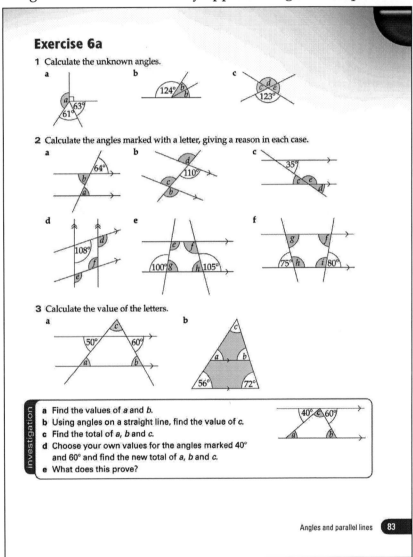

Extension

There are a few unusual angle rules/names. Investigate what is meant by **i** Exterior alternate angles (equal angles on either side of the transversal of a pair of parallel lines, lying outside the parallel lines rather than inside. Alternate angles are properly called interior alternate angles) **ii** Allied or consecutive interior angles (sum to 180°, on the same side of the transversal of a pair of parallel lines, lying inside the parallel lines.s) **iii** Complementary angles (angles that sum to 90°) **iv** Supplementary angles (angles that sum to 180°) (SM).

Exercise 6a commentary

Question 2 – Ask students to use sentences and explain which rule they have used, for example, 'angle *a* and 64 are corresponding angles and are therefore equal'.

Question 3 – Finding angle *c* requires the sum of angles in a triangle. Part **b**, may be made easier if the parallel lines are extended.

Investigation – Replace the two known angles with letters, what does this prove? Sum of angles in (any) triangle is 180°. Look at other proofs, for example, (1.4)

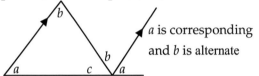

a is corresponding and *b* is alternate

Assessment Criteria – SSM, level 5: use language associated with angle and know and use the angle sum of a triangle and that of angles at a point. SSM, level 6: solve geometrical problems using properties of angles, of parallel and intersecting lines, and of triangles. SSM, level 6: identify alternate and corresponding angles: understand a proof that the sum of the angles in a triangle is 180°.

Links

Parallel lines are used in road markings. Yellow lines laid parallel to the kerb indicate no parking at certain times. Double yellow lines mean no waiting is permitted at any time. Red lines prevent all stopping, parking and loading. Double white lines down the centre of the road are used to prevent overtaking and reduce speeds. There is more information about road markings at http://www. direct.gov.uk/en/TravelAndTrans port/Highwaycode/Signsandmark ings/index.htm?IdcService=GET_FI LE&dID=95931&Rendition=Web

- Understand a proof that:
  - the angle sum of a triangles is 180° and of a quadrilateral is 360°
  - the exterior angle of a triangle is equal to the sum of the two interior opposite angle   (L6)
- Classify quadrilaterals by their geometric properties   (L6)

Useful resources
2 sets of congruent quadrilaterals.
Dictionaries

Starter – Triangle bingo

Ask students to draw a 3 × 3 grid and enter nine angles from this list:

30°, 35°, 40°, 45°, 50°, 55°, 60°, 65°, 70°, 7°, 80°, 85°, 90°, 95°, 100°, 105°, 110°, 115°, 120°, 125°.

Give two angles of a triangle, for example, 83° and 42°. If students have the third angle in their grid, 55°, they cross it out.

The winner is the first student to cross out all nine angles.

Teaching notes

If not already covered in spread **6a's investigation**, look at a proof of the interior angle sum of a triangle. Does this mean that you always need two angles to find a third? Counter this assertion by looking at examples of missing angles in isosceles triangles(RL) (1.2).

What is the interior angle sum for quadrilaterals? Show how this can be proved by splitting a quadrilateral into two triangles. Find the interior angle sum of another polygon using this method. Could you generalise? Interior angle sum of an n-sided polygon is $180(n - 2)$ (CT) (1.2).

What types of quadrilaterals can students recall? Instead of saying the name of the quadrilateral, ask students to identify some of its properties. Can the other students correctly identify it, either by describing it or naming it?

A list of the most common quadrilaterals is given in the student book.

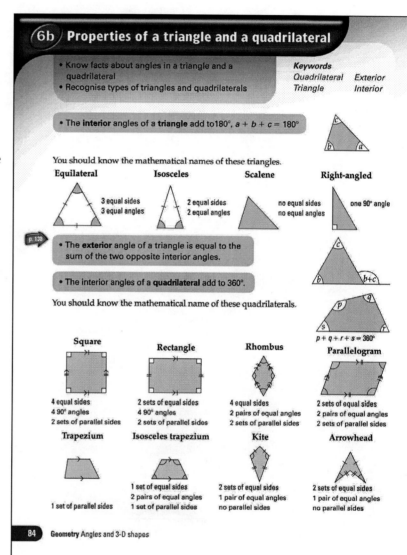

Plenary

Triangles can be further classified into acute angled and obtuse angled. What do these terms mean? How many different types of triangle can now be identified? (7) List them in a systematic way (CT) (1.1, 1.2).

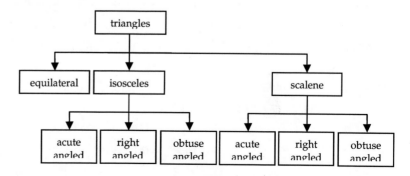

Simplification

Ensure checking strategies are used for the angle sum of triangles and quadrilaterals (RL).

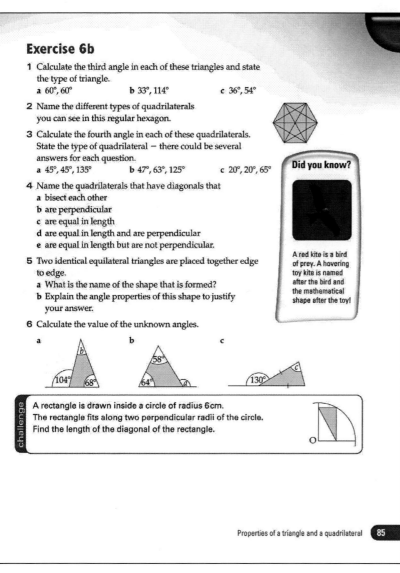

Exercise 6b

1 Calculate the third angle in each of these triangles and state the type of triangle.
   a 60°, 60°   **b** 33°, 114°   **c** 36°, 54°

2 Name the different types of quadrilaterals you can see in this regular hexagon.

3 Calculate the fourth angle in each of these quadrilaterals. State the type of quadrilateral — there could be several answers for each question.
   a 45°, 45°, 135°   **b** 47°, 63°, 125°   **c** 20°, 20°, 65°

4 Name the quadrilaterals that have diagonals that
   a bisect each other
   b are perpendicular
   c are equal in length
   d are equal in length and are perpendicular
   e are equal in length but are not perpendicular

5 Two identical equilateral triangles are placed together edge to edge.
   a What is the name of the shape that is formed?
   b Explain the angle properties of this shape to justify your answer.

6 Calculate the value of the unknown angles.

   a   **b**   **c**

Did you know?

A red kite is a bird of prey. A hovering toy kite is named after the bird and the mathematical shape after the toy!

challenge

A rectangle is drawn inside a circle of radius 6 cm. The rectangle fits along two perpendicular radii of the circle. Find the length of the diagonal of the rectangle.

Properties of a triangle and a quadrilateral   85

Extension

Using two congruent quadrilaterals, what types of quadrilateral can you construct? For example, two rhombuses can form a parallelogram. Students could use a set of shapes in this extension (CT, SM).

Exercise 6b commentary

All questions (1.2, 1.4)

Questions 1 and **3** – Encourage students to sketch their possible answers. (1.3)

Question 2 – Further investigation can be made if students construct the regular hexagon using six congruent equilateral triangles. There appears to be a square inside? Encourage students to prove or disprove, identifying equal sides may help (IE).

Question 4 and **5** – Ask students to check their ideas by drawing a reasonable sketch. Encourage the use of the standard labelling techniques for equal angles, lengths, *etc.*

Question 6 – Sketching the diagrams offers a good opportunity to explain how the missing angles are found. Students should also be encouraged to show their numerical working (1.3).

Challenge – This challenge may need careful explanation. The language is quite technical. Encourage students to identify all possible measurements.

Assessment Criteria – SSM, level 6: solve geometrical problems using properties of angles and of triangles and other polygons. SSM, level 6: classify quadrilaterals by their geometric properties.

Links

Provide dictionaries for the class. The word *isosceles* derives from the Greek *isos* meaning 'equal', and *skelos* meaning 'leg'. Ask the class to find other words beginning with *iso* that are related to the word equal. For example, *isobar* – a line on a map linking points of equal atmospheric pressure, *isometric* – having equal dimensions.

- Explain how to find, calculate and use:
  - the sums of the interior and exterior angles of quadrilaterals, pentagons and hexagons **(L6)**
  - the interior and exterior angles of regular polygons **(L6)**

Useful resources

Protractor
Scissors
Compasses
Tracing paper
List of polygon names
Chalk

Starter – One hundred and eighty!

Ask students questions based on the 180 times table (1.3). For example,

How many 180s in 1080? (6)

What is the angle sum of 8 triangles? (1440°)

How many triangles will give an angle sum of 900°? (5)

How many 180s are there in 4500? (25)

Teaching notes

Ask students if they have ever played the game 'tetris'? It is likely that many of them will have; generally it is played on a computer or mobile phone. Ask a student to describe how the game works. The goal is to tessellate the plane using the seven tetrominos. How can you prove that a particular shape will tessellate? What sort of shapes will tessellate? Ask students to make suggestions and put them into three categories: certainly does (square)/unsure (scalene triangle)/certainly does not (circle) (EP)

Explain what is meant by an exterior angle. It could be described as the angle you turn through to get onto the next edge. As a way to demonstrate the sum of interior angles, students could be taken outside and walk round the edge of a chalk drawn polygon. If the exterior angles are marked, students will be able to see that having turned each angle, they end up back at the start. Hence the exterior angles sum to 360° for any number of sides.

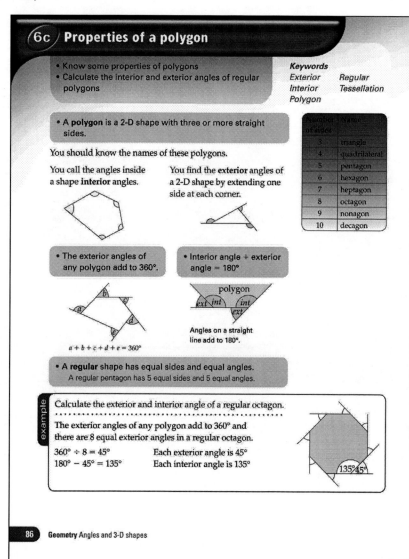

Plenary

Explore the list of names of polygons. What patterns can students spot in the language? Can students pronounce any of the more complex names? Who can memorise the first 20? Who can pronounce a polygon name that is not in the list by using the clues in the given list? (CT)

Simplification

Provide tracing paper to help tessellation. Encourage students to first try to tessellate without reflection. Provide students with diagrams of regular polygons (pentagon to decagon) with edges extended to illustrate exterior angles.

All questions (1.3)

Question 1 – Make sure students build in more than one direction to show convincingly that the shape tessellates.

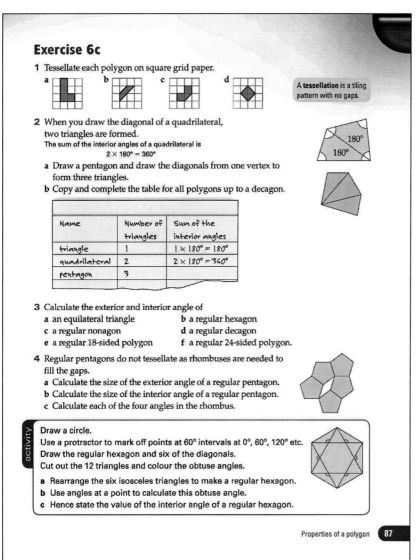

Exercise 6c

1 Tessellate each polygon on square grid paper.
a   b   c   d

A **tessellation** is a tiling pattern with no gaps.

2 When you draw the diagonal of a quadrilateral, two triangles are formed.
The sum of the interior angles of a quadrilateral is
$2 \times 180° = 360°$

180°
180°

a Draw a pentagon and draw the diagonals from one vertex to form three triangles.
b Copy and complete the table for all polygons up to a decagon.

Name	Number of triangles	Sum of the interior angles
triangle	1	$1 \times 180° = 180°$
quadrilateral	2	$2 \times 180° = 360°$
pentagon	3	

3 Calculate the exterior and interior angle of
a an equilateral triangle   b a regular hexagon
c a regular nonagon   d a regular decagon
e a regular 18-sided polygon   f a regular 24-sided polygon.

4 Regular pentagons do not tessellate as rhombuses are needed to fill the gaps.
a Calculate the size of the exterior angle of a regular pentagon.
b Calculate the size of the interior angle of a regular pentagon.
c Calculate each of the four angles in the rhombus.

activity

Draw a circle.
Use a protractor to mark off points at 60° intervals at 0°, 60°, 120° etc.
Draw the regular hexagon and six of the diagonals.
Cut out the 12 triangles and colour the obtuse angles.
a Rearrange the six isosceles triangles to make a regular hexagon.
b Use angles at a point to calculate this obtuse angle.
c Hence state the value of the interior angle of a regular hexagon.

Properties of a polygon   87

Extension

There is a special relationship between the interior and exterior angles of a triangle. Try to find it. The exterior angle of a triangle at any vertex is equal to the sum of the interior angles at the other two vertices. Once students have discovered this they could try to prove this rule. The following diagram could be given as a hint (CT) (1.4).

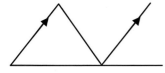

The same diagram as in the **investigation** in spread **6a**. The exterior angle is equal to $a + b$.

Exercise 6c commentary

Question 2 – Encourage students to look for a pattern in the results to speed up the process of finishing the table of results. Can they give the position-to-term rule for the linear sequence? ($180n - 360$) (CT) (1.1)

Question 3 – Which is easier to calculate first? Interior or exterior angle of a regular polygon? What check can be performed to check your answers? (sum to 180°) Can they find general formulae? (exterior = $360/n$, interior = $180 - 360/n$) (CT, RL) (1.1).

Question 4 – A sketch may prove useful here. Encourage students to label the information they find. Explain how the interior angle of a regular pentagon shows that it will not tessellate.

Activity – What makes the regular hexagon special? (can be formed from six congruent triangles). Does this work with other regular polygons? (IE) (1.1)

Assessment Criteria – SSM, level 6: understand a proof that the sum of the angles in a quadrilateral is 360°.

Links

The Giant's Causeway is a formation of thousands of columns of basalt which jut into the sea and resulted from a volcanic eruption 60 million years ago. The top surface of each column is polygonal, most columns having six sides but some having four, five, seven or eight sides. According to local legend, the Causeway was a bridge for two giants who wanted to cross the sea to do battle. There is more information at http://www.giantscausewayofficialguide.com/home.htm (EP).

- Know that if two shapes are congruent, corresponding sides and angles are equal (L6)

Useful resources
Tracing paper

Starter – Guess the polygons

I am a regular polygon that will not tessellate. (for example, pentagon)
Each of my internal angles is exactly 120°. (regular hexagon)
I have 1 pair of parallel lines and my angle sum is half of 720°. (trapezium)
I have 1 internal angle of 90°. All my other internal angles are less than this. (right-angled triangle)
My angle sum is 900°. (heptagon)
Can be extended with students own clues (IE) (1.4).

Teaching notes

Define the meaning of the word congruent. Are there some letters of the alphabet which might be congruent if they are drawn a certain way? For example, 'p' and 'd', 'W' and 'M'. How many examples can students find?

What can you say about the measurements on two congruent shapes? Look for responses that relate to the lengths of the sides and size of angles.

Combinations of certain congruent shapes can produce regular shapes. For example, two congruent isosceles right angled triangles can produce either a square or a larger isosceles right angles triangle depending on how they are joined. What other examples can students find?

A certain special shape can be formed from six congruent equilateral triangles. What shape is it? Encourage students to experiment with sketches. (regular hexagon) How can you be sure you have a *regular* hexagon?

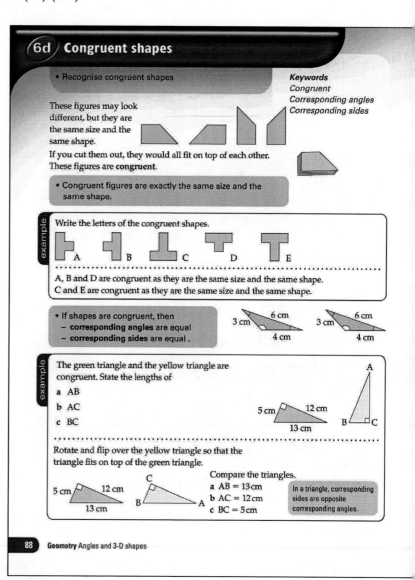

Plenary

The term *directly congruent* applies to shapes that have been translated and/or rotated to produce the second shape. The term *indirectly congruent* applies to shapes that have been reflected and may also have been translated and/or rotated. Look at the exercise again. Which shapes are directly and indirectly congruent? (1.2)

Simplification

Supply tracing paper to make the comparison of shapes easier. Use an enlarged copy of the exercise to allow for easier measurement.

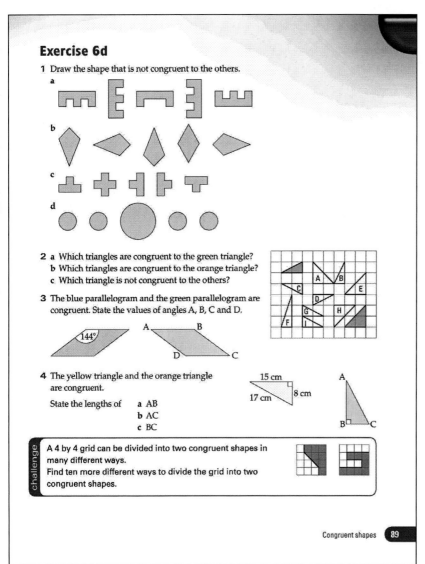

Exercise 6d

1 Draw the shape that is not congruent to the others.

a

b

c

d

2 a Which triangles are congruent to the green triangle?
  b Which triangles are congruent to the orange triangle?
  c Which triangle is not congruent to the others?

3 The blue parallelogram and the green parallelogram are congruent. State the values of angles A, B, C and D.

144°

A   B

D   C

4 The yellow triangle and the orange triangle are congruent.

  State the lengths of   a AB
                           b AC
                           c BC

15 cm

17 cm   8 cm

A

B   C

challenge

A 4 by 4 grid can be divided into two congruent shapes in many different ways.
Find ten more different ways to divide the grid into two congruent shapes.

Exercise 6d commentary

All questions (1.2)

Question 1 – Can a congruent shape be the same shape of a different size? If not, then is there another term to describe the relationship? (similar).

Question 2 – Can two non-congruent shapes have the same area and number of sides? (yes)

Question 3 – Can two congruent shapes ever have different angles from each other? If not, why?

Question 4 – Does it matter that one triangle is the reflection of the other? Are they still congruent?

Challenge – Make it clear that each grid shows two shapes that are congruent to each other. Some students may think that they are to compare the grids with other grids. Encourage the use of curves once lines are exhausted (SM, CT).

Links

Patchwork is a form of needlework in which pieces of different fabric are cut into shapes and then joined together to form a larger design. Congruent shapes are often used and tessellated to form decorative quilts. There are examples of quilt patterns using congruent shapes at http://quilting.about.com/od/pict uresofquilts/ig/Scrap-Quilts-Photo-Gallery/ (EP)

Extension

Consider four similarities between two shapes. **i** same number of sides **ii** same angles **iii** same perimeter **iv** same area. Is it possible to construct a pair of non-congruent shapes that still have all or some of these similarities? If so, which ones? Some possibilities: **i/ii/iii** only, **i/ii/iv** only, **i/iii/iv** only are all possible. **ii/iii/iv** only is impossible (IE, CT) (1.2).

6e 3-D shapes

• Visualise and use 2D representations of 3D shapes   (L6)

Useful resources
Card nets of common
    3D shapes
Card, rulers, scissors,
    glue for making nets.
Pentagon templates
Pipe cleaners

· ·

Starter – SHP!

Write words on the board missing out the vowels,
 for example, SHP).
Ask students for the original words – shape. Possible 'words':
NGL PRLLL RHMBS LTRNT RCTNGL DGNL SSCLS CTGN PRPNDCLR QLTRL
(angle parallel rhombus alternate rectangle diagonal isosceles octagon perpendicular equilateral).

Can be extended by asking students to make up their own examples.

Teaching notes

Using the resources detailed above get
students to draw one of the nets from
question **1**. Use a pentagon template
for the pyramid. Students will need to
think creatively about where they will
put the tabs for gluing together the
edges. Encourage students to think
about this before drawing out the net
(CT).

Challenge students to produce a net of
another 3D shape of their choice. Can
students tell how many faces, vertices
and edges the shape has from looking
at the net? Compare these answers
with the 3D model once it has been
constructed.

Is there more than one possible net for
the shapes in question **1**? If so,
challenge students to find alternative
representations for the nets. How can
you be certain they will work? Show
how labelling the faces of the net can
lead you to accept or reject it as a
possible solution. Normally begin by
labelling the middle one as the base
(1.2).

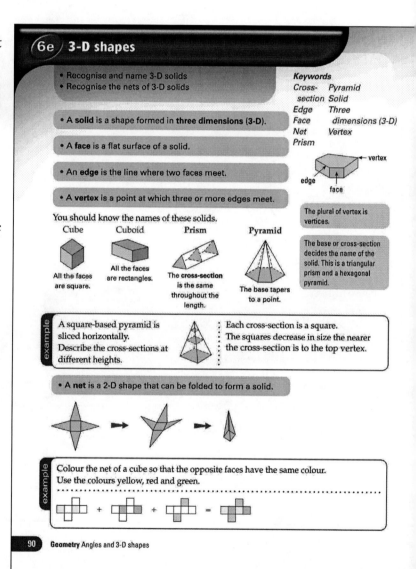

Plenary

Visit http://www.ac-noumea.nc/maths/amc/polyhedr/
index_.htm a French website with an English translation for
exploring polyhedra of many types (CT).

Simplification

Provide students with an enlarged copy of the exercise and encourage them to annotate the diagrams as they count the number of faces, edges and vertices. Provide pre-prepared nets for folding to help with the understanding of how the nets fold to produce the 3D shapes.

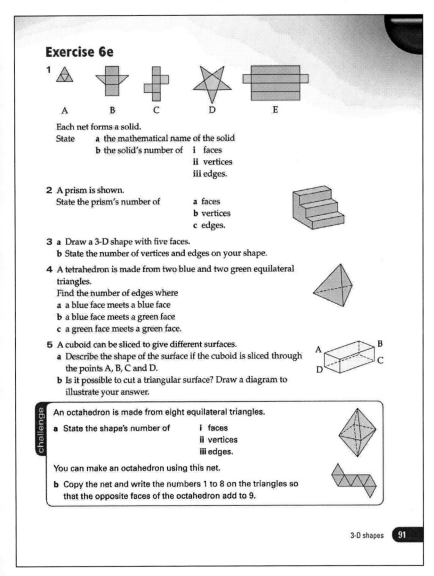

Exercise 6e

1

A   B   C   D   E

Each net forms a solid.

State   **a** the mathematical name of the solid
         b the solid's number of   **i** faces
                           ii vertices
                           iii edges.

2 A prism is shown.
   State the prism's number of   **a** faces
                                    b vertices
                                    c edges.

3 **a** Draw a 3-D shape with five faces.
   b State the number of vertices and edges on your shape.

4 A tetrahedron is made from two blue and two green equilateral triangles.
   Find the number of edges where
   a a blue face meets a blue face
   b a blue face meets a green face
   c a green face meets a green face.

5 A cuboid can be sliced to give different surfaces.
   a Describe the shape of the surface if the cuboid is sliced through the points A, B, C and D.
   b Is it possible to cut a triangular surface? Draw a diagram to illustrate your answer.

challenge

An octahedron is made from eight equilateral triangles.

a State the shape's number of   **i** faces
                                   ii vertices
                                   iii edges.

You can make an octahedron using this net.

b Copy the net and write the numbers 1 to 8 on the triangles so that the opposite faces of the octahedron add to 9.

Extension

A cube can be sliced in half to produce two congruent 3D shapes. How many different ways can this be done? (9) Encourage a new sketch to show each possibility. You could use the term *planes of symmetry* (CT) (1.1).

Exercise 6e commentary

All questions (CT) (1.1, 1.4)

Question 1 – Point students towards the description of the shapes in the student book, there is a clue to an alternative name for shape A elsewhere in the exercise. Can students find it?

Question 2 – Ask students to verbally describe the hidden faces in terms of faces, vertices, *etc.*

Question 3 – This shape is used as a dice in certain games. How do you think it is numbered and how is the score decided upon? One sophisticated option is shown here.

Question 4 – Does it matter how the blue and green faces are arranged? (no) Encourage students to think of a way to check their solution (RL).

Question 5 – Part **b** is very challenging. Students should construct their ideas using pipe cleaners for the shapes edges .

Challenge – Is there more than one way to number the octahedron? This could be used as a dice. Would it be a biased dice? (no) How would the roll be decided upon? Would there be a face you should obviously take as the roll? (the dice will lie flat on a surface and the opposite face will be on top and parallel to the surface, so it will be obvious (SM).

Assessment Criteria – SSM, level 6: visualise and use 2-D representations of 3-D objects.

Links

There is a collection of nets for paper models of more complex solids at http://www.korthalsaltes.com/index.html

- Analyse 3-D shapes through 2-D projections, including plans and elevations

(L6)

Useful resources
Isometric paper
Set of solid models of
3D shapes

Starter – Faceless

Ask students questions involving the numbers of faces, edges and vertices of 3-D shapes. For example,
The sum of faces on a cuboid and vertices on a triangular prism (12)
The product of edges on a cube and faces on a square based pyramid (60)
Subtract edges on a pentagonal pyramid from vertices on a cuboid (-2)

Teaching notes

Draw three views of a cuboid. Label them as the 'front elevation', 'side elevation' and 'plan view'. Is it possible to draw the resulting cuboid? Show how it can be drawn both on plain paper and on isometric paper.

Given a 3D object, attempt to construct the three views of it. A pentagonal prism in the standard shape of a house is a good example.

How is the sloping roof of the side elevation depicted?
How is the top of the roof to be shown on the plan view?
Why are elevations important to designers? Why can't you just draw a 3D picture of the shape you are describing?

Draw a plan view of a 3D shape, ask students to suggest what it might be? Now add the front elevation, does this make it completely clear? If not, add the side elevation (1.5).

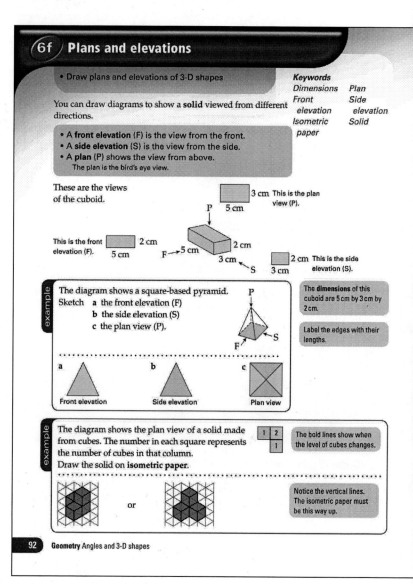

6f Plans and elevations

- Draw plans and elevations of 3-D shapes

Keywords
Dimensions Plan
Front   Side
elevation   elevation
Isometric   Solid
paper

You can draw diagrams to show a **solid** viewed from different directions.

- A **front elevation** (F) is the view from the front.
- A **side elevation** (S) is the view from the side.
- A **plan** (P) shows the view from above.
  The plan is the bird's eye view.

These are the views of the cuboid.

This is the front elevation (F).

3 cm This is the plan view (P).

The **dimensions** of this cuboid are 5 cm by 3 cm by 2 cm.

Label the edges with their lengths.

2 cm This is the side elevation (S).

The diagram shows a square-based pyramid.
Sketch a the front elevation (F)
        b the side elevation (S)
        c the plan view (P).

a Front elevation   b Side elevation   c Plan view

The diagram shows the plan view of a solid made from cubes. The number in each square represents the number of cubes in that column.
Draw the solid on **isometric paper**.

The bold lines show when the level of cubes changes.

or

Notice the vertical lines. The isometric paper must be this way up.

92   **Geometry** Angles and 3-D shapes

Plenary

Ask students to sketch a plan view of the ground floor of their house. Remind students they can't show height in any way. What are common ways that architects use for showing details like, windows, doors, *etc*? (EP).

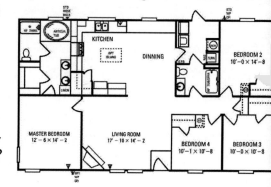

Simplification

Provide students with solid models of the 3D shapes used in the exercise. Advise students to look 'head on' at the models from a distance to give the idea of the elevated view.

All questions (IE) (1.1, 1.3)

Question 1 – Ask students what the dimensions are for the various views. A full size drawing will help to make the comparison between the views clearer.

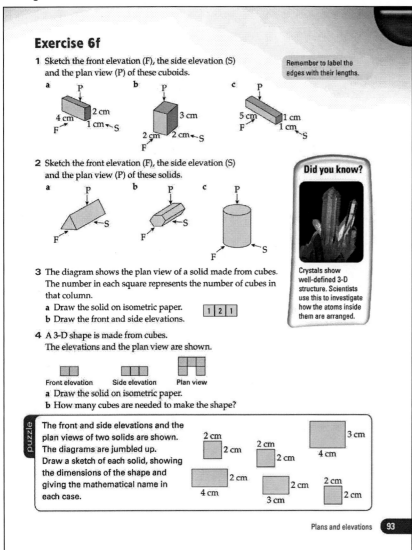

Exercise 6f

1 Sketch the front elevation (F), the side elevation (S) and the plan view (P) of these cuboids.

Remember to label the edges with their lengths.

a   4 cm   2 cm   1 cm

b   3 cm   2 cm   2 cm

c   5 cm   1 cm   1 cm

2 Sketch the front elevation (F), the side elevation (S) and the plan view (P) of these solids.

a   b   c

Did you know?

Crystals show well-defined 3-D structure. Scientists use this to investigate how the atoms inside them are arranged.

3 The diagram shows the plan view of a solid made from cubes. The number in each square represents the number of cubes in that column.
   a Draw the solid on isometric paper.   1 2 1
   b Draw the front and side elevations.

4 A 3-D shape is made from cubes. The elevations and the plan view are shown.

Front elevation   Side elevation   Plan view
   a Draw the solid on isometric paper.
   b How many cubes are needed to make the shape?

puzzle
The front and side elevations and the plan views of two solids are shown. The diagrams are jumbled up. Draw a sketch of each solid, showing the dimensions of the shape and giving the mathematical name in each case.

2 cm   2 cm
2 cm   2 cm   2 cm
2 cm   4 cm   3 cm
4 cm   3 cm   2 cm   2 cm   2 cm   2 cm

Plans and elevations   93

Extension

Attempt to draw plans and elevations of the five platonic solids. How do you decide which is the plan view? Students could be sent to investigate what they look like, or they could be provided with the sketches (SM).

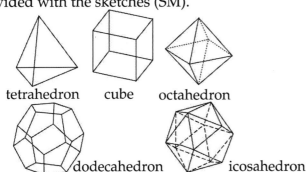

tetrahedron   cube   octahedron

dodecahedron   icosahedron

Exercise 6f commentary

Question 2 – Remind students that a depth is not shown in an elevation. A face that slopes away from you appears upright. Students maybe tempted to curve the edges of the cylinders side view.

Question 3 – Remind students that you can't join points both vertically and horizontally, they need to match the length to the horizontal direction. Allow students to decide which view to take as the front/side elevations.

Question 4 – Which views tells you the number of layers in the shape? Which view tells you the number of cubes that are used? Is there more than one possible solution? (no)

Puzzle – What solid shapes are likely to be used given the shape of all of the views? (cuboids or cubes) Students might try to sketch a cuboid from the given views, or sketch the cuboid first and then match the views to it. Which approach is easier? Is there only one possible solution? (yes) (1.5)

Assessment Criteria – SSM, level 6: visualise and use 2-D representations of 3D objects.

Links

Engineers and architects use drawings showing plan and elevation views of parts, products and buildings. Traditionally drawings were produced by hand but computers have revolutionised the process and most drawings are now produced using CAD (computer-aided design). There is an example of an engineering drawing showing plan and elevation views at http://en.wikipedia.org/wiki/Image:Schneckengetriebe.png (EP).

6 Consolidation

1 Calculate the angles marked with a letter, giving a reason in each case.

a

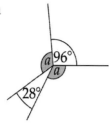

b

c

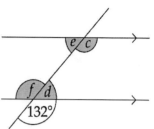

2 Find the value of **a** a
b b
c $a + b$

3 Calculate the value of the unknown angles.
Give a reason in each case.

a

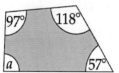

b

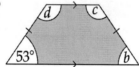

c

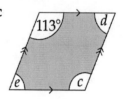

4 Two identical right-angled isosceles triangles are placed edge to edge.
Draw diagrams to show

a a square
b a right-angled isosceles triangle
c a parallelogram.

Use the properties of the right-angled triangles to show that each
shape is the required quadrilateral.

5 Calculate the value of the unknown angles.

a

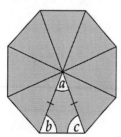

A regular octagon

b

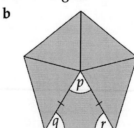

A regular pentagon.

6 a Copy these shapes and draw all the diagonals from each vertex.

b Copy and complete the table.

Polygon	Number of sides	Number of diagonals
triangle	3	0
quadrilateral	4	2
pentagon	5	

7 a Tessellate four congruent 'L' shapes on a 4 by 4 square grid.
b Draw a different arrangement using the same shapes on the grid.

8 On square grid paper, draw the net of a cuboid with dimensions 3 cm by 4 cm by 5 cm.

9 Which shapes are the net of a square-based pyramid?

 A B  C

10 On square grid paper, draw the front elevation (F), the side elevation (S) and the plan view (P) of each solid.

a 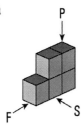 **b** 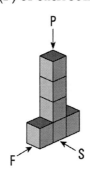 **c** 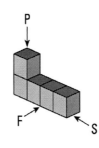 **d**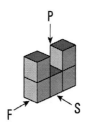

6 Summary

Assessment criteria

- Use language associated with angle and know and use the angle sum of a triangle and that of angles at a point — Level 5
- Classify quadrilaterals by their geometric properties — Level 6
- Solve geometrical problems using properties of angles, of parallel and intersecting lines, and of triangles and other polygons — Level 6
- Identify alternate and corresponding angles: understand a proof that the sum of angles of a triangle is 180° and of a quadrilateral is 360° — Level 6
- Visualise and use 2-D representations of 3-D objects — Level 6

Question commentary

Example

The example illustrates a question where students are asked to draw the plan and elevation views for a given shape. Emphasise that edges where levels change are shown with bold lines within the side view. Ask probing questions such as "How many faces does the shape have?" and "How will the views change if an additional white cube is placed on top of the centre grey cube?"

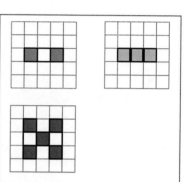

Past question

The question requires students to find the missing angles in a diagram. Some students may try to measure angles instead of calculate them. Emphasise that the words *work out* in the question mean that the drawing is not necessarily to scale. It may help some students to write on a copy of the diagram all the facts that they know or can derive. The next step to solving the unknown properties may then become clear. Angles a and b are found from the sum of the angles on a straight line. Angle d and the angle marked 70° are corresponding angles.

Answer

Level 6

2 $a = 110°$, $b = 130°$
$c = 50°$, $d = 70°$

Development and links

Students consider the symmetrical properties of quadrilaterals and apply knowledge of congruence to transformations and enlargements in Chapter 9. The topic of 3-D shapes is developed in chapter 14 when students will find the surface area and volume of a prism. They also construct triangles and quadrilaterals using a ruler and compasses.

Engineers and technicians in most technological fields use geometry. Carpenters use angles when making joints, engineers use angles when planning and constructing roads and lighting and acoustic engineers use angles to achieve the best effects. GPS systems and CAD software packages are based on geometric principles and most computer game software is written using geometry. The sum of angles at a point is important when working with bearings and maps in geography and when constructing and interpreting pie charts for statistical analysis. Angle work is especially important in physics when calculating forces. The properties of shapes are used in art and design to create geometric patterns and tessellations.

Objectives

- Construct and solve linear equations with integer coefficients (with and without brackets, negative signs anywhere in the equation, positive or negative solution) 6
- Find the inverse of a linear function 6
- Find the gradient of lines given by equations of the form $y = mx + c$, given values for m and c 6
- Construct functions arising from real-life problems and plot their corresponding graphs 6

Introduction

In this chapter, students review linear equations and extend techniques for solving them to include solving equations with a negative algebraic term on one or both sides of the equation. They find the inverse of a function and draw graphs of linear functions, recognising the equation of a straight-line graph and also quadratic functins. They learn to find the gradient and y-intercept of a straight-line and use this to find the equation of a straight-line in the form $y = mx + c$. The chapter concludes with finding the mid-point of a line segment defined by two coordinate pairs.

The student book discusses Robert Hooke and Hooke's Law. Hooke's Law is used to model the behaviour of a spring for small changes in length. Scientists use graphs and determine equations to describe and explain physical phenomena. Constructing and solving equations gives them the ability to understand and predict what is likely to happen in given circumstances. There is more information about Robert Hooke at http://en.wikipedia.org/wiki/Robert_Hooke and an animation illustrating Hooke's Law at http://webphysics.davidson.edu/Applets/animator4/demo_hook.html (EP).

⚡Fast-track
7b, d, e, e²

Level

MPA

1.1	7a, b, c, d, e, e², f
1.2	7a, c, e, e²
1.3	7a, b, c, d, e, e², f
1.4	7b, c, d, e, e², f
1.5	7a, b, c, d, e, e², f

PLTS

IE	7a, b, c, d, e, e², f
CT	7a, b, c, d, e, e², f
RL	7a, b, e, e², f
TW	7b, c, f
SM	7a, c
EP	7I, c, e, e², f

Extra Resources

- 7   Start of chapter presentation
- 7a   Animation: Balancing equations
- 7b   Starter: Simplifying algebra time challenge
- 7b   Worked solution: Q2
- 7d   Starter: Coordinates time challenge
- 7d   Animation: Straight line equations
- 7d   Animation: Plotting coordinates
- 7d   Consolidation sheet
- 7e   Animation: Straight line graphs
- 7e   Animation: Gradient and intercept
- 7e   Worked solution: Q2a
- 7e   Consolidation sheet

Assessment: chapter 7

- Construct and solve linear equations with integer coefficients (with and without brackets, positive or negative solution)

Useful resources

(L6)

• •

Starter − Algebra scores 72

Each consonant scores 2 and each vowel scores 1.

Multiply the total consonant score by the square of the total vowel score to get the word score.

Ask students to write down mathematical words and find their scores.

Bonus points for scores that equal 72.

Can be differentiated by the score allocated to a consonant or vowel.

Teaching notes

Using the idea of balancing scales, show how an equation can be solved by performing operations to both sides of the scales (equal sign). Use the example in the student book (1.2).

Show how equations can be solved algebraically without drawing balances, but strongly emphasise the need to show working on both sides.

Introduce the four basic methods of showing working, describe them as 'reverse' or 'inverse' operations. For example

$$x + 4 = 7 \qquad\qquad -2 = x - 3$$
$$\underline{-4 \quad -4} \qquad\qquad \underline{+3 \quad\quad +3}$$
$$x = 3 \qquad\qquad\quad 1 = x$$
$$3x = 1 \qquad\qquad\quad \tfrac{x}{4} = 2.5$$
$$\tfrac{3x}{3} = \tfrac{1}{3} \qquad\qquad 4 \times \tfrac{x}{4} = 2.5 \times 4$$
$$x = \tfrac{1}{3} \qquad\qquad\quad x = 10$$

Include examples where you need to perform two stages of operations. Progress onto examples that involve expanding brackets and having letters on both sides. Suggest that with letters on both sides, it is better to deal with the letters first. Note that students may well introduce an extra unnecessary step if they deal with the numbers first when solving an equation with letters on both sides.

Some students may need reminding of the rules for multiplying with negatives in order to be able to expand the brackets correctly.

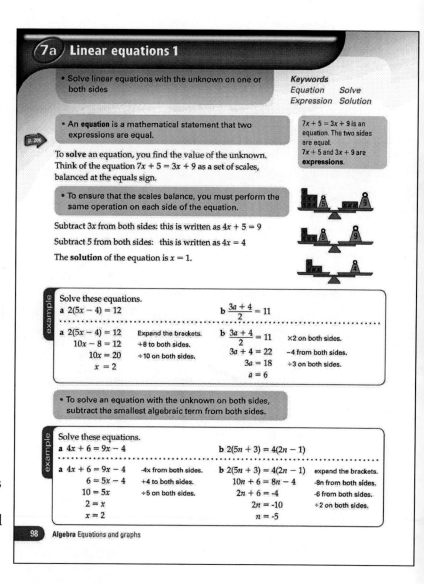

7a Linear equations 1

- Solve linear equations with the unknown on one or both sides

Keywords
Equation   Solve
Expression   Solution

- An **equation** is a mathematical statement that two expressions are equal.

$7x + 5 = 3x + 9$ is an equation. The two sides are equal.
$7x + 5$ and $3x + 9$ are **expressions**.

To **solve** an equation, you find the value of the unknown. Think of the equation $7x + 5 = 3x + 9$ as a set of scales, balanced at the equals sign.

- To ensure that the scales balance, you must perform the same operation on each side of the equation.

Subtract $3x$ from both sides: this is written as $4x + 5 = 9$

Subtract 5 from both sides: this is written as $4x = 4$

The **solution** of the equation is $x = 1$.

example

Solve these equations.
a $2(5x - 4) = 12$ b $\dfrac{3a + 4}{2} = 11$

a $2(5x - 4) = 12$ Expand the brackets.   b $\dfrac{3a + 4}{2} = 11$ ×2 on both sides.
$\quad 10x - 8 = 12$ +8 to both sides. $3a + 4 = 22$ −4 from both sides.
$\quad 10x = 20$ ÷10 on both sides. $3a = 18$ ÷3 on both sides.
$\quad x = 2$ $a = 6$

- To solve an equation with the unknown on both sides, subtract the smallest algebraic term from both sides.

example

Solve these equations.
a $4x + 6 = 9x - 4$ b $2(5n + 3) = 4(2n - 1)$

a $4x + 6 = 9x - 4$ -4x from both sides.   b $2(5n + 3) = 4(2n - 1)$ expand the brackets.
$\quad 6 = 5x - 4$ +4 to both sides. $10n + 6 = 8n - 4$ -8n from both sides.
$\quad 10 = 5x$ ÷5 on both sides. $2n + 6 = -4$ -6 from both sides.
$\quad 2 = x$ $2n = -10$ ÷2 on both sides.
$\quad x = 2$ $n = -5$

98   **Algebra** Equations and graphs

Plenary

Is there more than one solution for the isosceles triangle in question **6**? Yes, $x = 3, 4.5, 6$. are all correct Point out that the diagram can't be assumed to be drawn to scale. Write a similar question, but for an equilateral triangle (RL) (1.2).

Simplification

Pictorial representations of the equations through 'balances', where possible, may help to re-enforce understanding. The method of performing an operation to both sides of an equation can be compared to both the algebraic and pictorial approach. Students will however become aware of the disadvantages of the latter approach.

All questions (1.3)

Question 1 – In part **g**, encourage students to leave their answer as a simplified fraction; use a division line rather than ÷ to make the fractional solution more obvious.

Question 2 – Have some students got the correct answer through tackling the equation using steps in a different order. Who has the most efficient method? (1.5)

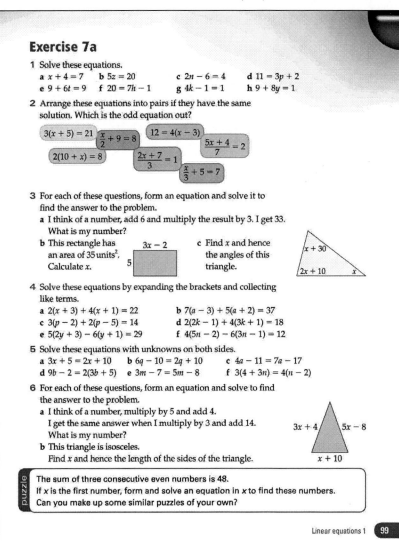

Question 3 – When forming an equation, each side can be expressed in words. Encourage students to think of this as two statements that amount to the same thing. Ask, what is the area of the rectangle? Say the area again in a different way (IE) (1.1).

Question 4 – Why is it important to simplify before solving the equations? Ask, what number is the bracket being multiplied by?

Question 5 – Ask, how many 'x's on each side? How many can you take off each side? Why do you need to remove brackets before you solve the equation?

Question 6 – In part **a**, are brackets needed? In part **b**, most students will assume that the base is the unique side of the isosceles triangle (IE) (1.1).

Puzzle – The term 'consecutive even' may need explaining. What is the connection between any even number and the even number after it? Allow struggling students to solve the problem using trial and improvement. Why is this an inefficient method? (IE, SM) (1.1)

Assessment Criteria – Algebra, level 6: construct and solve linear equations with integer coefficients, using an appropriate method.

Links

The human sense of balance is called equilibrioception. The brain collects information from a series of organs in the inner ear called the labyrinth and combines it with information from the other senses such as sight and touch to help prevent the body from falling over. There is more information at http://en.wikipedia.org/wiki/Equilibrioception

Extension

Write a set of identities for students to solve, but disguise them as equations. Ask students what problems they have encountered? What makes these questions special? For example, $3(2x - 4) = 4 + 2(x + 1) + 4x - 18$ (CT).

- Construct and solve linear equations with integer coefficients (with and without brackets, negative signs anywhere in the equation, positive or negative solution) (L6)
- solve linear equations that require prior simplification of brackets, including those with negative signs anywhere in the equation (L7)

Useful resources

Starter – Algebraic products

Draw a 4 × 4 table on the board.

Label the columns with the terms: $4a$, b, a^2, 7. Label the rows with the terms: a, $2ab$, b^2, $3c$.

Ask students to fill in the table with the products, for example, the top row in the table would read $4a^2$, ab, a^3, $7a$.

Can be differentiated by the choice of terms.

Teaching notes

Look at examples of equations that have a negative term. How can this be dealt with? Compare the way in which we solve examples like $2x - 3 = 5$ by $+3$ to each side (CT). Establish that adding the negative term to each side will 'improve' the equation.

$$25 - 2x = 7$$
$$+ 2x \quad + 2x$$
$$25 = 7 + 2x$$

Encourage students to always deal with the 'negative xs' as soon as possible.

Look at examples that have terms on both sides and include one or both as negative.

If both terms are negative, how much should you add onto each side? Try student's suggestions on an example and establish a good rule. Include examples that have brackets and/or fractions. For example,

$$\frac{14 - 2x}{3} = 2 \quad 3(1 - 2x) = 4x$$

Why is it not possible to $+2x$ to each side and deal with the negative x term immediately? What must the first step be in each case? (RL) (1.5)

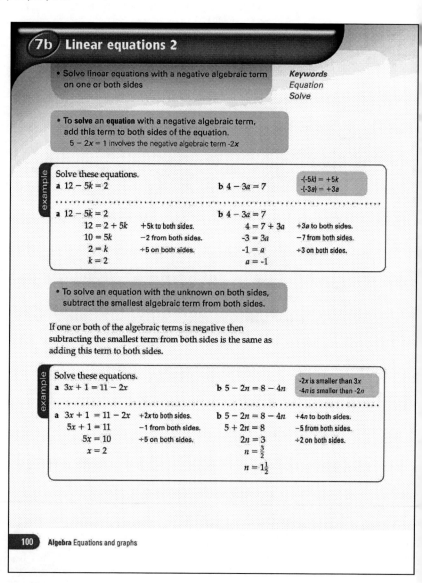

7b Linear equations 2

- Solve linear equations with a negative algebraic term on one or both sides

Keywords
Equation
Solve

- To **solve** an **equation** with a negative algebraic term, add this term to both sides of the equation.
  $5 - 2x = 1$ involves the negative algebraic term $-2x$

example

Solve these equations.
a $12 - 5k = 2$ b $4 - 3a = 7$

$-(-5k) = +5k$
$-(-3a) = +3a$

a $12 - 5k = 2$
$\quad 12 = 2 + 5k$ $+5k$ to both sides.
$\quad 10 = 5k$ -2 from both sides.
$\quad 2 = k$ $÷5$ on both sides.
$\quad k = 2$

b $4 - 3a = 7$
$\quad 4 = 7 + 3a$ $+3a$ to both sides.
$\quad -3 = 3a$ -7 from both sides.
$\quad -1 = a$ $÷3$ on both sides.
$\quad a = -1$

- To solve an equation with the unknown on both sides, subtract the smallest algebraic term from both sides.

If one or both of the algebraic terms is negative then subtracting the smallest term from both sides is the same as adding this term to both sides.

example

Solve these equations.
a $3x + 1 = 11 - 2x$ b $5 - 2n = 8 - 4n$

$-2x$ is smaller than $3x$
$-4n$ is smaller than $-2n$

a $3x + 1 = 11 - 2x$ $+2x$ to both sides.
$\quad 5x + 1 = 11$ -1 from both sides.
$\quad 5x = 10$ $÷5$ on both sides.
$\quad x = 2$

b $5 - 2n = 8 - 4n$ $+4n$ to both sides.
$\quad 5 + 2n = 8$ -5 from both sides.
$\quad 2n = 3$ $÷2$ on both sides.
$\quad n = \frac{3}{2}$
$\quad n = 1\frac{1}{2}$

Plenary

I think of a number, double it, add 6, then half the answer I have so far, finally I subtract the number I started with. What result do I get? (3). Why do you always get 3? Encourage students to try to explain in words. Is there an algebraic way to prove that the result is always 3? Encourage students to form the expression and simplify.

Simplification

Some students may find that using inverse operations is useful. Although this can be hard to use for negative terms. Continually emphasise the importance of removing the negative term to make the equation 'simpler'.

All questions (1.3)

Question 1 – Remind students of the rules of arithmetic for negative numbers.

Question 2 – What makes these equations more difficult to solve? Emphasise the importance of removing brackets and fractions. What part can be simplified after brackets are removed? Actually once one solution has been found the others can be checked by substitution.

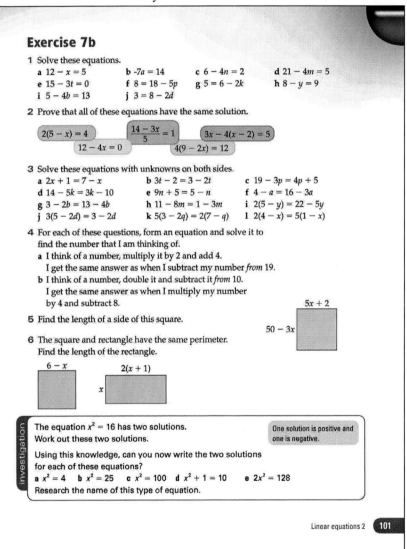

Extension

A rectangle is said to have sides $4 - x$ and $2 + 2x$. and perimeter i22 cm. Find x. (5). Is there anything wrong with your answer? Try finding the area? What can you say about the possible value of x? Look at the lengths of the sides. ($-1 < x < 4$). If the perimeter can't be 22, what values can it take? ($10 <$ perimeter < 20) (CT) (1.2, 1.5)

Exercise 7b commentary

Question 3 – With letters on both sides and negative terms, students may be unsure whether to add or subtract terms and by how much. Allow students to try their own ideas and reflect on its effectiveness and efficiency (1.4).

Question 4 – The wording needs to be carefully looked at to help form the equation. Encourage students to discuss with a partner whether they agree (IE, RL) (1.1, 1.5).

Question 5 – What properties does a square have? How can you form an equation? (IE) (1.1)

Question 6 – Do you need to expand the brackets to help find the perimeter of the rectangle? Some students may need help adding the negative x term for the perimeter of the square (IE) (1.1).

Investigation – What are the rules for multiplying with negative numbers? Encourage a mental approach rather than a formal algebraic method. An internet search will help students to identify the term 'quadratic' (CT) (1.4).

Assessment Criteria – Algebra, level 6: construct and solve linear equations with integer coefficients, using an appropriate method.

Links

The equals sign was first used by the Welsh mathematician and physician Robert Recorde in 1557 in his book The Whetstone of Witte. He used two parallel lines in the symbol because 'noe .2. thynges, can be moare equalle' However, other symbols for "is equal to" were still used until the 1700s including the Latin abbreviation *ae* or *oe* (for *aequalis* or equal) There is more information about Robert Recorde at http://en.wikipedia.org/wiki/Robert_Recorde (TW).

- Express simple functions algebraically and represent them in mappings (L5)
- Find the inverse of a linear function (L6)

Useful resources

Starter – Budgies and hamsters

Luxmi had some budgies and hamsters.

She counted the number heads and feet. There were 26 heads and 86 feet.

Ask students how many budgies and how many hamsters there were. (9 budgies, 17 hamsters)

Can be extended by asking students to make up their own bird and animal puzzles.

Teaching notes

A mathematical function is a rule that generates an output (answer) from a given input. The function normally has the same rule for every input value. Give examples of some common functions. Show how a table of values can be used to represent possible inputs and outputs. The function can be written as both an equation or as a mapping. Supply examples. The arrow in the mapping can be thought of as representing the words 'turns into'. Possible inputs and outputs can also be represented in a mapping diagram. Supply examples (1.1, 1.3).

Consider how to reverse a function. Give examples of functions and ask what steps are needed to change the output into the input. Arrow diagrams could be used to help reverse the operations. If the function is expressed as a formula, then the methods used in spread 5f for rearranging formulae could be used to find the inverse.

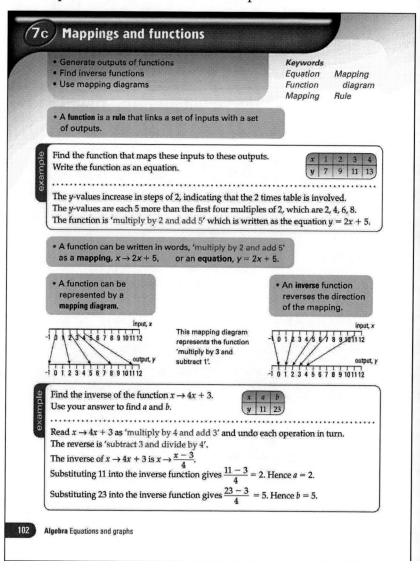

Plenary

Use two ovals for the input and output as an alternative mapping diagram. Discuss different types of mappings, that is, one-to-one, one-to-many, many-to-one and many-to-many. These formal terms need not be used, but the function types could be categorised and students could invent their own terminology (CT) (1.1, 1.4).

Examples of function types **i** one-to-one, $y = 2x - 1$ **ii** one-to-many, $y = \pm x + 5$ **iii** many-to-one, $y = x^2$ **iv** many-to-many $y^2 = x^2$.

Simplification

Write the mappings as equations beginning with '$y =$'. Ask, what is being done to x? Establish that the order of operations is vital. Encourage students to be able to express the function in words first.

All questions (1.1, 1.3)

Question 1 – Where there is more than one operation, students can use the rules of BIDMAS to help evaluate the function for different values.

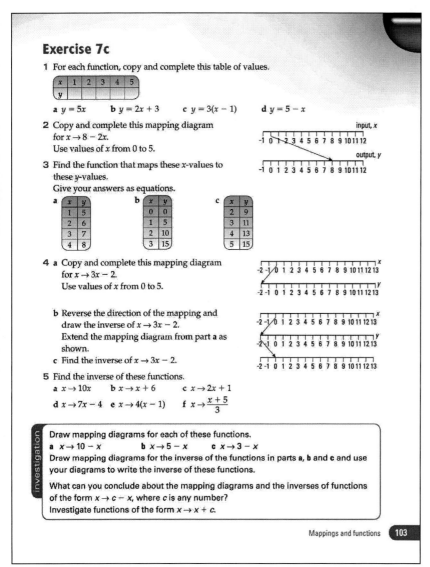

Extension

A mapping is described like this 'x is an integer that maps onto the next number greater than x that is a prime number.' Draw a mapping diagram for x from 0 to 10. Can you describe in words the inverse function? If the values of x continue after 10, how many lines is it possible to draw to the same output value from different input values? (SM, CT)

Exercise 7c commentary

Question 2 – Remind students that the term 'mapping' means the same as '$y =$'. Encourage a well spaced diagram to avoid untidy work.

Question 3 – Encourage students to look for simple rules initially. Part **c** has a two step rule, encourage students to investigate possibilities without giving a formal method involving differences.

Question 4 – What does the extension to the mapping diagram in part **b** show you? Students may need to be helped to understand what use this extension is.

Question 5 – A function machine with the direction of the arrows reversed may help in finding the inverse functions. How can the answer be checked? Encourage the use of at least one test value in the function and in its inverse.

Investigation – The investigation may need careful explaining as the 'constant c' will be an unfamiliar form of mathematical language. Students could work in pairs and share results in the last part of the investigation (IE, TW) (1.2, 1.5).

Links

In computing, input and output refer to the way the computer communicates with the outside world. Data is entered into the computer using an input device such as a keyboard or a mouse. The computer sends data to the outside world via an output device such as a printer, monitor or speaker. There is more information about PC Input/Output (I/O) at http://www.techweb.com/encyclopedia/defineterm.jhtml?term=PCinput%2Foutput (EP).

- Plot the graphs of linear functions, where y is given explicitly in terms of x, on paper **(L6)**
- Recognise that equations of the form y 5 mx 1 c correspond to straight-line graphs **(L6)**

Useful resources

Starter – £20 more

A cd player and batteries together cost £23.
The cd player cost £20 more than the batteries.
How much do the batteries cost? (£1.50)
Ask students to explain their methods.
Encourage the use of algebra.

Teaching notes

How can a function be represented as a diagram? Write a function as an equation and represent the input (x) and the possible outputs (y) on a set of Cartesian axes (1.1).

Show how the table of values used in the spread **7c** helps us to organise the possible points. What pattern do they seem to make? Ensure students extend their lines all the way through the axes and label the function.

How many points are needed if we believe the function will produce a straight line?

What do the functions y = a number and x = a number look like? Establish that they in fact go in the perpendicular direction to the y-axis and x-axis. Therefore, what are the equations of the x and y axes?

Is it possible to tell if an equation will produce a straight line or not? Use the previous spread as a guide, they all produce straight lines.

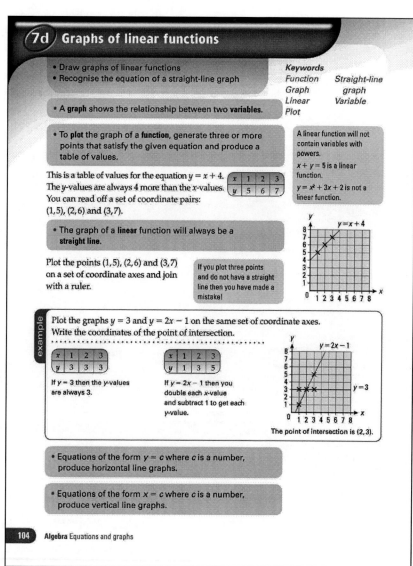

7d Graphs of linear functions

- Draw graphs of linear functions
- Recognise the equation of a straight-line graph

Keywords
Function   Straight-line
Graph   graph
Linear   Variable
Plot

- A **graph** shows the relationship between two **variables**.

- To **plot** the graph of a **function**, generate three or more points that satisfy the given equation and produce a table of values.

This is a table of values for the equation $y = x + 4$.
The y-values are always 4 more than the x-values.
You can read off a set of coordinate pairs:
(1,5), (2,6) and (3,7).

x	1	2	3
y	5	6	7

A linear function will not contain variables with powers.
$x + y = 5$ is a linear function.
$y = x^2 + 3x + 2$ is not a linear function.

- The graph of a **linear** function will always be a **straight line**.

Plot the points (1,5), (2,6) and (3,7) on a set of coordinate axes and join with a ruler.

If you plot three points and do not have a straight line then you have made a mistake!

Plot the graphs $y = 3$ and $y = 2x − 1$ on the same set of coordinate axes.
Write the coordinates of the point of intersection.

x	1	2	3
y	3	3	3

If $y = 3$ then the y-values are always 3.

x	1	2	3
y	1	3	5

If $y = 2x − 1$ then you double each x-value and subtract 1 to get each y-value.

The point of intersection is (2, 3).

- Equations of the form $y = c$ where c is a number, produce horizontal line graphs.

- Equations of the form $x = c$ where c is a number, produce vertical line graphs.

104 Algebra Equations and graphs

Plenary

Is this equation, $y = \sqrt{25 - x^2}$, going to produce a straight line? What shape might it produce? Try to complete this table of values and join the points.

x	-5	-4	-3	0	3	4	5
y							

Note that the square root sign strictly means the positive square root. The points produce a semi-circle when joined (CT) (1.1, 1.3).

Simplification

Provide students with examples of equation/table/graph for three different types of equation, $x = c$, $y = c$ and $y = mx + c$. Re-enforce the link between the three alternative ways of expressing the function algebraic/mapping diagram/graph.

All questions (1.1, 1.3)

Question 1 – Use the examples in the text to help match the cards and functions.

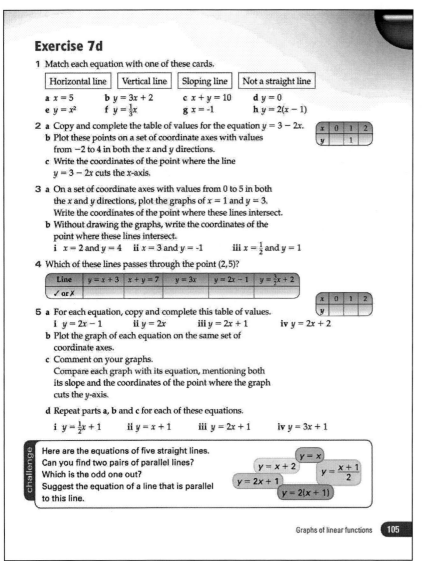

Exercise 7d

1 Match each equation with one of these cards.

Horizontal line	Vertical line	Sloping line	Not a straight line

- **a** $x = 5$
- **b** $y = 3x + 2$
- **c** $x + y = 10$
- **d** $y = 0$
- **e** $y = x^2$
- **f** $y = \frac{1}{3}x$
- **g** $x = -1$
- **h** $y = 2(x - 1)$

2 a Copy and complete the table of values for the equation $y = 3 - 2x$.

x	0	1	2
y		1	

- **b** Plot these points on a set of coordinate axes with values from −2 to 4 in both the x and y directions.
- **c** Write the coordinates of the point where the line $y = 3 - 2x$ cuts the x-axis.

3 a On a set of coordinate axes with values from 0 to 5 in both the x and y directions, plot the graphs of $x = 1$ and $y = 3$. Write the coordinates of the point where these lines intersect.

- **b** Without drawing the graphs, write the coordinates of the point where these lines intersect.
  - **i** $x = 2$ and $y = 4$
  - **ii** $x = 3$ and $y = -1$
  - **iii** $x = \frac{1}{2}$ and $y = 1$

4 Which of these lines passes through the point (2,5)?

Line	$y = x + 3$	$x + y = 7$	$y = 3x$	$y = 2x - 1$	$y = \frac{3}{2}x + 2$
✓ or ✗					

5 a For each equation, copy and complete this table of values.

x	0	1	2
y			

  - **i** $y = 2x - 1$
  - **ii** $y = 2x$
  - **iii** $y = 2x + 1$
  - **iv** $y = 2x + 2$
- **b** Plot the graph of each equation on the same set of coordinate axes.
- **c** Comment on your graphs. Compare each graph with its equation, mentioning both its slope and the coordinates of the point where the graph cuts the y-axis.
- **d** Repeat parts **a**, **b** and **c** for each of these equations.
  - **i** $y = \frac{1}{2}x + 1$
  - **ii** $y = x + 1$
  - **iii** $y = 2x + 1$
  - **iv** $y = 3x + 1$

challenge

Here are the equations of five straight lines. Can you find two pairs of parallel lines? Which is the odd one out? Suggest the equation of a line that is parallel to this line.

$y = x$
$y = x + 2$
$y = \frac{x + 1}{2}$
$y = 2x + 1$
$y = 2(x + 1)$

Graphs of linear functions **105**

Extension

Question **5d** has four lines that all intersect at the same point on the y-axis. Challenge students create four equations that produce lines that intersect at the same point on the x-axis. For a harder challenge, can they create four lines that intersect at a point not on either axis? Encourage students to discuss their approaches (CT) (1.5).

Question 2 – Some students may be confused by the $-2x$ term. Substitution and the rules of BIDMAS could be used to help in the evaluation. For example, $3 - 2x$ becomes $3 - 2 \times 2$. Why are three points needed in the table? (IE)

Question 3 – Why do some students mistake the horizontal and vertical directions of the $y = c$ and $x = c$ lines? (IE)

Question 4 – What does (2, 5) mean? It is not only the coordinates of a point but a pair of values for x and y. Does (2, 5) 'fit' any of the equations? What is meant by $\frac{3}{2}x$?

Question 5 – Parts **a-c**, what word describes the connection between the directions of the lines? (parallel). What part of the equation makes this happen? Part **d**, why aren't these lines parallel? Why do they all intersect at the same point? (IE, CT)

Challenge – The bracket and the fraction make this challenge more difficult. Can students suggest how to deal with this? What different ways can you express $x \div 2$? ($\frac{1}{2}x$ or $\frac{x}{2}$ or $0.5x$) (1.4)

Assessment Criteria – Algebra, level 6: plot the graphs of linear functions where y is given explicitly in terms of x. Algebra, level 6: recognize that equations of the form $y = mx + c$ correspond to straight-line graphs.

Links

The word *axes* is a heteronym as it can be pronounced in two different ways, each with a different meaning: the plural of axis or the plural of axe. Ask the class to try to list some other heteronyms. Some examples are minute, lead, wind, buffet, refuse, tear, wind, wound and sow.

- Find the gradient of lines given by equations of the form $y = mx + c$, given values for m and c   (L7)
- Understand that equations in the form $y = mx + c$ represent a straight line and that m is the gradient and c is the value of the y-intercept   (L6)
- Construct functions arising from real-life problems and plot their corresponding graphs   (L6)

Useful resources

Starter – ABCD

If $A = 3, B = 4, C = 7, D = 9$ ask students to form as many equations as they can in four minutes.

Score 1 point for each different operation or brackets and 2 points for each different letter used. For example, $2(B^2 - A) = AC + 5$ scores 11.

Teaching notes

Draw the lines with equations $y = 2x - 3$ and $y = -3x + 1$. What is meant by their gradients? *Gradient* is a measurement of the steepness of the slope. How can it be measured? Describe the method and give the formula gradient = $\frac{\text{height}}{\text{base}}$. It can be remembered by the fact that the 'height' goes 'high up' in the formula and the 'base' goes at the 'base'.

Find the gradients of the two lines. What major difference is there between the lines? One slopes uphill, the other downhill. How might this be represented in the value of the gradient? Discuss negative gradients.

An alternative way of looking at gradient is to see how far the line moves for every unit along. Test this on the two examples. The gradient is represented by the letter 'm'. The place where the line *intercepts* the y-axis is represented by the letter 'c'. Is there a link between the values of m and c for these two lines and their corresponding equations? Establish the general rule $y = mx + c$ (CT) (1.1).

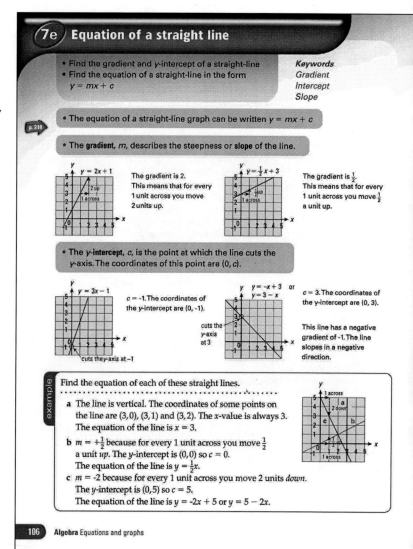

Plenary

Why do students think that 'm' and 'c' are used to represent the gradient and y-intercept? Why not use 'g' and 'i'? Unfortunately 'g' and 'i' are already taken to represent other values. In fact no one knows why 'm' is used.

Simplification

When using the equation of a line, consistently use the form $y = mx + c$ or $y = \dfrac{a}{b}x + c$. Show how equations can be re-written in this form if needed. This will help to reduce problems with distinguishing 'm' from 'c' and also help to find fractional gradients.

All questions (IE) (1.1, 1.3)

Question 1 –. Ask, what is x being multiplied by? What is the number that is on its own?

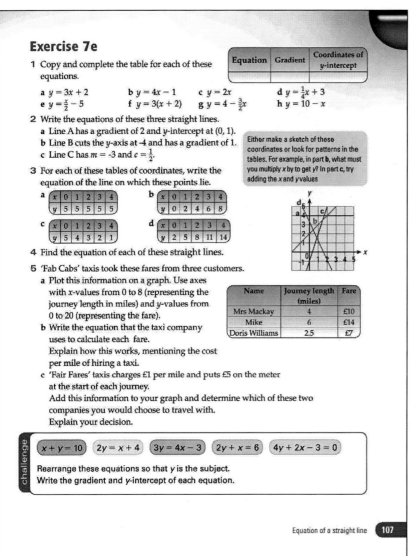

Extension

Give students examples of implicit straight line equations with negative y terms. Ask them to say what they think 'm' and 'c' are before drawing the lines. What method could be used? What about the method used in spread **7d**? How can the initial thoughts on the values of 'm' and 'c' be checked? If students made an error, can they say what made the equation difficult to read? Is there a way to find 'm' and 'c' correctly without drawing the line? How could the equation, for example $4x - 2y = 10$, be rearranged? (RL) (1.4, 1.5)

Exercise 7e commentary

Question 2 – Is there more than one way to express the solutions?

Question 3 – Not all straight lines are easily written in the form $y = mx + c$. Students should look for any relationship they can for x and y – part **c** in particular.

Question 4 – Which line will not have an equation that looks like $y = mx + c$? Are any of the gradients negative?

Question 5 – What do the values of the gradient and y-intercept mean in reality? Would you get in a taxi with a high value of 'c' and low value of 'm' ? (EP)

Challenge – Encourage students to rearrange the equations using a similar method to that of solving equations, that is, showing working on both sides. The fractional values of the gradient are likely to cause problems (1.2).

Assessment Criteria – Algebra, level 6: recognize that equations of the form $y = mx + c$ correspond to straight line graphs. Algebra, level 6: construct functions arising from real-life problems and plot their corresponding graphs.

Links

On maps, contour lines can be used to calculate the gradient of hills. Every point on a contour line is at the same height. The closer the contours are together, the steeper the slope. On roads a double arrow shows a gradient of 1 in 5 or steeper, that is, the road rises or falls 1 m in height for every 5 m in length, and a single arrow shows a gradient of 1 in 7 to 1 in 5. A map showing these features can be found using grid reference SS871466 at http://getamap.ordnancesurvey.co.uk/getamap/frames.htm (EP).

- Plot graphs of simple quadratic and cubic functions   (L7)   **Useful resources**
  'autograph'

Starter – Coordinates

Ask students to give three sets of coordinates that lie on the following lines:

$2y = 5x + 9$ for example (-1, 2) (1, 7) (3, 12)
$3x + y = -1$ for example (-1, 2) (-2, 5) (1, -4)
$y - x = 3$ for example (-1, 2) (1, 4) (-5, -2)

Encourage students to think of negative values.
Ask students what they notice when $x = -1$. (The lines intersect at (-1, 2).)

Teaching notes

Look at a table of values for a straight line (linear) graph. If the x values rise evenly, what do you notice about the y values? What would happen if the y values did not rise evenly? The graph would not be a straight line.

One particular group of non linear functions are known as the *quadratics*, they produce a type of graph known as a parabola. Give the students some examples of functions where all except one are quadratic. Can students tell which is the odd one out?

Establish what makes a quadratic function and look at how a table of values can be used to organise possible points on the graph. Why do you need so many points?

Look at the shape of the parabola, does it ever flatten out? Use the example of $y = x^2 - x$ and x values from -1 to 3. It appears that the curve is flat between $x = 0$ and $x = 1$. Is this the case? Taking x as 0.5 and using a calculator will help demonstrate that the curve continues to 'dip'. Is the curve symmetrical? (CT) (1.1, 1.4)

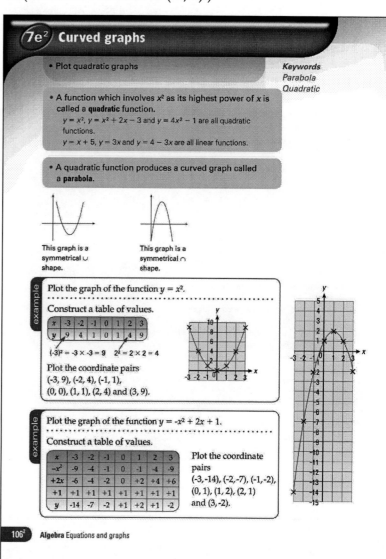

7e² Curved graphs

- Plot quadratic graphs

Keywords
Parabola
Quadratic

- A function which involves x^2 as its highest power of x is called a **quadratic** function.
  $y = x^2$, $y = x^2 + 2x - 3$ and $y = 4x^2 - 1$ are all quadratic functions.
  $y = x + 5$, $y = 3x$ and $y = 4 - 3x$ are all linear functions.

- A quadratic function produces a curved graph called a **parabola**.

This graph is a symmetrical ∪ shape.

This graph is a symmetrical ∩ shape.

example

Plot the graph of the function $y = x^2$.

Construct a table of values.

x	-3	-2	-1	0	1	2	3
y	9	4	1	0	1	4	9

$(-3)^2 = -3 \times -3 = 9$ $2^2 = 2 \times 2 = 4$

Plot the coordinate pairs
(-3, 9), (-2, 4), (-1, 1),
(0, 0), (1, 1), (2, 4) and (3, 9).

example

Plot the graph of the function $y = -x^2 + 2x + 1$.

Construct a table of values.

x	-3	-2	-1	0	1	2	3
$-x^2$	-9	-4	-1	0	-1	-4	-9
$+2x$	-6	-4	-2	0	+2	+4	+6
$+1$	+1	+1	+1	+1	+1	+1	+1
y	-14	-7	-2	+1	+2	+1	-2

Plot the coordinate pairs
(-3,-14), (-2,-7), (-1,-2),
(0, 1), (1, 2), (2, 1)
and (3,-2).

106² **Algebra** Equations and graphs

Plenary

Use a graphing package with the whole class. Ask students to suggest a quadratic equation that will pass between two given fixed points. Initial guesses can be further refined by editing the equation. This could be done in the context of a 'football' landing in a 'goal'. A further challenge could be set to obtain a quadratic curve that passes through two 'goals' (CT).

Simplification

The main assistance is needed in using the table of values. Encourage students to primarily use the positive x values. Once the graph is partly drawn, the negative x values can be checked to see if they fit the general shape of the curve.

All questions (CT) (1.1, 1.3)

Question 1 – When solving equations what do you do about brackets? (multiply them out) Encourage students to employ this tactic. Can students say any more than what type of graph each equation is? For example, a vertical line.

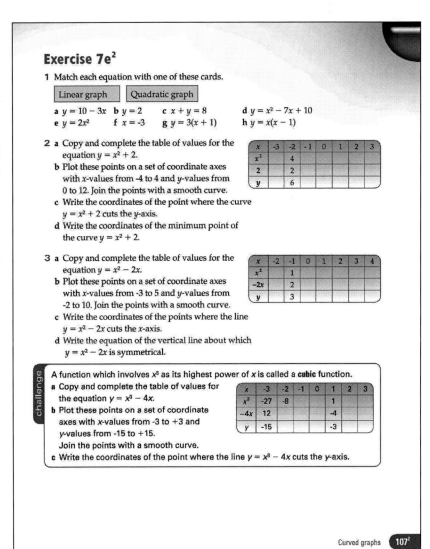

Exercise 7e²

1 Match each equation with one of these cards.

| Linear graph | Quadratic graph |

a $y = 10 - 3x$ b $y = 2$ c $x + y = 8$ d $y = x^2 - 7x + 10$
e $y = 2x^2$ f $x = -3$ g $y = 3(x + 1)$ h $y = x(x - 1)$

2 a Copy and complete the table of values for the equation $y = x^2 + 2$.
 b Plot these points on a set of coordinate axes with x-values from -4 to 4 and y-values from 0 to 12. Join the points with a smooth curve.
 c Write the coordinates of the point where the curve $y = x^2 + 2$ cuts the y-axis.
 d Write the coordinates of the minimum point of the curve $y = x^2 + 2$.

x	-3	-2	-1	0	1	2	3
x^2		4					
2		2					
y		6					

3 a Copy and complete the table of values for the equation $y = x^2 - 2x$.
 b Plot these points on a set of coordinate axes with x-values from -3 to 5 and y-values from -2 to 10. Join the points with a smooth curve.
 c Write the coordinates of the points where the line $y = x^2 - 2x$ cuts the x-axis.
 d Write the equation of the vertical line about which $y = x^2 - 2x$ is symmetrical.

x	-2	-1	0	1	2	3	4
x^2		1					
$-2x$		2					
y		3					

challenge

A function which involves x^3 as its highest power of x is called a **cubic** function.
a Copy and complete the table of values for the equation $y = x^3 - 4x$.
b Plot these points on a set of coordinate axes with x-values from -3 to +3 and y-values from -15 to +15. Join the points with a smooth curve.
c Write the coordinates of the point where the line $y = x^3 - 4x$ cuts the y-axis.

x	-3	-2	-1	0	1	2	3
x^3	-27	-8			1		
$-4x$	12				-4		
y	-15				-3		

Curved graphs   107²

Extension

Draw the graph of $y^2 = x$. How can you change the table of values to make this easier? How can you transform the graph of $y = x^2$ into $y^2 = x$? If chapter **9** has been covered, encourage the use of the language associated with reflection (CT) (1.1).

Exercise 7e² commentary

Question 2 – Some students maybe confused both by squaring a negative and by the third row requiring '2' to be repeated across the row. A simpler example could be used to demonstrate how the table works, for example, $y = 2x + 1$ (IE).

x	2	3
$2x$	4	6
1	1	1
$y = 2x + 1$	5	7

Question 3 – The subtraction of $2x$ may cause problems for students, especially with negative x values. Allow students to make errors in their table, but ask what type of graph they are expecting to get? Do the points they have found lie in a smooth U shape? Which points do they think are in error? (IE, RL) (1.2)

Challenge – Encourage students to discuss their table of results with their partners. What shape are they expecting for the graph? Is there any part of the graph that seems out of shape? (IE) (1.5)

Assessment Criteria – Algebra, level 7: plot graphs of simple quadratic and cubic functions.

Links

A television satellite dish is a type of parabolic antenna. The inside surface of the dish is parabolic in shape. The incoming radiation reflects off the inside of the dish and is focussed on to a central antenna called a feedhorn. The signal is then transmitted electrically from the feedhorn to the television. There is an applet demonstrating how parabolic reflectors work at http://www.analyzemath.com/parabola/parabola.html (EP).

- Find the mid-point of the line segment AB, given the coordinates of A and B (L6)

Useful resources
Graph paper
Graph paper on stiff card

Starter – Nested quadrilaterals

Ask students to draw a regular quadrilateral and then join the mid-points of neighbouring sides, what shape do they get?

Kite → rectangle,   Rectangle → rhombus,   rhombus → rectangle
Square → square,   parallelogram → parallelogram,   isosceles trapezium → kite

The procedure can be iterated to give a nested sequence of quadrilaterals. Repeating for a parallelogram results in a similar parallelogram of half the original size.

Teaching notes

Draw a diagonal line segment AB with given end coordinates (in the first quadrant) on a grid and ask students how they would find its mid-point. Can they do better than using a ruler to measure the distance along the line?

Suggest they look at the line from above, where would the end points of its shadow be: $(x_A, 0)$ and $(x_B, 0)$. Agree that to find the point half way between x_A and x_B you calculate $\frac{(x_A + x_B)}{2}$. Ask the students to do the same for the y-coordinate. Check understanding with a further numerical example (1.1, 1.4).

An alternate derivation follows by adding lines parallel to the axes at A, M and B and considering similar triangles.

Pose the problem: given a point A and a mid-point M, how would you find B? Two approaches are possible. Formally based on setting up and solving two linear equations ($x_B = 2x_M - x_A$ and $y_B = 2y_M - y_A$). Informally based on working out how far in x you have to go to get from x_A to x_M and then adding this onto x_M, likewise for y. Check understanding with a numerical example.

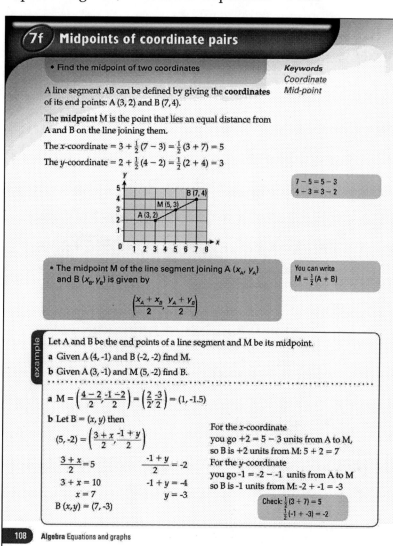

7f Midpoints of coordinate pairs

- Find the midpoint of two coordinates

Keywords
Coordinate
Mid-point

A line segment AB can be defined by giving the **coordinates** of its end points: A (3, 2) and B (7, 4).

The **midpoint** M is the point that lies an equal distance from A and B on the line joining them.

The x-coordinate $= 3 + \frac{1}{2}(7 - 3) = \frac{1}{2}(3 + 7) = 5$
The y-coordinate $= 2 + \frac{1}{2}(4 - 2) = \frac{1}{2}(2 + 4) = 3$

$7 - 5 = 5 - 3$
$4 - 3 = 3 - 2$

- The midpoint M of the line segment joining A (x_A, y_A) and B (x_B, y_B) is given by

$$\left(\frac{x_A + x_B}{2}, \frac{y_A + y_B}{2}\right)$$

You can write
$M = \frac{1}{2}(A + B)$

example

Let A and B be the end points of a line segment and M be its midpoint.
a Given A (4, -1) and B (-2, -2) find M.
b Given A (3, -1) and M (5, -2) find B.

a $M = \left(\frac{4 - 2}{2}, \frac{-1 - 2}{2}\right) = \left(\frac{2}{2}, \frac{-3}{2}\right) = (1, -1.5)$

b Let B = (x, y) then

$(5, -2) = \left(\frac{3 + x}{2}, \frac{-1 + y}{2}\right)$

$\frac{3 + x}{2} = 5$ $\frac{-1 + y}{2} = -2$

$3 + x = 10$ $-1 + y = -4$

$x = 7$ $y = -3$

B $(x, y) = (7, -3)$

For the x-coordinate
you go $+2 = 5 - 3$ units from A to M,
so B is $+2$ units from M: $5 + 2 = 7$
For the y-coordinate
you go $-1 = -2 - -1$ units from A to M
so B is -1 units from M: $-2 + -1 = -3$

Check: $\frac{1}{2}(3 + 7) = 5$
$\frac{1}{2}(-1 + -3) = -2$

108   **Algebra** Equations and graphs

Plenary

Pair students and ask them to set a question that gives A and M and asks you to find B. Swap with another pair and then check answers. As a class discuss cases where the pairs disagree or found a question hard (TW, RL) (1.5).

Simplification

Drawing the points on graph paper will help with the questions. Check students are confident plotting points in all four quadrants and with the rules for adding and subtracting negative numbers.

All questions (1.3)

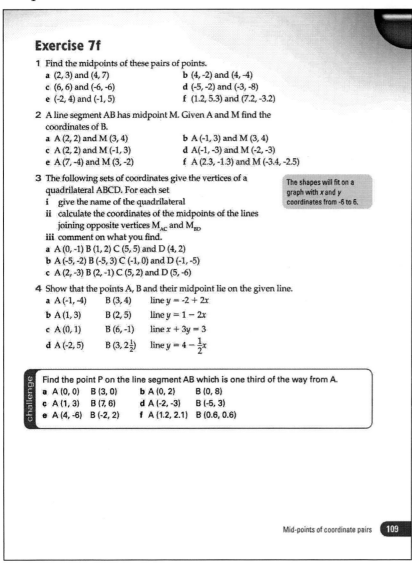

Exercise 7f

1 Find the midpoints of these pairs of points.
   a (2, 3) and (4, 7)
   b (4, -2) and (4, -4)
   c (6, 6) and (-6, -6)
   d (-5, -2) and (-3, -8)
   e (-2, 4) and (-1, 5)
   f (1.2, 5.3) and (7.2, -3.2)

2 A line segment AB has midpoint M. Given A and M find the coordinates of B.
   a A (2, 2) and M (3, 4)
   b A (-1, 3) and M (3, 4)
   c A (2, 2) and M (-1, 3)
   d A(-1, -3) and M (-2, -3)
   e A (7, -4) and M (3, -2)
   f A (2.3, -1.3) and M (-3.4, -2.5)

3 The following sets of coordinates give the vertices of a quadrilateral ABCD. For each set
   i give the name of the quadrilateral
   ii calculate the coordinates of the midpoints of the lines joining opposite vertices M_{AC} and M_{BD}
   iii comment on what you find.

   The shapes will fit on a graph with x and y coordinates from -6 to 6.

   a A (0, -1) B (1, 2) C (5, 5) and D (4, 2)
   b A (-5, -2) B (-5, 3) C (-1, 0) and D (-1, -5)
   c A (2, -3) B (2, -1) C (5, 2) and D (5, -6)

4 Show that the points A, B and their midpoint lie on the given line.
   a A (-1, -4)   B (3, 4)   line $y = -2 + 2x$
   b A (1, 3)   B (2, 5)   line $y = 1 - 2x$
   c A (0, 1)   B (6, -1)   line $x + 3y = 3$
   d A (-2, 5)   B $(3, 2\frac{1}{2})$ line $y = 4 - \frac{1}{2}x$

---

challenge

Find the point P on the line segment AB which is one third of the way from A.
   a A (0, 0)   B (3, 0)
   b A (0, 2)   B (0, 8)
   c A (1, 3)   B (7, 6)
   d A (-2, -3) B (-5, 3)
   e A (4, -6) B (-2, 2)
   f A (1.2, 2.1) B (0.6, 0.6)

Extension

A triangle ABC has coordinates A (2, 0) B (0, 4) and C (10, 8). Find the mid-points of the three sides, M_{AB}, M_{BC} and MC_A. Now find the point P which is one third of the way from M_{AB}, and the opposite vertex C. Likewise Q a third of the way from M_{BC} and A and R a third of the way from M_{CA} and B. The common point (4, 4) is the centre of gravity.

If the diagram is drawn on stiff card and cut out it should balance on a (pencil) point placed at P. Further if the shape is allowed to pivot freely about any point then P will hang directly below the pivot point (SM, EP) (1.3).

Exercise 7f commentary

Question 1 – Similar to part **a** of the example. Part **e** involves a fraction, part **f** involves a decimal – this will probably force the use of the formula.

Question 2 – Similar to part **b** of the example.

Question 3 – Students could be asked to generate their own quadrilaterals, including squares and rectangles, and check whether or not the diagonals bisect one another for their examples of the same shape or new shapes. Ask, is this a proof for all parallelograms, rhombuses, *etc*. (CT).(1.4)

Question 4 – All points should satisfy the given equation. Remind students that two points specify a line and so it is non-trivial that the third point lies on the line.

Challenge – The general formula is $M = \frac{2}{3}A + \frac{1}{3}B$. Can students find a point which is $\frac{1}{4}$, $\frac{1}{5}$, $\frac{1}{5}$, *etc.* of the way along a given line segment (IE, CT).

Links

René Descartes (1596–1650) was a polymath who made major contributions to several subjects. He developed a philosophy of knowledge starting from 'Je pense, donc je suis' (I think, therefore I am). In the sciences he showed that the angle between the centre and edge of a rainbow is 42°. Whilst in mathematics he is famous for *analytical geometry*, which combines geometry with algebra and is why we use the name Cartesian coordinates. For more information see the MacTutor site http://www-groups.dcs.st-and. ac.uk/~history/Mathematicians/ Descartes.html (TW).

1 Solve these equations.

   a $7x + 3 = 6x + 8$ **b** $6y + 9 = 4y + 17$

   c $2a + 5 = 5a - 7$ **d** $5b - 3 = 9b - 7$

   e $p + 24 = 7p$ **f** $4(q - 1) = 6q - 5$

   g $3(k - 4) = 2(4k - 1)$ **h** $\frac{2}{3}t - 2 = \frac{1}{3}t + 2$

2 For each of these questions, form an equation and solve it to find the answer to the problem.

   a Find the length of this rectangle.

        $3x + 2$

        $8(x - 1)$

   b The areas of these shapes are equal.

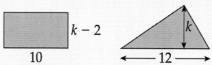

       Find k and hence the dimensions of each shape.

3 Solve these equations.

   a $10 - x = 7$ **b** $15 - 2y = 5$ **c** $11 = 21 - 5m$ **d** $0 = 18 - 6n$

   e $9 - 3d = 8$ **f** $4 - 7f = 11$ **g** $8 - 2k = 5$ **h** $12 - 3t = 7$

4 Solve these equations.

   a $4x + 3 = 8 - x$ **b** $2k + 5 = 17 - 4k$

   c $3p - 5 = 5 - 2p$ **d** $10 - 3t = t - 2$

   e $7 - a = 15 - 2a$ **f** $11 - 5b = 5 - 2b$

   g $8(3 - y) = 2 + 3y$ **h** $2(7 - 2g) = 3(4 - g)$

5 a Draw a mapping diagram for each of these functions.

   i

x	y
0	0
1	3
2	6
3	9

   ii

x	y
1	7
2	9
3	11
4	13

   b For each function in part **a**, write an equation that maps the x-values to the y-values.

6 Find the inverse of these functions.

   a $x \to x + 3$ **b** $x \to 5x$ **c** $x \to 4x - 2$ **d** $x \to \dfrac{x + 1}{6}$

7 **a** Copy and complete the table of values for the equation
$y = 2x + 1$.

b Plot these points on a set of coordinate axes with x and
y values from 0 to 8. Join your points with a straight line.

c On the same set of axes, plot the graph of $y = 7 - x$.

d Write the coordinates of the point of intersection of these graphs.

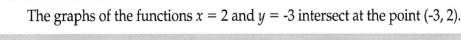

x	0	1	2
$2x$			
$+1$			
y	1		

8 True or false?
The graphs of the functions $x = 2$ and $y = -3$ intersect at the point $(-3, 2)$.

9 Write the gradient and y-intercept of these straight lines.

a $y = 2x + 1$ **b** $y = 3x - 2$

c $y = \frac{1}{2}x + 5$ **d** $y = 8x$

e $y = x - 2$ **f** $y = 4 - 3x$

g $y = 1 - \frac{1}{3}x$ **h** $y = 3(2 - x)$

10 Find the equation of each of these straight lines.

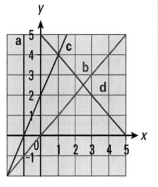

11 True or false?
The graph of the function $y = x^2 + 5x + 6$ passes through the point $(1, 12)$.
Explain your answer.

12 **a** Copy and complete the table of values for the equation $y = x^2 - x$.

b Plot these points on a set of coordinate axes with
x-values from -3 to 4 and y-values from -1 to 8.
Join the points with a smooth curve.

c Write the coordinates of the points where
the line $y = x^2 - x$ cuts the x-axis.

d Write the equation of the vertical line about which $y = x^2 - x$ is
symmetrical.

x	-2	-1	0	1	2	3
x^2	4					
$-x$	2					
y	6					

13 M is the midpoint of the line segment AB.
Find M or B given the following information.

a $A(4, 2)$ $B(6, 4)$ **b** $A(-1, 7)$ $B(3, 3)$

c $A(5, 6)$ $B(1, -2)$ **d** $A(-2, -3)$ $B(-4, 2)$

e $A(-2, -1)$ $M(0, 1)$ **f** $A(6, 4)$ $M(2, 2)$

7 Summary

Assessment criteria

- Construct and solve linear equations with integer coefficients, using an appropriate method **Level 6**
- Plot the graphs of linear functions, where y is given explicitly in terms of x **Level 6**
- Recognise that equations of the form $y = mx + c$ correspond to straight line graphs **Level 6**

Question commentary

Example	The example illustrates a problem where students are asked to construct and solve an equation. Ask questions such as "How do you decide where to start" and emphasise the importance of checking the final answer by substituting into the original equation.	$$5k - 60 = k$$ $$4k = 60$$ $$k = \frac{60}{4}$$ $$= 15$$

Past question	The question is a detailed question about the equation of a straight-line graph. In part **a**, emphasise that any straight line with gradient 1 is acceptable and encourage the use of a sharp pencil. In part **b**, students may substitute $x = 0$ in the equation, or may take the missing value directly from the equation as the y-intercept. In part **c**, students are asked to find the equation of a straight line. Some students may be unable to find the gradient. Encourage thorough reading of the question to determine that the line is parallel to a line with a gradient of 5. Some students may confuse the gradient and the y-intercept. Encourage students to think of the y-intercept as the value of y when $x = 0$ and to substitute $x = 0$ into the equation to check the value for y.	**Answer** **Level 6** **2 a** Any straight line parallel to the given line **b** $(0, 20)$ **c** $y = 5x + 10$

Development and links

This topic is developed further in Chapter 13 where students will solve further equations including those containing fractions, change the subject of further formulae, plot graphs of implicit functions and interpret and draw graphs arising from real-life situations.

The ability to solve equations and to find the equation of a graph is important in science, geography and technology where equations are used to model the behaviour of objects and phenomena in the real-world. Plotting and interpreting graphs has links to handling and interpreting data.

8 Calculations

Objectives

	Level
• Extend mental methods of calculation, working with decimals ..	5
• Use efficient written methods to add and subtract integers and decimals of any size...	5
• Multiply by decimals...	5
• Divide by decimals by transforming to division by an integer	5
• Use the sign change key (on a calculator)	5
• Use the function keys (on a calculator) for powers, roots and fractions	5
• Understand the order of precedence of operations, including powers..	5
• Use brackets (on a calculator)...	5
• Use rounding to make estimates..	6
• Extend knowledge of integer powers of 10	6
• Recognise the equivalence of 0.1, $\frac{1}{10}$ and 10^{-1}	6
• Multiply and divide by any integer power of 10...........................	6
• Make and justify estimates and approximations of calculations..	6
• Use ICT to estimate square roots and cube roots.........................	6
• Use a calculator efficiently and appropriately to perform complex calculations with numbers of any size...........................	6

Level

MPA

1.1 8b, c, e, g, i
1.2 8a, c, d, e, g, i
1.3 8a, b, c, d, e, f, g, h, i
1.4 8a, b, c, d, e, f, g, h, i
1.5 8a, b, c, d, e, f, i

PLTS

IE 8a, b, c, d, e, f, g, h, i
CT 8a, b, c, d, f, g, h, i
RL 8a, b, c, d, e, f, g, h, i
TW 8b, c, d, f, g, h
SM 8a, f, g
EP 8a, c, d, f, h

Introduction

The focus of this chapter is on reviewing and developing numerical methods. Students review mental and written methods for addition, subtraction, multiplication and division, practise rounding numbers to any power of ten, use rounding to make estimates and approximations and use the order of operations including brackets. They use a calculator to perform calculations involving fractions, powers and roots and learn to convert between units and interpret the display in different contexts.

The student book discusses the importance of calculation in engineering and specifically in a power station. Calculations surround our daily lives. We calculate when shopping, measuring, calculating taxes, working out calorie intake and calculating CO_2 emissions. Most people find it difficult to calculate mentally with long numbers because the human brain can only remember a few digits at a time. For large numbers, it is easier to use a written method or a calculator. There is more information about how calculators work at http://www.explainthatstuff.com/calculators.html

Extra Resources

8   Start of chapter presentation
8a Animation: Rounding
8b Starter: Addition with negatives matching
8b Consolidation sheet
8c Worked solution: Q2a
8d Animation: Multiplication
8d Animation: Multiplying decimals
8d Consolidation sheet
8e Consolidation sheet
8f Starter: Square and cube matching
8g Starter: Rounded decimal matching
8i Worked solution: Q2a
8i Consolidation sheet

Assessment: chapter 8

Fast-track
8a, c, d, e, g, h

- Round positive numbers to any given power of ten (L5)
- Round decimals to the nearest whole number or to one or two decimal places (L5)
- Use rounding to make estimates (L6)

••

Useful resources

Calculator

Number lines marked with thousands, hundreds etc

Internet access

Starter – What is my number

I am even but not square.
I am a multiple of 3.
I am greater than the number of days in November.
I am less than the product of 2^3 and 3^2.
I have 8 factors. (54)

Can be extended by asking students to make up their own puzzles.

Teaching notes

Many measurements can't be given exactly, so they are rounded. For example, your height maybe given as 167 cm, but this is only accurate to the nearest cm. In this case what must your height be between? Establish that it is between 166.5 cm and 167.5 cm. This can be illustrated on a number line. Many students will want to use 167.4 or 167.49 cm as the upper limit. Discuss why this is not possible and why the accepted method is to use 167.5 cm. (EP, RL) (1.5)

If a number has not yet been rounded, there are different methods of rounding that can be used. Look at examples that round off to the nearest 10, 100, *etc*. Include examples of decimal values.

Alternatively a number can be rounded off to a specific number of decimal places. Include awkward examples like 3.049604 rounded to 3 decimal places.

An alternative way of asking to round to 3 dp is to round to the nearest 0.001 or nearest thousandth.

In question **3** Brian the flea is taken from Robert Hooke's *Micrographia* (1665); see also page 97.

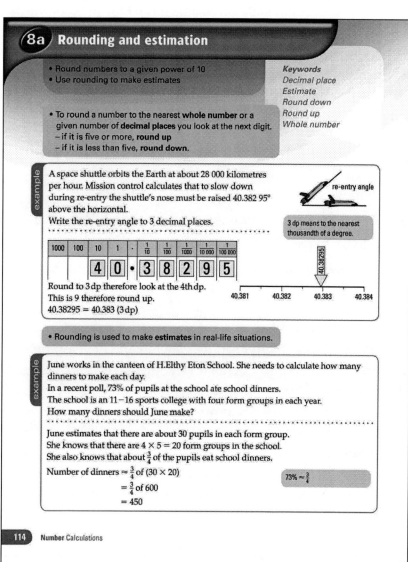

Plenary

When finding the maximum possible value of a rounded number, some measurements are treated differently. Discuss the difference between discrete and continuous measures. For example, the attendance at a sporting event is 4000 and the length of a rope is 4000 cm. Both measures have been rounded to the nearest thousand. (4499 people and 4500m) What other examples can students think of that need to be treated differently? (CT) (1.2, 1.5)

Simplification

Help students to visualise the numbers by referring to their place on a number line. Use pre-prepared lines marked with thousands, hundreds, *etc.*

All questions (1.3)

Question 1 – Can a number be rounded to zero? Why in real life examples do we tend not to round down to zero?

Question 2 – What happens when the decimal place you are rounding to is a '9' and you need to round up? For example, 0.954 or 0.995

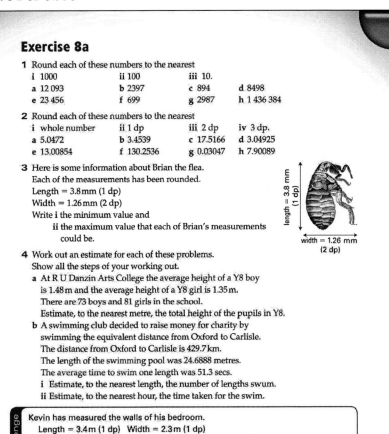

Exercise 8a

1 Round each of these numbers to the nearest
i 1000	ii 100	iii 10.	
a 12 093	b 2397	c 894	d 8498
e 23 456	f 699	g 2987	h 1 436 384

2 Round each of these numbers to the nearest
i whole number	ii 1 dp	iii 2 dp	iv 3 dp.
a 5.0472	b 3.4539	c 17.5166	d 3.04925
e 13.00854	f 130.2536	g 0.03047	h 7.90089

3 Here is some information about Brian the flea.
Each of the measurements has been rounded.
Length = 3.8 mm (1 dp)
Width = 1.26 mm (2 dp)
Write i the minimum value and
  ii the maximum value that each of Brian's measurements could be.

length = 3.8 mm (1 dp)
width = 1.26 mm (2 dp)

4 Work out an estimate for each of these problems.
Show all the steps of your working out.
a At R U Danzin Arts College the average height of a Y8 boy is 1.48 m and the average height of a Y8 girl is 1.35 m. There are 73 boys and 81 girls in the school. Estimate, to the nearest metre, the total height of the pupils in Y8.
b A swimming club decided to raise money for charity by swimming the equivalent distance from Oxford to Carlisle. The distance from Oxford to Carlisle is 429.7 km. The length of the swimming pool was 24.6888 metres. The average time to swim one length was 51.3 secs.
  i Estimate, to the nearest length, the number of lengths swum.
  ii Estimate, to the nearest hour, the time taken for the swim.

challenge
Kevin has measured the walls of his bedroom.
  Length = 3.4 m (1 dp) Width = 2.3 m (1 dp)
He buys a rectangular piece of carpet with an area of 7.9 m², in the same shape as his bedroom. However the piece of carpet is not long or wide enough!
Explain what has happened.

Rounding and estimation   115

Extension

Investigate the measurements of various famous heights. For example, Everest, Statue of Liberty, Burj Dubai (World's tallest building). What degree of accuracy is used in the sources you find? The answers for these examples are 8848 m, 46 m or 93 m (depending on how it is measured), 780 m (start 2009, under construction). Encourage the use of more than one source (IE, SM).

Exercise 8a commentary

Question 3 – Students are often reluctant to accept the maximum value of a continuous measurement, preferring to use a '9' or recurring '9's (CT) (1.2, 1.4, 1.5).

Question 4 – Use a calculator. Since students are asked to estimate and not calculate, students should use sensible rounded values. What degree of accuracy should be used? Encourage students to discuss this among themselves (CT) (1.2, 1.4).

Challenge – Why can't you calculate the exact area of the bedroom from the measurements given for length and width? When buying carpet what should you do to the measurements you make for length and width? (round them up and never down) What width and length do you think the carpet might be? (3.42 m × 2.31m 7.90 m² to 2dp) (CT, RL) (1.2, 1.4, 1.5)

Assessment Criteria – NNS, level 5: round decimals to the nearest decimal place. Calculating, level 5: approximate to check answers to problems are of the correct magnitude. Calculating, level 7: make and justify estimates and approximations of calculations.

Links

In parliamentary elections in Germany in 1992, a rounding error caused the wrong results to be announced. Under German law, a party can not have any seats in Parliament unless it has 5.0% or more of the vote. The Green Party appeared to have exactly 5.0%, until it was discovered that the computer that printed out the results only used one place after the decimal point and had rounded the vote up to 5.0%. The Green Party only had 4.97% of the vote and the results had to be changed (EP).

- Extend mental methods of calculation, working with decimals (L5)
- Use efficient written methods to add and subtract integers and decimals of any size (L5)

Useful resources

Starter – NMBR!

Write words on the board missing out the vowels, for example, nmbr.
Ask students for the original words (number). Possible 'words':

CHNC, DCML, HNDRDTH, PRBBLTY, LVN, FRCTN, MLLN, TNTH, PRCNTG, NT

(chance decimal hundredth probability eleven fraction million tenth percentage unit)

Can be extended by asking students to make up their own examples.

Teaching notes

Look at examples of decimal addition and subtraction that can be simply solved by using the method of 'partitioning'. Look at the method used in the student book as a guide. Introduce an example where partitioning is more difficult to use. Look at the method of 'compensation' and examples where it is useful.

Introduce an example where there is no obvious simple mental method. Look at the standard method of addition/subtraction in columns. How do you line up the numbers? Encourage the use of one digit to a square (on grid paper) or similar method to ensure a clear presentation to avoid errors. Include examples requiring trailing zeros to be added (1.4, 1.5).

What mistake might a student make with an example like $123.4 - 2.7 - 3.7 - 25.4$? Try to perform the calculation in one go with 4 rows of numbers. Discuss a better method. For example, summing the numbers that are to be subtracted and then performing a single subtraction (RL) (1.5).

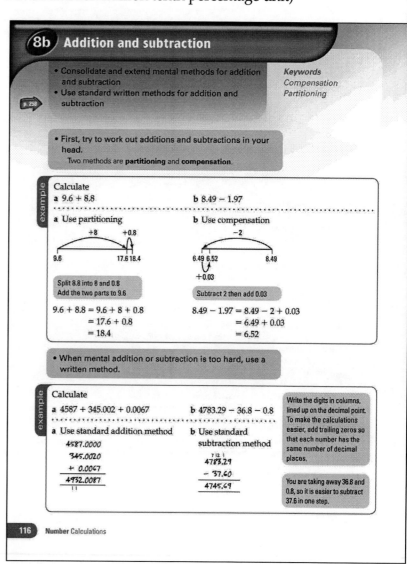

8b Addition and subtraction

- Consolidate and extend mental methods for addition and subtraction
- Use standard written methods for addition and subtraction

Keywords
Compensation
Partitioning

- First, try to work out additions and subtractions in your head.
  Two methods are **partitioning** and **compensation**.

Calculate
a $9.6 + 8.8$ b $8.49 - 1.97$

a Use partitioning

Split 8.8 into 8 and 0.8
Add the two parts to 9.6

$9.6 + 8.8 = 9.6 + 8 + 0.8$
$= 17.6 + 0.8$
$= 18.4$

b Use compensation

Subtract 2 then add 0.03

$8.49 - 1.97 = 8.49 - 2 + 0.03$
$= 6.49 + 0.03$
$= 6.52$

- When mental addition or subtraction is too hard, use a written method.

Calculate
a $4587 + 345.002 + 0.0067$ b $4783.29 - 36.8 - 0.8$

a Use standard addition method

```
  4587.0000
   345.0020
 +   0.0067
  4932.0087
    11
```

b Use standard subtraction method

```
  4783.29
 -   37.60
  4745.69
```

Write the digits in columns, lined up on the decimal point. To make the calculations easier, add trailing zeros so that each number has the same number of decimal places.

You are taking away 36.8 and 0.8, so it is easier to subtract 37.6 in one step.

116   Number Calculations

Plenary

Estimate the total mass of one each of the British coins in circulation; include the commemorative £5 coin. (A 10p weighs 6.5 g). Using mental, written or a combination of methods, calculate the total weight (83.21 g).

£5	£2	£1	50p	20p	10p	5p	2p	1p
28.28	12	9.5	8	5	6.5	3.25	7.12	3.56

How much would £1 million in 1p pieces weigh? (356 tonnes, roughly 20 double decker buses or six tanks.) (1.3)

Simplification

Students should focus on those parts that involve only two numbers. Encourage students to back up their mental answer with a written method. Students should not feel under pressure to get through lots of examples. It is better to focus on fewer questions and tackle them thoroughly.

All questions (1.3)

Question 1 – Encourage students to consider a mental approach first, before deciding on a written method. Ask students to discuss their method with a partner (TW).

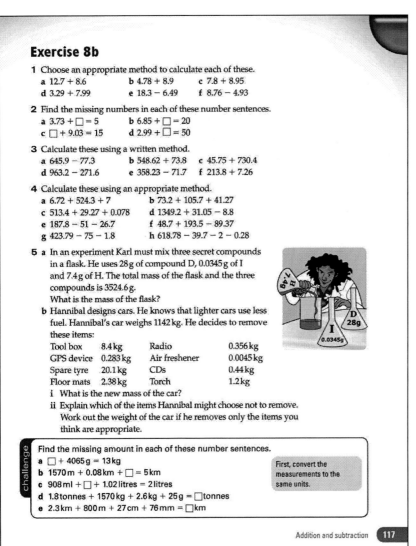

Exercise 8b

1 Choose an appropriate method to calculate each of these.
  a 12.7 + 8.6   b 4.78 + 8.9   c 7.8 + 8.95
  d 3.29 + 7.99   e 18.3 − 6.49   f 8.76 − 4.93

2 Find the missing numbers in each of these number sentences.
  a 3.73 + □ = 5   b 6.85 + □ = 20
  c □ + 9.03 = 15   d 2.99 + □ = 50

3 Calculate these using a written method.
  a 645.9 − 77.3   b 548.62 + 73.8   c 45.75 + 730.4
  d 963.2 − 271.6   e 358.23 − 71.7   f 213.8 + 7.26

4 Calculate these using an appropriate method.
  a 6.72 + 524.3 + 7   b 73.2 + 105.7 + 41.27
  c 513.4 + 29.27 + 0.078   d 1349.2 + 31.05 − 8.8
  e 187.8 − 51 − 26.7   f 48.7 + 193.5 − 89.37
  g 423.79 − 75 − 1.8   h 618.78 − 39.7 − 2 − 0.28

5 a In an experiment Karl must mix three secret compounds in a flask. He uses 28 g of compound D, 0.0345 g of I and 7.4 g of H. The total mass of the flask and the three compounds is 3524.6 g.
    What is the mass of the flask?
  b Hannibal designs cars. He knows that lighter cars use less fuel. Hannibal's car weighs 1142 kg. He decides to remove these items:

Tool box	8.4 kg	Radio	0.356 kg
GPS device	0.283 kg	Air freshener	0.0045 kg
Spare tyre	20.1 kg	CDs	0.44 kg
Floor mats	2.38 kg	Torch	1.2 kg

    i What is the new mass of the car?
    ii Explain which of the items Hannibal might choose not to remove. Work out the weight of the car if he removes only the items you think are appropriate.

challenge

Find the missing amount in each of these number sentences.
  a □ + 4065 g = 13 kg
  b 1570 m + 0.08 km + □ = 5 km
  c 908 ml + □ + 1.02 litres = 2 litres
  d 1.8 tonnes + 1570 kg + 2.6 kg + 25 g = □ tonnes
  e 2.3 km + 800 m + 27 cm + 76 mm = □ km

First, convert the measurements to the same units.

Extension

Calculate this series as far as you can.

12.8 − 6.4 + 3.2 − 1.6 + 0.8 − 0.4 + 0.2 − 0.1 +…

What do you think you get if you go on forever?

(6.4, 9.6, 8, 8.8, 8.4, 8.6, 8.5, 8.55, 8.525, 8.5375, 8.53125, 8.534375, 8.532813, 8.533594, 8.533203, 8.533398, 8.533301, 8.533350, 3.533325, 8.533337,…8$\frac{8}{15}$ = 8.53333…) (CT) (1.3)

Exercise 8b commentary

Question 3 – Beware of errors aligning the decimal points and adding trailing zeros. Encourage the occasional use of a checking procedure (RL).

Question 4 – Some students might try to use a single column of working. This will be very awkward unless all the numbers are added. Encourage students to think of ways to breakup the problem into stages (IE) (1.1).

Question 5 – Part **a** involves three trailing zeros and three sets of borrowing before the first digit can be calculated, this may cause confusion (RL).

Challenge – Students may need a reminder of the conversions. Which units do students think is the easiest to convert to? Why? (1.5)

Assessment Criteria – Calculating, level 4: use efficient methods of addition and subtraction. Calculating, level 4: use a range of mental methods of computation with all operations. Calculating, level 5: use known facts, place value, knowledge of operations and brackets to calculate including using all four operations with decimals to two places.

Links

The World's most fuel efficient car as of 2008 is the Volkswagen 285 MPG which uses 1 litre of fuel to drive 100 km (285 miles per gallon). The car body is made from reinforced carbon fibre and, to keep the car as light as possible, it is not even painted. Sleek aerodynamic design is used to reduce any air resistance. There is more information at http://gas2.org/2008/03/12/the-worlds-most-fuel-efficient-car-285-mpg-not-a-hybrid/comment-page-4/

- Extend knowledge of integer powers of 10   (L6)   *Useful resources*
- Recognise the equivalence of 0.1, 1/10 and 10^{-1} (L6)
- Multiply and divide by any integer power of 10   (L6)

Starter – Miss the multiples

Ask students to add up numbers you read out that are **not** multiples of 7. For example,
16, 21, 23, 7, 28, 34, 15, -3, 35, 11, 5, 14, -11, 49, 17 (total excluding multiples of 7 = 107)
Can be differentiated by choice of multiple and numbers.

Teaching notes

Look at the sequence created by descending power of 10, beginning with 10 cubed

$$\div 10 \quad \div 10 \quad \div 10 \quad \div 10 \quad \div 10 \quad \div 10$$
$$10^3 \to 10^2 \to 10^1 \to 10^0 \to 10^{-1} \to 10^{-2} \to 10^{-3}$$
$$1000 \quad 100 \quad 10 \quad 1 \quad 0.1 \quad 0.01 \quad 0.001$$

What happens when you multiply by a positive power of 10? Look at integer and decimal examples. What happens to a number when you multiply it by a number between 0 and 1? Establish that $\times 0.01$ is the same as $\times 10^{-2}$.

What happens when you divide by a positive power of 10? Look at integer and decimal examples. What happens to a number when you divide it by a number between 0 and 1? For example, $4 \div 0.01$. What does 0.01 represent? What does the question actually mean? How many hundredths in 4 units. Since the answer is 400, what effect does $\div 0.01$ have? Multiplication by 100. This question can also be written as $4 \div 10^{-2}$.

Question student's understanding of what is happening when multiplying or dividing by a number between 0 and 1. Discourage students from just slavishly following the rules (EP) (1.2).

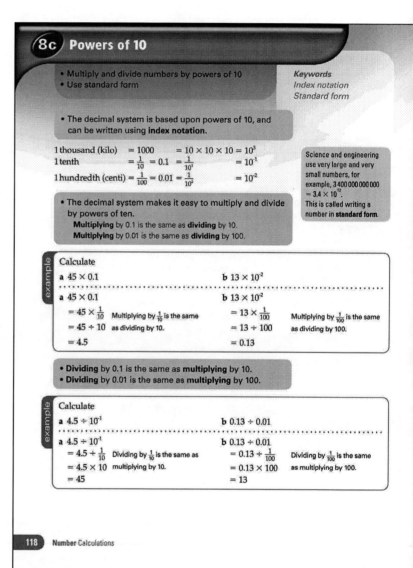

8c Powers of 10

- Multiply and divide numbers by powers of 10
- Use standard form

Keywords
Index notation
Standard form

- The decimal system is based upon powers of 10, and can be written using **index notation**.

1 thousand (kilo)	$= 1000$	$= 10 \times 10 \times 10 = 10^3$
1 tenth	$= \frac{1}{10} = 0.1$	$= \frac{1}{10^1} = 10^1$
1 hundredth (centi)	$= \frac{1}{100} = 0.01$	$= \frac{1}{10^2} = 10^2$

Science and engineering use very large and very small numbers, for example, $3\,400\,000\,000\,000 = 3.4 \times 10^{12}$. This is called writing a number in **standard form**.

- The decimal system makes it easy to multiply and divide by powers of ten.
   Multiplying by 0.1 is the same as **dividing** by 10.
   Multiplying by 0.01 is the same as **dividing** by 100.

example

Calculate
a 45×0.1 **b** 13×10^{-2}

a 45×0.1
$= 45 \times \frac{1}{10}$ Multiplying by $\frac{1}{10}$ is the same
$= 45 \div 10$ as dividing by 10.
$= 4.5$

b 13×10^{-2}
$= 13 \times \frac{1}{100}$ Multiplying by $\frac{1}{100}$ is the same
$= 13 \div 100$ as dividing by 100.
$= 0.13$

- **Dividing** by 0.1 is the same as **multiplying** by 10.
- **Dividing** by 0.01 is the same as **multiplying** by 100.

example

Calculate
a $4.5 \div 10^{-1}$ **b** $0.13 \div 0.01$

a $4.5 \div 10^{-1}$
$= 4.5 \div \frac{1}{10}$ Dividing by $\frac{1}{10}$ is the same as
$= 4.5 \times 10$ multiplying by 10.
$= 45$

b $0.13 \div 0.01$
$= 0.13 \div \frac{1}{100}$ Dividing by $\frac{1}{100}$ is the same
$= 0.13 \times 100$ as multiplying by 100.
$= 13$

118   Number Calculations

Plenary

This method can be used for writing very large numbers in a simpler way. For example, the world's population, to the nearest million, was estimated to be 6 684 000 000 (July 2008). In what ways could this be written using a power of ten?. Should you include the six zeros? Which is called the 'standard' way and is used around the world? Ask students for their views (CT) (1.3).

Simplification

It is very important that students 'understand' what is being asked and are not just getting answers correct by replicating a method. Focus on the simpler questions and ask students to show that they understand by explaining what is being asked for. Encourage the breaking up of a question into stages (EP).

All questions (1.3)

Question 1 – Ask students to try and explain the meaning of $\times 0.1$ and $\div 0.1$. For example, 26×0.1 is 26 lots of 0.1 making 2.6. What has happened to the starting number 26? For example, $388 \div 0.1$ is how many 0.1s or tenths in 388? (1.2)

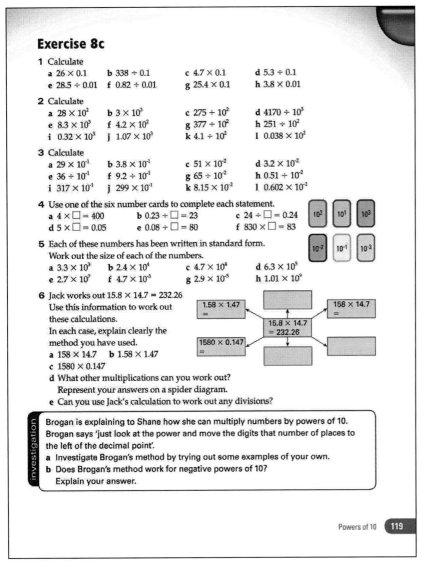

Exercise 8c

1 Calculate
  a 26×0.1 **b** $338 \div 0.1$ **c** 4.7×0.1 **d** $5.3 \div 0.1$
  e $28.5 \div 0.01$ **f** $0.82 \div 0.01$ **g** 25.4×0.1 **h** 3.8×0.01

2 Calculate
  a 28×10^2 **b** 3×10^3 **c** $275 \div 10^2$ **d** $4170 \div 10^3$
  e 8.3×10^3 **f** 4.2×10^2 **g** $377 \div 10^2$ **h** $251 \div 10^2$
  i 0.32×10^3 **j** 1.07×10^3 **k** $4.1 \div 10^2$ **l** 0.038×10^2

3 Calculate
  a 29×10^{-1} **b** 3.8×10^{-1} **c** 51×10^{-2} **d** 3.2×10^{-2}
  e $36 \div 10^{-1}$ **f** $9.2 \div 10^{-1}$ **g** $65 \div 10^{-2}$ **h** $0.51 \div 10^{-2}$
  i 317×10^{-1} **j** 299×10^{-1} **k** 8.15×10^{-2} **l** 0.602×10^{-2}

4 Use one of the six number cards to complete each statement.
  a $4 \times \square = 400$ **b** $0.23 \div \square = 23$ **c** $24 \div \square = 0.24$ 10^2 10^1 10^3
  d $5 \times \square = 0.05$ **e** $0.08 \div \square = 80$ **f** $830 \times \square = 83$

5 Each of these numbers has been written in standard form. Work out the size of each of the numbers. 10^{-2} 10^{-1} 10^{-3}
  a 3.3×10^3 **b** 2.4×10^4 **c** 4.7×10^4 **d** 6.3×10^5
  e 2.7×10^7 **f** 4.7×10^3 **g** 2.9×10^{-5} **h** 1.01×10^9

6 Jack works out $15.8 \times 14.7 = 232.26$
  Use this information to work out these calculations.
  In each case, explain clearly the method you have used.
  a 158×14.7 **b** 1.58×1.47
  c 1580×0.147
  d What other multiplications can you work out? Represent your answers on a spider diagram.
  e Can you use Jack's calculation to work out any divisions?

  [1.58×1.47 =] [15.8×14.7 $= 232.26$] [158×14.7 =] [1580×0.147 =]

investigation

Brogan is explaining to Shane how she can multiply numbers by powers of 10. Brogan says 'just look at the power and move the digits that number of places to the left of the decimal point'.
  a Investigate Brogan's method by trying out some examples of your own.
  b Does Brogan's method work for negative powers of 10? Explain your answer.

Powers of 10   **119**

Extension

Write the conversions for the standard metric measurements of length, mass and capacity using standard form. For example, 1×10^2 cm = 1m, 1×10^5 cm = 1 km, *etc.* (IE) (1.3)

Exercise 8c commentary

Questions 2 and **3** – Initially, encourage students to write out the question, replacing the power of ten with the number written in full., for example, 10^2 as 100 (1.1, 1.4).

Question 4 – Different approaches are possible. Encourage pairs of students to share their methods (TW, RL) (1.5).

Question 5 – Encourage students to use quick methods for writing ordinary numbers. What does the index tell you? How do you know whether to divide or multiply? (1.1)

Question 6 – Encourage students to look at the overall effect on the answer by changing both initial numbers. Emphasise the fact that multiplication and division cancel each other out (inverse operations). Ask students to explain the effect of changing the numerator and then the denominator (IE).

Investigation – Ask students what they think of this method of remembering how to multiply by powers of ten. What happens for division? Point out that in practice, we generally only multiply by powers of ten, so only one quick method is needed (1.1, 1.2, 1.4).

Assessment Criteria – NNS, level 5: use understanding of place value to multiply and divide whole numbers by 10, 100 and 1000 and explain the effect. Calculating, level 7: understand the effects of multiplying and dividing by numbers between 0 and 1.

Links

Number 10 Downing Street in London is the official residence of the First Lord of the Treasury, who is usually also the prime minister of Great Britain. See, http://www.number10.gov.uk/history-and-tour

- Extend mental methods of calculation, working with decimals (L5)
- Multiply by decimals (L5)
- Make and justify estimates and approximations of calculations (L6)

Useful resources

Starter – 105

Ask students to make 105 by

the product of two odd numbers (3 × 35)
the product of three odd numbers (3 × 5 × 7)
the product of four odd numbers (1 × 3 × 5 × 7)
the sum of a square number and a prime number (64 + 41)
the difference between two square numbers (169 − 64)

Can any be done in more than one way?

Teaching notes

Look at examples of multiplication that can be simply solved by using the method of 'factors'. Look at the method used in the student book as a guide. Introduce an example where factors are more difficult to use. Look at the method of 'partitioning' and examples where it is useful.

Look at the three most common methods of written multiplication.
i Long multiplication in rows **ii** box/lattice method **iii** grid method. The names of the last two methods are not helpful in differentiating between the two methods.

How can you use a written method to tackle decimal multiplication? Advise students to remove the decimal points from the calculation and insert it back in at the end. How can you tell where to put the decimal point? Would an estimate help? Conclude that it will help if an estimate is possible. For example, 4.3 × 8.34 is approximately 32, but 1.3 × 0.032 is harder to estimate, look at counting the number of digits after the decimal points (RL), (1.2, 1.5).

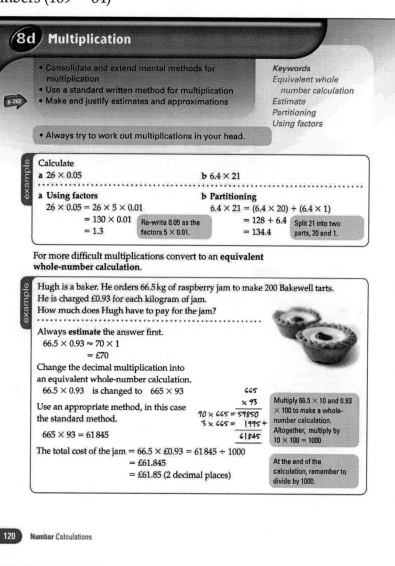

8d Multiplication

- Consolidate and extend mental methods for multiplication
- Use a standard written method for multiplication
- Make and justify estimates and approximations

Keywords
Equivalent whole number calculation
Estimate
Partitioning
Using factors

- Always try to work out multiplications in your head.

Calculate
a 26 × 0.05
b 6.4 × 21

a Using factors
26 × 0.05 = 26 × 5 × 0.01
= 130 × 0.01 Re-write 0.05 as the factors 5 × 0.01.
= 1.3

b Partitioning
6.4 × 21 = (6.4 × 20) + (6.4 × 1)
= 128 + 6.4 Split 21 into two parts, 20 and 1.
= 134.4

For more difficult multiplications convert to an **equivalent whole-number calculation**.

Hugh is a baker. He orders 66.5 kg of raspberry jam to make 200 Bakewell tarts. He is charged £0.93 for each kilogram of jam. How much does Hugh have to pay for the jam?

Always **estimate** the answer first.
66.5 × 0.93 ≈ 70 × 1
= £70

Change the decimal multiplication into an equivalent whole-number calculation.
66.5 × 0.93 is changed to 665 × 93

Use an appropriate method, in this case the standard method.

665
× 93
90 × 665 = 59850
3 × 665 = 1995 +
61845

Multiply 66.5 × 10 and 0.93 × 100 to make a whole-number calculation. Altogether, multiply by 10 × 100 = 1000

665 × 93 = 61 845

The total cost of the jam = 66.5 × £0.93 = 61 845 ÷ 1000
= £61.845
= £61.85 (2 decimal places)

At the end of the calculation, remember to divide by 1000.

120 Number Calculations

Plenary

Pull together the various methods that students have used in the exercise. Is there a common feeling for methods that are more or less effective? Does the choice of method depend on the question itself? Ask students to explain where they find the greatest difficulty (EP, RL) (1.5).

Simplification

Focus on a select few examples to illustrate mental short cut approaches. For example, questions **1d** and **2a**. Ask students to experiment with the different written methods for multiplication, perhaps trying different methods for the same question to see which method makes them feel most comfortable (1.5).

All questions (IE) (1.3)

Question 1 – Very few students will attempt these in their head. Encourage a mixture of written methods.

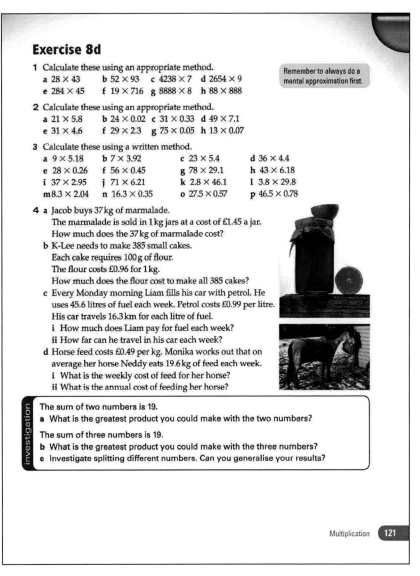

Exercise 8d

Remember to always do a mental approximation first.

1 Calculate these using an appropriate method.
a 28×43 b 52×93 c 4238×7 d 2654×9
e 284×45 f 19×716 g 8888×8 h 88×888

2 Calculate these using an appropriate method.
a 21×5.8 b 24×0.02 c 31×0.33 d 49×7.1
e 31×4.6 f 29×2.3 g 75×0.05 h 13×0.07

3 Calculate these using a written method.
a 9×5.18 b 7×3.92 c 23×5.4 d 36×4.4
e 28×0.26 f 56×0.45 g 78×29.1 h 43×6.18
i 37×2.95 j 71×6.21 k 2.8×46.1 l 3.8×29.8
m 8.3×2.04 n 16.3×0.35 o 27.5×0.57 p 46.5×0.78

4 a Jacob buys 37 kg of marmalade.
The marmalade is sold in 1 kg jars at a cost of £1.45 a jar.
How much does the 37 kg of marmalade cost?
b K-Lee needs to make 385 small cakes.
Each cake requires 100 g of flour.
The flour costs £0.96 for 1 kg.
How much does the flour cost to make all 385 cakes?
c Every Monday morning Liam fills his car with petrol. He uses 45.6 litres of fuel each week. Petrol costs £0.99 per litre. His car travels 16.3 km for each litre of fuel.
i How much does Liam pay for fuel each week?
ii How far can he travel in his car each week?
d Horse feed costs £0.49 per kg. Monika works out that on average her horse Neddy eats 19.6 kg of feed each week.
i What is the weekly cost of feed for her horse?
ii What is the annual cost of feeding her horse?

investigation

The sum of two numbers is 19.
a What is the greatest product you could make with the two numbers?

The sum of three numbers is 19.
b What is the greatest product you could make with the three numbers?
c Investigate splitting different numbers. Can you generalise your results?

Multiplication **121**

Extension

Work out one billion one million one thousand and one multiplied by one million one thousand and one. Why choose one particular method over another? What methods would prove too cumbersome? (1 002 003 003 002 001 (one quadrillion two trillion three billion three million two thousand and one) (RL) (1.5).

Exercise 8d commentary

Questions 2 and **3** – Ensure students are calculating the answer without the decimal point first. Ask them to explain how they know where to put the decimal point in the final answer (EP) (1.2).

Question 4 – How can you avoid using decimals when dealing with money in this question? Use pence instead of pounds. Did any student stick with pounds and find that they made an error, or that it was more difficult? (RL) (1.5)

Investigation – The terms 'product' and 'sum' may need explaining. Students may well restrict themselves to integers. Discuss this. When investigating for part **b**, allow the use of a calculator. Encourage a generalisation expressed in words for the maximum product. Ask students to test their ideas (CT) (1.4)

Assessment Criteria – Calculating, level 5: understand and use an appropriate non-calculator method for solving problems that involve multiplying any three digit number by any two digit number. Calculating, level 5: approximate to check answers to problems are of the correct magnitude. Calculating, level 7: make and justify estimates and approximations of calculations.

Links

The Ancient Babylonians used a number system based on 60. The large number of multiplication facts (60×60) made multiplication difficult so the Babylonians developed multiplication tables. The tables were written in cuneiform script on clay tablets and then baked. There is a picture of a Babylonian multiplication tablet for the 35 times table at http://it.stlawu. edu/ ~dmelvill/mesomath/tablets/ 36Times.html (TW)

- Extend mental methods of calculation, working with decimals (L5)
- Divide by decimals by transforming to division by an integer (L5)
- Make and justify estimates and approximations of calculations (L6)

Useful resources

Starter – Factor bingo

Ask students to draw a 3 × 3 grid and enter four factors of 48, three factors of 36 and two factors of 52.

Give possible answers, for example, 6.
The winner is the first student to cross out all their factors.
Can be differentiated by the choice of numbers.

Teaching notes

Look at examples of division that can be simply solved by using the method of 'factors'. Include examples with remainders if appropriate. Look at the method used in the student book as a guide. Introduce an example where factors are more difficult to use. Look at the method of 'partitioning' and examples where it is useful.

Look at the method of short division. For example 2399 ÷ 17. Why is it helpful to write down part of the times table? Show how this example can be extended to allow the solution to 1 d.p.

$$\begin{array}{r} 0141r2 \\ 17\overline{)23^69^19} \end{array}$$

$$1 \times 17 = 17$$
$$2 \times 17 = 34$$
$$4 \times 17 = 68$$
$$8 \times 17 = 136$$

Look at an example of division by a decimal. How can expressing the question as a fraction help to simplify the problem? Show how an equivalent fraction without a decimal denominator will be easier to solve. Will the numerator and denominator always have to be multiplied by a power of ten? Consider 56 ÷ 2.5.

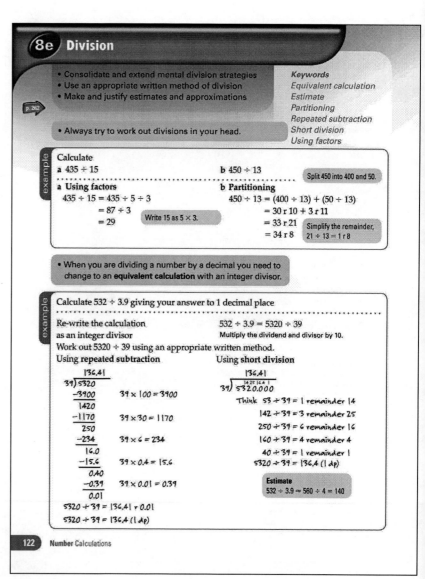

Plenary

What numbers were easier to divide by in the exercise? Why? (RL) (1.5). Before the invention of electronic calculators, division could take a very long time. Many clever inventions were made to help improve efficiency, look at some of them. For example, Napier's Bones (TW).

Simplification

Focus on a select few examples to illustrate mental short cut approaches. For example, questions **1a**, and **2h**. Ask students to experiment with the different written methods for division, trying different methods for the same question to see which method makes them feel most comfortable (1.5).

All questions (1.1, 1.3)

Questions 1 and **2** – Encourage a use of a variety of mental approaches. Students should share their method with a partner and discuss which methods work best (TW) (1.5). A common misconception is that division by 6 is equivalent to division by 3, followed by division by 3. Use a counter examples or factors of the divisor to counter this (RL).

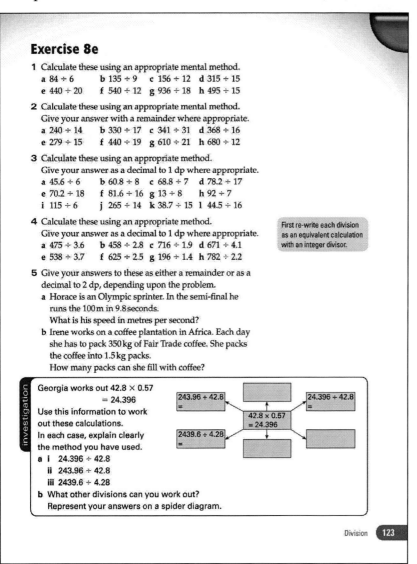

Extension

1 inch is exactly 25.4 mm. Without a calculator, convert 1 mm into inches. (0.039 370 078 740 157 5 to 16 dp) Can students express this as a fraction of an inch? Did any student divide by a number other than 254? (IE) (1.3)

Exercise 8e commentary

Question 3 – If the dividend is a decimal is it helpful to first change the numbers to integers? Ask students to show any additional working that is used. For example, part **e**, $18 \times 3 = 54$. Remind students to find the answer to 2 dp before rounding to 1 dp.

Question 4 – With a decimal divisor, is it helpful to first change the numbers to integers? Viewed as a fraction the division is easily converted.

Question 5 – What sort of questions require a decimal answer or a remainder? (RL)

Investigation – Think of division as a fraction. Ask questions like, if you multiply the denominator by 10, how will the answer change? Students often fail to appreciate the difference between altering the numerator and the denominator. Ask, what happens if you divide by a smaller number? For example, fewer people winning the lottery means bigger prizes (1.2, 1.4).

Assessment Criteria – Calculating, level 5: understand and use an appropriate non calculator method for solving problems that involve dividing any three digit number by any two digit number. Calculating, level 5: approximate to check answers to problems are of the correct magnitude. Calculating, level 7: make and justify estimates and approximations of calculations.

Links

Question **5** refers to Fair Trade coffee. Fair Trade is a trading partnership that ensures that farmers and producers in developing countries are paid a fair price for their goods. There is more information about Fair Trade at http://www.fairtrade.org.uk/

- Use ICT to estimate square roots and cube roots   (L6)   ***Useful resources***
  Scientific calculator

Starter – Double products

Draw a 4 × 4 table on the board.

Label the columns: 9, -4, 18, 11. Label the rows: 3, 7, 14, -5.

Ask students to fill in the table with the products (no calculators).

For example, the top row in the table would read 27, -12, 54, 33.

Are there any short cuts? Hint: 18 is double 9 and 14 is double 7.

Can be differentiated by the choice of numbers.

Teaching notes

Solve $x^2 = 71.4026$ by trial and improvement correct to 1dp.

x	8	8.5	8.4	8.45
x^2	64	72.25	70.56	71.4025
High/low	low	high	low	low

$8.5^2 = 72.25$ too high.

$72.25 - 71.4026 = \mathbf{0.8474}$ away from the required value.

$8.4^2 = 70.56$ too low.

$71.4026 - 70.56 = \mathbf{0.8426}$ away from the required value.

So $x = 8.4$ gives a closer answer to $x^2 = 71.4026$ than $x = 8.5$; can we conclude that $x = 8.4$ to 1 dp? We must make sure by looking half way between 8.4 and 8.5. That is, $8.45^2 = 71.4025$ too low.

So value of x lies just above 8.45 and so the answer is 8.5 to 1dp.

Conclusion, don't just use one decimal place, you need to go to the next decimal place to be sure of the answer (RL).

Explore the square root and cube root functions of calculators. Note that some students may not have a dedicated cube root button and will have to use the power root function.

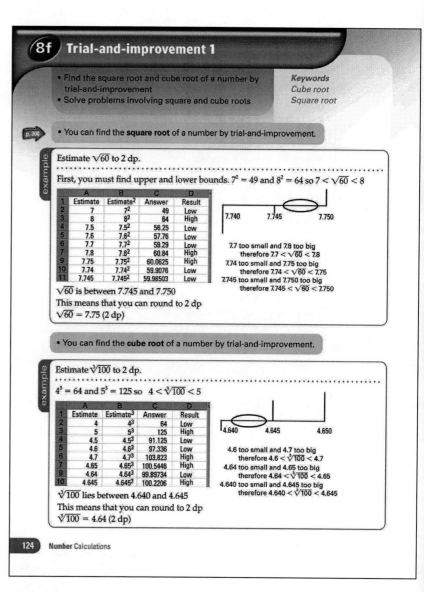

8f Trial-and-improvement 1

- Find the square root and cube root of a number by trial-and-improvement
- Solve problems involving square and cube roots

Keywords
Cube root
Square root

- You can find the **square root** of a number by trial-and-improvement.

example

Estimate $\sqrt{60}$ to 2 dp.

First, you must find upper and lower bounds. $7^2 = 49$ and $8^2 = 64$ so $7 < \sqrt{60} < 8$

	A	B	C	D
1	Estimate	Estimate²	Answer	Result
2	7	7²	49	Low
3	8	8²	64	High
4	7.5	7.5²	56.25	Low
5	7.6	7.6²	57.76	Low
6	7.7	7.7²	59.29	Low
7	7.8	7.8²	60.84	High
8	7.75	7.75²	60.0625	High
9	7.74	7.74²	59.9076	Low
10	7.745	7.745²	59.98503	Low

7.7 too small and 7.8 too big
therefore $7.7 < \sqrt{60} < 7.8$
7.74 too small and 7.75 too big
therefore $7.74 < \sqrt{60} < 7.75$
7.745 too small and 7.750 too big
therefore $7.745 < \sqrt{60} < 7.750$

$\sqrt{60}$ is between 7.745 and 7.750
This means that you can round to 2 dp
$\sqrt{60} = 7.75$ (2 dp)

- You can find the **cube root** of a number by trial-and-improvement.

example

Estimate $\sqrt[3]{100}$ to 2 dp.

$4^3 = 64$ and $5^3 = 125$ so $4 < \sqrt[3]{100} < 5$

	A	B	C	D
1	Estimate	Estimate³	Answer	Result
2	4	4³	64	Low
3	5	5³	125	High
4	4.5	4.5³	91.125	Low
5	4.6	4.6³	97.336	Low
6	4.7	4.7³	103.823	High
7	4.65	4.65³	100.5446	High
9	4.64	4.64³	99.89734	Low
10	4.645	4.645³	100.2206	High

4.6 too small and 4.7 too big
therefore $4.6 < \sqrt[3]{100} < 4.7$
4.64 too small and 4.65 too big
therefore $4.64 < \sqrt[3]{100} < 4.65$
4.640 too small and 4.645 too big
therefore $4.640 < \sqrt[3]{100} < 4.645$

$\sqrt[3]{100}$ lies between 4.640 and 4.645
This means that you can round to 2 dp
$\sqrt[3]{100} = 4.64$ (2 dp)

124   Number Calculations

Plenary

What is the drawback of a trial and improvement method? Discuss the method of bisection for finding accurate square roots of numbers. That is using half the interval each time. Is this a quicker method? Is this a more difficult method to use? (EP) (1.5)

Simplification

Use pre-prepared grids for the trial and improvement questions. Include some initial calculations.

All questions (1.3)

Questions 1 and **2** – Encourage students to have an informed initial guess. Stages of trials should be shown. Many students will not see the point of looking at the third decimal place, arguing that the answer to 2 dp is sufficient to find the closest approximation. Explain again that this will not always be certain (RL).

Exercise 8f

1 Lavina is working out $\sqrt{75}$ to 2 dp.
   Here is her working out.

Estimate	Estimate²	Answer	Result
8.6	8.6²	73.96	Low
8.7	8.7²	75.69	High
8.66	8.66²	74.996	Low
8.67	8.67²	75.169	High

   a Does she need to do any more working to find the answer? Explain your thinking.
   b Find $\sqrt{75}$ to 2 dp.
   c Continue Lavina's method to find $\sqrt{75}$ to 3 dp.

2 Use a trial-and-improvement method to find the square root of each of these numbers to 2 dp.
   a $\sqrt{30}$ b $\sqrt{70}$ c $\sqrt{145}$
   d $\sqrt{180}$ e $\sqrt{250}$ f $\sqrt{600}$
   Use the square root key on your calculator to check your answers.

3 Use a trial-and-improvement method to find the cube root of each of these numbers to 1 dp.
   a $\sqrt[3]{40}$ b $\sqrt[3]{200}$ c $\sqrt[3]{70}$ d $\sqrt[3]{13}$ e $\sqrt[3]{2000}$

Did you know?

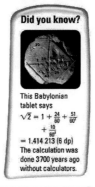

This Babylonian tablet says
$\sqrt{2} = 1 + \frac{24}{60} + \frac{51}{60^2} + \frac{10}{60^3}$
$= 1.414\ 213$ (6 dp)
The calculation was done 3700 years ago without calculators.

investigation

Yvette is trying to find $\sqrt{60}$ using a method called iteration. It takes an 'old' estimate and calculates an improved 'new' estimate.

Here is the formula she is using $\text{new} = \frac{1}{2} \times \left(\text{old} + \frac{60}{\text{old}}\right)$

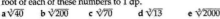

She tries 10 as her 'old' estimate.
She uses her 'new' estimate, 8, as the 'old' estimate. $\text{new} = \frac{1}{2} \times \left(10 + \frac{60}{10}\right) = 8$
She uses her 'new' estimate, 7.75, as the 'old' estimate, and repeats ... $\text{new} = \frac{1}{2} \times \left(8 + \frac{60}{8}\right) = 7.75$

   a Continue using Yvette's method for finding $\sqrt{60}$.
   b After a few goes, use your calculator to check the value of $\sqrt{60}$. Write what you notice.
   c Try finding $\sqrt{300}$ using the same method.
   d If you have access to a computer, use this formula in a spreadsheet.

Trial-and-improvement 1   125

Extension

Solve $10x^2 + 11x - 7 = 0$. Find x to 1 dp. Use trial and improvement. Tell students that there is more than one answer. (0.5 and -1.6) (SM, IE) (1.3)

Exercise 8f commentary

Question 3 – Some students may confuse cube root with division by 3. Consolidate understanding of cube root by using some simpler examples. For example, 2 cubed means $2 \times 2 \times 2 = 8$. Cube root of 8 means, what number do you cube to make 8? Some calculators do not have a dedicated cube root button. Introduction to the power root function maybe necessary.

Investigation – The method of (Newton-Raphson) iteration may need explaining carefully, as most students will not have come across it before. How many iterations do you need to do before your answer agrees with a calculator? (4) Does it depend on how close the starting guess is to the real answer? (yes). For example, if you start with 100, it takes 8 iterations, if you start with 7.7 it takes 3 iterations (CT) (1.4).

Try adaptng the method to find $\sqrt{2}$. Can you do better than the result on the Babylonian table tin the **Did you know?** (TW)

Assessment Criteria – Algebra, level 6: use systematic trial and improvement methods and ICT tools to find approximate solutions to equations such as $x^3 + x = 20$.

Links

The World Record for Mental Calculation is held by Alexis Lemaire. In July 2007 he found the 13th Root of a 200 digit number in 77.99 seconds without using a calculator, pen or paper. The solution has 16 digits. Lemaire already held one World record as in 2004, he found the 13th root of a 100-digit number in just 3.62 seconds.

- Use a calculator efficiently and appropriately to perform complex calculations (L6)
- Use the sign change key (L5)
- Use the function keys for powers roots and fractions (L5)
- Make and justify estimates and approximations of calculations (L6)

Useful resources
Scientific calculator

Starter – Crazy clocks

A clock chimes every 6 minutes. A second clock chimes every 7 minutes.
The clocks chime together. How many minutes before the clocks chime together again? (42 min)

What if a third clock chimes every 26 min? (5 hr 6 min)

Can be extended by asking how many times the clocks will chime together in 24 hours. (2 clocks 34 times, 3 clocks twice)

Teaching notes

Many of the calculator functions will have been used by students if they have tackled the previous chapters in the student book. Use examples to illustrate the use of the following functions/operations:

- the negative button (-) or +/−
- fractions, both mixed and vulgar
- square, cube and higher powers
- square root and cube root, using the power root function if necessary
- brackets for protecting fractions and negatives that are raised to a power

What use is the square root function? Look at the example of a square, how can the area be found? By squaring the side length. But suppose you know the area and want to find what was squared to make the area, that is, the side length of the square. This is the reverse process. The square root calculates what was squared to make the answer, it is known as the inverse of squaring.

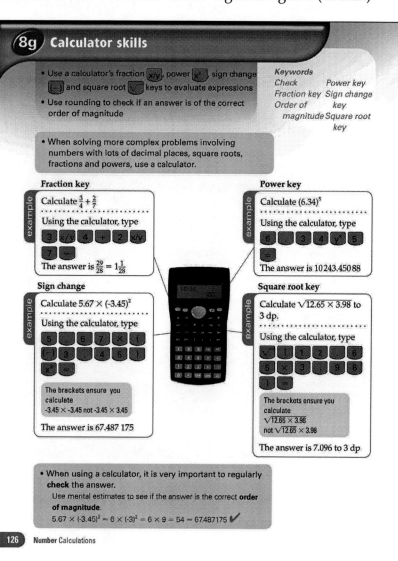

8g Calculator skills

- Use a calculator's fraction ☒, power ☒, sign change (-) and square root ☒ keys to evaluate expressions
- Use rounding to check if an answer is of the correct order of magnitude

Keywords
Check
Fraction key
Order of magnitude
Power key
Sign change key
Square root key

- When solving more complex problems involving numbers with lots of decimal places, square roots, fractions and powers, use a calculator.

Fraction key

example

Calculate $\frac{3}{4} + \frac{2}{7}$

Using the calculator, type

3 x/y 4 + 2 x/y 7 =

The answer is $\frac{29}{28} = 1\frac{1}{28}$

Power key

example

Calculate $(6.34)^5$

Using the calculator, type

6 . 3 4 x^y 5 =

The answer is 10243.45088

Sign change

example

Calculate $5.67 \times (-3.45)^2$

Using the calculator, type

5 . 6 7 × ((-) 3 . 4 5) x^2 =

The brackets ensure you calculate
-3.45 × -3.45 not -3.45 × 3.45

The answer is 67.487175

Square root key

example

Calculate $\sqrt{12.65} \times 3.98$ to 3 dp.

Using the calculator, type

√ (1 2 . 6 5 × 3 . 9 8) =

The brackets ensure you calculate
$\sqrt{12.65 \times 3.98}$
not $\sqrt{12.65} \times 3.98$

The answer is 7.096 to 3 dp.

- When using a calculator, it is very important to regularly **check** the answer.
  Use mental estimates to see if the answer is the correct **order of magnitude**.
  $5.67 \times (-3.45)^2 \approx 6 \times (-3)^2 = 6 \times 9 = 54 \approx 67.487175$ ✓

126 Number Calculations

Plenary

Investigate how to change hours, minutes and seconds into hours or visa versa. Make use of the D°M'S" and DEG functions. For example, 2.82 hr = 2hr 49min 12 sec (CT) (1.1).

Simplification

For estimations, encourage the use of rounding to one significant figure before calculation. Suggest a range of values that students can use to investigate the statements in question **3**.

All questions (1.3)

Question 1 – When using an estimate, is the estimate going to produce an answer greater or less than the true answer? What happens when you divide by a number between 0 and 1? Encourage using a calculator to check answers.

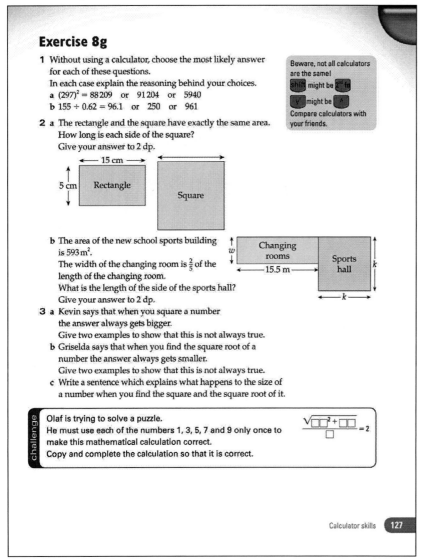

Extension

Using the fraction button on your calculator evaluate

$$\cfrac{1}{2+\cfrac{3}{4+\cfrac{5}{6+\cfrac{7}{8+9}}}} = \cfrac{1}{2+\cfrac{3}{4+\cfrac{5}{6+\cfrac{7}{17}}}} = \cfrac{1}{2+\cfrac{3}{4+\cfrac{85}{109}}} = \cfrac{1}{2\cfrac{327}{521}} = \cfrac{521}{1369}$$

Can the same be done using the negative integers from -1 to -9 instead of 1 to 9? That is, replace 1 will -1 and 2 with -2, *etc*. Will the answer just be the same but negative? No, the answer is 59/61 (IE) (1.3).

Exercise 8g commentary

Question 2 – Discourage the use of trial and improvement. Ask students to look for an alternative method. Use simpler areas of other squares to re-enforce the link between area and side length (1.4).

Question 3 – Ensure students give consideration to numbers between 0 and 1, -1 and 0, other negatives, the numbers 0 and 1. Does the student's conclusion cover all possible numbers? (CT, RL) (1.2)

Challenge – There are 5! = 120 different rearrangements of the numbers. The class could be split in order to divide the labour equally (TW, SM). Are there some short cuts you can make by excluding certain possibilities? For example, the number at the bottom can't be one. Reason, the number that is being square rooted would have to be equal to four (1.2).

Assessment Criteria – Calculating, level 5: approximate to check answers to problems are of the correct magnitude. Calculating, level 7: make and justify estimates and approximations of calculations.

Links

The first widely available hand-held battery-operated calculator was the Sharp LC-8 (also known as the EL-8) which was introduced in January 1971. The calculator measured 100 mm × 163 mm × 67 mm and was advertised as the world's smallest electronic calculator. Ask the class to compare the size of their own calculator. There is a video of an advertisement for the LC-8 at http://www.boreme.com/boreme/funny-2007/sharp-lc-8-p1.php and at http://www.youtube.com/watch?v=nCcgoTc8Aqc (TW).

- Enter numbers and interpret the display in different contexts (extend to time) (L6)
- Use a calculator efficiently and appropriately to perform complex calculations with numbers of any size, knowing not to round during intermediate steps of a calculation (L6)

Useful resources
Flow chart (see simplification)
Calculator

Starter – Pocket money

Anwar received £10 pocket money each week.

Bryony's pocket money started at £5 and increased by 50p each week:
£5 in week 1, £5.50 in week 2, *etc.*

Charlie said he would be happy if his pocket money started with1p and it doubled each week:
1p, 2p, 4p, *etc.*

Ask students who would get the most money after 10 weeks. (Anwar) How about 20 weeks? (Charlie) In which week will Charlie get more than £10? (week 11)

Teaching notes

Show a table of metric-metric, imperial-imperial and metric-imperial conversions with blanks. Ask students which they already know. Fill in as many of the blanks as possible. Are there some patterns in the answers that will make them easier to remember? For example, grams—kg—tonnes all go in thousands. Are there any rhymes or helpful tips that students know for remembering any other ones? For example, Two and a quarter pounds of jam is round about a kilogram.

Use a square metre to show that it is not the same as 100 square centimetres. Express the side length in cm to establish that $1 \text{ m}^2 = 10\,000 \text{ cm}^2$ (RL).

Use a calculator to show how units of time can be subdivided for examples like those in the student book.

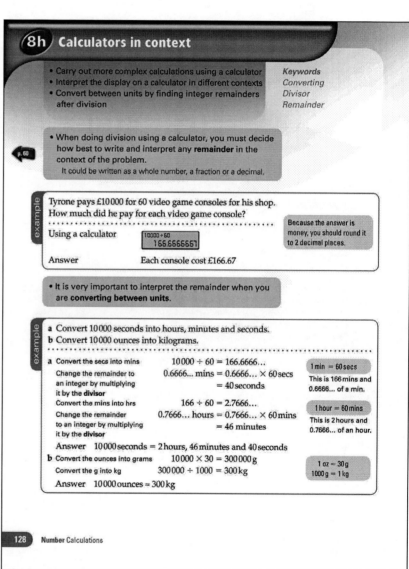

Plenary

Is there a quick way to convert from metres per sec to either km per hour or mph? Investigate (CT) ((1.4).

Simplification

For question **2**, a single flow diagram could be designed to help conversion from sec to min to hours to days to weeks to years that could be applied to all the parts. For example 4365 sec into hours, min, sec (1 hr 12 mins 45 secs)

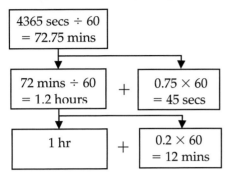

4365 secs ÷ 60 = 72.75 mins

72 mins ÷ 60 = 1.2 hours + 0.75 × 60 = 45 secs

1 hr + 0.2 × 60 = 12 mins

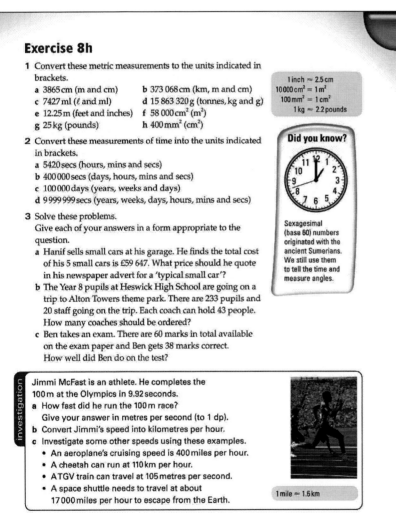

Exercise 8h

1 Convert these metric measurements to the units indicated in brackets.
   - **a** 3865 cm (m and cm)
   - **b** 373 068 cm (km, m and cm)
   - **c** 7427 ml (ℓ and ml)
   - **d** 15 863 320 g (tonnes, kg and g)
   - **e** 12.25 m (feet and inches)
   - **f** 58 000 cm² (m²)
   - **g** 25 kg (pounds)
   - **h** 400 mm² (cm²)

   1 inch ≈ 2.5 cm
   10 000 cm² = 1 m²
   100 mm² = 1 cm²
   1 kg ≈ 2.2 pounds

2 Convert these measurements of time into the units indicated in brackets.
   - **a** 5420 secs (hours, mins and secs)
   - **b** 400 000 secs (days, hours, mins and secs)
   - **c** 100 000 days (years, weeks and days)
   - **d** 9 999 999 secs (years, weeks, days, hours, mins and secs)

   Did you know?

   Sexagesimal (base 60) numbers originated with the ancient Sumerians. We still use them to tell the time and measure angles.

3 Solve these problems.
   Give each of your answers in a form appropriate to the question.
   - **a** Hanif sells small cars at his garage. He finds the total cost of his 5 small cars is £59 647. What price should he quote in his newspaper advert for a 'typical small car'?
   - **b** The Year 8 pupils at Heswick High School are going on a trip to Alton Towers theme park. There are 233 pupils and 20 staff going on the trip. Each coach can hold 43 people. How many coaches should be ordered?
   - **c** Ben takes an exam. There are 60 marks in total available on the exam paper and Ben gets 38 marks correct. How well did Ben do on the test?

   investigation

   Jimmi McFast is an athlete. He completes the 100 m at the Olympics in 9.92 seconds.
   - **a** How fast did he run the 100 m race? Give your answer in metres per second (to 1 dp).
   - **b** Convert Jimmi's speed into kilometres per hour.
   - **c** Investigate some other speeds using these examples.
     - An aeroplane's cruising speed is 400 miles per hour.
     - A cheetah can run at 110 km per hour.
     - A TGV train can travel at 105 metres per second.
     - A space shuttle needs to travel at about 17 000 miles per hour to escape from the Earth.

   1 mile ≈ 1.6 km

   Calculators in context   129

Extension

A light year, $9.46073047258 \times 10^{15}$ meters, is the distance that light travels in one year. Using appropriate units, what is the speed of light? A light year is based on a Julian year = 365.25 days. (299 792 458 m/s or 1 079 252 849 km/hr or 670 616 629 mph). These are the standard International Astronomical Union values, variants exist (EP).

Exercise 8h commentary

All questions (CT) (1.3)

Question 1 – Students may need reminders of metric and imperial measures and their conversions. Beware of students not making the distinction between length and area conversions

Question 2 – Encourage students to show all their working in breaking down the time measurements. The standard number of days in a year is 365; leap years are usually ignored in this type of calculation.

Question 3 – When solving these number problems, students will need to use percentages for some of the work. Students may need a reminder of the use of a calculator for percentages.

Investigation – using ratios offers a good approach here. Ask, what does speed in km per hour mean? How many km would be travelled if you ran at the same speed for one hour? In part **c**, give the students the option of what they want to convert the speeds into (IE, EP).

Assessment Criteria – Calculating, level 5: use known facts, place value, knowledge of operations and brackets to calculate including all four operations with decimals to two places.

Links

An abacus is a mechanical calculator that consists of a frame containing rows of beads threaded onto wires. Usually, two of the beads in each row are separated from the remaining five by a crossbar. Versions of the abacus are still widely used in the Far East and Africa. There is more information about the abacus and an online abacus at http://www.educalc.net /144267.page (TW)

- Understand the order of precedence of operations, including powers (L5)
- Use a calculator efficiently and appropriately to perform complex calculations (L6)
- Use the function key for powers and roots (L5)
- Use brackets (L5)

Useful resources
Scientific calculator

Starter – Amazing digits

Ask students to think of a four digit number (four different digits) for example, 4512

Ask them to reverse the digits, 2154.

Subtract the smaller number from the larger number, $4512 - 2154 = 2358$.

Add the answer digits together until a single digit obtained $2 + 3 + 5 + 8 = 18, 1 + 8 = 9$.
Repeat with another four digit number.

Ask students what they notice. (Always 9)

Teaching notes

Ensure students are familiar with all the main functions of their calculator. Previous exercises in this chapter and previous chapters will have already practiced the use of all the main functions (1.3).

Does a calculator follow the rules of BIDMAS? Establish that it does by using a few examples, $3 + 4 \times 5^2 = 103$. How can you evaluate expressions like $\dfrac{3 + 5^2}{1.6 \times 2.5}$?

What will happen if you type this into the calculator in one go? How will the calculator decide on the order of priority? $3 + 5^2 \div 1.6 \times 2.5 = 117.1875$. Check this answer by calculating the numerator and denominator of the original question and then dividing them. (4) Why has this gone wrong. Discuss what the calculator thinks is the correct calculation. How can you ensure that the correct calculation is performed? Discuss how brackets can be used to 'protect' the numerator and denominator.

What are the dis/advantages of using brackets around the numerator and denominator compared to working the top and bottom out separately?

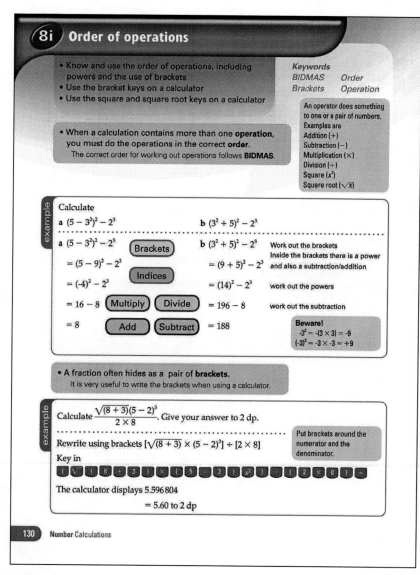

Plenary

Put brackets into the expression $2 + 3 \times 4 - 5$. What different answers can you make? Allow the use of one or more sets of brackets. (-5, -1, 9, 15)

Simplification

For question **1**, encourage students to use a calculator to find the correct answer. Reminding them that a calculator obeys the rules of BIDMAS. Then attempt to find how the incorrect answer is made by adjusting/removing some of the operations. Why do they think that mistake may have been made? Would they have been tempted to have made the same mistake without a calculator?

Exercise 8i

1 Fern and Caroline both sat a test but did not agree on the answers.

Question	Fern	Caroline
a $(3 + 4^2) \times 2$	38	
b $5 - 3^2 - 3$	1	98
c $6 - 5^2$	31	-7
d $(-5)^2 + 6$	31	-19
e $60 \div (4 + 8) - 7 + (5 - 2)^3$	25	-19
f $(3 \times 5^2) \div (3 \times 5)$	15	39
g $(3 \times 8)^2 \div (3 \times 2)$	96	5
		16

For each question, calculate the correct answer to see who is right.
Show your workings.
Explain the mistake made for each incorrect answer.

2 Calculate these giving your answer to 2 dp where appropriate.

a $\dfrac{(8-3)^2}{(5-2)^2}$ b $\dfrac{(3^2-1)(5-2)^2}{(9-4)^2}$ c $\dfrac{(7-3)^2\sqrt{(28-3)}}{(10-8)^3}$

3 Use a calculator to work out these calculations.
Give your answers to 2 dp where appropriate.

a $[2.5^2 + (5 - 2.8)]^2$ b $3.4 + [6.8 - (11.7 \times 3.2)]$

c $8 \times (2.5 - 4.6)^2$ d $\dfrac{4.37 \times 31.6}{1.09 \times (6.4 - 2.8)^2}$

e $\dfrac{3 \times \sqrt{(4.3^2 + 6^2)}}{5}$ f $\dfrac{(5^2 + 2)^2}{6 \times \sqrt{(7.8^2 - 9)}}$

investigation

a Jackie and Vlad are working out this calculation. $\left(\dfrac{5}{3}\right)^2$
Jackie types $\dfrac{5}{3}$ into her calculator and squares it.
Vlad works out 5^2 and divides by 3^2.
They both get the same answer.
Explain how and why both methods work.

b Investigate
  i $3^2 \times 5^2$ **ii** $\sqrt{12} \times \sqrt{3}$ **iii** $\sqrt{12} \div \sqrt{3}$

Exercise 8i commentary

All questions (1.1, 1.3)

Question 1 – Encourage students to calculate the answer setting out workings down the page, performing one calculation at a time, at least initially. Allow the use of a calculator (RL) (1.5).

Question 2 – Students should use the rules of BIDMAS without a calculator until it comes to the division.

Question 3 – Allow students to try more than one way of calculating the answer. The safest method may be to work out separate parts of the question. A more difficult method may be to try and find the answer in just one calculation. Challenge students to try both methods (1.4).

Investigation –Ask students to hypothesise how part b can be simplified. Test their ideas. Can they generalise? (CT) (1.2)

Assessment Criteria – Calculating, level 5: use knowledge of operations and brackets to calculate including all four operations.

Links

Bring in some dictionaries for the class to use. The word *order* can have several meanings and can be used as a noun or a verb. In which curriculum subject would each sense of the word most likely be used?

Extension

Use the digits 1, 2, 3, 4, 5 each only once. Use the operation $+$, $-$, $\times$, $\div$, cube and one set of brackets to make the answer -23. You could hint that the answer is in the style of question **2b**
Answer, $\dfrac{4 - 5 + 3}{(1 - 2)^3}$ (IE).

8a

1 Round each of these numbers to the nearest
  i whole number   **ii** 1 dp   **iii** 2 dp   **iv** 3 dp.
  a 6.1583   **b** 4.5648   **c** 18.6262   **d** 4.154 94
  e 3.909 09   **f** 9.999 99   **g** 87.654 32   **h** 0.000 707

2 Work out an estimate for each of these problems.
  Show all the steps of your working out.
  a The average height of a man in Scotland is 1.78 m. There are
     662 954 people living in Glasgow, of whom 49% are men.
     Estimate the combined height of all the men in Glasgow.
     Give your answer to the nearest kilometre.
  b Giuseppe runs the marathon which is 42.195 km in length.
     He covers each km in 3 mins 48 secs.
     Estimate the time it will take Giuseppe to complete the race.
     Give your answer to the nearest minute.

8b

3 Calculate these using an appropriate method.
  a $7.6 + 4.3 + 11$ **b** $79 + 115.6 + 41$ **c** $9.27 + 0.9 + 9 + 0.95$
  d $999.9 + 99.99 + 0.099$ **e** $33.3 + 333.3 - 3.33$ **f** $2473.5 + 40.79 - 4.6$

8c

4 Calculate
  a 39×10^3 **b** 7×10^2 **c** $416 \div 10^1$ **d** $3703 \div 10^2$
  e 5.3×10^1 **f** 7.7×10^1 **g** $562 \div 10^3$ **h** $327 \div 10^3$
  i 0.49×10^2 **j** 2.7×10^1 **k** $6.4 \div 10^2$ **l** 0.057×10^2

5 Each of these numbers has been written in standard form.
  Work out the size of each of the numbers.
  a 4.7×10^3 **b** 3.9×10^2 **c** 8.2×10^4 **d** 2.9×10^5
  e 7.3×10^6 **f** 8.07×10^4 **g** 6.3×10^5 **h** 2.05×10^7

8d

6 Calculate these using a written method.
  Remember to do a mental approximation first.
  a 82×0.65 **b** 64×0.57 **c** 82×91.3 **d** 93×26.5
  e 36×1.86 **f** 72×9.51 **g** 16×2.19 **h** 8.3×86.7
  i 63.7×0.91 **j** 38.4×0.69 **k** 57.2×0.61 **l** 93.9×0.93

7 Calculate these using an appropriate method.
Give your answer as a decimal to 1 dp where appropriate.
- **a** 48.6 ÷ 6
- **b** 67.4 ÷ 8
- **c** 82.8 ÷ 7
- **e** 38.5 ÷ 14
- **e** 62.5 ÷ 15
- **f** 31.2 ÷ 16
- **g** 327 ÷ 4.6
- **h** 912 ÷ 5.6
- **i** 304 ÷ 2.4
- **j** 441 ÷ 2.1
- **k** 327 ÷ 8.2
- **l** 955 ÷ 3.7

8 Use a trial and improvement method to find the square root of each of these numbers to 2 dp.
- **a** $\sqrt{45}$
- **b** $\sqrt{13}$
- **c** $\sqrt{361}$
- **d** $\sqrt{876}$
- **e** $\sqrt{2640}$

Use the square root key on your calculator to check your answers.

9 Use a trial and improvement method to find the cube root of each of these numbers to 1 decimal place.
- **a** $\sqrt[3]{95}$
- **b** $\sqrt[3]{300}$
- **c** $\sqrt[3]{10}$
- **d** $\sqrt[3]{999}$
- **e** $\sqrt[3]{87654}$

10 Use your calculator to work out the answer to these sets of instructions.
- **a** Input the number 12. Square your answer. Add 23.
  Find the square root. Add -8. Cube your answer.
- **b** Input the fraction $\frac{7}{8}$. Square your answer. Divide by 2.
  Add 14. Square root your answer.
- **c** Write the sets of instructions in parts **a** and **b** as calculations using the correct order of operations.

11 Solve these problems.
Give each of your answers in a form appropriate to the question.
- **a** Jasmine's syndicate wins £3 454 123.23 on the Euro millions. There are 17 people in the syndicate. How much does each person receive?
- **b** The population of Smalltown is 48. Each year the population is predicted to increase by 6%. What will the population be in one year's time?

12 Calculate these, giving your answer to 2 dp where appropriate.

a $\dfrac{(7-2)^3}{(8-3)^2}$

b $\dfrac{(4^2-1.2)(7-2.5)^2}{(9-4.1)^3}$

c $\dfrac{(3^2-2)^2\sqrt{(31-2^3)}}{(17-5)^2}$

13 Use a calculator to work out these calculations.
Give your answers to 2 dp where appropriate.

a $[1.8^3+(17-2.3^2)]^2$

b $8.2+[3.7^2-(12.7\div2.6)]$

c $9.2\times(1.05-2.1)^3$

d $\dfrac{5.03\times1.9^3}{4.23\times(8.7-3.3)^2}$

8 Summary

Assessment criteria

- Use efficient methods of addition and subtraction — Level 4
- Use a range of mental methods of computation with all operations — Level 4
- Round decimals to the nearest decimal place — Level 5
- Approximate to check answers to problems are of the correct magnitude — Level 5
- Use known facts, place value, knowledge of operations and brackets to calculate including using all four operations with decimals to two places — Level 5
- Use understanding of place value to multiply and divide whole numbers by 10,100 and 1000 and explain the effect — Level 5
- Understand and use an appropriate non-calculator method for solving problems that involve multiplying or dividing any three digit number by any two digit number — Level 5
- Use systematic trial and improvement methods and ICT tools to find approximate solutions to equations such as $x^3 + x = 20$ — Level 6
- Make and justify estimates and approximations of calculations — Level 7
- Understand the effect of multiplying and dividing by numbers between 0 and 1 — Level 7

Question commentary

Example The example illustrates a question about multiplying and dividing by negative powers of ten. Emphasise the use of an equivalent calculation in each part. Encourage students to compare the size of the answer with the original value to emphasise the effect of multiplying and dividing by numbers between 0 and 1.	**a** $4.8 \div 100 = 0.048$ **b** $\dfrac{6}{1} = 6$ **c** $3.4 \div 0.01 = 3.4 \times 100$ $= 340$

Past question The question requires students to round a value for π to 4 dp and then to choose a calculation to give a value closest to π. Students should take care to enter numbers into the calculator correctly and to square the entire value of $\frac{16}{9}$, not just the denominator. Three of the four calculations give an answer oft 3.14 to 2 dp Encourage students to compare their answers with the given value for π, digit by digit.	**Answer** **Level 6** **2 a** 3.1416 **b** $\dfrac{355}{113}$

Development and links

The methods of calculation discussed in this chapter are applied to problem solving in Chapter 17 and consolidated and practised in Chapter 16. Students will find square and cube roots using a calculator in Chapter 10. Multiplication and division are important in the topic of ratio and proportion in Chapter 12.

Students will have opportunities to perform calculations, round numbers to make estimations and approximations and use standard form across the curriculum, but particularly in science, technology and geography.

Transformations

Geometry

Objectives

- Recognise that translations, rotations and reflections preserve length and angle, and map objects on to congruent images **6**
- Use the coordinate grid to solve problems involving translations, rotations, reflections and enlargements **6**
- Explore and compare mathematical representations of combinations of translations, rotations and reflections of 2-D shapes **6**
- Enlarge 2-D shapes, given a centre of enlargement and a positive integer scale factor **6**
- Identify the scale factor of an enlargement as the ratio of the lengths of any two corresponding segments **6**
- Use and interpret maps and scale drawings in the context of mathematics and other subjects **6**
- Recognise that enlargements preserve angle but not length, and understand the implications of enlargement for perimeter... **7**

Level

MPA

1.1 9a, a^2, b, c, c^2, d, CS
1.2 9a, a^2, b, c, c^2, d, CS
1.3 9a, a^2, b, c, c^2, d, CS
1.4 $9a^2$, c, d, CS
1.5 9a, a^2, c, CS

PLTS

IE 9a, a^2, b, d, CS
CT 9a, a^2, b, c, c^2, d, CS
RL 9a, b, c, c^2, CS
TW 9I, a, a^2, CS
SM $9a^2$, b, d, CS
EP 9a, a^2, b, c, d, CS

Introduction

This chapter builds on knowledge of transformations and symmetry gained in Year 7. Students review reflections, rotations and translations, considering the congruence and similarity of the transformed shapes; review line and rotational symmetry of 2-D shapes; and use combinations of transformations to produce tessellations. The topic of enlargement is extended to include the enlargement of a shape using a centre of enlargement and either a positive whole number scale factor or a fractional scale factor. The chapter concludes with the interpretation of scale drawings using ratios.

The student book discusses the complex geometric shapes and constructions found in crop circles. Students will encounter geometric pattern design in Art and in Design and Technology. Crop circles appear suddenly, usually overnight, in fields of cereal crops. The plants in the field are flattened into the shape of a circle or other more complex design. Some crop circles are definitely the work of pranksters but others are unexplained. There is a collection of photographs of crop circles at http://www.visiblesigns.de/index.php?id=e-kk-main-laender (TW).

Extra Resources

9 Start of chapter presentation
9a Animation: Transformations
9a Worked solution: Q2
$9a^2$ Animation: Transformations 2
$9a^2$ Consolidation sheet
9b Animation: Symmetry
9b Animation: Symmetry 2
9c Animation: Enlargements
9c Worked solution: Q2a
9c Consolidation sheet
$9c^2$ Animation: Scale factors
9d Consolidation sheet
 Maths life: Patchwork

 Assessment: chapter 9

Fast-track

$9a^2$, c, c^2, d

- Transform 2-D shapes by rotation, reflection and translation   (L5)
- Recognise that translations, rotations and reflections preserve length and angle, and map objects in to congruent shapes   (L6)
- Use the coordinate grid to solve problems involving translations, rotations and reflections   (L6)

Useful resources
Tracing paper
Image of 2 faces/a vase
Mirrors

Starter – Palindromic dates

First November 2010 is palindromic if written using two digits for the day, month and year: 01.11.10

Ask students to find other palindromic dates occurring within the next 50 years. (11.11.11, 21.11.12, 02.11.20, 12.11.21, *etc*)

Teaching notes

What are the four main ways in which a shape can be transformed? Translation, Rotation, Reflection, Enlargement. What do students think is meant by a translation? Give an example of a shape and its translated image. Ask students to describe the transformation. Note that some students mistakenly count the gap between the two shapes rather than count the distance that a common point has moved (EP, RL).

How should a rotation be described? For example, is rotate 90 degrees a clear instruction that will give a unique answer? Establish that an angle, direction and centre of rotation are all needed to define the rotation properly.

Allow students to use tracing paper to help perform and describe rotations including finding the centre of rotation through trial and improvement.

How can diagonal reflections be performed? Use an example and demonstrate the method of counting perpendicular to and across the mirror line. What alternative method of counting is useful? Look at counting vertically and horizontally either side of the mirror line.

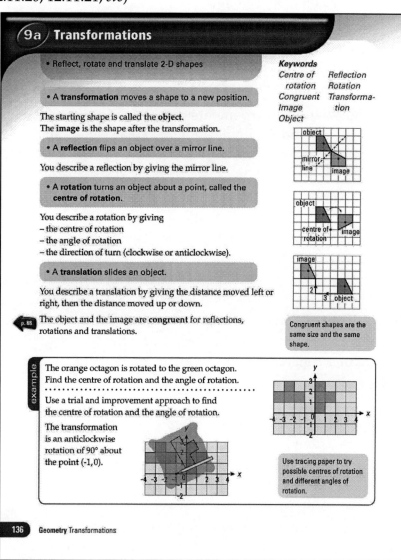

Plenary

Look at question **4** again. What other shapes can be made from rotating other types of triangle. If time allows, consider all classification of triangle, there are seven: scalene (acute angled, right angled, obtuse angled), isosceles (acute angled, right angled, obtuse angled) and equilateral. The class could be divided to spread the work load. (IE, TW) (1.1)

Simplification

Allow the use of mirrors to help with reflections. For those with poor motor skills, use enlarged copies of the exercise and tracing paper that already has the vertices of the original shape drawn on. Allow the students to add the edges.

Question 1 – When describing transformations, encourage students to write as complete answers as possible, for example, reflect in a vertical line, or rotate 90° clockwise, or move a given number of squares in specific directions.

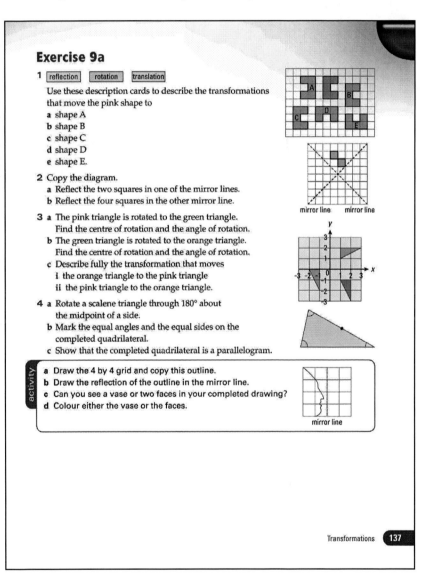

Extension

Use four mirror lines, $y = 0$, $x = 0$, $y = x$, $y = -x$. Draw a simple shape that actually crosses over one of the mirror lines. Reflect the shape in each of the lines. Challenge a partner to the same problem and see if there is agreement as to the solution (CT, RL) (1.5).

Exercise 9a commentary

Question 2 – Many students find diagonal reflection tricky. Ask students if they have different ways of counting the squares. Ask them to share their methods with a partner. Some may count perpendicular to the mirror line, some may count along to the mirror line and then down. (TW, EP) (1.3, 1.5)

Question 3 – Students need to realise the importance of an accurate tracing of the triangle. Encourage the use of a sharp pencil and perhaps a ruler. When trying different possible centres of rotation, make certain students are aware that they should position their pencil point as accurately as possible (1.2).

Question 4 – Students may find it helpful to label the angles *a*, *b*, *c*. Encourage the use of the standard method of labelling equal sides, that is, single/double lines (1.3).

Activity – Before commencing this activity, the class could be shown the completed picture for a few seconds and asked to write down the very first thing they see. What proportion of the class see two faces/a vase? (1.3)

Assessment Criteria – SSM, level 5: reason about position and movement and transform shapes. SSM, level 6: know that translations, rotations and reflections preserve length and angle and map objects onto congruent images.

Links

In photography reflections are used to add interest. Examples can be found at http://photography. nationalgeographic.com/photography/photos/patterns-nature-reflections.html and at http:// www.danheller.com/mirrors.html (EP).

- Explore and compare mathematical representations of combinations of translations, rotations and reflections of 2-D shapes

(L6)

Useful resources
Isometric paper
Tracing paper
Coloured pencils
Mirrors

Starter – Moving triangles

Ask students to plot (or imagine) a triangle with vertices at (1, 1) (2, 1) (1, 5).

Then ask students to imagine the x-coordinates are multiplied by -1, that is, (-1, 1) (-2, 1) (-1, 5).

What transformation has taken place? (reflection in *y*-axis)

What if the *x* and *y* coordinates are reversed? (reflection in $x = y$)

What transformation has taken place if the coordinates are (-1, 3) (0, 3) (-1, 7)?

Teaching notes

Students may already be familiar with the term tessellation from work in spread **6c**. If not then follow the second example as a way to introduce tessellation.

Look at examples of repeated transformations like the first example. Will two reflections always be able to be represented by a single transformation? Investigate.
(A rotation centred on where the mirror lines cross, through twice the angle between the lines. Or if the mirror lines are parallel a translation perpendicular to and through twice the separation between the mirror lines) Encourage students to consider vertical/horizontal/diagonal lines of refection. What difference if any would it make if the mirror line passes through the shape being reflected? What sort of shape should be used for the investigation?

Encourage students to share their findings with others and try to convince their neighbours of their conclusions (CT, EP) (1.4, 1.5).

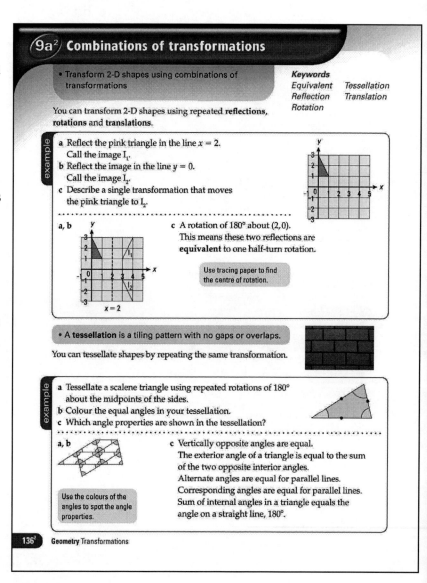

Plenary

What words in the English language read the same when they are rotated 180°? Use only capital letters. Begin by examining what letters make sense when rotated 180°. Examples are SIS, MOW, SWIMS, NOON. These are known as a type of ambigram. These could be further researched. (IE)

Simplification

Allow the use of mirrors to help with reflections. For those with poor motor skills, use enlarged copies of the exercise and tracing paper that already has the vertices of the original shape drawn on. Allow the students to add the edges.

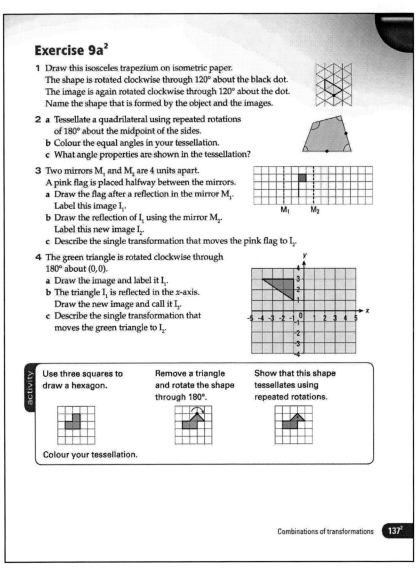

Exercise 9a²

1 Draw this isosceles trapezium on isometric paper. The shape is rotated clockwise through 120° about the black dot. The image is again rotated clockwise through 120° about the dot. Name the shape that is formed by the object and the images.

2 a Tessellate a quadrilateral using repeated rotations of 180° about the midpoint of the sides.
   b Colour the equal angles in your tessellation.
   c What angle properties are shown in the tessellation?

3 Two mirrors M_1 and M_2 are 4 units apart. A pink flag is placed halfway between the mirrors.
   a Draw the flag after a reflection in the mirror M_1. Label this image I_1.
   b Draw the reflection of I_1 using the mirror M_2. Label this new image I_2.
   c Describe the single transformation that moves the pink flag to I_2.

4 The green triangle is rotated clockwise through 180° about (0,0).
   a Draw the image and label it I_1.
   b The triangle I_1 is reflected in the x-axis. Draw the new image and call it I_2.
   c Describe the single transformation that moves the green triangle to I_2.

activity

Use three squares to draw a hexagon.

Remove a triangle and rotate the shape through 180°.

Show that this shape tessellates using repeated rotations.

Colour your tessellation.

All questions (CT) (1.2, 1.3)

Question 1 – Students may need to be helped in understanding that the isometric paper allows for the rotation of 60° at a time. Can students see why?

Question 2 – Some students may prefer to label the equal angles, a, b, c, d. Will all quadrilaterals tessellate using this method of rotation? (1.1)

Question 3 – Ensure students use the correct language to describe the translation in part **c** rather than just say 'slide'.

Question 4 – Encourage students to name the mirror line in part **c**. Is there more than one name for the line? (y-axis or $x = 0$, both are acceptable)

Activity – Does it matter if the shape is not rotated and just used in the same orientation?

Links

Islamic art does not use images of living things, but instead uses geometric patterns and tessellations. The Alhambra palace in Granada, Spain is richly decorated with Islamic art. For more information about the Palace see http://en.wikipedia.org/wiki/Alhambra

There are examples of the patterns found at Alhambra at http://www2.spsu.edu/math/tile/grammar/moor.htm (TW).

Extension

Is it possible to perform a reflection, then a rotation, then a translation to return at the end to the starting shape? (yes) Is it always possible, or does it depend on the type of shape you begin with? (it depends) Will the original order of the transformations make any difference? (CT, SM)

- Identify all the symmetries of 2D shapes   (L5)

Useful resources
Protractor
Tracing paper
Mirrors
Cut out copy of a parallelogram

Starter – Hexominoes

Ask students to draw hexominoes that will fold up to form a cube (CT).

How many can they find? (11 possible nets)
How many nets show line symmetry?
How many nets show rotation symmetry?

Teaching notes

When a parallelogram is rotated about its centre, will its edges and angles appear in exactly the same place more than once when it has completed a full turn? If so how many times? (twice) Introduce the term 'order of rotational symmetry'. A parallelogram is said to have order of rotational symmetry 2.

Look at some other common 2D shapes and comment on their orders of rotational symmetry. What order do shapes that have no rotational symmetry have? (order 1)

How many lines of symmetry do rhombuses and parallelograms have? Demonstrate that a parallelogram has no lines of symmetry by attempting to fold a cut out copy. Consider rectangles and squares, is there a connection between the number of lines of symmetry and the order of rotational symmetry? They are the same value. However, consider rhombuses and parallelograms, they contradict the rule (RL) (1.2, 1.5).

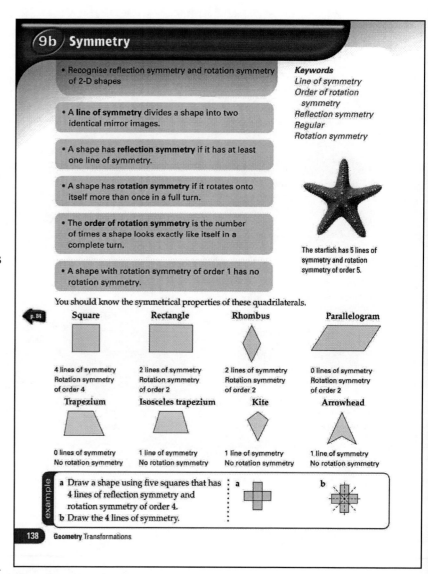

Plenary

A cuboid can be sliced in half to produce two 3D shapes that are reflections of each other. The 'slice' acts like a mirror. How many different ways can this be done? Encourage a new sketch to show each possibility. Three if no faces are square, or five if two opposite faces are square, or nine if it is in fact a cube. You could use the term 'planes of symmetry' (CT).

Simplification

Provide tracing paper to help identify rotational symmetry.
Provide mirrors to help identify line symmetry.

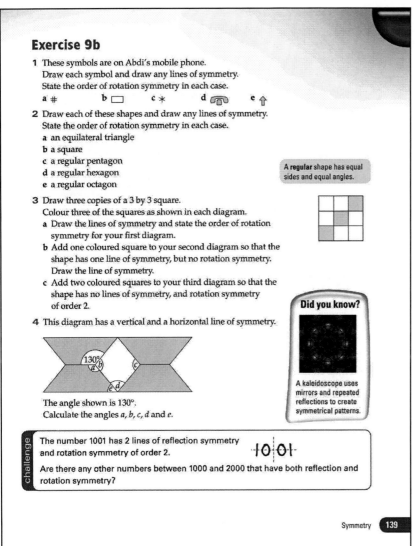

Exercise 9b

1 These symbols are on Abdi's mobile phone.
Draw each symbol and draw any lines of symmetry.
State the order of rotation symmetry in each case.

a ⌗   b ☐   c ✳   d ☎   e ⇧

2 Draw each of these shapes and draw any lines of symmetry.
State the order of rotation symmetry in each case.
a an equilateral triangle
b a square
c a regular pentagon
d a regular hexagon
e a regular octagon

*A **regular** shape has equal sides and equal angles.*

3 Draw three copies of a 3 by 3 square.
Colour three of the squares as shown in each diagram.
a Draw the lines of symmetry and state the order of rotation symmetry for your first diagram.
b Add one coloured square to your second diagram so that the shape has one line of symmetry, but no rotation symmetry. Draw the line of symmetry.
c Add two coloured squares to your third diagram so that the shape has no lines of symmetry, and rotation symmetry of order 2.

4 This diagram has a vertical and a horizontal line of symmetry.

The angle shown is 130°.
Calculate the angles *a, b, c, d* and *e*.

Did you know?

A kaleidoscope uses mirrors and repeated reflections to create symmetrical patterns.

challenge

The number 1001 has 2 lines of reflection symmetry and rotation symmetry of order 2.

I0I0I

Are there any other numbers between 1000 and 2000 that have both reflection and rotation symmetry?

Symmetry **139**

Extension

If possible construct hexagons that have 0, 1, 2, 3, 4, 5 lines of
symmetry. Hint that 0, 1, 2 are certainly possible (CT, SM).

Exercise 9b commentary

All questions (CT)

Question 1 – Encourage the use of dashed lines of symmetry to avoid confusion with the diagram itself.

Question 2 – Students could make accurate drawings of the regular shapes using a protractor and given the interior angles. Alternatively a reasonable sketch could be used. What do you notice about regular polygons? (1.3)

Question 3 – Students need to be aware that colours need to match up when considering symmetry (1.3).

Question 4 – Ask students to recall the angle rules they know. Which ones are useful here? Sum of interior angles in a quadrilateral is 360°. What shapes have been used in the diagram? Rhombus and (isosceles?) trapezium. (IE) (1.1, 1.2)

Challenge – What must students first ascertain? The digits which have rotational and reflective symmetry. Pose questions like, can you find all possible solutions? Are there solutions under 1000? Can a number have four lines of symmetry? (IE)

Assessment Criteria – SSM, level 5: identify all the symmetries of 2-D shapes.

Links

The kaleidoscope was invented in 1816 by David Brewster in Scotland. Kaleidoscopes are usually thought of as toys but are also used by designers and artists. There are instructions for making a simple kaleidoscope at http://www. zefrank.com/dtoy_vs_byokal/ index.html and an interactive kaleidoscope at http://www. kaleidoscopesusa.com/makeAscope. htm (EP).

- Enlarge 2D shapes, given a centre of enlargement and a positive integer scale factor **(L6)**
- Identify the scale factor of an enlargement as the ratio of the lengths of any two corresponding line segments **(L6)**
- Use the coordinate grid to solve problems involving enlargements **(L6)**

Useful resources
Isometric paper with lines drawn

Starter – Order 6

Ask students to draw (CT) (1.2)

shapes that have rotation symmetry of order six but no reflection symmetry
shapes that have rotation symmetry of order six and do have reflection symmetry.

Ask students how many lines of symmetry these shapes have.

Can be extended using different orders of symmetry.

Teaching notes

How can an enlargement be described? Discuss the term 'scale factor'. What scale factors are likely to be used in questions? (2, 3, 1.5, 2.5, 0.5) Do negative scale factors exist? (yes but normally covered in year 10.)

Why is a scale factor not enough to tell you all you need to know about the image? Because the position has not been stated.

Describe how a slide projector works. Describe how the light from the bulb strikes the slide and continues in 'rays' to the screen. The centre of enlargement is like a light source with the rays of light coming out to strike at the vertices of the shape. Use an example on coordinate axes and show how a scale factor of 2 is produced (EP). Emphasise that the distance from the centre of enlargement to the corners of the original shape has doubled. Note that many students double the distance from the vertex of the original shape rather than from the centre of enlargement (RL).

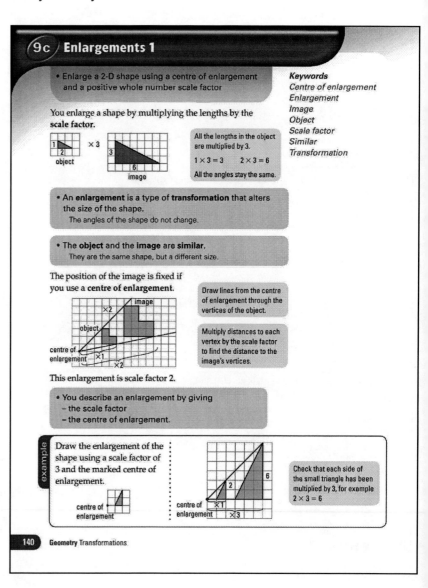

Plenary

If a shape is enlarged using the origin as the centre of enlargement, what pattern can you establish when comparing the original and new coordinates of the vertices of the shape? Answer, each *x* and *y* coordinate has been multiplied by the scale factor. What do you expect if the centre of enlargement had been somewhere else, for example, (1, 0)? (CT) (1.4)

Simplification

Provide students with enlarged copies of the shapes from the exercise.

All questions (1.3)

Question 1 – This should be attempted without a calculator. Ask students to check that the enlargement is possible. That is, the same scale factor is used for both dimensions.

Question 2 – Remind students that the centre of enlargement can be on the edge or inside a shape. Ask students to check that all dimensions have been enlarged by the same scale factor. Students should get used to counting squares when using construction lines, rather than use a ruler.

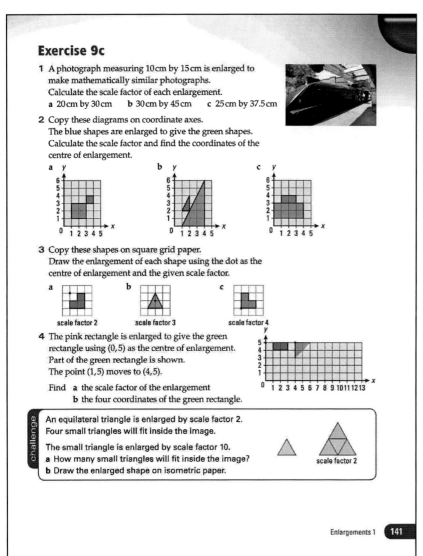

Exercise 9c

1 A photograph measuring 10cm by 15cm is enlarged to make mathematically similar photographs.
Calculate the scale factor of each enlargement.
  a 20cm by 30cm   b 30cm by 45cm   c 25cm by 37.5cm

2 Copy these diagrams on coordinate axes.
The blue shapes are enlarged to give the green shapes.
Calculate the scale factor and find the coordinates of the centre of enlargement.
  a   b   c

3 Copy these shapes on square grid paper.
Draw the enlargement of each shape using the dot as the centre of enlargement and the given scale factor.
  a   b   c
  scale factor 2   scale factor 3   scale factor 4

4 The pink rectangle is enlarged to give the green rectangle using (0,5) as the centre of enlargement.
Part of the green rectangle is shown.
The point (1,5) moves to (4,5).

Find a the scale factor of the enlargement
      b the four coordinates of the green rectangle.

challenge
An equilateral triangle is enlarged by scale factor 2.
Four small triangles will fit inside the image.

The small triangle is enlarged by scale factor 10.
a How many small triangles will fit inside the image?
b Draw the enlarged shape on isometric paper.
  scale factor 2

Enlargements 1   **141**

Extension

Explore enlargements of shapes that include arcs. Once students have decided on a shape, challenge them to enlarge it from different centres of enlargement. Advise students to keep their shape simple to begin with.

Exercise 9c commentary

Question 3 – Is it necessary to enlarge each vertex of the original shape? Some students may feel more comfortable doing this, but many maybe able to enlarge one point and then draw the enlarged shape in the correct way.

Question 4 – Many students might see this as a scale factor of 3 since the point has moved 3 squares on. Remind students that they are comparing the distance from the centre of enlargement of a point on the original shape, with a point on the enlarged shape. Comparing 1 square away with 4 squares away, that is, 4 times as far (1.1).

Challenge – What short cut methods can students find for adding up the total number of triangles? Can students generalise the number of triangles for any scale factor? Can the generalisation be explained? Re-enforce with an example of the area of a rectangle. Students may need to be convinced that counting area in triangles is just as valid, but more unusual than counting area in squares (CT) (1.1).

Assessment Criteria – SSM, level 6: enlarge 2-D shapes, given a centre of enlargement and a positive whole-number scale factor

Links

Magnifying glasses and microscopes are used to make objects appear larger. The magnification value is the scale factor. There are microscope images at different magnification values at http://micro.magnet.fsu.edu/primer/java/scienceopticsu/virtual/magnifying/index.html (EP).

- Enlarge 2D shapes using positive, fractional scale factors (L7)
- Recognise that enlargements preserve angle but not length, and understand the implications of enlargement for perimeter (L7)

Useful resources
Multilink cubes

• Starter – Jumbled up

Write a list of anagrams on the board and ask students to unscramble them and then make their own anagrams or word search. Possible anagrams are

ATTORNIO, SATTINAROL, AGEMI, GRONNTUCE, INFLEETOR, JOTBEC, TRYSMYME, DERRO, GLAMENNTREE, RECENT

(rotation, translation, image, congruent, reflection, object, symmetry, order, enlargement, centre)

Teaching notes

What do enlargements by scale factors 1 and 2 mean? Establish that scale factor 1 will keep a shape the same size in the same position. What must a scale factor or 1.5 or $\frac{1}{2}$ represent? What mistake is common when performing an enlargement by scale factor $\frac{1}{2}$? Enlarging by scale factor 1.5 rather than reducing the lengths to half the size (RL).

Look at an example of an enlargement between 0 and 1 on coordinate axes. Consider putting the centre of enlargement inside the original shape. How can the enlargement be reversed to return to the original shape? Is there a connection between the 2 scale factors that would be used? They are reciprocals (CT).

How could you enlarge a circle or ellipse? What ideas do students have? Which point is the most important one to enlarge? (centre point)

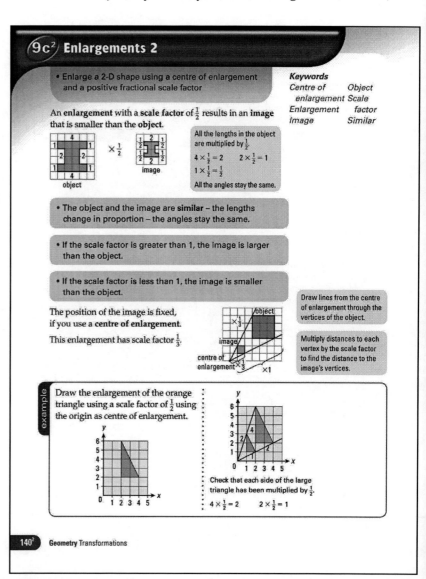

Plenary

If a 3D shape is enlarged, what happens to its volume? Experiment with cuboids initially. What conclusion do students reach? This could be made more interesting by using multilink cubes. Students could build small shapes and then an enlarged shape using a specified scale factor. How has the volume changed? (CT) (1.2)

Simplification

Provide students with enlarged copies of the shapes from the exercise. Remind students to keep measuring/counting from the centre of enlargement every time.

All questions (1.3)

Question 1 – The term 'enlargement' may cause confusion when the shapes are in fact being reduced in size. Discuss this problem with the language if necessary. Will the angles remain the same in the enlargement?

Question 2 – Encourage students to start with the easiest vertex. How far is it from the centre of enlargement? Students should count both vertically and horizontally in squares. Students often make errors by counting diagonally (RL).

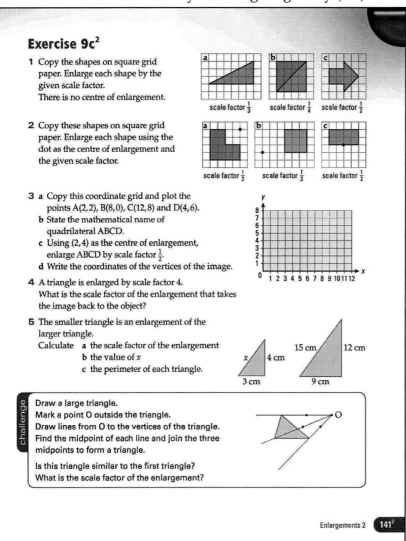

Extension

Set questions involving fractional scale factors greater than 1. If students tried the previous extension, can they apply fractional scale factors to shapes with arcs? (CT)

Exercise 9c² commentary

Question 3 – Students may only identify the shape as a quadrilateral. How can one pair of the lines be shown to be parallel? Look at the gradients (1.1).

Question 4 – Encourage students to make an initial guess. How can they check their idea? (RL)

Question 5 – What information is needed to find the scale factor? A pair of matching lengths. What relationship do you expect between the areas of the two shapes? Check your idea by calculation.

Challenge – Will this method always produce the same effect? What if the centre of enlargement were on the edge of the shape, or inside the shape?

Assessment Criteria – SSM, level 7: enlarge 2-D shapes, given a centre of enlargement and a fractional scale factor. SSM, level 7: recognise the similarity of the resulting shapes.

Links

Pictures can be copied and enlarged or reduced using a device called a pantograph. A pantograph consists of several hinged rods joined together in a parallelogram shape with extended sides. One end is traced over the image and a pencil attached to the other end reproduces the image to the desired scale. Pantographs are often sold as toys. There is more information about pantographs at http://en.wikipedia. org/wiki/Pantograph and an interactive pantograph at http://www.ies.co.jp/math/java/geo/panta/panta.html

- Use and interpret maps and scale drawings in the context of mathematics and other subjects (L6)

Useful resources
Calculator

• •

Starter – Shape bingo

Ask students to draw a 3 × 3 grid and enter nine quadrilaterals or polygons. Give properties, For example,

A regular shape with six lines of symmetry. (hexagon)
Two pairs of equal sides with perpendicular diagonals. (kite)

The winner is the first student to cross out all nine shapes.

Teaching notes

Show how a scale can be represented in words, for example, 2 cm represents 1 m. How can this be represented by a ratio? Show how the units would be removed on the ratio written in its simplest form.

A map scale might be written as 1 : 100 000. What does this actually mean? Is this a useful way to think of the scale if you are trying to measure distances on a map? Write this ratio in words.

A model maker of sailing ships knows the area of canvas needed for the sails of the full size ship. He is building a model using the ratio 1 : 100. How can he work out the area of the canvas he needs to use in the model? Are the areas and lengths of a scale drawing in the same ratio? Use two rectangles in the scale 1 : 3. What are their corresponding areas when their lengths are in the ratio 1 : 3? (1 : 9) How can this help the model maker? (CT) (1.2)

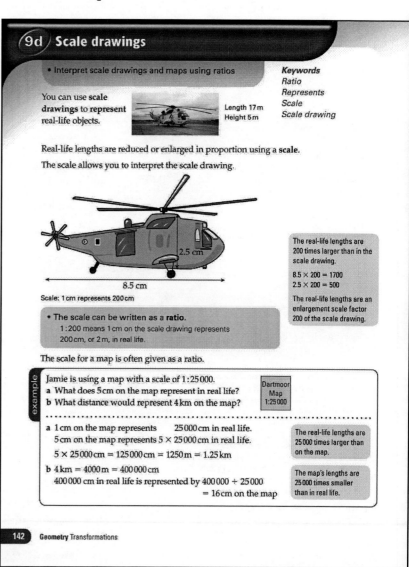

Plenary

Investigate the different scales used on ordnance survey maps. You can visit the site leisure.ordnancesurvey.co.uk to see the different scales and types of maps available.

Simplification

Treat the ratio similarly to the way an equation is treated. Show working on each side to create an equivalent ratio. Ask, what does the ratio tell you initially? What length are you trying to represent? How can the ratio be changed to get the number you want? For example 1 : 50 000 tells you 1 cm represent 50 000 cm. If you want to find 5 cm, you multiply each side by 5.

$$1 : 50\,000$$
$$\times 5 \qquad\qquad \times 5$$
$$5 : 250\,000$$

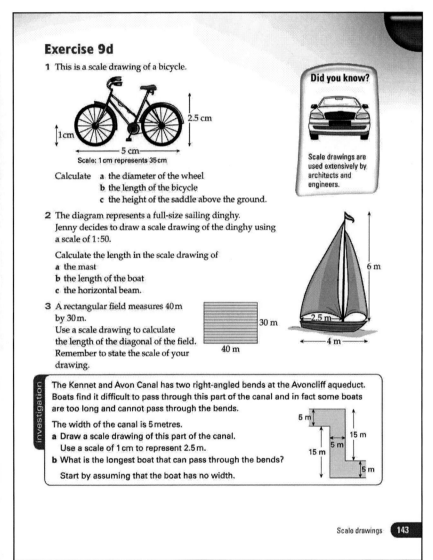

Exercise 9d

1 This is a scale drawing of a bicycle.

2.5 cm

1 cm

5 cm

Scale: 1 cm represents 35 cm

Calculate **a** the diameter of the wheel
  b the length of the bicycle
  c the height of the saddle above the ground.

2 The diagram represents a full-size sailing dinghy. Jenny decides to draw a scale drawing of the dinghy using a scale of 1 : 50.

Calculate the length in the scale drawing of
a the mast
b the length of the boat
c the horizontal beam.

6 m

2.5 m

4 m

3 A rectangular field measures 40 m by 30 m. Use a scale drawing to calculate the length of the diagonal of the field. Remember to state the scale of your drawing.

30 m

40 m

investigation

The Kennet and Avon Canal has two right-angled bends at the Avoncliff aqueduct. Boats find it difficult to pass through this part of the canal and in fact some boats are too long and cannot pass through the bends.

The width of the canal is 5 metres.
a Draw a scale drawing of this part of the canal. Use a scale of 1 cm to represent 2.5 m.
b What is the longest boat that can pass through the bends?

Start by assuming that the boat has no width.

5 m

15 m

5 m

15 m

5 m

Did you know?

Scale drawings are used extensively by architects and engineers.

Scale drawings **143**

Extension

The most popular map scales are 1 : 25 000 and 1 : 50 000 for walking. What length on each map represents a mile? Give your answer both in cm and inches. (6.437376 cm or 2.5344″ and 3.218688 cm or 1.2672″ respectively) (EP) (1.3).

Exercise 9d commentary

All questions (1.3)

Question 1 – Students should show their working. Why might some students have slightly different answers?

Question 2 – What units should the scale drawing be measured in? What is the reverse/inverse of multiplication?

Question 3 – Most students will use 4 cm by 3 cm. How can the scale be expressed? Some students may want to use the method of expression shown in question **1**, others may use 1 : 100. Would a larger scale drawing help to find the diagonal length more accurately?

Investigation – What shape can be used to initially represent the boat? A straight line. How can the longest possible boat be found? Encourage alternative approaches to the problem. Some students may try to 'push' different length lines around the bends. Others might make measurements at key points on the canal bends.

When refining the problem further, how wide should you make your representative shape? In reality 2.5 to 4 m is a common range. (SM, IE, CT) (1.1)

Links

Model railways are available in different gauges. OO gauge means that the model is built to a scale of 1 : 76, or 1 cm on the model represents a distance of 76 cm in real life. 1 cm on an N-gauge model represents a distance of 146 cm. If an N-gauge model locomotive is 5 cm long, how long is the real-life locomotive? There are pictures of different gauge model locomotives at http://ngaugesociety.com/modelling/scales/scales.htm (EP).

1 Copy the diagram on square grid paper.
Describe fully the transformation that moves the pink shape to
  a shape A
  b shape B
  c shape C.

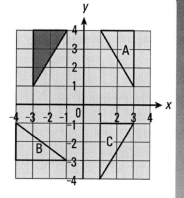

2 Copy the diagram on square grid paper.
  a Reflect the green hexagon in the line $y = x$.
   Colour the image orange.
  b Describe a different transformation that moves the green hexagon to the orange hexagon.

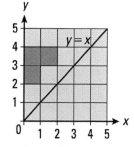

3 a Tessellate a regular hexagon using repeated translations.
  b Which other repeated transformations can you use to tessellate a regular hexagon?

4 The pink triangle is rotated clockwise through 90° about (0,0).
  a Draw the image and label it I_1.
  b The triangle I_1 is reflected in the y-axis.
   Draw the new image and call it I_2.
  c The triangle I_2 is reflected in the x-axis.
   Draw the new image and call it I_3.
  d Describe the single transformation that moves the pink triangle to I_3.

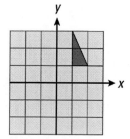

5 Draw these currency symbols.
Draw any lines of reflection symmetry and state the order of rotation symmetry for each symbol.
  a €   **b** $ **c** S   **d** ¥   **e** ₦

6 This triangle has one vertical line of symmetry.
  a State the values of a and b.
  b Explain your reasoning.

65° b a

7 Copy the shapes on square grid paper.

Draw the enlargement of each shape using the dot as the centre of enlargement and the given scale factor.

a

b

c

scale factor 3   scale factor 2   scale factor 4

8 a Plot the points A (4,0)' B (7,0) and C (4,6) on the coordinate axes.

b State the mathematical name of the shape ABC.

c Using (1,3) as the centre of enlargement, enlarge the shape ABC by scale factor $\frac{1}{3}$.

d Write down the coordinates of the image A'B'C'.

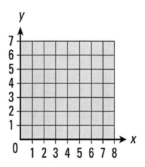

9 The Naze Tower in Essex is 26 metres high and 6 metres wide.

a Draw a scale drawing of the tower using a scale of 1 : 500.

Show your calculations for the height and the width of the tower in a scale drawing.

b Estimate the height of the person in the photograph.

c Calculate the height of the person in the scale drawing and draw the person on your scale drawing.

10 Jules is using a map with a scale of 1 : 50 000.

What is the actual distance in kilometres, if the length on the map is

a 1 cm   **b** 5 cm   **c** 1.5 cm   **d** 3.5 cm   **e** 4.8 cm?

- Pose questions and make convincing arguments to justify generalisations or solutions　(L6)
- Generate fuller solutions by presenting a concise, reasoned argument using symbols, diagrams, graphs and related explanations　(L7)

Useful resources
Examples of patchwork
Isometric paper

Background

Patchworks are mainly done as hobbies these days. In times of hardship, patchworks have been used as a way of recycling old clothes to make blankets and such like. Patchworks are often quite geometric in design. A person making the patchwork needs to consider how shapes fit together and often uses a template to make the pieces consistent sizes and shapes. Similar considerations apply to designs using paving stones (TW). This case study uses this geometric nature of patchworks to look at a shapes' internal angles and consider how these determine if a given shape will tessellate (EP).

Teaching notes

Introduce the idea of patchworks and remind students about tessellation. Look at the shapes that are used in typical patchworks and discuss what makes the shapes suitable for this purpose.

Look at the case study, focusing initially on the magazine and its free templates. What do you notice about the sizes of the templates? Agree that their dimensions are such that any shape will fit exactly with another. How long do you think the rectangle is compared with its width? Establish that it is twice as long as it is wide so that it can be used alongside two squares or other shapes. How do you think the lengths of the sides of the trapezium relate to each other? The longer side is twice as long as the shorter sides, which are all the same length as each other. Why do you think the rhombus and the trapezium have both been made with an angle of 60°? Establish that the equilateral triangle has to have an angle of 60°

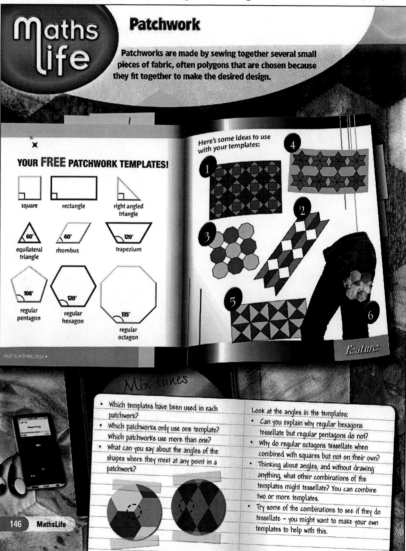

and that if the rhombus and trapezium are going to fit with the triangle, they too have to have an angle of 60° (CT) (1.4).

Now look at the example patchworks and ask students to think about which templates have been used in each patchwork. Give the students a few minutes to note their answers to this before discussing answers. When you check answers, some students might have considered the white spaces in patchworks 2, 3 and 4 as gaps while others might have included them as shapes and named their templates (1.5).

Teaching notes continued

Use the questions in the notebook below the magazine to initiate thinking about the angles in shapes and how these determine whether the shape will tessellate. Ask questions such as, why will some shapes tessellate and others not? Is it just to do with the length of their sides or is it also to do with their angles? What is it about the angles of some shapes that allow them to be used on their own? (CT)

Ask students to find the internal angles in regular polygons, from equilateral triangle to dodecagon. (60°, 90°, 108°, 120°, 128 4/7°, 135°, 140°, 144°, 147 3/11°, 150°) Using knowledge of these angles ask students to see how many polygons of one type they can fit exactly around a point. (6 equilateral triangles; 4 squares ; 3 hexagons). If you can use two polygons how many possibilities are there now? (2 squares and 3 equilateral triangles (two ways); 1 or 2 hexagons and 4 or 2 equilateral triangles; 2 octagons and 1 square; 2 dodecagons and 1 equilateral triangle) Can you use this knowledge to create six semiregular tessellations. Can you find the other two semiregular tessellations? (based on 1 equilateral triangle, 2 squares and 1 hexagon or 1 square, 1 hexagon and 1 dodecagon) (IE) (1.1, 1.2, 1.3)

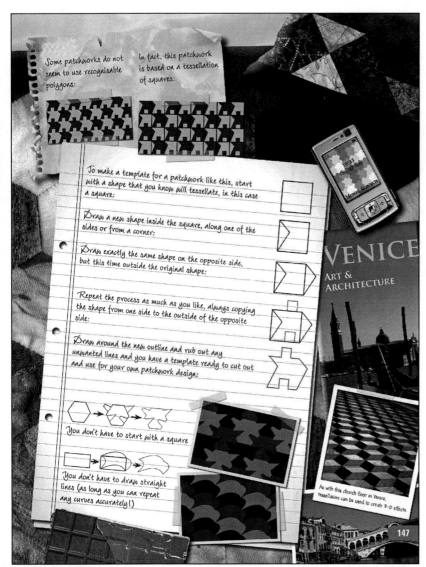

Now look at the tessellation on the right hand page. This uses a template that is not a regular polygon. To make a template based on a square follow the instructions. Make sure that students understand how the method requires a new shape to be drawn **inside** the shape on one side and **outside** the shape on the other, and that the two shapes are aligned with each other (RL).

Look at the two tessellation examples at the end of the instructions to see how the original shape doesn't have to be a square. What shapes could you start with? Establish that the initial shape needs to be one that tessellates.

Look also at how the rectangle has been changed to produce a template that has curved sides. Students should experiment with this method of creating templates. They should then choose one or two of their templates to produce a tessellation (CT) (1.3).

Extension

Ask students to try to tessellate irregular convex and concave ('tick shaped') quadrilaterals. If necessary suggest rotating the shape about the midpoint of each side. Can students show that the angles at a point add up to 360° (SM) (1.4).

Students could research the work of the Dutch artist M C Esher and identify any of his work that they think is based on tessellation (TW, EP).

9 Summary

Assessment criteria

• Reason about position and movement and transform shapes	Level 5
• Identify all the symmetries of 2-D shapes	Level 5
• Know that translations, rotations and reflections preserve length and angle and map objects onto congruent images	Level 6
• Enlarge 2-D shapes, given a centre of enlargement and a positive whole-number scale factor	Level 6
• Enlarge 2-D shapes using a centre of enlargement and a fractional scale factor	Level 7
• Recognise the similarity of the resulting shapes	Level 7

Question commentary

Example

The example illustrates a problem on congruence. Ask questions such as "When are two shapes congruent?" and "How do you know that two shapes are congruent?" Emphasise that congruent shapes are the same size and shape, so corresponding lengths and angles will be equal. Emphasise that, to answer the question, students need to identify which lengths and which angles are equal on the two triangles.

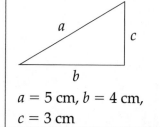

$a = 5$ cm, $b = 4$ cm, $c = 3$ cm

Past question

The question requires students to enlarge a shape using a given centre of enlargement and scale factor. Encourage students to think about strategies to make sure that the enlargement fits onto the piece of paper. Some students may position the enlarged image incorrectly. Encourage students to check their drawing by measuring corresponding lengths and angles on the image and the original. In part **b**, students are asked to find two missing lengths and a missing angle on a sketch of an enlargement with a fractional scale factor. Some students will multiply the angle by the scale factor as well as the lengths. Ask probing questions such as "What changes when you enlarge a shape? What stays the same?"

Answer

Level 6

2 a

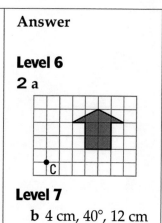

Level 7

b 4 cm, 40°, 12 cm

Development and links

The use of a scale factor links with work on ratio and proportion in Chapter 12 and scale drawing is used in work on loci in Chapter 14. Enlargement and Transformations are developed further in Year 9.

Reflection and line symmetry is important in physics when studying the properties of light, and in biology where symmetry occurs in nature. Most rotating mechanical parts used in design technology exploit the property of rotational symmetry and students rotate pictures and drawings using computer programs in ICT. Enlargement also links to resizing images in ICT. Symmetry and tessellations are important in art and design, particularly in Roman and Islamic art. Students will draw and use scale drawings in technology when creating design plans, and in geography when using maps.

10 Sequences and roots

Algebra

Objectives

Level

- Extend mental methods of calculating, working with powers and roots 5
- Generate terms of a sequence using term-to-term and position-to-term rules 6
- Generate sequences from practical contexts and write and justify an expression to describe the nth term of an arithmetic sequence 6
- Use the function keys (on a calculator) for powers and roots 6
- Use index notation for integer powers and simple instances of the index laws 6
- Distinguish the different roles played by letter symbols in equations, identities, formulae and functions 6
- Substitute numbers into expressions and formulae 6

MPA

1.1	10a, b
1.2	10b, c
1.3	10a, c, d, e
1.4	10a, b, c, e
1.5	10a, c

PLTS

IE	10a, b
CT	10a, b, c, d, e
RL	10c, d, e
TW	10I, a, e
SM	10a, b
EP	10b, d, e

Introduction

In this chapter, students review and extend Year 7 work on sequences and extend knowledge of powers and indices from Chapter 5. The chapter begins by generating terms of sequences using term-to-term and position-to-term rules and develops to finding the position-to-term rule of a sequence, justifying its form from the practical context. The work on squares and cubes from Chapter 1 is extended to finding powers and roots using the function button on a calculator. Students develop their use of index notation to using simple instances of the index laws. The chapter concludes by distinguishing between equations, identities and formulae.

The student book discusses the Italian mathematician Fibonacci and his work on sequences. Fibonacci was also known as Leonardo of Pisa where he was born in 1170. He described his model of the rabbit population in his book Liber Abaci in 1202 which introduced the Hindu-Arabic number system to Europe. Students may encounter Fibonacci sequences in unexpected places, in nature, in music, in art and in games and puzzles. There is a comprehensive description of Fibonacci's model of a rabbit population at http://www.mcs.surrey.ac.uk/Personal/R.Knott/Fibonacci/fibnat.html (I).

Extra Resources

10	Start of chapter presentation
10a	Animation: Sequences
10a	Animation: Sequences 2
10a	Worked solution: Q3a
10b	Worked solution: Q3a
10b	Consolidation sheet
10c	Starter: Arithmetic sequence multichoice
10d	Starter: Square and cube matching
10d	Worked solution: Q4a
10d	Consolidation sheet

Assessment: chapter 10

Fast-track

10a, b, c, d

- Generate terms of a sequence using term-to-term and position-to-term rules (L6)

Useful resources

•••

Starter − Connections

Ask students to give three sets of coordinates that lie on the following curves:

$y = x^2 + 3$ for example (0, 3) (-1, 4) (2, 7)

$y = x^2 + 3x + 3$ for example (0, 3) (1, 7) (-2, 1)

$y = 3 - x - x^2$ for example (0, 3) (2, -3) (-2, 1)

Ask students what they notice when $x = 0$.

(The point (0, 3) lies on all three curves.)

Teaching notes

Give the first few terms of a sequence. Can students spot the next two terms in the sequence by first describing the term-to-term rule? Do students know the name of the type of sequence? Give examples of

- Linear sequences, ascending and descending
- Square number sequence
- Triangular number sequence
- Fibonacci sequence
- Prime number sequence

A sequence can be defined by giving the first term and the term to term rule or by giving a position to term rule. We normally let the letter 'n' stand for the position of the term in the sequence. Examine the sequences generated by various position-to-term rules. The position-to-term rule is known as the nth term and can be written as $T(n)$. What is meant by $T(6)$? What is the advantage of the nth over the term to term rule? (1.1, 1.5)

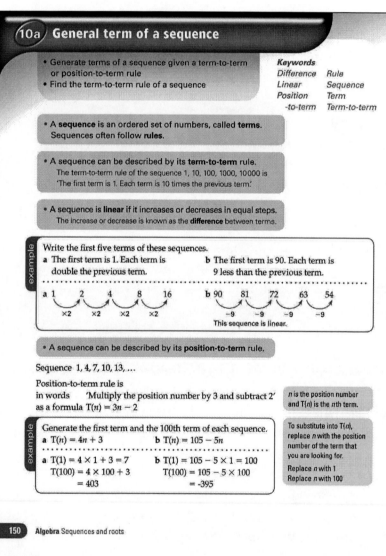

10a General term of a sequence

- Generate terms of a sequence given a term-to-term or position-to-term rule
- Find the term-to-term rule of a sequence

Keywords
Difference   Rule
Linear   Sequence
Position   Term
-to-term   Term-to-term

- A **sequence** is an ordered set of numbers, called **terms**. Sequences often follow **rules**.

- A sequence can be described by its **term-to-term** rule. The term-to-term rule of the sequence 1, 10, 100, 1000, 10000 is 'The first term is 1. Each term is 10 times the previous term.'

- A sequence is **linear** if it increases or decreases in equal steps. The increase or decrease is known as the **difference** between terms.

example

Write the first five terms of these sequences.

a The first term is 1. Each term is double the previous term.

b The first term is 90. Each term is 9 less than the previous term.

a 1   2   4   8   16
    ×2   ×2   ×2   ×2

b 90   81   72   63   54
     −9   −9   −9   −9
This sequence is linear.

- A sequence can be described by its **position-to-term** rule.

Sequence 1, 4, 7, 10, 13, ...

Position-to-term rule is

in words   'Multiply the position number by 3 and subtract 2'

as a formula $T(n) = 3n - 2$

n is the position number and $T(n)$ is the nth term.

example

Generate the first term and the 100th term of each sequence.

a $T(n) = 4n + 3$ b $T(n) = 105 - 5n$

a $T(1) = 4 \times 1 + 3 = 7$
   $T(100) = 4 \times 100 + 3$
         $= 403$

b $T(1) = 105 - 5 \times 1 = 100$
   $T(100) = 105 - 5 \times 100$
         $= -395$

To substitute into $T(n)$, replace n with the position number of the term that you are looking for.

Replace n with 1
Replace n with 100

150   Algebra Sequences and roots

Plenary

How is question **6** related to drawing graphs. Make the analogy with graphs of the form $y = mx + c$ and $y = x^2$. Experiment by drawing some of the graphs. What does the x-axis represent? (position) What does the gradient and y-intercept represent? (*m* represents the term-to-term rule, *c* represents the independent number in the $T(n)$ rule) (1.1)

Simplification

Provide a copy of the exercise and encourage students to annotate the sequences to help show the term-to-term rule. Alternatively, provide students with tables so they can insert the sequences and organise their results more clearly.

A calculator is not necessary. All questions (CT) (1.3)

Question 1 – Ask students what patterns they look for. They should share their approaches with each other (TW) (1.5).

Question 2 – Encourage the use of fractions if necessary.

Question 3 – Encourage students to check their theory for the term-to-term rule on every term. Is it possible that more than one rule may work? (1.4)

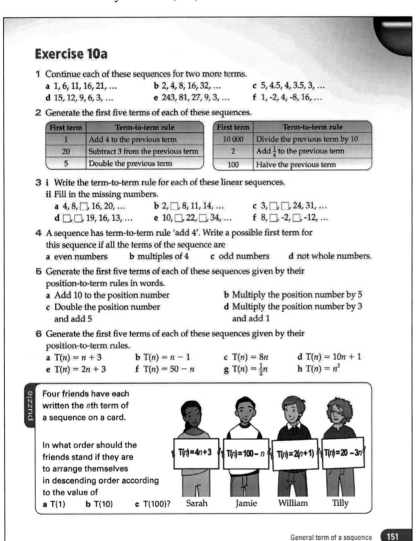

Exercise 10a

1 Continue each of these sequences for two more terms.
  a 1, 6, 11, 16, 21, …   **b** 2, 4, 8, 16, 32, …   **c** 5, 4.5, 4, 3.5, 3, …
  d 15, 12, 9, 6, 3, …   **e** 243, 81, 27, 9, 3, …   **f** 1, -2, 4, -8, 16, …

2 Generate the first five terms of each of these sequences.

First term	Term-to-term rule	First term	Term-to-term rule
1	Add 4 to the previous term	10 000	Divide the previous term by 10
20	Subtract 3 from the previous term	2	Add $\frac{1}{4}$ to the previous term
5	Double the previous term	100	Halve the previous term

3 **i** Write the term-to-term rule for each of these linear sequences.
  ii Fill in the missing numbers.
  a 4, 8, ☐, 16, 20, …   **b** 2, ☐, 8, 11, 14, …   **c** 3, ☐, ☐, 24, 31, …
  d ☐, ☐, 19, 16, 13, …   **e** 10, ☐, 22, ☐, 34, …   **f** 8, ☐, -2, ☐, -12, …

4 A sequence has term-to-term rule 'add 4'. Write a possible first term for this sequence if all the terms of the sequence are
  a even numbers   **b** multiples of 4   **c** odd numbers   **d** not whole numbers.

5 Generate the first five terms of each of these sequences given by their position-to-term rules in words.
  a Add 10 to the position number   **b** Multiply the position number by 5
  c Double the position number   **d** Multiply the position number by 3
     and add 5   and add 1

6 Generate the first five terms of each of these sequences given by their position-to-term rules.
  a $T(n) = n + 3$ **b** $T(n) = n - 1$ **c** $T(n) = 8n$ **d** $T(n) = 10n + 1$
  e $T(n) = 2n + 3$ **f** $T(n) = 50 - n$ **g** $T(n) = \frac{1}{2}n$ **h** $T(n) = n^2$

puzzle

Four friends have each written the nth term of a sequence on a card.

In what order should the friends stand if they are to arrange themselves in descending order according to the value of
  a T(1)   **b** T(10)   **c** T(100)?

$T(n) = 4n + 3$ $T(n) = 100 - n$ $T(n) = 2(n + 1)$ $T(n) = 20 - 3n$

Sarah   Jamie   William   Tilly

General term of a sequence   **151**

Extension

Set students questions similar to those in question **6** but that require the terms to be left in fractional form, for example, $T(n) = \dfrac{n}{n+1}$. Do not allow a calculator to be used (IE) (1.3).

Exercise 10a commentary

Question 4 – Can students generalise about the first term in each case. Encourage them to write down this generalisation in words.

Question 5 – Encourage students to use a table, listing the position numbers first. Draw an analogy with a table of values for the coordinates of a straight line graph.

Question 6 – What does 'n' represent in $T(n)$?. Use a table as described in question **5**.

Puzzle – Encourage students to show their workings in an organised way. Each solution is possible without using a calculator. Will the position they stand in ever change after T(100)? Does drawing a graph help? (1.1)

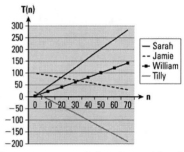

Assessment Criteria – Algebra, level 6: generate terms of a sequence using term-to term and position-to-term definitions of the sequence.

Links

The Look and Say sequence is a famous non-linear sequence that sometimes appears in puzzle books. The first seven terms are 1, 11, 21, 1211, 111221, 312211, 13112221, 1113213211. What is the rule for moving from one term to the next? (Describe the previous term in words and then write it in numbers, so one one; two ones; one two, two ones etc). Try starting the sequence with 2 or 3 instead of 1. See, http://en.wikipedia.org/wiki/Look_and_say_sequence (CT).

- Generate sequences from practical contexts and write and justify an expression to describe the nth term of an arithmetic sequence   (L6)

Useful resources

Starter – Connections

If $x = -2$, $y = -5$ and $z = 7$ ask students to write down ten equations connecting x, y and z. For example, $x - 2y = z + 1$ Encourage students to use all three letters in their rules.

Teaching notes

Write a linear sequence and ask students for the term-to-term rule. Show the term-to-term rule as the differences between successive terms and write the positions of the terms under the term values. For example,

$$\begin{array}{cccccc} & +3 & +3 & +3 & +3 \\ 5, & 8, & 11, & 14, & 17 \\ \text{positions} \quad 1 & 2 & 3 & 4 & 5 \end{array}$$

Is there a link between the positions and the value of the terms? Hint that the rule has something to do with the term-to-term rule. Establish that you need to multiply the positions by 3 to get close, but an extra +2 is needed in each case.

This rule is known as the 'position-to-term rule' or '*n*th term'. What letter is normally used for the positions? How is this rule written in algebra? ($3n + 2$) Will this approach work for all sequences? Will it depend on the type of sequence? Try a linear and non-linear sequence to establish the answer.

Look at an example of a linear sequence constructed from a series of diagrams. For example, triangles made from matchsticks. How can the number of 'matchsticks' be found for the 80th diagram? What sort of rule for the sequence will be most helpful in finding the answer? (CT)

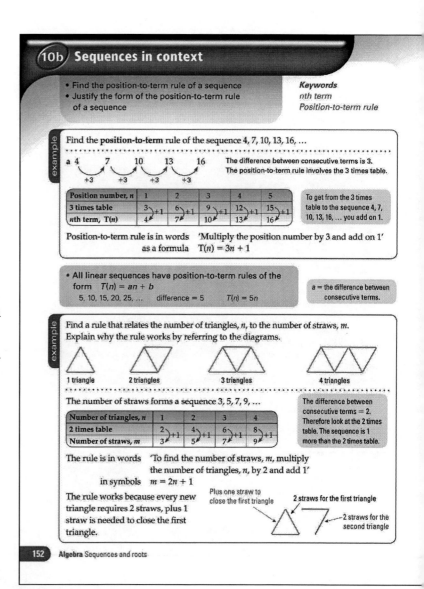

Plenary

When dealing with the *n*th term in a linear sequence, how can you quickly tell what *n* needs to be multiplied by? Look at the term-to-term rule. Is there a quick way, which does not involve a table of values, to tell what number to add? Using any linear sequence from the exercise, extend it backwards from the first term. Can anyone spot a connection? Why can you use the 'zeroth' term? (CT) (1.2)

Simplification

Provide a copy of the sequences in tables and encourage students to annotate the sequences in the way shown in the student book example. Encourage the use of arrows to show the thinking behind the patterns.

All questions (CT) (1.1, 1.4)

Question 1 – Encourage the use of the table. Some students maybe eager to race ahead, but more difficult sequences are likely to cause problems. How 'close' do you get to the sequence numbers when you multiply the positions by the term-to-term rule?

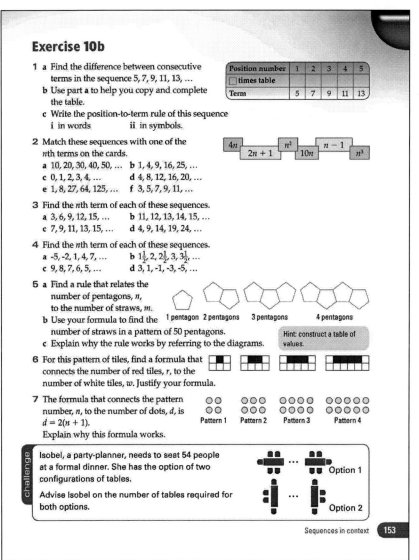

Exercise 10b

1 a Find the difference between consecutive terms in the sequence 5, 7, 9, 11, 13, …
   b Use part **a** to help you copy and complete the table.
   c Write the position-to-term rule of this sequence
      i in words   ii in symbols.

Position number	1	2	3	4	5
☐ times table					
Term	5	7	9	11	13

2 Match these sequences with one of the nth terms on the cards.
   a 10, 20, 30, 40, 50, …   b 1, 4, 9, 16, 25, …
   c 0, 1, 2, 3, 4, …   d 4, 8, 12, 16, 20, …
   e 1, 8, 27, 64, 125, …   f 3, 5, 7, 9, 11, …

   $4n$ $2n + 1$ n^2 $10n$ $n - 1$ n^3

3 Find the nth term of each of these sequences.
   a 3, 6, 9, 12, 15, …   b 11, 12, 13, 14, 15, …
   c 7, 9, 11, 13, 15, …   d 4, 9, 14, 19, 24, …

4 Find the nth term of each of these sequences.
   a -5, -2, 1, 4, 7, …   b $1\frac{1}{2}, 2, 2\frac{1}{2}, 3, 3\frac{1}{2}, …$
   c 9, 8, 7, 6, 5, …   d 3, 1, -1, -3, -5, …

5 a Find a rule that relates the number of pentagons, n, to the number of straws, m.
   b Use your formula to find the number of straws in a pattern of 50 pentagons.
   c Explain why the rule works by referring to the diagrams.

   1 pentagon 2 pentagons 3 pentagons 4 pentagons

   Hint: construct a table of values.

6 For this pattern of tiles, find a formula that connects the number of red tiles, r, to the number of white tiles, w. Justify your formula.

7 The formula that connects the pattern number, n, to the number of dots, d, is $d = 2(n + 1)$.
   Explain why this formula works.

   Pattern 1   Pattern 2   Pattern 3   Pattern 4

challenge

Isobel, a party-planner, needs to seat 54 people at a formal dinner. She has the option of two configurations of tables.

Advise Isobel on the number of tables required for both options.

Option 1

Option 2

Sequences in context 153

Extension

How many squares in each of these patterns?

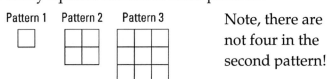

Pattern 1   Pattern 2   Pattern 3

Note, there are not four in the second pattern!

Give students a few minutes to search for the number of squares in the nth pattern. Ask them to see if $\dfrac{n(n+1)(2n+1)}{6}$ works (IE, SM).

Question 2 – For the cards that give 'simple' sequences, can you say what the term-to-term rule is? Students only need to write out the first couple of terms

Question 3 – Encourage the approach in question **1**. Some students may jump straight to the answer. Ensure this is checked against at least two of the terms.

Question 4 – Can students adopt the same method as used in questions **1** and **3**? Students often incorrectly think of 'divide' rather than 'multiplying a negative'.

Question 5 – Why might some people think that the term-to-term rule is 'add 5'? Reinforce that the number of pentagons just represents the term number (1.2).

Question 6 – In this case, students might like to try an alternative approach. Is there a quick way of counting the number of white tiles from the number of red tiles? (1.2)

Question 7 – What shapes are we dealing with here? Encourage students to think about area, as measured in small circles (1.2).

Challenge – How will students deal with spare chairs/tables? Do both arrangements take up the same area? Is there a formula which could be used to help (EP).

Assessment Criteria Algebra, level 6: write an expression to describe the nth term of an arithmetic sequence.

Links

Chronophotography is the art of taking a sequence of photographs of a moving object at regular time intervals. It was very popular with the Victorians. There are examples at http://www.sequences.org.uk/chrono1/0000.html

- Extend mental methods of calculating, working with powers and roots (L6)
- Use index notation with fractional powers (L7)
- Use the function keys (on a calculator) for powers and roots (L7)

Useful resources
Scientific calculator

Starter – Strange sequences

Write the following sequences on the board:
51, 48, 42, 33, 21… J, F, M, A, M… 3, -6, 12, -24, 48…2, 5, 10, 17, 26… S, M, T, W, T…
Ask students for the next two terms in each sequence.
Next terms are: 6, -12; J (June), J (July); -96, 192 (previous term ×-2); 37, 50; F (Friday), S (Saturday).
Can be extended by students making their own 'strange sequences'.

Teaching notes

What is meant by the 'square' and 'cube' of a number? Look at how these are written both for positive and negative values squared and cubed. What is the meaning of a square root? For example, what is $\sqrt{25}$ actually asking you to work out? What number do you square to get 25? Use arrow diagrams to show that squaring and square rooting are reverse processes. Use the same explanation to discuss the meaning of a cube root.

Find the square, cube, square root and cube root functions on students calculators. Note that some may need to use the power root function for cube roots.

What if a different power from 2 or 3 is needed? The calculator has a dedicated power button, this can appear as x^y , y^x , $\wedge$, x^n .
Experiment with its use. Try to solve a problem involving an unknown power. This may lead to the discussion of a non-integer power.

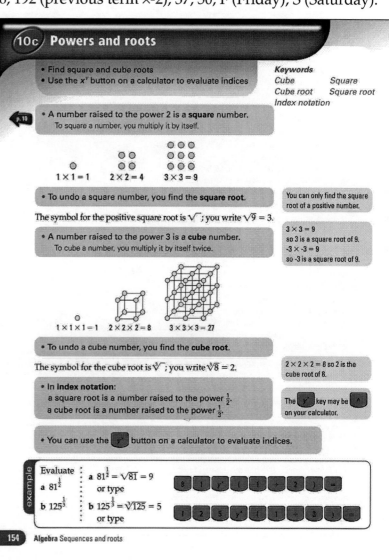

Plenary

Look at the sequence of Powers of 9 from 9^3 down to 9^0. What is the term-to-term rule? Answer, divide by 9. Fit $9^{1/2}$ into the pattern. It falls between 9^1 and 9^0. What should its value be to preserve the pattern? Does this help explain the meaning of a half power? (1.2)

$$\div 9 \qquad \div 9 \qquad \div? \qquad \div?$$
$$9^3 = 729 \rightarrow 9^2 = 81 \rightarrow 9^1 = 9 \rightarrow 9^{1/2} = 3 \rightarrow 9^0 = 1$$

Simplification

Help students to use their calculators efficiently by writing down the key strokes for obtaining the powers and roots required for this exercise for their calculator. This may involve the more complex power/root function. For finding roots, encourage students to write the question in an alternative way to help re-enforce understanding before trying the question. For example, $\sqrt[3]{125}$ means $x \times x \times x$ makes 125, what is x?

All questions (1.3)

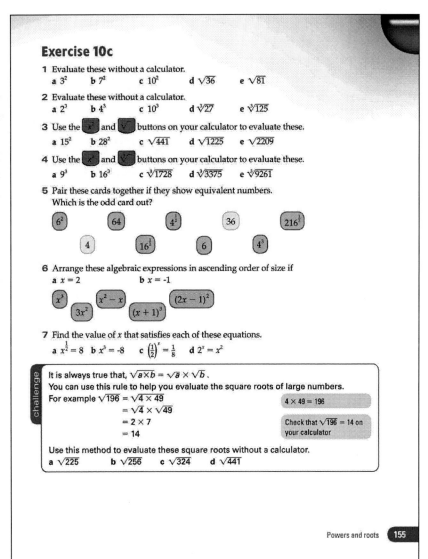

Extension

Can cube roots be simplified in the same way as the square roots in the challenge in the student book? For example, $\sqrt[3]{216} = \sqrt[3]{8 \times 27} = \sqrt[3]{8} \times \sqrt[3]{27} = 2 \times 3 = 6$. Set students other cube roots to practice simplifying. For example, 512, 1000, 1728. Students may be able to use product of prime factors to help (CT).

Exercise 10c commentary

Question 1 and **2** – Watch for students performing $\times 2$ or $\times 3$ rather than squaring or cubing. Ask students why they think their answers to parts **d** and **e** are correct? (RL) (1.2).

Question 3 and **4** – Be aware than some calculators do not have cube or cube root function keys. Some students may have to use the power or power root function. How can you check your answers to parts **c–e**?

Question 5 – Students are likely to need a reminder of the fractional index representation of square and cube roots.

Question 7 – In part **b**, remind students of the rules of arithmetic for negative numbers.

Question 7 – A calculator is an option in this question, depending on the level of difficulty required. Encourage students to use a variety of methods including trial and improvement (1.5).

Challenge – Students may need a few further examples of simple square roots before attempting the challenge. For example, $\sqrt{16}, \sqrt{36}, \sqrt{64}, \sqrt{81}$ (CT) (1.4).

Links

The sugar cube was invented in 1841 by Jakub Kryštof Rad in Dačice, Bohemia (now the Czech Republic). At this time, sugar was produced in a large, solid cone shape and had to be cut for the customer. Rad made his invention after his wife cut her finger slicing sugar. Sugar cubes first appeared in shops in Vienna in 1843. A granite monument of a sugar cube stands in the Town Square in Dačice. See, http://www.radio.cz/pictures/czech/dacice_cukr.jpg

- Use index notation for integer powers and simple
  instances of the index laws

Useful resources

(L7)

Starter – Power bingo

Ask students to draw a 3 × 3 grid and enter 9 numbers that are
square numbers (up to 144), cube numbers (up to 125) or triangular
numbers (up to 55).

Give possible numbers, for example, 6^2, second cube number,
fourth triangular number, *etc.*

Winner is the first student to cross out all their numbers.

Teaching notes

Why are powers useful in
mathematics? Discuss the way in
which they show repeated
multiplication. How are negative
numbers raised to a power? Stress the
importance of brackets because of the
BIDMAS rules. Remind students of
the power function on their
calculators, covered in the previous
spread.

How can indices be simplified? Look
at questions like those in the second
example from the student book. In the
case of multiplication, establish that
the indices are not multiplied. Show
this by writing out the meaning of the
calculation. Use a similar explanation
for division.

What happens to powers of different
bases? For example, $3^4 \times 2^5 \times 3^2 \times 2$.

What happens when a number is
already raised to a power and then is
powered again? Can this be
simplified? For example, $(5^3)^4$. Expand
the question and establish the
solution. Is there a convenient rule
that can be used?

Summarise the rules for indices.

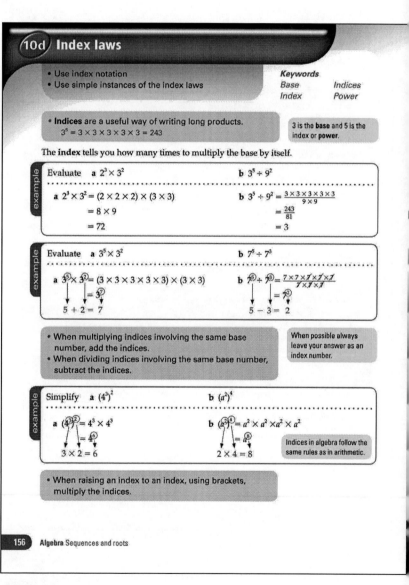

Plenary

Discuss the power to a power rule for question **5**. At this
stage it is probably unnecessary to look at the rule formally.
Discuss the type of errors students might make when tacking
questions like this, for example, $(3t^5)^2 = 6t^{10}$ (wrong!) (CT, RL)
(1.4)

Simplification

Although time consuming, encourage students to write out questions like **3** in full, at least initially. This may help to re-enforce why the rules of indices operate in the way they do. Students must not be allowed to just 'apply' the rules and make no attempt to understand 'why' they work.

All questions (1.3)

Question 1 – Encourage students to check their answers by evaluating them on a calculator, once in non simplified form and then using the power.

Question 2 – Some students may still be thinking of repeated addition. Why is writing out the question using multiplication signs not a good idea for every question?

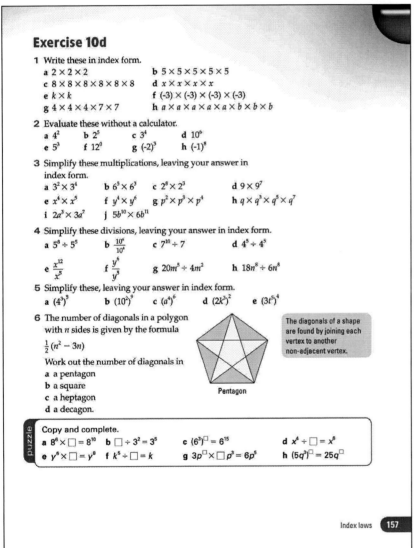

Exercise 10d

1 Write these in index form.
   a $2 \times 2 \times 2$
   b $5 \times 5 \times 5 \times 5 \times 5$
   c $8 \times 8 \times 8 \times 8 \times 8 \times 8$
   d $x \times x \times x \times x \times x$
   e $k \times k$
   f $(-3) \times (-3) \times (-3) \times (-3)$
   g $4 \times 4 \times 4 \times 7 \times 7$
   h $a \times a \times a \times a \times a \times b \times b \times b$

2 Evaluate these without a calculator.
   a 4^2 b 2^5 c 3^4 d 10^6
   e 5^3 f 12^0 g $(-2)^3$ h $(-1)^8$

3 Simplify these multiplications, leaving your answer in index form.
   a $3^2 \times 3^4$ b $6^5 \times 6^3$ c $2^8 \times 2^3$ d 9×9^7
   e $x^4 \times x^5$ f $y^4 \times y^6$ g $p^2 \times p^3 \times p^4$ h $q \times q^3 \times q^5 \times q^7$
   i $2a^3 \times 3a^7$ j $5b^{10} \times 6b^{11}$

4 Simplify these divisions, leaving your answer in index form.
   a $5^8 \div 5^5$ b $\frac{10^6}{10^4}$ c $7^{10} \div 7$ d $4^5 \div 4^5$
   e $\frac{x^{12}}{x^5}$ f $\frac{y^6}{y^5}$ g $20m^8 \div 4m^2$ h $18n^8 \div 6n^8$

5 Simplify these, leaving your answer in index form.
   a $(4^3)^5$ b $(10^2)^9$ c $(a^4)^6$ d $(2k^3)^2$ e $(3t^5)^4$

6 The number of diagonals in a polygon with n sides is given by the formula
   $\frac{1}{2}(n^2 - 3n)$
   Work out the number of diagonals in
   a a pentagon
   b a square
   c a heptagon
   d a decagon.

The diagonals of a shape are found by joining each vertex to another non-adjacent vertex.

Pentagon

puzzle

Copy and complete.
   a $8^6 \times \square = 8^{10}$ b $\square \div 3^2 = 3^5$ c $(6^3)^\square = 6^{15}$ d $x^4 \div \square = x^6$
   e $y^6 \times \square = y^8$ f $k^5 \div \square = k$ g $3p^\square \times \square p^3 = 6p^5$ h $(5q^3)^\square = 25q^\square$

Index laws   157

Extension

What is $(-1)^{20}$ and $(-1)^{25}$? What can you deduce about -1 to the power of any positive whole number? What about -1 to the power of a negative whole number? Would the plenary from exercise **10c** be of any help? Yes, replace 9 with -1 and look for a pattern in the results beyond zero (CT).

Exercise 10d commentary

Question 3 – Students maybe tempted to multiply the indices. Students should try to explain why you add the powers. In parts **i** and **j**, ask the students if the parts of the term can be 'moved around'. Which bits are calculated first?

Question 4 – Students may be tempted to divide the indices. Ask students to try to explain why you subtract the indices. In parts **g** and **h**, why do you subtract the indices, but divide the number?

Question 5 – Encourage students to first write out the question in expanded form. For example, $(3t^5)^4 = 3t^5 \times 3t^5 \times 3t^5 \times 3t^5$. Leave discussion of a new rule to the plenary.

Question 6 – No calculator. Some students might need to be reminded of the number of sides on a heptagon, or possibly a decagon.. Ask students to find the number of sides on a polygon that has 49 985 000 diagonals. A calculator would be needed. (10 000 a myriagon)

Puzzle – When finding the missing term, encourage students to check their solution using the rules from the exercise. Part **d** is particularly tricky. Can students see why? Can any of these be solved using similar methods to those of solving linear equations?

Links

In 1965 Gordon Moore the cofounder of the computer company Intel, made a prediction that the number of transistors that manufacturers could fit onto a silicon chip would double every two years. This means that every two years, computers become twice as powerful and computing costs get cheaper. A graph of Moore's law is at, http://en.wikipedia.org/wiki/Image:Moores_law.svg (EP).

- Distinguish the different roles played by letter symbols in equations, identities, formulae and functions (L6)
- Substitute numbers into expressions and formulae (L6)

Useful resources
Scientific calculator
for the plenary

Starter – All the nines!

Write the following five calculations on the board:

99×999, 99^3, $\sqrt{999999}$, $9(99 + 999)$, $\sqrt{99} \times 99^2$.

Ask students to estimate the answers and arrange them in order of size, smallest first.

Challenge students to explain their methods.

Correct order: $\sqrt{999999}$, $9(99 + 999)$, $\sqrt{99} \times 99^2$, 99×999, 99^3.

Teaching notes

Can students offer a solution for $3x + 4 = x + 4 + 2x$? Discuss the problems this causes. Why has this happened? Since both sides have exactly the same number of xs and the same constant value of 4, the two sides are 'identically equal'. This is known as an 'identity'. It is true for all x values.

What is the difference between an equation and an identity? Does an equation have to have only one solution? Does it have to have any solutions? Discuss this point and use examples to illustrate that equations can have no or a number of solutions. For example, $x = -1$, $x^2 = 25$. $(x - 1)(x - 2)(x - 3) = 0$.

Recap the methods of solving linear equations covered in spreads **7a** and **7b**. Continue to emphasise the importance of showing working on both sides and 'improving' the equation at every stage.

Recap the rules of BIDMAS to help with algebraic substitution, use examples like those in question **3**.

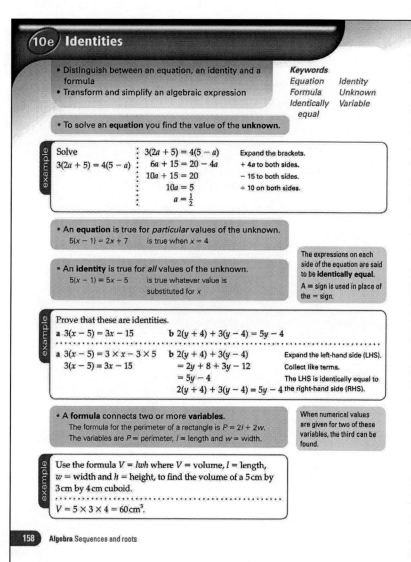

10e Identities

- Distinguish between an equation, an identity and a formula
- Transform and simplify an algebraic expression

Keywords
Equation   Identity
Formula   Unknown
Identically   Variable
equal

- To solve an **equation** you find the value of the **unknown**.

example

Solve	$3(2a + 5) = 4(5 - a)$	Expand the brackets.
$3(2a + 5) = 4(5 - a)$	$6a + 15 = 20 - 4a$	$+ 4a$ to both sides.
	$10a + 15 = 20$	$- 15$ to both sides.
	$10a = 5$	$\div 10$ on both sides.
	$a = \frac{1}{2}$	

- An **equation** is true for *particular* values of the unknown.
$5(x - 1) = 2x + 7$ is true when $x = 4$

- An **identity** is true for *all* values of the unknown.
$5(x - 1) \equiv 5x - 5$ is true whatever value is substituted for x

The expressions on each side of the equation are said to be **identically equal**.
A $\equiv$ sign is used in place of the $=$ sign.

example

Prove that these are identities.
a $3(x - 5) \equiv 3x - 15$ b $2(y + 4) + 3(y - 4) \equiv 5y - 4$

a $3(x - 5) = 3 \times x - 3 \times 5$ b $2(y + 4) + 3(y - 4)$ Expand the left-hand side (LHS).
$3(x - 5) \equiv 3x - 15$ $= 2y + 8 + 3y - 12$ Collect like terms.
                        $= 5y - 4$ The LHS is identically equal to
          $2(y + 4) + 3(y - 4) \equiv 5y - 4$ the right-hand side (RHS).

- A **formula** connects two or more **variables**.
The formula for the perimeter of a rectangle is $P = 2l + 2w$.
The variables are P = perimeter, l = length and w = width.

When numerical values are given for two of these variables, the third can be found.

example

Use the formula $V = lwh$ where V = volume, l = length, w = width and h = height, to find the volume of a 5 cm by 3 cm by 4 cm cuboid.

$V = 5 \times 3 \times 4 = 60 \text{ cm}^3$.

158   **Algebra** Sequences and roots

Plenary

There are some identities that use calculator functions that students probably have not come across before. Ask students to try to find the value of $(\sin x)^2 + (\cos x)^2$. What identity does this lead to? $(\sin x)^2 + (\cos x)^2 \equiv 1$ (CT).

Simplification

These identities can be checked by substituting two values into each side. Encourage students to use this method if it is more comfortable. If students are going to try to expand the brackets, suggest they attempt those involving '+' in front of a bracket rather than '−', at least initially.

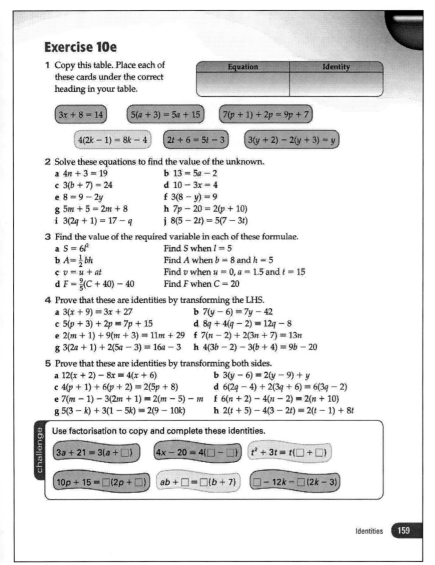

Exercise 10e

1 Copy this table. Place each of these cards under the correct heading in your table.

Equation	Identity

$3x + 8 = 14$

$5(a + 3) = 5a + 15$

$7(p + 1) + 2p = 9p + 7$

$4(2k − 1) = 8k − 4$

$2t + 6 = 5t − 3$

$3(y + 2) − 2(y + 3) = y$

2 Solve these equations to find the value of the unknown.
- **a** $4n + 3 = 19$
- **b** $13 = 5a − 2$
- **c** $3(b + 7) = 24$
- **d** $10 − 3x = 4$
- **e** $8 = 9 − 2y$
- **f** $3(8 − y) = 9$
- **g** $5m + 5 = 2m + 8$
- **h** $7p − 20 = 2(p + 10)$
- **i** $3(2q + 1) = 17 − q$
- **j** $8(5 − 2t) = 5(7 − 3t)$

3 Find the value of the required variable in each of these formulae.
- **a** $S = 6l^2$ — Find S when $l = 5$
- **b** $A = \frac{1}{2}bh$ — Find A when $b = 8$ and $h = 5$
- **c** $v = u + at$ — Find v when $u = 0$, $a = 1.5$ and $t = 15$
- **d** $F = \frac{9}{5}(C + 40) − 40$ — Find F when $C = 20$

4 Prove that these are identities by transforming the LHS.
- **a** $3(x + 9) \equiv 3x + 27$
- **b** $7(y − 6) \equiv 7y − 42$
- **c** $5(p + 3) + 2p \equiv 7p + 15$
- **d** $8q + 4(q − 2) \equiv 12q − 8$
- **e** $2(m + 1) + 9(m + 3) \equiv 11m + 29$
- **f** $7(n − 2) + 2(3n + 7) \equiv 13n$
- **g** $3(2a + 1) + 2(5a − 3) \equiv 16a − 3$
- **h** $4(3b − 2) − 3(b + 4) \equiv 9b − 20$

5 Prove that these are identities by transforming both sides.
- **a** $12(x + 2) − 8x \equiv 4(x + 6)$
- **b** $3(y − 6) \equiv 2(y − 9) + y$
- **c** $4(p + 1) + 6(p + 2) \equiv 2(5p + 8)$
- **d** $6(2q − 4) + 2(3q + 6) \equiv 6(3q − 2)$
- **e** $7(m − 1) − 3(2m + 1) \equiv 2(m − 5) − m$
- **f** $6(n + 2) − 4(n − 2) \equiv 2(n + 10)$
- **g** $5(3 − k) + 3(1 − 5k) \equiv 2(9 − 10k)$
- **h** $2(t + 5) − 4(3 − 2t) \equiv 2(t − 1) + 8t$

challenge

Use factorisation to copy and complete these identities.

$3a + 21 \equiv 3(a + \square)$

$4x − 20 \equiv 4(\square − \square)$

$t^2 + 3t \equiv t(\square + \square)$

$10p + 15 \equiv \square(2p + \square)$

$ab + \square \equiv \square(b + 7)$

$\square − 12k \equiv \square(2k − 3)$

Identities **159**

Extension

Create identities that involve fractions. Challenge a partner to check them. Challenge students to involve algebra in the denominator if possible (CT, TW).

Exercise 10e commentary

All questions (1.3)

Question 1 – Some students may think they need to solve the equations/identities. Ask, what happens when you try to solve an identity? (1.4)

Question 2 – Make reference to the methods used in spreads **7a** and **7b**. Students should still be encouraged to show working on both sides.

Question 3 – Students may need reminding of the rules of BIDMAS. Encourage students to break up the calculation into stages.

Questions 4 and **5** – When simplifying, students should show intermediate steps of working. Mistakes may well be made when brackets are multiplied by a negative coefficient. Ask, what number is multiplying the bracket? Since each part is to be proved as an identity, students should look for their mistakes when their working seems to contradict this (RL).

Challenge – Students should check their answers by expanding the brackets. Have the expressions been factorised using the largest possible factor? Are several answers possible?

Assessment Criteria – Algebra, level 5: Use simple formulae involving one or two operations. Algebra, level 7: substitute numbers into expressions and formulae.

Links

Equations are used in Chemistry to describe reactions. The chemicals that react are on one side of the equation and the chemicals that they produce are on the other. A balanced equation has equal numbers of each type of atom on each side of the equation. There is a calculator to balance chemical equations at www.webqc.org/balance.php (EP).

(10) Consolidation

1 Continue each of these sequences for two more terms.

   a 3, 6, 9, 12, 15, …   **b** 2, 5, 8, 11, 14, …

   c 1, 10, 100, 1000, 10 000, …   **d** 50, 44, 38, 32, 26, …

   e $1, 1\frac{1}{2}, 2, 2\frac{1}{2}, 3,$ …   **f** 1024, 512, 256, 128, 64, …

   g 2, 1.8, 1.6, 1.4, 1.2, …   **h** 1, 8, 27, 64, 125, …

2 **i** Write the term-to-term rule for each of these linear sequences.

   ii Fill in the missing numbers.

   a 4, ☐, 14, 19, 24, …   **b** 2, ☐, ☐, 14, 18, …

   c ☐, ☐, -1, -4, -7, …   **d** 5, ☐, 19, ☐, 33, …

3 Generate the first five terms of each of these sequences given by their position-to-term rules.

   a $T(n) = n + 10$ **b** $T(n) = 2n$

   c $T(n) = n - 5$ **d** $T(n) = \frac{n}{3}$

   e $T(n) = 2n + 1$ **f** $T(n) = 10 - n$

   g $T(n) = 5n - 2$ **h** $T(n) = 23 - 3n$

4 Find the nth term of each of these sequences.

   a 5, 10, 15, 20, 25, …   **b** 1, 4, 7, 10, 13, …

   c -2, 0, 2, 4, 6, …   **d** 5, 4, 3, 2, 1, …

5 **a** For this pattern of tiles, find a rule that relates the pattern number, n, to the number of tiles, t.

   b Use your formula to find the number of tiles in pattern number 100.

   c Explain why your rule works by referring to the diagrams.

  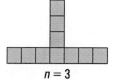

         $n = 1$ $n = 2$ $n = 3$

6 **a** For this pattern of tiles, find a rule that relates the number of red tiles, r, to the number of white tiles, w.

   b Use your formula to find the number of tiles in pattern number 100.

   c Explain why your rule works by referring to the diagrams.

  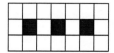

7 Evaluate these without a calculator.

    a 4^2 **b** 3^3 **c** 8^2 **d** 5^3 **e** 12^2

8 Evaluate these without a calculator.

    a $\sqrt{25}$ **b** $\sqrt{49}$ **c** $\sqrt[3]{8}$ **d** $\sqrt{121}$ **e** $\sqrt[3]{64}$

9 Find the value of x that satisfies each of these equations.

    a $x^{\frac{1}{2}} = 6$ **b** $64^x = 4$ **c** $x^{0.5} = 10$ **d** $\left(\frac{1}{4}\right)^x = \frac{1}{16}$

10 Simplify these, giving your answer in index form.

    a $2^3 \times 2^5$ **b** $4^8 \times 4^2$ **c** 7×7^4 **d** $5^7 \times 5^2$

    e $a^4 \times a^6$ **f** $b^3 \times b^2 \times b$ **g** $2x^7 \times 5x^2$ **h** $3y^3 \times 4y^8$

11 Simplify these, giving your answer in index form.

    a $6^7 \div 6^4$ **b** $10^6 \div 10$ **c** $\dfrac{8^4}{8^3}$

    d $\dfrac{p^{10}}{p^3}$ **e** $16k^8 \div k^6$ **f** $12t^8 \div 6t^8$

12 Simplify these, giving your answer in index form.

    a $\left(3^5\right)^2$ **b** $\left(12^3\right)^5$ **c** $\left(m^4\right)^9$ **d** $\left(n^2\right)^7$ **e** $\left(4d^5\right)^3$

13 Prove that these are identities by transforming the LHS.

    a $4(x + 7) \equiv 4x + 28$ **b** $6(2y - 5) \equiv 12y - 30$

    c $2m + 5(m - 3) \equiv 7m - 15$ **d** $10(n + 1) + 3(n - 4) \equiv 13n - 2$

    e $4(3k - 5) + 5(k + 4) \equiv 17k$ **f** $8(2t - 1) - 5(3t + 2) \equiv t - 18$

14 Prove that these are identities by transforming both sides.

    a $3(x + 5) + 7x \equiv 5(2x + 3)$ **b** $8(2y - 1) \equiv 12y + 4(y - 2)$

    c $15a - 3(a - 4) \equiv 12(a + 1)$ **d** $4(b + 1) + 2(3b + 4) \equiv 2(5b + 6)$

    e $3(3p + 4) - 2(4p - 1) \equiv 2(p + 7) - p$ **f** $4(3 - q) - 10(1 - 2q) \equiv 2(8q + 1)$

10 Summary

Assessment criteria

- Generate terms of a linear sequence using term-to-term and position-to-term definitions of the sequence   Level 6
- Write an expression to describe the nth term of an arithmetic sequence   Level 6

Question commentary

Example	The example illustrates a question on using index notation. Discuss how the index laws could be used to answer this question. Emphasise that the answer should state clearly the values of p, q and r.	**a** $p = 2 + 5 = 7$ **b** $q = 6 - 2 = 4$ **c** $r = 4 \times 2 = 8$

Past question	The question requires students to match generated terms of a sequence with the general term. Students may find this daunting as three of the four sequences are quadratic and so the descriptions will be unfamiliar. Encourage a logical approach, substituting $n = 1$, $n = 2$, $n = 3$, *etc.* into each description for the nth term and comparing the results with the given number sequences. Part **b** asks students to generate terms of a cubic sequence.	**Answer**
		
		Level 7
		2 a $4n$ 4, 8, 12, 16, …
		     $(n + 1)^2$ 4, 9, 16, 25, …
		     $n^2 + 3$ 4, 7, 12, 19, …
		     $n(n + 3)$ 4, 10, 18, 28, …
		 b 4, 11, 30, 67

Development and links

The topic of sequences links with work on proportion in Chapters 12 and 13 and is developed further in Year 9.

Sequences are found in all subjects of the curriculum: in the study of the natural world in science, in musical scales, in patterns in art and design, in tool sizes in technology, in sequences of dates in history and in sequences of instructions in ICT. Square and cube roots are used to find distances from known areas or volumes, for example the diagonal of a square piece of wood in technology.

11 Collecting and representing data

Statistics

Objectives

- Identify possible primary or secondary sources **6**
- Design a survey or experiment to capture the necessary data from one or more sources **6**
- Design, trial and if necessary refine data collection sheets **6**
- Determine the sample size and most appropriate degree of accuracy **6**
- Construct tables for gathering large discrete and continuous sets of raw data, choosing suitable class intervals **6**
- Select, construct and modify, on paper and using ICT, suitable graphical representations to progress an enquiry and identify key features present in the data. Include
  – line graphs for time series **6**
- Suggest a problem to explore using statistical methods, frame questions and raise conjectures **7**

Level

MPA

1.1	11a, d, e, f, g
1.2	11a, b, c, d, f, g
1.3	11d, e, f
1.4	11a, b, c, e, f, g
1.5	11a, b, c, d, e, f, g

PLTS

IE	11a, b, c, d, f, g
CT	11a, b, c, d, e, f, g
RL	11a, b, d, e, f
TW	11a, b, c, e, f, g
SM	11c, d
EP	11I, a, b, c, d, e, f, g

Introduction

The focus of this chapter is on the methods used in statistical enquiries to collect and represent data and begins by discussing the data-handling cycle. Students plan how to collect data, identifying areas for research and sources of data, consider methods of collecting data including the effect of sample size and construct frequency tables for large sets of discrete and continuous data. They construct stem-and-leaf diagrams and other graphical representations and charts, considering the advantages and disadvantages of different types of chart. The chapter extends to interpreting time series and comparative bar charts.

The student book discusses organisations that collect data and carry out surveys to inform their decisions. Statistical surveys and censuses are carried out for many reasons. They may provide factual information about the population or they may ask for opinions. They may ask the entire population or a representative sample of the population. They may be conducted by telephone, by questionnaire, online, at home, in the street, or information may be gathered from use of a loyalty card. The Data Protection Act states that the information can only be used for the specific purpose for which it was collected (EP).

Extra Resources

11	Start of chapter presentation
11b	Starter: Statistics multichoice
11c	Consolidation sheet
11d	Consolidation sheet
11f	Worked solution: Q1
11f	Consolidation sheet
	Assessment: chapter 11

Fast-track

11a, b, c, d, e, g

- Discuss a problem that can be addressed by statistical methods and identify related questions to explore (L6)

Useful resources

Starter – Today's number is ...72

Ask questions based on 'Today's number', for example,

What is one third of 72 and add 3? (27)

What is the nearest prime number to 72? (73)

How many factors of 72 are square numbers? (4)

What is 17.5% of 72? (12.6)

The square root of 72 lies between which two whole numbers? (8, 9)

Teaching notes

Discuss an issue that is relevant at the students' school/college. If students' views were to be sought in a survey, what factors would be of importance/relevance?

What sort of information would you need to collect? For example, age, ethnicity, gender. Are these factors relevant to the issue being discussed? Consider a wide range of factors.

Pick a completely different issue that is unrelated to the school, but relevant to young people. What factors are relevant in this case? (TW) (1.5)

Will it be possible to collect information from people relating to these factors? Can students see any potential problems? For example, is some of the information of a personal nature? Can students suggest a way round this? A confidential questionnaire or response sections that include a range of responses, for example, income £20–30 per week.

When collecting this information, will it be easy to analyse it? Can it be averaged or easily to put categories? (1.2)

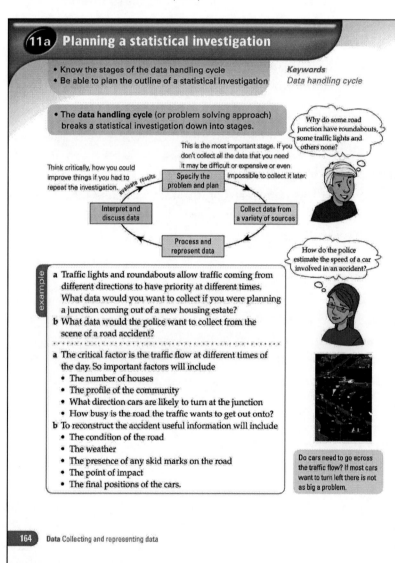

Plenary

With the whole class, look at the Office for National Statistics (ONS) website. What sort of information can be found? Encourage students to suggest a common line of enquiry and see if the ONS website can offer any data to help investigate further. (EP, TW)

Simplification

Suggest a number of possible responses to the questions. Which do students think are most appropriate?

Exercise 11a

1. A psychologist wants to look at factors affecting memory. She thinks gender is likely to be a factor, that is, males and females might be different.
   a How could the psychologist test her theory?
   b Write down any other factors which you think might make a difference to memory.

2. A road safety organisation is concerned about the speeds of cars on the road. They want to plan an advertising campaign to target groups of drivers. They plan to do some research to find out what types of drivers, or types of cars, are particularly bad about speed on the roads.
   Suggest categories of people or types of cars which you think they should look at.

3. A medical student is doing some research into the effects of alcohol on people's reaction times. He plans to measure their reaction times without taking any alcohol, and also after taking 1, 2 and 3 units of alcohol. A friend tells him that alcohol affects women more.
   Suggest other factors which might make a difference to the effect of the alcohol.

4. A transport manager has to estimate how long it will take his drivers to make deliveries to clients so he can plan the work.
   Apart from the distance to the client, what other factors should he take into consideration in estimating the time for each delivery?

> **discussion**
> Look back at the different factors you have suggested in each of the investigations. Would you be able to collect data on each of them easily?

Extension

If you want to discover if GCSE results have improved over the last five years at your school, how would you look at the data? Could you just see how many students passed? If possible, obtain the results and analyse them. Why are you unlikely to be provided with the students names? (confidential data) (EP) (1.1)

Exercise 11a commentary

All questions (IE, CT, EP) (1.1, 1.2)

Question 1 – Discuss the students' tests from the point of view of the answers they may give. In part **b**, students should restrict themselves to factors that can be measured and have a likely bearing on memory. Do not allow factors like 'favourite movie', 'hair length' (1.5).

Question 2 – This question suggests that 'research' is to be undertaken. Students need to bear this in mind when they are deciding what categories to use.

Question 3 – Students should try to keep the factors to those that can be measured. Focus on physical factors of the subject involved.

Question 4 – Some members of the class may have experience in making deliveries. What factors can they think of that effected delivery time?

Discussion – In the light of this discussion, would it be sensible to adjust any of your answers? (RL) (1.4, 1.5)

Assessment Criteria – HD, level 5: ask questions, plan how to answer them and collect data required.

Links

The traffic light was invented before the motor car. In 1868 a gas-powered lantern was used to control the horse-drawn and pedestrian traffic at a junction outside the Houses of Parliament in London. The lantern had rotating red and green lamps which were turned manually to face the oncoming traffic. The lantern exploded on January 2, 1869 and injured its operator. There is more information about traffic lights at http://www.bbc.co.uk/dna/h2g2/A9559407

- Suggest a problem to explore using statistical methods, frame questions and raise conjectures   (L7)

Useful resources

Starter – Distribution

Ask students to find six non-zero single digits that have the same value for the mean, median, mode and range.
(possible answer: 3, 5, 6, 6, 7, 9 average = 6)
What other mean values can they make?)

Teaching notes

Define a hypothesis as 'a statement that you believe is true, that can be tested using evidence'. What conclusions might you arrive at about a hypothesis?

Ask students to write a hypothesis relating to height and weight. What mistake might some students make? They write a question rather than a statement (RL) (1.5).

What data would need to be collected to test the hypothesis? How could you ask for someone's weight without making it too personal a question? Discuss the way in which a grouped response section can be used. Look at the problem of overlapping groups.

Look at the example; discuss the need to choose people from different categories if you feel that certain factors need to be looked at. Can students offer alternative answers to the example? Based on current experience, what conclusion do students think would be reached relating to this hypothesis? (TW, EP)

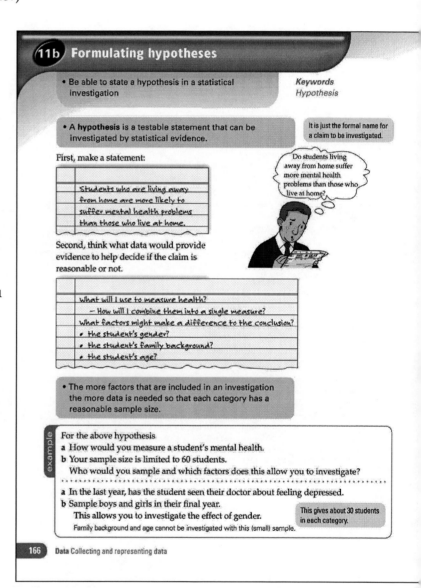

Plenary

Look back at question **3**. How can you compare the speed and speed limit? Encourage the use of both **i** difference **ii** percentage increase (IE).

Simplification

Allow students to work in pairs and make use of each others answers for question **2**. Encourage students to discuss why they are choosing a particular factor to be sampled (TW) (1.5).

Exercise 11b

1 For each of the following situations, write a formal hypothesis.
   a Do males have better memories than females?
   b Does memory get worse as you get older?
   c Do people under 22 drive faster than older people?
   d Do drivers of performance cars drive faster than drivers of family cars?
   e Does the same amount of alcohol have a bigger effect on people who do not normally drink alcohol?
   f Does the time of day affect how long it will take to make a delivery to a client?

2 Look back at the factors you considered in questions 1–4 in the previous spread. If your sample will only be large enough to allow you to consider two factors in each case, write down the factors you think should be taken.

3 Look at the data collection sheet below, which shows the first three records in a large set. Write down three hypotheses which could be investigated using this data set.

The legal limit for alcohol level when driving is 80 mg/100 millilitres of blood.

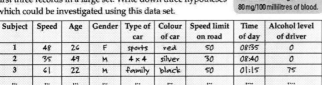

Subject	Speed	Age	Gender	Type of car	Colour of car	Speed limit on road	Time of day	Alcohol level of driver
1	48	26	F	sports	red	50	08:35	0
2	35	49	M	4 × 4	silver	30	08:40	0
3	61	22	M	family	black	50	01:15	75
...	...	...	...	...	...	...	...	...

discussion

A More males smoke than females.
B There is no difference in smoking between males and females.

Both the above hypotheses relate to the numbers of males and females who smoke.
Is there any difference between them?
Is one better than the other?

Formulating hypotheses **167**

Extension

A manufacturer claims that there are 40 matches on average in a box. What is the alternative to this hypothesis? There are less than 40 matches on average. Why does the alternative not include more than 40 matches?

A manufacturer claims that their nails are 3.2 cm long on average. What is the alternative to this hypothesis? The nails are not 3.2 cm long on average. Why does the alternative include both longer and shorter nails? (CT) (1.2)

Exercise 11b commentary

All questions (IE) (1.2, 1.4)

Question 1 – Encourage students to write the hypothesis that they believe is true. Verbally, can they suggest why? Ensure full sentences are used.

Question 2 – Why did students make these choices? (1.5)

Question 3 – Assume there will be a large data set. Which categories are not likely to be useful? Colour of car; although some students may try to argue the contrary.

Discussion – Discuss what the truth might be for male and female smokers. That is **i** More males smoke than females **ii** No difference between number of male and female smokers **iii** More females smoke than males. What is the alternate to the first hypothesis? What is the alternative to the second hypothesis? (1.5)

Assessment Criteria – HD, level 7: suggest a problem to explore using statistical methods, frame questions and raise conjectures.

Links

In 1811, the Italian scientist Amedeo Avogadro made a famous hypothesis that equal volumes of gases, at the same temperature and pressure, contain equal numbers of molecules. His work was ignored during most of his lifetime as the scientific community did not agree with his hypothesis. However, the hypothesis was later proved correct and is now known as Avogadro's Law. (TW, EP)

- Decide which data to collect to answer a question and the degree of accuracy needed (L6)
- Identify possible primary or secondary sources (L6)

Useful resources

Starter – Numbered cubes

Ask students to imagine a bag containing 10 cubes numbered 1, 2 or 5.
Cubes are drawn out of the bag and replaced each time.
Write numbers on the board, for example,
5, 1, 5, 5, 2, 2, 2, 5, 2, 5, 2, 2, 2, 2, 5, 2, 2, 2, 5, 2
Ask students to estimate how many of each number there are in the bag?
(for example, 1 × 1, 2 × 6, 5 × 3)
What is the average of the numbers pulled out? (3)

Teaching notes

Collecting data is a multi-million pound international business. Why is collecting data so important to so many companies? Discuss what companies do with their data. For example, design new products, improve their advertising methods, open new branches.

Some data is difficult to collect. Ask students for examples of types of data would be difficult for the following reasons, take too long, cost too much, too much effort, too personal/confidential, access would be denied, can't be measured effectively.

In each case suggest a way in which an attempt could be made to collect the data. For example, using a convenience sample to cut down on cost or applying to the police for data to help in your investigation.

What are students' experiences of taking part in surveys? How were they approached? What tactics do street surveyors use to try to stop people and encourage them to take part in a survey? (EP)

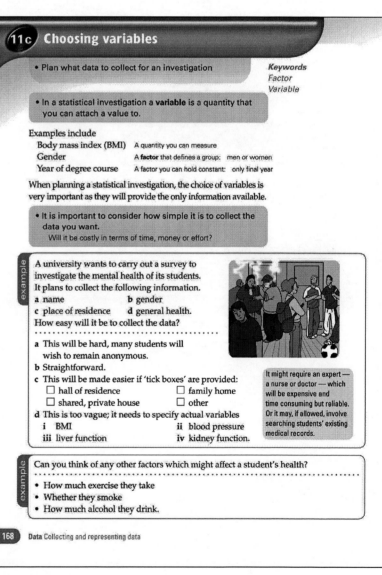

Plenary

Ask the class for their ideas on the relative importance of the factors in either **1a** or **1b**. Is there much agreement between the pupils? Is there a good statistical way to measure the amount of agreement between the students? (CT) (1.5)

Simplification

Rather than writing multiple detailed response sections to collect data, encourage students to give an example of a possible response box to show how responses might be collected.

Exercise 11c

1 For the following situations, say whether you think data could be collected on each of the variables, and if so how.

Some data is easy to collect. Some is very difficult or expensive to collect. Some requires special powers, such as only the police have.

a Volunteers are being used to investigate the effects of alcohol on reaction times. The variables being considered are
 i   age
 ii gender
 iii weight
 iv how used to drinking alcohol is the person
 v   are they taking medication
 vi how tired the person feels.

b A large teaching hospital is planning to conduct a study on the factors leading to increased risk of heart disease. The variables being considered are
 i   age   ii gender
 iii weight   iv blood pressure
 v   amount smoked   vi alcohol consumption

c A major study into the mental health of students is commissioned by the government. The variables being considered are
 i   age   ii   gender
 iii whether living at home   iv   amount of student debt
 v   in a stable relationship vi   family economic circumstances
 vii general health   viii academic performance.

2 A botanist wants to investigate the best conditions for growing a particular species. Make a list of variables which you think are factors he should consider and say how each might be measured.

discussion

Government need to have information about people to make decisions about health, education, policing and many other policies. People have a right to privacy about their own affairs if they are not breaking any laws. Sometimes these two considerations are in conflict.
When they conflict, which should be regarded as the more important?

Choosing variables **169**

Extension

Investigate different methods of sampling, for example, systematic, convenience, quota, cluster, random. A GCSE Statistic text book is a good reference to use if available (IE, SM).

Exercise 11c commentary

All questions (IE) (1.2, 1.5)

Question 1 – What sort of questions could be asked to get a reliable result? Focus particularly on the more difficult variables, such as, how tired someone feels.

Question 2 – The term 'botanist' may need explaining. Encourage students to be imaginative if they lack the botanical knowledge necessary. For example, moisture in the soil, hours of sunlight, distance from nearest plant, noise level (CT).

Discussion – Discuss the use of the national census. How often is it carried out? (every 10 years) When is the next one? (2011) What questions does it ask? Who is allowed to look at it? Is there a restriction on what information you can access? Can you look at all the information from very old ones? If so, how far back? (TW, EP)

Assessment Criteria – HD, level 6: design a survey or experiment to capture the necessary data from one or more sources

Links

Body Mass Index (BMI) is a relationship between weight and height that is associated with total body fat content for adults. BMI is calculated as body weight (kg) divided by the square of height (m). A person with a BMI of over 25 is considered overweight and can have an increased risk of disease such as heart disease and type II diabetes. There is a BMI calculator at http://www.nhsdirect.nhs.uk/magazine/interactive/bmi/index.aspx (EP)

- Design a survey or experiment to capture necessary data from one or more sources (L6)
- Design, trial and if necessary refine data collection sheets (L6)
- Determine the sample size and most appropriate degree of accuracy (L6)

Useful resources

Starter – Student survey

Draw a Venn diagram on the board with three different attributes, for example, brown eyes, cereal for breakfast, did homework last night.

Enter possible numbers or enter students' own data and ask questions. For example, how many students have brown eyes, did not have cereal for breakfast and did their homework last night?

Teaching notes

Suppose you wish to find out if men or woman are more likely to pass their driving test first time. What information do you need to have? Is it necessary to design a questionnaire and print one for every person you ask? Establish that you are simply collecting very basic data and a single 'record sheet' of all your results will supply you with all the relevant information. Show how this record sheet could be drawn up as a two-way table (1.3).

Suppose you wish to investigate if men or woman are safer drivers. What sort of information do you need to have? Discuss. In this case a carefully designed questionnaire is needed. Discuss the rules for designing good questions

- Questions must be very clear what they are asking, unambiguous
- Questions must not be too personal/rude
- Questions must have a clear set of possible responses, for example, scale 1–5
- Questions must not be biased/leading towards a specific response

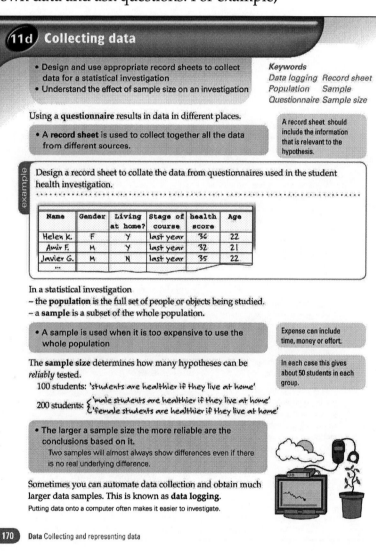

Plenary

Carry out the collection of data for ten random members of the class. How can people be chosen randomly? An internet search for a random number generator will allow the selection of a number to match the class register. Can any of the hypothesis suggested for question **2** be tested against the collected data? Is a sample of ten reliable?(IE, RL) (1.5)

Simplification

Provide students with an outline of a questionnaire and a data record sheet for question **1** to help emphasise the difference. Allow the students to select the appropriate detail.

Exercise 11d

1 Katie wants to investigate how long pupils sleep on nights before schooldays. She thinks that there may be differences between boys and girls, that it may change with age and that it may be different for single children and those with brothers or sisters.

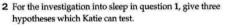
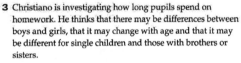
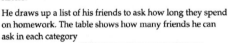

Questionnaire reminders

- Ask relevant questions.
- Avoid biased questions.
- Make questions and answer options unambiguous.
- Make it easy to complete; use 'tick boxes' and include an 'other' option.
- Avoid personal questions.

  a Design a short questionnaire she could use to collect the information she is interested in from each person.

  b Design a record sheet to show all the data together.

2 For the investigation into sleep in question **1**, give three hypotheses which Katie can test.

3 Christiano is investigating how long pupils spend on homework. He thinks that there may be differences between boys and girls, that it may change with age and that it may be different for single children and those with brothers or sisters.

He draws up a list of his friends to ask how long they spend on homework. The table shows how many friends he can ask in each category

	Age 12	Age 13	Age 14	Age 15
Boys, only child	7	8	2	1
Girls, only child	5	5	0	1
Boys with siblings	12	16	5	2
Girls with siblings	10	13	3	3

  a Make one criticism of how Christiano plans to collect the data other than some sample sizes.

  b The small numbers in some of the groups means that Christiano will not be able to answer all of the questions he was interested in. What would he have enough information to investigate?

task
How could Christiano improve the survey described in question **3**?

Collecting data **171**

Extension

What are the advantages/disadvantages of the following methods of data collection, postal questionnaire, telephone canvassing, email questionnaires, asking people in the street, asking your friends. How do companies improve the response rate for each of these methods? (EP, RL) (1.4, 1.5)

All questions (CT)

Question 1 – The questionnaire should be able to be filled in by the pupil you are collecting data for. Each question needs to make sense and a clear space needs to be made for the possible responses. The data record sheet is used for collecting data for lots of students. Look at the example as a possible guide (1.1).

Question 2 – The hypothesis should be able to be tested using the data collected in question **1**. Encourage students to write hypothesis they think are true (1.1, 1.2).

Question 3 – The main criticism relates to using 'convenient' data. Why is this a problem? This may need careful discussion. Use more obvious examples of convenience data being biased. For example, a professional footballer wants to investigate people's average salary (RL) (1.5).

Discussion – What sample sizes are reliable? If we accept that Christiano needs to ask people other than his friends, how can he choose the people? (RL) (1.5)

Assessment Criteria – HD, level 6: design, trial and if necessary refine data collection sheets.

Links

The UK Census has been held every ten years since 1801. It covers the entire population of the UK on one particular day. Information from a past census is useful to people trying to research their family history as it lists all the people living in a particular household on the day the census was taken. Information from censuses taken up until 1901 can be viewed at http://www.nationalarchives.gov.uk/census/ (EP).

- Construct tables for gathering large discrete and continuous sets of raw data, choosing suitable class intervals

Useful resources

(L6)

Starter – Favourite crisps

A pie chart shows the favourite crisps of 60 students.

The flavours and angles are: onion, chicken, plain, prawn, salt & vinegar, 30°, 36°, 60°, 90° and 144°.

25% of students preferred prawn.

Twice as many preferred salt & vinegar to chicken.

$\frac{1}{10}$ preferred plain.

Ask students to match angles and flavours. How many students prefer each flavour? What percentage of students prefer onion? (40%)

Teaching notes

Look at a set of ordered, raw, skewed data. How can the data be represented in a grouped frequency table? How many groups would be sensible? As a guide suggest between 4 and 8. Ask students to suggest group widths. How can the group widths/class intervals be written in so that overlapping does not occur? Make use of inequality signs if necessary.

Would a frequency table have been of more use in the case of this data? Which of these two types of table would be more useful for representing the number of goals scored by a single player over an entire season? Hint that they are only likely to have ever scored between 0 and 4 goals in a match.

How can the group/interval containing the median result be found for the first set of data? Hopefully if the data is skewed it will not lie in the middle interval. Discuss the method of counting through the data to the 'middle'.

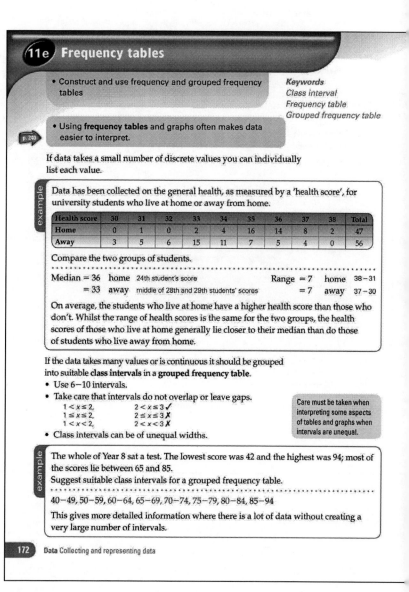

11e Frequency tables

- Construct and use frequency and grouped frequency tables

Keywords
Class interval
Frequency table
Grouped frequency table

- Using **frequency tables** and graphs often makes data easier to interpret.

If data takes a small number of discrete values you can individually list each value.

example

Data has been collected on the general health, as measured by a 'health score', for university students who live at home or away from home.

Health score	30	31	32	33	34	35	36	37	38	Total
Home	0	1	0	2	4	16	14	8	2	47
Away	3	5	6	15	11	7	5	4	0	56

Compare the two groups of students.

Median = 36   home   24th student's score   Range = 7   home   38−31
        = 33   away   middle of 28th and 29th students' scores   = 7   away   37−30

On average, the students who live at home have a higher health score than those who don't. Whilst the range of health scores is the same for the two groups, the health scores of those who live at home generally lie closer to their median than do those of students who live away from home.

If the data takes many values or is continuous it should be grouped into suitable **class intervals** in a **grouped frequency table**.
- Use 6–10 intervals.
- Take care that intervals do not overlap or leave gaps.

$1 < x \leq 2,$ $2 < x \leq 3$ ✓
$1 \leq x \leq 2,$ $2 \leq x \leq 3$ ✗
$1 < x < 2,$ $2 < x < 3$ ✗

Care must be taken when interpreting some aspects of tables and graphs when intervals are unequal.

- Class intervals can be of unequal widths.

example

The whole of Year 8 sat a test. The lowest score was 42 and the highest was 94; most of the scores lie between 65 and 85.
Suggest suitable class intervals for a grouped frequency table.

40−49, 50−59, 60−64, 65−69, 70−74, 75−79, 80−84, 85−94

This gives more detailed information where there is a lot of data without creating a very large number of intervals.

172   Data Collecting and representing data

Plenary

Discuss the various strategies used by members of the class to handle large amounts of data. What did students find successful and unsuccessful? Is there a broad agreement in as to the most efficient method? (EP, RL) (1.5)

Simplification

Provide students with a copy of the data to allow them to cross off the data as they go. Ask students to check with partners to see if they agree on the number of data results in each interval. Can they work together efficiently? (TW)

Question 1 – The inequality signs may need explaining. To minimise errors encourage a two step, rather than one step approach,: make a tally chart taking results in order then addi them Test both methods: in pairs, each student adopts one of the methods to complete part **a**. How long did each student take? Whose results were more accurate? Collate the whole class results. Which method has proved more reliable? When finding the class interval containing the median result, many students are tempted to choose the median class interval, 65–69. Why? (RL, TW) (1.3, 1.5)

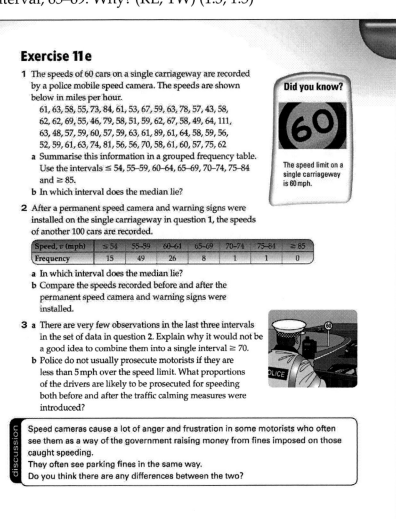

Exercise 11e commentary

Question 2 – The concept behind the position of median result in a frequency table can be difficult. Often the results can be more easily understood when seen in a long line. Why is this not always practical? (1.3,1.4, 1.5)

Question 3 – What is the advantage of having more/less intervals? (more detailed/manageable data). What is the ideal number of intervals? (roughly between 5 and 8) (1.3, 1.4).

Discussion – Are parking fines and speed cameras necessary? Can speed cameras cause accidents? How do average speed cameras work? Are they a better safety feature than speed cameras? (EP)

Assessment Criteria – HD, level 6: Construct tables for gathering large discrete and continuous sets of raw data, choosing suitable class intervals.

Links

Ask the class if they know the location of any speed cameras in the local area. There is a map showing the location of all speed cameras in the UK at http://www.speedcameramap.co.uk/

Are any shown locally on the map that the class didn't know were there?

Extension

Challenge students with a data set that does not lend itself easily to be converted into a grouped frequency table. For example, a skewed data set. What solutions can they come up with? For example, variation in group width (CT) (1.1).

- Select, construct and modify, on paper and using ICT, suitable graphical representations to progress an enquiry and identify key features present in the data. (L6)
- Include
  - pie charts for categorical data (L6)
  - bar charts and frequency diagrams for discrete and continuous data (L6)
  - stem-and-leaf diagrams (L6)

Useful resources

Speadsheet for help with discussion at end of exercise

Calculator

Starter – Data handling jumble

Write a list of anagrams on the board and ask students to unscramble them.

Possible anagrams are

VURSEY, DOME, TAAD, ATORSIINENQUE, UNNSUITCOO, NAME, MAPLES, CERTSIDE

(survey, mode, data, questionnaire, continuous, mean, sample, discrete)

Can be extended by asking students to make a data handling word search.

Teaching notes

Look at a set of data. Is it clear how many results are in the 20s, 30s, *etc*. Is the way that the data is spread obvious? Look at the way in which a stem-and-leaf diagram is constructed. The example illustrates this.

Encourage an unordered stem-and-leaf diagram as a first draft, putting in the data as it appears in the raw list. Next, convert to an ordered diagram. Why is this a good approach? Show how the key is used to explain the value of the data entries. What can you tell about the spread of the data from the diagram? (1.1, 1.5)

Discuss the difference between a bar chart and a comparative bar chart. For example, percentage of people who smoke in different age categories (bar chart) and percentage of males and females who smoke in different age categories (comparative bar chart)

Remind students of the method of finding the angle for the sectors of a pie chart.

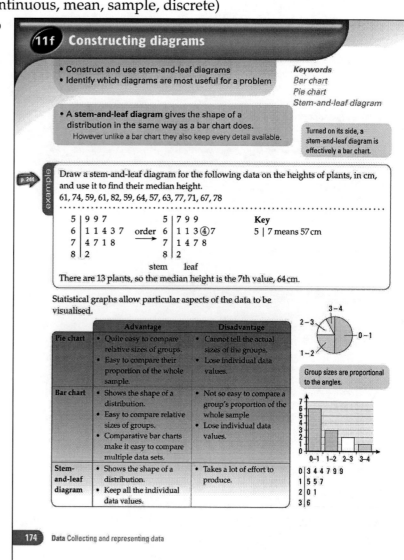

Plenary

Look at some examples of frequency graphs on the internet (search on 'frequency diagrams'). Discuss which graphs give clear information and which do not. Which types were not covered in the exercise? Can students make guesses into how they work? For example, cumulative frequency graphs (EP) (1.1, 1.5).

Simplification

Provide students with a copy of the data to allow them to cross off the data as they go. Encourage students to check with partners to see if they agree on the ordering of the data. Can they work together efficiently? (TW)

All questions (IE) (1.1, 1.3)

Question 1 – Before constructing a stem-and-leaf diagram, what do you need to find from your data? (minimum and maximum values). Consider repeating the approach of question **1** in spread **11e**: half the class enter the data one after the other and then order the other half search the list for entries in one row and enter hem in an order. Which method is quicker? More reliable? (RL) (1.5)

Exercise 11f

1 Car speeds recorded on a motorway are shown below.

61, 63, 72, 78, 73, 84, 68, 53, 74, 83, 79, 58, 77, 82, 91, 67, 58, 77, 89, 68, 61, 64, 68, 59, 73, 71, 81, 61, 63, 74

Show this information in a stem-and-leaf diagram.

2 The gender and age of the 36 members of a golf club who expressed interest in taking part in a charity golf event are shown below.

M35, F37, M41, M39, F55, M44, F47, M31, M41, F61, M29, M46, F42, F49, M36, M32, F39, M46, M61, M35, M51, F38, F57, M43, F52, F47, M37, M49, M45, F41, F49, M34, F63, M57, F34, M60

M35 means a man aged 35

a Draw a stem-and-leaf diagram to show the ages of the males.
b Draw a stem-and-leaf diagram to show the ages of the females.
c Find the median age of each group.
d Make any comparisons you can between the males and females who express interest.

3 The table below gives data on the number of pupils in four schools who achieve different levels in Intermediate Maths Challenge.

School	No award	Bronze	Silver	Gold	Total
A	53	22	12	4	91
B	37	28	18	9	92
C	44	21	16	7	88
D	41	25	17	5	88

For the following draw a pie chart, a bar chart or a comparative bar chart, choosing whichever is most appropriate.

a To compare the numbers at different levels in schools A and D.
b To see the proportions at different levels in school B.
c To see the numbers at different levels in school C.

> **discussion**
> If you drew a comparative bar chart to show the data on all four schools, you would have 16 bars. If there was data on 10 schools you would have 40 bars. How many schools do you think you can draw on a comparative bar chart and still make sense of the graph?

Extension

Challenge students with more difficult data sets, for example, including decimals to various orders of accuracy. Ask them to construct a stem-and-leaf diagram. They may need to consider rounding data (CT) (1.1).

Exercise 11f commentary

Question 2 – A back-to-back stem-and-leaf diagram could be used. Ask students to make use of both the median and the range when making comparisons (CT) (1.2).

Question 3 – Students could be told that each type of graph is used only once. The term 'proportions' may need explaining for part **b**. The pie chart has both an advantage and a disadvantage. What are they? Advantage, they can show the amount of results in each group in relation to the other groups without having to use a scale, that is, they show proportions. Disadvantage, they do not tell you the actual number of results in each group (RL) (1.5).

Discussion – Use an excel spread sheet to view a comparative bar chart for different numbers of schools. Ask the class to give their opinion on the most appropriate number of bars (EP)

Assessment Criteria – HD, level 6: Select, construct and modify, on paper and using ICT:
– pie charts for categorical data
– bar charts and frequency diagrams for discrete and continuous data
and identify which are most useful in the context of the problem.

Links

The first known use of a pie chart was in 1801 by William Playfair. He was a Scottish engineer who also invented the bar chart and line graph. There is a copy of one of his pie charts at http:// en.wikipedia.org/wiki/ Image: Playfair-piechart.jpg Stem-and-leaf diagrams are a much later innovation, being invented in 1969 by American statistician John Wilder Tukey (TW).

- Select, construct and modify, on paper and using ICT, suitable graphical representations to progress an enquiry and identify key features present in the data. Include
  – line graphs for time series   (L6)

Useful resources

Starter – Temperatures

Write a list of times and temperatures on the board:
6 a.m. -2°; 9 a.m. 9°; 12 noon 17.5°; 3 p.m. 14°; 6 p.m. 10.5°; 9 p.m. 8°.
Give students quick-fire questions, for example,

What is the biggest temperature difference?

By how much did the temperature change between 9 a.m. and 12 noon?

Can be differentiated by the choice of temperatures.

Teaching notes

Ask students how they think life expectancies have changed since 1900; will they be different for men and women? Ask them to sketch a graph to illustrate their ideas and then see how this compares to that given (EP).

Look at the comparative bar chart in the example in the student book. Describe the trends that can be seen in the graph. Initially confine the answers to specific parties. Then try to draw conclusions about the relationship between the votes of two parties over the time period. Should the graph be extended over 12 months? Discuss problems arising from too much information. What solution could be considered for examining a 12 month period? Consider grouping 2 or 3 months of results together (TW) (1.5).

Does the comparative bar chart show very great difference between the number of people voting for the parties? Are the variations significant? Point out that because the number of people who were polled is not given, thaty is, **sample size**, it is difficult to comment on the significance of the variation.

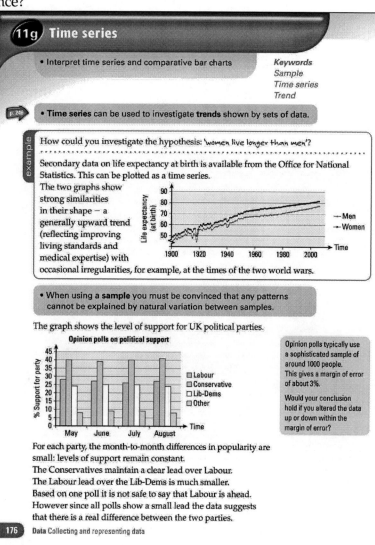

11g Time series

- Interpret time series and comparative bar charts

Keywords
Sample
Time series
Trend

- **Time series** can be used to investigate **trends** shown by sets of data.

How could you investigate the hypothesis: 'women live longer than men'?

Secondary data on life expectancy at birth is available from the Office for National Statistics. This can be plotted as a time series.

The two graphs show strong similarities in their shape – a generally upward trend (reflecting improving living standards and medical expertise) with occasional irregularities, for example, at the times of the two world wars.

- When using a **sample** you must be convinced that any patterns cannot be explained by natural variation between samples.

The graph shows the level of support for UK political parties.

Opinion polls on political support

Opinion polls typically use a sophisticated sample of around 1000 people. This gives a margin of error of about 3%.

Would your conclusion hold if you altered the data up or down within the margin of error?

For each party, the month-to-month differences in popularity are small: levels of support remain constant.
The Conservatives maintain a clear lead over Labour.
The Labour lead over the Lib-Dems is much smaller.
Based on one poll it is not safe to say that Labour is ahead.
However since all polls show a small lead the data suggests that there is a real difference between the two parties.

176   Data Collecting and representing data

Plenary

Carry out a confidential survey into the percentage of students in the class who have dropped litter during yesterday. Ask students to note yes/no and male/female and hand in their folded answers. Ask the class to suggest hypotheses. For example, over 50% of the class have dropped litter yesterday, or more boys than girls dropped litter yesterday. What do the actual results reveal? Can the results be trusted, will people have been honest? (IE, EP, TW) (1.1, 1.4, 1.5)

Simplification

Some students may find it difficult to write down their observations. Encourage them to verbalise their conclusions to the teacher. Allow students to make very short sentences if they need to, that is, just statements.

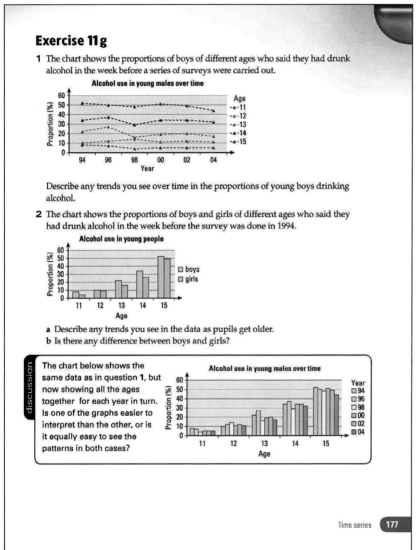

Exercise 11g

1 The chart shows the proportions of boys of different ages who said they had drunk alcohol in the week before a series of surveys were carried out.

Alcohol use in young males over time

Describe any trends you see over time in the proportions of young boys drinking alcohol.

2 The chart shows the proportions of boys and girls of different ages who said they had drunk alcohol in the week before the survey was done in 1994.

Alcohol use in young people

a Describe any trends you see in the data as pupils get older.
b Is there any difference between boys and girls?

discussion

The chart below shows the same data as in question 1, but now showing all the ages together for each year in turn. Is one of the graphs easier to interpret than the other, or is it equally easy to see the patterns in both cases?

Alcohol use in young males over time

Extension

How do you predict the data will change during the years following 15 years of age in question **1**. A google search under images and 'alcohol use in young people graph' will provide some interesting information. Can students find a graph that supports their prediction? (IE, EP) (1.2)

Exercise 11f commentary

All questions (CT) (1.2)

Question 1 – Initially, encourage responses that look only at specific elements of the data. For example, results for 12 year olds. Then, for more involved comparisons, look at how the differences between two consecutive age groups have changed over time. An overall comparison is quite difficult.

Question 2 – Students need to be aware that they can draw conclusions over just a few years, and do not need to base their answers on all the age ranges available. For example, from 13 to 15 the difference between the proportion of girls and boys who have drunk alcohol has decreased. That is, as the girls get older they 'catch up' with the boys.

Discussion – Which comparisons are most informative? For example, alcohol consumption of 11 year olds over the years or alcohol consumption of ages 11 to 15 in a particular year? Is alcohol consumption for 11 to 15 year olds going up or down? Which graph more clearly shows this? (1.5)

Assessment Criteria – HD, level 6: select, construct and modify, on paper and using ICT simple time graphs for time series.

Links

For every 100 girls born in the UK, there are around 105 boys. What ratio is this of male to female? What percentage of all babies born in the UK are boys? In 2001 the population of the UK was 28.6 million males and 30.2 million females. What percentage of the population is male? Why is this different to the percentage at birth? (life expectancy for females is longer than for males) (EP)

1 A drug company wants to test the effectiveness of different doses of a new drug and whether the drug will affect some groups of people differently.

Suggest at least six ways to group people you think might react differently to the drug, for example, by gender if you think males and females might react differently.

> A patient's general health is important when taking medication.
> You may wish to consider factors affecting general health.

2 For each of the groups you suggested in question **1**, write down a hypothesis which could be investigated.

3 a Make a list of the variables the company will need to collect data on in order to investigate these hypotheses.

b If the initial trials are to be done with groups of volunteers, say how easy you think it will be to get the information for each variable.

c Are there any of the variables you think will be harder to get information on when the people involved are not volunteers?

4 Part of the data record sheet for the drug trial might look like this.

Patient identifier	Gender	Age	......	......	Dosage	Treatment outcome
0001	M	56			xxxx	xxxx
0002	M	24			xxxx	xxxx
0003	F	37			xxxx	xxxx

Create a record sheet for the variables you have chosen to consider, and fill in (as for gender and age) examples of the values those variables might take for the first three patients.

5 Drug companies try to justify the price of new drugs by saying that the development costs are very high and only a small proportion of drugs they test end up with approval to go on the open market.

For the initial trials the company say they will only consider a maximum of four variables by which to group people. Which four of the variables you chose in question **1** would you recommend they consider?

6 The ages of a group of patients in a nursing home who were given the drug are given below.

67, 63, 52, 49, 71, 82, 71, 59, 61, 57, 64, 72, 56, 48, 59, 64, 70, 53, 49, 67,
81, 80, 56, 53, 59, 63, 67, 64, 47, 51, 60, 76, 70, 61, 53, 52, 59, 72, 86, 49,
73, 71, 59, 62, 57, 46, 62, 70, 49, 57, 62, 70, 49, 80, 66, 47, 55, 90, 53, 61

a Summarise this information in a grouped frequency table using intervals ≤ 54, 55–59, 60–64, 65–69, 70–74, 75–84, ≥ 85.

b In which interval does the median lie?

c Give two reasons, apart from the size of the group, why this group of patients would not be a good sample on its own to investigate the effectiveness of the drug.

7 A sample of half the population used in question **6** is taken.

a Draw a stem and leaf diagram to show the ages of these patients.

b Hence find the median of this group.

> 67, 63, 52, 49, 71, 82, 71, 59,
> 61, 57, 81, 80, 56, 53, 59, 63,
> 67, 64, 47, 51, 73, 71, 59, 62,
> 57, 46, 62, 70, 49, 57

8 a The left hand chart shows the recorded rates of treatment (per 1000 people) of different age groups of females between 1994 and 1998.

  i Describe any trends you see over the period 1994 to 1998.

  ii Describe any differences you see between the different age groups.

b The right hand chart shows the same data for males, using the same scale for comparison.

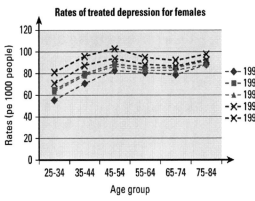

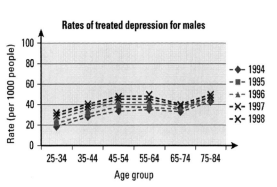

Describe any differences you see between males and females

11 Summary

Assessment criteria

- Ask questions, plan how to answer them and collect the data required — Level 5
- Design a survey or experiment to capture the necessary data from one or more sources — Level 6
- Design, trial and if necessary refine data collection sheets — Level 6
- Construct tables for large discrete and continuous sets of raw data, choosing suitable class intervals — Level 6
- Select, construct and modify, on paper and using ICT:
  - pie charts for categorical data
  - bar charts and frequency diagrams for discrete and ontinuous data
  - simple time graphs for time series
  and identify which are most useful in the context of the problem — Level 6
- Suggest a problem to explore using statistical methods, frame questions and raise conjectures — Level 7

Question commentary

Example

The example illustrates a problem on designing a data collection sheet. Ask students "What would be a good way to organise the data?" "How can you cope with an answer which isn't on your list of types of transport?" "What criteria should the distance intervals satisfy?"

Distance (km)	Walk	Car	Bus	Tram	Other
$0 < d \leq 1$					
$1 < d \leq 2$					
$2 < d \leq 3$					
$3 < d \leq 4$					
$4 < d \leq 5$					
5+					

Past question

The question requires students to interpret a time series graph. Emphasise the need to give a clear explanation for each answer. In case of difficulty in part **b**, use an analogy and ask students if what they eat for lunch today means that they will eat the same for lunch tomorrow. Emphasise that time series graphs can show past trends, but can not predict with certainty what will happen in the future.

Answer

Level 6

2 a False, with a correct explanation
  b Cannot be certain, with a correct explanation

Development and links

This topic is developed further in Chapter 15 where students will analyse and interpret data and compare distributions using statistics, charts, graphs and diagrams.

The methods of collecting and representing data encountered in this chapter are important in geography, where statistical information is presented in many forms of chart and graph. Charts and graphs are used in Science to present and analyse results of experiments. In everyday life, students will be bombarded with requests for their opinion, either online, by telephone, in the street or on printed surveys and questionnaires.

12 Ratio and proportion

Number

Objectives

Level

- Compare two ratios 6
- Interpret and use ratio in a range of contexts 6
- Use proportional reasoning to solve problems, choosing the correct numbers to take as 100%, or as a whole 6
- Solve problems involving percentage changes 6
- Recognise when fractions or percentages are needed to compare proportions 6

Introduction

This chapter builds on the ideas of ratio and proportion introduced in Year 7 and on the work on percentages in Chapter 4. Students simplify ratios, compare ratios, divide a quantity in a given ratio, recognise when two quantities are in direct proportion and solve ratio and direct proportion problems. The topic develops to solving problems using percentage change, using the equivalence of percentages, fractions and decimals to compare proportions and writing one number as a percentage of another.

The student book discusses maps of different scales. Proportional reasoning has many applications in everyday life including mixing paint colours, mixing screen wash and antifreeze with water in a car, calculating medicine doses in proportion to the weight of a patient, creating metal alloys, adapting recipes for larger or smaller numbers, making scale models and converting currencies. There is a comparison of maps of different scales at http://www.ordnancesurvey.co.uk/oswebsite/freefun/chooserightmap/(EP).

Fast-track

12b, c, d, e

MPA

1.1	12a, b, c, d, e, f, CS
1.2	12a, b, c, e, f, CS
1.3	12a, b, c, d, e, f, CS
1.4	12a, b, c, e, f, CS
1.5	12a, b, c, CS

PLTS

IE	12a, b, c, d, e, f, CS
CT	12a, b, c, e, CS
RL	12d, e, CS
TW	12a, b, CS
SM	12b, d, e, CS
EP	12I, a, b, c, d, e, f, CS

Extra Resources

12	Start of chapter presentation
12a	Animation: Ratios
12b	Worked solution: Q2b
12b	Worked solution: Q1a
12b	Consolidation sheet
12c	Starters: Ratio matching
12c	Consolidation sheet
12d	Animation: Ratios 2
12e	Worked solution: Q1a
12f	Consolidation sheet
	Maths life: Food crops
	Assessment: chapter 12

- Use ratio notation (L4) ***Useful resources***
- Simplify ratios, including those expressed in different units, recognising the link with fraction notation (L5)
- Compare two ratios (L6)

Starter – 9999

Ask students to make as many numbers as possible between 1 and 20 inclusive using four nines and any operation(s), for example,

$1 = (9 + 9) ÷ (9 + 9)$.

Hint: $\sqrt{9} = 3$

Teaching notes

Ratio is always used to compare amounts to each other. Give examples of ratios that can be simplified to their simplest forms. Remind students that ratios do not give the 'value' of a particular measurement, but allow for comparisons only. Express a ratio in words. For example, £10 : £15 = 2 : 3, 'for every £2 of the first amount there are £3 for the second amount'.

Look at examples were the units are different and show how converting to a convenient common unit allows us to do away with the units. Include examples of triple ratios.

Sometimes it is helpful to express a ratio in an alternative form to the simplest one.

For example, £10 : £15 = 1 : 1.5. This tells us that every £1 compares to £1.50. This form in known as the 1 : n. It can be an easier way to compare amounts and solve ratio problems (1.5).

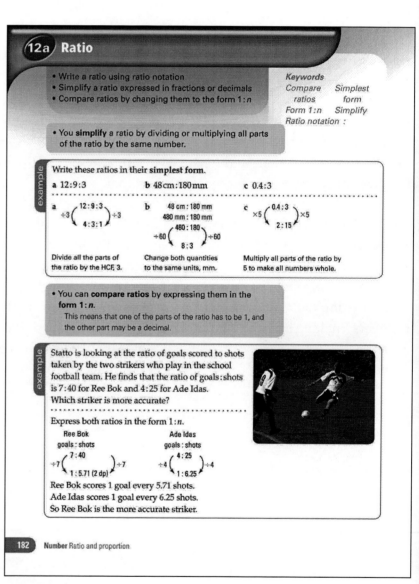

Plenary

Write the answers to question **3** using mixed fractions instead of decimals. What advantage does this give? A calculator would not be needed (CT) (1.5).

Simplification

Allow students to simplify their ratio without having to find the simplest form, for example, 8 : 20 to 4 : 10. If no calculator is used for the initial simplification, a calculator could then be used to go back over their answers and try to find the most simplified form.

All questions (1.3)

Question 1 – Encourage students to show working on both sides of the ratio. Do you need to use the highest common factor? Only if you want to simplify in one step. If a calculator is not used, then product of prime factors is very useful.

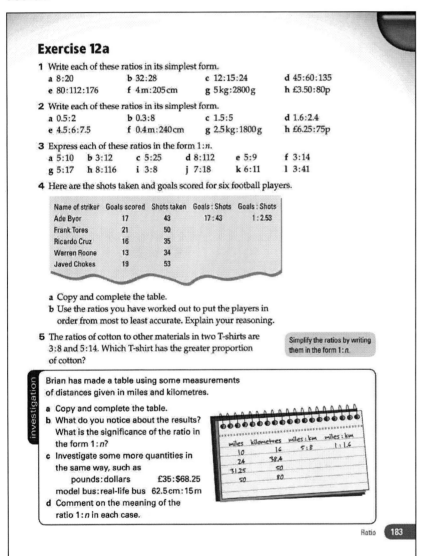

Exercise 12a

1 Write each of these ratios in its simplest form.
  a 8:20   **b** 32:28   **c** 12:15:24   **d** 45:60:135
  e 80:112:176   **f** 4m:205cm   **g** 5kg:2800g   **h** £3.50:80p

2 Write each of these ratios in its simplest form.
  a 0.5:2   **b** 0.3:8   **c** 1.5:5   **d** 1.6:2.4
  e 4.5:6:7.5   **f** 0.4m:240cm   **g** 2.5kg:1800g   **h** £6.25:75p

3 Express each of these ratios in the form 1:n.
  a 5:10   **b** 3:12   **c** 5:25   **d** 8:112   **e** 5:9   **f** 3:14
  g 5:17   **h** 8:116   **i** 3:8   **j** 7:18   **k** 6:11   **l** 3:41

4 Here are the shots taken and goals scored for six football players.

Name of striker	Goals scored	Shots taken	Goals : Shots	Goals : Shots
Ade Byor	17	43	17 : 43	1 : 2.53
Frank Tores	21	50		
Ricardo Cruz	16	35		
Warren Roone	13	34		
Javed Chokes	19	53		

  a Copy and complete the table.
  b Use the ratios you have worked out to put the players in order from most to least accurate. Explain your reasoning.

5 The ratios of cotton to other materials in two T-shirts are 3:8 and 5:14. Which T-shirt has the greater proportion of cotton?

> Simplify the ratios by writing them in the form 1:n.

investigation

Brian has made a table using some measurements of distances given in miles and kilometres.
  a Copy and complete the table.
  b What do you notice about the results? What is the significance of the ratio in the form 1:n?
  c Investigate some more quantities in the same way, such as
        pounds:dollars   £35:$68.25
        model bus:real-life bus 62.5cm:15m
  d Comment on the meaning of the ratio 1:n in each case.

miles	kilometres	miles:km	miles:km
10	16	5:8	1:1.6
24	38.4		
31.25	50		
50	80		

Ratio 183

Extension

Examine the ratio of the lengths of students little fingers to their middle fingers. Give answers to the nearest cm. Is the ratio the same for everyone? If the measurement was made to the nearest 2 cm, would that change the conclusions? (TW) (1.2, 1.3)

Exercise 12a commentary

Question 2 – What is the simplest way to eliminate the decimals? Encourage students to check for further simplification once decimals are eliminated.

Question 3 – Allow the use of a calculator when needed. What accuracy would be sensible? Can students think of any examples of where a scale of 1 : n is used? (model making or maps)

Question 4 – Use a calculator. What does 1 : 2.53 actually mean? Can you tell who is the best player? Did they all play the same number of games? Against a similar standard of opposition? (EP) (1.4)

Question 5 – Use a calculator if needed. How does converting the ratio to 1 : n help? And what does it mean? Encourage students to say the meanings: every one part of cotton has 2.66 parts of other material in the T-shirt (EP) (1.4).

Investigation – A calculator is not required. Students may need to increase the numbers in the ratio before simplifying them, as in question **2**. Why is the ratio 1 : n helpful? When would the ratio n : 1 be useful? (IE, EP) (1.1, 1.4, 1.5)

Assessment Criteria – NNS, level 5: understand simple ratio.

Links

The aspect ratio of a screen or an image is the ratio of its width to its height. HD televisions and monitors have an aspect ratio of 16 : 9 (also known as 1.78 : 1) but older style screens use 4 : 3 (1.33 : 1) Common cinema film ratios are 1.85 : 1 and 2.35 : 1. When an image filmed in one aspect ratio is displayed on a screen with a different aspect ratio, the image has to be cropped or distorted (EP).

- Divide a quantity into two or more parts in a given ratio (L6)
- Interpret and use ratio in a range of contexts (L6)

Useful resources
Spreadsheet to show results for investigation

Starter – Countdown

Ask students for six numbers between 1 and 10, and one from 25, 50, 75 and 100.

Write the numbers on the board.

Throw a die three times to generate a three digit target number.

Challenge students to calculate this target number (or get as close as possible to it) using the five numbers and any operations.

Teaching notes

An amount can be split up/divided up in a certain ratio. First, identify how many parts the amount is being split up into. Two or three people may be sharing the amount, but that does not mean it is being split into two or three parts. Look at the total of all the parts of the ratio. Ask, what is one part worth? This is called the unitary method because it finds the value of one unit/part first. How many parts does each person receive? Use multiplication to find the amounts that are to go to each person. Look at examples that have integer solutions and include triple ratios.

An alternative way of looking at ratio is to ask what fraction/proportion each person receives of the whole amount. Look at the parts of the ratio in order to decide. Then that fraction/proportion of the total amount can be calculated. Look at the second example (1.5).

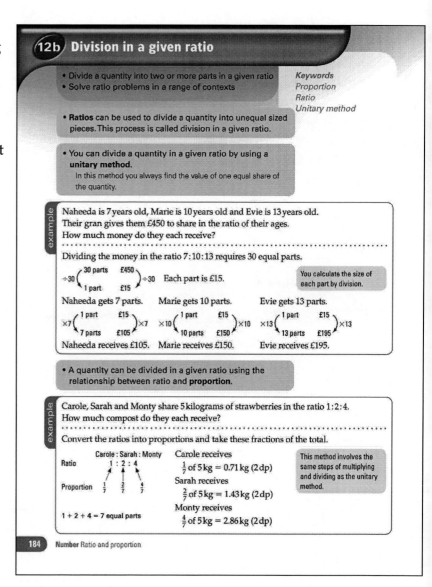

Plenary

Investigate the ratio of elements in various alloys. For example, 'Nickel Silver' is 65 : 18 : 17 copper : nickel : zinc. Wikipedia 'list of alloys' is a useful site. The ratios tend to be given as percentages, can any of the ratios looked at be simplified? (SM, EP)

Simplification

Keep the language of ratio in terms of 'parts' of the whole amount. Ask, 'how much is there to begin with?' 'How many groups is it being split into?' 'How many parts are their all together?' 'What is each part worth?' When solving a question, help students to correctly label what they have found, for example, 1 part = 16 cakes for question **1a**.

All questions (EP) (1.3)

Question 1 – No calculator. How many parts is the amount to be split up into? Students need to think initially in terms of adding the parts. For part **a**, use language like 'person A gets 2 parts and person B gets 3 parts'. What is each part worth? Students need to think in terms of division. How many parts does the first person get? How much is this worth?

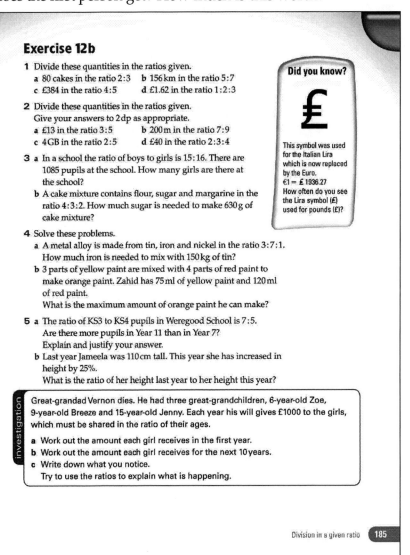

Exercise 12b

1 Divide these quantities in the ratios given.
  a 80 cakes in the ratio 2:3 **b** 156 km in the ratio 5:7
  c £384 in the ratio 4:5 **d** £1.62 in the ratio 1:2:3

2 Divide these quantities in the ratios given.
  Give your answers to 2 dp as appropriate.
  a £13 in the ratio 3:5 **b** 200 m in the ratio 7:9
  c 4 GB in the ratio 2:5 **d** £40 in the ratio 2:3:4

3 a In a school the ratio of boys to girls is 15:16. There are 1085 pupils at the school. How many girls are there at the school?
  b A cake mixture contains flour, sugar and margarine in the ratio 4:3:2. How much sugar is needed to make 630 g of cake mixture?

4 Solve these problems.
  a A metal alloy is made from tin, iron and nickel in the ratio 3:7:1. How much iron is needed to mix with 150 kg of tin?
  b 3 parts of yellow paint are mixed with 4 parts of red paint to make orange paint. Zahid has 75 ml of yellow paint and 120 ml of red paint.
  What is the maximum amount of orange paint he can make?

5 a The ratio of KS3 to KS4 pupils in Weregood School is 7:5.
  Are there more pupils in Year 11 than in Year 7?
  Explain and justify your answer.
  b Last year Jameela was 110 cm tall. This year she has increased in height by 25%.
  What is the ratio of her height last year to her height this year?

investigation

Great-grandad Vernon dies. He had three great-grandchildren, 6-year-old Zoe, 9-year-old Breeze and 15-year-old Jenny. Each year his will gives £1000 to the girls, which must be shared in the ratio of their ages.

a Work out the amount each girl receives in the first year.
b Work out the amount each girl receives for the next 10 years.
c Write down what you notice.
  Try to use the ratios to explain what is happening.

Did you know?

£

This symbol was used for the Italian Lira which is now replaced by the Euro.
€1 = £1936.27
How often do you see the Lira symbol (£) used for pounds (£)?

Division in a given ratio **185**

Extension

In the **investigation,** how old would the girls have to be so that they all receive the same amount of money? A trial and improvement approach is likely to be the most effective; a linear equation could be formed but is very difficult to solve at this level. (999 997, 1 000 000 and 1 000 006) (IE, SM) (1.3)

Exercise 12b commentary

Question 2 – Calculator needed. Adopt the same method as question **1**. Why might the amounts not add up to the original total?

Question 3 – Calculator needed.

Question 4 – Calculator needed. These questions are more difficult as you are not always given the full total amount. Encourage students to change the ratios they have into they required ratio.

Question 5 – If there are the same number in each year, what would you expect the ratio of KS3 to KS4 pupils to be? (3 : 2). What assumption could you make? Assume there are the same number in year 7/8/9 and the same number in 10/11, then the ratio for each year would be $2\frac{1}{3} : 2\frac{1}{3} : 2\frac{1}{3} : 2\frac{1}{2} : 2\frac{1}{2}$ (1.2).

Investigation – A spreadsheet is a useful way of calculating the figures that the girls have each year. Why are they getting closer? Why is the eldest getting less each year? Why is the youngest getting more each year? Will the amounts ever be the same? (CT, SM) (1,1, 1.4)

Assessment Criteria – Calculating, level 6: divide a quantity into two or more parts in a given ratio and solve problems involving ratio and direct proportion.

Links

The Golden Ratio, 1 : 1.618 (to 3 dp), occurs in mathematics, art and in nature. It can be used to divide an object into two parts so that the ratio of the smaller part to the larger part is the same as the ratio of the larger part to the whole object. The ratio is used in architecture to produce buildings of aesthetically pleasing proportions. There are pictures of buildings built on the Golden Ratio at http:// goldennumber.net/ architecture.htm (TW)

- Use the unitary method to solve problems involving ratio and direct proportion (L6)
- Use proportional reasoning to solve problems, choosing the correct number to take as 100%, or as a whole (L6)

Useful resources

Starter – Grandad Bob

Bob wanted to share £5555 between his four grandchildren.

He decided give the money in the ratio of their ages.
Simon was 16, Lucy and Jo were both 12 and Steven was 10.

Ask students how much money each grandchild received.
(Simon £1777.60, Lucy £1333.20, Jo £1333.20, Steven £1111)

Can be extended by students making up their own ratio problems.

Teaching notes

Describe situations where two quantities are in direct proportion. What can be said about how the two amounts change? They rise and fall by the same factor. If one amount was zero, what would the other amount be?

Direct proportion and ratio are really the same thing. The unitary method (from the previous spread) can still be used, but another method maybe of more use. Look at examples that make easy use of the scaling method but would be more awkward when using the unitary method. For example, 6 pens cost 34p, the number of pens and cost are in direct proportion. What is the cost of 15 pens? Show how this problem can be scaled down and then up to the required solution. Illustrate this additionally using ratio notation. Ask students which of the methods of calculation and presentation would they be likely to use in this case. (1.5)

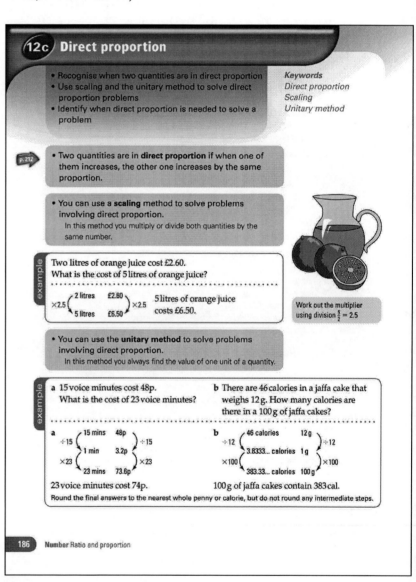

Plenary

Without a calculator, why would the unitary method be a poor choice for solving this question? 21 pencils can be purchased for £4.90. How much would 45 pencils cost? (Assume cost ∝ number of pencils). What non calculator approach could be used? What is the advantage of pence rather than pounds? Is it helpful to represent this question using ratio? (CT) (1.2, 1.5)

Simplification

Expressing the proportional questions as ratios may be an easier way to approach this exercise. How can the ratio be changed into the numbers asked for? Do you need two steps to achieve the result you want? This could lead the way to the unitary method with the use of a calculator.

All questions (IE, EP) (1.1, 1.3)

Question 1 – No calculator needed. Students may find it convenient to set out the proportions as ratios. How can you change the initial proportions into the ones asked for? Initially, encourage students to look for simple integer methods, for example, ÷ 2 and × 5 rather than × 2.5.

Exercise 12c

1 Use direct proportion to solve each of these problems.
   a 5 kg of pears cost 195p. What is the cost of 15 kg of pears?
   b 40 g of breakfast cereal contain 128 calories.
      How many calories are there in 100 g of breakfast cereal?
   c A recipe for six people uses 750 ml of stock.
      What amount of stock is needed for four people?

2 Solve each of these problems, giving your answers to an appropriate degree of accuracy.
   a 5 litres of oil cost £4.79. What is the cost of 18 litres of oil?
   b There are 12 biscuits in a packet. The packet weighs 200 g.
      What is the weight of 23 biscuits?
   c A car's petrol tank when full holds 48 litres of petrol. On a full tank of petrol Jake can drive 650 km.
      i How far could Jake's car travel on 20 litres of petrol?
      ii How much petrol would he need to travel 130 km?
   d £10 is worth 92.27 Croatian kuna.
      i How much is £325 worth in Croatian kuna?
      ii How much is 1000 Croatian kuna worth in pounds?

3 Here are three offers for text messages on a mobile phone. In which of these offers are the numbers in direct proportion? In each case, explain and justify your answers.

investigation

Use **direct proportion** to copy and complete this conversion table for kilograms and pounds. Write the ratio in its simplest form.

a Write anything you notice. What do these results tell you about the relationship between pounds and kilograms?

b How could you quickly change from kilograms to pounds using what you've found out?

Kilograms (kg)	Pounds (lb)	Pounds ÷ Kilograms	Ratio Pounds : Kilograms
1			
	4.4		
5	11		
10			
23			
	110		

c What about changing from pounds to kilograms?

Direct proportion 187

Extension

If the exchange rate for £ : $ is 1 : 1.79 and £ : euros is 0.79 : 1, find the exchange rate for $: euros in the three forms **i** 1 : n **ii** n : 1 **iii** simplest. (1.41 : 1 (2.dp), 1 : 0.71 (2d.p), 14 141 : 10 000) Are these exchange rates still accurate? The website www.xe.com is useful for current exchange rates (EP) (1.3).

Exercise 12c commentary

Question 2 – Calculator needed. Many students will use the unitary method here. To avoid confusion, ask students to show their working as they scale each side of the proportion. How can you tell which side of the proportion to make '1'?

Question 3 – Calculator needed. Ask, how much for one text? Does it depend on the number of messages you send? Some students may like to use a multiplier to see if the number of messages and price are in the same ratio (1.4).

Investigation – Encourage students to think about simple mental methods rather than multiplication. For example, converting from kg to pounds: add together the two results you get from **i** doubling and **ii** doubling and dividing by ten. Ask students to convert their own weight to pounds or kg if they know it.

Assessment Criteria – Calculating, level 5: solve simple problems involving ratio and direct proportion. Calculating, level 6; Use proportional reasoning to solve problems, choosing the correct number to take as 100%, or as a whole

Links

As part of the design process for a product, manufacturers draw up a 'parts list' of all the components used in the assembled product. The manufacturer decides how many of the product he is going to build and then orders the number of parts required. The number he needs is in direct proportion to the number on the parts list. There are examples of parts lists at http://www.turbocharged.com/catalog/parts_list.html and at http://www.wellsdental.com/Techbull/U801/u801.htm (EP).

- Apply understanding of the relationship between ratio and proportion
  (L6)

Useful resources

• •

Starter – Emergency!

Ask students find as many ways as possible of arranging the digits 1 to 9 to make three three digit numbers that will add up to give 999. (One possible way is 498 + 375 + 126 = 999)

Can a similar kind of puzzle be made using subtraction?

Teaching notes

Ratio can be used to compare the proportions of amounts to each other. For example, Mr A is 20 years old and Mr B is 35 years old. What proportion is Mr A's age of Mr B's age? How can their ages be compared to begin with? Ratio 20 : 35. Is this satisfactory? Simplifying the ratio gives 4 : 7. Therefore Mr A is $\frac{4}{7}$ of Mr B's age. Verify this from their actual ages. What fraction is Mr B's age of Mr A's age? What sort of answer is expected? Greater than one, actually $\frac{7}{4}$. Can this be expressed as a percentage?

Ratio can also be used to find the total amount. Look at examples where the ratio is given and the quantity of one side of the ratio is known. Consider examples like those in question **3**.

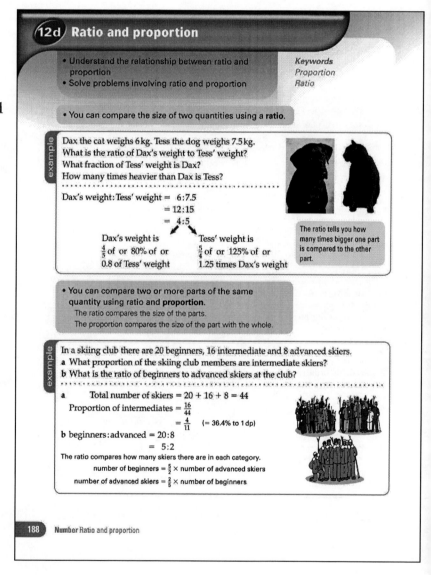

12d Ratio and proportion

- Understand the relationship between ratio and proportion
- Solve problems involving ratio and proportion

Keywords
Proportion
Ratio

• You can compare the size of two quantities using a **ratio**.

example

Dax the cat weighs 6 kg. Tess the dog weighs 7.5 kg.
What is the ratio of Dax's weight to Tess' weight?
What fraction of Tess' weight is Dax?
How many times heavier than Dax is Tess?

Dax's weight : Tess' weight = 6 : 7.5
= 12 : 15
= 4 : 5

Dax's weight is $\frac{4}{5}$ of or 80% of or 0.8 of Tess' weight

Tess' weight is $\frac{5}{4}$ of or 125% of or 1.25 times Dax's weight

The ratio tells you how many times bigger one part is compared to the other part.

• You can compare two or more parts of the same quantity using ratio and **proportion**.
The ratio compares the size of the parts.
The proportion compares the size of the part with the whole.

example

In a skiing club there are 20 beginners, 16 intermediate and 8 advanced skiers.
a What proportion of the skiing club members are intermediate skiers?
b What is the ratio of beginners to advanced skiers at the club?

a   Total number of skiers = 20 + 16 + 8 = 44
Proportion of intermediates = $\frac{16}{44}$
= $\frac{4}{11}$ (= 36.4% to 1 dp)

b beginners : advanced = 20 : 8
= 5 : 2

The ratio compares how many skiers there are in each category.
number of beginners = $\frac{5}{2}$ × number of advanced skiers
number of advanced skiers = $\frac{2}{5}$ × number of beginners

Plenary

The dimensions of a football pitch for international games must be 100 to 120 m long by 70 to 80 m wide. What ratios can be created from the possible pitch sizes? Simplify each answer (1.3).

Simplification

Ask students to explain verbally what they understand by the information given. Allow students to draw sketches to visualise how the ratio is dividing the amounts. Allow the explanation and clear understanding of a question to stand as a substitute to answering it in some cases.

All questions (1.3)

Question 1 – Students need to recognise that when taking about the whole shape, the fraction is out of 36. Confusion can come from misunderstanding when the whole shape or just one colour is being referred to. In part **iii**, can the × sign be thought of in another way? Students may need reminding that 'of' and '×' mean the same thing with fractions (RL).

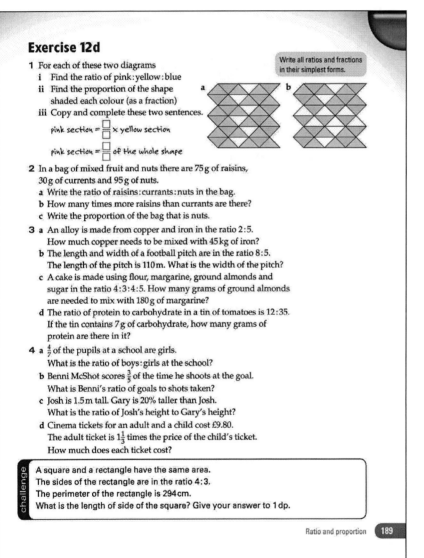

Exercise 12d

1 For each of these two diagrams
   i Find the ratio of pink:yellow:blue
   ii Find the proportion of the shape shaded each colour (as a fraction)
   iii Copy and complete these two sentences.

   Write all ratios and fractions in their simplest forms.

   a   b

   pink section = □/□ × yellow section

   pink section = □/□ of the whole shape

2 In a bag of mixed fruit and nuts there are 75 g of raisins, 30 g of currents and 95 g of nuts.
   a Write the ratio of raisins:currants:nuts in the bag.
   b How many times more raisins than currants are there?
   c Write the proportion of the bag that is nuts.

3 a An alloy is made from copper and iron in the ratio 2:5. How much copper needs to be mixed with 45 kg of iron?
   b The length and width of a football pitch are in the ratio 8:5. The length of the pitch is 110 m. What is the width of the pitch?
   c A cake is made using flour, margarine, ground almonds and sugar in the ratio 4:3:4:5. How many grams of ground almonds are needed to mix with 180 g of margarine?
   d The ratio of protein to carbohydrate in a tin of tomatoes is 12:35. If the tin contains 7 g of carbohydrate, how many grams of protein are there in it?

4 a $\frac{4}{7}$ of the pupils at a school are girls. What is the ratio of boys:girls at the school?
   b Benni McShot scores $\frac{3}{5}$ of the time he shoots at the goal. What is Benni's ratio of goals to shots taken?
   c Josh is 1.5 m tall. Gary is 20% taller than Josh. What is the ratio of Josh's height to Gary's height?
   d Cinema tickets for an adult and a child cost £9.80. The adult ticket is $1\frac{1}{3}$ times the price of the child's ticket. How much does each ticket cost?

challenge

A square and a rectangle have the same area.
The sides of the rectangle are in the ratio 4:3.
The perimeter of the rectangle is 294 cm.
What is the length of side of the square? Give your answer to 1 dp.

Ratio and proportion 189

Extension

£140 is shared between Mr A, Mr B and Mr C in the ratio $x : x + 2 : x - 3$. The second largest share of the money is £49. How much does each person get? Many approaches are possible. Some students may want to try different values for x, ($x = 7$ in fact). Others may want to try using algebra, although this is difficult. (49 : 63 : 28) (IE) (1.3)

Exercise 12d commentary

Question 2 – Students must take care to differentiate between comparisons between parts of the ratio and to the whole ratio (EP).

Question 3 – How can the ratio be changed into the amount you want? Encourage students to write down the initial ratio and then try to convert it. This is likely to lead to fewer errors by confusing when to multiply and when to divide (EP).

Question 4 – Once students have answered the question, encourage them to read through again and check the statement from the question matches their answer. Again, confusion is possible between comparisons of the overall total and the separate parts of the ratio (EP).

Challenge – Calculator needed. Rather than, 'how can I answer the question?' Ask students to think 'what can I work out?' What can be discovered about the rectangle? Some students may need to use trial and improvement rather than understand the square root for the side length of the square. In this case, a nearest integer solution will suffice (IE, SM) (1.1).

Assessment Criteria – Calculating, level 6: divide a quantity into two or more parts in a given ratio and solve problems involving ratio and direct proportion.

Links

Proportional representation is a system of election where the number of seats given to a particular party is proportional to the number of votes that it receives. In an election in the UK, only the winning candidate in each constituency becomes a Member of Parliament. Smaller parties might win a sizeable proportion of the vote without winning any seats.

- Solve problems involving percentage changes (L7)
- Calculate an original amount when given the transformed amount after a percentage change (L8)

Useful resources
Calculator

Starter – Percentage pairs

Write the following list of percentage calculations on the board:

7% of 200, 30% of 75, 15% of 70, 90% of 25, 20% of 75, 1% of 350, 56% of 25, 200% of 18.5, 60% of 25, 35% of 10, 25% of 148, 42% of 25.

Challenge students to match up the pairs in the shortest possible time.

Hint: 90% of 25 = 25% of 90

Can be differentiated by the choice of percentages.

Teaching notes

Recap the work covered in spread **4e** for performing percentage increases and decreases using a single multiplier. Remind students of the inverse process of reversing a percentage change. Use arrow diagrams to help reinforce the understanding.

Ensure students are confident expressing percentages as decimals. Why do you multiply by a number greater than one for a percentage increase? When an increase takes place, your answer will represent more than 100% (or one unit).

What percentage is VAT currently running at? How can you add VAT onto an amount? How can you remove the VAT from an amount that includes VAT?

Discuss a simple way to find the VAT on an amount using a mental method: ÷10 (10%) then divide 10% ÷ 2 (5%) then 5% ÷ 2 (2.5%), then sum 10%, 5% and 2.5%.

Is there a simple mental method for removing VAT from an amount? One possibility is to divide by 47 then multiply by 40 (EP) (1.3).

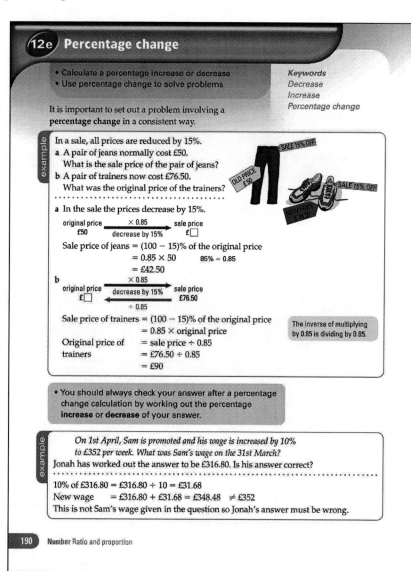

Plenary

Discuss ways in which a calculator can be used to effectively perform two successive percentage changes. Make use of the squared button. Can this be applied in reverse? What about three or four repeated percentage changes? (CT) (1.3)

Simplification

Initially allow students to find the amount of change using a method they are comfortable with. For example, question **1a**, $60 \div 10 = £6$ (10%). $6 \div 2 = £3$ (5%). $6 + 3 = £9$ (15%), add on £9 to £60. Progress students into finding the amount of change using a decimal multiplication: $60 \times 0.15 = 9$. Avoid original amount questions until students are confident using a single decimal multiplication for percentage change.

All questions (EP) (1.3)

Question 1 – Encourage students to some use of the single multiplication method. Allow students to still use the method of finding the amount to be increased/ decreased by and then adding or subtracting.

Exercise 12e

1 Calculate these percentage changes.   *Give answers to 2 dp where appropriate.*
   a Increase £60 by 15%.   b Decrease £270 by 8%.
   c Increase 350 km by 12%.   d Decrease 530 m by 55%.
   e Increase 25 kg by 3%.   f Decrease £450 000 by 2.5%.

2 Samina decides to increase the prices of all the items in her shop by 10%. Copy and complete her new price list.

Item	Original price	New price
Greeting card	£2.40	
Wrapping paper(per roll)		£3.19
Tape roll	78p	
Mug		£1.76

3 a Kelvin weighs 65 kg. He decides to go on a diet and 1 month later his weight has decreased by 7%. What is Kelvin's new weight?
   b In a sale, all prices are reduced by 21%. A DVD costs £11.50 before the sale. What is the sale price of the DVD?
   c A computer costs £340. At the checkout, VAT is added at 17.5%. What is the total price of the computer including the charge for VAT?

4 a Melvin decides to go on a diet and 1 month later his weight has decreased by 5%. Melvin now weighs 57 kg. What was Melvin's weight before the diet?
   b In a sale all prices are reduced by 15%. A CD costs £10.20 in the sale. What was the cost of the CD before the sale?
   c A computer costs £329 including VAT at 17.5%. What was the price of the computer before VAT was added?

5 a This week Shabana scored 54 marks in a geography test. Her teacher said that this was a 12.5% improvement on her last score. What was Shabana's score in her last geography test?
   b A packet of biscuits is increased in size by 20%. The new packet weighs 216 g. What was the weight of the original packet?

investigation

The population of Mathstown in the year 2008 was 88 400.

a If the population of the town has increased by approximately 3% a year, what was the population of the town in   i 2007   ii 2006?
b What would you expect the population of Mathstown to be in   i 2009   ii 2010?
c In what year did the population of Mathstown reach 50 000?
d In what year will the population of Mathstown reach 100 000?
e Investigate the population of Mathstown in different years.

Percentage change   191

Extension

Has the population of the earth been growing at a steady rate of ≈1% per year? Students will need to decide on what data they need. Current/initial population, ≈ 6.2 billion, 2(?) How can you increase by 1%? How can you use a calculator or spread sheet to help see how many years this will take? (2197 years, rounded up). So not true (IE, SM) (1.2, 1.3).

Exercise 12e commentary

Question 2 – Some students maybe use ×0.90 to find the original price after a 10% increase. Emphasise using the correct inverses (RL).

Question 3 – In part **b**, £9.085 will need to be rounded; should the price be rounded up or down?

Question 4 – Ask, how were the new amounts calculated? Ask students to think of the single multiplication that is needed to make the change. How can this be reversed?

Investigation – When having to do repeated percentage change, students should question whether using decimal multiplication and division is the best method. Part **c** requires a number of repeated steps, encourage students to use the previous calculator display rather than rounding off the decimals after every new year.

Assessment Criteria – Calculating: level 6: calculate percentages and find the outcome of a given percentage increase or decrease. Calculating, level 7: calculate the result of any proportional change using multiplicative methods. Calculating, level 8: calculate the original quantity given the result of a proportional change.

Links

A map of the percentage change in the number of people over the state pension age (65/60 for men/ women) by area of the UK can be found at http://www.statistics .gov.uk/cci/nugget.asp?id=875. What two factors could make the population of retired people in an area increase? (More people over the state pension age move into the area, perhaps to retire, or younger people leave the area, perhaps to find work elsewhere) (1.1, 1.4).

- Recognise when fractions or percentages are needed to compare proportions   (L6)
- Use proportional reasoning to solve problems, choosing the correct number to take as 100% or as a whole   (L6)

Useful resources
Calculator

Starter – Paper round

Sam earns £25 a week doing a paper round. As a bonus Sam was offered a choice of three options

- an extra lump sum of £10 for one week
- an extra £2 each week for five weeks
- a pay rise of 50% for one week followed by a pay cut of 50% the following week.

Ask students what choice Sam should make and why?

What should the pay cut be? ($33\frac{1}{3}$ %)

Teaching notes

A proportion of the whole amount can be expressed as a fraction or percentage. Look at examples that convert easily to denominators of 100 and other examples that require a calculator to change a fraction into a decimal. Recap equivalence between decimals and percentages. Encourage students to recognise a decimal as a percentage rather than rely on multiplying by 100.

Look at examples of finding the percentage change. Give the original and new amounts. Before finding the percentage change, what needs to be calculated first? The change itself. Is the change that has happened out of the new amount or out of the **original**? Establish that the change has come out of the original amount. Use the formula

percentage change $= \frac{\text{change}}{\text{original}}$
(expressed as a decimal)

Include examples that can be solved mentally (denominators can be easily converted to 100) and those require a calculator.

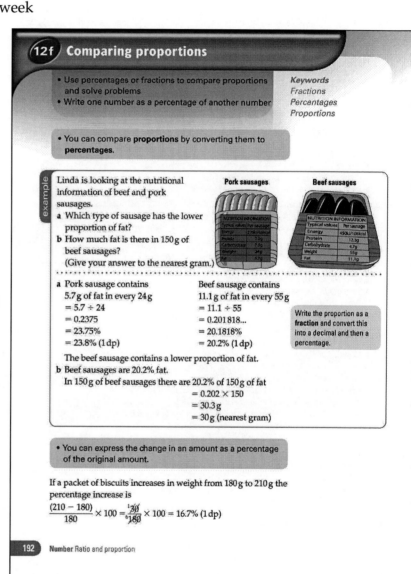

12f Comparing proportions

- Use percentages or fractions to compare proportions and solve problems
- Write one number as a percentage of another number

Keywords
Fractions
Percentages
Proportions

- You can compare **proportions** by converting them to **percentages**.

Linda is looking at the nutritional information of beef and pork sausages.

a Which type of sausage has the lower proportion of fat?
b How much fat is there in 150 g of beef sausages?
(Give your answer to the nearest gram.)

Pork sausages   Beef sausages

a Pork sausage contains
5.7 g of fat in every 24 g
= 5.7 ÷ 24
= 0.2375
= 23.75%
= 23.8% (1 dp)

Beef sausage contains
11.1 g of fat in every 55 g
= 11.1 ÷ 55
= 0.201818...
= 20.1818%
= 20.2% (1 dp)

Write the proportion as a **fraction** and convert this into a decimal and then a percentage.

The beef sausage contains a lower proportion of fat.
b Beef sausages are 20.2% fat.
In 150 g of beef sausages there are 20.2% of 150 g of fat
= 0.202 × 150
= 30.3 g
= 30 g (nearest gram)

- You can express the change in an amount as a percentage of the original amount.

If a packet of biscuits increases in weight from 180 g to 210 g the percentage increase is
$\frac{(210 - 180)}{180} \times 100 = \frac{30}{180} \times 100 = 16.7\%$ (1 dp)

192 **Number** Ratio and proportion

Plenary

Explore examples of expressing one number as a percentage of another where division in either direction is meaningful. Use non calculator methods. For example, Mr A is 20 years old and Mr B is 25 years old. What is Mr A's age as a percentage of Mr B's age? (80%) and vise-versa (125%) Use equivalent fractions to convert to a fraction out of 100. What do these results mean in words? Mr A is 80% of Mr B's age. Is there a connection between the two numbers? Explore other examples that can be done without a calculator (1.3).

Simplification

Write one amount as a fraction of another amount before calculating the fraction. This may make it easier to perform the division in the correct direction. Ask students to say what they are calculating in words, for example, question **2a** 5.5 out of 21 as a percentage. Encourage students to have an idea about the approximate value of the answer.

All questions (1.3)

Exercise 12f

1 Express each of your answers
  i as a fraction in its simplest form **ii** as a percentage (to 1 dp).
  a Four out of every 500 drawing pins produced by a machine are rejected. What proportion of drawing pins are rejected?
  b In a survey, 23 out of 40 cats preferred chicken flavour cat food. What proportion of the cats surveyed preferred chicken flavour cat food?
  c In class 8X1 there are 35 pupils. 21 of these pupils are boys. What proportion of the class are girls?

2 This table shows the number of grams of fat in different chocolate bars.
  a Copy and complete the table.
  b Which is the least healthy bar to eat? Explain and justify your answer.
  c How many grams of fat would there be in 150g of each chocolate bar? (Give your answers to the nearest gram.)

Chocolate	Weight (grams)	Fat content (grams)	% fat
Kit Kit	21	5.5	
Malties	37	8.5	
Venus bar	65	11.4	
Cream egg	39	6.2	
Twicks	62	14.9	

3 Many food labels give the proportion of energy, protein, carbohydrate, fat, fibre and salt that the product contains.
  a Which cereal contains the least amount of fat? Explain and justify your answer.
  b Which is the healthiest cereal to eat? Explain your answer.
  c How much fat is there in a 40g serving of each cereal?

2.2g fat per 100g
Fruity Fruit Cereal
NUTTY Fruit Flakes
oat bran

problem solving

In 1997 about 45% of the tropical rain forests had been destroyed around the world. Since then about 175 000 square kilometres have been destroyed every year, which represents about 1.1% of the remainder.

  a Estimate the original area of rain forest.
  b Estimate the current area.
  c Estimate when the rain forest will disappear.

Comparing proportions **193**

Extension

A pub landlord purchases 50 000 litres of lemonade for £1500. She sells the lemonade at £2.10 per pint. What is the percentage profit? How do you interpret an answer (much) greater than 100%? Will the same answer be achieved regardless of whether the numbers are converted to pints or litres? 1 litre $\approx 1\frac{3}{4}$ pints; a useful rhyme is 'a litre of water's a pint and three quarters!'. Answer, buy at 3p/litre sell at 367.5p/litre or buy at £1500 and sell at £183 750, percentage profit is 12 150% (IE) (1.3).

Exercise 12f commentary

Question 1 – Ask, what does the line between the numerator and denominator mean in a fraction? Establish that apart from separating the parts of the fraction, it also means divide. Rather than multiply the decimal equivalent by 100, encourage students to recognise the decimal as a percentage.

Question 2 – Which way round is the division to be performed? Why that way? (1.4)

Question 3 – Ask students for their initial thoughts as to the least amount of fat without complex calculations.

Problem solving – Students need to identify what percentages are represented by the figures. What was the size in percentage terms of the rain forests in 1997 compared to a time before forest destruction? Why do you not use repeated percentage change after 1997 to find the current area? Area is changing by a fixed amount (IE) (1.1).

Assessment Criteria – NNS, level 6: use the equivalence of fractions decimals and percentages to compare proportions. Calculating, level 6: use proportional reasoning to solve a problem, choosing the correct numbers to take as 100%, or as a whole.

Links

Chocolate is made from the beans of the tropical cacao tree and was prized as a drink by the Aztecs. The first eating chocolate was produced by Joseph Fry in Bristol in 1848. On average, each person in the UK eats 10 kg of chocolate each year. The population of The United Kingdom is approximately 60 million. How many tonnes of chocolate are eaten in the UK each year? (600 000). If chocolate is ≈10% fat, how many tonnes of fat is this? (60 000) (EP)

12 Consolidation

1 Write each of these ratios in its simplest form.

a 0.4:3	**b** 0.6:5	**c** 1.2:4	**d** 2.5:4
e 1.8:2.8	**f** 3.2:4:4.8	**g** 2:3:4.5	**h** 1.6:2.4:6.4
i 0.6m:360cm	**j** 2.2kg:1100g	**k** £3.75:90p	**l** 440ml:1.4litres

2 Express each of these ratios in the form 1:n.

a 3:15	**b** 8:12	**c** 10:25	**d** 9:12
e 15:21	**f** 5:19	**g** 6:21	**h** 15:100
i 7:12	**j** 26:9100	**k** 3.4:68000	**l** 2.5cm:75m

3 Divide these quantities in the ratios given.

    a Divide 140 km in the ratio 2:5   **b** Divide £640 in the ratio 3:5

    c Divide $728 in the ratio 6:7   **d** Divide 30 cm in the ratio 4:3

    e Divide 7 MB in the ratio 8:7   **f** Divide €3000 in the ratio 4:2:1

4 a In a school, the ratio of boys to girls is 7:9. There are 371 boys at the school. How many girls are there at the school?

    b A metal alloy is made from zinc and iron in the ratio 7:2.
How much iron is needed to make 792 kg of the alloy?

    c Gina draws a pie chart to show how the pupils in her school travel home.
The pupils travel home by walking, bus or car in the ratio 7:3:2.
How big are the angles she needs to draw for each of the three sectors?

5 a 7 litres of petrol cost £7.91. What is the cost of 35 litres of petrol?

    b There are 15 cakes in a box. The cakes weigh 420 g.
What is the weight of 25 cakes?

    c Rene's mobile phone contract means she pays £3.60 for 150 text messages.
    i How much would Rene pay for 500 text messages?
    ii How many text messages could she have for £2?

6 a An alloy is made from lead and iron in the ratio 4:7.
How much lead needs to be mixed with 8.4 kg of iron?

    b The length and width of a netball court are in the ratio 9:5. The length of the court is 40.5 m. What is the width of the court?

    c The ratio of pop music to rock music CDs in Jermal's collection is 4:11.
If there are 28 pop music CDs, how many rock music CDs does Jermal have in his collection?

7 a $\frac{2}{9}$ of the pupils at a school gym club are boys.
What is the ratio of boys to girls at the gym club?

b Roldova scores $\frac{7}{11}$ of the time he shoots at the goal.
What is Roldova's ratio of goals to missed shots?

c Hannah is 1.75 m tall. Ursula is 20% shorter than Hannah.
What is the ratio of Hannah's height to Ursula's height?

d A bow and set of arrows costs £40.50. The bow is $1\frac{1}{4}$ times the price of
the arrows. How much did the bow cost?

8 a Sam weighs 84 kg. He decides to go on a diet for three
months. At the end of the three months his weight
has decreased by 8%.
What is Sam's new weight?

> Give your answers to 2 dp where appropriate.

b In a sale, all prices are reduced by 22%. A sofa costs £1349 before the
sale. What is the cost of the sofa during the sale?

c A car costs £7300. On the bill, VAT is added at 17.5%.
What was the total price of the car including VAT?

9 a Steve decides to go on a diet but unfortunately three months later his
weight has increased by 3.5%. Steve now weighs 74.52 kg.
What was Steve's weight before the diet?

b In a sale, all prices are reduced by 12%. A sofa costs £1188 in the sale.
What was the cost of the sofa before the sale?

c A car costs £19 328.75 including VAT at 17.5%.
What was the price of the car before VAT was added?

10 a Copy and complete the table.

b Which is the least healthy food to eat? Explain and justify your answer.

c Which is the most healthy food to eat? Explain and justify your answer.

Type of food	Weight (grams)	Fat content (grams)	%fat
Lamb chops	28	5	
Chocolate bar	26	4.3	
Crisps	35	11.6	
Burger and bun	215	23	
Peas	60	0.4	

d How many grams of fat
would there be in 250 g of each food?
(Give your answers to the nearest gram.)

- Represent problems and synthesise information in
  algebraic, geometric or graphical form   (L6)
- Review and refine own findings and approaches on
  the basis of discussions with others   (L6)

Useful resources

Background

Many students will be aware of the rising use of biofuels through hearing about cars that run on chip fat and other oils. Some may have experienced it or know adults who use biofuels. Running cars in this way is often portrayed as being 'alternative' and 'green'. Students might also be aware that prices for wheat and other crops have recently been rising quite rapidly and know that there is a shortage of food crops in some parts of the world.

This case study focuses on production figures for wheat and biodiesel to raise the possibility that there could be a partial link between the increasing use of biodiesel and the increasing price and shortage of wheat (EP).

Teaching notes

Introduce the case study and look at the spreadsheet shown at the top left. Discuss what is meant by 'produced', 'consumed' and 'stocks' and look at the first two columns to see how the figures relate to each other by asking questions such as, If the value for stocks for 03/04 wasn't given, how could you work out that the stocks would be 129 million tonnes given the other figures for the first two years? Discuss how you have to find the surplus or deficit of production compared with consumption and then adjust the stocks level accordingly. Give the students a few minutes to work out the missing values on the spreadsheet and answer the related questions (1.3).

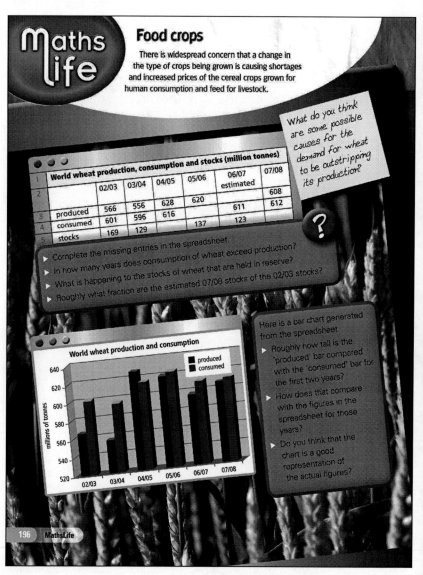

When complete, discuss the answers and then look together at the bar chart produced from the spreadsheet. When the students have considered the questions relating to this bar chart, discuss their opinions about the reasonableness or otherwise of the vertical scale. For example, the differences would be very hard to determine if the vertical axis started at zero. However, starting the axis at 520 million tonnes means that the shortfall between wheat production and consumption appears exaggerated. In the first two columns the production appears, to provide only about half the amount of wheat that is needed. (RL) (1.1, 1.2, 1.4)

Teaching notes continued

Having established that consumption is tending to outstrip production, discuss how this produces shortages which are then likely to cause a rise in prices. Look at the graph showing wheat prices for the past few years. What do you notice about the graph? The most obvious thing is that the prices rise very rapidly in the last two years shown on the graph. Students should then work through the questions about the graph. When the have had time to consider the questions, discuss the answers, especially talking about how the time for prices to double has become very much shorter (EP) (1.5).

Look again at the wheat production graph as well as the wheat price graph and discuss how the drop in production is not as dramatic as the rise in prices. Ask, do you think that the shortfall in production can be the only reason that prices have increased so much in the last few years? Discuss how there might be other factors also affecting the price. Look at the final graph on the spread that shows figures for biodiesel production in Europe. Do you notice anything familiar about this graph? Elicit that the shape is very similar to the shape of the wheat price graph, increasing only slowly for a while and then increasing much more rapidly but note that it doesn't increase quite as rapidly as the price graph does. Look at the questions relating to the biodiesel figures. Ensure that students understand how to find the percentage increase by firstly finding the increase and then expressing this as a percentage of the original value (1.3).

Draw all parts of the case study together by considering whether the production of biofuels could be having an influence on the cost of wheat and other crops. Discuss things such as different use of land for other crops such as oilseed rape will be taking away some of the land traditionally used for food crops and also the fact that some crops that in the past have been used solely for food are now being partially used to produce biofuels (CT).

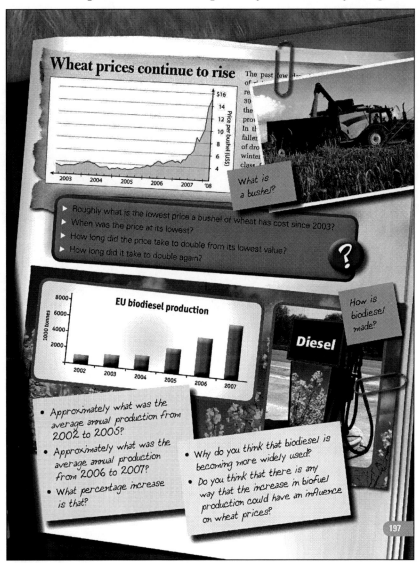

Extension

Students should be encouraged to look in more detail at the range of crops that are being used for various purposes and research the effects this is having worldwide on food prices and levels of availability (IE, SM). There is much useful data on the internet, for example,

> www.hgca.com,
> www.ukagriculture.com/crops/crops.cfm   and
> www.direct.gov.uk/en/Environmentandgreenerliving/Greenertravel/DG_171015

Students could be organised to research different aspects to bring together as a class display (TW).

12 Summary

- Understand simple ratio   Level 5
- Solve simple problems involving ratio and direct proportion   Level 5
- Divide a quantity into two or more parts in a given ratio and solve problems involving ratio and direct proportion   Level 6
- Use proportional reasoning to solve a problem, choosing the correct numbers to take as 100%, or as a whole Level 6
- Calculate percentages and find the outcome of a given percentage increase or decrease   Level 6
- Use the equivalence of fractions, decimals and percentages to compare proportions   Level 6
- Calculate the result of any proportional change using multiplicative methods   Level 7
- Calculate the original quantity given the result of a proportional change   Level 8

Question commentary

<table>
<tr><td>Example</td><td>The example illustrates a question requiring the use of proportional reasoning. In parts **a** and **b**, students may have difficulty identifying which quantity represents 100%. Ask questions such as "Which are the key words in this problem?" and "How do these words help you to decide what to do?" A unitary method could be used here. Emphasise that working must be shown and that in part **c**, the answer to the question should be clearly stated.</td><td>**a** $\dfrac{47}{254} = 18.5\,\%555$

b $\dfrac{28.75}{256.21} = 11.2\%$

c $\dfrac{73.47}{93} = 0.79$

$\dfrac{50.88}{53} = 0.96$</td></tr>
<tr><td>Past question</td><td>This is a problem about dividing a quantity into a given ratio. Students may use the unitary method or convert the ratio into proportions and take fractions of the total weight. Some students may confuse ratio with proportion. Emphasise that ratio compares the sizes of parts, whereas proportion compares the size of the part to the size of the whole.</td><td>**Answer**

Level 6
2 125 g</td></tr>
</table>

Development and links

This topic is developed in Chapter 13 where students will use algebraic methods to solve problems involving direct proportion and use conversion graphs. Proportional reasoning is used to solve problems in Chapter 16. The topic of ratio and proportion is developed further in Year 9.

Ratio and proportion are important in many areas of the curriculum. Students will use ratio and proportion when scaling formulae in science, converting recipe quantities in food technology, mixing paint colours in art and working with maps in geography. Percentage increase is used in business studies and economics to calculate price rises and VAT.

13 Algebra

Objectives

	Level
• Use systematic trial and improvement methods and ICT tools to find approximate solutions to equations such as $x^2 + x = 20$	**6**
• Construct functions arising from real-life problems and plot their corresponding graphs	**6**
• Interpret graphs arising from real situations, e.g. time series graphs	**6**
• Add simple algebraic fractions	**7**
• Use formulae from mathematics and other subjects	**7**
• In simple cases, change a formula's subject	**7**
• Interpret the meaning of various points and sections of straight-line graphs, including intercepts and intersections, e.g. solving simultaneous linear equations	**7**
• Generate points and plot graphs of linear functions, where y is given implicitly in terms of x (e.g. $ay + bx = 0$, $y + bx + c = 0$), on paper and using ICT	**7**
• Use algebraic methods to solve problems involving direct proportion	**7**
• Use compound measures to compare in real-life contexts	**7**

Level

MPA

1.1	13a, b, c, d, e, f, g, h
1.2	13a, b, c, d, e, f, g, h
1.3	13a, b, c, d, e, f, g, h
1.4	13a, c, d, e, f, g, h
1.5	13a, b, c, e, f, g, h

PLTS

IE	13a, b, c, e, f
CT	13a, b, c, d, e, f, g, h
RL	13a, b, c, d, e
TW	13c, e, h
SM	13f
EP	13I, a, c, d, f, g, h

Introduction

The aim of this chapter is to consolidate and extend knowledge of algebra topics introduced in earlier chapters. Students write and simplify expressions, rearrange and substitute values into formulae, and solve further linear equations including those involving fractions. They use trial and improvement methods to solve equations, plot linear graphs where y is given implicitly in terms of x and solve proportion problems using algebraic methods. The topic concludes by plotting and interpreting graphs arising from real-life situations including conversion graphs and distance-time graphs.

The student book discusses how computers perform calculations. Computer programmers use a programming language to write instructions to tell the computer how to deal with input values. In the same way, the language of algebra is used to write expressions that give instructions on how to deal with input values. Using certain rules, the expressions can be rearranged and manipulated without needing to know the input values. There is more information about computer programming at http://computer.howstuffworks.com/program1.htm (EP).

Extra Resources

13	Start of chapter presentation
13a	Starter Brackets T or F
13b	Consolidation sheet
13c	Consolidation sheet
13d	Worked solution: Q1i
13d	Consolidation sheet
13e	Worked solution: Q1
13e	Consolidation sheet
13g	Animation: Proportion graphs
13g	Consolidation sheet
13h	Animation: Interpreting graphs
13h	Animation: Real-life graphs
13h	Consolidation sheet

Assessment: chapter 13

Fast-track

13b, c, d, e, f, g, h

- Simplify or transform linear expressions by collecting like terms (L6)
- Multiply a single term over a bracket (L6)

Useful resources

Starter – Calculate 100

Ask students to calculate 100 using the digits 1 to 9 and any operation(s). For example, $123 - 4 - 5 - 6 - 7 + 8 - 9 = 100$.

Students score a point for each different calculation. Bonus points if the digits are kept in numerical order as in the example!

Teaching notes

Recapitulate work covered in spreads **5b** and **5c**. Give examples of addition and subtraction of terms including two variables. Ask students to fill in the missing terms to make a simplification complete. For example, $3x + ? - 5 = 7x - 8$. Include examples that involve adding and subtracting negatives.

Give examples of multiplication of terms including two variables and squared terms.

Look at the use of brackets in practical contexts, for example, for expressing the area of a shape (EP).

Look at examples of the expansion of a single bracket, include calculations that involve negatives and squaring terms.

Look at an example of the area of a triangle. This will allow exploration of division in algebra. Can the expression be simplified?

Look back at the expressions discussed. Can any of them be factorised?

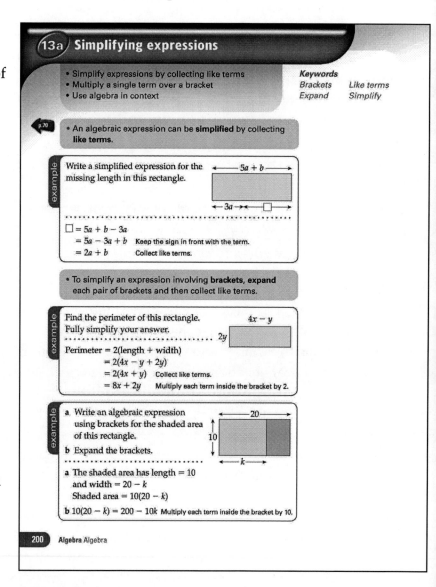

13a **Simplifying expressions**

- Simplify expressions by collecting like terms
- Multiply a single term over a bracket
- Use algebra in context

Keywords
Brackets   Like terms
Expand   Simplify

p.70
- An algebraic expression can be **simplified** by collecting **like terms**.

Write a simplified expression for the missing length in this rectangle.
$5a + b$
$3a$

$\square = 5a + b - 3a$
$= 5a - 3a + b$ Keep the sign in front with the term.
$= 2a + b$ Collect like terms.

- To simplify an expression involving **brackets, expand** each pair of brackets and then collect like terms.

Find the perimeter of this rectangle. Fully simplify your answer.
$4x - y$
$2y$

Perimeter $= 2(\text{length} + \text{width})$
$= 2(4x - y + 2y)$
$= 2(4x + y)$ Collect like terms.
$= 8x + 2y$ Multiply each term inside the bracket by 2.

a Write an algebraic expression using brackets for the shaded area of this rectangle.
b Expand the brackets.
20
10
k

a The shaded area has length $= 10$ and width $= 20 - k$
Shaded area $= 10(20 - k)$
b $10(20 - k) = 200 - 10k$ Multiply each term inside the bracket by 10.

200   Algebra Algebra

Plenary

How can the magic square in question **2** be used to create a non-algebraic magic square? Substitute values for a and b. How can the magic square be adapted to create another algebraic magic square? Add or subtract the same terms to each square.

Simplification

Encourage students to circle the like terms and join them, perhaps using colours for questions **1** and **2**.

All questions (1.3)

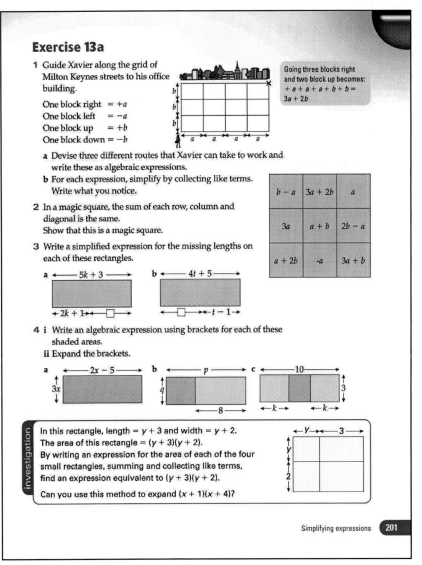

Extension

Set questions similar to question **4** involving compound shapes including right angled triangles. Find possible values of the unknowns if the area is given (IE).

Exercise 13a commentary

Question 1 – encourage students to choose routes that involve both positive and negative terms. Why do they all simplify to the same answer? (1.1)

Question 2 – How many checks do you have to make? Is it possible to work out possible values for a and b? No, they can be any value (1.1, 1.2).

Question 3 – Most students are likely to see what else is needed to make the whole length of the rectangle. Can the answer be found by subtraction? Encourage students to check their solution by summing (RL).

Question 4 – Encourage students to sketch the rectangles and fill in missing lengths where necessary. In part **a**, students may need help when multiplying $2x$ by $3x$.

Investigation – Some students may think it possible to collect the terms in y^2 and y. Make up a value for y and show that this does not work. Encourage students to make a guess as to the simplification of $(x + 1)(x + 4)$ before trying a diagram approach (CT, RL) (1.4).

Links

The city of Milton Keynes in the UK is laid out in a grid system with ten horizontal roads (Ways) at 1 km intervals and eleven vertical roads (Streets), also at 1 km intervals. Milton Keynes was designed as a new town and construction began in 1967. The roads are numbered with H or V numbers for horizontal or vertical, for example, H6 Childs Way. There is more information about the Milton Keynes grid system at http://www.road-to-nowhere.co.uk/features/milton_keynes.html (EP) (1.1).

- Add simple algebraic fractions

(L7) *Useful resources*

Starter – Algebraic differences

Draw a 4 × 4 table on the board to form 16 cells.

Label the columns with the terms, x, $3x$, $2y$, $-4x$, label the rows with the terms, $-2x$, $3y$, $5x$, $-y$.

Ask students to fill in the table by subtracting the left label term from the top label term. For example, the top row in the table would read $3x$, $5x$, $2y + 2x$, $-2x$.

Can be differentiated by the choice of terms.

Teaching notes

Recapitulate the methods of addition and subtraction of fractions covered in spread **4b**. The methods that apply to numbers can be extended to apply to algebra. Look at different ways of expressing a fraction of a term, for example, one and a half x, $1\frac{1}{2}x$, $\frac{3}{2}x$, $\frac{3x}{2}$

Which is the most common method of representation? What does $\frac{x}{5}$ actually mean? Discuss the fact that something that is cut into 5 is actually just one fifth.

Look at examples of adding and subtracting simple algebraic fractions with common denominators. Can any of the examples be simplified?

How can algebraic fractions be simplified if the denominators are different? Use the idea of equivalent fractions used for non algebraic fractions. Is it possible to simplify the final answers?

Consider looking at examples that include **i** a mixed fractional part of a term, **ii** the combination of algebraic and non algebraic fractions, **iii** three algebraic fractions with different denominators.

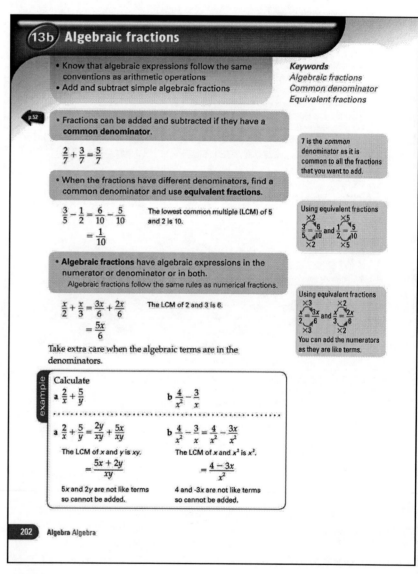

Plenary

Ask students to suggest a pair of equivalent fractions, similar to those in question **3**. Encourage students to be creative and think of complex possibilities. Does the rest of the class agree with the suggestions? (CT) (1.5)

Simplification

Use diagrams to re-enforce what is happening when fractions are added and subtracted. Rectangles, subdivided into squares, are a convenient way of explaining the process for questions **1** and **4** (1.1).

All questions (1.3)

Question 1 – Why are these fractions simple to add or subtract? Denominators are the same. Watch for students incorrectly summing the denominators (RL).

Question 2 – Are parts **d** and **e** different from the other parts of the question? How can they those parts be pronounced? What do they mean?

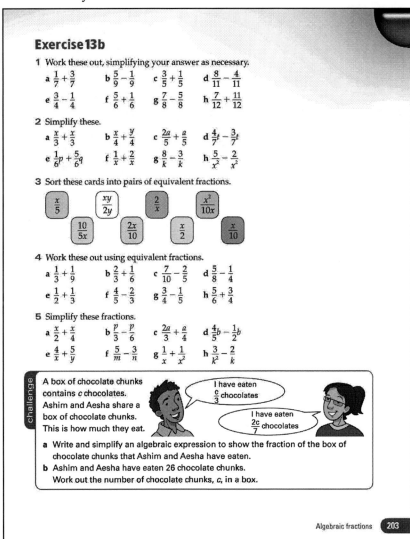

Exercise 13b commentary

Question 3 – Encourage students to write out the algebraic fractions in full, splitting up x^2 ($x \times x$) and 10 (2×5). This may make it easier to see how the fractions simplify.

Question 4 – Urge students to look for the lowest common denominator, rather than just use the product of the denominators. Why is this a good idea? (1.5)

Question 5 – How can the denominators be made to be the same? Compare the methods used in question **4** with those needed in this question. Part **d** could be re-written in the format of the other parts to make it easier to manipulate (CT) (1.2).

Challenge – What does $\frac{c}{3}$ mean if there are c chocolates in the box? How can the total number of chocolates eaten be worked out if c were known? When finding c, students might form an equation and solve it, however, many students are likely to try a different approach. Encourage the use of trial and improvement methods or the use of a fractional comparison, For example, $\frac{13}{21}$ of the box represents 26 chocolates, what is $\frac{1}{21}$ of the box? (IE) (1.1).

Links

In chemistry, a fraction is a mixture of liquids with similar boiling points. The fractions in crude oil have individual names, (diesel, kerosene, petrol, *etc.*) and have different properties and uses. They are separated using a fractionating column. There is more information about oil fractions at http://www.bbc.co.uk/schools/gcsebitesize/science/edexcel/oneearth/fuelsrev3.shtml

Extension

Introduce mixed algebraic fraction questions. Begin with simple examples and ask if the fractions need to be converted into top heavy fractions or not. For example, $1\frac{x}{3} + x\frac{2}{3} = \frac{?}{3}$

- Use formulae from mathematics and other subjects   (L7)
- In simple cases, change (a formula's) subject   (L7)

Useful resources
Calculator for checking solutions

Starter – Five, one, four

Write F I V E
− O N E
F O U R

Ask students to find what digits the letters
E, F, I, N, O, R, U and V represent so that
the calculation is true

(One possible solution is E = 7, F = 1, I = 4, N = 5, O = 2, R = 0, U = 3, V = 8)

How many ways can they find? Can they make other word to number puzzles?

Discuss strategies used (EP).

Teaching notes

Recapitulate work on substituting values in formulae, covered in spreads **5e**, **8i** and **10e**, and work on rearranging formulae, covered in spread **5f**. Look at examples like those in questions **1** and **2**. Here you are given a formula and some values to substitute, but the equation does not have the correct subject. Tackle the examples in two ways. First, rearrange to get the correct subject, then substitute in the values. Then try the same example, but substitute in the values first and then solve the resulting equation. Ask students to compare the two methods and say which they find most convenient? Will it depend of the complexity of the formulae?

Continue to emphasise the importance of showing working on both sides, whether rearranging or solving equations. Remind students to eliminate negative terms of the subject in question and expand brackets when necessary.

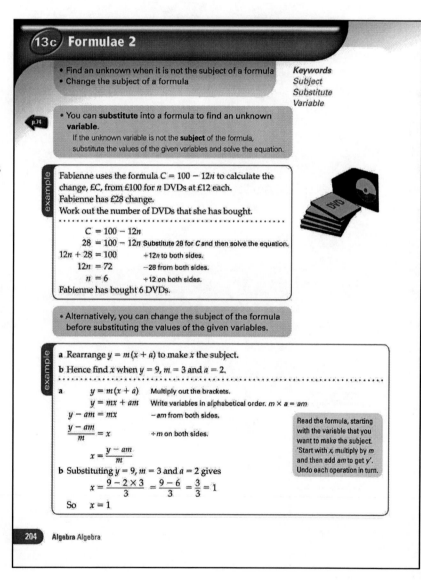

Plenary

Look at question **4** again. Examine correct answers that students obtained that look different to each other. For example, part **a**, $\frac{a}{b} - y$ or $\frac{a - by}{b}$. How can we show that they are the same? Is either one simpler? (1.5)

Simplification

An arrow diagram maybe useful for some of the rearrangements. By reversing the processes the new subject could be found. For example, question **4a** (1.2)

$$x \;\rightarrow\; +y \;\rightarrow\; \times b \;=\; a$$
$$a \;\rightarrow\; \div b \;\rightarrow\; -y \;=\; x$$
$$x = \frac{a}{b} - y$$

No question requires a calculator, but one could be allowed as a checking tool (RL). All questions (1.3)

Question 1 – Encourage the approach: write the question/ substitute in values/ expand brackets/rearrange. With a calculator, ask students to check that both sides of the original formulae give the same value using their answers.

Exercise 13c

1 By substituting the given values to form an equation, find the required variable in each of these formulae.

   a $m = \frac{c}{100}$ Find c when $m = 3.2$

   b $A = \frac{1}{2}bh$ Find h when $A = 27$ and $b = 6$

   c $P = 2(l + w)$ Find w when $P = 22$ and $l = 8$

   d $s = \left(\frac{u + v}{2}\right)t$ Find t when $s = 180$, $u = 0$ and $v = 24$

2 The area, A, of a trapezium is given by the formula
   $A = \frac{1}{2}(a + b)h$ where a, b and h are the lengths as shown on the diagram.

   a By forming and solving an equation, find h when $A = 12$, $a = 2$ and $b = 6$.

   b By forming and solving an equation, find a when $A = 24$, $b = 7$ and $h = 4$.

3 The surface area, S, of a cuboid is given by the formula
   $S = 2lw + 2hw + 2hl$ where l is the length, w is the width and h is the height.

   a By forming and solving an equation, find w when $S = 76$, $l = 4$ and $h = 5$.

   b Find the length of a cuboid with a surface area of 94, a width of 3 and a height of 4.

   c Explain why this formula works.

4 Make x the subject of each of these formulae.

   a $a = b(x + y)$ **b** $p(w + x) = q$

   c $t = m(x - n)$ **d** $x(a + b) = c$

   e $k^2 = t(m + x)$ **f** $t = \frac{1}{2}(x + y)$

   g $r^2 = \frac{1}{3}(x - p)$ **h** $pq(x - p) = r$

   challenge

   a Make x the subject of these formulae.

   i $\frac{a}{x} = b$ **ii** $p + q = \frac{r}{x}$

   b Create some more formulae involving x as the denominator of a fraction and challenge your partner to rearrange your formulae to make x the subject. Discuss your methods.

Extension

Try questions **1–3** by substituting fractions rather than integers. Set this challenge without a calculator. Use vulgar fractions initially, but could be made more challenging by using mixed fractions.

Question 2 – Students may find is awkward to get rid of the $\frac{1}{2}$. If the R.H.S. is thought of as half of $(a + b) \times h$, then what can be done to remove the half? ($\times 2$) (1.1).

Question 3 – Draw on previous work from spread **13a** to simplify terms that are added. Adopt the same approach as question **1** to work methodically through to the solution. A diagram may help to explain how the surface area formula is derived (1.1).

Question 4 – Some students may feel that this question does not give 'an answer' since it does not result in a numerical value.

Challenge – How can you remove the x from the denominator? Draw a comparison to simplifying the algebraic fractions in spread **13b** question **3**. When looking at the final answer, can you see what has 'swapped round'? (IE, TW) (1.5)

Assessment Criteria – Algebra, level 7: use formulae from mathematics and other subjects. Algebra, level 7: derive a formula and, in simple cases, change its subject.

Links

The formula $V = IR$ is called Ohm's Law and was discovered by the German physicist George Ohm who published the results of his work in 1827. At first, other German scientists did not accept his work and it was only after the Royal Society in London awarded Ohm a medal in 1841 that he became a professor at the university in Munich. There is more information about Georg Ohm at http:// en.wikipedia.org/wiki/ Georg_Ohm (EP).

• Solve linear equations with in one unknown with integer and fractional coefficients

Useful resources

(L7)

Starter – Twins

Siobhan and Rachel are twins. Siobhan multiplied her age by 3 and subtracted 6 Rachel got the same answer when she multiplied her age by 2 and added 6.

Ask students to work out the age of the twins by forming an equation and solving it. (12 years)

Challenge students to make up their own puzzles.

Teaching notes

Recapitulate work covered for solving equations in exercises **7a** and **7b**. Focus on equations that have fractions. Include examples of different types and discuss the best steps to find solutions. Remind students to eliminate negative terms of the unknown value as soon as possible. For example,

$$\frac{x}{3} + 5 = 12, \quad \frac{5(3 - 2x)}{4} = 3, \quad \frac{7}{x} = 8,$$

$$5 - \frac{3x}{2} = 7, \quad \frac{2}{x} + 7 = 18, \quad \frac{10}{x + 1} = 4$$

How can the fractions be eliminated? Should you multiply both sides by the denominator as the first step in every case? Encourage students to look for ways to simplify the equation by adding or subtracting from both sides if possible.

Look at an equation of the type in question **3**. What will happen if you multiply both sides by one of the denominators? When a fraction is multiplied, which part of the fraction changes? Top, bottom, both? Look at the example of $\frac{1}{4} \times 3 = \frac{3}{4}$. Only the top is multiplied. Perform two multiplications to eliminate both denominators. Ask, could this have been achieved in one step? Discus the method of cross multiplying.

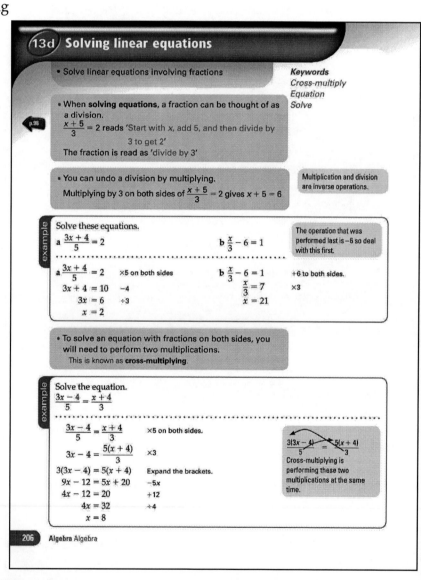

Plenary

Challenge students to construct a question similar to question **5**. Area or perimeter could be used. Can the rest of the class answer some of the proposed questions? Is it possible to construct this sort of question and end up with an impossible answer? For example, a negative area or length of a side (CT) (1.2).

Simplification

This is a challenging exercise: direct students to those parts that only involve a simple denominator, for example, questions **1**, **2a–g**. Writing out all workings should be encouraged. Cross multiplication is often very poorly recalled and confused with addition/subtraction and multiplication of ordinary fractions. In question **3**, part **a**, start students off by writing $4x = 2(x + 6)$.

All questions (1.3)

Question 1 – Some students may multiply by the denominator as the first step. Is this a good idea for every part? For example, parts **a** and **e**. The most likely error is to forget to multiply each term by the denominator, (RL).

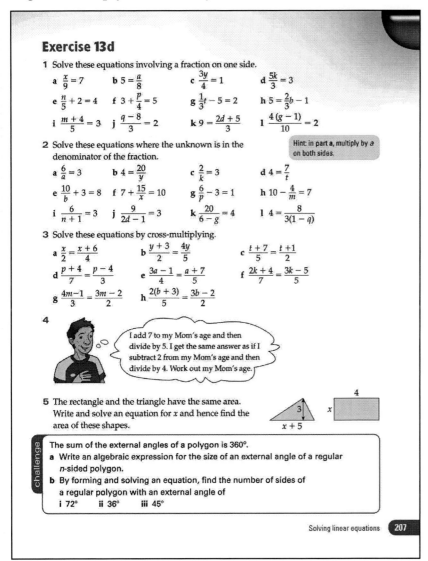

Exercise 13d

1 Solve these equations involving a fraction on one side.

a $\frac{x}{9} = 7$ b $5 = \frac{a}{8}$ c $\frac{3y}{4} = 1$ d $\frac{5k}{3} = 3$

e $\frac{n}{5} + 2 = 4$ f $3 + \frac{p}{4} = 5$ g $\frac{1}{3}t - 5 = 2$ h $5 = \frac{2}{3}b - 1$

i $\frac{m+4}{5} = 3$ j $\frac{q-8}{3} = 2$ k $9 = \frac{2d+5}{3}$ l $\frac{4(g-1)}{10} = 2$

2 Solve these equations where the unknown is in the denominator of the fraction.

> Hint: in part **a**, multiply by *a* on both sides.

a $\frac{6}{a} = 3$ b $4 = \frac{20}{y}$ c $\frac{2}{k} = 3$ d $4 = \frac{7}{t}$

e $\frac{10}{b} + 3 = 8$ f $7 + \frac{15}{x} = 10$ g $\frac{6}{p} - 3 = 1$ h $10 - \frac{4}{m} = 7$

i $\frac{6}{n+1} = 3$ j $\frac{9}{2d-1} = 3$ k $\frac{20}{6-g} = 4$ l $4 = \frac{8}{3(1-q)}$

3 Solve these equations by cross-multiplying.

a $\frac{x}{2} = \frac{x+6}{4}$ b $\frac{y+3}{2} = \frac{4y}{5}$ c $\frac{t+7}{5} = \frac{t+1}{2}$

d $\frac{p+4}{7} = \frac{p-4}{3}$ e $\frac{3a-1}{4} = \frac{a+7}{5}$ f $\frac{2k+4}{7} = \frac{3k-5}{5}$

g $\frac{4m-1}{3} = \frac{3m-2}{2}$ h $\frac{2(b+3)}{5} = \frac{3b-2}{2}$

4

> I add 7 to my Mom's age and then divide by 5. I get the same answer as if I subtract 2 from my Mom's age and then divide by 4. Work out my Mom's age.

5 The rectangle and the triangle have the same area. Write and solve an equation for *x* and hence find the area of these shapes.

challenge

The sum of the external angles of a polygon is 360°.
a Write an algebraic expression for the size of an external angle of a regular *n*-sided polygon.
b By forming and solving an equation, find the number of sides of a regular polygon with an external angle of
   i 72°   ii 36°   iii 45°

Solving linear equations **207**

Extension

Challenge students with examples that include three fractions. How can the denominators be removed? Can cross multiplication still be used? If so, how? Are the methods used in spread **13b** helpful? For example, $\frac{x}{5} + \frac{2x}{3} = \frac{1}{2}$ (CT) (1.1).

Question 2 – For the more challenging parts, the use of brackets is essential. Encourage simplifying before multiplying.

Question 3 – Encourage students to use brackets for the first stage of cross-multiplication.

Question 4 – Ensure students use the fractional notation for division and not a '÷' symbol. Why is cross multiplication useful here? (1.1)

Question 5 – Some students may need reminding of the area of a triangle formula. The concept of forming an equation could be helped by asking, what is the area of each shape? What does the question tell us about the two areas? Make sure students find the area, not just *x* (1.1).

Challenge – Use a regular hexagon to establish that the first statement in the challenge is true, and that all the exterior angles are equal (1.4).

Links

There is no proof for the existence of extra-terrestrial life, but in 1960 scientist Frank Drake invented a famous equation to estimate the number (N) of civilisations in our galaxy who might be capable of communicating with us. The equation is $N = R \times f_p \times n_e \times f_l \times f_i \times f_c \times L$ where, for example, R is the rate of formation of stars, f_p is the fraction of stars with planets, n_e is the number of planets per star capable of sustaining life, f_l is is the fraction of those planets where life develops, f_i is the fraction of f_l where intelligent life develops, f_c is the fraction of f_i where technology develops and L is the length of time that civilizations release radio waves into space. Find out more at http://www.pbs.org/wgbh/nova/origins/drak-flash.html (EP).

- Use systematic trial and improvement methods and ICT tools to find approximate solutions to equations such as $x^2 + x = 20$ (L6)

Useful resources
Scientific calculator

Starter – Think of a number

Ask students to write equations for 'Think of a number' problems and find the starting numbers, For example,

I multiply by 3 and subtract 7. I get the same answer if I double and add 2. (9)

I double my number, add 14 and divide by 2. I get the same answer if I double and subtract 5. (12)

Teaching notes

Recap work on trial-and-improvement covered previously in spread **8f**. Remind students that the x in the examples that gives the closest estimate is not necessarily the correct answer. The mid point of the x values **must** be checked and then the correct x value decided upon.

Look at alternative approaches to constructing a table to record the trials. The example uses two additional columns of working for x^2 and $\frac{1}{x}$. Are these necessary? Encourage students to give advantages and disadvantages to showing this extra working. Which students in the class feel more comfortable showing all the working? (1.4, 1.5)

Solving equations like $x^4 = 60$ can be made much easier by using the power function on a calculator. Ensure all students are aware of how it is displayed on their own calculator, appearing as any of x^y y^x $\wedge$ x^n (1.3).

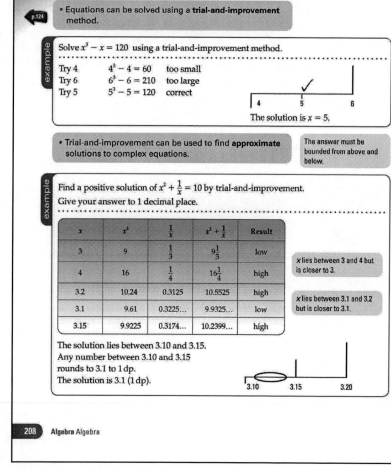

13e Trial-and-improvement 2

- Use systematic trial-and-improvement methods to find solutions or approximate solutions to equations

Keywords
Approximate
Trial-and-improvement

- Equations can be solved using a **trial-and-improvement** method.

Solve $x^3 - x = 120$ using a trial-and-improvement method.

Try 4 $4^3 - 4 = 60$ too small
Try 6 $6^3 - 6 = 210$ too large
Try 5 $5^3 - 5 = 120$ correct

The solution is $x = 5$.

- Trial-and-improvement can be used to find **approximate** solutions to complex equations.

The answer must be bounded from above and below.

Find a positive solution of $x^2 + \frac{1}{x} = 10$ by trial-and-improvement. Give your answer to 1 decimal place.

x	x^2	$\frac{1}{x}$	$x^2 + \frac{1}{x}$	Result
3	9	$\frac{1}{3}$	$9\frac{1}{3}$	low
4	16	$\frac{1}{4}$	$16\frac{1}{4}$	high
3.2	10.24	0.3125	10.5525	high
3.1	9.61	0.3225...	9.9325...	low
3.15	9.9225	0.3174...	10.2399...	high

x lies between 3 and 4 but is closer to 3.

x lies between 3.1 and 3.2 but is closer to 3.1.

The solution lies between 3.10 and 3.15.
Any number between 3.10 and 3.15 rounds to 3.1 to 1 dp.
The solution is 3.1 (1 dp).

208   Algebra Algebra

Plenary

The equation $x^3 - 4x = 0$ has three solutions (0, ±2). Find all of them using trial-and-improvement. What value of x should you begin with? What are the limitations of the method of trial and improvement? (RL) (1.2)

Simplification

Prepare the table of values for some of the questions and include an initial close estimation. Allow students to work to the nearest integer rather than 1 dp for questions **4–6**, but point out that they must still check half of the final interval.

All questions (IE) (1.1, 1.3)

Question 1 – Insist students show all their working to demonstrate how they bound the solution. Some may be tempted to ignore a trial if it gives a poor result.

Question 2 – Encourage a similar layout to that used in question 1. Part **d** may need some explaining. Some students may know how to use the power function, though this is not essential.

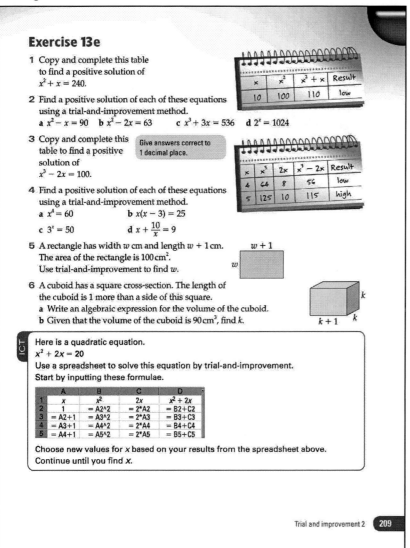

Extension

Solve these problems using trial and improvement and the power button on the calculator.

$9^x = 3$, $100^x = 10$, $36^x = 6$, $8^x = 2$, $1000^x = 10$, $125^x = 5$

What does a power of $\frac{1}{2}$ or $\frac{1}{3}$ do to a number? (square and cube root) (CT) (1.3, 1.4)

Exercise 13e commentary

Question 3 – Challenge students to say when they feel it is appropriate to stop the trials. Some students may incorrectly try to achieve 100 to 1 dp. Other students are very likely to accept an answer without bisecting the final interval (RL).

Question 4 – Parts **a** and **c** that used powers may need some further explanation. The power button on the calculator will be needed for part **c**. Some students may question the meaning of 3 to a decimal power.

Questions 5 and **6** – Encourage students to write an equation before using trial and improvement. Why can't these problems be solved by just trying a few values? How can you choose a good starting value? (1.5)

ICT – Some students will have had little experience using spread sheets or formulae. An explanation of the power and multiplication symbols may be needed. Students could be put in mixed experience pairs (TW).

Assessment Criteria – Algebra, level 6: use systematic trial and improvement methods and ICT tools to find approximate solutions to equations such as $x^3 + x = 20$.

Links

Trial by ordeal is an ancient form of trial practised by the Anglo-Saxons up until the Middle Ages. The defendant was forced to walk over red-hot coals/plunge their hand into boiling water/be thrown into a river or pond to see if they sank/take part in a fight (trial by fire/hot water/cold water/combat). In each case, it was believed that God would intervene to protect the innocent.

Useful resources

- Generate points and plot graphs of linear functions, where y is given implicitly as a function of x (e.g. $ay + bx = 0$, $y + bx + c = 0$) on paper and using ICT (L7)
- Interpret the meaning of various points and sections of straight-line graphs, including intercepts and intersections, e.g. solving simultaneous linear equations (L7)

Starter – Pigeons and rabbits

Gareth was watching some pigeons and rabbits. He counted the number of heads and feet. There were 26 heads and 74 feet.

How many pigeons and how many rabbits there were. (15 pigeons, 11 rabbits)

Can be extended by asking students to make up their own bird and animal puzzles.

Teaching notes

Recapitulate work covered previously on rearranging formulae in spreads **5f** and **13c**. Continue to insist on working being shown on both sides. Keep comparing with the method of solving linear equations. Look briefly at examples that include all four operations (1.2).

Recapitulate work on drawing graphs of linear functions covered previously in spread **7d**. Previously the equation was given 'explicitly', that is, it began with $y =$. Look at examples of 'implicit' linear functions. How can a table of values be completed for these? Encourage different approaches. First, by choosing different x or y values, can the matching y or x value be found to make the equation 'correct'? What difficulties does this create? Some values maybe hard to find or give decimal/fractional answers that will difficult to plot. Second, if explicit functions are easier to work with, what other method might be useful? Rearrange the function to make y the subject first (1.4, 1.5).

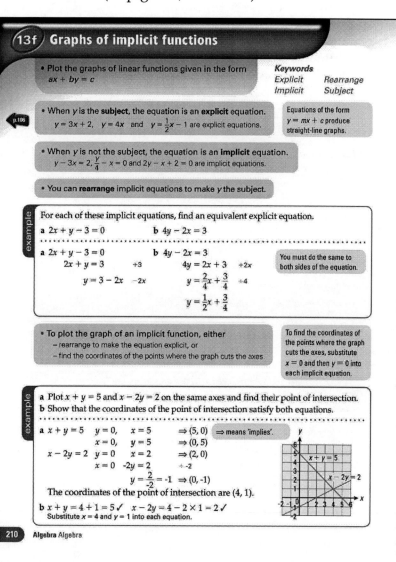

13f Graphs of implicit functions

- Plot the graphs of linear functions given in the form $ax + by = c$

Keywords
Explicit   Rearrange
Implicit   Subject

- When y is the **subject**, the equation is an **explicit** equation.
  $y = 3x + 2$, $y = 4x$ and $y = \frac{1}{2}x - 1$ are explicit equations.

  Equations of the form $y = mx + c$ produce straight-line graphs.

- When y is not the subject, the equation is an **implicit** equation.
  $y - 3x = 2$, $\frac{y}{4} - x = 0$ and $2y - x + 2 = 0$ are implicit equations.

- You can **rearrange** implicit equations to make y the subject.

example

For each of these implicit equations, find an equivalent explicit equation.
a $2x + y - 3 = 0$ **b** $4y - 2x = 3$

a $2x + y - 3 = 0$ **b** $4y - 2x = 3$
  $2x + y = 3$ $+3$ $4y = 2x + 3$ $+2x$
  $y = 3 - 2x$ $-2x$ $y = \frac{2}{4}x + \frac{3}{4}$ $\div4$
                              $y = \frac{1}{2}x + \frac{3}{4}$

You must do the same to both sides of the equation.

- To plot the graph of an implicit function, either
  – rearrange to make the equation explicit, or
  – find the coordinates of the points where the graph cuts the axes.

To find the coordinates of the points where the graph cuts the axes, substitute $x = 0$ and then $y = 0$ into each implicit equation.

example

a Plot $x + y = 5$ and $x - 2y = 2$ on the same axes and find their point of intersection.
b Show that the coordinates of the point of intersection satisfy both equations.

a $x + y = 5$ $y = 0$, $x = 5$ $\Rightarrow (5, 0)$ $\Rightarrow$ means 'implies'.
                   $x = 0$, $y = 5$ $\Rightarrow (0, 5)$
   $x - 2y = 2$ $y = 0$ $x = 2$ $\Rightarrow (2, 0)$
                 $x = 0$ $-2y = 2$ $\div -2$
                 $y = \frac{2}{-2} = -1$ $\Rightarrow (0, -1)$
The coordinates of the point of intersection are (4, 1).

b $x + y = 4 + 1 = 5$✓ $x - 2y = 4 - 2 \times 1 = 2$✓
Substitute $x = 4$ and $y = 1$ into each equation.

Plenary

Is it possible to tell if a function will be linear before you draw it? Ask the students to suggest some functions they believe are linear. Encourage different looking functions. Can students suggest some that are not linear? (1.4)

Simplification

When rearranging implicit functions, it may be helpful to use arrow diagrams that show the function beginning with y. Then by reversing the operations y can be made the subject.

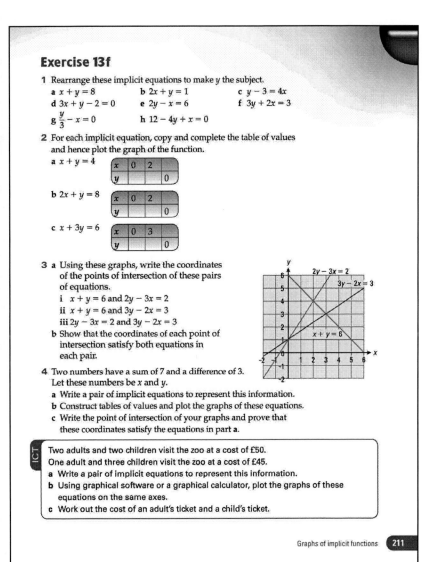

Exercise 13f

1 Rearrange these implicit equations to make y the subject.
- **a** $x + y = 8$
- **b** $2x + y = 1$
- **c** $y - 3 = 4x$
- **d** $3x + y - 2 = 0$
- **e** $2y - x = 6$
- **f** $3y + 2x = 3$
- **g** $\frac{y}{3} - x = 0$
- **h** $12 - 4y + x = 0$

2 For each implicit equation, copy and complete the table of values and hence plot the graph of the function.

a $x + y = 4$

x	0	2
y		0

b $2x + y = 8$

x	0	2
y		0

c $x + 3y = 6$

x	0	3
y		0

3 a Using these graphs, write the coordinates of the points of intersection of these pairs of equations.
  - **i** $x + y = 6$ and $2y - 3x = 2$
  - **ii** $x + y = 6$ and $3y - 2x = 3$
  - **iii** $2y - 3x = 2$ and $3y - 2x = 3$

  b Show that the coordinates of each point of intersection satisfy both equations in each pair.

4 Two numbers have a sum of 7 and a difference of 3. Let these numbers be x and y.
  - **a** Write a pair of implicit equations to represent this information.
  - **b** Construct tables of values and plot the graphs of these equations.
  - **c** Write the point of intersection of your graphs and prove that these coordinates satisfy the equations in part **a**.

ICT

Two adults and two children visit the zoo at a cost of £50. One adult and three children visit the zoo at a cost of £45.
  - **a** Write a pair of implicit equations to represent this information.
  - **b** Using graphical software or a graphical calculator, plot the graphs of these equations on the same axes.
  - **c** Work out the cost of an adult's ticket and a child's ticket.

Extension

Plot linear functions that are expressed implicitly, but do not have a convenient set of integer solutions. For example, $3x + 4y = 7$. If an accurate drawing is required, how can the points and scale be chosen to avoid the need for decimals? For this example use seven intervals per unit on each axis (CT).

Exercise 13f commentary

All questions (1.1, 1.3)

Question 1 – Encourage the same approach as solving linear equations; perform an operation to both sides. Ask, how do you get the y on its own? Part **h** has a negative y term, how can this be dealt with?

Question 2 – Some students may want to make y the subject, is this necessary?

Question 3 – Some students may need reminding how to express coordinates. For part **b**, students should prove that the coordinates work by substitution and subsequent working (1.4).

Question 4 – There are two possible solutions for x and y since $x - y = 3$ or $y - x = 3$. In part **c** prove your answers are correct by showing the working (IE, CT) (1.4).

ICT – For those without access to a graphing program, how can the equation $2a + 2c = 50$ be simplified? Can you find the cost of a child's ticket by comparing the two equations now? That is, $a + c = 25$ and $a + 3c = 45$? What is the difference between the two equations? (IE, CT, EP, SM) (1.4)

Assessment Criteria – Algebra, level 7: use algebraic and graphical methods to solve simultaneous linear equations in two variables.

Links

An oscilloscope is a test instrument often used to troubleshoot electrical equipment that is malfunctioning. The instrument has a screen which can display a graph of voltage against time for the part of the circuit that is being tested. There is more information about oscilloscopes at http://en.wikipedia.org/wiki/Oscilloscope (EP).

- Use algebraic methods to solve problems involving direct proportion

Useful resources

(L7)

Starter – Algebraic jumble

Write a list of anagrams on the board and ask students to unscramble them and then make up their own anagrams. Possible anagrams are

MIFLIPSY, RABAGEL, AQUITONE, SPERENXIOS, CARKBEST, DPAXEN, OURFLAM, ENISERV, VELOS, OURFLAME

(simplify, algebra, equation, expression, brackets, expand, formula, inverse, solve, formulae)

Teaching notes

Recapitulate the definition of direct proportion covered in spread **12c**. Ask students to suggest two quantities that are in direct proportion. What does a graph of direct proportion look like? Ask students for their suggestions based on the types of quantities already discussed. Establish that it is represented by a line that passes through the origin. Ratio can be used to compare two quantities that in direct proportion. What will happen when the ratio of different amounts of the same two quantities are simplified to the form 1 : *n*? They will give the same ratio.

Which method, plotting a graph or comparing ratio will be more useful in establishing whether two quantities are in direct proportion. How many pairs of results will you need in each case? Two pairs of results, since the straight line on the graph must also pass through the origin (CT) (1.1, 1.4).

The man on the 100NZ$ note is Lord Rutherford who was instrumental in establishing the view of the atom suggested in the **Did you know?** in spread **1a**.

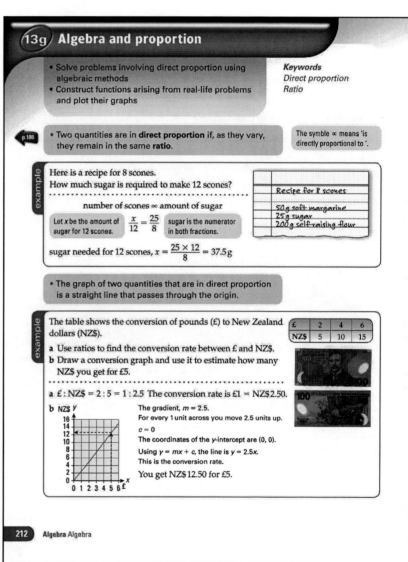

- Solve problems involving direct proportion using algebraic methods
- Construct functions arising from real-life problems and plot their graphs

Keywords
Direct proportion
Ratio

p.186
- Two quantities are in **direct proportion** if, as they vary, they remain in the same **ratio**.

The symble ∝ means 'is directly proportional to'.

Here is a recipe for 8 scones.
How much sugar is required to make 12 scones?

number of scones ∝ amount of sugar

Let *x* be the amount of sugar for 12 scones. $\frac{x}{12} = \frac{25}{8}$ sugar is the numerator in both fractions.

sugar needed for 12 scones, $x = \frac{25 \times 12}{8} = 37.5\,g$

Recipe for 8 scones
50 g soft margarine
25 g sugar
200 g self-raising flour

- The graph of two quantities that are in direct proportion is a straight line that passes through the origin.

The table shows the conversion of pounds (£) to New Zealand dollars (NZ$).

£	2	4	6
NZ$	5	10	15

a Use ratios to find the conversion rate between £ and NZ$.
b Draw a conversion graph and use it to estimate how many NZ$ you get for £5.

a £ : NZ$ = 2 : 5 = 1 : 2.5 The conversion rate is £1 = NZ$2.50.

b
The gradient, *m* = 2.5.
For every 1 unit across you move 2.5 units up.

c = 0
The coordinates of the *y*-intercept are (0, 0).
Using *y* = *mx* + *c*, the line is *y* = 2.5*x*.
This is the conversion rate.
You get NZ$12.50 for £5.

212 Algebra Algebra

Plenary

Look at the examples in question **1**. What suggestions can be made about how the variables are connected? Which are in direct proportion? Which are in a linear relationship? What about the others? Would sketch graphs help to decide on the type of relationship? Suggest possible sketches (1.1, 1.4).

Simplification

Allow students to solve problems using a non-algebraic method, for example, using ratio and converting to the required solution. Why is this method not always going to be useful? It may take longer to find the solution and be more difficult to use with more awkward numbers (1.5).

All questions (1.1, 1.3)

Question 1 – Ask, if you double one of the variables, do you double the other? If one of the variables is zero, will the other be zero? Would a graph of one variable plotted against the other produce a straight line through the origin? (EP) (1.2, 1.4)

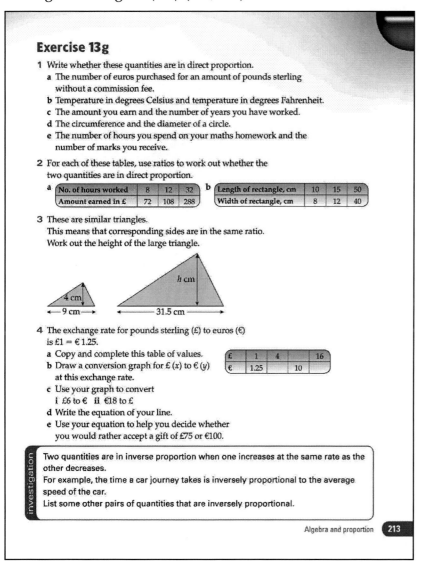

Exercise 13g

1 Write whether these quantities are in direct proportion.
  a The number of euros purchased for an amount of pounds sterling without a commission fee.
  b Temperature in degrees Celsius and temperature in degrees Fahrenheit.
  c The amount you earn and the number of years you have worked.
  d The circumference and the diameter of a circle.
  e The number of hours you spend on your maths homework and the number of marks you receive.

2 For each of these tables, use ratios to work out whether the two quantities are in direct proportion.

a

No. of hours worked	8	12	32
Amount earned in £	72	108	288

b

Length of rectangle, cm	10	15	50
Width of rectangle, cm	8	12	40

3 These are similar triangles.
  This means that corresponding sides are in the same ratio.
  Work out the height of the large triangle.

4 cm
9 cm
h cm
31.5 cm

4 The exchange rate for pounds sterling (£) to euros (€) is £1 = € 1.25.
  a Copy and complete this table of values.
  b Draw a conversion graph for £ (x) to € (y) at this exchange rate.

£	1	4		16
€	1.25		10	

  c Use your graph to convert
    i £6 to €   ii €18 to £
  d Write the equation of your line.
  e Use your equation to help you decide whether you would rather accept a gift of £75 or €100.

investigation
Two quantities are in inverse proportion when one increases at the same rate as the other decreases.
For example, the time a car journey takes is inversely proportional to the average speed of the car.
List some other pairs of quantities that are inversely proportional.

Algebra and proportion **213**

Extension

Work out some values for the example of speed/time from the **investigation**. Choose a convenient value for the fixed distance travelled. Draw the graph of the inverse proportion. What do you notice about the graph? It is curved and does not cross either axis, though it gets closer and closer (1.1, 1.4).

Exercise 13g commentary

Question 2 – Simplify each ratio, encourage students to 'knock off zeros' where possible to speed up the simplification process. Does it matter which way round the ratios are written?

Question 3 – Use the method of the first example. Some students may find cross multiplication useful if it has already been covered.

Question 4 – An equation of a line normally begins with $y =$. What is represented by the y-axis? How are the Euros calculated from the pounds? Advise students to draw their scale from 0 to 100 on each axis (EP).

Investigation – It is not easy to think up other examples. Encourage students to think of variables that have a negative correlation to begin with. For example, age and value of a car. Is this inverse proportion? Many of the best examples come from physics (CT, EP).

Assessment Criteria – NNS, level 7: understand and use proportionality.

Links

In finance, the exchange rate between two currencies is the price at which one country's currency can be exchanged to another currency. Most of the rates change daily although some exchange rates are fixed. Current exchange rates and a conversion calculator can be found at http://uk.finance.yahoo.com/ currency-converter?u and at http://www.x-rates.com/calculator.html How many Euros can be bought with £10 at today's exchange rate? (EP)

- Construct functions arising from real-life problems and plot their corresponding graphs; interpret graphs arising from real situations   (L6)
- Interpret graphs arising from real situations, e.g. time series graphs   (L6
- Use compound measures to compare in real-life contexts (e.g. travel graphs)   (L7)

Useful resources

Starter – Containers

Ask students to imagine two unmarked containers. One holds exactly 3 litres; the other holds exactly 5 litres. Jamie says he can use these containers to get exactly 4 litres. Ask students to work out how this can be done. How about 1 litre?

What if the capacities are 5 litres and 7 litres?

Teaching notes

Look at a distance time graph for a swimmer that is doing laps in a pool. Use the vertical axis for the distance from the start point. Show variations in speed and points were the swimmer stops. Ask students to suggest explanations for the shape of the graph.

Draw the graph of another swimmer on top of the previous graph. Use an example that shows the second swimmer initially swimming faster, but ultimately swimming the same distance in a slower time. Ask, who is the faster swimmer? Discuss the parts of the graph that provide us with the evidence (TW) (1.4).

Look at an example of the depth/time graph for filling a container at a constant rate. Use an example such as

How can the change in the speed of the increase of depth be shown in the graph? (CT)

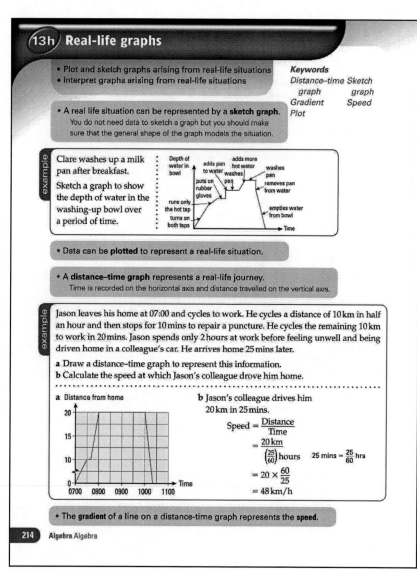

Plenary

What would a speed/time graph look like for the journey in question **3**? What scales are needed on the axes? Between the distance/time and speed/time graphs, which gives a clearer representation of the journey? (1.4) (1.5)

Simplification

Ask students to explain verbally what is happening at the various parts of the graphs. Encourage use of words like, 'increasing more and more'.

All questions (CT, EP) (1.1, 1.2, 1.4)

Question 1 – To begin with, students could match the statements and points of the graph that show an increase/decrease/constant depth and then investigate further to put the statements in order.

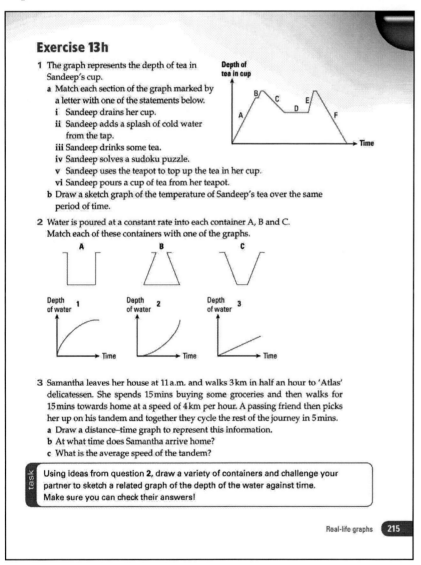

Exercise 13h

1 The graph represents the depth of tea in Sandeep's cup.
   a Match each section of the graph marked by a letter with one of the statements below.
   i Sandeep drains her cup.
   ii Sandeep adds a splash of cold water from the tap.
   iii Sandeep drinks some tea.
   iv Sandeep solves a sudoku puzzle.
   v Sandeep uses the teapot to top up the tea in her cup.
   vi Sandeep pours a cup of tea from her teapot.
   b Draw a sketch graph of the temperature of Sandeep's tea over the same period of time.

2 Water is poured at a constant rate into each container A, B and C. Match each of these containers with one of the graphs.

3 Samantha leaves her house at 11 a.m. and walks 3 km in half an hour to 'Atlas' delicatessen. She spends 15 mins buying some groceries and then walks for 15 mins towards home at a speed of 4 km per hour. A passing friend then picks her up on his tandem and together they cycle the rest of the journey in 5 mins.
   a Draw a distance–time graph to represent this information.
   b At what time does Samantha arrive home?
   c What is the average speed of the tandem?

> **task**
> Using ideas from question **2**, draw a variety of containers and challenge your partner to sketch a related graph of the depth of the water against time. Make sure you can check their answers!

Real-life graphs **215**

Extension

Draw a speed time graph for the journey in question **3**. Find the area underneath the graph. Look at the graph in question **3** again. Can you see what the value of the area represents in this journey? (CT) (1.1)

Exercise 13h commentary

Question 2 – Ask students to describe what happens when they fill a water bottle from the tap at home. The bottle fills up much quicker in the last few moments. Why?

Question 3 – What scale is needed on each axis? Which axis should time be plotted on? When finding average speed from the graph, ask, how far could he go in an hour? Remind students that car journeys tend to measure speed in mph or km/h meaning how far you would go in an hour. Since the graph does not always show a full hour, students will have to consider how they can work out an hour's worth of journey time (1.3).

Task – Ensure the containers are not too complicated, combinations of the ones used in question **2** will work well (TW).

Assessment Criteria – Algebra, level 6: construct functions arising from real-life problems and plot their corresponding graphs. Algebra, level 6: interpret graphs arising from real situations. SSM, level 7: understand and use measures of speed to solve problems.

Links

Racing drivers use real life graphs to analyse their own driving skills and the performance of the car during a race. The graphs can show features such as the engine speed and degree of steering as the car progresses around the bends in the track. There are examples of graphs used in motor sports at http:// autospeed.com/cms/A_108255/ article.html and at http://www. advantagemotorsports.com/ WS.htm (EP).

1 Write an algebraic expression for each missing length on this rectangle.

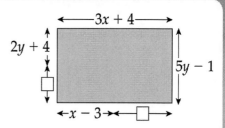

2 i Write an algebraic expression using brackets for the shaded areas in these rectangles.

ii Expand the brackets.

a

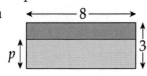

b

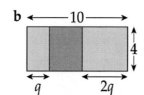

3 Simplify these expressions.

a $\dfrac{x}{5} + \dfrac{2x}{5}$ b $\dfrac{p}{8} - \dfrac{q}{8}$ c $\dfrac{5}{9}a - \dfrac{1}{9}a$ d $\dfrac{10}{t} - \dfrac{3}{t}$

4 Simplify these using equivalent fractions.

a $\dfrac{k}{4} + \dfrac{k}{8}$ b $\dfrac{2y}{5} - \dfrac{y}{100}$ c $\dfrac{3}{8}m + \dfrac{1}{2}m$ d $\dfrac{3}{10}n - \dfrac{1}{8}n$

e $\dfrac{3}{a} + \dfrac{2}{b}$ f $\dfrac{6}{p} - \dfrac{1}{q}$ g $\dfrac{10}{t} - \dfrac{7}{t^2}$ h $\dfrac{5}{xy} - \dfrac{3}{x}$

5 Jolyon decides to spend his £80 birthday money on CDs.
He uses the formula

$$P = 80 - 9x$$

to calculate P, the amount of money that he has left after buying x CDs.

a Write the cost of each CD.   b Jolyon has £26 left.
Write and solve an equation to calculate x, the number of CDs that Jolyon has bought.

6 Make x the subject of these formulae.

a $m = 3(x + n)$ b $k = \dfrac{1}{10}(c + x)$ c $p = q(x - t)$ d $k(x - r) = d^2$

7 Solve these equations.

a $\dfrac{a}{3} = \dfrac{a + 4}{5}$ b $\dfrac{b - 1}{3} = \dfrac{2b}{7}$ c $\dfrac{x + 5}{3} = \dfrac{x + 11}{5}$

d $\dfrac{y + 6}{9} = \dfrac{y - 2}{5}$ e $\dfrac{2p - 1}{9} = \dfrac{p - 3}{2}$ f $\dfrac{5q - 1}{4} = \dfrac{7q - 5}{5}$

g $\dfrac{3m + 1}{7} = \dfrac{5m - 6}{4}$ h $\dfrac{3n - 2}{5} = \dfrac{5n - 8}{6}$

8 Copy and complete this table to find a positive solution of $x^3 - x = 50$, correct to 1 dp.

x	x^3	$x^3 - x$	Result
4	64	60	high
3	27	24	low

9 a Copy and complete the tables and plot the graphs of these implicit functions on the same set of axes.

$x + y = 5$

x	0	1	2
y			

$5x - y = 1$

x	0	1	2
y			

b Write the coordinates of the point of intersection of these graphs.

c Show that the coordinates of the point of intersection satisfy each equation.

10 To convert miles to kilometres, you use the direct proportion relationship

$$5 \text{ miles} = 8 \text{ kilometres}$$

a Copy and complete this table of values.

b Draw a graph to convert miles to kilometres.

Miles	5	7.5		20
Kilometres	8		16	

c Use your graph to estimate how many kilometres are equivalent to 7 miles.

d Write the equation of your line.

11 Patrick leaves his home at 08:00. He jogs 3 km in 20 mins and then stops for 30 mins to have breakfast at a local café. Patrick sprints home in 10 mins. Patrick's wife, Giselle, leaves home at 08:15. She runs to the same café as Patrick in 15 mins and joins her husband for breakfast. Giselle leaves at the same time as Patrick and quickly walks back home, arriving at 09:15.

a Draw each of these journeys on the same distance–time graph.

b How long did Patrick and Giselle spend together over breakfast?

c Calculate the average speed at which
  i Patrick ran home
  ii Giselle walked home.

13 Summary

Assessment criteria

- Use systematic trial and improvement methods and ICT tools to find approximate solutions to equations such as $x^3 + x = 20$ — Level 6
- Construct functions arising from real-life problems and plot their corresponding graphs — Level 6
- Interpret graphs arising from real situations — Level 6
- Use formulae from mathematics and other subjects — Level 7
- Derive a formula and, in simple cases, change its subject — Level 7
- Use algebraic and graphical methods to solve simultaneous linear equations in two variables — Level 7
- Understand and use proportionality — Level 7
- Understand and use measures of speed to solve problems — Level 7

Question commentary

Example

The example illustrates a problem on using trial and improvement to solve an equation. Ask questions such as "How do you go about choosing a value of x to start?" Some students may confuse $2x^2$ with $(2x)^2$. Others may find that the answer is between 6.5 and 6.6 and so assume that the answer is 6.5 to 1 dp. Use of a number line will help to illustrate that this assumption is incorrect. Ask students if the equation can be solved by any other method.

x	$2x^2$	Comment
6	72	low
7	98	high
6.5	84.5	low
6.6	87.12	high
6.55	85.805	low

$x = 6.6$ to 1 dp

Past question

The question asks students to add lines representing different speeds to a distance-time graph. Encourage the use of a sharp pencil. Ask questions such as "What do the axes represent?" In part **b**, the distance axis does not extend to 120 km. Emphasise speed measured in km/hour as the distance travelled in an hour. Ask what distance will be travelled in half an hour. Encourage students to check their work by calculating the distance travelled in an hour, 30 minutes and 15 minutes at each speed and checking that the resulting points lie on the line drawn.

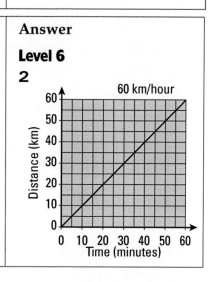

Answer

Level 6

2

Development and links

Students will interpret more real-life graphs in Chapter 15. The topics covered in this chapter are developed further in Year 9.

The ability to solve equations and rearrange and use formulae is important in science and engineering, particularly in physics. Students will derive and use formulae when creating spreadsheets in ICT. They will plot and interpret linear and non-linear graphs to analyse the results of experiments in science. Graphs are also important in other curriculum areas, particularly in geography.

Geometry

Objectives

- Use straight edge and compasses to construct triangles, given right angle, hypotenuse and side (RHS) **6**
- Know and use the formulae for the circumference and area of a circle **6**
- Visualise and use 2-D representations of 3-D objects **6**
- Find the locus of a point that moves according to a simple rule, by reasoning **7**
- Calculate the surface area and volume of right prisms **7**

Introduction

The focus of this chapter is on accurate construction techniques and further work on shapes. Students develop their skills in constructing triangles and bisectors from Year 7 and extend these to drawing triangles given a right angle, hypotenuse and side (RHS), and to constructing the perpendicular to and from a point on a line. Students apply their construction skills to describing the locus of a moving point and use bearings to specify direction. Shape work is extended to finding the circumference and area of a circle, the surface area of a prism and the volume of simple right prisms.

The student book discusses the use of triangles in surveying. Surveyors use a method called triangulation. The area to be surveyed is divided up into triangles and the surveyor measures the length of one side of a triangle and the angles that it makes with the other two sides. From this, they can calculate the lengths of the other two sides. Modern mobile phones use a similar method to locate their position by sending and receiving a signal from three nearby phone masts. More information on triangulation and map making can be found at http://en.wikipedia.org/wiki/Triangulation

⚡Fast-track

14a, b, c, d, e, g, h

Level

MPA

1.1	14a, b, c, g, h
1.2	14a, b, c, d, e
1.3	14a, b, c, d, e, f, g, h
1.4	14b, e, g
1.5	14b, d

PLTS

IE	14b, c, d, f, g, h
CT	14a, c, d, e, f, g, h
RL	14a, b, c, d, e, f
TW	14b, e
SM	14c, h, g
EP	14a, b, c, d, e, f

Extra Resources

14	Start of chapter presentation
14a	Starter: Missing angle bingo
14a	Animation: Drawing triangles
14a	Animation: Angles in a triangle
14b	Animation: Constructing triangles
14b	Animation: Drawing triangles 2
14b	Consolidation sheet
14c	Animation: Bisectors
14c	Animation: Finding perpendicular points
14d	Animation: loci
14d	Animation: Loci 2
14d	Consolidation sheet
14e	Animation: Bearings
14e	Consolidation sheet
14f	Worked solution: Q1a
14h	Worked solution: Q3
14h	Animation: Volume of a prism
14h	Consolidation sheet
	Assessment: chapter 14

- Use a ruler and protractor to
  - measure and draw line to the nearest millimeter and angles to the nearest degree (L5)
  - construct a triangle given two sides and the included angle (SAS) or two angles and the included side (ASA) (L6)

Useful resources

Angle measurer
Ruler

Starter – How many angles?

Two lines meet exactly at a point. Excluding reflex angles, one angle is made.
Ask students how many non-reflex angles will be made if three lines meet at a point. (3)
What if four lines meet at a point? (6) five lines? (10) *n* lines? $\left(\frac{n(n-1)}{2} \right)$

Teaching notes

Recapitulate the sum of the interior angles of a triangle and quadrilateral covered previously in spread **6b**.

Look at the proper use of an angle measurer (protractor). What mistakes do many students make when measuring and drawing angles? Invite comments from students. These may include: placing the centre of the base of the 180° protractor at the vertex of the angle, rather than the marked cross, a 360° angle measurer will remove this error. Not lining up zero degrees with one of the arms of the angle, but squaring the angle measurer to the page instead. Reading the angle measurer in the wrong direction and finding the supplementary angle. Taking insufficient care over accuracy and misreading by more than 1° (RL).

Ask students to construct this triangle as carefully and accurately as possible.

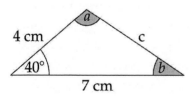

Measure the missing values; good accuracy has been achieved if:
$a \in (72, 74)°$, $b \in (66, 68)°$ and $c \in (4.6, 4.8)$ cm (1.3).

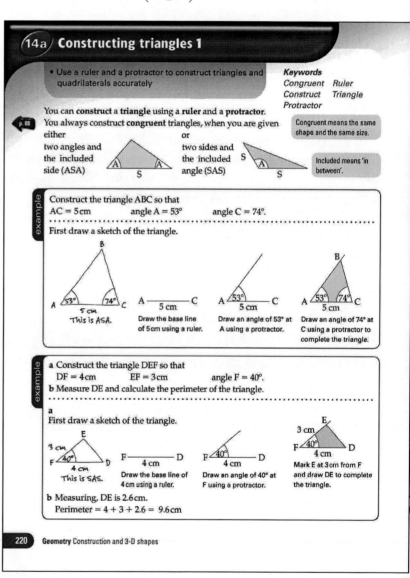

14a Constructing triangles 1

- Use a ruler and a protractor to construct triangles and quadrilaterals accurately

Keywords
Congruent   Ruler
Construct   Triangle
Protractor

You can **construct** a **triangle** using a **ruler** and a **protractor**.
You always construct **congruent** triangles, when you are given either

Congruent means the same shape and the same size.

two angles and the included side (ASA)

or

two sides and the included angle (SAS)

Included means 'in between'.

Construct the triangle ABC so that
AC = 5 cm   angle A = 53°   angle C = 74°.

First draw a sketch of the triangle.

This is ASA.

Draw the base line of 5 cm using a ruler.

Draw an angle of 53° at A using a protractor.

Draw an angle of 74° at C using a protractor to complete the triangle.

a Construct the triangle DEF so that
DF = 4 cm   EF = 3 cm   angle F = 40°.
b Measure DE and calculate the perimeter of the triangle.

a
First draw a sketch of the triangle.

This is SAS.

Draw the base line of 4 cm using a ruler.

Draw an angle of 40° at F using a protractor.

Mark E at 3 cm from F and draw DE to complete the triangle.

b Measuring, DE is 2.6 cm.
Perimeter = 4 + 3 + 2.6 = 9.6 cm

220   Geometry Construction and 3-D shapes

Plenary

How much information is needed in order to draw a unique triangle? Try to find all the combinations of sides and angles. For example are three angles and one side needed, or can just two angles and one side be given? This could lead to a discussion of ambiguous triangles, for example, the ASS triangle 30° – 8 cm – 5 cm. Missing side/angles: 9.9 cm – 53° – 97° or 3.9 cm – 127° – 23° (CT) (1.2).

Simplification

Provide students with the base of the triangle drawn accurately on a worksheet. Leave adequate space for them to layout all their solutions. Ask students to initially label the vertices of the base of the triangle.

Remind students to use a sharp pencil and to be accurate to the nearest mm and degree. Examiners will generally allow tolerances of 1 mm and 1° either way. All questions (1.1, 1.3)

Question 1 – The diagrams in the exercise are roughly to scale. Does the student's answer look similar? Most common error is likely to be reading 95° as 85°.

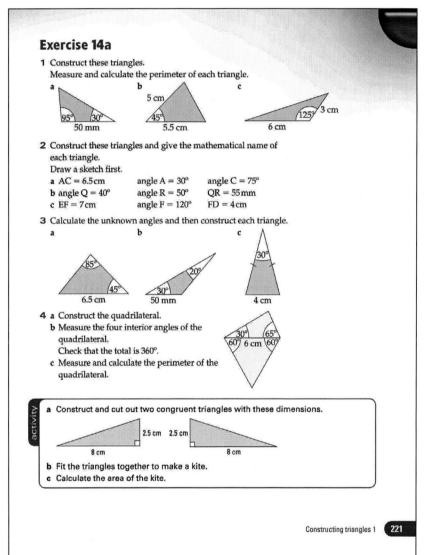

Exercise 14a

1 Construct these triangles.
  Measure and calculate the perimeter of each triangle.

  a   b   c
  95° 30°   5 cm   125° 3 cm
  50 mm   45°   6 cm
       5.5 cm

2 Construct these triangles and give the mathematical name of each triangle.
  Draw a sketch first.
  a AC = 6.5 cm   angle A = 30°   angle C = 75°
  b angle Q = 40°   angle R = 50°   QR = 55 mm
  c EF = 7 cm   angle F = 120°   FD = 4 cm

3 Calculate the unknown angles and then construct each triangle.

  a   b   c
  85°   30°
  45°   20°
  6.5 cm   30°   4 cm
       50 mm

4 a Construct the quadrilateral.
  b Measure the four interior angles of the quadrilateral.
    Check that the total is 360°.
  c Measure and calculate the perimeter of the quadrilateral.

    30° 65°
    60° 6 cm 60°

  activity

  a Construct and cut out two congruent triangles with these dimensions.

    2.5 cm 2.5 cm
    8 cm   8 cm

  b Fit the triangles together to make a kite.
  c Calculate the area of the kite.

Constructing triangles 1   **221**

Extension

Triangle ABC has AC = 8 cm, BC = 6 cm and angle A = 30°. One person says angle B is 42° and another says angle C is 12°. How could they both be correct? Encourage students to sketch the triangle, then draw it accurately. There are in fact two possible triangles, angles B and C could 42° and 108° or 138° and 12° (RL) (1.2).

Exercise 14a commentary

Question 2 – Does it matter which corner has which label? No, angles and lengths will still be the same. Encourage students to make their rough sketches similar to the accurate diagrams, at least an obtuse angle should appear as such.

Question 3 – Why is it necessary to find the unknown angles? Students may need help recalling the meaning of the marks on the side of the triangle in part **c.**.

Question 4 – Are there any sides that can be calculated without an accurate drawing? Yes, the bottom triangle is equilateral. After measuring the sum of the interior angles, what if you do not get 360°? Does this mean you have made an error? No, not if you are 1° out.

Activity – Is there more than one way to make a kite? (No) Some students might use the formula for the area of a triangle. Is there a simpler method? The kite has the same area as a rectangle.

Assessment Criteria – SSM, level 5: measure and draw angle to the nearest degree, when constructing models and drawing or using shapes. SSM, level 6: use straight edge and compasses to do standard constructions.

Links

A Geodesic Dome is a structure comprised of a network of triangles that form a surface shaped like a piece of a sphere. Geodesic domes are very strong but are lightweight and can be built very quickly. There are famous geodesic domes at the Eden Project in Cornwall and at the Epcot Centre in Florida There are pictures of geodesic domes at http://www.geo-dome.co.uk/ and at http://en.wikipedia.org/wiki/Geodesic_dome (EP).

- Use straight edge and compasses to construct a triangle, given three sides (SSS) **(L6)**
- Use straight edge and compasses to construct triangles, given right angle, hypotenuse and side (RHS) **(L6)**

Useful resources

Ruler
Compasses
Angle measurer

Starter – Take three

Ask students to make triangles from six rods that are exactly 1 cm, 2 cm, 3 cm, 4 cm, 5 cm and 6 cm long (only 1 of each rod). How many different triangles can they find? (7) Which rod does not get used at all? (1 cm) Why? What if there was a seventh rod 7 cm long?

Teaching notes

Look at the proper use of a pair of compasses. What mistakes do many students make when drawing arcs and circles? Invite comments from students. These may include (RL)

- Holding the compass poorly so that the point moves around.
- Using a loose compass so the arms move and the arc is not accurate.
- Measuring the radius of the arc for the compass on a ruler by starting at the end of the ruler rather than a few mm in where the zero maker on the ruler lies.

Look at the method described in the student book. Since you can't be sure where the 5 cm and 4 cm sides go draw a picture of possible locations for each side.

Ask students to construct this triangle as carefully and accurately as possible using a compass and ruler. Which side should be constructed first?

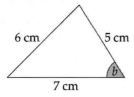

Measure the angle *b*, if it is between 56° and 58° then good accuracy has been achieved (1.3).

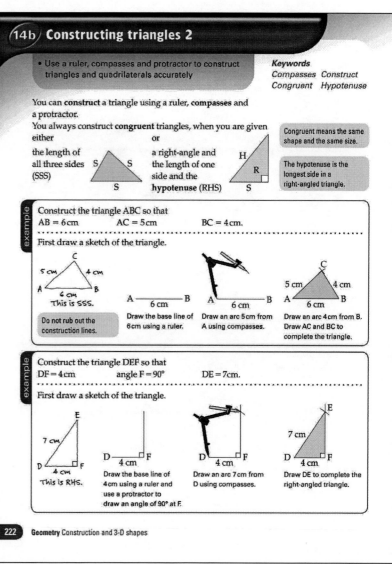

Plenary

Discuss real life examples of when a scale drawing is necessary. For example, when designing a new product that you intend to sell, when landscaping your garden, when demonstrating team tactics for a ball game to your team, drawing pictures to help with the construction of something you have purchased like a chest of drawers (EP).

Simplification

Provide students with the base of the triangle drawn accurately on a worksheet. Leave adequate space for them to layout all their solutions. Ask students to initially label the vertices of the base of the triangle. In question **2** draw the lines BC, PR, EF and label the vertices to assist with the initial stages of the triangle construction.

Remind students to use a sharp pencil and be accurate to the nearest mm and degree. They will also need to ensure their compasses are properly tightened to improve accuracy. Many students find using compasses awkward; allow them plenty of time to get used to using them (RL). All questions (1.3).

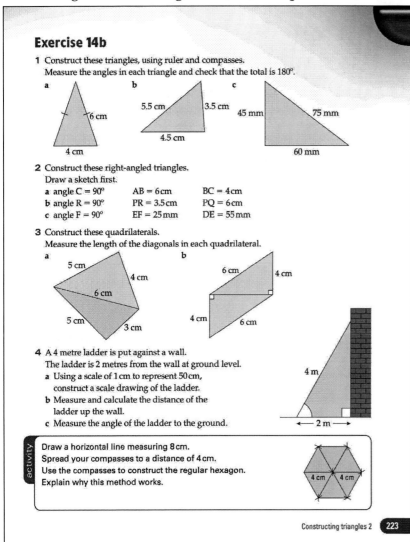

Exercise 14b

1 Construct these triangles, using ruler and compasses.
   Measure the angles in each triangle and check that the total is 180°.

   a   6 cm   4 cm

   b   5.5 cm   3.5 cm   4.5 cm

   c   45 mm   75 mm   60 mm

2 Construct these right-angled triangles.
   Draw a sketch first.
   a angle C = 90°   AB = 6cm   BC = 4cm
   b angle R = 90°   PR = 3.5cm   PQ = 6cm
   c angle F = 90°   EF = 25mm   DE = 55mm

3 Construct these quadrilaterals.
   Measure the length of the diagonals in each quadrilateral.

   a   5 cm   4 cm   6 cm   5 cm   3 cm

   b   6 cm   4 cm   4 cm   6 cm

4 A 4 metre ladder is put against a wall.
   The ladder is 2 metres from the wall at ground level.
   a Using a scale of 1cm to represent 50cm, construct a scale drawing of the ladder.
   b Measure and calculate the distance of the ladder up the wall.
   c Measure the angle of the ladder to the ground.

   4 m   2 m

   activity
   Draw a horizontal line measuring 8cm.
   Spread your compasses to a distance of 4cm.
   Use the compasses to construct the regular hexagon.
   Explain why this method works.

   4 cm   4 cm

   Constructing triangles 2   223

Extension

Construct an isosceles trapezium and an arrowhead accurately. Measure all the sides and angles to see how good your drawing is. What equipment is necessary? If three students are attempting this, allow each a ruler and then one has just compasses, one has just a protractor, one has both a protractor and compasses. Who has the most accurate drawing? What conclusions can you draw? (TW) (1.3)

Exercise 14b commentary

Question 1 – Encourage students to begin with the base of the triangle, as this is generally the easiest part. Also encourage students to extend their arcs to make absolutely sure they intersect.

Question 2 – Make sure the sketches look similar to the intended accurately drawn triangle. Which side should you take as the base? This is not immediately obvious. Encourage students to try the other side if they initially get stuck RL) (1.5).

Question 3 – Which side should you begin with? Does it make any difference?

Question 4 – In parts **b** and **c**, would a larger scale lead to more accurate answers? (**b** yes, **c** no) (IE, EP) (1.2).

Activity – What sort of triangles have been constructed? Encourage students to look at the angles formed inside the hexagon. What are the exterior angles? What can every regular hexagon be formed from? Six congruent equilateral triangles. (IE) (1.1, 1.4)

Assessment Criteria – SSM, level 6: use straight edge and compass to do standard constructions.

Links

A hexaflexagon is a flat hexagon-shaped paper toy that can be folded or flexed along its folds to reveal and conceal its faces alternately. It was invented in 1939 in the USA by Arthur Stone and its construction is based on equilateral triangles. There are instructions to make a hexaflexagon at http://hexaflexagon.sourceforge.net/ and at http://www.flexagon.net/flexagons/hexahexaflexagon-c.pdf (EP).

- Use straight edge and compasses to construct
  - the midpoint and perpendicular bisector of a line segment   (L6)
  - the bisector of an angle   (L6)
  - the perpendicular from a point to a line   (L6)
  - the perpendicular from a point on a line   (L6)

Useful resources
Ruler
Angle measurer
Compasses

Starter – Quad bingo

Ask students to draw a 3 × 3 grid and enter nine angles from the following list:

30°, 35°, 40°, 45°, 50°, 55°, 60°, 65°, 70°, 75°, 80°, 85°, 90°, 95°, 100°, 105°, 110°, 115°, 120°, 125°.

Give questions, for example, one of the angles in a rhombus is 135°, what is the smallest angle?

The winner is the first student to cross out all nine angles.

Teaching notes

If available, use the compass tool on an interactive whiteboard to demonstrate the method of constructing

- the perpendicular bisector of a line
- the perpendicular of a line through a point on a line
- the perpendicular of a line through a point off the line
- the angle bisector

Use a pre-prepared worksheet to give students an opportunity to try each of the four constructions in turn once they have seen a demonstration. Remind students to make sure their compasses are extended to over half the length of the line in the case of the perpendicular bisector. Highlight the similarities between the first three constructions, the second and third construction in fact being perpendicular bisectors of a 'shortened line'. In the case of the angle bisector, warn students against using the ends of the arms of the angle to create their 'middle point'. Point out that the ends of the arms are not necessarily equidistant form the vertex of the angle. Two equidistant points should be found using the compass.

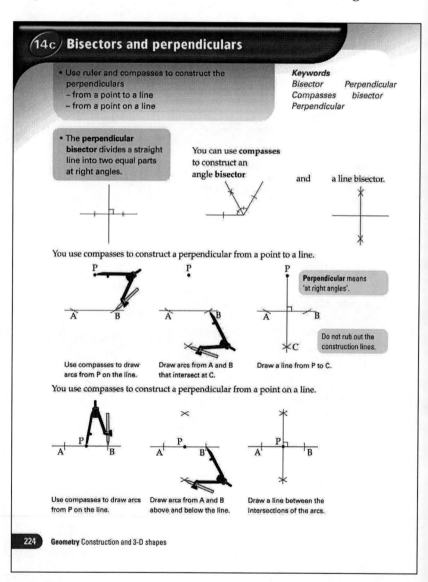

14c Bisectors and perpendiculars

- Use ruler and compasses to construct the perpendiculars
  - from a point to a line
  - from a point on a line

Keywords
Bisector   Perpendicular
Compasses   bisector
Perpendicular

- The **perpendicular bisector** divides a straight line into two equal parts at right angles.

You can use **compasses** to construct an angle **bisector**   and   a line bisector.

You use compasses to construct a perpendicular from a point to a line.

Perpendicular means 'at right angles'.

Do not rub out the construction lines.

Use compasses to draw arcs from P on the line.   Draw arcs from A and B that intersect at C.   Draw a line from P to C.

You use compasses to construct a perpendicular from a point on a line.

Use compasses to draw arcs from P on the line.   Draw arcs from A and B above and below the line.   Draw a line between the intersections of the arcs.

224   **Geometry** Construction and 3-D shapes

Plenary

Do the perpendicular bisectors of the sides of an isosceles triangle cross at the same point? If instead you join the midpoint of each side to the opposite vertex do the lines cross at the same point? Is it the same point? Are either of these points the centre of gravity of the triangle? Can this be tested with an actual triangle? (CT)

Simplification

Use a prepared worksheet with the first line and, if appropriate, the first intersection of arcs to help with the construction. With this initial assistance for the first few questions, it might help students to feel more confident to try the latter questions on their own.

Use plane rather than square paper so that the grid can not be used to draw perpendiculars. All questions (1.1, 1.3)

Question 1 – Some students will feel the need to enlarge their compass to the length of the line, this may mean that an intersection point is off the page. Others may not enlarge their compasses far enough and the arcs might not cross (RL).

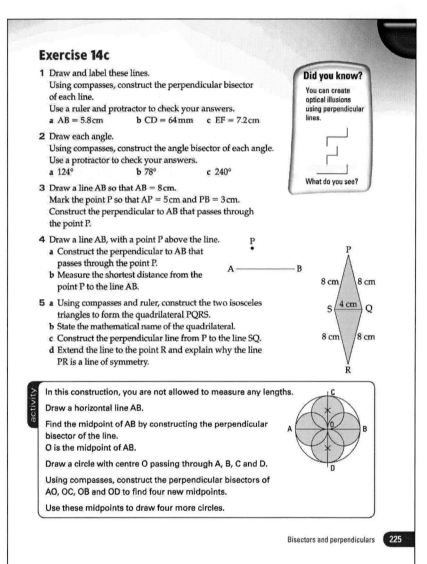

Exercise 14c commentary

Question 2 – Students may well make the arms of the angle the same length. This will mean that the ends of the arms could be used to construct the middle point. Ask students to make the arms of different lengths.

Question 4 – Use the method detailed in the student book. Will the shortest distance from a point to a line always be perpendicular? (Yes) (1.2)

Question 5 – Use the methods practiced in spread **14b** for constructing a triangle using a ruler/compass. The term diamond might be used, but encourage the use of the term rhombus. How many lines of symmetry does a rhombus have?

Activity – Ensure students draw a sufficiently large diagram. Encourage the use of different ways of showing the lines and the circles to add clarity to the diagram, for example, colours or solid and dashed lines/circles.

Assessment Criteria – SSM, level 6: use straight edge and compasses to do standard constructions.

Links

Perpendicular recording is a new technology that increases the storage capacity of hard drives. It is predicted that perpendicular recording will allow information densities of up to around 1000 Gbit/in² compared with 100–200 Gbit/in² using conventional technology. There is an amusing video describing perpendicular recording at http://www.hitachigst.com/hdd/ research/recording_head/pr/ PerpendicularAnimation.html

Extension

The perpendicular bisectors of the sides of an equilateral triangle all pass through the same point. Is this true of all triangles? (IE, SM) (1.2, 1.3)

- Find the locus of a point that moves according to a simple rule, by reasoning (L7)

Useful resources
Ruler
Compasses
Angle measurer
Tracing paper

Starter – Clock angles

Ask students to give the angle between the hour and minute hands at the following times: 7.00, 4.00, 9.30, 1.30, 3.15 and 4.45.

Hint: The hour hand moves as well as the minute hand!

(150° or 210°, 120°, 105°, 135°, 7.5° and 127.5°)

Teaching notes

Look back at the initial work from the previous spread. In the case of the perpendicular bisector, where would you have to stand in order to be an equal distance (equidistant) from the two end points of the line? On the perpendicular bisector. In the case of the angle bisector, where would you have to stand in order to be equidistant from the two lines? On the angle bisector.

The word locus (singular) or loci (plural) comes from the Latin word for 'position' or 'place'. So, 'find the locus' reads 'find the place'.

What does the locus of the points an equal distance around the outside of a rectangle look like? Invite students' comments and then look carefully at the solution. Why are the corners 'rounded off'? What would the locus around an equilateral triangle look like? (EP) (1.5)

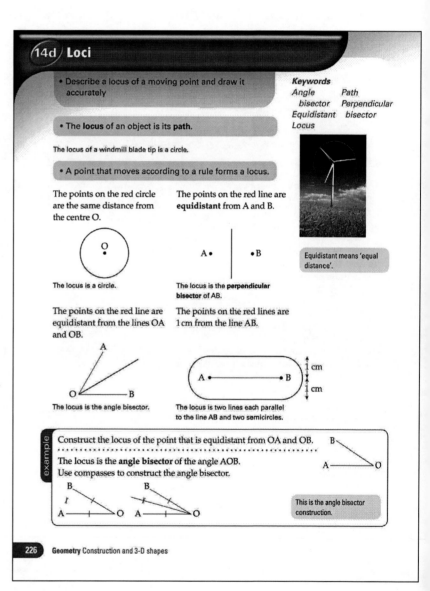

Plenary

Examine the locus of points that can be reached by a dog on a lead when tied to different positions along two walls at right angles. Look at solutions that involve being tied at one point and other solutions that allow the dogs lead to move along a rail on the wall. Include problems that let the dog go round to the next wall, thereby 'shortening' the lead and resulting in an arc of smaller radius (CT) (1.2).

Simplification

Use a prepared worksheet with the question already drawn in place and, if appropriate the first intersection of arcs to help with the construction. With this initial assistance for the first few questions, it might help students to feel more confident to try the latter questions on their own.

All questions (CT) (1.2, 1.3)

Question 1 – Allow students to extend the line and not concern themselves with it being 'too long'. It shows the direction of the angle bisector. Ensure students do not use the end points of the arms, as they are likely to be different distances from the vertex (RL).

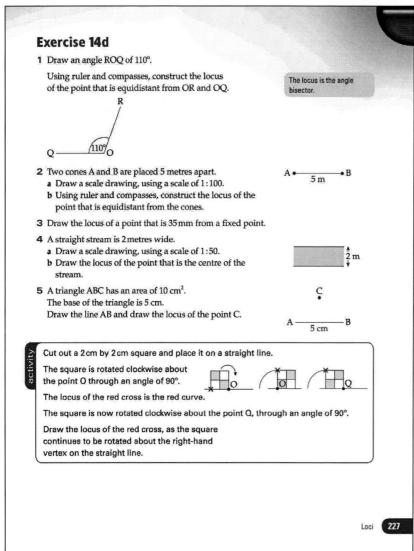

Exercise 14d

1 Draw an angle ROQ of 110°.

Using ruler and compasses, construct the locus of the point that is equidistant from OR and OQ.

R

Q ——— 110° O

The locus is the angle bisector.

2 Two cones A and B are placed 5 metres apart.
 a Draw a scale drawing, using a scale of 1:100.
 b Using ruler and compasses, construct the locus of the point that is equidistant from the cones.

A •——— 5 m ———• B

3 Draw the locus of a point that is 35 mm from a fixed point.

4 A straight stream is 2 metres wide.
 a Draw a scale drawing, using a scale of 1:50.
 b Draw the locus of the point that is the centre of the stream.

2 m

5 A triangle ABC has an area of 10 cm².
The base of the triangle is 5 cm.
Draw the line AB and draw the locus of the point C.

C•

A ——— 5 cm ——— B

---

activity

Cut out a 2 cm by 2 cm square and place it on a straight line.

The square is rotated clockwise about the point O through an angle of 90°.

The locus of the red cross is the red curve.

The square is now rotated clockwise about the point Q, through an angle of 90°.

Draw the locus of the red cross, as the square continues to be rotated about the right-hand vertex on the straight line.

Extension

Construct perimeters around shapes that are equidistant at all points from the shape. Include challenging shapes like concave polygons and compound shapes made from arcs and straight lines (IE, CT).

Exercise 14d commentary

Question 2 – Since you are drawing a line that is equidistant from two points, what is it know as? The perpendicular bisector of the line joining the two points.

Question 3 – How can you move so that you always remain the same distance from a certain point? Move in a circle around the point.

Question 4 – Encourage students to be accurate. Measuring the distance to the centre of the stream at either end will lead to a more accurate diagram. Plane paper rather than squared will also make this a more useful task.

Question 5 – The formula for the area of a triangle may need to be recalled. This question relies on the student realising that perpendicular height is fixed. The triangle does not have to be isosceles as might at first appear to be the only option. Some students may realise that point C could be underneath the line AB.

Activity – The activity could be aided by the use of tracing paper. Ask students to anticipate what they think will be the shape of the path. Is the final answer a surprise?

Assessment Criteria – SSM, level 7: find the locus of a point that moves according to a given rule, by reasoning.

Links

Spirograph is a toy invented by the British engineer Denys Fisher in 1965. The pattern drawn is the locus of a pen attached to one circle rolling around the inside circumference of another and is called a Hypotrochoid. There is an interactive spirograph at http://perl.guru.org/lynn/apps/index.html (EP).

• Use bearings to specify direction

(L6) Useful resources
Enlarged copy of
question 1
Angle measurer

Starter – Triangles from squares!

Ask students to find a triangle where all the angles are square numbers. (100°, 64°, 16°)
Can they find any quadrilaterals where all the angles are square numbers?
(144°, 100°, 100°, 16° and others)
Any pentagons? (196, 144, 100, 64, 36)

Teaching notes

What does a bearing measure? An angle. Where do the arms that make the angle of the bearing go? One always points to the North, the other points in the direction of the point you are finding the bearing of. Where do you always begin counting from? The North line. Which direction do you count in? Always clockwise. How many digits are there in a bearing? Three.

Remind students of the common mistakes made using angle measurers, see notes in spread **14a**. How can bearings be measured if they are over 180°? (RL)

Use a pre-prepared worksheet to check student's accuracy in measuring bearings.

Ensure students draw in the North line at B. Encourage students to label the bearing on the diagram and show the direction in which it was measured. For example

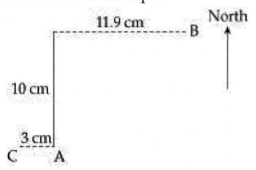

Measure the bearing of B from A (050°). Measure the bearing from B to C (236°). Allow 1° either side (1.3).

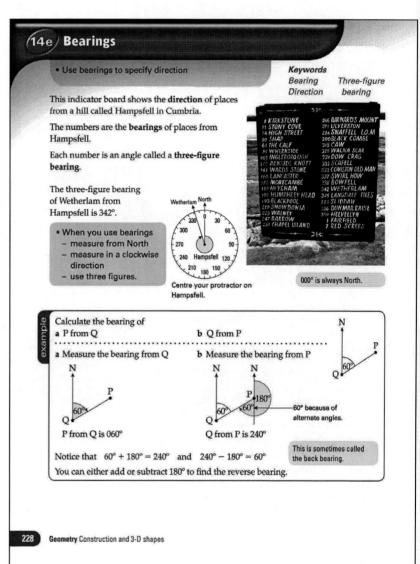

Plenary

Suppose a ship is in a storm and is attempting to transmit its bearing from a lighthouse over the radio. If the radio communication fails part of the way through the message, what possible bearing could the ship be on? Use examples and invite students to give possible solutions. *'we are on bearing 2……..!'* Some students may give the solution 20 or 25, is this possible? Is it clearer now why three figures are used by everyone around the world? For clarity and safety the first figure is always the hundreds (EP).

Simplification

Consider giving students two copies of question **1** to allow them to add in the arc for the bearings without over complicating the diagram.

Provide students with accurate drawing of question **2** as well as a copy of the exercise. Ask students to try to use the printed exercise to find the other angles in the question, but check their answers using the scaled copy.

All questions (IE, EP) (1.2, 1.3).

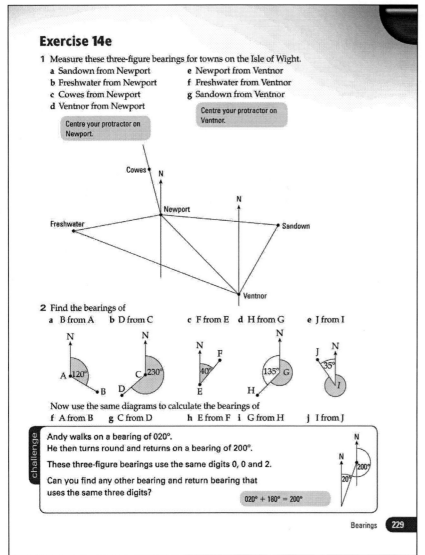

Extension

In question **2** the bearing from A to B was 120°, the bearing from B to A (known as a back bearing) was 300°. By examining the bearings and back bearings of each point in question **2**, write a formula that connects the bearing and back bearing. If the bearing is < 180°, then back bearing 5 bearing 1 180°, if bearing is ≥180° then back bearing = bearing 2 180°. Note, a bearing of 360° is not used, instead 000° is used for North (CT) (1.4).

Question 1 – Encourage students to add the arc to show the bearing. Remind students that they need to measure the bearing to within 1° to get full marks. Watch for students who forget to use three figures for the bearings.

Question 2 – The diagrams are not drawn to scale. If a student just records the angle written in the question, ask, which way round are bearings always measured? For the reverse (or back bearings) begin by extending North lines at both points. Then ask the students to fill in any angles they can from the information provided in the question. Next, can they find any alternate angles? This gradual approach is likely to be of more use than trying to memorise a formula.

Challenge – Begin with bearings restricted to below 180°. From the given example students are likely to notice that you add 180° to get the bearing back the other way. This can become a number problem rather than a bearing problem needing drawing: abc 1 180 5 'abc' but a, b, c can be in any order. For example, 020° 1 180° 5 200°. Encourage students to experiment or divide the work among themselves to examine different possible solutions (TW).

Links

Magnetic compasses measure bearings in relation to the Magnetic North Pole rather than the geographical North Pole. The Earth's magnetic field changes and the position of the Magnetic North Pole moves about 40 km each year. There is more information about the Magnetic North Pole at http://en.wikipedia.org/wiki/Magnetic_north_pole (EP).

• •

Starter – Directions

Ask students to visualise the following shape.

A line 5 cm long towards N, then 4 cm on a bearing of 140°, then 4 cm on a bearing of 040°, finally 5 cm on a bearing of 180°.

Ask students to sketch what they have visualised. (The letter M)

Ask students to make up directions for other letters.

Teaching notes

Recapitulate the work covered previously in spreads **2e** and **2f**. Can students recall the formulae for the area and circumference of a circle? If appropriate, use the rhyme from spread **2f**.

Use 3.14 as an approximation for π during the exercise. Remind students how to use the formula to find area and circumference by looking at an example. Is it possible to work out the diameter of a circle if you know the circumference? Ask students for their ideas? Test the students' ideas by rearranging the formula for circumference to make the diameter the subject (EP).

Can the area be found by knowing only the circumference of the circle? Encourage students to explain their ideas. Can a new formula be constructed to for the area in terms of the circumference? Hint that the circumference formula can be written as $C = 2\pi r$ (CT).

$$\text{Area} = \frac{C^2}{4\pi}$$

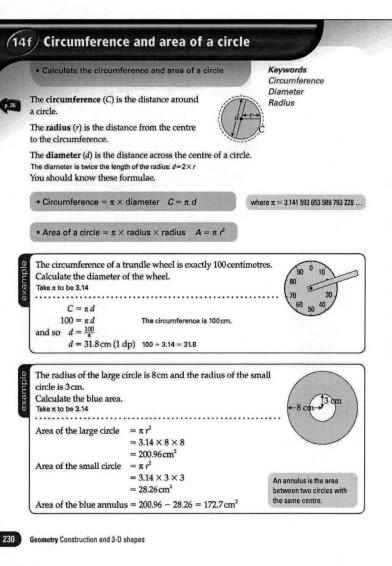

14f Circumference and area of a circle

- Calculate the circumference and area of a circle

Keywords
Circumference
Diameter
Radius

The **circumference** (C) is the distance around a circle.

The **radius** (r) is the distance from the centre to the circumference.

The **diameter** (d) is the distance across the centre of a circle.
The diameter is twice the length of the radius: $d = 2 \times r$
You should know these formulae.

- Circumference = π × diameter $C = \pi d$

where π = 3.141 592 653 589 793 228 …

- Area of a circle = π × radius × radius $A = \pi r^2$

example
The circumference of a trundle wheel is exactly 100 centimetres.
Calculate the diameter of the wheel.
Take π to be 3.14
. . . .
$C = \pi d$
$100 = \pi d$ The circumference is 100 cm.
and so $d = \frac{100}{\pi}$
$d = 31.8\,\text{cm}$ (1 dp)   100 ÷ 3.14 = 31.8

example
The radius of the large circle is 8 cm and the radius of the small circle is 3 cm.
Calculate the blue area.
Take π to be 3.14
. . . .
Area of the large circle $= \pi r^2$
                           $= 3.14 \times 8 \times 8$
                           $= 200.96\,\text{cm}^2$
Area of the small circle $= \pi r^2$
                           $= 3.14 \times 3 \times 3$
                           $= 28.26\,\text{cm}^2$
Area of the blue annulus $= 200.96 - 28.26 = 172.7\,\text{cm}^2$

An annulus is the area between two circles with the same centre.

230   Geometry Construction and 3-D shapes

Plenary

What is the formula for the area of a square? Look at question **4** again. Is there another formula for the area of a square? Yes, area = (diagonal length)² ÷ 2 (CT).

Simplification

Initially use arrow diagrams to help with the calculations of area and circumference. The arrow diagrams could be even more useful when using the formulae for reverse problems.

All questions (IE) (1.3).

Question 1 – Strongly encourage the process of writing formula/substituting in values/working out answer. Some students might be tempted to calculate $(3.14 \times r)^2$; remind students of the rules of BIDMAS if necessary (RL).

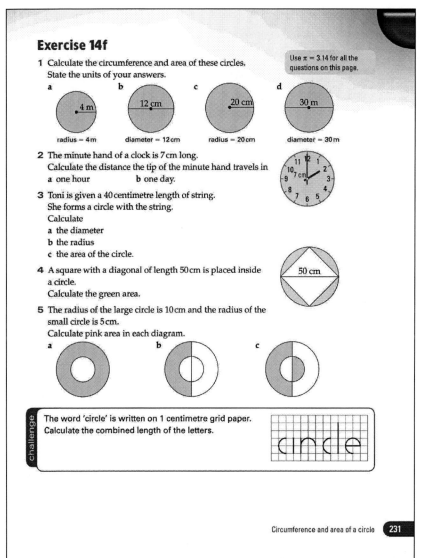

Extension

How can the circumference be calculated from the area? Set students questions of this type. They will need an awareness of the square root function (IE) (1.3).

Exercise 14f commentary

Question 2 – What needs to be calculated first? Encourage students to break the problem down into smaller parts, rather than just leap to the solution (1.1).

Question 3 – Encourage the approach used in the example. Students should write the formula they need to use first.

Question 4 – How can the area of the square be found? Students might begin by trying to find the side lengths of the square. Is there another way? How can the two triangles that the square has been subdivided into help?

Question 5 – Encourage students to organise their findings and carefully represent each part of the diagram.

Challenge – Encourage students to think about a strategy before they begin their calculations. Perhaps separating the parts of the word into straight lines and arcs.

Assessment Criteria – SSM, level 6: know and use the formula for the circumference and area of a circle.

Links

Pompoms are sometimes used to decorate clothing such as hats and scarves. Pompoms can be made by wrapping wool around two annulus shapes cut from cardboard. When the central hole is completely filled with wool, the wool is cut around the outer circle edges. Another piece of wool is then threaded between the two pieces of cardboard, the pompom tied off and the cardboard removed. There are full details on how to make pompoms at http://www.kid-craft-central.com/ pom-poms.html

- Visualise and use 2D representations of 3D objects (L6)
- Calculate the surface area of right prisms (L7)

Useful resources
Multilink cubes

Starter – Puzzle pairs

Write the following lists on the board.

Measurements in cm: 15 and 9; 7 and 6; 12 and 7; 12 and 9; 7 and 7; 14 and 2.5.
Areas in cm²: 84, 54, 135, 21, 24.5, 35.

The measurements are either the lengths and widths of rectangles or the bases and heights of triangles. Ask students to match up the triangles and rectangles with their areas and then make their own puzzle.

Teaching notes

Use multilink cubes to build a cuboid from 24 cubes. Count the area of each of the six faces/surfaces in square faces of the multilink cubes. What is the total? This is known as the surface area. Is it possible to construct the cuboid in such a way as to make the surface area equal to any of these values 52, 56, 68, 70, 76, 98?

Look at a sketch of a cuboid. How can the surface area be found? Encourage students to look for an efficient means of calculating. What units are likely to be used?

Draw a net for the example just looked at. Is it possible to tell the surface area from the net? Would drawing in the squares on the net be helpful?

Recap the formula for the area of a triangle. What can students recall about the definition of a prism? Use the term cross-section to describe the ends of the prism.

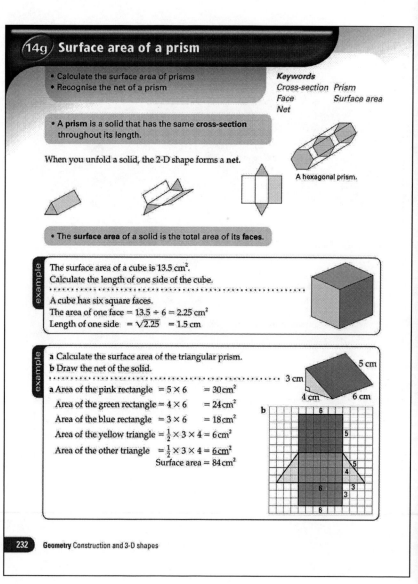

14g Surface area of a prism

- Calculate the surface area of prisms
- Recognise the net of a prism

Keywords
Cross-section Prism
Face   Surface area
Net

- **A prism** is a solid that has the same **cross-section** throughout its length.

When you unfold a solid, the 2-D shape forms a **net**.

A hexagonal prism.

- The **surface area** of a solid is the total area of its **faces**.

example

The surface area of a cube is 13.5 cm².
Calculate the length of one side of the cube.
....
A cube has six square faces.
The area of one face = 13.5 ÷ 6 = 2.25 cm²
Length of one side = √2.25 = 1.5 cm

example

a Calculate the surface area of the triangular prism.
b Draw the net of the solid.
....
a Area of the pink rectangle = 5 × 6 = 30 cm²
  Area of the green rectangle = 4 × 6 = 24 cm²
  Area of the blue rectangle = 3 × 6 = 18 cm²
  Area of the yellow triangle = ½ × 3 × 4 = 6 cm²
  Area of the other triangle = ½ × 3 × 4 = 6 cm²
                    Surface area = 84 cm²

232 Geometry Construction and 3-D shapes

Plenary

Calculate the surface area of a prism with a circular cross section. Can a formula be constructed for the surface area of these types of prisms? Explore different ways of expressing the formulae (CT) (1.1, 1.4).

Simplification

Set students to initially work out surface area of cuboids that have integer length sides. Show how the faces can be split into unit squares. This 'counting' method may help to re-enforce the more general method of finding the surface area.

A calculator would be useful for the exercise, but is not essential. For a more demanding exercise students could attempt some or all of the questions without a calculator.

All questions (1.1, 1.3)

Question 1 – Encourage students to write down not only their calculations, but also which face they are calculating.

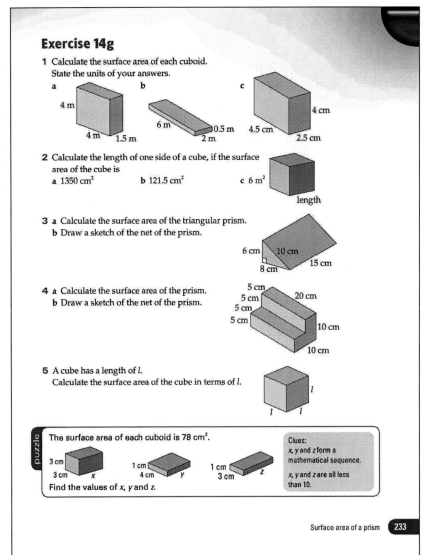

Exercise 14g

1 Calculate the surface area of each cuboid. State the units of your answers.

a   4 m   4 m

b   6 m   0.5 m   1.5 m

c   4 cm   4.5 cm   2.5 cm   2 m

2 Calculate the length of one side of a cube, if the surface area of the cube is
a 1350 cm²   b 121.5 cm²   c 6 m²

length

3 a Calculate the surface area of the triangular prism.
  b Draw a sketch of the net of the prism.

6 cm   10 cm   15 cm   8 cm

4 a Calculate the surface area of the prism.
  b Draw a sketch of the net of the prism.

5 cm   5 cm   5 cm   5 cm   20 cm   10 cm   10 cm

5 A cube has a length of *l*.
  Calculate the surface area of the cube in terms of *l*.

l   *l*   *l*

puzzle

The surface area of each cuboid is 78 cm².

3 cm   3 cm   *x*
1 cm   4 cm   *y*
1 cm   3 cm   *z*
Find the values of *x*, *y* and *z*.

Clues:
x, *y* and *z* form a mathematical sequence.
x, *y* and *z* are all less than 10.

Surface area of a prism   233

Extension

A cuboid has integer lengths for its sides. The ratio of surface area to volume is 13 : 6. Suggest possible dimensions for the cuboid. One possible solution is 2 × 3 × 4. Other solutions might be possible. One possible strategy could be to write an equivalent ratio to 13 : 6 and look for possible values of the sides that have a product of the volume (IE, SM).

Exercise 14g commentary

Question 2 – Given the entire surface area of the cube, what can be initially calculated? The area of one face. How can this help to find the length of the side of one face? Allow students to come up with a solution without thinking explicitly in terms of square roots.

Question 3 – What shape is the sloping face of the prism? How many faces does the prism have? A number of nets are possible.

Question 4 – Encourage students to identify which part they are calculating. This may help to reduce the risk of one of the faces being excluded.

Question 5 – What is the area of each face? How can this be simply expressed? (1.4)

Puzzle – Encourage students to use a variety of methods. What can they initially work out? Some students may be able to form an equation. Others may want to experiment with different possible values. Make sure students look at the clues given in the question.

Assessment Criteria – SSM, level 6: visualize and use 2-D representations of 3-D objects. SSM, level 6: calculate surface areas of cuboids. SSM, level 7: calculate lengths and areas in right prisms.

Links

Human skin has a total surface area of about 1.8 m². It accounts for between 15% and 20% of the total weight of the human body and helps to protect the body from the environment. It constantly renews itself. Over 90% of common house dust is made up of dead skin cells. For more information see http://yucky.discovery.com/flash/body/pg000146.html

- Calculate the volume of right prisms   (L7)   ***Useful resources***
                                                                 Calculator
                                                                 Multilink cubes

Starter – Costly solids

A face cost 7p, an edge cost 8p and a vertex cost 9p.

Ask students to find the cost of different solids, for example, a cuboid, a square based pyramid and a pentagonal prism. (£2.10, £1.44 and £2.59)

Ask students to find a shape that costs £1.61? (triangular prism)

Teaching notes

Construct a cuboid from multilink cubes. How can the number of cubes be found without having to count every single one? Establish that multiplication can find the area on the end 'slice' of the cuboid, and a final multiplication by the number of 'slices' can find the number of cubes.

Generalise this to produce a formula for the volume of a cuboid: volume = length × width × height or volume = area of the cross section × length.

Look at the volume of a right angled triangular prism. Can its volume be found in a similar way to that of the cuboid? Try using the second formula. This gives half the answer that the cuboid formula would give, is this correct?

Establish that the cross section can be of any shape, as long as it is continuous (same size and shape all the way along) to produce a prism.

volume of a prism = area of the cross section × length.

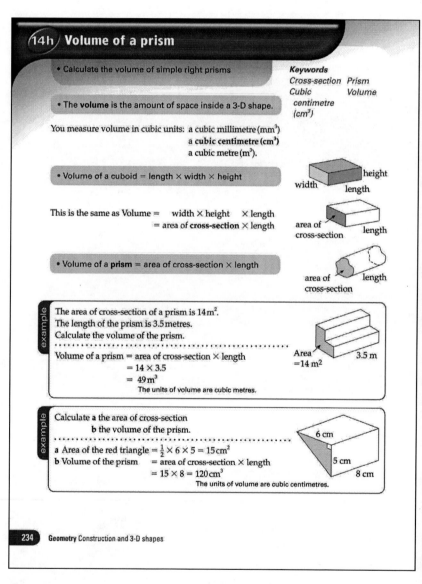

Plenary

Look at question **4** again. Is it possible to predict the volume from the net? Look at other nets of 3D shapes, beginning with cuboids, can students imagine the net being folded and calculate the volume? (CT) (1.1)

Simplification

Set students to initially work out volumes of cuboids that have integer length sides. Show how the faces can be split into unit squares. This 'counting' method may help to re-enforce the more general method of finding the volume. Possibly use simple prisms in the same way, showing how the cubes are subdivided.

All questions (IE) (1.1, 1.3)

Question 1 – Challenge students to explain in their own words why they are multiplying the side lengths.

Question 2 – How can the green shape be split? In terms of cubes, what does the area of the cross section represent? How long is the prism? Why is multiplication needed?

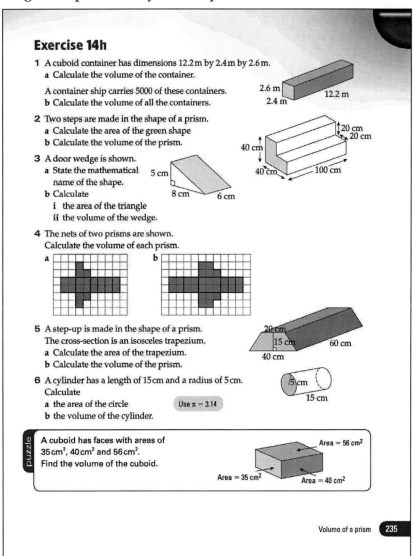

Exercise 14h

1 A cuboid container has dimensions 12.2 m by 2.4 m by 2.6 m.
   a Calculate the volume of the container.
   A container ship carries 5000 of these containers.
   b Calculate the volume of all the containers.

   2.6 m
   2.4 m
   12.2 m

2 Two steps are made in the shape of a prism.
   a Calculate the area of the green shape
   b Calculate the volume of the prism.

   20 cm
   20 cm
   40 cm
   40 cm
   100 cm

3 A door wedge is shown.
   a State the mathematical name of the shape.
   b Calculate
      i the area of the triangle
      ii the volume of the wedge.

   5 cm
   8 cm
   6 cm

4 The nets of two prisms are shown. Calculate the volume of each prism.
   a   b

5 A step-up is made in the shape of a prism. The cross-section is an isosceles trapezium.
   a Calculate the area of the trapezium.
   b Calculate the volume of the prism.

   20 cm
   15 cm
   40 cm
   60 cm

6 A cylinder has a length of 15 cm and a radius of 5 cm. Calculate
   a the area of the circle
   b the volume of the cylinder.

   Use π = 3.14

   5 cm
   15 cm

puzzle
A cuboid has faces with areas of 35 cm², 40 cm² and 56 cm². Find the volume of the cuboid.

   Area = 56 cm²
   Area = 35 cm²
   Area = 40 cm²

Volume of a prism   235

Extension

Find the volume of a regular hexagonal prism. Students may need reminding that six congruent equilateral triangles form a regular hexagon. Can students construct a formula? Without the use of Pythagoras students will have to consider the height of the triangles separately from the base (CT).

Exercise 14h commentary

Question 3 – Can the name of the shape be given using these terms? prism, triangular, right angled, right, scalene. What do they mean?

Question 4 – Some students may be tempted to calculate the volume from the net. Encourage students to sketch the 3D prism before deciding on the volume. When 'folding' the net, advise students to use the central face of the net as the base of the 3D sketch.

Question 5 – Students may not know the formula for the area of a trapezium, therefore look at ways in which the trapezium can be cut up to form rectangles and triangles.

Question 6 – Students may need reminding of the formula for the area of a circle, covered in spread 14f. What does the area of the end circle represent? Compare with the same question that was suggested in question 2 about the green shape.

Puzzle – What assumption could be made about the lengths of the sides to help find an easy solution? They are integers. Which of the faces has the fewest possible integer solutions for its sides? (35 cm²) Is the solution unique? (Yes) (SM).

Assessment Criteria – SSM, level 6: calculate volumes of cuboids. SSM, level 7: calculate lengths, areas and volumes in right prisms.

Links

The largest building in the World by volume is the Boeing aircraft factory at Everett, Washington in the USA. The volume of the building is 13.3 million m³ and it has a floor area of 398 000 m² or 98 acres. There is more information about the factory at http://www.boeing.com/commercial/facilities/index.html

14a

1 Construct these triangles.

a 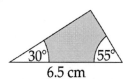 b 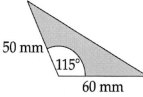 c

14b

2 Construct these nets, using ruler and compasses.
Each triangle is equilateral.
State the name of the 3-D shape formed by the net.

a  b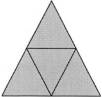

14c

3 Draw a horizontal line and a point P above the line.
a Using compasses, construct the perpendicular to the line passing through P.
b Label your diagram A, B, P and C as shown.
c What is the mathematical name of the quadrilateral APBC?
d Explain why this construction gives a perpendicular line.

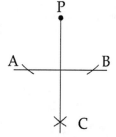

14d

4 A goat is tethered to a post with a 3 metre length of rope.
a Using a scale of 1:100, draw a scale drawing showing all the grass the goat can reach to eat.
b The goat is now tethered with the same rope to a wall. Draw another scale drawing with the same scale, showing all the grass the goat can now eat.

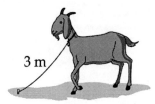

5 The map shows three villages in Derbyshire.
Measure the bearing of
a Baslow from Bakewell
b Ashford from Bakewell
  Centre your protractor at Bakewell.

c Baslow from Ashford
  Centre your protractor at Ashford.

d Bakewell from Baslow
e Ashford from Baslow.
  Centre your protractor at Baslow.

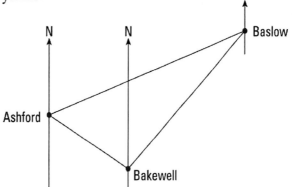

6 A circle has a circumference of 3 metres.
Calculate the diameter of the circle.
Give your answer to a suitable degree of accuracy.

Use $\pi = 3.14$

7 Calculate the shaded areas.

a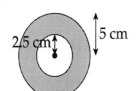
2.5 cm   5 cm

b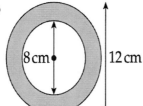
8 cm   12 cm

8 a Find the nine possible cuboids that can be made using 48 one-
  centimetre cubes.
b Calculate the surface area of each cuboid.
c Which cuboid has the largest surface area?
d Which cuboid has the smallest surface area?

9 A chocolate box has a cross-section of an equilateral triangle.
a State the mathematical name of the solid.
b Draw a sketch of the net, showing the dimensions.
c Calculate
  i the surface area
  ii the volume of the solid.

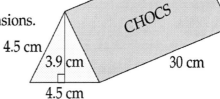
4.5 cm
3.9 cm
4.5 cm
30 cm
CHOCS

14 Summary

Assessment criteria

- Measure and draw angles to the nearest degree, when constructing models and drawing or using shapes — Level 5
- Use straight edge and compasses to do standard constructions — Level 6
- Know and use the formulae for the circumference and area of a circle — Level 6
- Find the locus of a point that moves according to a given rule, by reasoning — Level 7
- Calculate lengths, areas and volumes in right prisms — Level 7

Question commentary

Example

The example illustrates a question where students are asked to find the volume of a triangular prism. Encourage a step-by-step approach as shown. Emphasise that correct units must be given with the final answer. Ask questions such as "What would the volume be if the shape were a cuboid with the same dimensions?"

$$40 \times \frac{1}{2} \times 12 \times 8$$
$$= 40 \times 48$$
$$= 1920 \text{ cm}^3$$

Past question

The question is a challenging problem that requires students to find the area of a specified part of a square. Encourage a step-by-step approach, writing down all known lengths. Students may not spot that the length of the side of the square is found from the radii of the circles. Emphasise the need to show all working and to give correct units with the final answer.

Answer

Level 7
2 60.8 cm²

Development and links

This topic is developed further in Year 9.

The ability to construct shapes accurately is important in design technology and in some forms of art. Bearings are used in navigation and link to the geography curriculum. Students will use volumes and surface areas in science when dealing with solids, liquids and gases, and in food technology and design technology to calculate required quantities of ingredients or materials.

15 Analysing and interpreting data

Data

Objectives

- Calculate statistics and select those most appropriate to the problem or which address the questions posed **6**
- Interpret graphs and diagrams and make inferences to support or cast doubt on initial conjectures **6**
- Select, construct and modify suitable graphical representations to progress an enquiry and identify key features present in the data. Include:
  - line graphs for time series
  - scatter graphs to develop further understanding of correlation **6**
- Have a basic understanding of correlation **6**
- Compare two or more distributions and make inferences, using the shape of the distributions and appropriate statistics **7**

Introduction

The focus of this chapter is on comparing distributions and identifying trends. The chapter begins by calculating statistics from a frequency table, including the mean, and students construct stem-and-leaf diagrams. They learn to interpret comparative charts, compare groups of data on a scatter graph, identify forms of correlation and identify trends in time series data. The chapter concludes with comparing distributions using statistical measures.

The student book discusses the UK government census that has been carried out every ten years since 1801. The UK Statistics Authority summarises, interprets and presents the collected data so that users can understand and improve the economy and society of the UK. Data is summarised and presented in many forms and in daily life, students are bombarded with statistics in the media. A clear understanding of how statistics are calculated and the features of different types of statistical chart will help students to make informed decisions and prevent them from being mislead by biased reports (EP).

◴ast-track
All spreads

Level

MPA

1.1	15a, b, c, d, e, CS
1.2	15a, b, c, d, e, f, CS
1.3	15a, b, c, d, e, f, CS
1.4	15a, c, e, f, CS
1.5	15a, b, c, d, e, f, CS

PLTS

IE	15b, c, d, f, CS
CT	15a, b, c, d, f, CS
RL	15a, b, c, d, e, f, CS
TW	15a, c, e, f, CS
SM	15d, e, CS
EP	15I, a, b, c, d, e, f, CS

Extra Resources

- 15   Start of chapter presentation
- 15a   Starter: Statistics multichoice
- 15a   Animation: Mode, median, mean and range
- 15a   Animation: Median, mean and range
- 15b   Animation: Averages and range
- 15b   Consolidation sheet
- 15e   Consolidation sheet
- 15e   Simulation: Correlations
- 15f   Consolidation sheet
      Maths life: Energy in the home

    Assessment: chapter 15

- Calculate statistics for small sets of discrete and continuous data, including with a calculator   (L6)

Useful resources
Copy of exercise

Starter – Today's number is ...111

Ask questions based on 'Today's number'. For example,

What is 25% of 111? (27.75)

What is the closest square number to 111? (121)

What is 400 subtract 111? (289)

111 is a multiple of 3. True or false? (T)

What are the prime factors of 111? (3, 37)

Teaching notes

Recapitulate the work on medians and ranges looked at previously in spreads **11e** and **11f**. Recall work in year seven on the mode (modal average). Why can't the mode or median actually be found from a grouped frequency table? Ask, what is the modal class interval? Which interval contains the median? (EP)

How can the median be roughly located in a grouped table? Show a list of raw data and clearly identify the median. Then put the data into a grouped frequency table. Ensure the median does not lie in the middle interval. Show how you can count through the data to find the 'middle' data value. What should you know before you start counting through the table? The number of data values.

Discuss where exactly the middle data value lies for an odd or even number of data values. The method of adding 1 and dividing by 2 to find the position of the median value could be used.

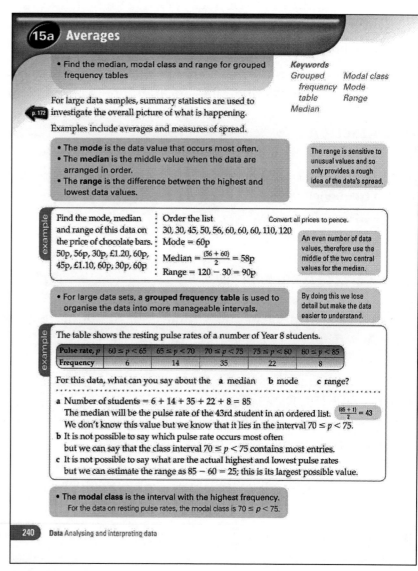

Plenary

If the interval widths were not all of the same size, would it still make sense to find the modal class interval and the interval containing the median? No. What other type of average have students come across? Mean average. Why is it not possible to find the (exact) mean average from a grouped frequency table? (CT) (1.2)

Simplification

Provide students with a list of the raw data for question **2** and the outline of the grouped frequency table for question **3**. Encourage students to explain how the raw data and grouped data both help to find the mode and median in different ways (EP).

All questions (EP) (1.1, 1.3)

Question 1 – What makes this question slightly more awkward? Units are different. Encourage students to order the data before deciding on the answers.

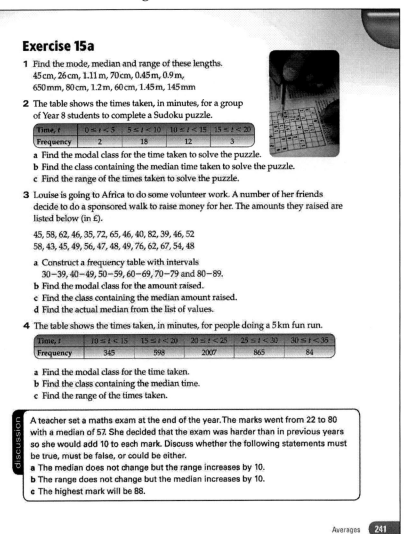

Exercise 15a

1 Find the mode, median and range of these lengths.
45 cm, 26 cm, 1.11 m, 70 cm, 0.45 m, 0.9 m,
650 mm, 80 cm, 1.2 m, 60 cm, 1.45 m, 145 mm

2 The table shows the times taken, in minutes, for a group of Year 8 students to complete a Sudoku puzzle.

Time, t	$0 \leqslant t < 5$	$5 \leqslant t < 10$	$10 \leqslant t < 15$	$15 \leqslant t < 20$
Frequency	2	18	12	3

  a Find the modal class for the time taken to solve the puzzle.
  b Find the class containing the median time taken to solve the puzzle.
  c Find the range of the times taken to solve the puzzle.

3 Louise is going to Africa to do some volunteer work. A number of her friends decide to do a sponsored walk to raise money for her. The amounts they raised are listed below (in £).

45, 58, 62, 46, 35, 72, 65, 46, 40, 82, 39, 46, 52
58, 43, 45, 49, 56, 47, 48, 49, 76, 62, 67, 54, 48

  a Construct a frequency table with intervals
    30–39, 40–49, 50–59, 60–69, 70–79 and 80–89.
  b Find the modal class for the amount raised.
  c Find the class containing the median amount raised.
  d Find the actual median from the list of values.

4 The table shows the times taken, in minutes, for people doing a 5 km fun run.

Time, t	$10 \leqslant t < 15$	$15 \leqslant t < 20$	$20 \leqslant t < 25$	$25 \leqslant t < 30$	$30 \leqslant t < 35$
Frequency	345	598	2007	865	84

  a Find the modal class for the time taken.
  b Find the class containing the median time.
  c Find the range of the times taken.

> **discussion**
>
> A teacher set a maths exam at the end of the year. The marks went from 22 to 80 with a median of 57. She decided that the exam was harder than in previous years so she would add 10 to each mark. Discuss whether the following statements must be true, must be false, or could be either.
> **a** The median does not change but the range increases by 10.
> **b** The range does not change but the median increases by 10.
> **c** The highest mark will be 88.

Averages   241

Extension

Look again at question **2**. Find a good estimate for the median from the table. How many results are there? (35) Which result is the median? (18th result) Where exactly might you find the 18th result? What assumption would you have to make? That the 18 results in the second interval were evenly spread. (9. 4/9 min = 9.4 min to 1 dp). (CT)

Exercise 15a commentary

Question 2 – In parts **a** and **b** check students do not state the frequency. Why can't the range be stated exactly? Can students say what the largest and smallest possible values will be? What estimate of the range could be made? (RL)

Question 3 – Encourage students to use a tally at first to ensure they put all the data results into the correct intervals, rather than 'scan' the list. Once most students in the class have tried this question, see which students have made an error. Does this help the students to decide on an appropriate method? (RL) (1.5)

Question 4 – How many people took part in the race? In part **b**, many students maybe tempted to answer 20–25; discuss why some students do this. When finding the range, tell students that the world record is just under 13 min.

Discussion – If necessary examine the affect of adding ten to a small data set, what has changed? Is this a sensible method of adjusting the grades of students in a test? What problems could it cause? What about students who scored zero or over 90 marks? What happens to the range and median if all the data results are multiplied by 2? (1.2, 1.4)

Assessment Criteria – HD, level 7: Estimate the median and range of a set of grouped data and determine the modal class.

Links

The word *average* comes from the French word *averie* which means "damage sustained at sea". Costs of losses at sea were shared between the ship owners and the cargo owners and the calculations used to assess the individual contributions gave rise to the modern sense of the word *average* (TW).

- Calculate statistics and select those most appropriate to the problem or which address the question posed (L6)

Useful resources
Calculator

Starter – DVDs

Ask students to calculate the mean, median and range of the playing times of the following DVDs:

Harry Potter and the Chamber of Secrets 2 hours 34 minutes
Lord of the Rings   3 hours 21 minutes
Toy Story 2   1 hour 29 minutes
Spiderman   2 hours   1 minute
Billy Elliot   1 hour 46 minutes
Batman Begins   2 hours 20 minutes

(Mean = 2hr 15min 10sec, median = 2hr 10min 30sec, range = 1hr 52min)

Teaching notes

Work through an example like question **1** involving a change of units. Emphasise that you add up the values and divide by the number of values. Then give a long (~30 items) list of discrete values and ask students to find the mean. Can they think of ways of organising the calculation? Suggest putting the data in order (always useful for finding the mode and median) can any one spot how multiplication might help? Show how the calculation can be set out in a table. Again emphasis that you divide the total of the values by the number of values and **not** the number of 'intervals'. (CT, RL) (1.5)

Consider splitting the class in two for question **3a**. One half to first tally the values, the second half to 'scan' the data and go straight to finding the frequency. Which group was more successful getting the right answer? Can any errors be traced to getting the frequencies wrong? (RL)

15b More averages

- Find the mean for a list of numbers
- Find the mean from a frequency table

Keywords
Frequency table
Mean

- The **mean** is the total of the data values divided by the number of values.

example

Calculate the mean of these lengths.
1.05 m, 102 cm, 99 cm, 1050 mm, 0.98 m, 103 cm

Number of measurements = 6
  Sum of lengths = 105 + 102 + 99 + 105 + 98 + 103 = 612 cm
    Mean = $\frac{612}{6}$ cm
         = 102 cm

Use the same units for all measurements.

Sometimes it is easier to do the calculation by subtracting a common value.
  Mean = $100 + \frac{(5 + 2 - 1 + 5 - 2 + 3)}{6}$ = $100 + \frac{12}{6}$ = 102 cm

When you have a lot of data it is helpful to organise it using a **frequency table**.

example

The list shows the number of radios that are in the homes of Mrs Bowler's Year 8 form class.

2, 3, 1, 2, 0, 1, 5, 2, 3, 1, 2, 3, 2, 1, 0,
0, 2, 3, 1, 1, 1, 1, 2, 5, 2, 3, 2, 0, 2, 3

Calculate the mean number of radios per household.

Number of radios, n	Tally	Frequency, f	$n \times f$
0	IIII	4	0
1	IIII III	8	8
2	IIII IIII	10	20
3	IIII I	6	18
4		0	0
5	II	2	10
Total		30	56

Mean = $\frac{\text{total number of radios}}{\text{total number of households}}$
     = $\frac{56}{30}$
     = $1.8\dot{6}$ = 1.9 (1 dp)

242 Data Analysing and interpreting data

Plenary

Look back at the data in exercises **15a** and **15b**. What is the best average to use to represent the data? Is there more than one good option? Can students think of examples where each of the averages would be appropriate/inappropriate? For example, a professional footballer scores the following number of goals in five matches, 0, 1, 0, 2, 3. His modal score is zero, is he a good player by this measure of average? (1.5)

Simplification

Provide students with a separate copy of the grouped tables with space to include a further row for frequency × value. Also make a further box for the total frequency to reduce the risk of division by the number of intervals rather than the total frequency (RL).

All questions (IE) (1.1, 1.3)

Question 1 – What makes this question a little awkward? Some students may need reminding of the conversion factor for kg and g. Ensure students find the total sum of the data before dividing by 6. Some students may forget to press '=' before performing the division.

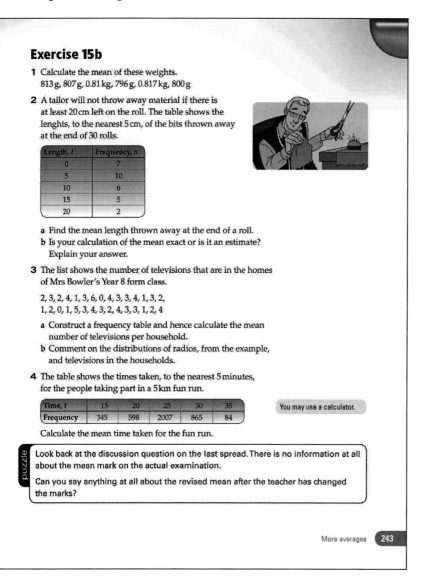

Exercise 15b

1 Calculate the mean of these weights.
813 g, 807 g, 0.81 kg, 796 g, 0.817 kg, 800 g

2 A tailor will not throw away material if there is at least 20 cm left on the roll. The table shows the lenghts, to the nearest 5 cm, of the bits thrown away at the end of 30 rolls.

Length, l	Frequency, n
0	7
5	10
10	6
15	5
20	2

a Find the mean length thrown away at the end of a roll.
b Is your calculation of the mean exact or is it an estimate? Explain your answer.

3 The list shows the number of televisions that are in the homes of Mrs Bowler's Year 8 form class.

2, 3, 2, 4, 1, 3, 6, 0, 4, 3, 3, 4, 1, 3, 2,
1, 2, 0, 1, 5, 3, 4, 3, 2, 4, 3, 3, 1, 2, 4

a Construct a frequency table and hence calculate the mean number of televisions per household.
b Comment on the distributions of radios, from the example, and televisions in the households.

4 The table shows the times taken, to the nearest 5 minutes, for the people taking part in a 5 km fun run.

Time, t	15	20	25	30	35
Frequency	345	598	2007	865	84

You may use a calculator.

Calculate the mean time taken for the fun run.

puzzle
Look back at the discussion question on the last spread. There is no information at all about the mean mark on the actual examination.

Can you say anything at all about the revised mean after the teacher has changed the marks?

Extension

Construct a grouped frequency table with more than ten results that has the modal class interval, class interval containing the median and the mean all occurring in different class intervals. Note, students should try to keep the class intervals the same width if possible.

Exercise 15b commentary

Question 2 – Part **a**, students need to show the calculations they are performing. In an exam, this type of question may be worth 3 to 4%. One small error and no working will lose all the marks. In part **b**, ask what might be the effect of rounding measurements to the nearest 5 cm?

Question 3 – In part **a**, encourage a two-step approach to constructing a frequency table: first tally then add. Check that students divide by 30, not 7. In part **b** students should definitely compare means but could also plot bar charts and look at distributions (CT) (1.5).

Question 4 – This will necessitate the use of a calculator.

Puzzle – Encourage students to test their theory on a small set of data. What happens to the mean value when 10 is added to each data value? (CT) (1.2)

Assessment Criteria4 – HD, level 7: estimate the mean of a set of grouped data.

Links

The average at rest pulse for an adult human is about 70 beats per minute but animals have widely differing pulse rates depending on their size. Smaller animals usually have faster pulse rates. An elephant has a pulse rate of about 25 beats per minute, a dog's pulse is 90–100 beats per minute, while a shrew's pulse rate is over 600 beats per minute. However an elephant has a much longer life span than a shrew, so the total number of heart beats in both animals' life span is roughly the same. What does this tell you about size and heart rate? (EP)

- Select, construct and modify, on paper and using ICT, suitable graphical representations to progress an enquiry and identify key features present in the data (L6)
- Include
  - pie charts for categorical data
  - stem-and-leaf diagrams (L6)
- Interpret graphs and diagrams and make inferences to support or cast doubt on initial conjectures (L6)

Useful resources
Calculator
Protractor

Starter – Missing numbers

Ask students to find

Four numbers with a mean of 15 and a range of 11 (11, 12, 15, 22)

Four numbers with a mean of 16 and a range of 14 (9, 13, 19, 23)

Five numbers with a mean of 14, a median of 12 and a range of 9 (10, 12, 12, 17, 19)

Possible solutions given, there are others.

Teaching notes

Recapitulate the method of finding the angles of the sectors for a pie chart previously covered in spread **11f**. Advise students to write their angles to 1 dp and then decide how to round them in case rounding leads to the sum not equalling 360°. For example, 1800 people are asked which party they will vote for, the votes for parties A, B and C are 267, 632 and 901. Once the angles are calculated you obtain 53.4°, 126.4° and 180.2°. What problem has this created? How can it be solved?

If the pie chart is shown without any numbers, does it demonstrate a large support for party C? Discuss the fact that the pie chart does not say the number of people it represents, it might only be a very small survey, and therefore unreliable.

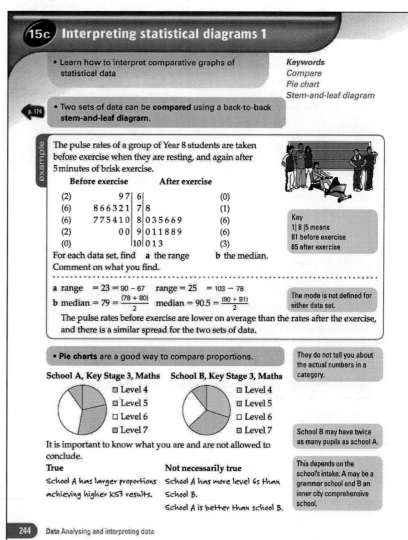

15c Interpreting statistical diagrams 1

- Learn how to interpret comparative graphs of statistical data

Keywords
Compare
Pie chart
Stem-and-leaf diagram

p. 174

- Two sets of data can be **compared** using a back-to-back **stem-and-leaf diagram**.

The pulse rates of a group of Year 8 students are taken before exercise when they are resting, and again after 5 minutes of brisk exercise.

Before exercise			After exercise
(2)	9 7	6	(0)
(6)	8 6 6 3 2 1	7	8 (1)
(6)	7 7 5 4 1 0	8	0 3 5 6 6 9 (6)
(2)	0 0	9	0 1 1 8 8 9 (6)
(0)		10	0 1 3 (3)

Key
1 | 8 | 5 means
81 before exercise
85 after exercise

For each data set, find **a** the range **b** the median. Comment on what you find.

a range $= 23 = 90 - 67$ range $= 25 = 103 - 78$

b median $= 79 = \frac{(78 + 80)}{2}$ median $= 90.5 = \frac{(90 + 91)}{2}$

The mode is not defined for either data set.

The pulse rates before exercise are lower on average than the rates after the exercise, and there is a similar spread for the two sets of data.

- **Pie charts** are a good way to compare proportions.

They do not tell you about the actual numbers in a category.

School A, Key Stage 3, Maths
- Level 4
- Level 5
- Level 6
- Level 7

School B, Key Stage 3, Maths
- Level 4
- Level 5
- Level 6
- Level 7

School B may have twice as many pupils as school A.

It is important to know what you are and are not allowed to conclude.

True
School A has larger proportions achieving higher KS3 results.

Not necessarily true
School A has more level 6s than School B.

School A is better than school B.

This depends on the school's intake: A may be a grammar school and B an inner city comprehensive school.

244 Data Analysing and interpreting data

Plenary

Statistical graphs can be used to mislead people. In what ways can this be done? For example, change class widths on grouped frequency tables, omit the scale on a bar chart, record results over selected time periods, *etc.* (EP, TW) (1.5)

Simplification

Provide students with a copy of the data from the exercise to allow them to cross off values as they go. If necessary, begin the formation of the pie chart and stem-and-leaf diagram. Create extra rows for the data in question **3** to allow for the calculations of the angles for the pie charts. Give these rows headings.

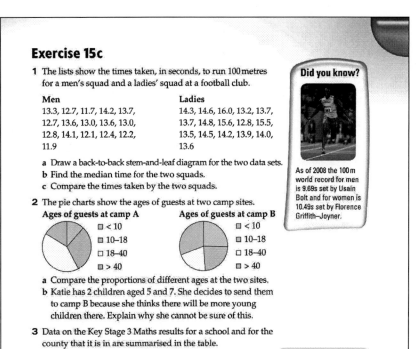

Exercise 15c

1 The lists show the times taken, in seconds, to run 100 metres for a men's squad and a ladies' squad at a football club.

Men	Ladies
13.3, 12.7, 11.7, 14.2, 13.7,	14.3, 14.6, 16.0, 13.2, 13.7,
12.7, 13.6, 13.0, 13.6, 13.0,	13.7, 14.8, 15.6, 12.8, 15.5,
12.8, 14.1, 12.1, 12.4, 12.2,	13.5, 14.5, 14.2, 13.9, 14.0,
11.9	13.6

Did you know?

As of 2008 the 100 m world record for men is 9.69s set by Usain Bolt and for women is 10.49s set by Florence Griffith–Joyner.

  a Draw a back-to-back stem-and-leaf diagram for the two data sets.
  b Find the median time for the two squads.
  c Compare the times taken by the two squads.

2 The pie charts show the ages of guests at two camp sites.

Ages of guests at camp A   Ages of guests at camp B
☑ < 10   ☑ 10–18   ☐ 18–40   ☑ > 40

  a Compare the proportions of different ages at the two sites.
  b Katie has 2 children aged 5 and 7. She decides to send them to camp B because she thinks there will be more young children there. Explain why she cannot be sure of this.

3 Data on the Key Stage 3 Maths results for a school and for the county that it is in are summarised in the table.

	Level 4	Level 5	Level 6	Level 7
School	15	45	25	35
County	254	481	180	134

Hint: for each level, write the number of entries as a fraction of the total and take this proportion of 360°.

  a Draw pie charts to show the school's results and the county's results.
  b Compare the performance of the school in maths with the general performance in the county.

discussion

The actual numbers for the pie charts in the example on the page opposite are given in the table.

	Level 4	Level 5	Level 6	Level 7	Total
School A	26	38	45	12	121
School B	22	25	19	8	74

Can you think of how you might draw pie charts which would allow you to compare not only the proportions but also the actual numbers at the different levels?

Interpreting statistical diagrams 1   245

Extension

Draw pie charts to show comparisons between the times for the men and woman in question **1**. How should the data be grouped to be able to show a clear comparison? Use exactly the same intervals, ensuring that each data set has at least one result in the intervals chosen. How many intervals should be used? Rough estimate maybe over 2 and under 7 (IE) (1.1).

Exercise 15c commentary

All questions (1.3)

Question 1 – Remind students that the 'leaf' can only hold one digit. Can students comment on the 'shape' of the data? For example, tends to group towards the quicker times or roughly evenly spread over the times (IE) (1.1).

Question 2 – Draw comparisons between each of the age groups. Encourage students to make comparisons over two combined age groups if possible. Can an overall comparison be made between the two camps? (RL) (1.2)

Question 3 – The total for the school is a convenient number (120), but the total for the county is not (1049). Encourage students to draw the pie chart for the school first. Try to employ the same method for the county, although the numbers are more awkward (IE) (1.1).

Discussion – What detail does a pie chart lack that makes it less informative? Where would it be convenient to add this detail? (CT)

Assessment Criteria – HD, level 6: Select, construct and modify, on paper and using ICT:
– pie charts for categorical data.

Links

The history of the World record for running the 100 m can be found at http://en.wikipedia.org/wiki/World_record_progression_100_metres_men and http:// en.wikipedia.org/wiki/World_record_progression_100_metres_women This data could be used to produce time series graphs. Can students explain why there are 'steps'? Can they make predictions for what the records will be in 2050? (CT, EP) (1.4)

- Select, construct and modify, on paper and using ICT, suitable graphical representations to progress an enquiry and identify key features present in the data (L6)

Useful resources

- Include
  - simple scatter graphs
  - line graphs for time series (L6)
- Interpret graphs and diagrams and make inferences to support or cast doubt on initial conjectures (L6)

Starter – House numbers

Seven consecutive house numbers add up 280.
Ask students what are the numbers and the mean house number?
(34, 36, 38, 40, 42, 44, 46; mean=40)
Eight consecutive house numbers add up to 1024.
What are the numbers and the median house number?
(121, 123, 125, 127, 129, 131, 133, 135; median=128)

Teaching notes

Look at the scatter graph example. This plots the 100 m and 200 m times for people from two different backgrounds. Ask students to suggest other pairs of data that could be plotted on a scatter diagram, encourage students to make suggestions that are likely to produce a similar pattern to that of the athletes and footballers. For example, exam performance in English and History, peoples height and weight, *etc.*

Can students suggest pairs of data where the pattern will be in the opposite direction? (EP)
For example, time for 100 m and age (for ages between 30 and 50). What might happen to the data outside these age ranges?

Look at the time series example. Why is there a seasonal variation? How can you compare your electricity use over the three years? Which parts of the graph can be compared? (CT)

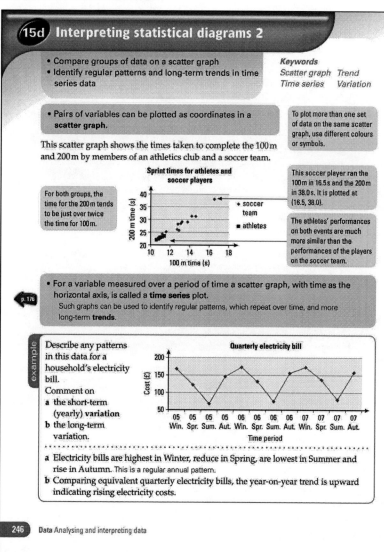

15d Interpreting statistical diagrams 2

- Compare groups of data on a scatter graph
- Identify regular patterns and long-term trends in time series data

Keywords
Scatter graph Trend
Time series Variation

- Pairs of variables can be plotted as coordinates in a **scatter graph**.

To plot more than one set of data on the same scatter graph, use different colours or symbols.

This scatter graph shows the times taken to complete the 100 m and 200 m by members of an athletics club and a soccer team.

Sprint times for athletes and soccer players

For both groups, the time for the 200 m tends to be just over twice the time for 100 m.

This soccer player ran the 100 m in 16.5 s and the 200 m in 38.0 s. It is plotted at (16.5, 38.0).

The athletes' performances on both events are much more similar than the performances of the players on the soccer team.

- For a variable measured over a period of time a scatter graph, with time as the horizontal axis, is called a **time series** plot.
  Such graphs can be used to identify regular patterns, which repeat over time, and more long-term **trends**.

example

Describe any patterns in this data for a household's electricity bill.
Comment on
a the short-term (yearly) **variation**
b the long-term variation.

Quarterly electricity bill

a Electricity bills are highest in Winter, reduce in Spring, are lowest in Summer and rise in Autumn. This is a regular annual pattern.
b Comparing equivalent quarterly electricity bills, the year-on-year trend is upward indicating rising electricity costs.

246 **Data** Analysing and interpreting data

Plenary

A company that produces ice creams wants to look at how its sales have changed over the past few years. They are also interested in their Summer sales over the past few years. They have monthly sales data. What graph(s) should they plot and what should they look for? (EP, RL)

Simplification

Provide students with the outline of a scatter diagram and a suggestion of an appropriate scale. Perhaps indicate where the intervals on the axes could lie without inserting the actual numbers except the starting value.

All questions (1.1)

Question 1 – Encourage students to think about the scales on the axes by looking at both data sets before beginning the graph. Ensure a sensible scale is being used that will mean the graph is not too small (IE) (1.3).

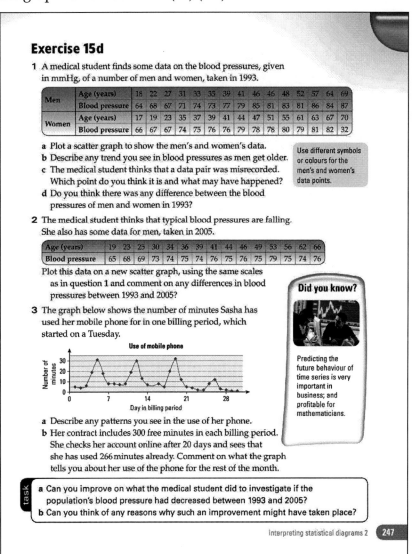

Exercise 15d

1 A medical student finds some data on the blood pressures, given in mmHg, of a number of men and women, taken in 1993.

Men	Age (years)	18	22	27	31	33	35	39	41	46	46	48	52	57	64	69
	Blood pressure	64	68	67	71	74	73	77	79	85	81	83	81	86	84	87
Women	Age (years)	17	19	23	35	37	39	41	44	47	51	55	61	63	67	70
	Blood pressure	66	67	67	74	75	76	76	79	78	78	80	79	81	82	32

a Plot a scatter graph to show the men's and women's data.
b Describe any trend you see in blood pressures as men get older.
c The medical student thinks that a data pair was misrecorded. Which point do you think it is and what may have happened?
d Do you think there was any difference between the blood pressures of men and women in 1993?

> Use different symbols or colours for the men's and women's data points.

2 The medical student thinks that typical blood pressures are falling. She also has some data for men, taken in 2005.

| Age (years) | 19 | 23 | 25 | 30 | 34 | 36 | 39 | 41 | 44 | 46 | 49 | 53 | 56 | 62 | 66 |
| Blood pressure | 65 | 68 | 69 | 73 | 74 | 75 | 74 | 76 | 75 | 76 | 75 | 79 | 75 | 74 | 76 |

Plot this data on a new scatter graph, using the same scales as in question 1 and comment on any differences in blood pressures between 1993 and 2005?

3 The graph below shows the number of minutes Sasha has used her mobile phone for in one billing period, which started on a Tuesday.

Use of mobile phone

a Describe any patterns you see in the use of her phone.
b Her contract includes 300 free minutes in each billing period. She checks her account online after 20 days and sees that she has used 266 minutes already. Comment on what the graph tells you about her use of the phone for the rest of the month.

task
a Can you improve on what the medical student did to investigate if the population's blood pressure had decreased between 1993 and 2005?
b Can you think of any reasons why such an improvement might have taken place?

> **Did you know?**
> Predicting the future behaviour of time series is very important in business; and profitable for mathematicians.

Interpreting statistical diagrams 2　247

Extension

A line of best fit could be drawn through the scatter diagrams, but it is sometimes difficult to do an accurate job in placing it. A useful aid is to find what is know as the mean point. Find the mean age and the mean blood pressure. Add this 'new mean person' to the scatter diagram and make the line of best fit pass through this point as well as roughly passing through the trend of the other points (CT, SM).

Exercise 15d commentary

Question 2 – Encourage students to look at the trend rather than the individual results. Is the sample large enough to feel confident about your conclusions? (IE) (1.3)

Question 3 – Why is the graph rising at the four peaks? Hint that each mark represents a day and the first represents Tuesday. Invite more detailed answers about the end of the month than just 'she reduces her time on the phone' (CT) (1.2).

Task – Is there a way to find the 'average blood pressure'? Would the total of the ages and the blood pressures help in drawing a conclusion? Does it matter that the ages of the people were not the same in the two surveys? Are 15 people enough to ask? (1.5)

Assessment Criteria – HD, level 6: Select, construct and modify, on paper and using ICT:
– simple line graphs for time series
– scatter graphs.

Links

A Hertzsprung-Russell diagram is a scatter graph showing the connection between the luminosity of a star and its temperature. The position of each star on the chart depends on its age. The diagram is named after the Danish astronomer Ejnar Hertzsprung (1873–1967) and the American astronomer Henry Norris Russell (1877–1957). There is more information about the Hertzsprung-Russell diagram at http://en. wikipedia.org/wiki/Hertzsprung-Russell_diagram and an interactive version at http://aspire.cosmic-ray. org/labs/star_life/hr_diagram.html (EP)

- Select, construct and modify, on paper and using ICT, suitable graphical representations to progress an enquiry and identify key features present in the data (L6)
- Include
  - scatter graphs to develop further understanding of correlation (L6)
- Have a basic understanding of correlation (L6)

Useful resources
Calculator
Spread sheet

Starter – Data bingo

Ask students to draw a 3 × 3 grid and enter nine numbers between 15 and 40 inclusive

Give two numbers and ask students to give the mean or range of the numbers, for example, range of 17, 41; mean of 11, 25.

The winner is the first student to cross out all their numbers.

Teaching notes

If there is a pattern in the results then we say that there is a correlation, if no pattern is obvious then there is no correlation. If the rough pattern lies in a straight line then there is a linear correlation. The type of linear correlation depends on the direction of the line. Ask students what they think would be a good name for the increasing and decreasing lines. You could hint that this is related to the equations of straight lines. Establish that, like gradients, you have positive and negative correlation.

Emphasise that the strength of a correlation relates to how closely the data clusters about a line, not how steep the line is (RL) (1.5).

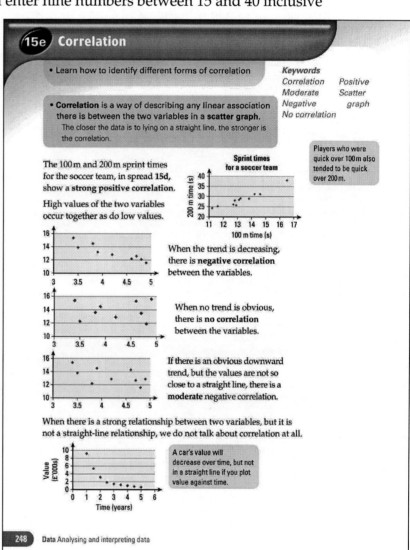

Plenary

Draw a scatter diagram showing a strong correlation between two obviously unconnected variables. For example, a persons height (between birth and the age of ten) and the price of a pint of milk. Ask the students, what can you say about the correlation? (Positive) Does this mean that the increase in one of the variables is causing an increase in the other? Although there is correlation, this does not automatically mean that the two variables are connected, we need to use common sense as well. (RL) (1.5)

Simplification

Help students by outlining the axes needed for the scatter diagram in question 3.

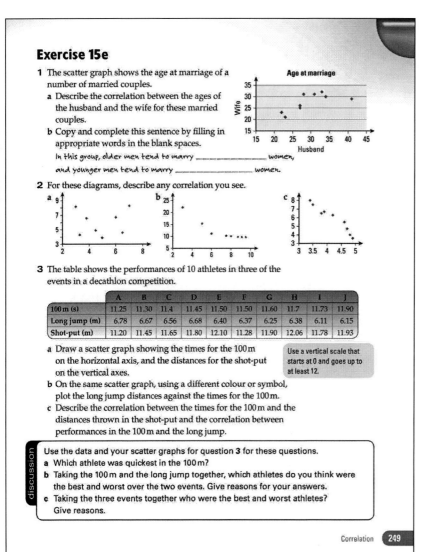

Exercise 15e

1 The scatter graph shows the age at marriage of a number of married couples.
   a Describe the correlation between the ages of the husband and the wife for these married couples.
   b Copy and complete this sentence by filling in appropriate words in the blank spaces.
   In this group, older men tend to marry _____ women, and younger men tend to marry _____ women.

2 For these diagrams, describe any correlation you see.
   a   b   c

3 The table shows the performances of 10 athletes in three of the events in a decathlon competition.

	A	B	C	D	E	F	G	H	I	J
100 m (s)	11.25	11.30	11.4	11.45	11.50	11.50	11.60	11.7	11.73	11.90
Long jump (m)	6.78	6.67	6.56	6.68	6.40	6.37	6.25	6.38	6.11	6.15
Shot-put (m)	11.20	11.45	11.65	11.80	12.10	11.28	11.90	12.06	11.78	11.93

   a Draw a scatter graph showing the times for the 100 m on the horizontal axis, and the distances for the shot-put on the vertical axes.
   Use a vertical scale that starts at 0 and goes up to at least 12.
   b On the same scatter graph, using a different colour or symbol, plot the long jump distances against the times for the 100 m.
   c Describe the correlation between the times for the 100 m and the distances thrown in the shot-put and the correlation between performances in the 100 m and the long jump.

discussion

Use the data and your scatter graphs for question 3 for these questions.
   a Which athlete was quickest in the 100 m?
   b Taking the 100 m and the long jump together, which athletes do you think were the best and worst over the two events. Give reasons for your answers.
   c Taking the three events together who were the best and worst athletes? Give reasons.

Correlation **249**

Extension

The official points system for the decathlon uses the following formulae.

100 m: $\quad$ points $= 25.4347(18 - \text{time (s)})^{1.81}$

long jump: $\quad$ points $= 0.14354(\text{distance (cm)} - 220)^{1.4}$

shot putt: $\quad$ points $= 51.39(\text{distance (m)} - 1.5)^{1.05}$

The points are rounded down to the nearest integer. Calculate athletes' scores from question 3 and then rank them in descending order (A, B, D, C, E, H, F, G, I, J). This could be done using a spread sheet (EP. SM) (1.3)

Exercise 15e commentary

All questions (1.1, 1.4)

Question 1 – Should one result influence your view of the trend in a set of results? An unusual result is normally called at 'outlier'. Describe the relationship in words before stating the type of correlation.

Question 2 – Encourage the use of descriptive terms: strong, weak, curved as well as positive/negative correlation.

Question 3 – What type of correlation do students expect to find for these athletes? It might be necessary to explain what a decathlete is (1.2, 1.3).

Discussion – Encourage students to explain why they pick certain athletes. Which athlete seems to be doing the best over all three events? If someone in the class has tried the extension, compare their findings (TW) (1.2, 1.5).

Assessment Criteria – HD, level 6: select, construct and modify, on paper and using ICT: scatter graphs. HD, level 6: communicate interpretations and results of a statistical survey using selected tables, graphs and diagrams in support.

Links

Bring in some advertisements for the class to use from local car dealers showing prices for second hand cars. Alternatively prices can be found at http://www.autotrader.co.uk/ or http://www.exchangeandmart.co.uk/iad Choose a particular brand of car and find prices for models of different ages. Is there any correlation between the age of the car and the price? What other factors affect the price of the car? (mileage, model, condition) (EP)

- Compare two or more distributions and make inferences, using the shape of the distributions and appropriate statistics (L7)

Useful resources

Starter – More jumble

Write a list of anagrams on the board and ask students to unscramble them and then make their own anagrams or word search. Possible anagrams are AGRAVEE, CQUEENFRY, GAREN, TRAINCOROLE, CASTISITT, EDAMIN, MISTIREESE (2 words), ACIPERTH (2 words) (average, frequency, range, correlation, statistic, median, time series, pie chart)

Teaching notes

Look at the example for the high tide depths. When trying to compare the average high tide, why is the median a more reliable measure than the mean? Discuss the fact that the mean is calculated from all the results, so one unusual result will have an effect on the mean, but not on the median.

What type of measure is the range? Establish that it gives an idea of the degree of variation in the data. Is the range a reliable measure of the overall degree of variation in the results? Establish that the range is also affected by one extreme result that might not reflect the rest of the data. In more advanced statistics, there are better measures of the variation that are not affected so extremely by one result (RL) (1.5).

Recall the method of finding the interval that contains the median result from a grouped frequency table, previously covered in spreads **11e, 11f** and **15a**.

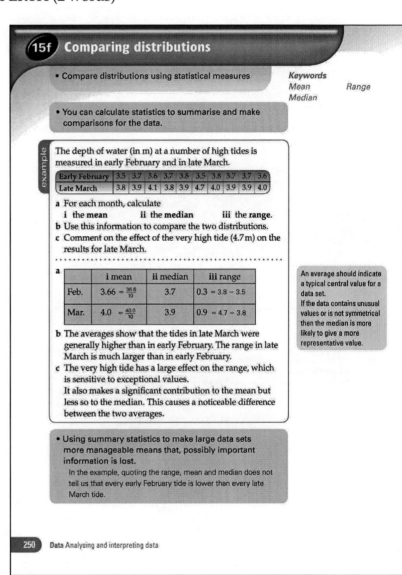

15f Comparing distributions

- Compare distributions using statistical measures

Keywords
Mean
Median
Range

- You can calculate statistics to summarise and make comparisons for the data.

example

The depth of water (in m) at a number of high tides is measured in early February and in late March.

| Early February | 3.5 | 3.7 | 3.6 | 3.7 | 3.8 | 3.5 | 3.8 | 3.7 | 3.7 | 3.6 |
| Late March | 3.8 | 3.9 | 4.1 | 3.8 | 3.9 | 4.7 | 4.0 | 3.9 | 3.9 | 4.0 |

a For each month, calculate
  i the mean   ii the median   iii the range.
b Use this information to compare the two distributions.
c Comment on the effect of the very high tide (4.7 m) on the results for late March.

a

	i mean	ii median	iii range
Feb.	$3.66 = \frac{36.6}{10}$	3.7	$0.3 = 3.8 - 3.5$
Mar.	$4.0 = \frac{40.0}{10}$	3.9	$0.9 = 4.7 - 3.8$

b The averages show that the tides in late March were generally higher than in early February. The range in late March is much larger than in early February.
c The very high tide has a large effect on the range, which is sensitive to exceptional values.
It also makes a significant contribution to the mean but less so to the median. This causes a noticeable difference between the two averages.

An average should indicate a typical central value for a data set.
If the data contains unusual values or is not symmetrical then the median is more likely to give a more representative value.

- Using summary statistics to make large data sets more manageable means that, possibly important information is lost.
  In the example, quoting the range, mean and median does not tell us that every early February tide is lower than every late March tide.

250 Data Analysing and interpreting data

Plenary

Look at a frequency polygon for the data in question **3**. Would it have been possible to make the same conclusions from these graphs as from the data in the table? (1.1)

Simplification

Provide students with ordered data for question **2**. Keep emphasising the type of response needed when comparing the sets of data. Give examples like 'women perform better' rather than 'women have a higher average'.

All questions (IE, CT, EP) (1.2 1.4, 1.5)

Question 1 – Students need to comment on the changes in the mean and the range, and interpret what this tells us about the training, rather than their numeric values. In part **b**, ask students to take into account sample size and the participants' familiarity with the test.

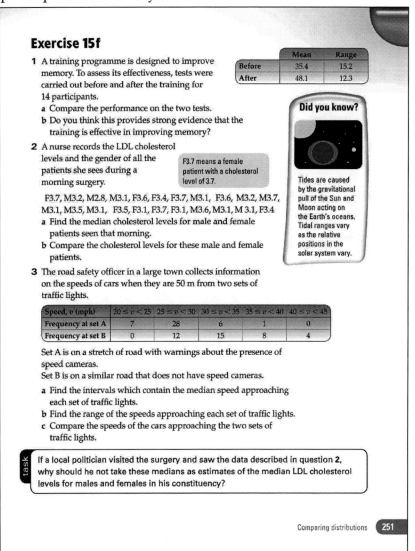

Exercise 15f

1 A training programme is designed to improve memory. To assess its effectiveness, tests were carried out before and after the training for 14 participants.

	Mean	Range
Before	35.4	15.2
After	48.1	12.3

  a Compare the performance on the two tests.
  b Do you think this provides strong evidence that the training is effective in improving memory?

2 A nurse records the LDL cholesterol levels and the gender of all the patients she sees during a morning surgery.

F3.7 means a female patient with a cholesterol level of 3.7.

F3.7, M3.2, M2.8, M3.1, F3.6, F3.4, F3.7, M3.1, F3.6, M3.2, M3.7, M3.1, M3.5, M3.1, F3.5, F3.1, F3.7, F3.1, M3.6, M3.1, M 3.1, F3.4

  a Find the median cholesterol levels for male and female patients seen that morning.
  b Compare the cholesterol levels for these male and female patients.

Did you know?

Tides are caused by the gravitational pull of the Sun and Moon acting on the Earth's oceans. Tidal ranges vary as the relative positions in the solar system vary.

3 The road safety officer in a large town collects information on the speeds of cars when they are 50 m from two sets of traffic lights.

Speed, v (mph)	$20 \leq v < 25$	$25 \leq v < 30$	$30 \leq v < 35$	$35 \leq v < 40$	$40 \leq v < 45$
Frequency at set A	7	28	6	1	0
Frequency at set B	0	12	15	8	4

Set A is on a stretch of road with warnings about the presence of speed cameras.
Set B is on a similar road that does not have speed cameras.

  a Find the intervals which contain the median speed approaching each set of traffic lights.
  b Find the range of the speeds approaching each set of traffic lights.
  c Compare the speeds of the cars approaching the two sets of traffic lights.

task If a local politician visited the surgery and saw the data described in question **2**, why should he not take these medians as estimates of the median LDL cholesterol levels for males and females in his constituency?

Comparing distributions   251

Extension

In question **2**, instead of comparing the ranges (max. – min), compare the difference between the results that are a quarter and three quarters of the way through the data. Does this change the conclusions? Range = 0.6 females, 0.9 males; conclude that there is more variation of cholesterol levels in males. IQR =0.3 females 0.25 males; conclude that there is no real difference in the variation of cholesterol levels between men and women. Why is this second measurement a more reliable one? It is not affected by extreme results (RL) (1.5).

Exercise 15f commentary

Question 2 – When drawing a comparison, encourage students to make use of both the median and the range. Ensure comments relate to the differences rather than just the numerical results (1.3).

Question 3 – When finding the interval containing the median, many students may pick the middle interval (30 – 35). Why is this wrong? What assumption could be made when arriving at a measure for the range? (1.3)

Discussion – The term constituency may need explaining. What would you need to know about the patients in order to decide if they were a typical cross section of people from the area? Is it likely that people who have gone to see the nurse have typical levels of cholesterol?

Assessment Criteria – HD, level 7: compare two or more distributions and make inferences, using the shape of the distributions and measures of average and range.

Links

The highest tides in the U.K. are in the Bristol Channel where in extreme cases the water can rise up to 15 m between low and high tide. Before Bristol's floating harbour was built at the beginning of the 19th century, boats unloading at Bristol were stranded in the mud for a considerable length of time at low tide. Boats had to be in good condition to withstand the stresses and strains this caused and originated the phrase "shipshape and Bristol fashion". A graph showing current tide information for Bristol can be found at http://www.bbc.co.uk/weather/coast/tides/west.shtml. Predicting tides is a very important problem (EP, TW).

1 Two friends wash cars on Saturday mornings, charging £2 for small cars and £3 for larger cars. These are the amounts (in £) they collect over a six-month period.

| 48, 54, 82, 75, 64, 41, |
| 85, 76, 34, 48, 46, 71, |
| 63, 86, 71, 59, 64, 38, |
| 47, 51, 56, 78, 83, 57, |
| 53, 46 |

a Construct a frequency table with amounts 30−39, 40−49, 50−59, 60−69, 70−79 and 80−89.

b Find the modal class for the amount they collect.

c Find the class containing the median amount collected.

d Find the actual median from the list of values.

2 The table shows the times taken, in minutes, for a group of Year 8 students to complete a cross-country run.

Time, t	$10 \leq t < 12$	$12 \leq t < 14$	$14 \leq t < 16$	$16 \leq t < 18$	$18 \leq t < 20$
Frequency	7	24	15	6	2

a Find the modal class for the time taken for the run.

b Find the class containing the median time taken for the run.

c Find the range of the times taken for the run.

3 Sally sells some raffle tickets. Using the table calculate the mean number sold per person.

Number of tickets	1	2	3	4	5
Frequency	8	5	2	1	9

4 Data is collected on the distances in miles driven in a week by a number of people.

Females
97, 82, 86, 89, 92, 77, 104, 85, 84, 91, 80, 86, 95, 101

Males
102, 121, 93, 86, 112, 100, 107, 109, 109, 103, 117, 94, 93, 114, 91, 98

a Draw a back-to-back stem-and-leaf diagram for these two data sets.

b Find the median distance driven for females and males.

c Compare the distances driven by females and males.

5 100 people in London and in Belfast were asked to choose which food they preferred. The results are shown in the pie charts.

London

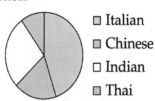

☐ Italian
☐ Chinese
☐ Indian
☐ Thai

Belfast

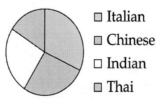

☐ Italian
☐ Chinese
☐ Indian
☐ Thai

Compare the food preferences of people in London and Belfast.

6 Karim runs a newsagent which sells CDs. The time series graph shows the number sold recently in each quarter. Describe two features of the graph.

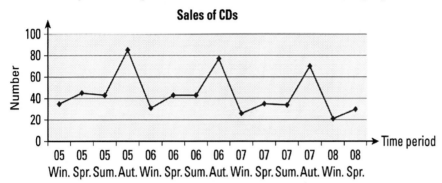

7 Sketch three scatter graphs showing these types of correlation.
  a strong negative   **b** none   **c** weak positive

8 The scatter graph shows the marks scored by a number of pupils in examinations in maths and in biology.
  a Describe the correlation between the marks obtained in the two subjects.
  b Copy and complete the following sentence by filling in appropriate words in the blank spaces.

  In this group of pupils, those who score high marks in maths tend to score _____ marks in biology and pupils who score low marks in maths tend to score _____ marks in biology.

Examination Marks

9 A training programme is designed to improve a school athlete's technique in the javelin. The table shows a summary of samples of 10 throws taken before and after the athlete follows the training programme.
  a Compare his performance before and after the training.
  b Do you think this provides strong evidence that the training is effective in improving his technique?

	Mean	Range
Before	51.3	4.2
After	56.4	3.1

10 A careers teacher has collected data from some sixth form pupils who left school to start a job on whether they did A-level maths and their starting salary (in £'000s).
  a Find the median starting salaries for the two groups.
  b Is it reasonable to say that on average people with an A-level in maths earn more than those without one?

Y15.7, N13.7, Y13.5, Y14.2,
N14.0, Y14.8, Y13.9, N13.7,
Y13.9, N14.2, Y14.6, Y13.9,
N13.8, N14.3, Y14.8, Y13.9,
Y15.1, N13.6, Y14.3, Y14.1

Y15.7 means yes did A-level maths, starting salary £15.7k.

- Break down substantial tasks to make them more manageable (L6)
- Justify the mathematical features drawn from a context and the choice of approach (L6)

Useful resources

Background

With energy prices rising rapidly and environmental concerns about the climate, there is much interest in reducing energy use around the house and obtaining energy in a cheaper or cleaner way.

This case study looks at a number of things that can be done to a house to make it more energy efficient. It looks at them in terms of how much they could reduce the cost of energy used over a year at current costs and considers their cost effectiveness by working out how long it would take for the savings to pay back the cost of purchase and installation of the items (EP).

Teaching notes

Look at the case study and explain that the house shows ways of either saving energy or of providing the energy in a different way. Ask the students some general questions such as: which items would save energy and which are alternative sources of energy? Do you have any of these things in your house? Why do you think that there is so much interest in saving energy these days? Establish that rising energy costs and concerns for the environment can both drive people to think about the way they use energy (TW).

Look at the information about loft insulation. What do you notice about the information that is given? (The cost is greater than or equal to the saving, depending on which figures you take.) Roughly how long would it take for the savings in costs to repay the cost of installing the insulation? Discuss how figures for items such as this are often given as ranges, as the actual figure will vary from house to house depending on its size, type and construction. Discuss how you could take an average 'middle' value for the cost and the savings or you could try to work out the maximum and minimum pay back times. Whichever you do, ask, do you think that is a reasonable time in which to recoup the cost? What will happen for every year after that? Now look at the information for the A rated boiler and ask similar questions. The pay back time is considerably longer. Discuss whether this is cost effective by asking questions such as, if you have a perfectly good working boiler at the moment, do you think that it would be worth paying to have it changed for a new one? If you needed to change your current boiler, would it be worth having an A rated boiler as the replacement? (1.3, 1.5)

Teaching notes continued

You might discuss whether their answers might change depending on how long they were staying in their house. Ask students to find the minimum (lowest cost and highest saving) and maximum (highest cost and lowest saving) payback times for the nine energy saving suggestions on the green labels. Discuss students' answers to the questions, which is the most/least cost effective? Why might some items be more cost effect for a new build? What would you install if money were no object? (1.2)

Look at the information about the energy saving light bulbs. Use the 100W bulb to make sure that pupils understand the units involved. What is 1kW? (1000 Watts) One kWh is the amount of electricity needed to run something that uses 1000W for 1 hour. How many kW is a 100W bulb? (0.1) So the bulb uses 0.1kWh. How long will the bulb run on 1kW of electricity? (10 hours) How much would it cost to run the bulb for 10 hours? (11p) What savings might be made by replacing one or all the incandescent bulbs in a house with energy efficient ones? Is there another way money might be saved? Energy efficient light bulbs tend to have a longer life than standard bulbs, so offsetting some of their initial cost (CT) (1.1).

Likewise, work through the section about the photovoltaic panels. Note how the possibly unusual unit kWp (peak kW) can be replaced by the more familiar 750kWh for the initial calculation. When discussing answers, ensure that students comment on the fact that the pay back time might shorten due to the electricity costs of supplied electricity increasing over time thereby increasing the annual savings.

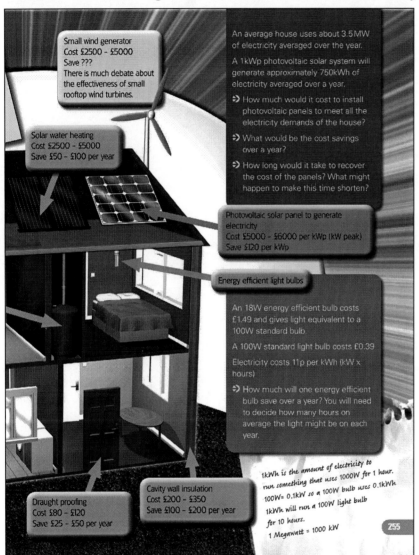

Small wind generator
Cost £2500 – £5000
Save ???
There is much debate about the effectiveness of small rooftop wind turbines.

Solar water heating
Cost £2500 – £5000
Save £50 – £100 per year

An average house uses about 3.5MW of electricity averaged over the year.

A 1kWp photovoltaic solar system will generate approximately 750kWh of electricity averaged over a year.

→ How much would it cost to install photovoltaic panels to meet all the electricity demands of the house?

→ What would be the cost savings over a year?

→ How long would it take to recover the cost of the panels? What might happen to make this time shorten?

Photovoltaic solar panel to generate electricity
Cost £5000 – £6000 per kWp (kW peak)
Save £120 per kWp

Energy efficient light bulbs

An 18W energy efficient bulb costs £1.49 and gives light equivalent to a 100W standard bulb.

A 100W standard light bulb costs £0.39

Electricity costs 11p per kWh (kW x hours)

→ How much will one energy efficient bulb save over a year? You will need to decide how many hours on average the light might be on each year.

Draught proofing
Cost £80 – £120
Save £25 – £50 per year

Cavity wall insulation
Cost £200 – £350
Save £100 – £200 per year

1kWh is the amount of electricity to run something that uses 1000W for 1 hour. 100W= 0.1kW so a 100W bulb uses 0.1kWh 1kWh will run a 100W light bulb for 10 hours. 1 Megawatt = 1000 kW

255

Extension

The information about the wind turbine is left deliberately vague in the case study as there are many discussions about how effective small home turbines are. The table illustrates the basic relationship between the average power output of a turbine as a function of the average wind speed (cubic) and blade diameter (quadratic). Students could be asked to investigate the relationship and make predictions for other turbines (IE, CT, SM) (1.4).

There is much more detail about wind power, including information about how the height above ground affects the power output, at: http://www.scoraigwind.com/ and http://windmeasurement.co.uk/wind_shade.html

		Average wind speed (m/s)			
		3	4.5	6	9
Blade diam (m)	1	4	13	30	106
	2	15	51	121	408
	3	34	115	272	919
	4	60	204	483	1625

15 Summary

Assessment criteria

- Select, construct and modify, on paper and using ICT:
  - pie charts for categorical data
  - simple line graphs for time series
  - scatter graphs   Level 6
- Communicate interpretations and results of a statistical survey
  using selected tables, graphs and diagrams in support   Level 6
- Estimate the mean, median and range of a set of grouped data
  and determine the modal class   Level 7
- Compare two or more distributions and make inferences, using
  the shape of the distributions and measures of average and range   Level 7

Question commentary

Example The example illustrates a problem about calculating a mean from a frequency table. In part **a**, some students may confuse the number of flowers with the number of plants. Similarly in part **b**, some students may add the numbers in the first column to find the total number of flowers. Encourage students to add an extra column to the table for the total number of flowers on the plants for each category. Encourage students to check that the value of their final answer is reasonable.	**a** $20 - (2 \times 3 + 3 \times 3 + 4 \times 1)$ $\qquad = 20 - 19$ $\qquad = 1$ **b** $\dfrac{20}{8} = 2.5$
Past questions The question requires students to interpret a scatter graph. In part **a**, students may wrongly give the highest single score instead of the highest combined score. In part **b**, emphasise the need to show working to explain the answer.	**Answer** **Level 6** **2 a** N **b** True, Coursework range = 40, Test range = 30

Development and links

This topic will be developed further in Year 9.

Students will read and interpret statistics and statistical diagrams across the curriculum, particularly in geography but also in science, physical education, history, economics and citizenship. In everyday life, students are surrounded by charts and graphs in magazines, newspapers and on television. Writing about the results of a statistical enquiry has links with report writing in English.

Objectives

- Extend mental methods of calculation, working with decimals **5**
- Use efficient written methods to add and subtract integers and decimals of any size **5**
- Break down substantial tasks to make them more manageable **6**
- Multiply decimals **5**
- Divide by decimals by transforming to division by an integer **5**
- Check results using appropriate methods **5**
- Calculate accurately, selecting mental methods or calculating devices as appropriate........................ **5**
- Solve problems mentally **6**
- Make and justify estimates and approximations of calculations.. **6**
- Record methods, solutions and conclusions............. **6**

Level

MPA

1.1	16a, b, c, d, e
1.2	16a, b, c, d, e
1.3	16a, b, c, d, e
1.4	16a, c, d, e
1.5	16a, b, c, d, e

PLTS

IE	16a, b, c, d, e
CT	16a, b, c, d, e
RL	16a, b, c, d, e
TW	16d, e
SM	16a, b, e
EP	16I, a, b, c, d, e

Introduction

The focus of this chapter is on using efficient strategies to solve problems involving calculations. Students will identify the information necessary to solve a problem, break the problem down into smaller steps, make approximations, consolidate mental, written and calculator methods for addition, subtraction, multiplication and division, record and check working and check answers using a variety of methods.

The student book discusses the importance for traders in financial markets of being able to calculate quickly and accurately. Accurate calculation depends on being able to apply mathematical techniques with speed and confidence. Most people find it difficult to calculate mentally with large numbers because the human brain can only remember a few digits at a time. For large numbers, it is easier to use a written method. A calculator can store many more digits than the human brain, but can only give the answer to a calculation. Extracting the information and solving the problem is still up to the human operator! There is an explanation of shares and how the stock market works at http://www.thisismoney.co.uk/help-and-advice/advice-banks/article.html?in_advicepage_id=124&in_article_id=394209&in_page_id=90 (EP).

Extra Resources

- 16   Start of chapter presentation
- 16a   Starter: BIDMAS multichoice
- 16c   Starter: Multiplying with negatives T or F
- 16c   Worked solution: Q1
- 16e   Starter: Rounded decimal matching

     Assessment: chapter 16

⇥Fast-track

No spreads

- Extend mental methods of calculation, working with decimals (L5)
- Solve problems mentally (L6)
- Make and justify estimates and approximations of calculations (L6)

Useful resources

Starter – Estimate

Ask students

to estimate the number of seconds in July
to calculate the number of seconds in July (2 678 400)

How close were their estimates? What was the average error?
Are older students more likely to be accurate than younger students.
Are girls more accurate then boys?

Teaching notes

Recall work previously covered in spread **8b**. Ask students what number bonds they use to help with addition, such as, $4 + 6 = 10$, $8 + 7 = 15$. When summing decimals, ask students to describe any mental methods they use, for example, $6.9 + 12.3 = (7 + 12.3) - 0.1$, $3.42 + 5.5 = (3 + 5) + (0.42 + 0.5)$. When subtracting decimals, ask students for their strategies, for example, $4.24 - 1.98 = (4.42 - 2) + 0.02$ Look at the distance chart in the student book. Choose two distances from the chart and challenge students to find the sum and difference using a mental method. When adding or subtracting with different units, what strategies do students use? For example, 1.23 m $+ 43$ cm $+ 0.54$ m. When summing a long line of figures, what strategies can be used? For example, 2, **5**, 7, 2, 9, 12, 3, 6, 4, 9, 7, 1, 4, 10, 3, 12, **5**, 4, 6 looking through the list in order, focusing on the units you can see: $(5 + 5) + (7 + 3) + (9 + 1) + (3 + 7) + (6 + 4) + (4 + 6) + (2 + 2 + 2 + 4) + 9 + 2 + 3 \times 10 = 111$. Alternatively, you could add the numbers in pairs making, $7 + 9 + 21 + 9 + 13 + 8 + 14 + 15 + 9 + 6$ then repeat $16 + 30 + 21 + 29 + 15$ and finally sum the units and tens separately (EP) (1.5).

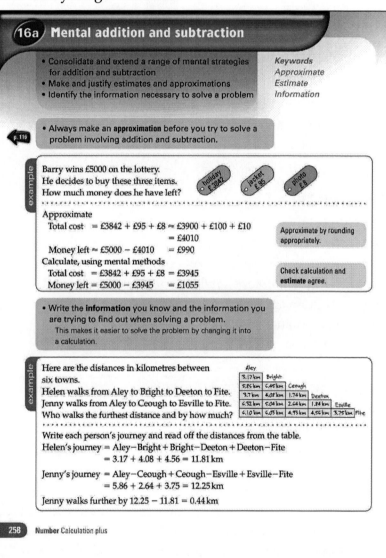

16a **Mental addition and subtraction**

- Consolidate and extend a range of mental strategies for addition and subtraction
- Make and justify estimates and approximations
- Identify the information necessary to solve a problem

Keywords
Approximate
Estimate
Information

- Always make an **approximation** before you try to solve a problem involving addition and subtraction.

Barry wins £5000 on the lottery.
He decides to buy these three items.
How much money does he have left?

holiday £3842   jacket £95   photo £8

Approximate
Total cost = £3842 + £95 + £8 ≈ £3900 + £100 + £10
= £4010
Money left ≈ £5000 − £4010 = £990

Approximate by rounding appropriately.

Calculate, using mental methods
Total cost = £3842 + £95 + £8 = £3945
Money left = £5000 − £3945 = £1055

Check calculation and estimate agree.

- Write the **information** you know and the information you are trying to find out when solving a problem.
  This makes it easier to solve the problem by changing it into a calculation.

Here are the distances in kilometres between six towns.
Helen walks from Aley to Bright to Deeton to Fite.
Jenny walks from Aley to Ceough to Esville to Fite.
Who walks the furthest distance and by how much?

Aley					
3.17 km	Bright				
5.85 km	6.45 km	Ceough			
3.7 km	4.08 km	1.74 km	Deeton		
6.32 km	5.04 km	2.64 km	1.84 km	Esville	
6.10 km	6.03 km	4.93 km	4.56 km	3.75 km	Fite

Write each person's journey and read off the distances from the table.
Helen's journey = Aley–Bright + Bright–Deeton + Deeton–Fite
= 3.17 + 4.08 + 4.56 = 11.81 km

Jenny's journey = Aley–Ceough + Ceough–Esville + Esville–Fite
= 5.86 + 2.64 + 3.75 = 12.25 km

Jenny walks further by 12.25 − 11.81 = 0.44 km

258   Number Calculation plus

Plenary

How can you represent the information for the distances between the six towns in the student book example as a diagram? Use this diagram to ask questions relating to shortest distances. This could include visiting all or some of the towns, possibly in a specified order. Consider excluding a few towns in order to shorten the problem (CT) (1.1)

Simplification

Assist students with the ordering of the information. Help them to arrange the most direct route in question **1**. Help them to identify the order in which the information needs to be taken in question **2**.

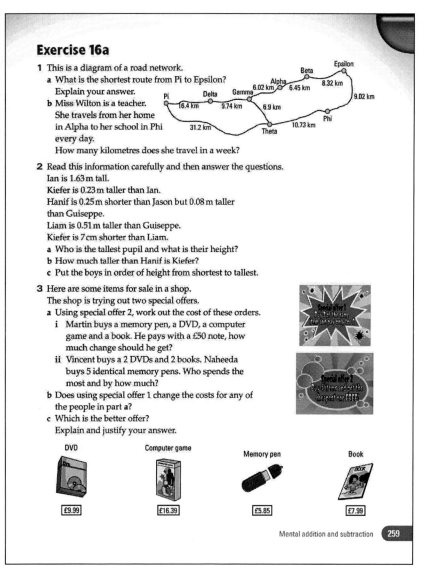

Exercise 16a

1 This is a diagram of a road network.
  a What is the shortest route from Pi to Epsilon? Explain your answer.
  b Miss Wilton is a teacher. She travels from her home in Alpha to her school in Phi every day. How many kilometres does she travel in a week?

2 Read this information carefully and then answer the questions.
  Ian is 1.63 m tall.
  Kiefer is 0.23 m taller than Ian.
  Hanif is 0.25 m shorter than Jason but 0.08 m taller than Guiseppe.
  Liam is 0.51 m taller than Guiseppe.
  Kiefer is 7 cm shorter than Liam.
  a Who is the tallest pupil and what is their height?
  b How much taller than Hanif is Kiefer?
  c Put the boys in order of height from shortest to tallest.

3 Here are some items for sale in a shop.
  The shop is trying out two special offers.
  a Using special offer 2, work out the cost of these orders.
   i Martin buys a memory pen, a DVD, a computer game and a book. He pays with a £50 note, how much change should he get?
   ii Vincent buys a 2 DVDs and 2 books. Naheeda buys 5 identical memory pens. Who spends the most and by how much?
  b Does using special offer 1 change the costs for any of the people in part **a**?
  c Which is the better offer? Explain and justify your answer.

DVD £9.99   Computer game £16.39   Memory pen £5.85   Book £7.99

Mental addition and subtraction **259**

Extension

Look at question **1** again. Begin at Alpha. You want to visit all the cities in the order Alpha, Beta, Gamma, Delta, Epsilon, Theta, Pi, Phi. What path should you take in order to minimise your distance? Note, you will have to pass through some cities again to get to your destination. A-B-A-G-D-G-A-B-E-PH-T-PI-T-PH. What is the total distance? (152.07 km) (CT, SM) (1.1, 1.3)

Exercise 16a commentary

All questions (IE) (1.1, 1.3)

Question 1 – Remind students that the diagram is not drawn to scale, so they will have to look carefully to find the shortest distance. Encourage students to show all their workings, rather than just a final answer (EP) (1.4).

Question 2 – Encourage the students to write down the information they know in an ordered way. Some may want to draw sketches of the people. Which piece of information is initially most valuable? Watch for students making errors due to confusion over units (RL) (1.2).

Question 3 – Some students may be confused by the fact that 'offer 1' does not apply to all purchases in part **b**. What items are unlikely to benefit from 'offer 1'? Ensure students layout their working to clearly show what values are being added (EP).

Assessment Criteria – Calculating, level 4: use a range of mental methods of computation with all operations. Calculating, level 5: approximate to check answers to problems are of the correct magnitude. Calculating, level 7: make and justify estimates and approximations of calculations.

Links

The world record for adding 100 single digit numbers randomly generated by a computer is 19.23 seconds and is held by Alberto Coto from Spain. Details of other mental calculation World records can be found at http://www.recordholders.org/en/list/memory.html#adding10digits

- Use efficient written methods to add and subtract integers and decimals of any size (L5)
- Break down substantial tasks to make them more manageable (L6)

Useful resources

••

Starter – How many sweets?

Seven students estimated the number of sweets in a jar.
Their estimates were: 135, 139, 141, 145, 149, 158 and 162.
The errors in their estimates (not necessarily in the same order) were: 2, 6, 7, 11, 15, 17 and 21.

Ask students how many sweets were in the jar. (156)

Can be extended by asking students to explain their strategies and making their own puzzles (1.5).

Teaching notes

Recall work previously covered in spread **8b**. What errors might students make when adding a column of decimals? Discuss problems of getting the decimal point in the correct place and forgetting about carry marks. Do you need to insert extra trailing zeros to make all the numbers have the same number of decimal places? Discuss.

What errors might students make when subtracting with decimals? Discuss the problems of blank spaces created by mismatched numbers of decimal places. Show that a calculation is incorrect by using the inverse operation of adding. For example,

$$
\begin{array}{r}
79.8 \\
-\ \ 6.54 \\
\hline
73.34
\end{array}
\qquad
\begin{array}{r}
73.34 \\
+\ \ 6.54 \\
\hline
79.88
\end{array}
$$

Therefore an error has occurred. How can the calculation be performed correctly? Try the calculation again with a trailing zero after the '8'.

What strategy can be employed to calculate questions like 12.43 – 2.12 – 4.32 – 3.075? Will this work in one long column? Is there a simple alternative? (EP, RL) (1.5).

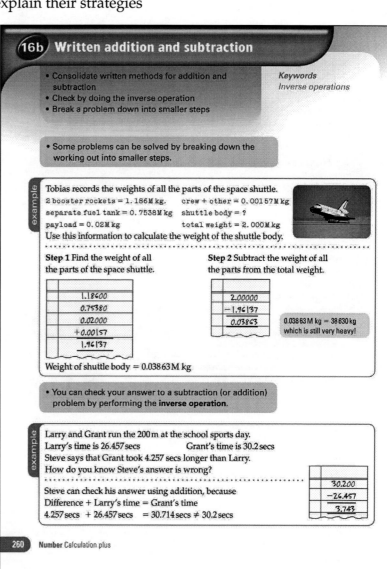

16b Written addition and subtraction

- Consolidate written methods for addition and subtraction
- Check by doing the inverse operation
- Break a problem down into smaller steps

Keywords
Inverse operations

- Some problems can be solved by breaking down the working out into smaller steps.

example

Tobias records the weights of all the parts of the space shuttle.
2 booster rockets = 1.186 M kg.   crew + other = 0.00157 M kg
separate fuel tank = 0.7538 M kg   shuttle body = ?
payload = 0.02 M kg   total weight = 2.000 M kg
Use this information to calculate the weight of the shuttle body.

Step 1 Find the weight of all the parts of the space shuttle.

$$
\begin{array}{r}
1.18600 \\
0.75380 \\
0.02000 \\
+0.00157 \\
\hline
1.96137
\end{array}
$$

Step 2 Subtract the weight of all the parts from the total weight.

$$
\begin{array}{r}
2.00000 \\
-1.96137 \\
\hline
0.03863
\end{array}
$$

0.03863 M kg = 38 630 kg which is still very heavy!

Weight of shuttle body = 0.03863 M kg

- You can check your answer to a subtraction (or addition) problem by performing the **inverse operation**.

example

Larry and Grant run the 200 m at the school sports day.
Larry's time is 26.457 secs   Grant's time is 30.2 secs
Steve says that Grant took 4.257 secs longer than Larry.
How do you know Steve's answer is wrong?

Steve can check his answer using addition, because
Difference + Larry's time = Grant's time
4.257 secs + 26.457 secs = 30.714 secs ≠ 30.2 secs

$$
\begin{array}{r}
30.200 \\
-26.457 \\
\hline
3.743
\end{array}
$$

Plenary

Discuss the strategies used in questions **3** and **4**. In question **4**, how does one diagram help add meaning to the next one? In question **3**, what can be calculated first from knowing the entire perimeter? (RL, EP) (1.1, 1.5)

Simplification

Provide students with pre-drawn columns for writing in decimal numbers. This may help students to keep their decimal points lined up and assist with subtraction and addition.

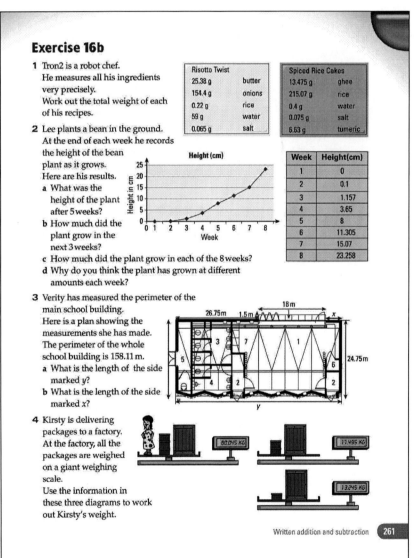

Exercise 16b

1 Tron2 is a robot chef.
He measures all his ingredients very precisely.
Work out the total weight of each of his recipes.

Risotto Twist	
25.38 g	butter
154.4 g	onions
0.22 g	rice
59 g	water
0.065 g	salt

Spiced Rice Cakes	
13.475 g	ghee
215.07 g	rice
0.4 g	water
0.075 g	salt
6.63 g	tumeric

2 Lee plants a bean in the ground.
At the end of each week he records the height of the bean plant as it grows. Here are his results.
a What was the height of the plant after 5 weeks?
b How much did the plant grow in the next 3 weeks?

Height (cm)

Week	Height(cm)
1	0
2	0.1
3	1.157
4	3.65
5	8
6	11.305
7	15.07
8	23.258

c How much did the plant grow in each of the 8 weeks?
d Why do you think the plant has grown at different amounts each week?

3 Verity has measured the perimeter of the main school building.
Here is a plan showing the measurements she has made.
The perimeter of the whole school building is 158.11 m.
a What is the length of the side marked y?
b What is the length of the side marked x?

26.75 m   1.5 m   18 m   x
24.75 m   y

4 Kirsty is delivering packages to a factory.
At the factory, all the packages are weighed on a giant weighing scale.
Use the information in these three diagrams to work out Kirsty's weight.

80.045 KG   11.495 KG   13.245 KG

Written addition and subtraction   261

Extension

An unusual plant keeps increasing in size. At the end of the first day after germinating it is 0.1 cm high, at the end of the next four days it is 0.2, 0.4, 0.7, 1.1 cm high. The pattern of growth forms a mathematical sequence. (compare. triangular numbers: $0.1[1+\frac{1}{2} n(n-1)]$)How long before the plant grows to over 100 cm? (46 days, 103.6 cm) (CT, SM) (1.3)

Exercise 16b commentary

All questions (IE) (1.1, 1.3)

Question 1 – Ensure students are very careful when lining up the digits in their correct place value. Urge students to show carry marks.

Question 2 – Students will have to take care to insert zeros after the decimal places when performing subtractions (RL).

Question 3 – A sketch of the rectangle representing the building maybe useful. What can you say about the sides of the building? Encourage students to fill in what they know from the diagram on their sketch.

Question 4 – Which two scales are the most similar? What can you tell about the difference between these two scales? Encourage students to say what they can work out rather than worry about how to solve the whole problem (1.2).

Assessment Criteria – Calculating, level 4: use efficient methods of addition and subtraction. Calculating, level 5: use known facts, place value, knowledge of operations and brackets to calculate including using all four operations with decimals to two places. UAM, level6: solve problems and carry through substantial tasks by breaking them into smaller more manageable tasks, using a range of efficient techniques, methods and resources.

Links

By 2008 over 120 US space shuttle flights have been made since the space shuttle Columbia made its first test flight into space in 1981. There is more information about the US space shuttle at http://www.nasa.gov/mission_pages/shuttle/main/index.html

- Extend mental methods of calculation, working with decimals (L5)
- Break down substantial tasks to make them more manageable (L6)
- Make and justify estimates and approximations of calculations (L6)

Useful resources

Starter – Sums and products

Ask students for

Three numbers where the sum is the same as the product. $(1 + 2 + 3 = 1 \times 2 \times 3)$
Four numbers where the sum is the same as the product. $(1 + 1 + 2 + 4 = 1 \times 1 \times 2 \times 4)$
Five numbers where the sum is the same as the product. $(1 + 1 + 2 + 2 + 2 = 1 \times 1 \times 2 \times 2 \times 2)$

Is there more than one solution? Hint: the same number may be used more than once.

Teaching notes

Recall work previously covered in spread **8d**. When solving problems involving multiplication, what mental and short cut strategies do students use? Suggest examples and examine various possibilities. For example,

$12 \times 34 = 10 \times 34 + 68$
$92 \times 66 = 100 \times 66 - 10 \times 66 + 2 \times 66$

Encourage students to consider estimates before they perform a calculation. What would the estimates be for the examples considered so far?

When a number of figures need to be multiplied together, is there a useful strategy than can be adopted? For example, $7 \times 5 \times 12 \times 2 \times 4 \times 7$. Pick the numbers that are easiest to work with $(5 \times 4) \times (12 \times 2) \times (7 \times 7) = 20 \times 24 \times 49 = 480 \times 49$. Now look at a strategy for multiplying by 49.

$480 \times 100 = 48000$

$480 \times 50 = 24000$

$480 \times 49 = 24000 - 480 = 23520$.

Look at examples of division that can be cancelled down significantly by writing the division as an equivalent fraction (EP) (1.4, 1.5).

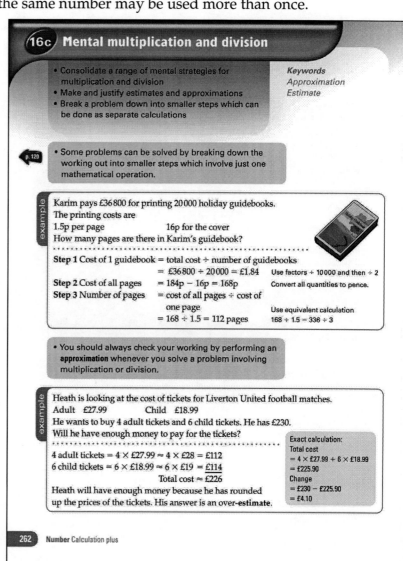

Plenary

Discuss mental methods for calculating multiples of common prices charged in shops. For example, $7 \times £8.99$ or $8 \times £4.98$ or $3 \times £899$. What are common prices for cars and houses? For example £11 995 or £195 000. How can you mentally calculate multiples of these amounts? (EP) (1.3, 1.5)

Simplification

Encourage students to make suggestions as to ways in which they might use short cut/mental methods. Discuss possible miscomprehensions, for example, $13 \times 24 = (10 \times 20) + (3 \times 4)$ (RL). If necessary allow students to work with suitable approximations to make calculations more manageable.

All questions (IE) (1.1, 1.3)

Question 1 – Encourage the use of a mental/short cut method where possible. For example, for 83×15 use $83 \times 10 = 830$ so 83×5 is half that answer 415, add results together. Encourage students to write down their methods.

Exercise 16c

1 Joachim is trying to improve his fitness levels. Here is how fast his heart beats per minute for three activities.
cycling 83   running 91   swimming 75
Each day Joachim cycles for 15 mins, runs for 13 mins and swims for 17 mins.
In which activity does Joachim's heart beat the greatest number of times in total?
Explain and justify your answer.

2 Derek pays £9750 for printing 15 000 holiday guidebooks.
The printing costs are
2.5p per page   25p for the cover
How many pages are there in Derek's guidebook?

3 'Nut-e-nuts' is an online retailer.
Work out, using an approximation, if each of these people has enough money for the cost of their orders.
Explain and justify your answers.
  a Marge orders 3 kg of almonds, 2 kg of peanuts and 4 kg of walnuts. She has £75.
  b Jameela orders 8 kg of walnuts and 15 kg of pecans. She has £300.
  c Bert orders 17 kg of almonds, 15 kg of peanuts and 12 kg of pecans. He has £350.

Almonds £7.95
Peanuts £4.85
Pecans £14.38
Walnuts £9.99
(Prices per kilogram)

4 Every person is recommended to consume 5 portions of fruit and vegetables every day. A 150 ml glass of fruit juice counts as one daily portion. A carton of fruit juice normally contains 1000 ml (= 1 litre). This week the fruit juice is in special Xtra packs with 15% extra free.
  a How many recommended daily portions of fruit juice are there in one Xtra carton?
  b A family of 4 decide to each drink 150 ml of fruit juice every day.
    i How much fruit juice will they drink in 1 week?
    ii How many Xtra cartons of fruit juice will they need to buy?
  c A carton of Xtra fruit juice costs £1.80. What is the approximate cost in a year for the family of 4 to each drink 150 ml of fruit juice a day?

Mental multiplication and division   263

Extension

Set students divisions that can be solved more simply by using product of prime factors. Students may find it useful to set out the division as a fraction first. For example, $315 \div 126$
$$\frac{315}{126} = \frac{3 \times 3 \times 7 \times 5}{2 \times 3 \times 3 \times 7} = \frac{5}{2} = 2.5 \text{ (CT) (1.5)}.$$

Exercise 16c commentary

Question 2 – Encourage students to view divisions with large numbers as a simplifiable fraction.
$$\frac{9750}{15000} = \frac{975}{1500} = \frac{195}{300} = \frac{39}{60} = \frac{13}{20} = \frac{65}{100} =$$
0.65 or 65 p (1.2).

Question 3 – Encourage use of a range of strategies: repeated addition for small multiples or multiplication by 15 as described in question **1**. Students should write down any approximation used.

Question 4 – When multiplying more than two numbers together, ask students to consider which order is the easiest to multiply in. Emphasise that repeated addition can be used to give an answer to a division. For example, $4200 \div 1150$, $1150 + 1150 + 1150 = 3450$, will not be able to get another 1150 into 4200, so answer is 3 and a bit extra.

Assessment Criteria – Calculating, level 4: use a range of mental methods of computation with all operations. Calculating, level 5: approximate to check answers to problems are of the correct magnitude. UAM, level6: solve problems and carry through substantial tasks by breaking them into smaller more manageable tasks, using a range of efficient techniques, methods and resources. Calculating, level 7: make and justify estimates and approximations of calculations.

Links

The cost of football tickets for all Premiership clubs can be found at http://www.footballticketprices.co.uk/index.php/premier-league
Find the cost of three adult tickets at the most/least expensive clubs and compare with the cost in the example. Is £115 enough to buy three adult tickets?

- Multiply decimals   (L5)   ***Useful resources***
- Divide by decimals by transforming to division by
  an integer   (L5)
- Check results using appropriate methods   (L6)

Starter – Last minute?

Write the following list of times on the board:

3 days, 192 hours, 1 fortnight, 47 hours, 24 600 seconds, 8 days,
1 leap year, 17 hours, 12 300 minutes, 1020 minutes, 169 200 seconds,
8784 hours, 336 hours, 4320 minutes, 410 minutes, 205 hours.

Challenge students to match up eight pairs in the shortest possible time.

Teaching notes

Recall work previously covered in spread 8d. What written methods are students most confident using? For example, diagonal grid method over long multiplication or using short division with part of the times table copied out (see the notes for spread 8e).

How can decimal multiplication be dealt with? Should the decimal point be removed? If so, how can you tell where it is to be placed at the end of the calculation? Discuss the use of estimates to help place the decimal point. Is this the only way to tell?

How can you divide by a decimal? Can the decimal point be removed and inserted later? Will an estimate help to place the decimal point correctly? Is there a good alternative? Discuss eliminating the decimal from the denominator by a suitable multiplication to give an equivalent fraction (RL, EP) (1.4, 1.5).

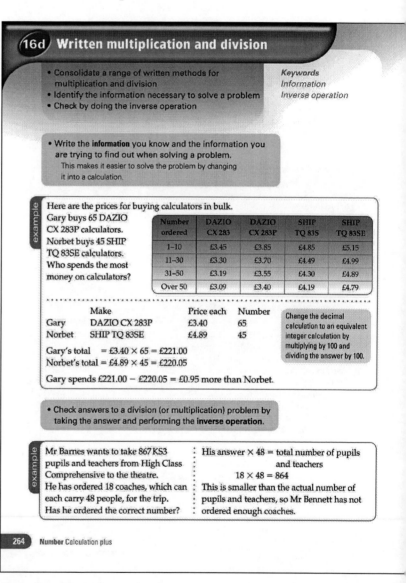

Plenary

Discuss the methods that students used for multiplying with decimals. Did any students attempt to multiply with the decimals still in place? Did this lead to any incorrect answers? Ask the same question with respect to division with decimals (RL, EP) (1.4, 1.5).

Simplification

To help students with multiplications or divisions involving decimals, use a simple approximation to judge the order of magnitude. Discourage multiplication and division methods that include calculations with decimals in. Encourage students to remove decimals before calculating.

All questions (IE, EP) (1.1, 1.3)

Question 1 – Encourage students to work without decimals. How many times larger/smaller will the 'integer' answer be than the real answer? Challenge students to explain their written method of multiplication: in long multiplication why add zeros at the start of some lines? (1.5)

Exercise 16d

1 Here are the offers from three phone companies for text messages.

Number ordered	CO2	Yello	Four	Skyte
1–9	4.25p	4.5p	4.25p	4.8p
10–49	4.2p	4.3p	4.15p	4.35p
50–99	4.15p	4.1p	4.05p	3.9p
Over 100	4.1p	3.9p	3.95p	3.45p

  a Karl buys 35 text messages from CO2. How much money would he save if he switched to Four to buy his text messages?
  b Zak buys 160 text messages a week from Yello.
    i How much money would he save each week if he switched to Skyte?
    ii How much money would he save in a year if he switched?
  c Which phone company would you recommend to these people?
    i Pete spends about £1.50 a week on text messages
    ii Josh spends about £3 a week on text messages
    iii Kath spends about £5 a week on text messages
    In each case, explain and justify your choice.

2 Maude is working out the costs of her motoring each week.
Petrol costs £1.18 a litre.
Maude's car travels 9.8 km for each litre of petrol.
Each week Maude travels 343 km in her car.
  a How much money does Maude spend on petrol each week?
  b How much money would you expect Maude to spend on petrol in a year? Explain your answer.

3 a Roger drives on the motorway at an average speed of 64 mph for 1.2 hours. Sarah completes the same journey in 1.6 hours. At what speed does Sarah drive?
  b Isobel travels at 60 mph for 6 hours. Investigate other speeds and the time it would take to complete the same journey.

4 a Miss McCloud wants to take 650 KS3 pupils and teachers to a football match. She orders 11 coaches, which can each carry 58 people. Has she ordered the correct number? Explain your answer.
  b Mr Kinsella wants to organise the 250 pupils in Year 8 into nine maths groups. There are supposed to be no more than 28 pupils in any class. Can Mr Kinsella fit the pupils into the 9 groups? Explain your thinking.

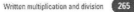

Extension

Look at question **3a** again. What is the percentage increase in the journey time? What happens to the speed? (-25%) Can students see any connection between these two percentages? Try other examples. The time increased by $\frac{1}{3}$, that is, $\times \frac{4}{3}$. The speed decreased to $\frac{3}{4}$ of the original, the fraction is inverted This is difficult; encourage a range of responses (CT) (1.2, 1.4).

Exercise 16d commentary

Question 2 – This is quite challenging. Students may be able to divide by 98, but are more likely to be successful at simplifying $\frac{3430}{98}$ by using prime factor decomposition for simplification. The factor of 7 being hard to spot in the numerator.

Question 3 – Some students may need help with linking speed, distance and time. The S/D/T triangle might be useful here.

Question 4 – Ask students to consider tackling these questions both by division and multiplication. Can students write down the required working for both methods and then choose the easiest approach? (1.4, 1.5)

Assessment Criteria – Calculating, level 5: understand and use an appropriate non-calculator method for solving problems that involve multiplying and dividing any three digit number by any two digit number. Calculating, level 5: apply inverse operations and approximate to check answers to problems are of the correct magnitude. Calculating, level 7: make and justify estimates and approximations of calculations.

Links

The division symbol ÷ is called an obelus. The symbol was originally used in manuscripts to mark passages containing errors, but first appeared as a division symbol in a book called *Teutsche Algebra* by Johann Rahn in 1659. In Denmark, the obelus was used to represent subtraction. There is more information about mathematical symbols at http://members.aol.com/jeff570/operation.html (TW).

- Calculate accurately, selecting mental methods or calculating devices as appropriate (L5)
- Record methods, solutions and conclusions (L6)
- Check results using an appropriate method (L6)

Useful resources
Calculator

Starter – Same digit

Ask students to find pairs of numbers that will give the same digit when one of the numbers is divided by the other, for example.

$385 \div 50 = 7.7$
$33 \div 6 = 5.5$
$3000 \div 9 = 333.33333\ldots$

Can they find pairs of numbers that multiply to give the same digit? (for example $7.4 \times 6 = 44.4$) Can be extended by asking students to explain any methods they have used.

Teaching notes

Use a calculator for this problem. A window cleaner has to clean an office block. He cleans at a speed of $1m^2$ per minute. The office block has 20 floors with windows on each side. On each floor on one side of the building there are four identical windows. They each measure 3.4 m by 140 cm. The building is 58 m high. The cleaners works from 9 am to 5 pm with an hour break for lunch and two half hour breaks one in the morning and one in afternoon. How long will it take the cleaner to clean all the windows?

What information do you need to use in order to find the answer? Will a sketch of the building help to make sense of the problem? Discuss students' methods of dissecting the problem. Is any given information irrelevant? (EP) (1.5)

Solutions, 320 windows, 1523.2 m² total area, 25 hours 23 min 12 sec time (encourage students to use a sensible rounded value for time). 6 hours work a day. Finish about 10:30 am on the fifth day.

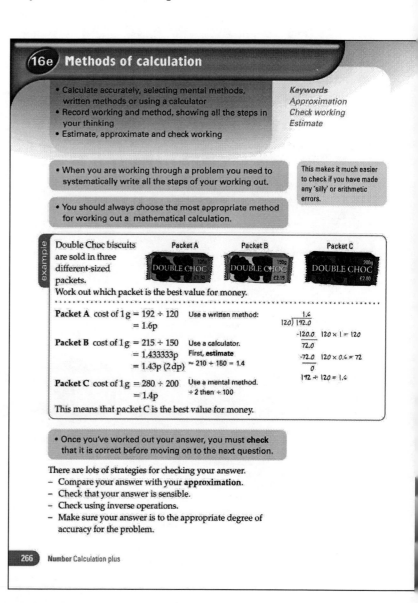

Plenary

What conclusions did students come to for question **3**? Examine the different costs and attitudes to convenience and reliability. Do students think that the estimates of the car costs are realistic? (Do not include the costs of parking, repairs or new tyres, *etc.*) Suppose Jordan already has a car, how could this change your report? Many of the costs will have to be met anyway for her to run a car even if she does not take it to work. If Jordan plans to sell her car, how might this change the report? (Probably unchanged) (CT)

Simplification

Ask students to explain what they think their calculation will represent. Ensure that students write down their calculations. Can students explain why they are choosing a particular operation? For example, division instead of multiplication.

All questions (IE, EP) (1.1, 1.3)

Question 1 – Is it easy to convert each sack to a common number of kg? If no obvious number of kg can be used, how can you convert all the sacks to 1 kg?

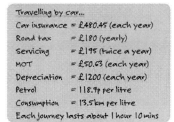

Exercise 16e

1 Wheat is sold in three different-sized sacks.
Work out which size of sack is the best value for money.
Explain your answer.

Sack A   Sack B   Sack C

2 Solve each problem using the most appropriate method.
Explain your choice of method.
a Marek saves £48 a week for 24 weeks. He takes his money on holiday.
How much money would he have to spend each day if his holiday lasted
i 16 days   ii 7 days   iii 30 days?
Investigate his daily spending money for other lengths of holiday.
b Otis goes on a sponsored charity walk from Blackburn to Cardiff dressed as a giant bear. He takes 12 days to complete the walk. Each day he walks the same distance. He returns by car along the same route in 3.2 hours at an average speed of 60 mph. He raises £38.95 for charity for each mile he walks.
i How far did Otis travel each day on his charity walk?
ii How much money did Otis raise for charity by completing his walk?

1 mile = 1.6 km

3 Jordan travels 42 miles to work each day. She is trying to decide whether it is better to travel to work by car or by train. Here are some ideas she has written down.

Travelling by car...
Car insurance = £480.45 (each year)
Road tax = £180 (yearly)
Servicing = £195 (twice a year)
MOT = £50.63 (each year)
Depreciation = £1200 (each year)
Petrol = 118.9p per litre
Consumption = 13.5 km per litre
Each journey lasts about 1 hour 10 mins

Travelling by train...
Monthly season ticket = £730
Daily return ticket = £42.50
Home to station = 18 mins walk
Journey on train = 31 mins
Station to work = 19 mins walk

Jordan works for 44 weeks a year.
She has a 4-week holiday in August.
Write a short report recommending which form of transport Jordan should take. Explain and justify your answer.

Methods of calculation   267

Extension

Carry out a short survey into the costs of students in the class getting to school. Assumptions will have to be made for some forms of transport. For example, cycling, costs for helmet, tyres, lock, *etc.* Also assumptions about the average cost of fuel will have to be made for an 'average' car. The data in question 3 could be used for all cars (SM, IE) (1.1).

Exercise 16e commentary

Question 2 – For part **a**, encourage students to first try a mental division. If the answer is clearly not an integer, then what approach would be useful? In part **b** students may need reminding that d = v × t. In part **ii**, beware of students using their answer from part **i**. Encourage students to make clear what each calculation represents (RL).

Question 3 – To convert km/litre to miles/litre, suggest dividing by 1.6. In the reports, encourage students to explain their answers without showing all the working, but by summarizing their findings. Suggest commenting on cost, time, convenience and reliability (SM) (1.2, 1.4)

Assessment Criteria – Calculating, level 5: apply inverse operations and approximate to check answers to problems are of the correct magnitude. UAM, level 6: present a concise, reasoned argument, using symbols, diagrams, graphs and related explanatory text. Calculating, level 7: make and justify estimates and approximations of calculations.

Links

Before electronic calculators became widely available in around 1974, slide rules were widely used to perform multiplication and division calculations. A slide rule is a mechanical device shaped like a large ruler with two or more scales that can slide against each other. Using a slide rule converted a multiplication or division into an addition or subtraction. There is more information about slide rules at http://en.wikipedia.org/wiki/Slide_rule and at http://www.sliderulemuseum.com/ (TW)

16 Summary

Assessment criteria

- Use a range of mental methods of calculation with all operations — Level 4
- Use efficient methods of addition and subtraction — Level 4
- Apply inverse operations and approximate to check answers to problems are of the correct magnitude — Level 5
- Use known facts, place value, knowledge of operations and brackets to calculate including all four operations with decimals to two places — Level 5
- Understand and use an appropriate non-calculator method for solving problems that involve multiplying and dividing any three digit number by any two digit number — Level 5
- Solve problems and carry through substantial tasks by breaking them into smaller, more manageable tasks, using a range of efficient techniques, methods and resources — Level 6
- Present a concise reasoned argument using symbols, diagrams, graphs and related explanatory text. — Level 6
- Make and justify estimates and approximations of calculations — Level 7

Question commentary

Example

The example illustrates a problem involving proportional reasoning. Emphasise the importance of recording all working and giving a clear answer with correct units. A unitary method can be used as an alternative to that shown. In part c, emphasise that the ratio has to be calculated using the amount of salt in equal weights of cereal.

a $\dfrac{0.5}{30} \times 6 = 0.01666.. \times 6$
$= 0.1$

b $\dfrac{0.24}{36} = 0.00666$
whole wheat

c $5 : 2$

Past question

The question is a more demanding question about percentages and proportional reasoning. Ask questions such as "What do you see as the main steps in solving this problem?" and "What information do you have?" Some students may get as far as working out the number of drivers who used three 50p coins and then calculate the incorrect percentage. Emphasise the need to show all steps clearly as partial marks are often awarded for correct method.

Answer

Level 7
2 15%

Development and links

Students will continue to practise their calculation and problem-solving skills in Year 9.

Students need to perform calculations in many areas of the curriculum, particularly in science, technology and geography. The skills and techniques practised in this chapter can be applied to a variety of problems and puzzles in daily life.

17 Functional Maths

Objective

- Break down substantial tasks to make them more manageable **6**
- Calculate accurately, selecting mental methods or calculating devices as appropriate **6**
- Recognise the impact of constraints or assumptions **6**
- Use connections with related contexts to improve the analysis of a situation or problem **6**
- Represent problems and synthesise information in algebraic, geometric or graphical form **6**
- Estimate, approximate and check working **6**
- Make accurate mathematical diagrams, graphs and constructions on paper and on screen **6**
- Look for and reflect on other approaches and build on previous experience of similar situations and outcomes **7**
- Pose questions and make convincing arguments to justify generalizations or solutions **7**

Introduction

The chapter consists of a sequence of five spreads based on the theme of a year 8 school camping trip to France. This allows questions to cover a wide range of topics taken from algebra, statistics, geometry and number. The questions are word-based and often do not directly indicate what type of mathematics is involved. Therefore students will need to work to identify the relevant mathematics and in several instances which of a variety of methods to apply before commencing. This approach is rather different from the previous topic based spreads and students may require additional support in this aspect of functional maths.

🗲ast-track
All spreads

Level

MPA

1.1	17a, b, c, d, e
1.2	17a, b, c, d, e
1.3	17a, b, c, d, e
1.4	17a, b, c, d, e
1.5	17a, b, c, d, e

PLTS

IE	17a, b, c, d, e
CT	17a, b, c, d, e
RL	17a, b, c, d, e
TW	17a, c, d, e
SM	17a, b, c, d, e
EP	17a, b, c, d, e

Extra Resources

17 Start of chapter presentation

Assessment: chapter 17

- Breakdown substantial tasks to make them more manageable (L6)
- Calculate accurately, selecting mental methods or calculating devices as appropriate (L6)

Useful resources
Calculators
Travel brochures

Background

This spreads focuses on the logistics and finances of the trip and largely exercises number skills. Issues surrounding costs, deposits and exchange rates may be familiar to some students from family holidays and this knowledge can be used to both enliven discussion and provide a source of illustrative examples (EP).

An aspect of camp life is giving awards for various types of achievement, see spread **17e**. This could be mirrored throughout this chapter with, for example, bronze, silver and gold awards being given to students in recognition of their 'effort', 'achievement' and 'support to others' (TW, SM).

Teaching notes

Invite pairs of students to imagine that they are a teacher planning a school trip and ask them to suggest what they need to consider. Focus on the costs involved: how should they calculate deposits, deal with exchange rates, *etc.* The student book can be used as a prompt. The subsequent discussion should concentrate on generic approaches, what is required and a suitable method, rather than specific details (TW).

Supply students with some example calculations and ask them to explain how they would complete them. Total cost £3782, 20 students: cost per student, 15% deposit, £435 to be paid in Euros at £1= €1.28. Ask how they decide whether to use mental, written or calculator methods: can they give two pros and two cons for each method? (EP) (1.5)

Also ask how they would go about checking their answers (against an approximation, using an inverse operation, is it reasonable, is it to an appropriate degree of accuracy?) (RL).

Ask students if they can supply some handy hints for doing calculations, especial using mental methods. These can be collected on the board as a reminder for students as they work through the spread (1.5).

.

Maths life — 17a Planning the trip to France

Miss Perry is planning a trip for 50 year 8 students. They will travel from Birmingham to Sarlat in France.

She has to decide whether to travel by coach or train.

Coach	£3560
Ferry berths	£975
Accommodation	£1475
Food	£1450
Insurance	£516
Activities	£1700

Train	£6000
Accommodation	£1550
Food	£1450
Insurance	£500
Activities	£1700

The students would spend 4 days travelling and have 5 days of activities.

The students would spend 3 days travelling and have 6 days of activities.

1 a For each possibility work out
  i the total cost of the trips
  ii the costs per student.
    Round the costs to the nearest whole pound (£).

  b Which is the most expensive way to travel and by how much?

2 Miss Perry wants to show parents the difference in cost as a percentage of the total cost of the coach trip.
Do the calculation for her giving your answer to the nearest whole percent.

3 By working out the daily cost for each student say which transport method gives the best value for money.
Include only the number of days spent doing activities, and justify your choice.

270 **Functional maths** Problem solving

Simplification

Provide students with a reminder of some of the mathematics they will need during the problem solving exercise. For example

$$\text{percentage difference} = \frac{\text{difference}}{\text{original}} \times \text{percentage}$$

$$\text{speed} = \frac{\text{distance}}{\text{time}}$$

All questions (IE) (1.1, 1.3, 1.4)

Question 1 – (spreads 8a, b, e, 16a-d) Encourage student to make a rough estimate before they do an exact calculation. Do their totals look about right? Encourage students to check their calculations at least twice (RL).

Extension

Flying turns out to be 80% more expensive than taking the coach. Would it be good value for money though? What measure can you use to decide? Look at question **3** again. Based on only two days travelling it's approximately £50 per day per student. Can you suggest possible answers for the other questions if you fly, or at least if the answers will be lower, higher or the same (1.2).

Exercise 17a commentary

Question 2 – (spreads 4f, 8a,) Does it matter if you use the cost of the whole trip or the student's individual cost to find the percentage difference? What will the figure tell you? Encourage students to write down the calculation they are using. If the train is 15% more expensive than the coach, then is the coach i15% cheaper than the train?

Question 3 – (spreads 12c, f) Can proportion or ratio be used here to work out value for money? Why is it awkward to compare the total cost per student? Suggest using the unitary method.

Question 4 – What part of the timetable do you need to begin by looking at? Is there more than one option? Why are some trains have very long journey times? Can you foresee any problems in the timings, for example, long delays? (Three and a half hours in London in the middle of the night!) (CT)

Question 5 – (spread 8h) When totalling the time, encourage students to show how they are summing the hours and minutes. What time is it in the UK when you arrive at Sarlat? Do you include the waiting time in your answer?

Question 6 – (spreads 2b) When converting units, ensure that the result feels right. Note that km are a bit shorter than miles.

Question 7 – (spread 13h) Will you include the waiting time in your speed calculation?

Assessment criteria – UAM, level6: solve problems and carry through substantial tasks by breaking them into smaller more manageable tasks, using a range of efficient techniques, methods and resources, including ICT.

The group decide to travel by train. Their journey starts in Birmingham.

These tables show the train times from Birmingham to London, and London to Sarlat (in France)

Depart St Pancras	Arrive Sarlat
04.30	16.50
08.26	18.55
11.05	20.55

Birmingham	23.00	23.00	00.10	05.40	06.40
London	06.50	01.02	07.00	07.00	08.09

When deciding on their schedule they have to take into account these factors.

- When the group arrive in Sarlat they will have to drive for 20 minutes to reach the campsite.
- They have to set-up their tents and this will take about one hour.
- The sun sets at about 8 p.m.
- To be safe, the party will need at least 1 hour to transfer between stations in London.

4 Which trains will the party need to take?

5 What will be their total journey time to the nearest hour? Remember that French time is one hour ahead of UK time.

From London to Birmingham is about 120 miles.
From London to Sarlat is about 1300 km.

6 What is the total distance between Birmingham and Sarlat stations?
Write your answer in miles or kilometres to the nearest whole unit.

To convert between kilometres (k) and miles (m) use

$$m = \frac{5 \times k}{8}$$

or

$$k = 1.6 \times m$$

7 Using your answers to questions **5** and **6** to calculate the average speed for the whole journey in kilometres per hour or in miles per hour.

Planning the trip to France

- Recognise the impact of constraints or assumptions (L6)
- Use connections with related contexts to improve the analysis of a situation or problem (L6)

Useful resources
Local area map
Small name cards

Background

This spread takes up the theme of the school trip and arriving at the camp where they have to organise the accommodation and familiarise themselves with the campsite. The mathematics involves areas of rectangles and compound shapes, arithmetic with decimals, the use of six-figure coordinates (with direct cross-curricular links to geography) and logical reasoning (EP).

Teaching notes

The first question involves the multiplication and division of decimals. It will be useful revision to ask students to explain how to do this and how to check their answer. Test their understanding by asking them to calculate the area of a rectangular tent. Ask how they think this is related to how many people the tent will comfortably sleep Is the ground area the only thing that needs to be considered? What about the tent's shape? (CT) (1.3)

Question **2** is likely to be new to the students in the context of mathematics. It may help to provide a similar example and ask students to provide a 'method' for solving the puzzle and for verifying any solution (IE, RL) (1.4).

Questions **3** to **6** involve interpreting a map and finding locations. Using a local area map, ask students to specify the positions of local landmarks. Can they do this is such a way that they don't refer to other locations on the map? This may be familiar from geography and the method used in the questions is easily tied in with the use of coordinates in mathematics. The map is also a scale drawing and students could be asked to think about how they could calculate real-life distances based on either the local area or campsite maps. One way to approach this is by asking students to say how they would go about creating an accurate map of the school (SM). (1.2, 1.5). This could be a teamwork activity (TW).

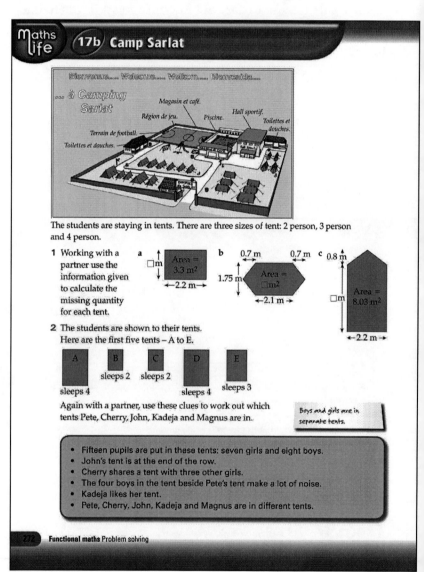

17b Camp Sarlat

The students are staying in tents. There are three sizes of tent: 2 person, 3 person and 4 person.

1 Working with a partner use the information given to calculate the missing quantity for each tent.

a Area = 3.3 m² □m ←2.2 m→

b 0.7 m 0.7 m Area = □m² 1.75 m ←2.1 m→

c 0.8 m Area = 8.03 m² □m ←2.2 m→

2 The students are shown to their tents. Here are the first five tents – A to E.

A sleeps 4   B sleeps 2   C sleeps 2   D sleeps 4   E sleeps 3

Again with a partner, use these clues to work out which tents Pete, Cherry, John, Kadeja and Magnus are in.

Boys and girls are in separate tents.

- Fifteen pupils are put in these tents: seven girls and eight boys.
- John's tent is at the end of the row.
- Cherry shares a tent with three other girls.
- The four boys in the tent beside Pete's tent make a lot of noise.
- Kadeja likes her tent.
- Pete, Cherry, John, Kadeja and Magnus are in different tents.

272   Functional maths Problem solving

Simplification

For question **1**, provide integer dimensions and possibly draw in the squares to allow the link between multiplication and counting squares to be reinforced. For question **2**, consider providing students with five counters, these could be labelled with the students names to allow them to be arranged to solve the problem.

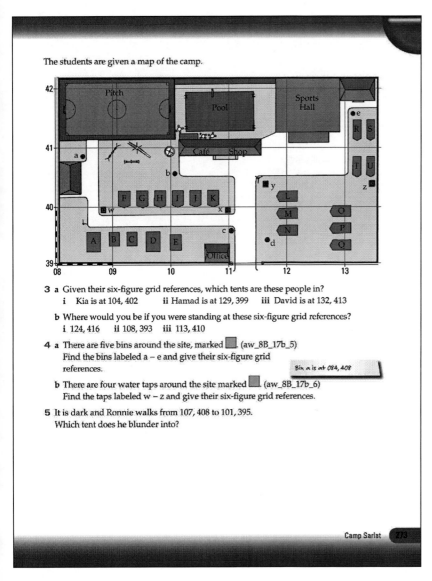

The students are given a map of the camp.

3 a Given their six-figure grid references, which tents are these people in?
   i Kia is at 104, 402   **ii** Hamad is at 129, 399   **iii** David is at 132, 413

   b Where would you be if you were standing at these six-figure grid references?
   i 124, 416   **ii** 108, 393   **iii** 113, 410

4 a There are five bins around the site, marked ▪. (aw_8B_17b_5)
   Find the bins labeled a – e and give their six-figure grid references.

   Bin a is at 084, 408

   b There are four water taps around the site marked ▫. (aw_8B_17b_6)
   Find the taps labeled w – z and give their six-figure grid references.

5 It is dark and Ronnie walks from 107, 408 to 101, 395.
   Which tent does he blunder into?

Camp Sarlat 273

Extension

Ask students to write their own logic puzzle, similar to that in question **2**. How should you begin designing the problem? How can you make sure you give enough information to solve the problem? Try the problem on a partner. (CT)

Exercise 17b commentary

All questions (CT) (1.1)

Question 1 – (spreads 2c, d) What shapes can you split the tent up into? How do you find the area of a triangle? Is there a way to find a missing length when you know the area without using trial and improvement? Consider looking at an arrow diagram to show how area is calculated for a rectangle (1.3).

Question 2 – Encourage students to look at all the information to begin with. Which piece is immediately useful? Can students rule out certain answers using the available information? Drawing a sketch my well help solve the problem (IE).

Questions 3 – (spread 7d) Six-figure grid references are more commonly used in geography rather than maths. What tends to be used in maths to describe position? Coordinates and bearings (1.3).

Questions 4 – (spread 7d) Encourage students to be as accurate as possible, using a ruler to mentally subdivide the specific grid into ten equal parts. Is it necessary to draw in the subdivided grid lines? (1.3)

Questions 5 – (spread 7d) What assumption will you have to make about Ronnie's walk? That he walks in a straight line (1.2, 1.3).

Assessment criteria – UAM, level6: use logical argument to establish the truth of a statement. UAM, level 6: interpret discuss and synthesise information presented in a variety of mathematical forms. UAM, level 7: justify generalizations, arguments or solutions.

- Represent problems and synthesise information in algebraic, geometric or graphical form (L6)
- Look for and reflect on other approaches and build on previous experience of similar situations and outcomes (L7)

Useful resources
Large copies of question 2 table

Background

The sports day theme can be made even more real for the students if data from sports competitions in which they are involved can be used as illustrations or to replace numeric values in the questions (EP).

A large range of mathematics is encountered in this spread broadly on the theme of statistics, including: interpreting and drawing pie charts, reading data and finding summary statistics, solving 'algebraic' problems, calculating perimeters of shapes involving circles.

Teaching notes

Given the breadth of knowledge being tested here it will be most useful to focus attention on those areas which are likely to cause the students most difficulty, rather than try to address all potential issues.

A majority of the class is likely to be familiar with scoring in football. Using results from the school or an international competition will allow several of the issues associated with question 2 to be discussed. In particular, cover how to interpret the results in the summary table.

Put students into groups and pose a question similar to 5. Ask students for their ideas on how to go about solving it; did they get it right? How do they know? Several approaches are possible and it will be instructive to get students to compare their relative merits (TW, EP) (1.4, 1.5).

In question 7, students are asked to calculate the 'stagger' on a running track, is this something a mathematician become involved in? How accurate do the distances need to be measured if times are measured to one hundredth of a second? (Assume sprinters run at 10 m/s) Distances need to be measured to at least 10 cm accuracy!

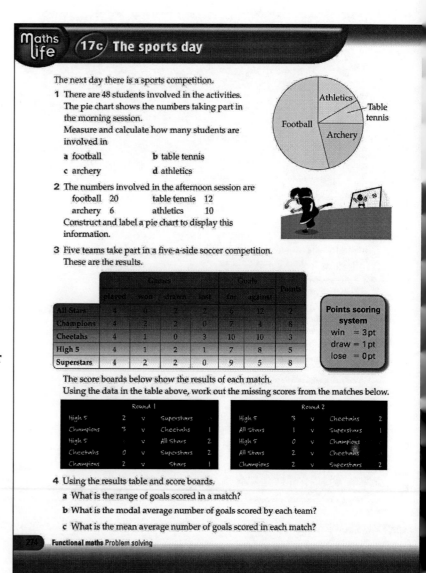

Maths life — **17c The sports day**

The next day there is a sports competition.

1 There are 48 students involved in the activities. The pie chart shows the numbers taking part in the morning session.
Measure and calculate how many students are involved in

   a football   **b** table tennis

   c archery   **d** athletics

2 The numbers involved in the afternoon session are
football 20   table tennis 12
archery 6   athletics 10
Construct and label a pie chart to display this information.

3 Five teams take part in a five-a-side soccer competition. These are the results.

	Games				Goals		Points
	played	won	drawn	lost	for	against	
All Stars	4	0	2	2	6	12	2
Champions	4	2	2	0	7	4	8
Cheetahs	4	1	0	3	10	10	3
High 5	4	1	2	1	7	8	5
Superstars	4	2	2	0	9	5	8

Points scoring system
win = 3 pt
draw = 1 pt
lose = 0 pt

The score boards below show the results of each match.
Using the data in the table above, work out the missing scores from the matches below.

Round 1

High 5	2	v	Superstars
Champions	3	v	Cheetahs 1
High 5		v	All Stars 2
Cheetahs	0	v	Superstars 2
Champions	2	v	Stars 1

Round 2

High 5	3	v	Cheetahs 2
All Stars	1	v	Superstars 1
High 5	0	v	Champions
All Stars	2	v	Cheetahs
Champions	2	v	Superstars 2

4 Using the results table and score boards.

   a What is the range of goals scored in a match?

   b What is the modal average number of goals scored by each team?

   c What is the mean average number of goals scored in each match?

274   **Functional maths** Problem solving

Simplification

Provide students with a reminder of some of the mathematics they will need during the spread. For example,

$$\text{angle in pie chart} = \frac{\text{number in single group}}{\text{number in all groups}} \times 360°$$

circumference of circle = π × diameter

definitions of range, mode, median and mean.

All questions (IE, CT, SM) (1.1, 1.3)

Question 1 – (spread 15c) What fraction of the circle is taken up by each of the sports? Encourage students to measure the angle as carefully as possible. What methods do students have for finding a fraction of 48? How would you cope with a fraction answer?

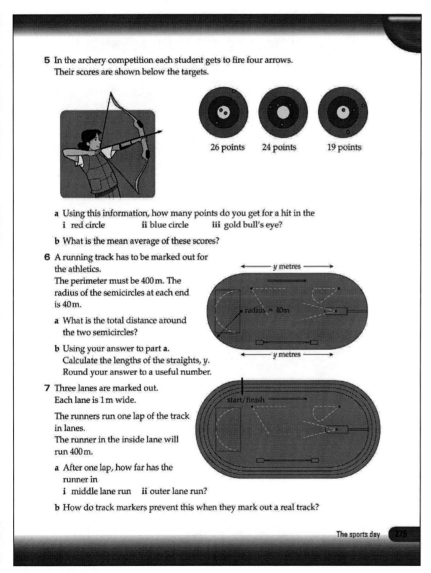

5 In the archery competition each student gets to fire four arrows. Their scores are shown below the targets.

26 points   24 points   19 points

a Using this information, how many points do you get for a hit in the
   i red circle   ii blue circle   iii gold bull's eye?

b What is the mean average of these scores?

6 A running track has to be marked out for the athletics.
The perimeter must be 400 m. The radius of the semicircles at each end is 40 m.

← y metres →

radius = 40 m

a What is the total distance around the two semicircles?

b Using your answer to part a. Calculate the lengths of the straights, y. Round your answer to a useful number.

← y metres →

7 Three lanes are marked out. Each lane is 1 m wide.

The runners run one lap of the track in lanes.
The runner in the inside lane will run 400 m.

start/finish

a After one lap, how far has the runner in
   i middle lane run   ii outer lane run?

b How do track markers prevent this when they mark out a real track?

The sports day   275

Extension

Look again at question **7**. Can students work out the area of one running track? Encourage the use of a diagram to help support their answer. (403m² to 3 s.f, using the pi button (or 3.14) and full calculator displays. Rounding during the intermediate steps may lead to the solution 402m²) (1.2, 1.3)

Exercise 17c commentary

Question 2 – (spreads 11f, 15c) What fraction are taking part in each of the sports? What information needs to be put on a pie chart? Encourage students to show both the name of the activity, and the number taking part.

Question 3 – The terms goals 'for' and 'against' may need explaining. Which data entries are the most useful when finding the missing values? What checks can students make against the other data values? For example, is the number of points gained correct? (RL)

Question 4 – (spreads 15a, b, f) Do you need to use both the table and scoreboard? Is the mean or mode a better estimate in this case?

Question 5 – (spreads 13f, 15b) What information does the centre target immediately give you? Can you make up any equations for the other two targets? How are the other two targets different? Can you assume the scores are integers? What is the highest/lowest score that gold/ blue could be? Encourage students to check any solution for all targets (1.2).

Question 6 – (spreads 2e, 14f, 16b) What do the two ends of the track form? What value should you take for pi? Ask students to draw a sketch showing the values used in their proposed solution.

Question 7 – (spreads 2e, 14f) Encourage students to adapt their sketch to show the effect of including an extra lane: each new lane increases the diameter by 2m.

Assessment criteria – UAM, level 6: interpret discuss and synthesise information presented in a variety of mathematical forms. UAM, level 7: refine or extend the mathematics used to generate fuller solutions.

- Represent problems and synthesise information in algebraic, geometric or graphical form (L6)
- Estimate, approximate and check working (L6)

Useful resources
Protractor
Ruler

Background

Students who are involved in the Duke of Edinburgh award scheme, Boy Scouts, Girl Guides, Woodcraft Folk, Combined Cadet Force, *etc.* may have direct experience of going on expeditions. Sailors and orienteers may also have knowledge of navigation. These students' experiences of how mathematics can be applied should be used to enliven and inform classroom discussion (EP) (1.2).

The mathematics in this spread is broadly on the theme of geometry and includes giving compass bearings, measuring angles and measuring distances on scale drawings, as well as averages, time scales and finding proportions. There are direct links to the geography syllabus.

Teaching notes

In question **1c**, the mean can be thought of as a 'balance point' for the distribution of students' weights. This provides a means of checking the answer: The sum of the differences between individual students' weights and the mean should be zero. This provides a more formal definition of 'it should be in the middle' (RL).

Question **2** has obvious links to geography with directions being specified by three-figure bearings, whilst in question **4**, angles are measured in degrees. Why are different approaches used? (EP) (1.5).

A further option is to show how locations can be 'triangulated': what place is on a bearing 045° as seen from point A and 030° as seen from point B? (castle/chateau) Can students provide their own examples, perhaps using a different base-line that requires larger angles to be measured? This could even be used as a challenge: can students produce an accurate scale drawing given the line AB and pairs of bearings for other locations? Distance can then be measured with a ruler and converted into a real-life distance using a scale; this skill is required for question **6** (CT).

The first part of question **3** is likely to cause trouble due to the lack of a year zero – which some students might not appreciate. This is most easily clarified using small values and a number line.

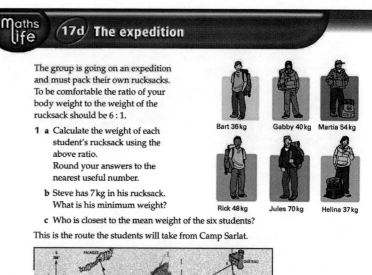

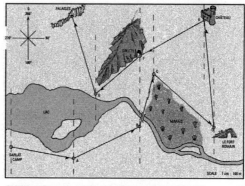

Maths life 17d The expedition

The group is going on an expedition and must pack their own rucksacks. To be comfortable the ratio of your body weight to the weight of the rucksack should be 6 : 1.

Bart 36 kg   Gabby 40 kg   Martia 54 kg
Rick 48 kg   Jules 70 kg   Helina 37 kg

1 a Calculate the weight of each student's rucksack using the above ratio.
Round your answers to the nearest useful number.

b Steve has 7 kg in his rucksack. What is his minimum weight?

c Who is closest to the mean weight of the six students?

This is the route the students will take from Camp Sarlat.

2 Using the scale on the map copy and complete this table of distances and bearings.

3 a In the cave there are drawings that were made in 2150 B.C. How many years ago is this?

b The Roman fort was occupied between 74 B.C. and 48 A.D. How many years is this?

Section	3-figure bearing	Distance (m)
A to B	070°	350
B to C		
C to D		
D to E		
E to F		
F to G		

Functional maths Problem solving

Simplification

For question **1**, consider making the weight of the students all multiples of 6 or possibly 3 to make calculation easier. For question **2**, ask students to identify with an arc the bearings they are intending to measure. Check with the teacher that they are in the correct position before measuring them.

All questions (1.1, 1.3)

Question 1 – (spreads 4c, 12c, 15b) How can the ration 6 : 1 be converted so that it changes into the persons weight? What can be done to both sides of a ratio so that it remains in the same proportions? Consider alternative ways of looking at the question. For example, for every 6kg you weigh, you can carry 1kg. How many 6kg make up each person?

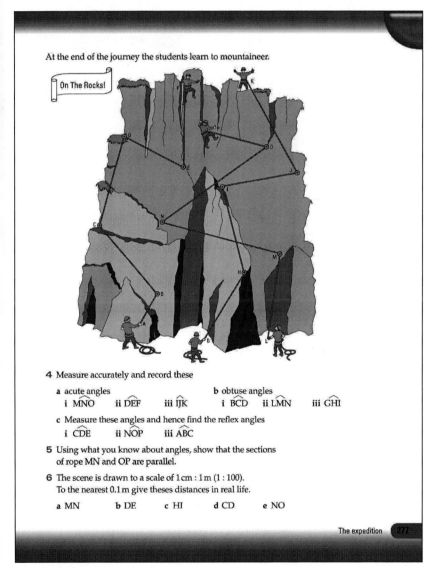

At the end of the journey the students learn to mountaineer.

On The Rocks!

4 Measure accurately and record these

   a acute angles   **b** obtuse angles
     i $M\widehat{N}O$ **ii** $D\widehat{E}F$ **iii** $I\widehat{J}K$ **i** $B\widehat{C}D$ **ii** $L\widehat{M}N$ **iii** $G\widehat{H}I$

   c Measure these angles and hence find the reflex angles
     i $C\widehat{D}E$ **ii** $N\widehat{O}P$ **iii** $A\widehat{B}C$

5 Using what you know about angles, show that the sections of rope MN and OP are parallel.

6 The scene is drawn to a scale of 1 cm : 1 m (1 : 100). To the nearest 0.1 m give theses distances in real life.

   a MN   **b** DE   **c** HI   **d** CD   **e** NO

The expedition **277**

Exercise 17d commentary

Question 2 – (spreads 9d, 14e) Students may need reminding of the method for measuring bearings. Is it possible for students to work it out themselves from the example given in the question? How can a 180 degree angle measurer be used to measure reflex angles?

Question 3 – (spreads 1a, 16a, b) It might be helpful to look at the sketch of a timeline to establish that this is similar to negative numbers (TW, 1.2).

Question 4 – The terms acute, obtuse and reflex may need recapping. Encourage students to measure as accurately as possible. Ask students to consider if their answer is reasonable, have they read the angle measurer in the correct direction?

Question 5 – (spread 6a) Suggest drawing the section MNOP out separately and labelling the angles. What angle rule is this? Extend each line to create corresponding and vertically opposite angles if need be to illustrate that OP and MN are parallel (1.4).

Question 6 – (spread 9d) If 1cm represents 1m and you want answers accurate to 0.1m, how accurately do you have to measure the lines with your ruler? (1.2, 1.4)

Assessment criteria – UAM, level 6: give solutions to an appropriate degree of accuracy. UAM, level 6: interpret discuss and synthesise information presented in a variety of mathematical forms.

Extension

Draw a polygon by joining the following vertices. Cliffs - Sarlat Camp – A – B – C – D – E – F – G – Cliffs. Find an approximation for the area. What shapes can you approximate with? For example, triangles FDE and ABG and trapeziums FCBG and AG 'cliffs' 'camp' (IE, SM).

- Make accurate mathematical diagrams, graphs and constructions on paper and on screen (L6)
- Pose questions and make convincing arguments to justify generalizations or solutions (L7)

Useful resources
Graph paper
Tracing paper
Calculator

Background

The spread has a loose focus on incidents that occur in the life of Miss Perry and the students. It allows a breadth of mathematics to be covered including: finding areas, applying algebra, rotations, using systematic approaches to problem solving and the speed-distance-time relationship (EP).

As suggested in spread **17a**, an aspect of camp life is giving awards for various types of achievement. Now is a natural opportunity to make presentations and to also analyse the class's results. For example, producing graphs of boys' and girls' achievements in the various prize categories (TW, SM).

Teaching notes

Question **1** involves finding areas. It may be instructive to ask students to explain where the formula for the area of a triangle comes from. Can they use this argument to simplify calculating the area of the two end triangles?

Question **2** should be tackled using algebra. Supply two similar simultaneous equations, for example $4A + 3B = 25$ and $A + 7B = 25$, and ask students to explain how they would solve these equations. Also ask how they could check that their answer is correct (RL).

Question **3** may prove confusing to students given the apparent diagonal axes. It will be useful to get students

Maths life **17e** Camp life

The day started badly for Miss Perry — her tent leaked in the night and she is not pleased. She asks Mr Powell to waterproof the tent for her.

1 The tent is made from a large rectangle and two triangles.

a Calculate the area of   i the rectangle   ii a triangle.

b use you answers to part a to find the total surface area of the tent.

c How many cans of Seal It! will be needed to spray the whole tent if it takes 250 ml to waterproof every 5 m².

Ms. Perry refuses to use the showers — they are just too dirty for her! She has a private shower made for her.

2 The students have to carry the water to her shower in containers. Meg and Leroy use different sized containers. They empty their containers in to the shower and fill it exactly.

= 50 litres

Leroy empties container A three times and Meg empties container B once. They refill the shower and again fill it exactly.

= 50 litres

This time they use 1 A container and 7 B containers. Work out how much water each container holds.

Functional maths Problem solving

to explain their methods for how to rotate a shape, drawn on a grid, through a right-angle. Do they get the same result if the same problem were posed but with the axes in a different orientation? In fact, are axes required at all? Would it make a difference if you turned the book through 45°? (CT)

Question **4**, requires students to work systematically through the possible combination of weights. Ask students to explain their methods for listing and testing the various possibilities

Question **5** involves the speed-distance-time relationship in a new form. This can be left for students to reason through what is required using common sense and experience or a simple example could be discussed to demonstrate how they should proceed (CT).

Simplification

For question **1**, consider giving students the net for the tent and asking them to add the dimensions onto the net. For question **2**, provide students with the 3 times table up to 3 × 20 and the 7 times table up to 7 × 10. For question **5**, consider altering the wind speed slightly from 10 m.p.h. to 42 m.p.h. This gives a journey time of 6.25 hours which is more easily seen to be 6 hours and 15 minutes.

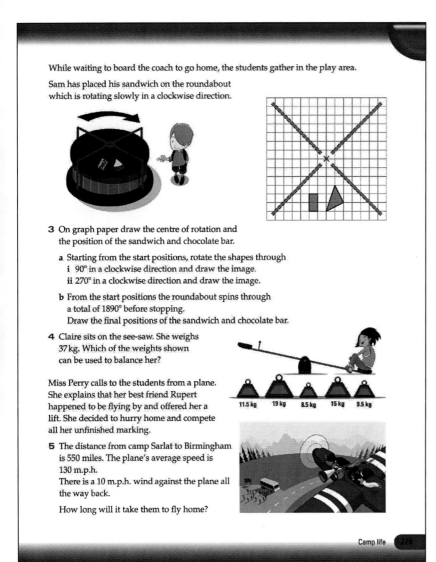

While waiting to board the coach to go home, the students gather in the play area.

Sam has placed his sandwich on the roundabout which is rotating slowly in a clockwise direction.

3 On graph paper draw the centre of rotation and the position of the sandwich and chocolate bar.

   a Starting from the start positions, rotate the shapes through
   i 90° in a clockwise direction and draw the image.
   ii 270° in a clockwise direction and draw the image.

   b From the start positions the roundabout spins through a total of 1890° before stopping.
   Draw the final positions of the sandwich and chocolate bar.

4 Claire sits on the see-saw. She weighs 37 kg. Which of the weights shown can be used to balance her?

11.5 kg   19 kg   8.5 kg   15 kg   9.5 kg

Miss Perry calls to the students from a plane. She explains that her best friend Rupert happened to be flying by and offered her a lift. She decided to hurry home and compete all her unfinished marking.

5 The distance from camp Sarlat to Birmingham is 550 miles. The plane's average speed is 130 m.p.h.
There is a 10 m.p.h. wind against the plane all the way back.

How long will it take them to fly home?

Camp life   279

Extension

Suppose that in question **2** you were told information such that 3A + B = 50 and A + 7C = 50. How many sets of integer solutions can you find? (A, B, C) = (15, 5, 5) or (8, 26, 6) or (1, 47, 7) Students will need to use a systematic way of listing the possibilities. Consider putting the results in a table (SM, CT).

Exercise 17e commentary

All questions (CT, IE) (1.1, 1.3).

Question 1 – (spreads 2c, 14g) Students may find it useful to draw the net of the tent and a 3D sketch showing the hidden lines. Which measurements are not needed for the calculation of the area of the triangle? Encourage students to write down their workings. What if you need a decimal number of cans of 'Seal It'? (1.4, 1.5)

Question 2 – (spread 13f) Ask students to suggest certain possible solutions that give the correct mathematical value and seem sensible in practice. Do you think B is smaller than A? Why? Are the diagrams drawn to scale?

Question 3 – (spread 9a) When performing a rotation what resource could you use? (tracing paper) What sort of triangle is the sandwich? How can you find the number of full turns from the total angle if it's over 360°? (1.2, 1.4)

Question 4 – To begin consider two weights, how many combinations are there? (ten to check) and three weights? (Also ten) Does it make a difference where the weights are placed on the slide? (1.2)

Question 5 – (spreads 8h, 13h) Students may need reminding of the formula for speed-distance-time. What is the effect of a head wind? How can a decimal number of hours be converted in minutes? Look at the effective use of the calculator when converting 4.583333.hr to hrs and mins.

Assessment criteria – UAM, level 6: present a concise, reasoned argument, using symbols, diagrams, graphs and related explanatory text. UAM, level 7: solve increasingly demanding problems and evaluate solutions.

17 Summary

- Solve problems and carry through substantial tasks by breaking them into smaller more manageable tasks, using a range of efficient techniques, methods and resources, including ICT   Level 6
- Use logical argument to establish the truth of a statement   Level 6
- Interpret discuss and synthesise information presented in a variety of mathematical forms   Level 6
- Give solutions to an appropriate degree of accuracy   Level 6
- Present a concise, reasoned argument, using symbols, diagrams, graphs and related explanatory text   Level 6
- Justify generalizations, arguments or solutions   Level 7
- Refine or extend the mathematics used to generate fuller solutions   Level 7
- Solve increasingly demanding problems and evaluate solutions   Level 7

Development and links

Students will continue to practise functional mathematics throughout Year 9.

The student book start of chapter suggests five areas of everyday life where aspects of the ability to apply mathematical ideas prove highly valuable.

Using mathematical reasoning: the most efficient way to lay out a pattern on a piece of cloth is an example of an optimisation problem. Similar problems have to be solved when arranging files on a hard drive so as to minimize wasted space or packing oranges in a box so as reduce the need for packaging.

Representing: scale drawings based on careful measurements and 3-D reasoning are used throughout building and engineering to plan projects. Many of the same ideas are used to produce the graphics in computer games.

Using mathematical procedures: spreadsheet type programs are often used to help compile business accounts. However, to check and understand what they are doing you often need to be able to do simpler versions of the calculations yourself

Interpreting and evaluating: distribution centres face a difficult task in planning the best routes, loads and timetables. To guide them, they collect data on fuel cost, journey times, stock shortages, *etc*, and by carefully looking at this data can monitor and improve their performance.

Communicating: it isn't always enough to just find the correct answer to a problem, often you have to be able to convince other people using appropriately chosen graphs and mathematical explanations

Student book answers

Chapter 1

Check in   page 1

1 a -6   **b** -25   **c** 5   **d** -8

2 a -20   **b** 15   **c** 24

   d -5   **e** 6   **f** -4

3 a 1, 2, 3, 4, 5, 6, 10, 12, 15, 20, 30, 60

   b 1, 2, 3, 4, 6, 11, 12, 22, 33, 44, 66, 132

   c 1, 3, 5, 9, 15, 25, 45, 75, 225

4 a HCF = 4 LCM = 24

   b HCF = 5 LCM = 60

   c HCF = 9 LCM = 54

5 a 30   **b** 36   **c** 350

6 a $2 \times 2 \times 2 \times 3$

   b $2 \times 2 \times 2 \times 5$

   c $2 \times 2 \times 3 \times 7$

7 a 81   **b** 169   **c** 1225

   d 125   **e** 3375

Exercise 1a   page 3

1 a <   **b** >   **c** >

   d <   **e** >   **f** <

2 a -3, -2, -1.8, 1.5, 5,

   b -3.8, -3.4, -3.2, -3, -2.7,

   c -5.3, -5.28, -5.25, -5.2, 5.4,

3 a -4   **b** -21   **c** 7

   d 9   **e** -34   **f** 6

   g -5   **h** -7   **i** -7

4 a -36   **b** -180   **c** 84   **d** 105

   e 50   **f** -51   **g** 23   **h** -32

5 a 8   **b** -2   **c** 15

   d -91   **e** -16   **f** -14

   g -30   **h** -6   **i** 24

6 a $-4x \div x, x \neq 0$

   b $x - (x + 10), \forall x$

   c $x + (12 - x), \forall x$

   d $(36 \div x) \times x, x \neq 0$

   e one unknown must be zero

   f $x + (-x), \forall x$

7 -9, -8, -7

Investigation

×	8	2	-7	-3
-6	-48	-12	42	18
-5	-40	-10	35	15
4	32	8	-28	-12
-9	-72	-18	63	27

×	8	2	-7	-3
-6	-48	-12	42	18
-5	-40	-10	35	15
4	32	8	-28	-12
-9	-72	-18	63	27

Exercise 1b   page 5

1 a Yes $385 \div 5 = 77$

   b No $746 \div 3 = 248 \text{ r } 2$

   c No $164 \div 7 = 23 \text{ r } 3$

   d Yes $3234 \div 11 = 294$

   e No $458 \div 12 = 38 \text{ r } 2$

   f Yes $2010 \div 15 = 134$

   g Yes $1926 \div 18 = 107$

   h Yes $2712 \div 24 = 113$

2 a 1, 2, 4, 5, 10, 20, 23, 46, 92, 115, 230, 460

   b 1, 2, 3, 4, 6, 8, 9, 12, 16, 18, 24, 27, 32, 36, 48, 54, 72, 96, 108, 144, 216, 288, 432, 864

   c 1, 5, 25, 125, 625

   d 1, 2, 3, 4, 6, 7, 11, 12, 14, 21, 22, 28, 33, 42, 44, 66, 77, 84, 132, 154, 231, 308, 462, 924

   e 1, 2, 4, 8, 16, 32, 64, 128, 256, 512, 1024

   f 1, 5, 7, 25, 35, 49, 175, 245, 1225

3 a Yes   **b** No $161 \div 7 = 23$

   c No $221 \div 13 = 17$ **d** Yes

   e No $301 \div 7 = 43$ **f** Yes

4 10 007, 10 009, 10 037, 10 039

5 a 1, 7, 19, 37

   b 61, 91

   c All prime numbers except 1 and 91

   d $3n^2 - 3n + 1$ generates some more prime numbers: 127, $n = 7$, 271, $n = 10…$

Investigation

a 7, 13, 19, 25 = 5×5, 31, 37, 43, 49 = $7 \times 7,…$

b 5, 11, 17, 23, 29, 35 = 3×7, 41, 47,… All primes fall into one of these two sequences.

c 41, 43, 47, 53, 61, 71,… Found by Euler in 1772; first fails for $n = 41$ (gives 41×41)

d $M_2 = 3$, $M_3 = 7$, $M_5 = 31$, $M_7 = 127$, $M_{13} = 8191$, $M_{17} = 131071$, $M_{19} = 524287$, $M_{31} = 2147483647,…$
Known as Mersenne primes, n must be prime.

Exercise 1c   page 7

1 a 60   **b** 28   **c** 90   **d** 700

   e 220   **f** 252   **g** 104   **h** 252

   i 4200   **j** 880

2 a 2×3^2 **b** $2 \times 3 \times 7$ **c** $2^4 \times 5$

   d 2×3^3 **e** 2^7 **f** $2^2 \times 3 \times 5 \times 7$

   g $2^3 \times 5^2$ **h** $5^2 \times 7$ **i** $2^3 \times 3^2 \times 5$

   j $2^5 \times 3 \times 5$ **k** $2^6 \times 3^2$ **l** $2^3 \times 3^3 \times 5$

   m $2^3 \times 3^2 \times 5 \times 7$ **n** $2^4 \times 3^4$ **o** $3^4 \times 5^2$

3 a $9 \times 13 = 117$ not 126

     $55 \times 49 = 2695$ not 2646

   b $12\,600 = 2^3 \times 3^2 \times 5^2 \times 7$

     $26\,460 = 2^2 \times 3^3 \times 5 \times 7^2$

   c Students' answers

4 a 1, 2, 4, 5, 8, 10, 16, 20, 40, 80

   b 1, 2, 3, 4, 5, 6, 9, 10, 12, 15, 18, 20, 30, 36, 45, 60, 90, 180 c 1, 2, 3, 5, 6, 9, 10, 15, 18, 25, 30, 45, 50, 75, 90, 150, 225, 450

d 1, 2, 3, 5, 6, 10, 11, 15, 22, 30, 33, 55, 66, 110,165, 330

e 1, 2, 3, 5, 6, 7, 10, 14, 15, 21, 30, 35, 42, 49, 70, 98, 105, 147, 210, 245, 294, 490, 735, 1470

f 1, 2, 4, 5, 8, 10, 20, 25, 40, 50, 100, 125, 200, 250, 500, 1000

5 a $2 \times 3 \times 5 = 30$, $2^2 \times 3 \times 5 = 60$, $2 \times 3^2 \times 5 = 90$, $2^3 \times 3 \times 5 = 120$, $2 \times 3 \times 5^2 = 150$ Multiples of $2 \times 3 \times 5 = 30$

b $204 = 2^2 \times 3 \times 17$

c $210 = 2 \times 3 \times 5 \times 7$

Investigation

$3 \times 5 \times 7$	$= 105$	$3^2 \times 5 \times 7$	$= 315$
5^3	$= 125$	7^3	$= 343$
$3^3 \times 5$	$= 135$	3×5^3	$= 375$
3×7^2	$= 147$	$3^4 \times 5$	$= 405$
$3^3 \times 7$	$= 189$	$3^2 \times 7^2$	$= 441$
$3^2 \times 5^2$	$= 225$	$3 \times 5^2 \times 7$	$= 525$
3^5	$= 243$	$3^4 \times 7$	$= 567$
5×7^2	$= 245$		

Exercise 1d　page 9

1 a 5　　**b** 5　　**c** 24

　d 19　　**e** 3　　**f** 8

2 a 30　　**b** 350　　**c** 340

　d 980　　**e** 210　　**f** 200

3 a 　　　　　　　　　　**b**

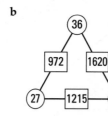

4 a HCF = 36, LCM = 432

b HCF = 40, LCM = 2520

c HCF = 55, LCM = 4620

d HCF = 63, LCM = 5733

e HCF = 120, LCM = 4320

f HCF = 180, LCM = 5040

g HCF = 7, LCM = 2520

h HCF = 15, LCM = 450

5 a $\frac{2}{3}$　　**b** $\frac{5}{9}$　　**c** $\frac{3}{4}$

　d $\frac{3}{5}$　　**e** $\frac{5}{8}$

6 a $\frac{7}{30}$　　**b** $\frac{53}{60}$　　**c** $\frac{47}{100}$　　**d** $\frac{161}{200}$

7 a 588 weeks

　b 21; 14 and 12 orbits respectively

Investigation

a $n \times 20$ and $m \times 20$ where the HCF of n and m is 1

b 1, 100;　2, 100;　4, 25;　5, 100;　10, 100; 20, 100;　50, 100

Exercise 1e　page 11

1 a 144　　**b** 361　　**c** 625　　**d** 343

　e 2197　　**f** 64　　**g** 1000　　**h** 12.25

　i 8000　　**j** 74.088　　**k** 1771.561　　**l** -125

2 a 8.4　　**b** 11.0　　　　**c** 4.1

d 14.1　　**e** not possible　　**f** -4.5

3 a 15　　**b** 18　　**c** 24

　d 6　　**e** 8　　**f** 36

4 a 94 and 95　　**b** 56,57 and 58　　**c** 8.4cm

5 Rounding error on calculator; $\sqrt{10}$ is a non-terminating decimal

Challenge

a 4.5, 9.7, 17.3　　　　**b** 4.6, 2.2, 11.7

Exercise 1f　page 13

1 a 125　　**b** 64　　**c** 27　　**d** 1

　e 1　　**f** 100 000　　**g** 2　　**h** 1

　i 0.01　　**j** 1331

2 $3^5 (= 243) < 2^8 = 4^4 (= 256) < 11^3 (= 1331)$

3 multiply 256 by $2 \times 2 = 1024$

4 a 1024　　**b** 16 384

5 a 4　　**b** 5　　**c** 6　　**d** 2

　e 5　　**f** 4　　**g** 8　　**h** -1

6 a 4^5　　**b** 3^6　　**c** 5^7　　**d** 4^7

　e 2^8　　**f** 4^3　　**g** 3^4　　**h** 5^2

　i 4^2　　**j** 2

7 a 200　　**b** 36　　**c** 48

　d 15.1875　　**e** 2^{-1}

8 a 3^7　　**b** 4^6　　**c** 10^9

　d 2^6　　**e** 4^3　　**f** 10^{-2}

Investigation

a 54

b 0 red 27, 2 red 36, 3 red 8

c 0 red $(n-2)^3$, 1 red $6(n-2)^2$, 2 red $12(n-2)$, 3 red 8, total n^3

Consolidation　page 14

1 a -3,　　-2,　　-0.5,　　0.5,　　2

　b -4.5,　　-3.5,　　-2.5,　　-1.5,　　-0.5

　c -5.2,　　-5,　　-4.6,　　-4.5,　　3

2 a -5　　**b** -24　　**c** 12　　**d** 7

　e -30　　**f** -6　　**g** -47　　**h** 3

　i 100　　**j** -72.5　　**k** -6　　**l** 10

3 a -63　　**b** -72　　**c** 77　　**d** 117

　e -180　　**f** -255　　**g** -234　　**h** 171

　i 345　　**j** -399　　**k** 25　　**l** -33

　m 27　　**n** 34　　**o** -31　　**p** 23

4 a 1, 2, 4, 5, 8, 10, 20, 25, 40, 50, 100, 200

　b 1, 2, 3, 4, 6, 8, 9, 12, 16, 18, 24, 32, 36, 48, 72, 96, 144, 288

　c 1, 17, 289

　d 1, 2, 3, 4, 5, 6, 10, 12, 15, 20, 25, 30, 50, 60, 75, 100, 150, 300

　e 1, 2, 4, 5, 8, 10, 11, 20, 22, 40, 44, 55, 88, 110, 220, 440

　f 1, 2, 4, 8, 16, 32, 64, 128, 256

　g 1, 2, 4, 5, 10, 20, 25, 50, 100, 125, 250, 500

　h 1, 3, 9, 71, 213, 639

　i 1, 3, 7, 21, 37, 111, 259, 777

　j 1, 3, 9, 27, 37, 111, 333, 999

　k 1, 2, 4, 5, 8, 10, 20, 25, 40, 50, 100, 125, 200, 250, 500, 1000

l 1, 2, 3, 4, 6, 8, 9, 12, 16, 18, 24, 32, 36, 48, 64, 72, 96, 128, 144, 192, 256, 288, 384, 576, 768, 1152, 2304

5 a Yes **b** No $413 \div 7 = 59$
  c Yes **d** No $437 \div 19 = 23$
  e No $451 \div 11 = 41$ **f** Yes

6 a 2×11 **b** 2×23 **c** $2^2 \times 3 \times 7$
  d 2×29 **e** $2^2 \times 3 \times 11$ **f** $2^3 \times 13$
  g 5×37 **h** $5^2 \times 17$ **i** 5×41
  j prime **k** $2 \times 3 \times 61$ **l** 3×103
  m 3×163 **n** $3^2 \times 5 \times 13$ **o** $3^2 \times 11^2$
  p $3^2 \times 281$ **q** $3^2 \times 5 \times 29$ **r** $5^2 \times 11^2$

7 a $2^2 \times 3 \times 5$: 1, 2, 3, 4, 5, 6, 10, 12, 15, 20, 30, 60
  b $2^5 \times 3$: 1, 2, 3, 4, 6, 8, 12, 16, 24, 32, 48, 96
  c $2 \times 5 \times 11$: 1, 2, 5, 10, 11, 22, 55, 110
  d $3 \times 5 \times 11$: 1, 3, 5, 11, 15, 33, 55, 165
  e $2 \times 5 \times 43$: 1, 2, 5, 10, 43, 86, 215, 430
  f $2^3 \times 3 \times 5^2$: 1, 2, 3, 4, 5, 6, 8, 10, 12, 15, 20, 24, 25, 30, 40, 50, 60, 75, 100, 120, 150, 200, 300, 600
  g $2 \times 5^2 \times 19$: 1, 2, 5, 10, 19, 25, 38, 50, 95, 190, 475, 950
  h $5^2 \times 7^2$: 1, 5, 7, 25, 35, 49, 175, 245, 1225
  i $2^2 \times 23^2$: 1, 2, 4, 23, 46, 92, 529, 1058, 2116
  j $2^2 \times 3^2 \times 7^2$: 1, 2, 3, 4, 6, 7, 9, 12, 14, 18, 21, 28, 36, 42, 49, 63, 84, 98, 126, 147, 196, 252, 294, 441, 588, 882, 1764
  k $2^4 \times 7^2$: 1, 2, 4, 7, 8, 14, 16, 28, 32, 49, 56, 64, 98, 112, 196, 224, 392, 448, 784, 1568, 3136
  l $3^4 \times 7^2$: 1, 3, 7, 9, 21, 27, 49, 63, 81, 147, 189, 441, 567, 1323, 3969

8 a HCF = 20, LCM = 600
  b HCF = 48, LCM = 576
  c HCF = 30, LCM = 1680
  d HCF = 42, LCM = 3024
  e HCF = 45, LCM = 3465
  f HCF = 56, LCM = 8008
  g HCF = 8, LCM = 2520
  h HCF = 16, LCM = 2640

9 a $\frac{5}{7}$ **b** $\frac{5}{6}$ **c** $\frac{3}{4}$ **d** $\frac{7}{8}$
  e $\frac{3}{5}$ **f** $\frac{6}{7}$ **g** $\frac{5}{9}$ **h** $\frac{2}{11}$
  i $\frac{9}{11}$ **j** $\frac{3}{13}$

10 a $\frac{9}{14}$ **b** $\frac{11}{16}$ **c** $\frac{7}{10}$ **d** $\frac{10}{13}$
  e $\frac{1}{30}$ **f** $\frac{103}{120}$ **g** $\frac{17}{24}$ **h** $\frac{101}{150}$

11 a 3.3 **b** 10.5 **c** 4.8
  d -10.4 **e** not possible **f** 4.5

12 a -11, -12, -13 **b** 42, 43 and -42, -43

13 a 16 **b** 21 **c** 27
  d 12 **e** 15 **f** 45

14 a 7 **b** 9 **c** 8 **d** 6
  e 0 **f** 5 **g** 0 **h** 5
  i 4 **j** -1

15 a 2^7 **b** 7^{12} **c** 4^{12} **d** 3^5

e 6^{10} **f** 2^2 **g** $2^0 = 1$ **h** 4^1
i 3^5 **j** 10^{-1}

16 a 5184 **b** 24 **c** 109
  d $256 = 4^4 = 2^8$ **e** 3^4

17 a 5^9 **b** 3^{15} **c** 10^{12}
  d 2^{12} **e** 5^9 **f** 8^0
  g 3^5 **h** 2^4 **i** 10^0

Summary   page 16

2 3, 6, 9, 18
  5, -3, **2**, **-15**
  -8, **3**, -5, **-24**

Chapter 2

Check in   page 17

1 a 74 **b** 0.39 **c** 60 **d** 0.25
2 a 15 **b** 54 **c** 165 **d** 12.1
3 a 28 **b** 0.8 **c** 300 **d** 9
4 a 26 m, 40 m²
  b 21 cm, 27 cm²
  c 75 mm, 312.5 mm²

Exercise 2a   page 19

1 a 300 000 – 3 000 000 litres **b** 30–120 cm
  c 500 cm² **d** 1–50 litres
  e 30–80 kg **f** 4000–11 000 km
  g 80–700 m **h** ≈ 50 g
  i ≈ 100 cm² **j** 200 ml or 20 cl

2 a 176 cm **b** 1760 mm

3 a 8375 g **b** 8.375 kg

4 4770 m

5 30 teaspoons

6 100 m by 100 m

7 a 400 mm **b** 200 g **c** 25 000 m² **d** 8500 m
  e 650 cl **f** 0.5 l **g** 6.3 t **h** 80 cm

Problem

1 cm = 100 sheets
Typically 150 cm = 15 000 sheets

Exercise 2b   page 21

1 a 13 200 inches, 1920 inches
  b 33 000 cm, 4800 cm
  c 330 m, 48 m

2 a 3.6 litres **b** 9.9 lbs **c** 45 litres
  d 112 km **e** 90 cm **f** 99 lbs
  g 1500 ml **h** 150 cm **i** 135 g

3 £5.58

4 5 miles per hour

5 a 12 inches **b** 7 pints **c** 7.5 miles
  d 0.5 pints **e** 9 gallons **f** 47 kg
  g 15 oz **h** 9.6 inches **i** 22 feet

6 912.5 – 1217 pints

7 a 11 t, 11 000 kg;   11.5 t, 11 500 kg

  b 8.6 cm, 86 mm;   9.2 cm, 92 mm

  c $2\frac{1}{4}$ inches or 2.25 inches; $2\frac{5}{8}$ inches or 2.625 inches

  d 0.4 l, 400 ml, 40 cl;   0.7 l, 700 ml, 70 cl

  e 0.8 kg, 800 g;   1.4 kg, 1400 g, 1 kg 400 g

  f $\frac{1}{4}$ gallon, 2 pint; $\frac{1}{2}$ gallon, 4 pints

Puzzle

a Appear different but same length in reality

b 3 cm

c 1.2 inches

Exercise 2c   page 23

1 a 20 cm, 18 cm²

  b 40 cm, 72 cm²

  c 30 cm, 26 cm²

2 a 18 cm² **b** 18.75 m² **c** 90 cm² **d** 4 m²

3 a $w = 3$ cm   **b** $w = 7.5$ mm

  c $b = 8$ cm   **d** $h = 7.2$ m

4 a 17 square units

  b 12 square units

  c 12.5 square units

5 $h = 9$ cm

Challenge

56.25 m²

Exercise 2d   page 25

1 a 432 cm² **b** 360 cm² **c** 6 m²

  d 36 cm² **e** 2.5 m² **f** 8 mm²

2 a $h = 2.5$ cm   **b** $h = 6$ m

  c $b = 5$ mm

3 a 340 m²   **b** 68 litres of paint

Challenge

Find values of a and b, with $a < b$, such that

$a + b = 10$,

e.g. $a = 1$ cm, $b = 9$ cm

Exercise 2e   page 27

1 d 3.142

2 a $r = 6.5$ mm, $d = 13$ mm

  b $r = 8.5$ mm, $d = 17$ mm

  c $r = 4$ mm, $d = 8$ mm

3 a 21.98 cm **b** 50.24 m **c** 62.8 cm **d** 15.7 m

4 a 40 cm   **b** 31.4 cm

  c The distance around the outside of the square is more than the distance around the circle.

Activity

$\pi = 3.14$ approximately

Exercise 2f   page 29

1 a 12.56 cm²   **b** 28.26 cm² **c** 50.24 cm²

2 a 153.86 cm²   **b** 200.96 cm²

3 a 39.25 cm²   **b** 100.48 cm² **c** 7.065 cm²

4 a 86 cm²   **b** 86 cm²

5 5481.25 cm²

Investigation

The area of the circle is 4 times larger.

Consolidation   page 30

1 50 lengths

2 a 8500 ml **b** 45.6 cm **c** 85 000 m²

  d 250 ml **e** 4200 kg

3 a 60.5 lbs   **b** 48 inches **c** 4.5 oz

  d 1.25 pints **e** 1360 km

4 a 0.3 cm, 3 mm; 0.8 cm, 8 mm

  b 0.3 kg, 300 g;   1.6 kg, 1600 g, 1 kg 600 g

  c 0.4 l, 400 ml, 40 cl;   0.8 l, 800 ml, 80 cl

5 18 cm²

6 a $h = 10$ cm   **b** $b = 16$ cm

  c $h = 12.5$ cm   **d** $h = 20$ cm

7 a 67.5 cm² **b** 336 cm² **c** 2.5 m²

8 $h = 4$ cm

9 a 40 cm **b** 125.6 cm **c** 376.8 cm **d** 3 times

10 37.68 cm

11 78.5 m²

12 2251 cm²

Summary   page 32

2 35 cm² (units must be given)

Chapter 3

Check in   page 33

1 a $\frac{3}{4}$ **b** $\frac{17}{20}$ **c** $\frac{2}{3}$

  d $\frac{3}{5}$ **e** $\frac{3}{5}$

2 a $\frac{1}{2}$ **b** 0.55   **c** $\frac{1}{2}$ **d** 70%

3 a $\frac{7}{16}$ **b** $\frac{11}{16}$ **c** $\frac{2}{3}$ **d** $\frac{71}{105}$

4

	Fraction	Percentage	Decimal
Liquorice	$\frac{1}{4}$	25%	0.25
Chocolate button	$\frac{7}{20}$	35%	0.35
Toffee	$\frac{3}{20}$	15%	0.15
Mint	$\frac{1}{8}$	12.5%	0.125
Jelly bean	$\frac{1}{8}$	12.5%	0.125

Exercise 3a   page 35

1 a TT, TH, HT, HH

  b i $\frac{1}{4}$ **ii** $\frac{1}{2}$ **iii** $\frac{1}{4}$

  c They add up to one.

2 a TTT, TTH, THT, THH, HTT, HTH, HHT, HHH

  b i 3   **ii** 4   **c** $\frac{3}{8}$

3 $4 \times (1 + 3) = 16$

4 (C cone, T tub) × (V vanilla, Sp strawberry) ×
(F flake only, Sp sprinkles only, B both, N neither)

CVF, CVSp, CVB, CVN,

CSF, CSSp, CSB, CSN,

TVF, TVSp, TVB, TVN,

TSF, TSSp, TSB, TSN

5 a

High	1	2	3	4	5	6
1	1	2	3	4	5	6
2	2	2	3	4	5	6
3	3	3	3	4	5	6
4	4	4	4	4	5	6
5	5	5	5	5	5	6
6	6	6	6	6	6	6

b $\frac{7}{36}$

Investigation

a $3 \times 4 \times 4 = 48$ **b** $3 \times 3 \times 3 = 27$

c $2 \times 1 \times 4 = 8$

Exercise 3b   page 37

1 a First   Second

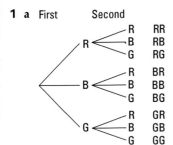

B   RR

b i $\frac{5}{9}$ **ii** $\frac{4}{9}$

2 a First   Second

b i $\frac{2}{3}$ **ii** $\frac{1}{3}$

3 a, b First   Second

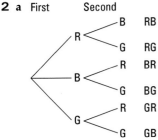

c i $\frac{60}{150} = \frac{2}{5}$ **ii** $\frac{(30+40)}{150} = \frac{7}{5}$ **iii** $\frac{20}{150} = \frac{2}{15}$

Discussion

Students' answers. In both cases the expectation is the same,

$(100 + 200 + 300) \times \frac{1}{3} = £200 = 0 \times \frac{1}{2} +$

$(200 + 400 + 600) \times \frac{1}{6}$

Exercise 3c   page 39

1 a No. These are extremely unlikely to happen in the same year but not impossible.

   b Yes. The only even prime is 2 and you can not get this as the sum of three dice.

   c No, if you take over a lifetime,
   Yes, in a single season.

2 a A and B, B and D, C and D

   b Students' answers: odd total and same score, odd and even, a 5 and less than 3, prime and   multiple of 4

3 a

	Even	Odd
Even	E, E	E, O
Odd	O, E	O, O

×	Even	Odd
Even	E	E
Odd	E	O

   b $\frac{3}{4}$ **c** $1 - \frac{3}{4} = \frac{1}{4}$

4 a   First   Second   Third

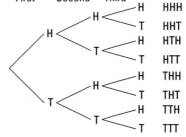

HHH

   b i $\frac{3}{8}$ **ii** $\frac{4}{8} = \frac{1}{2}$

   c i $\frac{4}{8} = \frac{1}{2}$ **ii** $1 - \frac{1}{2} = \frac{1}{2}$

Puzzle

a i $2^4 = 16$ **ii** 4

b i $2^5 = 32$ **ii** 5

c i $2^{10} = 1024$ **ii** 10

Exercise 3d   page 41

1 $\frac{4}{22} = \frac{2}{11}$

2 a

Vowel	a	e	i	o	u
Frequency	108	177	100	101	31

   b $\frac{158}{476} = 0.332$

3 a It is likely to be close, unlikely to be exactly the same because of sampling variability.

   b Students' answers.

   c Students' answer, likely to vary.

   d Make a larger sample by combining class results for non-duplicate pages.

4 a $\frac{8}{16} = \frac{1}{2}$

   b No, pages containing 1 are not evenly distributed, they in groups 10–19, 100–199

5 a Divide the number of people in UK struck by lightning in past 70 years by 60 million.

   Results may differ for other counties that are more or less prone to thunderstorms.

   b Use historical weather records for the given day, or group of days centred on the birthday.

   c Limited 'evidence' as only last 2–3 seasons relevant. Bookmakers odds may reflect a pool of peoples views (and the size of bets placed).

Discussion

Likely to be similar. Though in a children's book words like 'a' and 'the' may be more frequent and give a higher proportion of vowels.

Exercise 3e   page 43

1 a Students' answers. Outcomes HH, HT, TH, TT so P(1 head) $= \frac{2}{4} = \frac{1}{2} \neq \frac{1}{3}$

b Estimated probability $= \frac{21}{40} = 0.525$. Differs from $\frac{1}{3}$ by 0.19167 whilst a single event contributes $\frac{1}{40} = 0.025$. Therefore data provides strong evidence but it is not a proof.

2 Estimated rates of cure are: drug A $\frac{72}{96} = 0.750$ $\left(\frac{1}{96} = 0.010\right)$, drug B $\frac{7}{10} = 0.700$ $\left(\frac{1}{10} = 0.100\right)$, placebo $\frac{17}{36} = 0.472$ $\left(\frac{1}{36} = 0.0278\right)$. Both drugs appear beneficial but the results for drug B are less reliable. A better trial would randomly assign equal numbers of patients to the three groups with a larger test group.

3 a $\frac{12}{37} = 32.4\%$ for each group

b

	1–12	13–24	25–36	Total
1	38.3%	36.7%	25.0%	100%
2	28.3%	31.7%	36.7%	96.7%
3	26.7%	28.3%	45.0%	100%
4	33.3%	30.0%	36.7%	100%

c Wheel 3 gives a large number of high scores $\left(\frac{27}{60} - \frac{12}{37} = 0.126$ compared to $\frac{1}{60} = 0.017\right)$. Since cheaper to test than replace recommend more trials.

d Wheel 2, sum of probabilities $= \frac{58}{60}$; two 0s must have occurred (the house won twice).

Task

Students' answers
Not a proof but would provide much more compelling evidence. A list of outcomes/sample space or tree diagram could be used to give a proof.

Exercise 3e²   page 43²

1 Student answers

a Heads if tenths digit 0–4, else tails (expect ~5 heads)

b i Heads if first tenths 0–5, else tails (expect ~6 heads)

  ii Heads if tenths digit 0–2, tails if 3–9, else repeat (expect ~3 heads)

2 Students' answers

a Estimated P(heads) = no. heads ÷ 10 (expect 0.60 ± 0.15)

b Very, very unlikely given the random nature of coin tosses.

c Estimated P(heads) = total no. heads ÷ 100 (expect 0.60 ± 0.05)

3 a Students' answers $\left(\text{fair coin } P = \frac{1}{4} - \frac{1}{2^{10}}\right)$

b Probability to increase with P(heads)
P$(\geqslant 3 \text{ heads}) = p^2 \left[1 - (1-p)^{n-2}\right]$

4 Students' answers
Distribution is skewed towards low numbers of heads; suggests coin is biased P(heads) < 0.5. (Estimate P(heads) $= \frac{117}{300} = 0.39$, actual 0.4; compare $\frac{140}{300} = 0.47$ for fair coin)

Investigation

Students' answers
Reliable results will require repeat simulations for the same value of P(heads). Expect the centre of the distribution to be at $10 \times$ P(heads), with an increasingly asymmetric distribution as P(heads) moves away from 0.5.

Consolidation   page 44

1 a RR, RG, RW, GR, GG, GW, WR, WG, WW

b 2

c 5

2 a

×	1	2	3	4	5	6
1	1	2	3	4	5	6
2	2	4	6	8	10	12
3	3	3	9	12	15	18
4	4	8	12	16	20	24
5	5	10	15	20	25	30
6	6	12	18	24	30	36

b $\frac{8}{36} = \frac{2}{9}$

3 $3 \times 4 \times 2 = 24$ menu choices

4 First   Second

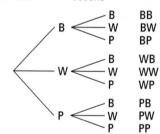

b i $\frac{2}{9}$ **ii** $\frac{3}{9} = \frac{1}{3}$

5 a Not mutually exclusive, (1,3) satisfies A and B.

b Not mutually exclusive, (1,2) satisfies B and D.

c Mutually exclusive, only (1,1) satisfies C and this is not in B.

6 a

	1	2	3	4	5	6	7	8
1	1,1	2,1	3,1	4,1	5,1	6,1	7,1	8,1
2	1,2	2,2	3,2	4,2	5,2	6,2	7,2	8,2
3	1,3	2,3	3,3	4,3	5,3	6,3	7,3	8,3
4	1,4	2,4	3,4	4,4	5,4	6,4	7,4	8,4

b i $\frac{8}{32} = \frac{1}{4}$ (Primes are 2, 3, 5 and 7 so there are 2 in every other row)

  ii $\frac{16}{32} = \frac{1}{2}$

c $1 - \left(\frac{1}{2} + \frac{1}{4}\right) = \frac{1}{4}$

7 a $\frac{4}{22} = \frac{2}{11}$

b By taking a larger sample on which to base the estimate.

8 a Count the relative frequency of the letter a amongst vowels in a typical piece of French text.

b Looking at the data (available on the internet) on how many times there has been a single jackpot. For a particular draw – once it is known whether it is a rollover, you could improve the estimates (in rollovers more people enter so the chance of a single winner is lower).

c You could run an experiment or a simulation a number of times. Or calculate: $6 \times 6 \times 6$ possibilities, $5 \times 5 \times 5$ contain a six, so $P = \frac{(216 - 125)}{216} = 1 - \left(\frac{5}{6}\right)^3 = \frac{91}{216}$.

9 No, if equal likely each first digit would occur ~11 times, whereas low digits occur more often.

10 a $P(1) = P(2) = P(3) = P(4) = \frac{1}{10}$, $P(5) = P(6) = \frac{3}{10}$

  Students' answers

  b Score 1 if tenths digit is 1, likewise 2, 3, 4; score 5 if 5, 6 or 7, score 6 if 8, 9 or 0

  c Expectation $\frac{129}{10}$

  d By taking more trials your estimate is more likely to be close to the true average.

Case study   page 46

1 Three sticks, scores 0, 1, 2 and 3

2 Four sticks, scores 0, 1, 2, 3 and 4

3 a Most likely score 2 ($P = \frac{6}{16}$)

  b Least likely scores 4, 6, 14, 15, 5, 10 ($P = \frac{1}{16}$)

  c Least likely scores all equally probable

4 a Five regular solids (tetrahedron, cube, octahedron, dodecahedron, icosahedron)

  b Yes

  c A fair die has equally probabilities of landing on the marked faces

  d Polygonal prisms

  e 8, 12 and 20 sided regular solids

  f It would be biased

Summary   page 48

2 Various possibilities, for example, 5 red, 10 white, 1 yellow, but white must be double red and P(red) > 0.25.

Chapter 4

Check in   page 49

1 a $1\frac{1}{2}$ **b** $\frac{39}{50}$ **c** $\frac{1}{8}$

2 a 0.7   **b** 1.35   **c** 0.52   **d** 0.875

3 a $\frac{13}{20}$ **b** $\frac{4}{21}$

4 a £65   **b** 350 kg

5 a $5\frac{5}{7}$ **b** 12

6

Fraction	Decimal	Percentage
$\frac{13}{20}$	0.65	65%
$\frac{1}{8}$	0.125	12.5%

Exercise 4a   page 51

1 a $\frac{2}{5}$ **b** $\frac{28}{25}$ **c** $\frac{9}{25}$

  d $\frac{49}{50}$ **e** $\frac{83}{500}$

2 a 0.3   **b** 1.15   **c** 0.76   **d** 1.26

  e 2.2   **f** 1.6   **g** 0.15   **h** 0.825

  i 0.875   **j** 1.0625

3 a 0.3125   **b** 0.09375   **c** 0.36364

  d 0.42857   **e** 2.83333

4 a <   **b** <   **c** >   **d** >

  e <   **f** >   **g** <   **h** >

5 a $0.425 < \frac{3}{7} < 0.43 < \frac{7}{16}$

  b $0.11 < \frac{1}{9} < 0.12 < \frac{1}{8}$

  c $\frac{4}{7} < \frac{571}{999} < \frac{19}{33} < 0.6$

6 a 0.5, 0.6, 0.7

  b 0.4, 0.5, 0.6, 0.7

7 a $0.\dot{1}\dot{8}$ **b** $0.\dot{2}\dot{7}$

  c $0.\dot{3}\dot{6}$ **d** $0.\dot{4}\dot{5}$

  e $0.\dot{5}\dot{4}$

Challenge

$\frac{13}{19}$

Exercise 4b   page 53

1 a $\frac{4}{7}$ **b** $\frac{1}{2}$ **c** $4\frac{1}{12}$ **d** $1\frac{2}{3}$

2 a $\frac{67}{72}$ **b** $1\frac{9}{77}$ **c** $\frac{27}{35}$ **d** $\frac{11}{195}$

  e $\frac{23}{255}$ **f** $\frac{305}{432}$ **g** $\frac{33}{208}$ **h** $\frac{43}{48}$

3 a $\frac{19}{30}$ **b** $1\frac{23}{60}$ **c** $\frac{29}{140}$ **d** $1\frac{17}{120}$

  e $\frac{47}{48}$ **f** $\frac{7}{32}$ **g** $1\frac{11}{60}$ **h** $\frac{53}{90}$

4 a i $\frac{37}{56}$ **ii** $\frac{19}{56}$

  b $1\frac{9}{16}$ kg

5 a $1\frac{7}{8}$ **b** $1\frac{7}{8}$ **c** $5\frac{1}{2}$ **d** $\frac{7}{10}$

  e $3\frac{55}{63}$ **f** $4\frac{4}{15}$ **g** $\frac{37}{40}$ **h** $3\frac{19}{21}$

6 a $16\frac{1}{6}$ inches   **b** $2\frac{19}{40}$ km

Investigation

a $2\frac{9}{16}$ kg   **b** $\frac{3}{4}$ kg and $\frac{3}{16}$ kg

c Students' answers

Exercise 4c   page 55

1 a $\frac{6}{7}$ **b** $\frac{4}{9}$ **c** $\frac{5}{8}$ **d** $\frac{9}{11}$

  e $\frac{5}{7}$ **f** $1\frac{7}{8}$ **g** $2\frac{2}{5}$ **h** $4\frac{3}{8}$

2 a 4   **b** $4\frac{1}{2}$ **c** $7\frac{1}{2}$ **d** $13\frac{3}{4}$

  e $5\frac{1}{4}$ **f** $7\frac{4}{5}$ **g** $22\frac{1}{2}$ **h** $2\frac{6}{7}$

3 a $3\frac{3}{4}$ feet   **b** 24

  c $5\frac{1}{3}$ inches   **d** $93\frac{1}{2}$ minutes

  e $35\frac{5}{8}$ GB   **f** 297 m

4 a $\frac{6}{35}$ **b** $\frac{5}{16}$ **c** $\frac{5}{12}$ **d** $\frac{1}{4}$

  e $\frac{1}{6}$ **f** $\frac{3}{8}$ **g** $\frac{4}{5}$ **h** $\frac{8}{35}$

5 a $34\frac{7}{8}$ inches^2 **b** $1\frac{23}{40}$ kg

6 i 250 g   **ii** $\frac{1}{4}$

7 a 6   **b** 10   **c** 15   **d** 21

  e $11\frac{1}{4}$ **f** $17\frac{1}{2}$ **g** $16\frac{1}{2}$ **h** $16\frac{1}{4}$

8 a $1\frac{1}{20}$ **b** $\frac{3}{4}$ **c** $1\frac{1}{6}$ **d** $\frac{49}{50}$

  e $2\frac{2}{15}$ **f** $\frac{2}{3}$ **g** $\frac{7}{16}$ **h** $\frac{2}{3}$

Challenge

$\frac{a}{b} \rightarrow \frac{b-a}{b+a} \rightarrow \frac{2a}{2b} = \frac{a}{b}$

Exercise 4d page 57

1 **a** £10.50 **b** 45 m **c** 45.24 kg **d** 84 ml

  e £61.38 **f** 29.75 GB **g** $26.10 **h** 98.01 m

  i 3.6 mm **j** 43.75 MB **k** 0.11 m **l** £1282.50

  m 147 km **n** 698.25 g **o** 0.66 tonnes **p** £50 000

2 Paying in instalments costs more (£317.70)

3 **a** £44.80 **b** £284.40 **c** 50.4 km **d** 30.6 mm

  e 147.5 kg **f** £2405 **g** £22.33 **h** 64.94 kJ

4 **a** 48.6 kg **b** £9.10 **c** 46 marks **d** £184.80

5 **a** 319 225 **b** 250 000

Problem solving

a 98.1 cm **b** 127.0 cm

c 213.1 cm

d No. His growth rate will increase at puberty and tail off to zero afterwards.

Exercise 4e page 59

1

Name	Old Wage	New Wage
James	300	312
Bernie	275	286
Vikki	500	520
Rufus	350	364

2 **a** £120 **b** £460 **c** 240 g

3 **a** £20 **b** 500 g

4 **a** £150 **b** £120 **c** £105

Investigation

a 6518.6 million **b** 5788.4 million

c Students' answers

Exercise 4f page 61

1

Fraction	Decimal	Percentage
$\frac{7}{40}$	0.175	17.5%
$\frac{7}{100}$	0.07	7%
$\frac{27}{20}$	1.35	135%
$\frac{7}{12}$	0.5833	58.33%
$\frac{19}{400}$	0.0475	4.75%

2 **a**

Engineering	37.5%	(P)
Maths	35%	(P)
Media	80.4%	(P)
German	36.7%	(P)
Art	34.3%	
Geography	34.7%	
Sports Studies	34%	

  b Sports Studies

  c Sports Studies, Art, Geography, Maths, German, Engineering, Media

3 **a** 15% **b** 3% **c** 5%

4 **a** 9%

  b Students' answers e.g. cracked pipes; ice floats

Investigation

Object	% increase/decrease
House	747.8% increase
Salary	228.6% increase
TV	50% decrease
Petrol	205.9% increase
Marz bars	181.3% increase
Milk	80% increase
Season ticket	582.8% increase
Music player	75% decrease

b Students' answers

c Students' answers e.g. inflation

Consolidation page 62

1 **a** 0.5625 **b** 0.29412 **c** 0.23077

  d 0.85714 **e** 0.57895

2 **a** < **b** < **c** > **d** >

3 **a** $\frac{8}{13} < 0.623 < \frac{5}{8} < 0.63$

  b $0.229 < 0.23 < \frac{3}{13} < \frac{4}{17}$

4 **a** $\frac{37}{90}$ **b** $1\frac{23}{75}$ **c** $1\frac{13}{54}$ **d** $\frac{5}{6}$

  e $1\frac{13}{80}$ **f** $\frac{71}{140}$ **g** $\frac{83}{108}$ **h** $\frac{3}{4}$

5 $3\frac{1}{10}$ litres

6 **a** $2\frac{8}{15}$ **b** $\frac{5}{8}$ **c** $5\frac{1}{15}$ **d** $\frac{17}{24}$

7 **a** $3\frac{3}{4}$ yards **b** 25 kg **c** 7.5 mm

  d 12 km **e** $52\frac{1}{2}$ miles **f** 775 m²

  g $481\frac{2}{3}$ ml **h** 332 years

8 **a** $\frac{20}{21}$ **b** $\frac{3}{20}$ **c** $\frac{2}{3}$ **d** $\frac{21}{32}$

  e $\frac{8}{25}$ **f** $\frac{12}{49}$ **g** 3 **h** 1

9 **a** 7 **b** 9 **c** 18 **d** 14

  e $6\frac{3}{5}$ **f** 8 **g** $16\frac{1}{2}$ **h** 26

10 **a** $\frac{32}{35}$ **b** $\frac{7}{9}$ **c** $\frac{32}{33}$ **d** $1\frac{1}{13}$

  e $1\frac{7}{8}$ **f** $1\frac{1}{2}$ **g** $\frac{5}{8}$ **h** $1\frac{1}{4}$

11 **a** £64 **b** £352 **c** 190.8 km

  d 260.55 mm **e** 91.8 kg **f** £8 892 000

12 **a** £36.40 **b** £10.62

13 **a** £550 **b** £16 700

14 **a** £80 **b** 320 g

15

Fraction	Decimal	Percentage
$\frac{7}{15}$	0.4667	46.67%
$\frac{199}{200}$	0.995	99.5%
$\frac{1}{8}$	0.125	12.5%
$\frac{4}{13}$	0.3077	30.77%
$1\frac{377}{10000}$	1.0377	103.77%

16 **a** 12% **b** 5%

Summary   page 64

2 a $1\frac{4}{5}$

b 20

c 4 with correct working

Chapter 5

Check in   page 65

1 a -5 **b** -3 **c** 10 **d** -9
e -20 **f** -7 **g** 42 **h** 6

2 a 10 **b** 8 **c** 17 **d** 16
e 10 **f** 12 **g** 25 **h** 4

3 a $2x$ **b** $3y$ **c** $3a$ **d** $2b$
e $5p + q$ **f** $8k - 3$ **g** $5x + y$ **h** $4m - 3n$

Exercise 5a   page 67

1 a 9 **b** 64 **c** 100 000 **d** 1
e 0 **f** 1 **g** -1 **h** 81

2 a $\frac{1}{16}$ **b** $\frac{1}{36}$ **c** $\frac{1}{125}$ **d** 1
e 32 **f** 27 **g** $\frac{81}{16}$ **h** $\frac{81}{16}$

3 a True **b** False, $x^3 = x \times x \times x$ **c** True
d True **e** True
f False, $y - 4 = -4 + y$ **g** True
h False, $(3b)^2 = 9b^2$ **i** False, $-n \times -n = n^3$

4 $a^3 = -27 < 4a = -12 < a^{-2} = \frac{1}{9} < a^0 = 1 < 2a^2$
    $= 18 < (2a)^2 = 36$

5 a 128 **b** -125 **c** 40 **d** 64
e 31 **f** 21 **g** -20 **h** 81

6 a 144 cubic units **b** 1152 cubic units
c $42\frac{2}{3}$ cubic units **d** $341\frac{1}{3}$ cubic units

Investigation

a 2^6 **b** 3^8 **c** 4^{15}
    Rule is $(2^m)^n = 2^{m \times n}$

Exercise 5b   page 69

1 a

Can be simplified	Cannot be simplified
$p^2 + p^2 = 2p^2$	$4x + 1$
$3g \times 8h = 24gh$	$5a^2 - 2a$
$6m - 3m + n =$ $3m + n$	$\frac{2k + k^2}{2}$
$\frac{14b}{7} = 2b$	
$ab + 3ba = 4ab$	

2 a $3x$ **b** $12m$

c $7t$ **d** a^2
e $3p^2 + 9p$ **f** $7k + 3 - 2k^2$
g $5ab + 6bc - 1$ **h** $g^3 + 5p^2 - 2p$
i $x^2 + 2x + 3$

3 $4 \times a \times a$ pairs with $4a^2$
$4a^2b^2$ pairs with $2ab \times 2ba$
$4a \times 2$ pairs with $8a$
$8ab$ pairs with $2a \times 4b$

4 a $\frac{x}{3}$ **b** $4a$ **c** p **d** 4
e $5g$ **f** $5b$ **g** $5pq$ **h** $3n$
i $a + 2$ **j** $3 - k$

5 a $8a^3$ **b** $30p^2q$

Puzzle

a   **b**

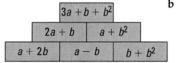

Exercise 5c   page 71

1 a $3x + 12$ **b** $8f - 4$ **c** $t^2 + 9t$ **d** $mn - 7m$
e $10p - pq$ **f** $3a^2 + 3ab$ **g** $-32 + 16y$ **h** $-x^2 + 10$

2 a $5(3x - 4) = 15x - 20$
b $p(2p + q) = 2p^2 + pq$

3 a $7x + 23$ **b** $11p + 19$ **c** $21a - 6$ **d** $t + 6$
e $2k + 17$ **f** $y - 8$ **g** $2m + 19$ **h** $4n$

4 $6(k - 1) + k(k + 5) = k^2 + 11k - 6$

5 $p^3 + p^2$

6 $x(x + 1) + 2(x - 5)$ pairs with $x(x + 5) - 2(x + 5)$
$2x(x - 2) + 3(2 - x)$ pairs with $5x(x + 1) -$
$3x(x + 4) + 6$
$3(x + 2) - 2x(2 - x)$ is the odd one out.

Challenge

a x **b** 4 **c** 2
d k and 3 **e** 3 and 5 **f** 5 and $3a$

Exercise 5d   page 73

1 a 2 **b** 3 **c** 6 **d** 5
e $3x$ **f** 4 **g** $6p$ **h** $2t$

2 a $3(x + 2)$ **b** $4(a - 3)$ **c** $3(4b - 5)$ **d** $5(2k + 3)$
e $2(8 - 3p)$ **f** $7(1 - t)$ **g** $m(n + 2)$ **h** $2(4a - b)$
i $5pq + 2$ **j** $6x(y - 3)$

3 a Mum's age $= 4(a - 3)$
b $4a - 12 = 4(a - 3)$
c 44

4 a Factor should be $3x$
b Factor should be $2a$
c Factor should be $8k$
d Second term in bracket is $15t \div 3t = 5$
e Need to leave a 1 as the first term
f Second term in bracket is $10x^2 \div 5x = 2x$

5 $x = 3$

$x = (32 - 20) \div 4 = 32 \div 4 - 5$

Challenge

a $5(x + 2)$ **b** $3(x - 2)$

c $5(x + 2) - 3(x - 2) = 2x + 16 = 2(x + 8)$
which is always even.

Exercise 5e   page 75

1 a 28   **b** 48   **c** 86   **d** 25

2 Route B $(14 < 16\,\text{km})$

3 a 15   **b** 5050

4 a i $C = 20h + 35$ where $C =$ total cost and $h =$ hours worked

  ii $C = 15h + 50$ where $C =$ total cost and $h =$ hours worked

  b i Mike ($75 < 80$)

  ii Phil ($125 < 135$)

  c 3

5 a The $4l$ part gives the number of red squares that touch the inside square edge to edge.
The $+ 4$ part adds on the four red squares in the corners.

  b 44

Task

a Perimeter of a square

b Speed given distance and time

c Temp in °F given °C

d Distance travelled given constant acceleration, initial velocity and time

Exercise 5f   page 77

1 a $x = a - b$ **b** $x = y + t$ **c** $x = q + r - p$

  d $x = p - y - z$ **e** $x = 3y$ **f** $x = m^2 + n$

  g $x = c - ab$ **h** $x = pq$

2 a Twice the length of one of the equal sides, a, plus the base, b.

  b $b = P - 2a$

  c 9

3 a $y = \dfrac{z}{x}$ **b** $y = \dfrac{q + r}{p}$ **c** $y = \dfrac{a + c}{b}$

  d $y = \dfrac{a - r}{x}$ **e** $y = \dfrac{p - 2m}{n}$ **f** $y = \dfrac{f}{d}$

  g $y = \dfrac{p}{xz}$ **h** $y = \dfrac{m + n}{kl}$

4 $a = bx + by,\ a - bx = by,\ \dfrac{a - bx}{b} = y$

5 a Perimeter, P, is equal to twice the length, l, plus twice the width, w.

  b $w = \dfrac{P - 2l}{2}$

  c 5

  d $P = 8a$ where width $= a$

6 a $x = P - y - z$ **b** $l = \dfrac{P}{4}$ **c** $l = \dfrac{A}{w}$

  d $b = \dfrac{P - 2a}{2}$ **e** $r = \dfrac{C}{2\pi}$ **f** $m = \dfrac{y - c}{x}$

  g $t = \dfrac{v - u}{a}$ **h** $a = 2m - b$

Challenge

a i $x = a - b$ **ii** $x = \dfrac{p - r}{q}$

b Student's answers

Consolidation   page 78

1 a 25   **b** 81   **c** 256   **d** 1

  e $\dfrac{1}{64}$ **f** $\dfrac{1}{64}$ **g** 128   **h** $\dfrac{16}{9}$

2 a 9   **b** -8   **c** 54   **d** 24

  e 16   **f** 25   **g** 12   **h** 25

3 a $9x$ **b** $8a^2$ **c** $5m + 4n$

  d $4p^2 - 3p + 8$ **e** $7ab$ **f** $2g^2 - g^3$

4 a $4x$ **b** 3   **c** $3p$ **d** $\dfrac{5}{3}k$

  e $\dfrac{3}{2}gh$ **f** $b + 4$

5 $x(x + 5) = x^2 + 5x$

6 a $8a + 22$ **b** $24x - 3$ **c** $5p + 16$

  d $7b - 12$ **e** $2m + 25$ **f** $4n - 2$

  g $x^2 + 7x - 8$ **h** $y^2 - 2y$

7 a $2(x + 2)$ **b** $5(y + 4)$ **c** $2(3g - 1)$

  d $4(2t - 3)$ **e** $3(6 - 5k)$ **f** $5(2p + 3q)$

  g $a(7 + b)$ **h** $3n(5m - 3)$

8 a $n + (n + 1) + (n + 2) = 3n + 3$

  b $3n + 3 = 3(n + 1)$

9 a £14

  b $C = 3.5n$

  c $C = 2.5n + 10$

  d As a non-member cost is £42. As a member cost is £40. Just worth it!

10 a $r = 2w + 6$

  b Twice the white tiles gives the tiles directly above and below and plus 6 gives the left and right ends.

  c 206

11 a $x = p - r$ **b** $x = a + b + c$

  c $x = z - 3y$ **d** $x = 2p$

  e $x = a + a^2$ **f** $x = p + 2mn$

12 a $y = \dfrac{m}{n}$ **b** $y = \dfrac{a}{b^2}$

  c $y = \dfrac{p + 3}{q}$ **d** $y = \dfrac{g - h}{f}$

  e $y = \dfrac{x}{ab}$ **f** $y = \dfrac{r}{\pi + 2}$

Summary   page 80

2 $2n + 4, n + 2, n$

Chapter 6

Check in   page 81

1 a 45°, acute **b** 115°, obtuse **c** 295°, reflex

2 a $a = 36°$ **b** $b = 18°$ **c** $c = 24°$

Exercise 6a   page 83

1 a $a = 146°$ **b** $b = 28°$

  c $c = 57°, d = 123°, e = 57°$

2 a $a = 64°$ (corr.), $b = 64°$ (vert. opp.)

  b $b = 110°$ (corr.), $c = 110°$ (vert. opp.), $d = 110°$ (vert. opp.)

c $c = 35°$ (alt.), $d = 35°$ (vert. opp.), $e = 145°$ (ang. on st. line)

d $d = 108°$ (corr.), $e = 108°$ (corr.), $f = 108°$ (alt.)

e $e = 100°$ (alt.), $f = 105°$ (alt.), $g = 80°$ (ang. on st. line), $h = 75°$ (ang. on st. line)

f $f = 80°$ (alt.), $g = 75°$ (alt.), $h = 105°$ (ang. on st. line), $i = 100°$ (ang. on st. line)

3 a $a = 50°$, $b = 60°$, $c = 70°$

b $a = 56°$, $b = 72°$, $c = 52°$

Investigation

a $a = 40°$, $b = 60°$

b $c = 80°$

c $180°$

d $180°$

e Angles in a triangle add to $180°$

Exercise 6b   page 85

1 a $60°$, equilateral

b $33°$, isosceles

c $90°$, right-angled

2 Isosceles trapezium, rectangle, kite, rhombus, trapezium, arrowhead

3 a $135°$, isosceles trapezium, rhombus, parallelogram

b $125°$, kite

c $255°$, arrowhead

4 a Square, rectangle, rhombus, parallelogram, isosceles trapezium

b Square, rhombus, kite

c Square, rectangle, isosceles trapezium

d Square

e Rectangle, isosceles trapezium

5 a Rhombus

b 4 equal sides, opposite angles are equal ($60°$ and $120°$), opposite sides are parallel.

6 a $b = 36°$ **b** $a = 122°$ **c** $c = 65°$

Challenge

6 cm (draw the other diagonal)

Exercise 6c   page 87

1 a   **b**

c   **d**

2 a Students' drawings

b

name	no. triangles	sum int. angles
pentagon	3	$3 \times 180° = 540°$
hexagon	4	$4 \times 180° = 720°$
heptagon	5	$5 \times 180° = 900°$
octagon	6	$6 \times 180° = 1080°$
nonagon	7	$7 \times 180° = 1260°$
decagon	8	$8 \times 180° = 1440°$

3 a $120°$, $60°$ **b** $60°$, $120°$ **c** $40°$, $140°$

d $36°$, $144°$ **e** $20°$, $160°$ **f** $15°$, $165°$

4 a $72°$ **b** $108°$ **c** $36°$, $36°$, $144°$, $144°$

Activity

a    **b** $120°$ **c** $120°$

Exercise 6d   page 89

1 a The non-E shape   **b** The rhombus

c The + shape   **d** The large circle

2 a B, C, D, G, I   **b** A, E, H   **c** F

3 A = $36°$, B = $144°$, C = $36°$, D = $144°$

4 a AB = 15 cm   **b** AC = 17 cm

c BC = 8 cm

Challenge

Exercise 6e   page 91

1 a A tetrahedron, B triangular prism, C cube, D pentagonal pyramid, E cuboid

b i 4, 5, 6, 6, 6 faces

ii 4, 6, 8, 6, 8 vertices

iii 6, 9, 12, 10, 12 edges

2 a 10 faces   **b** 16 vertices   **c** 24 edges

3 a square-based pyramid or triangular prism

b 5 vertices, 8 edges or 6 vertices, 9 edges

4 a 1 edge   **b** 4 edges   **c** 1 edge

5 a rectangle   **b** Yes. Cut one corner off.

Challenge

a i 8 faces   **ii** 6 vertices   **iii** 12 edges

b various answers e.g.

Exercise 6f   page 93

1 a

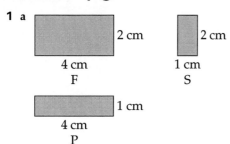

b

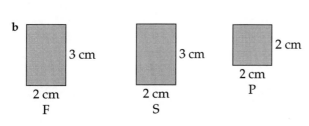

c

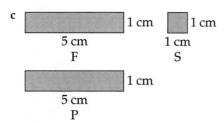

2 a

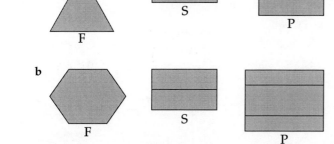

b

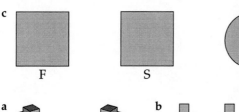

c

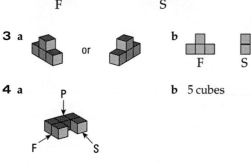

3 a 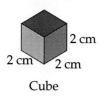 or   **b**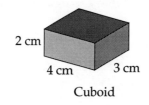

4 a   **b** 5 cubes

Puzzle

cube; cuboid

Cube   Cuboid

Consolidation   page 94

1 a $a = 118°$ Angles at a point add to 360°.
 b $b = 46°$ Angles on a straight line add to 180°.
 c $c = 132°$ Corresponding angles are equal.
  $d = 48°$ Angles on a straight line add to 180°.
  $e = 48°$ Various.
  $f = 132°$ Vertically opposite angles are equal.

2 a $a = 50°$ **b** $b = 60°$ **c** $a + b = 110°$

3 a $a = 88°$ Angle sum of a quadrilateral is 360°.
 b $b = 53°$ Isosceles trapezium.
  $c = 127°,\ d = 127°$ Angle sum of a quadrilateral and
          isosceles trapezium angle properties.
 c $c = 113°$ Opposite angles of a parallelogram are equal
  $d = 67°,\ e = 67°$ Angle sum of a quadrilateral and
          parallelogram angle properties.

4 a

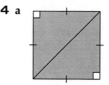

4 equal sides and
2 right angles,
45° + 45° = 90°. Must be
a square.

b

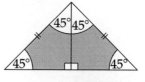

2 equal sides and 45° + 45° =
90°. Must be a right-angled
isosceles triangle.

c

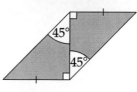

45° + 90° = 135° for both
opposite angles. Two sets
of equal sides. Must be a
parallelogram.

5 a $a = 45°, b = 67.5°, c = 67.5°$
 b $b = 72°, c = 54°, d = 54°$

6 a Students' drawings
 b

Name	No. sides	No. diagonals
triangle	3	0
quadrilateral	4	2
pentagon	5	5
hexagon	6	9
heptagon	7	14
octagon	8	20
	n	$n(n - 3)/2$

7 a   **b**

8

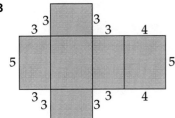

9 A and B

10 a

 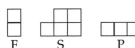

F S P

b

 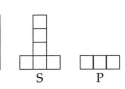

F S P

c

F S P

d

F S P

Summary   page 96

2 $a = 110°$, $b = 130°$, $c = 50°$, $d = 70°$

Chapter 7

Check in   page 97

1 a $x = 5$ **b** $y = 4$ **c** $p = 6$ **d** $k = 3$

2 a $2a + 10$ **b** $3b - 30$ **c** $x^2 + 2x$ **d** $ab - 3a$

e $3t^2 - 3t$ **f** $6pq + 8p$ **g** $9k + 2$ **h** $7n + 12$

3 a

x	0	2	3
y	1	3	4

b The y-coordinate is equal to the x-coordinate $+ 1$.

c $y = x + 1$

Exercise 7a   page 99

1 a $x = 3$ **b** $z = 4$ **c** $n = 5$ **d** $p = 3$

e $t = 0$ **f** $h = 3$ **g** $k = \frac{1}{2}$ **h** $y = -1$

2 $3(x + 5) = 21$ pairs with $\frac{5x + 4}{7} = 2$

$\frac{x}{2} + 9 = 8$ pairs with $\frac{2x + 7}{3} = 1$

$12 = 4(x - 3)$ pairs with $\frac{x}{3} + 5 = 7$

The odd one out is $2(10 + x) = 8$

3 a The number is 5   **b** $x = 3$

c $x = 35$. The angles are $35°$, $65°$ and $80°$.

4 a $x = 2$ **b** $a = 4$ **c** $p = 6$

d $k = 1$ **e** $y = 5$ **f** $n = 7$

5 a $x = 5$ **b** $q = 5$ **c** $a = 2$

d $b = 4$ **e** $m = \frac{1}{2}$ **f** $n = -4$

6 a $5n + 4 = 3n + 14$, $n = 5$

b $x = 6$ and the sides are 22, 22, 16

$x = 3$ and the sides are 13, 7, 13

$x = 4.5$ and the sides are 17.5, 14.5, 14.5

Puzzle

$x + (x + 2) + (x + 4) = 3x + 6 = 48$ hence $x = 14$

Exercise 7b   page 101

1 a $x = 7$ **b** $a = -2$ **c** $n = 1$ **d** $m = 4$

e $t = 5$ **f** $p = 2$ **g** $k = 0.5$ **h** $y = -1$

i $b = -2$ **j** $d = 2.5$

2 The solution is $x = 3$ for all.

3 a $x = 2$ **b** $t = 1$ **c** $p = 2$ **d** $k = 3$

e $n = 0$ **f** $a = 6$ **g** $b = 5$ **h** $m = 2$

i $y = 4$ **j** $d = 3$ **k** $q = \frac{1}{8}$ **l** $x = -1$

4 a $2n + 4 = 19 - n$, $n = 5$

b $10 - 2n = 4n - 8$, $n = 3$

5 The length is 32 ($x = 6$)

6 The length is 6 ($x = 2$)

Investigation

$x = \pm 4$

a $x = \pm 2$ **b** $x = \pm 5$ **c** $x = \pm 10$

d $x = \pm 3$ **e** $x = \pm 8$

Quadratic equation

Exercise 7c   page 103

Mapping diagrams to appear as in exercise

1 a

x	1	2	3	4	5
y	5	10	15	20	25

b

x	1	2	3	4	5
y	5	7	9	11	13

c

x	1	2	3	4	5
y	0	3	6	9	12

d

x	1	2	3	4	5
y	4	3	2	1	0

2

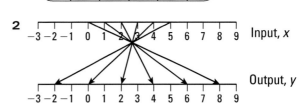

Input, x

Output, y

3 a $y = x + 4$ **b** $y = 5x$ **c** $y = 2x + 5$

4 a, b

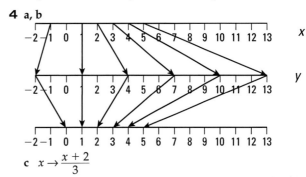

x

y

c $x \rightarrow \dfrac{x + 2}{3}$

5 a $x \to \dfrac{x}{10}$

b $x \to x - 6$

c $x \to \dfrac{x-1}{2}$

d $x \to \dfrac{x+4}{7}$

e $x \to \dfrac{x}{4} + 1$

f $x \to 3x - 5$

Investigation

a

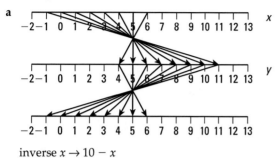

inverse $x \to 10 - x$

b

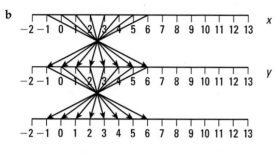

inverse $x \to 5 - x$

c

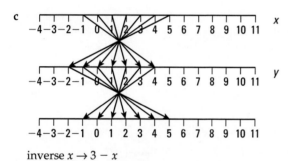

inverse $x \to 3 - x$

All these functions are self-inversing.

Inverse of $x \to x + c$ is $x \to x - c$.

Exercise 7d　page 105

1 a Vertical line
　b Sloping line

　c Sloping line
　d Horizontal line

　e Not a straight line
　f Sloping line

　g Vertical line
　h Sloping line

2 a

x	0	1	2
y	3	1	-1

b

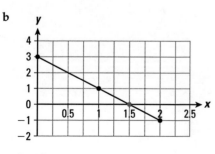

c $\left(1\tfrac{1}{2}, 0\right)$

3 a

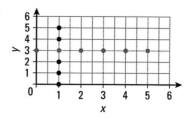

b i $(2, 4)$　**ii** $(3, -1)$　**iii** $\left(\tfrac{1}{2}, 1\right)$

4

Line	$y = x + 3$	$x + y = 7$	$y = 3x$	$y = 2x - 1$	$y = \tfrac{3}{2}x + 2$
✓ or ✗	✓	✓	✗	✗	✓

5 a i

x	0	1	2
y	-1	1	3

ii

x	0	1	2
y	0	2	4

iii

x	0	1	2
y	1	3	5

iv

x	0	1	2
y	2	4	6

b

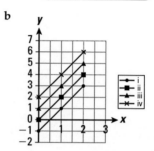

c The graphs are all parallel.

All graphs have the same slope and the y-intercept for each graph is given by the '$+ c$' part of the equation.

d i

x	0	1	2
y	1	$1\tfrac{1}{2}$	2

ii

x	0	1	2
y	1	2	3

iii

x	0	1	2
y	1	3	5

iv

x	0	1	2
y	1	4	7

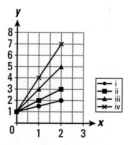

The graphs all have different slopes.

The y-intercept for each graph is given by the '$+ c$' part of the equation.

For each graph it is '$+1$' and all the graphs cut at $(0, 1)$.

Challenge

$y = x$ pairs with $y = x + 2$

$y = 2x + 1$ pairs with $y = 2(x + 1)$

The odd equation out is $y = \dfrac{x + 1}{2}$

An equation that pairs with the odd equation out is of the form

$y = \dfrac{1}{2}x + c$ where c is a number.

Exercise 7e   page 107

1

Equation	Gradient	Coordinate of y-intercept
$y = 3x + 2$	3	(0, 2)
$y = 4x - 1$	4	(0, -1)
$y = 2x$	2	(0, 0)
$y = \frac{1}{4}x + 3$	$\frac{1}{4}$	(0, 3)
$y = \frac{1}{2}x - 5$	$\frac{1}{2}$	(0, -5)
$y = 3(x + 2)$	3	(0, 6)
$y = 4 - \frac{3}{2}x$	$-\frac{3}{2}$	(0, 4)
$y = 10 - x$	-1	(0, 10)

2 a $y = 2x + 1$ **b** $y = x - 4$

c $y = \dfrac{1}{2} - 3x$

3 a $y = 5$ **b** $y = 2x$

c $x + y = 5$ **d** $y = 3x + 2$

4 a $y = 4$ **b** $y = x + 2$ **c** $y = 3x - 1$

5 a, c

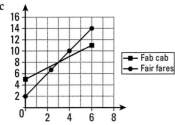

b $y = 2x + 2$ so company charges £2 per mile and puts £2 on the meter at the start of the journey.

c If the mileage is less than 3, use Fab Cabs.

If the mileage is more than 3, use Fair Fares.

If the mileage is equal to 3, choose either taxi company.

Challenge

Equation	Gradient	Coordinate of y-intercept
$y = 10 - x$	-1	(0, 10)
$y = \frac{1}{2}x + 2$	$\frac{1}{2}$	(0, 2)
$y = \frac{4}{3}x - 1$	$\frac{4}{3}$	(0, -1)
$y = 3 - \frac{1}{2}x$	$-\frac{1}{2}$	(0, 3)
$y = \frac{3}{4} - \frac{1}{2}x$	$-\frac{1}{2}$	$(0, \frac{3}{4})$

Exercise 7e²   page 107²

1 a Linear   **b** Linear   **c** Linear   **d** Quadratic

e Quadratic **f** Linear   **g** Linear   **h** Quadratic

2 a

x	-3	-2	-1	0	1	2	3
x^2	9	4	1	0	1	4	9
+2	2	2	2	2	2	2	2
y	11	6	3	2	3	6	11

b

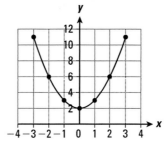

c (0, 2)   **d** (0, 2)

3 a

x	-2	-1	0	1	2	3	4
x^2	4	1	0	1	4	9	16
-2x	4	2	0	-2	-4	-6	-8
y	8	3	0	-1	0	3	8

b

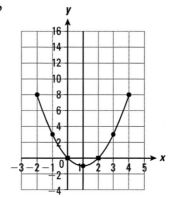

c (0, 0) and (2, 0)   **d** $x = 1$

Investigation

a

x	-3	-2	-1	0	1	2	3
x^3	-27	-8	-1	0	1	8	27
-4x	12	8	4	0	-4	-8	-12
y	-15	0	3	0	-3	0	15

b

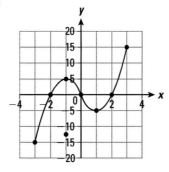

c (0, 0)

Exercise 7f   page 109

1 a (3, 5)   **b** (4, -3)   **c** (0, 0)

d (-4, -5)   **e** $\left(-1\frac{1}{2}, 4\frac{1}{2}\right)$ **f** (4.2, 1.05)

2 a (4, 6)   **b** (7, 5)   **c** (-4, 4)

d (-3, -3)   **e** (-1, 0)   **f** (-9.1, 3.7)

3 a Parallelogram, $M_{AB} = (2\frac{1}{2}, 2) = M_{CD}$, diagonals bisect one another

b Rhombus, $M_{AB} = (-3, -1) = M_{CD}$, diagonals bisect one another

c Isosceles trapezium, $M_{AB} = (3\frac{1}{2}, -\frac{1}{2})$ $M_{CD} = (3\frac{1}{2}, -3\frac{1}{2})$, the lines do not bisect one another but they lie on a line parallel to the edges of the trapezium.

4 a M(1,0)　　**b** M($1\frac{1}{2}$, 4)　　**c** M(3,0)　　**d** M$\left(\frac{1}{2}, 3\frac{3}{4}\right)$

Challenge

a (1, 0)　　**b** (0, 4)　　**c** (3, 4)

d (-3, -1)　　**e** (-2, -$3\frac{1}{3}$)　　**f** (1, 1.6)

Consolidation　page 110

1 a $x = 5$　　**b** $y = 4$　　**c** $a = 4$　　**d** $b = 1$

e $p = 4$　　**f** $q = \frac{1}{2}$　　**g** $k = -2$　　**h** $t = 12$

2 a $3x + 2 = 8(x - 1)$, $x = 2$ so the length of the rectangle is 8

b $10(k - 2) = 6k$, $k = 5$ so the rectangle has length = 10 and width = 3 and the triangle has base = 12 and height = 5

3 a $x = 3$　　**b** $y = 5$　　**c** $m = 2$　　**d** $n = 3$

e $d = \frac{1}{3}$　　**f** $f = -1$　　**g** $k = 1\frac{1}{2}$　　**h** $t = 1\frac{2}{3}$

4 a $x = 1$　　**b** $k = 2$　　**c** $p = 2$　　**d** $t = 3$

e $a = 8$　　**f** $b = 2$　　**g** $y = 2$　　**h** $g = 2$

5 a i

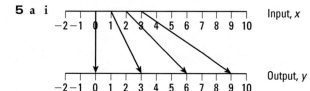

ii

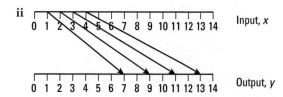

b i $y = 3x$　　　　**ii** $y = 2x + 5$

6 a $x \rightarrow x - 3$　　　　**b** $x \rightarrow \frac{x}{5}$

c $x \rightarrow \dfrac{x + 2}{4}$　　　　**d** $x \rightarrow 6x - 1$

7 a

x	0	1	2
$2x$	0	2	4
$+1$	1	1	1
y	1	3	5

b, c

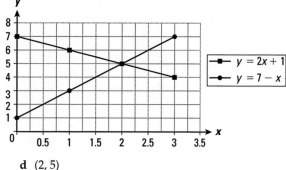

d (2, 5)

8 False, intersect at (2, -3)

9

Equation	Gradient	Coordinate of y-intercept
$y = 2x + 1$	2	(0, 1)
$y = 3x - 2$	3	(0, -2)
$y = \frac{1}{2}x + 5$	$\frac{1}{2}$	(0, 5)
$y = 8x$	8	(0, 0)
$y = x - 2$	1	(0, -2)
$y = 4 - 3x$	-3	(0, 4)
$y = 1 - \frac{1}{3}x$	$-\frac{1}{3}$	(0, 1)
$y = 3(2 - x)$	-3	(0, 6)

10 a $x = -1$　　　　**b** $y = x$

c $y = 2x + 2$　　　　**d** $x + y = 5$

11 True, $y = 1^2 + 5 \times 1 + 6 = 12$

12 a

x	-2	-1	0	1	2	3
x^2	4	1	0	1	4	9
$-x$	2	1	0	-1	-2	-3
y	6	2	0	0	2	6

b

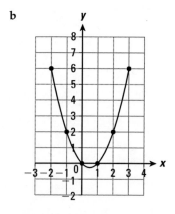

c (0, 0) and (1, 0)　　　　**d** $x = \frac{1}{2}$

13 a M(5, 3)　　**b** M(1, 5)　　**c** M(3, 2)

d M(-3, -$\frac{1}{2}$)　　**e** B(2, 3)　　**f** B(-2, 0)

Summary　page 112

2 a Any straight line parallel to the given line

b (0, 20)　　　　**c** $y = 5x + 10$

Chapter 8

Check in　page 113

1 a i 6　　　　**ii** 6.1

b i 16　　　　**ii** 15.5

c i 217　　　　**ii** 217.4

2 a 12.1　　**b** 8.41　　**c** 38.16　　**d** 3.81

3 a 120　　**b** 3.8　　**c** 0.037　　**d** 480

4 a 58.8　　**b** 1645.8

5 a 18.6　　**b** 7.7

6 a 28　　**b** 17　　　　**c** 104

Exercise 8a　page 115

1 i　　　　　　　**ii**　　　　　　　**iii**

a 12 000　　　　12 100　　　　12 090

b 2000   2400   2400
c 1000   900   890
d 8000   8500   8500
e 23000   23500   23460
f 1000   700   700
g 3000   3000   2990
h 1436000   1436400   1436380

2   **i**   **ii**   **iii**   **iv**

	i	ii	iii	iv
a	5	5.0	5.05	5.047
b	3	3.5	3.45	3.454
c	18	17.5	17.52	17.517
d	3	3.0	3.05	3.049
e	13	13.0	13.01	13.009
f	130	130.3	130.25	130.254
g	0	0.0	0.03	0.003
h	8	7.9	7.90	7.90

3 **i**   length 3.75 mm   width 1.255 mm

   ii   length 3.85 (or   width 1.265 (or
     3.8499...) mm   1.26499...) mm

4 a Students' answers, e.g. $1.5 \times 70 + 1.4 \times 80 = 217$ m

   b Students' answers, e.g. $430000 \div 25 = 17200$ lengths;
     $17200 \times 50 = 860000$ s = 14333 min = 239 hours

Challenge

Students' answers, but essentially that Kevin has rounded his measurements so $3.4 \times 2.3 = 7.82$ m², which makes his piece look big enough; but when we take the max possible size of Kevin's room it is $3.45 \times 2.35 = 8.1075$ m², which means his piece is too small.

Exercise 8b   page 117

1 a 21.3   **b** 13.68   **c** 16.75
   d 11.28   **e** 11.81   **f** 3.83

2 a 1.27   **b** 13.15   **c** 5.97   **d** 47.01

3 a 568.6   **b** 622.42   **c** 776.15
   d 691.6   **e** 286.53   **f** 221.06

4 a 538.02   **b** 220.17   **c** 542.748   **d** 1371.45
   e 110.1   **f** 152.83   **g** 346.99   **h** 576.8

5 a 3489.1655 g
   b **i** 1108.8365 kg   **ii** Students' answers

Challenge

a 8.935 kg   **b** 3.35 km   **c** 0.072 litres = 72 ml
d 3.372625 tonnes   **e** 3.100346 km

Exercise 8c   page 119

1 a 2.6   **b** 3380   **c** 0.47   **d** 53
   e 2850   **f** 82   **g** 2.54   **h** 0.038

2 a 2800   **b** 3000   **c** 2.75   **d** 4.170
   e 8300   **f** 420   **g** 3.77   **h** 2.51
   i 320   **j** 1070   **k** 0.041   **l** 3.8

3 a 2.9   **b** 0.38   **c** 0.51   **d** 0.032
   e 360   **f** 92   **g** 6500   **h** 51
   i 31.7   **j** 29.9   **k** 0.0815   **l** 0.00602

4 a 10^2 **b** 10^{-2} **c** 10^2
   d 10^{-2} **e** 10^{-3} **f** 10^{-1}

5 a 3300   **b** 24000   **c** 47000
   d 630000   **e** 27000000   **f** 0.0047
   g 0.000029   **h** 1010000000

6 a 2322.6   **b** 2.3226   **c** 232.26
   d Students' answers   **e** Students' answers

Investigation

a Students' answers: it always works

b Students' answers: move the digits to the rights, equivalent to moving a negative number of places to the left

Exercise 8d   page 121

1 a 1204   **b** 4836   **c** 29666   **d** 23886
   e 12780   **f** 13604   **g** 71104   **h** 78144

2 a 121.8   **b** 0.48   **c** 10.23   **d** 347.9
   e 142.6   **f** 66.7   **g** 3.75   **h** 0.91

3 a 46.62   **b** 27.44   **c** 124.2   **d** 158.4
   e 7.28   **f** 25.2   **g** 2269.8   **h** 265.74
   i 109.15   **j** 440.91   **k** 129.08   **l** 113.24
   m 16.932   **n** 5.705   **o** 15.675   **p** 36.27

4 a £53.65   **b** £36.96
   c **i** £45.14   **ii** 743.28 km
   d **i** £9.60   **ii** £499.41

Investigation

a $\left(\frac{19}{2}\right)^2 = 90.25$ **b** $\left(\frac{19}{3}\right)^3 = 254.04$ (2 dps)

c Students' answers; largest value for equal divisions.

Exercise 8e   page 123

1 a 14   **b** 15   **c** 13   **d** 21
   e 22   **f** 45   **g** 52   **h** 33

2 a 17 r 2   **b** 19 r 7   **c** 11   **d** 23
   e 18 r 9   **f** 23 r 3   **g** 29 r 1   **h** 56 r 8

3 a 7.6   **b** 7.6   **c** 9.8   **d** 4.6
   e 3.9   **f** 5.1   **g** 1.6   **h** 13.1
   i 19.2   **j** 18.9   **k** 2.6   **l** 2.8

4 a 131.9   **b** 163.6   **c** 376.8   **d** 163.7
   e 145.4   **f** 250   **g** 140   **h** 355.5

5 a 10.20 m/s   **b** 233 packs, remainder 0.5 kg

Investigation

a **i** 0.57   **ii** 5.7   **iii** 570

b Students' answers

Exercise 8f   page 125

1 a Students' answers: yes, she must try 8.665 to decide between 8.66 and 8.67

   b 8.66   **c** 8.660

2 a 5.48   **b** 8.37   **c** 12.04
   d 13.42   **e** 15.81   **f** 24.49

3 a 3.4   **b** 5.8   **c** 4.1
   d 2.4   **e** 12.6

Investigation

a 7.745967742, 7.745966692, 7.745966692

b The same! **c** 17.32050808 **d** Students' answers

Exercise 8g page 127

1 a 88 209 **b** 250

2 a 8.66 cm

b Width of changing room = 6.2 m
Area of changing room = 96.1 m²
Areas of sports hall = 496.9 m²
Length of sports hall = 22.29 m

3 a Students' answers: numbers in (0, 1).

b Students' answers: numbers in (0, 1)

c Students' answers

Challenge

$$\sqrt{\frac{17^2 + 35}{9}} = 2$$

Exercise 8h page 129

1 a 38 m   65 cm

b 3 km   730 m   68 cm

c 7 litres   427 ml

d 15 tonnes   863 kg   320 g

e 490 inches = 40 feet, 10 inches

f 5.8 m² **g** 55 pounds **h** 4 cm²

2 a 1 hour, 30 mins, 20 secs

b 4 days, 15 hours, 6 mins, 40 secs

c 274 years, 37 weeks, 5 days

d 0 years, 16 weeks, 3 days, 17 hours, 46 mins, 39 secs

3 a £11 929.40 or more realistically 'under £12 000'

b 5.88 so they need to order 6 coaches

c $\frac{38}{60}$, which is about 63%

Investigation

a 10.1 m/s   **b** 36.3 kmph

c Students' answers:

400 mph = 640 kmph,
110 kmph = 30.6 m/s
105 m/s = 378 kmph = 236 mph
17 000 mph = 27 200 kmph = 7556 m/s

Exercise 8i page 131

1 a 38, $(3 + 4)^2 \times 2$ **b** -7, $(5 - 3)^2 - 3$

c -19, $6 + 5^2$ **d** 31, $-(5)^2 + 6$

e 25, $60 \div (4 + 8) + 7 + (5 - 2)^3$

f 5, $\frac{(3 \times 5)^2}{(3 \times 5)}$ **g** 96, $\left(\frac{3 \times 8}{3 \times 2}\right)^2$

2 a 2.78   **b** 2.88   **c** 10

3 a 71.40   **b** -27.24   **c** 35.28

d 9.78   **e** 4.43   **f** 16.88

Investigation

a Students' answers: $\left(\frac{a}{b}\right) \times \left(\frac{a}{b}\right) = \frac{a^2}{b^2}$

b i $3^2 \times 5^2 = (3 \times 5)^2 = 225$

ii $\sqrt{12} \times \sqrt{3} = \sqrt{12 \times 3} = \sqrt{(2 \times 3)^2} = 2 \times 3 = 6$

iii $\sqrt{12} \div \sqrt{3} = \sqrt{\frac{12}{3}} = \sqrt{2^2} = 2$

Consolidation page 132

	i	**ii**	**iii**	**iv**
1				
a	6	6.2	6.16	6.158
b	5	4.6	4.56	4.565
c	19	18.6	18.63	18.626
d	4	4.2	4.15	4.155
e	4	3.9	3.91	3.909
f	10	10.0	10.00	10.000
g	88	87.7	87.65	87.654
h	0	0.0	0.00	0.001

2 a 578 km   **b** 160 mins

3 a 22.9   **b** 235.6   **c** 20.12

d 1099.989   **e** 363.27   **f** 2509.69

4 a 39 000   **b** 700   **c** 41.6   **d** 37.03

e 0.53   **f** 77   **g** 0.562   **h** 0.327

i 0.0049   **j** 0.27   **k** 640   **l** 0.00057

5 a 4700   **b** 0.039   **c** 82 000   **d** 290 000

e 7 300 000   **f** 0.000807   **g** 630 000   **h** 20 500 000

6 a 53.3   **b** 36.48   **c** 7486.6   **d** 2464.5

e 66.96   **f** 684.72   **g** 35.04   **h** 719.61

i 57.967   **j** 26.496   **k** 34.892   **l** 87.327

7 a 8.1   **b** 8.4   **c** 11.8   **d** 2.8

e 4.2   **f** 2.0   **g** 71.1   **h** 162.9

i 126.7   **j** 210   **k** 39.9   **l** 258.1

8 a 6.71   **b** 3.61   **c** 19

d 29.60   **e** 51.38

9 a 4.6   **b** 6.7   **c** 2.2

d 10.0   **e** 44.4

10 a 119.3   **b** 3.79

c $\left(\sqrt{(12^2 + 23)} - 8\right)^3$, $\sqrt{(7 \div 8)^2 \div 2 + 14}$

11 a £203 183.72   **b** 51

12 a 5   **b** 2.55   **c** 1.63

13 a 307.72   **b** 17.01   **c** -10.65   **d** 0.28

Summary page 134

2 a 3.1416   **b** $\frac{355}{113}$

Chapter 9

Check in page 135

1 a 800 mm   **b** 200 m   **c** 350 cm

d 0.45 km   **e** 0.75 m   **f** 1.5 cm

2 a

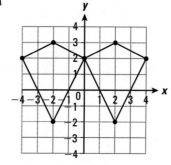

b (0, 2) (2, 3) (4, 2) (2, -2)

c y-axis, $x = 0$

Exercise 9a page 137

1 a reflection   **b** translation
  c translation   **d** rotation
  e rotation or reflection

2 a, b

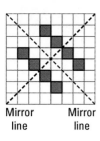

Mirror line   Mirror line

3 a (0, 0), 90° anticlockwise
  b (-1, 2), 90° clockwise
  c i translation of 3 to the left and 1 up
     ii translation of 3 to the right and 1 down

4 a, b

  c Opposite angles are equal, 2 sets of equal sides

     Must be a parallelogram

Activity

Students' drawing

Exercise 9a² page 137²

1 An equilateral triangle

2 a, b Check students' drawing

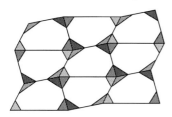

  c Alternate angles are equal for parallel lines.

     Sum of the angles in a quadrilateral is the same as the sum of the angles at a point.

3 a, b

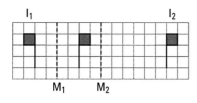

  c Translation of 8 to the right.

4 a, b

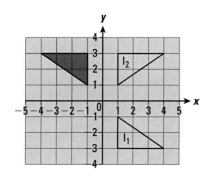

  c Reflection in the y-axis

Activity

Check students' drawing

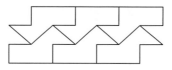

Exercise 9b page 139

1 a 4 lines, order 4

  b 2 lines, order 2

  c 6 lines, order 6

  d 1 line, order 1

  e 1 line, order 1

2 a 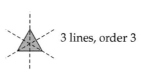 3 lines, order 3

  b 4 lines, order 4

  c 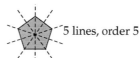 5 lines, order 5

  d 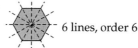 6 lines, order 6

  e 8 lines, order 8

3 a 2 lines, order 2

  b 1 line, order 1

  c no lines, order 2

4 $a = 130°$, $b = 100°$, $c = 100°$, $d = 80°$, $e = 50°$

Challenge

1111 and 1881

Exercise 9c page 141

1 a s.f. 2   **b** s.f. 3   **c** s.f. 2.5

2 a s.f. 2, centre (5, 5)   **b** s.f. 3, centre (1, 3)

  c s.f. 2, centre (2, 5)

3 a

scale factor 2

b
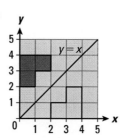
scale factor 3

c
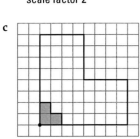
scale factor 4

4 a s.f. 4

  b (4, 5) (4, 1) (12, 1) (12, 5)

Challenge

a 100 small triangles

b Check student drawing.

Exercise 9c²   page 141²

1 a
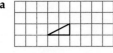

b

c

2 a   **b**   **c**
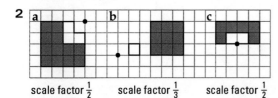
scale factor $\frac{1}{2}$ scale factor $\frac{1}{3}$ scale factor $\frac{1}{2}$

3 a, c
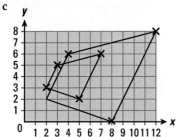

  b trapezium   **d** (2, 3) (5, 2) (7, 6) (3, 5)

4 s.f. $\frac{1}{4}$

5 a s.f. $\frac{1}{3}$ **b** $x = 5\,$cm   **c** 12 cm, 36 cm

Challenge

yes, s.f. $\frac{1}{2}$

Exercise 9d   page 143

1 a 70 cm   **b** 175 cm   **c** 87.5 cm

2 a 12 cm   **b** 8 cm   **c** 5 cm

3 50 m

Investigation

≈ 14 m, shorter for a non-zero width boat

Consolidation   page 144

1 a Reflection in the y-axis

  b Anticlockwise rotation of 90° about (0, 0)

  c Translation of 4 to the right and 5 down

2 a
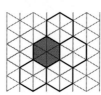
  b Rotation of 180° about (2, 2)

3 a
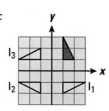
  b Reflections or rotations

4 a, b, c
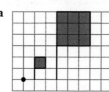
  d Anticlockwise rotation of 90° about (0, 0)

5 a ──€── 1 line, order 1

  b $ no lines, order 2

  c S   no lines, order 2

  d ¥   1 line, order 1

  e ₦   0 lines, order 2

6 a $a = 65°, b = 90°$

  b The two triangles are congruent and so $a = 65°$.

    Angles on a straight line add to 180° and so $2b = 180°$ and so $b = 90°$.

7 a

scale factor 3
  b scale factor 2

c
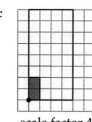
scale factor 4

8 a, c

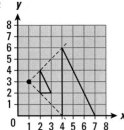

b Right-angled triangle

d (2, 2) (3, 2) (2, 4)

9 a Height 5.2 cm; width 1.2 cm

  b Students' answers

  c 1.5 − 1.6 m

10 a 500 m   **b** 2.5 km   **c** 750 m

    d 1.75 km **e** 2.4 km

Case study   page 146

1 1 square, right angled triangle

  2 isosceles trapezium [and rhombus]

  3 regular octagon [and square]

  4 rhombus

  5 right angled triangle

  6 regular hexagon

2 a [2, 3,] 4, 5, 6 **b** 1 [2, 3]

3 Sum to 360°

4 360 ÷ 60 = 6 an integer but 360 ÷ 108 = $3\frac{1}{3}$

  a fraction

5 360 ÷ 135 = $2\frac{2}{3}$ a fraction but 2 × 135 + 90 = 360

6 Students' answers

  Square and rectangle, regular octagon and right angled

  triangles, trapezium and regular hexagon, *etc.*

Summary   page 148

a

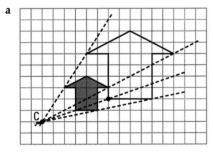

b 4 cm, 40°, 12 cm

Chapter 10

Check in   page 149

1 a 36, 42   **b** 28, 33   **c** 45, 36

    d 22.5, 11.25

2 a 4, 9, 14, 19, 24, ...   **b** 1, 3, 9, 27, 81, ...

    c 10, 5, 2.5, 1.25, 0.625, ...

3 a 64   **b** 196   **c** 343   **d** 1728

4 a 16   **b** 21   **c** 12   **d** 18

Exercise 10a   page 151

1 a 26, 31   **b** 64, 128   **c** 2.5, 2

    d 0, -3   **e** 1, $\frac{1}{3}$ **f** -32, 64

2 a 1, 5, 9, 13, 17, ...   **b** 20, 17, 14, 11, 8, ...

    c 5, 10, 20, 40, 80, ...   **d** 10 000, 1000, 100, 10, 1, ...

    e 2, $2\frac{1}{4}$, $2\frac{1}{2}$, $2\frac{3}{4}$, 3, ...   **f** 100, 50, 25, 12.5, 6.25, ...

3 a i Add 4 to the previous term   **ii** 12

  b i Add 3 to the previous term   **ii** 5

  c i Add 7 to the previous term   **ii** 10, 17

  d i Subtract 3 from the previous   **ii** 25, 22

      term

  e i Add 6 to the previous term   **ii** 16, 28

  f i Subtract 5 from the previous   **ii** 3, -7

      term

4 a Any even integer.   **b** Any multiple of 4

  c Any odd integer   **d** Any fraction

5 a 11, 12, 13, 14, 15   **b** 5, 10, 15, 20, 25

  c 7, 9, 11, 13, 15   **d** 4, 7, 10, 13, 16

6 a 4, 5, 6, 7, 8   **b** 0, 1, 2, 3, 4

  c 8, 16, 24, 32, 40   **d** 11, 21, 31, 41, 51

  e 5, 7, 9, 11, 13   **f** 49, 48, 47, 46, 45

  g $\frac{1}{2}$, 1, $1\frac{1}{2}$, 2, $2\frac{1}{2}$ **h** 1, 4, 9, 16, 25

Puzzle

a Jamie (99), Tilly (17), Sarah (7), William (4)

b Jamie (90), Sarah (43), William (22), Tilly (-10)

c Sarah (403), William (202), Jamie (0), Tilly (-280)

Exercise 10b   page 153

1 a 2

  b

Position number	1	2	3	4	5
2 times table	2	4	6	8	10
Term	5	7	9	11	13

  c i Multiply the position number by 2 and

      add 3.

    ii T(n) = 2n + 3

2 a 10n   **b** n^2 **c** n − 1

  d 4n   **e** n^3 **f** 2n + 1

3 a T(n) = 3n   **b** T(n) = n + 1

  c T(n) = 2n + 5   **d** T(n) = 5n − 1

4 a T(n) = 3n − 8   **b** T(n) = $\frac{1}{2}$n + 1

  c T(n) = 10n − 1   **d** T(n) = 5 − 2n

5 a m = 4n + 1   **b** 201

  c Each pentagon uses 4 straws plus one more is needed to

    close the last pentagon in each diagram.

6 w = r + 4

  Each diagram has the same number of white tiles as red

  plus 4 more at the ends (2 at the left, 2 at the right).

7 Consider each pattern as two rows of dots. The number of

  dots in each row is the pattern number plus 1. Then double

  this as there are two rows.

Challenge

Let p = number of people and t = number of tables.

The rule for option 1 is $p = 4t + 2$ and for option 2 is $p = 2t + 4$.

The number of tables for option 1 is 13 and for option 2 is 25.

Exercise 10c   page 155

1 a 9   **b** 49   **c** 100

  d 6   **e** 9

2 a 8   **b** 64   **c** 1000

  d 3   **e** 5

3 a 225   **b** 784   **c** 21

  d 35   **e** 47

4 a 729   **b** 4096   **c** 12

  d 15   **e** 21

5 6^2 pairs with 36

  $16^{\frac{1}{2}}$ pairs with 4

  4^3 pairs with 64

  $216^{\frac{1}{3}}$ pairs with 6

  The odd card out is $4^{\frac{1}{2}}$

6 a $x^2 - x = 2 < x^3 = 8 < (2x - 1)^2 = 9 < 3x^2 = 12 < (x + 1)^3 = 27$

  b $x^3 = -1 < (x + 1)^3 = 0 < x^2 - x = 2 < 3x^2 = 3 < (2x - 1)^2 = 9$

7 a $x = 64$ **b** $x = -2$ **c** $x = 3$ **d** $x = 2$ or 4

Challenge

a 15   **b** 16   **c** 18   **d** 21

Exercise 10d   page 157

1 a 2^3 **b** 5^5 **c** 8^6 **d** x^4

  e k^2 **f** $(-3)^4$ **g** $4^3 \times 7^2$ **h** $a^5 \times b^3$

2 a 16   **b** 32   **c** 81   **d** 1 000 000

  e 125   **f** 1   **g** -8   **h** 1

3 a 3^6 **b** 6^8 **c** 2^{11} **d** 9^8

  e x^9 **f** y^{10} **g** p^9 **h** q^{16}

  i $6a^{10}$ **j** $30b^{21}$

4 a 5^3 **b** 10^2 **c** 7^9 **d** 1

  e x^7 **f** y **g** $5m^3$ **h** 3

5 a 4^{15} **b** 10^{18} **c** a^{24} **d** $4k^6$

  e $81t^{20}$

6 a 5   **b** 2   **c** 14   **d** 35

Puzzle

a 8^4 **b** 3^7 **c** 5   **d** x^2

e y^2 **f** k^4 **g** 2, 2   **h** 2, 6

Exercise 10e   page 159

1

Equation	Identity
$3x + 8 = 14$	$5(a + 3) = 5a + 15$
$2t + 6 = 5t - 3$	$7(p + 1) + 2p = 9p + 7$
	$4(2k - 1) = 8k - 4$
	$3(y + 2) - 2(y + 3) = y$

2 a $n = 4$ **b** $a = 3$ **c** $b = 1$ **d** $x = 2$

  e $y = \frac{1}{2}$ **f** $y = 5$ **g** $m = 1$ **h** $p = 8$

  i $q = 2$ **j** $t = 5$

3 a $S = 150$ **b** $A = 20$ **c** $v = 22.5$ **d** $F = 68$

4 All proofs, LHS = RHS

5 All proofs, LHS = RHS

  a $4x + 24$ **b** $3y - 18$ **c** $10p + 16$ **d** $18q - 12$

  e $m - 10$ **f** $2n + 20$ **g** $18 - 20k$ **h** $10t - 2$

Challenge

$3a + 21 \equiv 3(a + 7)$, $4x - 20 \equiv 4(x - 5)$,

$t^2 + 3t \equiv t(t + 3)$ $10p + 15 \equiv 5(2p + 3)$,

$ab + 7a \equiv a(b + 7)$, $8k^2 - 12k \equiv 4k(2k - 3)$

Consolidation   page 160

1 a 18, 21   **b** 17, 20   **c** 100 000, 1 000 000

  d 20, 14   **e** $3\frac{1}{2}, 4$ **f** 32, 16

  g 1.0, 0.8   **h** 216, 343

2

	i	ii
a	Add 5 to the previous term	9
b	Add 4 to the previous term	6, 10
c	Subtract 3 from the previous term	5, 2
d	Add 7 to the previous term	12, 26

3 a 11, 12, 13, 14, 15   **b** 2, 4, 6, 8, 10

  c -4, -3, -2, -1, 0   **d** $\frac{1}{3}, \frac{2}{3}, 1, 1\frac{1}{3}, 1\frac{2}{3}$

  e 3, 5, 7, 9, 11   **f** 9, 8, 7, 6, 5

  g 3, 8, 13, 18, 23   **h** 20, 17, 14, 11, 8

4 a $T(n) = 5n$ **b** $T(n) = 3n - 2$

  c $T(n) = 2n - 4$ **d** $T(n) = 6 - n$

5 a $t = 3n + 1$ **b** 301

  c 3 tiles are added on each new diagram – one on each 'arm'.

  Then add on one for the central tile.

6 a $w = 5r + 3$ **b** 503

  c 5 white tiles in a 'C' shape for each red tile plus 3 tiles in a vertical line at the right-hand end.

7 a 16   **b** 27   **c** 64

  d 125   **e** 144

8 a 5   **b** 7   **c** 2

  d 11   **e** 4

9 a $x = 36$ **b** $x = \frac{1}{3}$ **c** $x = 100$ **d** $x = 2$

10 a 2^8 **b** 4^{10} **c** 7^5 **d** 5^9

  e a^{10} **f** b^6 **g** $10x^9$ **h** $12y^{11}$

11 a 6^3 **b** 10^5 **c** 8

  d $p7$ **e** $16k2$ **f** 2

12 a 3^{10} **b** 12^{15} **c** m^{36}

  d n^{14} **e** $64d^{15}$

13 All proofs, LHS = RHS

14 All proofs, LHS = RHS

  a $10x + 15$ **b** $16y - 8$ **c** $12a + 12$

  d $10b + 12$ **e** $p + 14$ **f** $16q + 2$

Summary   page 162

2 a $4n$ 4, 8, 12, 16, ..

   $(n + 1)^2$ 4, 9, 16, 25, ..

   $n^2 + 3$ 4, 7, 12, 19, ..

   $n(n + 3)$ 4, 10, 18, 28, ..

  b 4, 11, 30, 67

Chapter 11

Check in   page 163

1 Specific responses which cover all options without any
   overlap, for example

   i   at least once a week

   ii less than once a week but at least once a month

   iii sometimes but less than once a month

   iv never

2 None of these people will answer 'never' and those who
   go to the cinema regularly will be over-represented in the
   sample she takes.

Exercise 11a   page 165

The answers in this exercise should be taken as indicative of
the type of factors to consider rather than an exhaustive list of
all the possibilities.

1 General memory: age, intelligence, type of job, general
   health, specific brain diseases.

   Temporary effects: tiredness, alcohol or drug consumption.

2 Driving groups: young people – especially young males,
   business people late for a meeting, high mileage drivers.

   Types of car: sports performance models, convertibles,
   high-powered executive cars.

3 Body weight, age, whether the usual level of alcohol
   consumption, time since alcohol consumed, tiredness, time
   since last meal.

4 Time of day, type of roads on journey, any known
   bottlenecks, what is being delivered (time to load/unload),
   need for breaks, number of drivers per delivery.

Discussion

Students' answers.

1 Straightforward: gender, age, type of job. Difficult:
   intelligence, health (exam/medical records or tests).
   Controlled experiments: tiredness, alcohol consumption,
   drugs (legal?)

2 Use police records but would miss aware drivers who avoid
   speed traps. Observation on a road (without cameras or
   radar) would provide data on car types but not drivers.

3 In an experiment easy to measure body weight, gender
   and age and to control for time of eating and drinking and
   tiredness. Accurate self-reporting of how much people
   regularly drink may not be reliable (though the context is
   not judgemental).

4 Straightforward: type of road, known bottlenecks, type of
   load. Experiment: time of day, number of drivers.

Exercise 11b   page 167

Hypotheses can be expressed in several forms
($A = B$, $A > B$, $A \neq B$), so only examples are given.

1 a Males have better memories than females.

  b Older people have worse memories than young people.

  c People under 22 drive faster than older people.

  d Drivers of performance cars drive faster than drivers of
      family cars.

  e The same amount of alcohol has a bigger effect on people
      who do not normally drink alcohol.

  f The time of day affects how long it will take to make a
      delivery to a client.

2 Students' answers

3 People under 22 drive faster than older people.
   The time of day affects how fast people drive.
   Males drive faster than females.
   Drivers of performance cars drive faster than drivers of
   family cars
   The same proportion of people exceed the speed limit,
   whatever the limit is.
   The same proportion of males and females drive with some
   alcohol

Discussion

A specifies the direction any difference is likely to be (males >
females) whereas B allows either males > females or females
> males.

If there is a reason to thinking a difference should be only in
one direction (a drug causes an improvement; a diet leads to
weight loss) then a hypothesis like A is better, but if there is no
such reason then B is better.

Exercise 11c   page 169

1 a i   Ask them/birth records

   ii Observation

   iii Measure

   iv Ask them – may not be reliable

   v   Ask them – if confidential, probably reasonably reliable

   vi Ask them – very subjective descriptions

  b i   Measure

   ii Ask them – if confidential, probably reasonably reliable;
       also likely to be accurate

   iii Ask them – may not be reliable, also people
       misremember quantities

   iv Medical records/test

   v   Ask them – may not be reliable, patients may be
       unaware of family history

   vi Ask – reasonably reliable

  c i   Ask them/birth records

   ii,iii,vi,viii University administrative records

   iv,v,vii Ask them – not necessarily very reliable

2 Carry out a controlled greenhouse experiment not field
   observations
   Soil: acidity, amount of fertiliser, mineral content, type
   (clay/sandy/...)
   Amount of ground water – control
   Humidity – control
   Temperature – control
   Depth of planting – control

Discussion

Students' answers

Issues: could the information be used maliciously or illegally, is security guaranteed; how sensitive is the information personally; the purpose of the information – the fight against terrorism is a common rationale put forward, but how certain information helps in this needs to be kept secret to be effective, making the argument a very complex one.

Exercise 11d   page 171

1 a Gender   male/female

Age _____ years

Do you have any brothers or sisters? yes/no

How long did you sleep last night? _____ hours

b

Name	Gender (M/F)	Age (years)	Siblings (Y/N)	Sleep (hours)
Auther M.	M	12	N	7.5

2 Girls sleep longer than boys

Older children sleep less

Children with no brothers or sisters sleep longer than single children.

3 a Friends are a 'special group' who may act alike and not be typical also they may give answers they think he wants to hear.

b There are very few 14 or 15 year olds and the difference between 12 and 13 year olds is not likely to be big enough to show up, so looking at gender differences and whether siblings makes a difference are probably the best.

Task

Collect information from a large number of students aged 12 and aged 15 and select them randomly.

Exercise 11e   page 173

1 a

Speed	≤ 54	55–59	60–64	65–69	70–74	75–84	≥ 85
No cars	7	21	19	3	3	5	2

b 60–64

2 a 55–59

b Before, less than half the cars travelled at less than 60 mph and $\frac{10}{60} = 16.7\%$ travelled at over 70 mph. After, almost $\frac{2}{3}$ of cars respected the speed limit and only $\frac{2}{100} = 2\%$ travelled over 70 mph. Speeds have been reduced.

3 a The actual speed makes a big difference to the level of danger; combining a 73 mph and a 111 mph driver loses important information.

b Before $\frac{13}{60} = 26.7\%$, after $\frac{10}{100} = 10\%$.

Discussion

There is a major safety component in cameras for speeding (although there are arguments whether this is the main consideration in where cameras are placed), but not for parking. These are more social issues relating to keeping traffic moving. Fines are intended to act as a deterrent and cover the cost of running the detections services needed to make them work.

Exercise 11f   page 175

1 5 | 3 8 8 9
6 | 1 1 1 3 3 4 7 8 8 8
7 | 1 2 3 3 4 4 7 7 8 9
8 | 1 2 3 4 9
9 | 1

Key
7 | 1 means 71 mph

2 a **Males**
2 | 9
3 | 1 2 4 5 5 6 7 9
4 | 1 1 3 4 5 6 6 9
5 | 1 7
6 | 0 1

Key
5 | 1 means 51 years old

b **Females**
2 |
3 | 4 7 8 9
4 | 1 2 7 7 9 9
5 | 2 5 7
6 | 1 3

Key
5 | 2 means 52 years old

c Males 41, females 47

d There are more males than females and the males tend to be younger.

3 a Comparative bar chart for comparing numbers in groups – can be grouped in 2 ways either

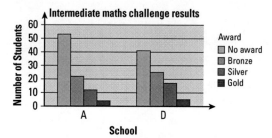

or

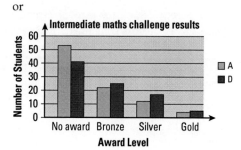

b Pie chart **Intermediate maths challenge for School B**

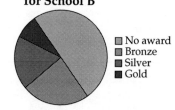

c Bar chart

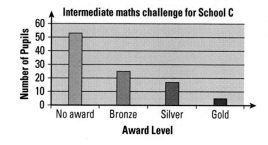

Discussion

To compare a large number of schools the second of the charts (showing all the schools results together) will make it easier to see what is going on. 6 or 7 schools is OK, 10 is quite a lot to work with and more than that gets difficult unless there are big differences.

Exercise 11g   page 177

1 There is some variation. There seems to have been a modest decrease in the proportions drinking at most ages (little change at 12 or 14).

2 a Higher proportions drinking among older children.

b Higher proportion of boys drinking than girls at all ages.

Discussion

Students' answers

The first graph lets you see much more easily that the pattern across age groups has stayed very similar. The second allows comparisons across time for any of the ages to be seen more easily.

Consolidation   page 178

1 Age, gender, body weight, how severe their illness is, any medication they already take, other health issues – do they smoke/drink (how much), lifestyle – how much exercise they take.

2 Students' answers

Hypotheses should be a clear statement about the effectiveness of the drug on different groups being equal (or giving a direction of expected difference – but this is much more difficult to do in this context without expert medical knowledge).

3 a Students' answers based on their choice of variables

b Drug trials are usually conducted through clinics or through GP surgeries so some medical background information is likely to be available; volunteers are likely to co-operate.
Age: ask/records – easy
Gender: observation/records – easy
Body weight: measure – relatively easy
Severity of illness: expert opinion – will depend on what the disease is.
Medication: medical records (reliable) or ask (reasonably reliable)
Other health issues: do they smoke/drink (how much), lifestyle – how much exercise they take.

c Even if they have not volunteered they probably have to agree to take part in the trial so there should not be too much difficulty here.

4 Students' answers

5 Age, gender, severity of illness, body weight have the advantage of being relevant and reasonably easy to identify – other choices are possible.

6 a

Age	≤ 54	55–59	60–64	65–69	70–74	75–84	≥ 85
No. patients	16	11	12	4	10	5	2

b 60–64 years

c All coming from the one nursing home suggests that they have other health problems as well, and being in the same place means other factors like the environment/nursing care *etc.* will not be typical of the range elsewhere.

7 a

```
4 | 6 7 9 9
5 | 1 2 3 6 7 7 7 9 9 9
6 | 1 2 2 3 3 4 7 7        Key
7 | 0 1 1 1 3              7|1 means 71 years old
8 | 0 1 2
```

b Median is 61.5 years

8 a i The recorded rates in all the age groups have increased steadily year on year.

ii In 1994 the rates of treatment for depression were lower for young females, but the rates of increase for younger females have been faster than for older females so now there is less of a difference between ages.

b The rates are much higher across all age groups for women. There is a similar pattern for males – that depression was treated much less frequently in young men in 1994 but the rate of increase has been faster and now there is much less difference across age groups for men.

Summary   page 180

2 a False with a correct explanation.

b Cannot be certain with a correct explanation.

Chapter 12

Check in   page 181

1 a 3 : 5   **b** 3 : 2   **c** 4 : 3   **d** 5 : 7

2 24 : 36

3 435 p

4 48 kg

5 a $\frac{1}{2}$ = 50%   **b** 5 : 2

6 £72

Exercise 12a   page 183

1 a 2 : 5   **b** 8 : 7   **c** 4 : 5 : 8   **d** 3 : 4 : 9
e 5 : 7 : 11   **f** 80 : 41   **g** 25 : 14   **h** 35 : 8

2 a 1 : 4   **b** 3 : 80   **c** 3 : 10   **d** 2 : 3
e 3 : 4 : 5   **f** 1 : 6   **g** 25 : 18   **h** 25 : 3

3 a 1 : 2   **b** 1 : 4   **c** 1 : 5   **d** 1 : 14
e 1 : 1.8   **f** 1 : 4.67   **g** 1 : 3.4   **h** 1 : 14.5
i 1 : 2.67   **j** 1 : 2.57   **k** 1 : 1.83   **l** 1 : 13.67

4

Name	Goals : Shots	1 : n
Ricardo	16 : 35	1 : 2.19
Frank	21 : 50	1 : 2.38
Ade	17 : 43	1 : 2.53
Warren	13 : 34	1 : 2.62
Javed	19 : 53	1 : 2.79

5 First T-shirt   1 : 2.66   or   0.375 : 1
Second T-shirt 1 : 2.8   0.357 : 1

Investigation

a all are $5:8$ $1:1.6$

b it is the conversion factor i.e. miles $\times 1.6 =$ km

c Students' answers

d n is the conversion factor

Exercise 12b page 185

1 a 32 cakes : 48 cakes **b** 65 km : 91 km

c £170.67 : £213.33 **d** 27 p : 54 p : 81 p

2 a £4.88 : £8.13 **b** 87.5 m : 112.5 m

c 1.14 GB : 2.86 GB **d** £8.89 : £13.33 : £17.78

3 a 560 girls **b** 210 g

4 a 350 kg **b** 175 ml

5 a Not enough information:
years 7 + 8 + 9 > year 10 + 11

b $1:1.25 = 4:5$

Investigation

Year	Zoe	Breeze	Jenny
1	6 £200.00	9 £300.00	15 £500.00
2	7 £212.12	10 £303.03	16 £484.85
3	8 £222.22	11 £305.56	17 £472.22
4	9 £230.77	12 £307.69	18 £461.54
5	10 £238.10	13 £309.52	19 £452.38
6	11 £244.44	14 £311.11	20 £444.44
7	12 £250.00	15 £312.50	21 £437.50
8	13 £254.90	16 £313.73	22 £431.37
9	14 £259.26	17 £314.81	23 £425.93
10	15 £263.16	18 £315.79	24 £421.05
11	16 £266.67	19 £316.67	24 £416.66

c ratios $n+6:n+9:n+15 \to 1:1:1$ as they get older

Exercise 12c page 187

1 a 585 p **b** 320 calories **c** 500 ml

2 a £17.24 **b** 383.3 g **c** 270.8 km : 9.6 litres

d i 2998.78 Croatian kuna **ii** £10.84

3 Offer A Direct proportion $(1:2.4)$
Offer B No
Offer C Direct proportion $(1:2.25)$

Investigation

Kilograms (kg)	Pounds (lb)	Pounds ÷ Kilograms	Ratio Pounds : Kilograms
1	2.2	2.2	11 : 5
2	4.4	2.2	11 : 5
5	11	2.2	11 : 5
10	22	2.2	11 : 5
23	50.6	2.2	11 : 5
50	110	2.2	11 : 5

a pounds ÷ kilograms = 2.2,
pounds : kilograms = 5 : 11

b kilograms = pounds ÷ 2.2

c pounds = kilograms × 2.2

Exercise 12d page 189

1 a i $2:1:3$

ii $\frac{1}{3}$ red; $\frac{1}{6}$ yellow; $\frac{1}{2}$ blue

iii Red = 2 × yellow
Red = $\frac{2}{6}$ or $\frac{1}{3}$ ×whole shape

b i $7:5:6$

ii $\frac{7}{18}$ red; $\frac{5}{18}$ yellow; $\frac{1}{3}$ blue

iii Red = $\frac{7}{5}$ × yellow
Red = $\frac{7}{18}$ × whole shape

2 a $15:6:19$ **b** 2.5 **c** $\frac{19}{40} = 47.5\%$

3 a 18 kg **b** 68.75 m **c** 240 g **d** 2.4 g

4 a $3:4$ **b** $3:5$ **c** $5:6$

d £4.20 child; £5.60 adult

Challenge

72.7 cm

Exercise 12e page 191

1 a £69 **b** £248.40 **c** 392 km **d** 238.5 m

e 25.75 kg **f** £438750

2

Item	Original	New
Card	£2.40	£2.64
Wrapping	£2.90	£3.19
Tape	78 p	86 p (rounded)
Mug	£1.60	£1.76

3 a 60.45 kg **b** £9.09 (nearest penny) **c** £399.50

4 a 60 kg **b** £12 **c** £280

5 a 48 marks **b** 180 g

Investigation

a i 85 825 **ii** 83 325

b i 91 052 **ii** 93 784

c 19 years earlier i.e. 1989

d 5 years later i.e. 2013

e in 2008 + n, population = 88 400 × 1.03^n

Exercise 12f page 193

1 a i $\frac{1}{125}$ **ii** 0.8%

b i $\frac{23}{40}$ **ii** 57.5%

c i $\frac{2}{5}$ **ii** 40%

2 a, c

Chocolate	% fat	Fat/150 g
Kit Kit	26.2%	39.3 g
Malties	23.0%	34.5 g
Venus bar	17.5%	26.3 g
Cream egg	15.9%	23.8 g
Twicks	24.0%	36.0 g

b Kit Kit is the least healthy as it has the highest proportion of fat.

3 a, c

Cereal	% fat	Fat/40 g
Fruity fruit	2.2%	0.9 g
Nutty fruit	3.3%	1.3 g
Nuts to nuts	3.6%	1.4 g

  b Fruity fruit is the healthiest as it contains the lowest proportion of fat.

Problem solving

a Original area = $175\,000 \div 0.011 \div (1 - 0.45)$
$= 28\,925\,619.83 = 29\,000\,000$ km²

b In 1997, area $= 175\,000 \div 0.011 = 15\,910\,000$ km²
in 1997 + n,   area $= 15\,910\,000 \times (1 - 0.011)^n$
(in 2009,   area $= 15\,560\,000$ km²)

c About 91 years after 1997   at a constant rate of loss

Consolidation   page 194

1 a $2:15$ b $3:25$ c $3:10$ d $5:8$
  e $9:14$ f $4:5:6$ g $4:6:9$ h $2:3:8$
  i $1:6$ j $2:1$ k $25:6$ l $11:35$

2 a $1:5$ b $1:1.5$ c $1:2.5$ d $1:3\dot{3}$
  e $1:1.4$ f $1:3.8$ g $1:3.5$ h $1:6.\dot{6}$
  i $1:1.71$ j $1:350$ k $1:20000$ l $1:3000$

3 a $40\,\text{km}:100\,\text{km}$ b $£240:£400$
  c $\$336:\$392$ d $17.1\,\text{cm}:12.9\,\text{cm}$
  e $3.7\,\text{MB}:3.3\,\text{MB}$
  f €1714.29; €857.14; €428.57

4 a 477 girls   b 176 kg
  c $210°, 90°, 60°$

5 a £39.55   b 700 g
  c i £12   ii 83 text messages

6 a 4.8 kg   b 22.5 m   c 77 CDs

7 a $2:7$ b $7:4$ c $5:4$ d £22.50

8 a 77.28 kg   b £1052.22   c £8577.50

9 a 72 kg   b £1350   c £16 450

10 a, d

Food	% fat	Fat/250 g
Chops	17.9%	45 g
Chocolate	16.5%	41 g
Crisps	33.1%	83 g
Burger	10.7%	27 g
Peas	0.7%	2 g

  b crisps are least healthy, they have the highest proportion of fat

  c peas are most healthy, they have the lowest proportion of fat

Case study   page 196

1 a

	02/03	03/04	04/05	05/06	06/07	07/08
Produced	566	556	628	620	597	608
Consumed	601	596	616	624	611	612
Stocks	169	129	141	137	123	119

b 5 years
  c Decreasing trend
  d $\frac{119}{169} \approx \frac{7}{10}$
  Students' answers
  Increases in the population; increase in popularity of wheat products, wheat growing land being switched to other uses, etc.

2 a Appears to be half the height

  b Should be 95% of the height.

  c Students' answers
  The suppressed zero make the size of the difference misleading but allows it to be seen.

3 a Just over $3   b May, 2004
  c $2\frac{1}{2}$ years   d $\frac{1}{2}$ year
  A bushel is a measure of dry volume equal to 8 (local) gallons.

4 a 2 million tonnes
  b 6 million tonnes
  c 200%
  d Students' answers
  It may be seen as more environmental friendly.
  e Students' answers
  Increase demand for bio-diesel may cause wheat producing land to be switched to other crops.
  Bio-diesel is made by converting fats, typically from soybeans or rapeseed, mixed with an alcohol into chains of alkyl-esters.

Summary   page 198

2 125 g

Chapter 13

Check in   page 199

1 a $P = 36$ b $k = 3.2$ c $V = 12$

2 a $\frac{3}{5}$ b $\frac{7}{9}$ c $\frac{3}{8}$ d $\frac{11}{15}$
  e $\frac{8}{9}$ f $\frac{7}{12}$ g $1\frac{3}{20}$ h $\frac{23}{24}$

3 a $24a + 16$ b $20b - 4$ c $k^2 - 4k$
  d $5x - xy$ e $10p^2 - 15p$ f $12 - 24q$
  g $-21 + 3m$ h $-10n + n^2$

4 a $x = 2$ b $y = 4$ c $m = 5$ d $n = 6$

Exercise 13a   page 201

1 a Three possible routes which all simplify to $4a + 3b$

  b All expressions simplify to $4a + 3b$

2 Each row, column and diagonal sums to $3a + 3b$

3 a $3k + 2$ b $3t + 6$

4 a i $3x(2x - 5)$ ii $6x^2 - 15x$
  b i $q(p - 8)$ ii $pq - 8q$
  c i $3(10 - 2k)$ ii $30 - 6k$

Investigation

$(y + 3)(y + 2) = y^2 + 3y + 2y + 6 = y^2 + 5y + 6$

$(x + 1)(x + 4) = x^2 + 1x + 4x + 4 = x^2 + 5x + 4$

Exercise 13b   page 203

1 a $\frac{4}{7}$ **b** $\frac{4}{9}$ **c** $\frac{4}{5}$ **d** $\frac{4}{11}$

   e $\frac{1}{2}$ **f** 1 **g** $\frac{1}{4}$ **h** $1\frac{1}{2}$

2 a $\frac{2x}{3}$ **b** $\frac{x + y}{4}$ **c** $\frac{3a}{5}$ **d** $\frac{t}{7}$

   e $\frac{1}{6}p + \frac{5}{6}q$ **f** $\frac{3}{x}$ **g** $\frac{5}{k}$ **h** $\frac{3}{x^2}$

3 $\frac{x}{5}$ pairs with $\frac{2x}{10}$ $\frac{x}{2}$ pairs with $\frac{xy}{2y}$

   $\frac{x}{10}$ pairs with $\frac{x^2}{10x}$ $\frac{2}{x}$ pairs with $\frac{10}{5x}$

4 a $\frac{4}{9}$ **b** $\frac{5}{6}$ **c** $\frac{3}{10}$ **d** $\frac{3}{8}$

   e $\frac{5}{6}$ **f** $\frac{2}{15}$ **g** $\frac{11}{20}$ **h** $1\frac{7}{12}$

5 a $\frac{3x}{4}$ **b** $\frac{p}{6}$ **c** $\frac{11a}{12}$ **d** $\frac{3b}{10}$

   e $\frac{5x + 4y}{xy}$ **f** $\frac{5n - 3m}{mn}$ **g** $\frac{x + 1}{x^2}$ **h** $\frac{3 - 2k}{k^2}$

Challenge

a $\frac{c}{3} + \frac{2c}{7} = \frac{13c}{21}$ **b** 42 chocolates

Exercise 13c   page 205

1 a $c = 320$ **b** $h = 9$ **c** $w = 3$ **d** $t = 15$

2 a $h = 3$ **b** $b = 5$

3 a $w = 2$ **b** $l = 5$

   c The formula finds the area of all six faces in three equal pairs.

4 a $x = \frac{a - by}{b}$ **b** $x = \frac{q - pw}{p}$

   c $x = \frac{t + mn}{m}$ **d** $x = \frac{c}{a + b}$

   e $x = \frac{k^2 - mt}{t}$ **f** $x = 2t - y$

   g $x = 3r^2 + p$ **h** $x = \frac{p^2 q + r}{pq}$

Challenge

a i $x = \frac{a}{b}$ **ii** $x = \frac{r}{p + q}$

b Students' answers

Exercise 13d   page 207

1 a $x = 63$ **b** $a = 40$ **c** $y = 1\frac{1}{3}$ **d** $k = 1\frac{4}{5}$
   e $n = 10$ **f** $p = 8$ **g** $t = 21$ **h** $b = 9$
   i $m = 11$ **j** $q = 14$ **k** $d = 11$ **l** $g = 6$

2 a $a = 2$ **b** $y = 5$ **c** $k = \frac{2}{3}$ **d** $t = 1\frac{3}{4}$
   e $b = 2$ **f** $x = 5$ **g** $p = 1\frac{1}{2}$ **h** $m = 1\frac{1}{3}$
   i $n = 1$ **j** $d = 2$ **k** $g = 1$ **l** $q = \frac{1}{3}$

3 a $x = 6$ **b** $y = 5$ **c** $t = 3$ **d** $p = 10$
   e $a = 3$ **f** $k = 5$ **g** $m = 4$ **h** $b = 2$

4 $m = 38$

5 $x = 3$, area $= 12$ units^2

Challenge

a $a = \frac{360°}{n}$ where a is the external angle and n is the number of sides.

b i 5   **ii** 10   **iii** 8

Exercise 13e   page 209

1 $x = 15$

2 a $x = 10$ **b** $x = 9$ **c** $x = 8$ **d** $x = 10$

3 $x = 4.8$ (1 dp)

4 a $x = 2.8$ (1 dp)   **b** $x = 6.7$ (1 dp)
   c $x = 3.6$ (1 dp)   **d** $x = 7.7$ or 1.3 (1 dp)

5 $w = 9.5$ (1 dp)

6 a $V = k^3 + k^2$ **b** $k = 4.2$ (1 dp)

ICT

$x = 3.6$ (1 dp)

Exercise 13f   page 211

1 a $y = 8 - x$ **b** $y = 1 - 2x$
   c $y = 4x + 3$ **d** $y = 2 - 3x$
   e $y = \frac{1}{2}x + 3$ **f** $y = 1 - \frac{2}{3}x$
   g $y = 3x$ **h** $y = \frac{1}{4}x + 3$

2 a

x	0	2	4
y	4	2	0

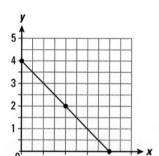

b

x	0	2	4
y	8	4	0

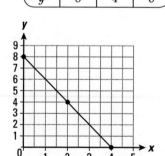

c

x	0	3	6
y	2	1	0

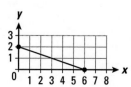

3 a i (2, 4)

   ii (3, 3)

   iii (0, 1)

  b i $2 + 4 = 6$ and $2 \times 4 - 3 \times 2 = 2$

   ii $3 + 3 = 6$ and $3 \times 3 - 2 \times 3 = 3$

   iii $2 \times 1 - 3 \times 0 = 2$ and $3 \times 1 - 2 \times 0 = 3$

4 a $x + y = 7$ and $x - y = 3$

  b $x + y = 7$

x	0	3	7
y	7	4	0

   $x - y = 3$

x	0	3	7
y	-3	0	4

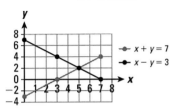

  c (5, 2)

    $5 + 2 = 7$ and $5 - 2 = 3$

ICT

a $2a + 2c = 50$, or $a + c = 25$, and $a + 3c = 45$

b

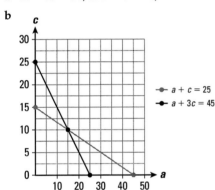

c Adult's ticket = £15 and child's ticket = £10

Exercise 13g   page 213

1 a Yes   **b** No   **c** No

  d Yes   **e** No

2 a Yes (1 : 9)   **b** Yes (1 : 0.8)

3 $h = 14$ cm

4 a

£	1	4	8	16
€	1.25	5	10	20

  b

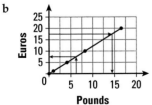

  c i €7.50   **ii** £14.40

  d $y = 1.25x$

  e €100

Investigation

Pressure − volume of a gas (Boyle's law)

Time taken to do a job − number of people working on it.

Length − width for a rectangle of constant area.

Exercise 13h   page 215

1 a A to vi   B to ii   C to iii

       D to iv   E to v   F to i

  b

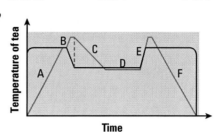

2 A to 3   B to 2   C to 1

3 a Distance–time graph   **b** 12:05   **c** 24 km/h

Task

Students answers; compare to question **2**.

Consolidation   page 216

1 a $3y - 5, 2x + 7$

2 a i $8(3 - p)$ **ii** $24 - 8p$

  b i $4(10 - 3q)$ **ii** $40 - 12q$

3 a $\dfrac{3x}{5}$ **b** $\dfrac{p - q}{8}$ **c** $\dfrac{4}{9}a$ **d** $\dfrac{7}{t}$

4 a $\dfrac{3k}{8}$ **b** $\dfrac{39y}{100}$ **c** $\dfrac{7m}{12}$ **d** $\dfrac{7n}{40}$

  e $\dfrac{2a + 3b}{ab}$ **f** $\dfrac{6q - p}{pq}$ **g** $\dfrac{10t - 7}{t^2}$ **h** $\dfrac{5 - 3y}{xy}$

5 a £9   **b** $80 - 9x = 26, x = 6$

6 a $x = \dfrac{m - 3n}{3}$ **b** $x = 10k - c$

  c $x = \dfrac{p + qt}{q}$ **d** $x = \dfrac{d^2 + kr}{k}$

7 a $a = 6$ **b** $b = 7$ **c** $x = 4$ **d** $y = 12$

  e $p = 5$ **f** $q = 5$ **g** $m = 2$ **h** $n = 4$

8 $x = 3.8$ (1 dp)

9 a $x + y = 5$ $5x - y = 1$

x	0	1	2
y	5	4	3

x	0	1	2
y	-1	4	9

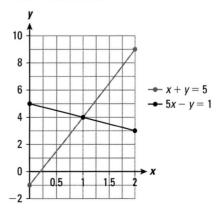

b (1, 4)   **c** 1 + 4 = 5 and 5 × 1 − 4 = 1

10 a

Miles	5	7.5	10	20
Kilometres	8	12	16	32

b

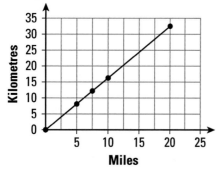

c 11.2 km

d If x is miles and y is km then $y = \frac{8}{5}x$

11 a

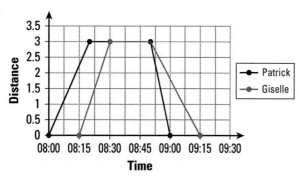

Distance-time Graphs

b 20 minutes

c i 18 km/h   **ii** 7.2 km/h

Summary   page 218

2

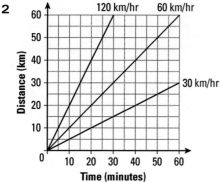

Chapter 14

Check in   page 219

1 a $a = 40°$ **b** $b = 140°$

2 a 50.27 cm   **b** 201.06 cm²

3 a 72 cm³   **b** 24 m³

Exercise 14a   page 221

1 Students' constructions

a 142 mm

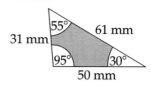

b 14.5 cm

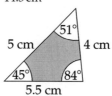

c 17.1 cm

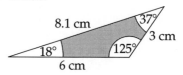

2 Students' constructions

a isosceles

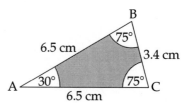

b right-angled

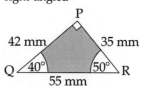

c scalene

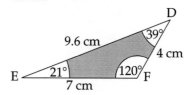

3 Students' constructions

a 50°

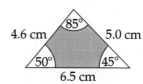

b 130°

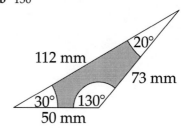

c 75°, 75°

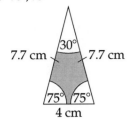

7.7 cm   30°   7.7 cm

75°   75°

4 cm

4 a Students' construction

b 60°, 85°, 90°, 125°

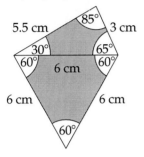

5.5 cm   85°   3 cm

30°   65°

60°   6 cm   60°

6 cm   6 cm

60°

c 20.5 cm

Activity

a Student activity

b

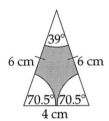

c 20 cm²

Exercise 14b   page 223

1 Students' constructions

a

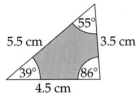

39°

6 cm   6 cm

70.5°   70.5°

4 cm

b

55°

5.5 cm   3.5 cm

39°   86°

4.5 cm

c

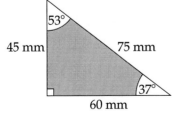

53°

45 mm   75 mm

60 mm   37°

2 Students' constructions

a

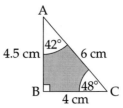

A

4.5 cm   42°   6 cm

B   48°   C

4 cm

b

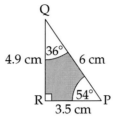

Q

4.9 cm   36°   6 cm

R   54°   P

3.5 cm

c

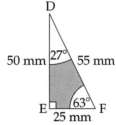

D

50 mm   27°   55 mm

E   63°   F

25 mm

3 Students' constructions

a 5.8 cm and 6 cm

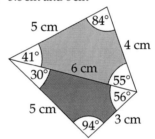

5 cm   84°

41°   4 cm

30°   6 cm   55°

       56°

5 cm   3 cm

94°

b 4.5 cm and 9.2 cm

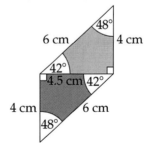

48°

6 cm   4 cm

42°

4.5 cm   42°

4 cm   6 cm

48°

4 a Students' constructions

b 6.9 cm representing 3.45 m

c 60°

Activity

Students' constructions
The hexagon is made from 6 equilateral triangles
of length 4 cm.
The construction of each triangle is SSS.

Exercise 14c   page 225

1 Students' constructions

2 Students' constructions

3 Students' constructions

4 a Students' constructions

  b Perpendicular distance on students' diagrams

5 a Students' constructions

  b Rhombus

  c Students' constructions

  d PR is the perpendicular bisector of SQ

Activity

Students' constructons

Exercise 14d   page 227

1 Students' constructions of the bisector of angle ROQ.

2 a AB = 5 cm

  b Students' constructions of the perpendicular bisector of AB.

3 Students' constructions of a circle of radius 35 mm.

4 a Students' drawings of two parallel lines, 4 cm apart

  b Students' drawings of a straight line parallel to the existing lines, 2 cm from each.

5 Students' constructions of a straight line parallel to AB, 4 cm from AB

Activity

Student activity

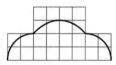

Exercise 14e   page 229

1 a 095° **b** 260° **c** 345° **d** 135°
  e 315° **f** 290° **g** 030°

2 a 120° **b** 230° **c** 040° **d** 225°
  e 325° **f** 300° **g** 050° **h** 220°
  i 045° **j** 145°

Challenge

130°, 310°;   131°, 311°;   132°, 312°;   133°, 313°;
134°, 314°;   135°, 315°;   136°, 316°;   137°, 317°;
138°, 318°;   139°, 319°

Exercise 14f   page 231

1 a 25.12 m,   50.24 m² **b** 37.68 cm,   113.04 cm²
  c 125.6 cm,   1256 cm² **d** 94.2 m,   706.5 m²

2 a 43.96 cm **b** 1055.04 cm

3 a 12.7 cm **b** 6.4 cm **c** 127.4 cm² or 128.6 cm²

4 712.5 cm²

5 a 235.5 cm² **b** 117.75 cm²

  c 157 cm² (Just a semicircle of radius 10 cm)

Challenge

24.13 cm

Exercise 14g   page 233

1 a 56 m² **b** 32 m² **c** 78.5 cm²

2 a 15 cm **b** 4.5 cm **c** 1 m

3 a 408 cm² **b**

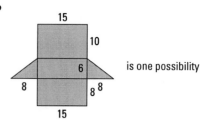

is one possibility

4 a 950 cm²

  b

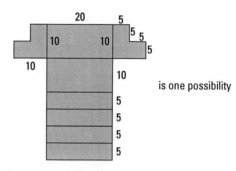

is one possibility

5 $6l^2$

Puzzle

$x = 5$ cm, $y = 7$ cm, $z = 9$ cm

Exercise 14h   page 235

1 a 76.128 m³ **b** 380 640 m³

2 a 1200 cm² **b** 120 000 cm³

3 a Triangular prism **b i** 20 cm² **ii** 120 cm³

4 a 6 cm³ **b** 10 cm³

5 a 450 cm² **b** 27 000 cm³

6 a 78.5 cm² **b** 1177.5 cm³

Puzzle

280 cm³

Consolidation   page 236

1 Students' constructions

  a

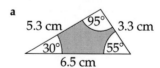

  b

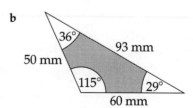

  c

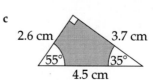

2 Students' constructions

  a Tetrahedron **b** Tetrahedron

3 a Students' constructions

  b Correct labelling of diagram

  c Rhombus

  d The diagonals of a rhombus are perpendicular.

4 a Students' constructions indicating the interior of a circle of radius 3 cm.

  b Students' constructions indicating the interior of a semicircle of radius 3 cm.

5 a 045° **b** 300° **c** 070°

  d 225° **e** 250°

6 95.5 cm

7 a 58.875 cm² **b** 62.8 cm²

8 a, b $1 \times 1 \times 48$ (194 cm²); $1 \times 2 \times 24$ (148 cm²); $1 \times 3 \times 16$ (134 cm²);

  $1 \times 4 \times 12$ (128 cm²); $1 \times 6 \times 8$ (124 cm²); $2 \times 2 \times 12$ (104 cm²);

  $2 \times 3 \times 8$ (92 cm²); $2 \times 4 \times 6$ (88 cm²); $3 \times 4 \times 4$ (80 cm²)

  c $1 \times 1 \times 48$ **d** $3 \times 4 \times 4$

9 a Triangular prism

  b

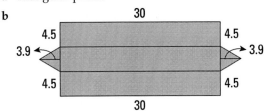

  c i 422.55 cm² **ii** 263.25 cm³

Summary   page 238

2 60.8 cm²

Chapter 15

Check in   page xx

1 a 6 **b** 5.5 **c** 5 **d** 5

2 a

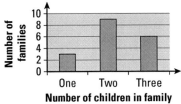

  b Number of children in family

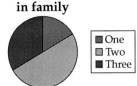

One
Two
Three

Exercise 15a   page 241

1 Mode = 45 cm, median = 67.5 cm, range = 130.5 cm

2 a $5 \le t < 10$

  b $5 \le t < 10$

  c $20 - 0 = 20$ min

3 a

Amount raised (£)	30–39	40–49	50–59	60–69	70–79	80–89
No. of friends	2	12	5	4	2	1

  b £40–49

  c £40−49

  d £49

4 a $20 \le t < 25$

  b $20 \le t < 25$

  c $35 - 10 = 25$ min

Discussion

a False, rank order the same, so same median person but mark increased by 10. Highest and lowest marks both increase by 10 so range stays the same.

b True

c False, highest mark = 80 + 10 = 90

Exercise 15b   page 243

1 $800 + \frac{43}{6} = 807.2$ g

2 a 7.5 cm **b** An estimate since lengths were rounded.

3 a

No. of t.v.s	0	1	2	3	4	5	6
Frequency	2	5	6	9	6	1	1

  Mean = $\frac{79}{30} = 2.6\dot{3} = 2.6$ (1 d.p.)

  b On average there are more televisions than radios per household, t.v. mean = 2.6 > radio mean = 1.9, and a greater variation in the distribution, t.v. range = 6 > radio range = 5.

4 Mean = $\frac{96\,200}{3899} = 24.7$ mins (1 d.p.)

Puzzle

The mean mark will increase by 10.

Exercise 15c   page 245

1 a

	Men		Ladies	
(2)	9 7	11		(0)
(6)	8 7 7 4 2 1	12	8	(1)
(6)	7 6 6 3 0 0	13	2 5 6 7 7 9	(6)
(2)	2 1	14	0 2 3 5 6 8	(6)
(0)		15	5 6	(2)
(0)		16	0	(1)

  key

  1|12|5 means   12.1 s for men   12.5 s for ladies

  b 12.9 s men,   14.1 s ladies

  c The ladies are typically a second slower than the men; the two distributions have similar shapes, with slightly more variation in the ladies times (a longer tail for longer times).

2 a There is a higher proportion of young children at B and of older children at A.

  b Only the proportion of young children is higher at camp B, there may be many more children at camp A.

3 a

School KS3 maths results

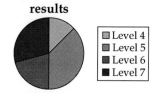

- Level 4
- Level 5
- Level 6
- Level 7

County KS3 maths results

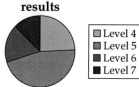

- Level 4
- Level 5
- Level 6
- Level 7

b The school has higher proportions of high levels, 6 and 7, in Maths than were found across the County: the proportion of level 7s is more than twice that achieved in the county.

Discussion

Students' answers.
Make the areas (radius squared) of the two pie charts proportional to the total number of entries in each pie chart. Sizes of the sectors would then reflect the absolute sizes of the catogory.

Exercise 15d   page 247

1 a

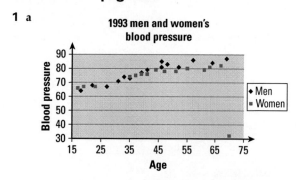

1993 men and women's blood pressure

b Blood pressure tends to be higher in older men.

c (70, 32), blood pressure and age may have been swapped.

d Women's blood pressure tend to increase less as they get older and becomes slightly less than men of the same age above 45.

2

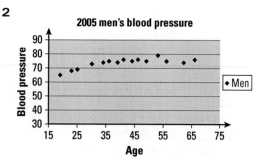

2005 men's blood pressure

The age—blood pressure relationship is similar for young men but does not increase as much with age as in 1993.

3 a Sasha's usage follows a weekly pattern; she uses her phone much more at the weekend, particularly on Saturdays.

b Near the end of the billing period she is using phone much less; presumably so she does not have to pay a lot extra than her minimum contract.

Task

Students' answers

a These are small samples: looking at more data would help identify whether these trends applied more widely than just these groups.

b NHS have made treatment of blood pressure a key indicator for GPs so there has been a particular focus on it.

Exercise 15e   page 249

1 a Moderate, positive correlation.

b Older, younger

2 a None

b None, there is a non-linear relationship

c Moderate, negative correlation.

3 a, b

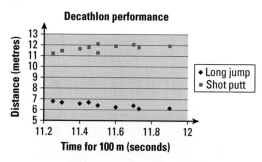

Decathlon performance

- Long jump
- Shot putt

c There is a moderate positive correlation ($\rho = 0.4$) between the time for 100 metres and distance thrown in the shot putt, and a strong negative correlation ($\rho = -0.8$) between time for 100 metres and distance in the long jump (this means fast sprinters jump further but do not throw the shot putt as far as slow sprinters).

Discussion

a A (11.25 s)

Student answers

b A – he came first in both events
I and J occupied the last two places in the two events. J performed worse in the 100 m compared to the general performance.

c Hard given negative correlation and absence of consistent standout performances in all three events. This is why the decathlon has a 'points' system of scoring for the 10 events. Contenders for best are A, B and E (best in shot, reasonable in other 2) and for worst are F, I and J (F is poor in shot, only reasonable in others).

Exercise 15f   page 251

1 a The difference in means (12.7) is substantial compared to the range of scores on the two tests, so this group have done much better on the test after the training.

b The improvement could be down to practice rather than training. The sample is small.
The time scale is important – if they were tested again in a year would they show the same improvement (if not, would you say the training was effective?).

2 a Male 3.1, female 3.55

b There are many more males with low cholesterol levels than females. Only 2 females below 3.4 and only 3 males above 3.4.

3 a A has median in $25 \leq v < 30$ mph and B is in $30 \leq v < 35$ mph

b Range = 20 mph for A and B.

c The speeds approaching B tends to be higher on average and more variable (although the range is the same for both) than A.

Task

Students' answers

The patients in a doctor's surgery are not representative of the general population – since cholesterol is an important health indicator this is a biased sample.

Consolidation   page 252

1 a

Amount (£)	30–39	40–49	50–59	60–69	70–79	80–89
No. of Weeks	2	6	6	3	5	4

b Bimodal (both 40–49 and 50–59 contain 6 entries)

c 50–59

d £58

2 a $12 \leq t < 14$ min

b $12 \leq t < 14$ min

c 10 min

3 a $\frac{73}{25} = 2.92$ min

4 a

	Females		Males	
(1)	7	7		(0)
(7)	9 6 6 5 4 2 0	8	6	(1)
(4)	7 5 2 1	9	1 3 3 4 8	(5)
(2)	4 1	10	0 2 3 7 9 9	(6)
(0)		11	2 4 7	(3)
(0)		12	1	(1)

key

1 | 9 | 5 means   91 miles for females   95 miles for males

b 87.5 females, 102.5 males

c Males tend to drive further than females on average and there is more variation in how far they drive (range = 35 males, 27 females).

5 Many way to talk about this:

Italian is more popular in London and Chinese is more popular in Belfast (others are similar).

In London, Italian is by far the most popular then Indian, Chinese, Thai. In Belfast Italian is slightly more popular than Chinese and Indian and Thai is the least popular.

6 Sales are reasonably consistent through the year with a peak in the autumn.

There has been a slight decline in sales over the 3 year period.

7 Students' answers

a
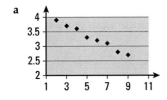

b
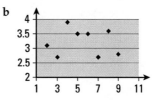

c
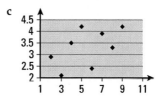

8 a Moderate, positive correlation

b High, low

9 a He is throwing further on average (by 5 metres) than before the programme and he is more consistent in how far he throws the javelin (smaller range)

b Although these are not big samples, they are both from the same athlete so there is fairly strong evidence of an improvement

10 a £13 800 without A-level Maths, £14 200 with it.

b This is just a small sample and it is only the starting salary, so while it is true for this group the statement is too strong for the evidence of this sample.

Case study   page 254

1 a

Item	cost (£)	yearly saving (£)	minimum pay back time (years)	maximum pay back time (years)
Loft insulation	200–350	100–200	1	3.5
Lagging hot water tank	15–20	40–50	0.3	0.5
Efficient A rated boiler	1500–2000	100–150	10	20
New heating controls	150	30–50	3	5
Ground based heat pump	7000–12 000	400–800	8.75	30
Double glazing	2500–3500	50–100	25	70
Draught proofing	80–120	25–50	1.6	4.8
Cavity wall insulation	200–350	100–200	1	3.5

b Lagging hot water tank, loft insulation, cavity wall insulation.

c Double glazing, efficient boiler, heat pump.

Students' answers

May not see the benefit, could increase the value of house.

e Availability of grants, disruptiveness of installation, time taken to recoup costs, sense of 'environmental duty', *etc.*

2 a $4\frac{2}{3}$ panels, cost £23 300 − £28 000

   b Saving = £560

   c $41\frac{2}{3}$ − 50 years

   d Electricity prices may rise, energy consumption may fall.

3 £3.29 per hour used each day; £13.17 for fours hours daily.

Summary   page 256

2 a N

   b True, Coursework range = 40, Test range = 30

Chapter 16

Check in   page 257

1 a 338.32   **b** 204.6   **c** 365.9   **d** 554.97

2 a 60.84   **b** 232.65   **c** 262.88   **d** 48.705

3 a 148.2   **b** 192.1   **c** 380   **d** 170

Exercise 16a   page 259

1 a Pi-Delta-Gamma-Alpha-Beta-Epsilon = 46.93 km

   b 236.5 km

2 a Liam 1.93 m   **b** 0.36 m

   c Giuseppe 1.42 m < Hanif 1.50 m < Ian 1.63 m < Jason 1.75 m < Kiefer 1.86 m < Liam 1.93 m

3 a i £34.37; change £15.63

     ii Vincent £27.97 and Naheeda £23.40; Vincent spends £4.57 more than Naheeda

   b Yes: Martin would have to pay an extra £5.85 for the memory pen.
Vincent would have to pay an extra £7.99 for book.

     No: Naheeda could now buy 6 memory pens and pay the same amount.

   c Students' answers

Exercise 16b   page 261

1 Risotto Twist   458.845 g

  Spiced Rice Cakes   635.25 g

2 a 8 cm

   b 15.258 cm

   c 0 cm; 0.1 cm; 1.057 cm; 2.493 cm; 4.35 cm; 3.305 cm; 3.765 cm; 8.188 cm

   d Students' answers
Availability of light, water and heat; number of leaves, *etc.*

3 a x = 8.055 m   **b** y = 52.805 m

4 58.3 kg

Exercise 16c   page 263

1 Cycling   1245 beats

  Running   1183 beats

  Swimming   **1275 beats**

2 16 pages

3 a Marge's order costs   £73.51; so she has enough money

   b Jameela's order costs   £295.77; so she has enough money

   c Bert's order costs   £380.58; so he has NOT got enough money

4 a 7 portions with 100 ml left over

   b i 4.2 litres   **ii** 4 cartons

   c £395

Exercise 16d   page 265

1 a 1.75p

   b i 72p   **ii** £37.44

   c i ≈36 texts, Four

     ii ≈77 texts, Skyte

     iii ≈145 texts, Skyte

2 a £41.30

   b about £2000 (she might not spend any on her holidays etc)

3 a 48 mph

   b t (hours) = 360/v (mph)

4 a No; 11 × 58 = 638 people

   b Yes; 250 ÷ 9 = 27.8, but this would mean all class sizes were nearly 28.

Exercise 16e   page 267

1 Sack A   £1.25/kg

  Sack B   £1.22/kg

  Sack C   £1.20/kg

2 a i £72/day

     ii £164.57/day

     iii £38.40/day

   b i 16 miles per day   **ii** £7478.40

3 Student answers

Car	fixed costs	£2301.08
	petrol	£1302.09
	total	£3603.17
	time	70 min
Train	season ticket	£8030
	daily ticket	£9350
	time	68 min

Summary   page 268

2 15%

Chapter 17

Exercise 17a   page 270

1 a i Coach: £9676   Train: £11 200

     ii Coach: £194   Train: £224

   b The train is the more expensive by £30

2 16%

3 Coach: £38.70 per day   Train: £37.33 per day

4 The 23:00 from Birmingham arrives at St. Pancras at 01:02 and the 04:30 from St. Pancras to arrive at Sarlat at 16:50

5 (17:10) hours.

6 1492 km or 933 miles

7 88 km or 55 mph

Exercise 17b   page 272

1 1.5 m   4.9 m²   3.25 m

2 A: John,   B: Pete,   C: Magnus,   D: Cherry,
E: Kadeja

3 a i J   **ii** O   **iii** R

b i Sports Hall   **ii** Office   **iii** Shop

4 a Bin a 084 408 **b**   Tap w 088 399
Bin b 101 405   Tap x 109 399
Bin c 111 379   Tap y 116 404
Bin d 117 394   Tap z 132 404
Bin e 132 416

5 Tent J

Exercise 17c   page 274

1 a Football   195° → 26 players

b Table Tennis   30° → 4 players

c Archery   75° → 10 players

d Athletics   60° → 8 players

2 Teacher to check charts:

a Football   150° → 20 players

b Table Tennis   90° → 12 players

c Archery   45° → 6 players

d Athletics   75° → 10 players

3

Round 1			
High 5	2	Superstars	4
Champions	3	Cheetahs	1
High 5	2	All Stars	2
Cheetahs	0	Superstars	2
Champions	2	All Stars	1

Round 2			
High 5	3	Cheetahs	2
All Stars	1	Superstars	1
High 5	0	All Stars	0
All Stars	2	Cheetahs	7
Champions	2	Superstars	1

4 a Range of goals = 7 goals

b Modal goal score = 2

c 3.9 goals

5 a i Red circle → 2 points

ii Blue circle → 6 points

iii Gold   → 9 points

6 a 251 m   **b** $y = 74$ m

7 a i 406.3 m   **ii** 412.6 m

b They stagger the start for races which involve using
curves.

Exercise 17d   page 276

1 a Bart 6 kg   **b** 42 kg   **c** Rick
Gabby 7 kg
Martia 9 kg
Rick 8 kg
Jules 12 kg
Helina 6 kg

2

Section	3 figure bearing	Distance (m)
A to B	065°	350
B to C	015°	250
C to D	131°	380
D to E	355°	500
E to F	242°	350
F to G	231°	275

3 a 2150 + current year. (e.g. if now 2009, then 2150 + 2009
= 4169)

b 122 years

4 a i 49°   **ii** 64°   **iii** 71°

b i 123°   **ii** 97°   **iii** 133°

c i 360° − 79° = 281°   **ii** 360° − 49° = 311°

iii 360° − 108° = 252°

5 Alternate angles are equal: $M\hat{N}O = N\hat{O}P = 49°$

6 a 5.8 m   **b** 3.2 m   **c** 4.1 m

d 4.3 m   **e** 6.1 m

Exercise 17e   page 278

1 a i 18 m²   **ii** 3.9 m²

b Total surface area
= 18 m² + 3.9 m² + 3.9 m² = 25.8 m²

c 6 cans

2 Carrier A holds 15 litres
Carrier B holds 5 litres

3 Teacher to check all three drawings for accuracy.

4 8.5 kg + 9.5 kg + 19 kg

5 4 hours 35 mins

Index

This scheme of work shows how MathsLinks can be used in a two-year Key Stage 3, and is linked to the sample medium-term plans for a condensed programme of study.

Book 8C contains most of the level 6/7 material needed for Year 2 of a condensed Key Stage 3.
You can supplement the material with Year 2 topics from 9C, to consolidate level 7 and stretch to level 8, as indicated in Table 2.

Table 1 shows how you can cover the condensed Key Stage 3 using Mathslinks in two different ways, depending on class ability.

	Y7	Y8	Y9
Fast-track route 1 **Book B**	Levels 4-5 Fast-track Year 1	Levels 5-6 Fast-track Year 1/2	Levels 5-7 Fast-track Year 2
Fast-track route 2 **Book C**	Levels 5-6 Fast-track Year 1	Levels 6-7 Fast-track Year 2	Levels 6-8 Fast-track Year 2

Table 2 shows how you can plan Year 2 for fast-track route 2, using books 8C (and 9C).

Medium-term plan unit	Recommended number of hours	8C lessons	content from 9C
		Autumn term	
A6	6	10a, 10b, 7d, 7e, 13h	quadratic sequences
N5	9	12b-12e, 9c, $9c^2$, 8a, 8g	enlargement and area/volume
S5	9	6a-c, 14a-d	Pythagoras (2 lessons)
D4	7	11a-e, 15c, 15d	
A7	6	5a, 13c, 13d, 13e	simultaneous equations (2 lessons)
		Spring term	
S6	5	2d, 14g+h	compound measures; dividing a line in a given ratio; conversion of units of area and volume
N6	8	4b, 4c, 8c, 8d, 8e, 8h	standard form; upper and lower bounds
A8	9	1c, 1e, $7e^2$, 10c, 10d, 13f, 13g	further index laws; further quadratic and cubic graphs
D5	3	3c-e	
S7	6	6d-f, $9a^2$, 9d	enlargement with fractional scale factor
		Summer term	
A9	7	5c, 5d, 5e+f, 7b, 13b	quadratic expansion and factorisation; inequalities including regions
D6	6	11g, 15a, 15b, 15e, 15f	estimation of median and quartiles for large sets of grouped data
SP2	12	17a-e	Y9 functional maths chapter (5 lessons); general problems (2 lessons)
S8	6	14e	congruence in triangles; further Pythagoras (inc context); basic circle theorems; trigonometry (2 lessons)
D7	6	3a, 3b	prediction and uncertainty; relative frequency; comparing experimental and theoretical probability; simulations
Total hours	**105 hours**	**72 hours**	**33 hours needed from 9C**